The Dog Shogun

Portrait of Tokugawa Tsunayoshi, reproduced courtesy of Hasedera, Nara. The box containing the portrait scroll has the name of the monk Ryūkei (1647–1717) written in black ink; hence the painting is believed to be contemporaneous.

The Dog Shogun

The Personality and Policies of Tokugawa Tsunayoshi

Beatrice M. Bodart-Bailey

University of Hawai'i Press • Honolulu

© 2006 University of Hawai'i Press
All rights reserved
Printed in the United States of America
11 10 09 08 07 06   6 5 4 3 2 1

Library of Congress Cataloging-in-Publication Data

Bodart-Bailey, Beatrice M.
  The dog shogun : the personality and policies of Tokugawa Tsunayoshi / Beatrice M. Bodart-Bailey.
    p.   cm.
  ISBN-13: 978-0-8248-2978-0 (hardcover : alk. paper)
  ISBN-10: 0-8248-2978-6 (hardcover : alk. paper)
  ISBN-13: 978-0-8248-3030-4 (pbk. : alk. paper)
  ISBN-10: 0-8248-3030-X (pbk. : alk. paper)
    1. Tokugawa, Tsunayoshi, 1646–1709.   2. Shoguns—Biography.   3. Japan—Politics and government—1600–1868.   I. Title.
  DS872.T634B63 2006
  952'.025092—dc22
                                                    2005036471

University of Hawai'i Press books are printed on acid-free paper and meet the guidelines for permanence and durability of the Council on Library Resources.

Designed by Lucie Aono

Printed by The Maple-Vail Book Manufacturing Group

To my daughter Mia

Contents

Acknowledgments ix
Conventions xi

1 Prologue 1
2 The Inheritance 10
3 When a Child's Nurse Ought to Be Male 21
4 Lord of Tatebayashi 37
5 Confucian Governance 50
6 A Great and Excellent Lord 69
7 The First Year of Government 79
8 The Rise and Fall of Hotta Masatoshi 90
9 The Shogun's New Men 103
10 The Laws of Compassion 128
11 The Dog Shogun 144
12 The Forty-Seven Loyal Samurai 161
13 Financial Matters 183
14 Producing Currency 197
15 The Two Wheels of a Cart 207
16 The Apprenticeship of Ogyū Sorai 230
17 The Final Years 255
18 The Legacy 278

Abbreviations 299
Notes 301
Glossary 345
Bibliography 351
Index 371

Acknowledgments

My research on the policies of the fifth shogun Tsunayoshi began when Syd Crawcour, then Professor of the Department of Far Eastern History, Research School of Pacific Studies of the Australian National University, suggested that I write a Ph.D. thesis on the political significance of the Grand Chamberlain Yanagisawa Yoshiyasu. It soon became apparent to me that Yoshiyasu's greatest political significance lay in faithfully executing the policies of the fifth shogun, and a significant part of my thesis dealt with these policies. Since this was some twenty-five years ago, the list of people I need to thank is long, and it will be impossible to mention all.

However, I do want to express my warm gratitude to my two thesis supervisors, Syd Crawcour and Andrew Fraser. They not only ensured successful completion of the thesis but also set me on the right path for future research. Further, they invited Japanese historians to Canberra from whose scholarship and support I profited greatly at the time and also on many occasions in Japan since. I am particularly indebted in this respect to Banno Junji, Kamiki Tetsuo, and Tsuji Tatsuya (in alphabetical order, here as elsewhere). Tom Harper helped with my first attempts at reading *Matsukage nikki,* the late Eugene Kamenka with Max Weber.

My warm gratitude goes to the late Julia Ching, for help with *kanbun* texts but even more important for being a caring friend and an inspiration and model with her hard work and determination from the very beginning of my studies in Australia.

Personal and teaching commitments meant that only sections of my thesis were published as articles. When I returned to full-time research, work on the documents of Engelbert Kaempfer occupied an unexpectedly long period. I would not advise young scholars to embark on a different topic before publishing their Ph.D. thesis as a book, but the research necessary to interpret Kaempfer's account of Japan greatly deepened my understanding of the period. Consequently those individuals and institutions whose assistance I acknowledge in *Kaempfer's Japan: Tokugawa Culture Observed* also need to be thanked here.

The detailed research that increasingly emboldened me to challenge established opinion, however, would have been difficult without living in Japan for the last seven years, within easy reach of archives, libraries and last but not least experts to consult. For this I need to thank Haga Toru, who recommended me for my position in the Department of Comparative Culture of Otsuma Women's University, as well as Nakagawa Hideyasu, then director of the university. Further, I would like to thank my colleagues, especially Hanada Fujio and Matsumura Hisashi, for generously giving their time to answer questions, as well as the office and library staff for their practical assistance.

While the department was under preparation, Kamiki Tetsuo invited me to teach at the Faculty of Economics, Kobe University. It was there that I researched the economic plight and policies of the fifth shogun's government. I remember with gratitude the warm reception and lasting friendship of my colleagues in this faculty.

Many years ago I received help with Dutch sources from Ruudje Laarhoven and more recently from Matsui Yōko and Matsukata Fuyuko of the Historical Institute, Tokyo University, and Isabel van Daalen of the Japan-Netherlands Institute, and I would like to express my appreciation. I would also like to thank all those who generously provided and assisted me with illustrations, especially Tokugawa Iehiro.

The help of many other individuals is acknowledged in the notes, but I would like especially to express thanks for frequent conversations generating new ideas with Derek Massarella and Watanabe Hiroshi. In Hawai'i Michael Cooper read the greater part of the manuscript, and my warm gratitude goes to him for helpful suggestions too many to detail.

I am grateful to University of Hawai'i Press for competently producing this volume, especially to executive editor Patricia Crosby, whose continued interest in the manuscript greatly encouraged its final completion, and to Susan Stone for catching many lapses as copy editor. I would also like to thank two anonymous readers for the press for helpful comments. Needless to say, any remaining mistakes are my own responsibility.

Earlier articles from which material has been used are listed below, and I thank the publishers for granting permission to use this material.

"The Laws of Compassion," *Monumenta Nipponica*, 40:2 (Summer 1985)
"A Case of Political and Economic Expropriation: The Monetary Reform of the Fifth Tokugawa Shogun," *Papers on Far Eastern History*, March 1989
"The Persecution of Confucianism in Early Tokugawa Japan," *Monumenta Nipponica*, 48:3 (Autumn 1993)
"The Economic Plight of the Fifth Tokugawa Shogun," *Kobe University Economic Review*, 44 (1998)
"The Early Economic Policies of the Fifth Tokugawa Shogun Tsunayoshi," *Kokumin keizai zasshi*, 179:3 (1999)

Conventions

Japanese year names are used in this book since they do not always accurately correspond to Western years. Thus while most of Genroku 15 corresponds to 1702, the revenge of the forty-seven masterless samurai of 15.12.Genroku 15 corresponds to February 1, 1703, of the Western calendar. To avoid visual confusion when several dates appear in the same sentence or note, I have closed the space between the month and the name of the year: for example, 1.20.Tenna 3.

Japanese ages have been calculated the Western way. Thus Ietsuna, born in 1641, was ten on the death of his father in 1651, and not eleven as Japanese works state. Some Western historians have used the ages as given in Japanese material; hence discrepancies might arise.

I have followed the Japanese custom of abbreviating modern names by using the family name only, while using the personal name with historical figures. Using the personal name for historical figures is necessary since many came from the same family and since Matsudaira was bestowed as family name on a great number of individuals. However, in the case of the forty-seven masterless samurai, the main actors Asano Naganori, Kira Yoshinaka and Ōishi Kuranosuke are commonly referred to by their family names (Asano, Kira, Ōishi), and I have followed that practice here. In the notes, family names are used in short citations for modern names and family and personal names for premodern individuals. Where the title of the work includes the name of the author, the title only is used (e.g., *Kaempfer's Japan*, *Arai Hakuseki nikki*). Where the work is better known than the author (e.g., *Hagakure*, *Matsukage nikki*), the work is cited under the title in the notes. This practice has also been adopted for edited sources, such as the *Deshima Diaries*.

English translations of Japanese titles in the text are an approximation only. Combinations of Japanese characters allow for multiple meanings and connotations, and these literary devices are frequently used. Thus *Matsukage nikki* literally means "diary written in the shade of a pine tree." The pine, however, is not just a symbol of prosperity and longevity, but also refers to the name of Matsudaira, which the head of the household, Yanagisawa Yoshiyasu, received from the shogun.

Japanese "n" has consistently been transcribed as "n." Thus, for instance, Enpō and Sunpu are used where some Western literature has Empō and Sumpu.

All translations of passages cited are my own unless otherwise stated. Where I have retranslated passages, reference to the Japanese original is given first and the existing translation is given in parentheses in the notes.

The crest used throughout the book is Tsunayoshi's version of the Tokugawa crest as it appears on the curtain of his portrait.

Prologue

From the beginning Heaven seemed to show its displeasure with the government of the fifth Tokugawa shogun Tsunayoshi. As the ceremonies on his accession were being held in the eighth intercalary month of Enpō 8 (1680), heavy rainstorms and earthquakes caused damage to roofs and walls at Edo castle, and a tidal wave brought death along the shore. Fire broke out in the city, and as the smoke rose, strange objects were seen flying in the sky. In the countryside storms and floods were devastating the harvest, causing rice prices to skyrocket and famine to inflict Japan.[1] When earthquakes and storms had abated, on a perfectly still day, the cross bar of the large stone gate at the Sanō shrine mysteriously collapsed, causing the stones to bleed. Some people, however, suggested that it was not the stones that were bleeding but the blood of bats crushed between the tumbling debris that tainted the earth.[2]

When Tsunayoshi's government came to an end nearly three decades later with his death on the tenth day of the first month of Hōei 6 (1709), opinions were similarly divided. Heavy downpours ended a long drought the very day he passed away, and continuous rain, sleet, and snow caused his funeral to be postponed. As if to inflict pain on the realm's dignitaries even in death, ceremonial garments were splashed with dirt and the muddy road proved extraordinarily dangerous when Tsunayoshi's funeral procession finally made its way from Edo castle to the ancestral temple at Ueno on the twenty-second day of the first month.[3]

Overwhelmed by grief, some courtiers following the procession had shaven their heads and donned monk's robes to show that their secular life had come to an end.[4] In the household of the grand chamberlain Yanagisawa Yoshiyasu, Machiko, the daughter of the Kyoto noble Ōgimachi Dainagon, was to compare the late shogun to the revered king Wen of ancient China. During the thirty years of his reign, she asserted, he did not make a single mistake. He never ceased caring for his people; till late into the night he had sat bent over his books to perfect the way of government.[5]

Others, however, were of very different opinion. On learning of the shogun's death, Konoe Motohiro wrote in his diary: "Indeed, in the entire thirty years of this shogun's government nothing good has happened. The complaints of the people have increased daily. His death will be the fulfillment of a long-cherished wish for his heir in the Western enceinte who has been waiting impatiently to succeed. When this sad news reaches the provinces will people secretly rejoice? It is better not to speak about it, better not speak about it."[6]

Motohiro was the father-in-law of Ienobu, Tsunayoshi's nephew, adopted son, and successor. As a man of forty-seven, Ienobu was no doubt anxiously waiting in the wings to take over the government of the country, and Motohiro's opinion might well have been colored by the desire to reap the benefits that would come to him once his son-in-law became shogun. But he was also one of those many high-ranking men whose expectations of promotion had been shattered with the accession of the fifth shogun. When the rule of precedent should have guaranteed Motohiro in Kyoto the high imperial appointment of *kanpaku* (regent) in Tenna 2 (1682), he was passed over at the instigation of the ruler at Edo, causing Motohiro and his family enormous grief and loss of face. It took eight further years until he finally obtained the coveted appointment.[7]

Motohiro's wholesale condemnation of the fifth shogun's thirty years of government was echoed many times over in the following decades and centuries. It also appears in the Dutch sources, where the diary of the Dutch factory at Deshima notes that "instead of mourning, there is a lot of joy at the Shogun's death and many lampoons circulate, especially about his avariciousness."[8]

The Story of the Three Kings

The essence of such lampoons is contained in *Sannō gaiki* (The unofficial record of the three kings), an anonymous piece of writing that circulated around Edo soon after the short-lived government of the sixth shogun and the even briefer one of his infant son, the seventh shogun Ietsugu. Parodying the government of the last three shoguns, it reserved the greatest flight of the imagination, derision, and mockery for that of the fifth shogun Tsunayoshi. He was described as the archetype of the corrupt and cruel ruler, given to bouts of anger during which he would kill members of his entourage with his sword. In an effort to distract him from such aggressive behavior, his grand chamberlain Makino Narisada urged him to call Confucian scholars and Buddhist monks, as well as *nō* actors, who performed "day and night." But the shogun's most notorious commands concerned the protection of dogs. Samurai, until then accustomed to cut down offending commoners, were no longer permitted to harm even a dog. Those who did forfeited their lives. Such shogunal orders, *Sannō gaiki* claimed, were not based on rational considerations. After Tsunayoshi's only son had died in childhood, a Buddhist priest had persuaded his superstitious mother that since the shogun was born in the astral Year of the Dog, the lack of an heir was due to offenses against dogs in his previous life. Only the protection of dogs would secure him the birth of the desired son. With his unnaturally strong attachment to his mother, *Sannō gaiki* continued, the shogun heeded this advice, and hence men were killed for the sake of dogs. This earned Tsunayoshi the title of "Dog Shogun" *(inu kubō)*, a name by which he is still popularly known today.[9]

The author of *Sannō gaiki* was widely believed to be the Confucian Dazai Shundai (1680–1747), but in a society where criticism of government incurred heavy punishment, it would have been unwise for him to attach his name to the outrageous and obviously spurious claims made in the text. Much as the contemporary Chikamatsu Monzaemon (1653–1724) transposed the plot of his puppet play satirizing Tsunayoshi's government, *Sagami nyūdō senbiki no inu* (The thousand dogs of the Sagami priest), to the Kamakura period in the hope of evading the censors, so in *Sannō gaiki* the scene was set in ancient China. Mocking Tsunayoshi's attempt to model himself on the three sage kings of ancient China, the work was given a solemn title and written in the style of the Chinese classics.[10]

With its erudite style of writing and contrasting outrageous statements, *Sannō gaiki* appealed to the humor of the times. Its popularity increased rapidly, and in its wake a number of other, similarly fictional works with sensational claims about the life and government of the fifth shogun and his chamberlains began to appear. By the nineteenth century the scholar Matsuura Seizan (1760–1841) felt cause to lament in his *Kasshi yawa* (Evening tales of months and years past) that while at first everybody knew the content of these works to be spurious, over the years people began to consider them true. He condemned Dazai Shundai for the spread of false scholarship and advised his readers to consult instead Machiko's *Matsukage nikki* (Diary written in the shade of a pine tree) to learn the truth about the government of the fifth shogun.[11]

Sannō gaiki cleverly mixes fact and fiction, often making it difficult to determine where one ends and the other begins. Tsunayoshi's laws for the protection of dogs are well documented, and so are death sentences for killing dogs. Yet the notion that these laws were due to the shogun's birth in the astral Year of the Dog finds no support in reliable sources, as will be shown in some detail later. Although this was pointed out by Miyazaki Eiga as early as the 1920s, most histories pay no attention to this fact. Scholars generally recognize that a number of events described in *Sannō gaiki*, such as the shogun's murder by his consort, are fiction, since other materials describe in great detail his infection with measles, which were epidemic at the time, and his failing health. But when *Sannō gaiki* seems to provide the outrageous specifics for vague, difficult-to-interpret remarks in reliable sources, many writers succumb to the temptation of livening up their accounts with citations from this work. Thus it has come to be used to impute meaning in generally reliable sources beyond that contained in the original text and is cited without further qualifications along with serious primary material. Even *Tokugawa jikki*, the official *bakufu* annals, generally regarded as a collation of reliable primary sources and a standard reference work of the period, on occasion cites *Sannō gaiki* without further explanation or warning.[12] In a curious fashion, a short piece of writing initially intended as a joke has come to color the image of the thirty-year government of the fifth Tokugawa shogun. A question that has so far not been adequately addressed is why the *bakufu*, which so effectively suppressed all other political criticism, permitted *Sannō gaiki* not only to circulate, but also to generate a large number of other, similarly libelous works about the period.

The Genroku Period

Yet even when strictly adhering to reliable, contemporaneous writings, the historian is left with a highly ambiguous picture of the period. While samurai sources often describe the period as one of suffering, the ebullient novels of the popular Ihara Saikaku (1642–1693) speak of unprecedented wealth and a rise in living standards. The Genroku period (1688–1704), forming the core of Tsunayoshi's thirty-year government, is recognized as one of unprecedented cultural flowering and good living. Such prosperity was not to be experienced in Japan again until the postwar boom of the Shōwa period, leading to the expression Shōwa-Genroku.[13]

The image of the downtrodden, suffering population is also contradicted by the detailed observations of a foreign visitor. Employed as physician by the Dutch East India Company for their settlement at Nagasaki, the German scholar Engelbert Kaempfer was able to survey living conditions during two trips from Nagasaki to Edo some ten years after the accession of the fifth shogun. Like his fellow residents on the small manmade island of Deshima in the harbor of Nagasaki, on which he was confined for the greater part of the time, Kaempfer was indignant about the prisonlike conditions suffered at the hands of the Japanese. Yet in spite of his complaints, Kaempfer's appraisal of Japanese society was positive. While fully aware of the shogun's infamous Laws of Compassion that forbade the killing of animals, he observed a well-functioning society, with none of the suffering so eloquently described in Japanese records. To the contrary, he praised the fifth shogun as a wise and compassionate ruler. Kaempfer's voluminous record became the standard reference work on Japan throughout Europe until the opening of the country in the middle of the nineteenth century and ironically secured for Tsunayoshi in Europe the praise as sage ruler he was denied by his own people.[14]

Judge in Hades

Now, for a long time, the historian has passed for a sort of judge in Hades, charged with meting out praise or blame to dead heroes. . . . When the

> passions of the past blend with the prejudices of the present, human reality is reduced to a picture in black and white.
> Marc Bloch, *The Historian's Craft*

The fifth shogun has been judged harshly by historians, but there have always been scholars who have attempted to paint a more differentiated picture by investigating what motivated the political actors of this period. Their explanations have had relatively little impact, however.

Condemnation of the fifth shogun invariably includes condemnation of his grand chamberlain Yanagisawa Yoshiyasu (1658–1714), often described as fawning minion, who encouraged the shogun in his vices while himself arbitrarily wielding the powers of government. Already at the end of the nineteenth century, the scholar Sakata Morotō in some thirty years of painstaking work examined all available documentation pertaining to these charges. He came to the conclusion that they were not justified and that Yoshiyasu was, to the contrary, one of the most enlightened ministers of his age. Yet in spite of its meticulous scholarship the work remains unpublished.[15]

Towards the turn of the twentieth century, Japanese scholars were attempting to gain a more comprehensive view of the Tokugawa era, and the theory of alternating periods of strong and weak government evolved. In this analysis the early reforms of Tsunayoshi were ascribed to his early grand councilor Hotta Masatoshi and seen as strong government, while the later period under Yanagisawa Yoshiyasu was seen as weak.[16] The standard histories that appeared in the first half of the twentieth century, such as Ikeda Kōen's *Tokugawa bakufu jidai shi* (History of the era under the Tokugawa *bakufu*), Tokutomi Iichirō's (Sohō) *Kinsei nihon kokumin shi* (History of the Japanese people of the premodern era), and Mikami Sanji's *Edo jidai shi* (History of the Edo period), all basically conform to this view.[17] Primary sources are generally quoted at length, especially in Tokutomi's impressive multivolume work, but no consideration is given to the writers' intent or other circumstances that might have colored their contents. Thus Tokutomi describes *Sannō gaiki* as a bold, outspoken account containing the unadorned truth and cites it at length when it suits his argument. Where fabrications are all too obvious, as in the matter of Tsunayoshi's death, Tokutomi reverts to reliable material, qualifying his citation of *Sannō gaiki* by noting that it was understandable that such rumors circulated among the populace.[18] Quoting "sources" selectively in this fashion with the preconceived idea of the evil ruler, the picture of Tsunayoshi as the corrupt oppressor of a hapless population is not difficult to corroborate.

While the above scholars demonstrated a genuine concern to adhere to "sources," other publications in reputable journals took even greater liberties. In 1903 an article titled "About the Mental State of Tokugawa Tsunayoshi" in the venerable *Journal of the National Medical Association* (of Japan) by the scholar Irizawa Tatsukichi suggested that Tsunayoshi suffered from an illness for which the author used the high-sounding German term *zoophilomanie*.[19] And even in 1970 an article in the scholarly journal *Japanese History* claimed that under the fifth shogun some three hundred people were executed daily for offenses against dogs.[20]

At about the same time that Miyazaki Eiga attempted to refute the myth of Tsunayoshi having protected dogs on account of personal superstitions, another scholar, Kurita Mototsugu, argued in a series of articles that Tsunayoshi's government was one of the high points of the Tokugawa period. Tracing a change from militarism *(budan shugi)* to civil administration *(bunji/bunchi shugi)*, he suggests that the administration of the fifth shogun made an important contribution to this process.[21] Excerpts from Sakata's painstaking work also became available to the public in a book-length work on Yanagisawa Yoshiyasu by Hayashi Masaru, where long passages were quoted verbatim without acknowledgment of the source.[22] The shogun's much maligned chamberlain was also reappraised by Tsuji Zennosuke, paying special attention to his religious and philosophical ideals and activities.[23] Zennosuke's son, Tsuji Tatsuya, accorded Tsunayoshi's administration new importance by pointing out how some of its political strategies prepared the ground for the Kyōhō era reforms under the eighth shogun Yoshimune.[24] Tsuji Tatsuya's important contribution in the *Cambridge History of Japan* makes some of his scholarship available to those without Japanese language skills. In English the work of Donald H. Shively and Harold Bolitho deserves mention as well.[25]

The most detailed work on the government of the fifth shogun has been done by Tsukamoto Manabu, who since the 1970s has been publishing first articles and later books dealing mainly with the much maligned Laws of Compassion. In 1998 he published a monograph on the personality and government of the fifth shogun, and, as is evident from the notes, my work makes ample use of Tsukamoto's research.

The image of the fifth shogun has thus become a far more differentiated one over the years. Japan's school history books, however, still maintain that he protected dogs on account of his love for this animal, based on his birth in the Year of the Dog of the Chinese calendar.[26] Most modern publications still decry his administration as corrupt. Even Tsukamoto Manabu, though dismissing much criticism in the sources as libel, concludes his study on an ambivalent note.[27]

One criticism that surfaces repeatedly is that Tsunayoshi was greatly attached to his mother, who came to exercise undue influence over him and hence over the politics of the country. Documentation well supports his strong bonding to his mother, a woman born as a commoner. Her influence over the shogun is generally viewed as simply yet another flaw in his degenerate character. I would argue, however, that the mother's influence presents a more complex question and that it constitutes a "blind spot" in the appraisal of the government of the fifth shogun.

Blind Spots

"The individual is the carrier of both his species and his culture. Cultural practices, like genetic traits, are transmitted from individual to individual," notes the anthropologist B. F. Skinner.[28] Yet Erik H. Erikson has pointed out that scholars have not always paid heed to this fact, especially with regard to the legacy from the mother. He has labeled this "the blind spot" and argues: "Historians and philosophers recognize a 'female principle' in the world, but not the fact that man is born and reared by women."[29]

Such arguments assume importance in an analysis of the personality and policies of the fifth shogun. Here an unusually strong bond existed with the mother, an outsider, who had spent her early formative years as member of a class with cultural practices differing widely from that into which Tsunayoshi was born. Other Japanese rulers had mothers of low social status. This was acceptable in a society where the woman was merely considered to provide the womb carrying the baby, and attachment of the young samurai to the mother was strictly avoided. Tsunayoshi was different in being permitted by a quirk of fate to form a deep mental bond with his mother, and he thus not only inherited her genetic traits, but also some of the culturally conditioned values of her class. I believe that these traits and the worldview of the mother, transmitted surreptitiously from the time of early mother-child bonding, resulted in Tsunayoshi's rebellion against the values of the samurai environment in which he was otherwise raised. This shaped the administration of his domain even before his succession as the country's ruler, and the unorthodoxy of these early policies, duly recognized as such at the time, accounts for the opposition to his succession on the death of his elder brother.

Tsunayoshi's mother Keishō-in is traditionally described as an uneducated, credulous, and superstitious woman. There is no evidence to support this image. To the contrary, the little reliable material available shows a resolute woman, with high expectations of her son and his government. It is likely that these expectations were transmitted early to the child and over time came to generate the image of the sage ruler Tsunayoshi attempted to model himself on. The ideal of the benevolent autocrat was confirmed in the Confucian classics he studied from a young age, where rulers governed a rural population with the help of well-trained and obedient ministers. In this utopian society of Chinese antiquity, feudal-type lords and samurai subjecting hapless commoners to their wishes, as happened in Japan, did not exist.

Tsunayoshi's strong attachment to and esteem for his mother could not but result in respect and sympathy for the class from which she came. Such sentiments, however, entailed a drastic change in government ideology and policy that hitherto had permitted the samurai to discount commoners' rights and arbitrarily exercise power over the commoners, even at a time when it was no longer military battles but production and trade that shaped everyday life.

The shogun found justification for his political ideology not only in the rapidly changing social environment of Japan, but also in the events on the continent. While he grew up, discontented commoners in China greatly aided the fall of the Ming dynasty, demonstrating the dangers of government ignoring the plight of the greater part of the population. Chinese Confucian scholars seeking refuge in Japan persuasively argued for the ideal of benevolent administration for the masses.

Political ideology according greater respect and rights to the common population entailed by necessity a reduction of the privileges, freedom, and status of the ruling class, the samurai. The opposition of the latter was inevitable, and so was the resulting struggle for authority between the shogun and the traditional holders of political power. I argue that all the policies of the fifth shogun, including the protection of dogs, are the outcome of and are consistently shaped by this struggle between a shogun relentlessly pursuing his political ideals and a military aristocracy equally fiercely defending their traditional rights.

In light of the suffering Tsunayoshi's policies inflicted on the samurai, the nature and purpose of composition of source materials must be given careful consideration. This has not always been done with sufficient rigor, and I see this omission as a further blind spot in the analysis of the personality and government of the fifth shogun. The sources consist overwhelmingly of accounts written by samurai for samurai, upholding and reflecting the samurai point of view, selectively preserved and edited by a totalitarian government for political expediency.[30] When expressions such as *tenka* (lit.: all under Heaven) appear in the sources, they have been taken to mean "all the Japanese population," while in fact in the majority of cases they meant "everybody that mattered," namely, the samurai population. "Popular lampoons" cited in samurai records were popular among the samurai class and not necessarily the rest of the population. Policies criticized by samurai writers as bringing suffering to "the whole country" were often of benefit to the commoners making up by far the largest part of the population.

How research based on conditions in farming communities fundamentally alters the picture of the period is apparent in the writings of Ōishi Shinzaburō. In his earlier work he roundly condemned the government of the fifth shogun in line with most of his colleagues. Yet after a detailed study of the economic progress in rural communities during his government, Ōishi completely changed his opinion and has since praised the fifth shogun as one of the most enlightened rulers of the Tokugawa period.[31] But even Ōishi cannot come to terms with the Laws of Compassion. Since this area is beyond his field of specialization, he uncritically accepts the evidence and verdict of other historians.

In this volume I attempt to show that once these "blind spots" are taken into consideration, rather than illustrating the mindset of a madman, Tsunayoshi's policies bear testimony to great political skill by which, without the use of military backing or financial reserves, the ruler succeeded in imprinting new standards of behavior upon the samurai. When the political changes under Tsunayoshi are examined in the light of Max Weber's theory of political dominance *(Herrschaftstheorie)*, the important role his government played in the development of the modern Japanese state becomes evident. Acceptance that the government of the fifth shogun, rather than evil and corrupt, was to an unusual degree competent and progressive permits a new reading of Ogyū Sorai's work and the realization that his political philosophy owes much to this shogun. To understand how a future military ruler was permitted to come under the sway of a greengrocer's daughter and to espouse an ideology much to the detriment of the military class, I will begin by examining Tsunayoshi's unusual inheritance on both his father's and his mother's side.

The Inheritance

Tsunayoshi was born in Shōhō 3 (1646), just over four decades after his great-grandfather Ieyasu had obliged the emperor to confer upon him and his descendants the title of shogun, thus establishing the Tokugawa hegemony.

The First Shogun Ieyasu

Tokugawa Ieyasu (1542-1616) has gone down in history as one of Japan's great unifiers, the third and last of three generals who ended over a century and a half of sporadic local warfare and ushered in some two and a half centuries of unbroken peace. Yet while in hindsight we recognize in Ieyasu the first of an unbroken line of fifteen Tokugawa shoguns, the future of Tokugawa rule looked much less certain to his contemporaries.

"His Majesty . . . has reasons to fear for his life, for there is the example of his predecessors. This kind of empire is only acquired by force of arms and is retained by the use of tyranny," mused the Spaniard Rodrigo de Vivero y Velasco (1564-1636) when he visited Ieyasu at his retirement seat at Sunpu.[1] The future viceroy of Mexico, who had been shipwrecked in Japan en route to his appointment, marveled at the strength of the fortifications of Ieyasu's castle, only outdone by those of Edo, where Ieyasu's son, Hidetada, was conducting the government. In Edo some twenty thousand men were, in de Vivero's estimation, assigned to duty between the outer defenses ringed by the moat and the inner palace of the ruler, but he noted that Ieyasu at Suruga had a larger contingent of troops stationed nearby.[2]

Life had presented Ieyasu with plenty of opportunity to observe the dangers befalling a ruler. Born as the son of a minor feudal lord in a period known as the "Warring States," he had spent his youth as hostage to a neighboring clan. Though the emperor was still residing in unbroken lineage at his capital of Kyoto, political authority was split between a large number of military houses, attempting to enlarge their sphere of influence or simply to survive. The bond between lord and retainer was feudal in character, but considerations of loyalty were all too often eclipsed by strategic interests. This lack of loyalty was so prominent that the Jesuit Alessandro Valignano (1539-1606) considered it one of the two greatest defects of the Japanese. He ranked it second only to their sexual promiscuity.³ Hence the period is characterized by the phrase *gekokujō*, "inferiors overthrowing superiors."

In this turmoil of small-scale wars, Ieyasu eventually managed to establish a power base and joined the most successful of those competing for political authority over the country, Oda Nobunaga (1534-1582). Nobunaga succeeded in unifying the country, but as this brilliant military strategist was beginning to lay the groundwork for long-term hegemony, he was assassinated by a dissatisfied retainer at his temporary quarters in a Kyoto temple. One of his most astute generals, Toyotomi Hideyoshi (1536-1598), seized the occasion not only to avenge his lord, but also to usurp the power of the Oda clan. Ieyasu transferred his allegiance to the most successful party, but not without commanding a price of extensive landholdings for his submission. This included the large plain where Tokyo is situated today, then a marshy backwater with a small castle.

Hideyoshi continued the work of Oda Nobunaga in overcoming military opposition to a central hegemony, and when this was achieved, he sent his generals to Korea to exercise their swords against a foreign enemy. Simultaneously he laid the social foundations for long-term hegemony. The most important of his measures were his large-scale land surveys that tied the tillers to the soil and his sword hunts that deprived them of their weapons.

Pragmatically Ieyasu sacrificed his first two sons to his overlords. His eldest, Nobuyasu (1559-1579), had been betrothed to Oda Nobunaga's daughter Tokuhime. But when Tokuhime accused her husband of treason, Ieyasu obliged by ordering his son to disembowel himself. After Nobunaga's fall, Hideyoshi sought to ensure Ieyasu's loyalty by requesting his second son in adoption. Reluctantly Ieyasu acceded to the request. In recognition of their alliance, the boy was given the name of Hideyasu, combining the names of his real and adopted fathers but placing the latter first.⁴ When eventually a son was born to Hideyoshi late in life, Hideyasu was once more sent away in adoption, this time to the Yūki family of Echizen. Some eighty years later, Hideyasu's grandson was to be one of the first to experience Tsunayoshi's wrath and sense of justice, which, as he was to proclaim, made no distinction between "the high and the lowly," nor did it spare blood relatives.

Hideyoshi attempted to cement his alliance with Ieyasu further by offering him as wife his half-sister, Asahime, a married lady in her forties. Unable to refuse this gift, Ieyasu agreed on the condition that whatever other sons might be born to him, his third son, later known as Hidetada (1579-1632), should succeed him.⁵

Hideyoshi's first son died in infancy. But two years later, in 1593, his mother, Hideyoshi's favorite concubine, Yodogimi (1567-1615), produced a second son, Hideyori. Ironically Yodogimi's mother had been the younger sister of Oda Nobunaga. When Yodogimi's father, the daimyo Asai Nagamasa (1545-1573), was eliminated by Nobunaga, the mother had fled the burning castle with her three young daughters. But when her second husband was also under siege, this time by Toyotomi Hideyoshi, she decided to die with her husband, sending her daughters into the victor's care.

At the birth of Hideyori, Hideyoshi was a man of fifty-seven. Ruthlessly he had eliminated his real or imaginary enemies, down to his own half-brother and his nephew, whom prior to the birth of his second son he had named his successor.[6] Fearful that he might die before his son was old enough to uphold authority, he attempted to establish all possible safeguards to ensure the continuation of the Toyotomi hegemony. One of these was the appointment of a council of five elders, pledged to act as guardians and protectors of the child, with Ieyasu as the senior member.[7] Another was marrying the younger sister of Yodogimi, usually known by her posthumous name of Sūgen-in (1573–1626), to Ieyasu's son Hidetada, even though she had been given away in marriage twice previously and was six years older than the sixteen-year-old groom. Finally, before Hideyoshi's death, a daughter of this union was promised as bride to Hideyori, a marriage between cousins.[8]

Ieyasu carried out the promised marriage arrangements and eventually gave his six-year-old granddaughter Senhime—later to be known by her Buddhist name of Tenju-in (1597–1666)—in marriage to Hideyori.[9] In more important matters, however, Ieyasu was less punctilious in carrying out Hideyoshi's wishes. Rather than support Hideyoshi's heir, Ieyasu strove to establish his own power base, which led to military clashes with Hideyori's supporters. These culminated in the summer of 1615, when under Ieyasu's siege, Hideyori and his mother Yodogimi committed suicide as their fortress, Osaka castle, went up in flames. Even some seventy-five years later, when the German physician Engelbert Kaempfer visited Japan at the time of Tsunayoshi's government, this event had neither been forgotten nor whitewashed by Tokugawa supremacy. Kaempfer was told and he recorded that Ieyasu "seized" political power.[10]

Ieyasu died one year after the siege of Osaka, satisfied that he had eliminated the most dangerous challenge to the Tokugawa hegemony. Before his death he established three younger sons in large strategic domains, designated as the Three Related Houses *(gosanke)*, eligible to provide successors should the family's main line lack an heir. Furthermore, he had made it clear that in the succession primogeniture was to be strictly observed, regardless of which son appeared more promising. With this act he had unwittingly set in motion a chain of events that was to shape the unusual personality and government of the fifth shogun.

The Second Shogun Hidetada and His Sons

"Now among the good qualities that are known about this prince is that he does not use more than one woman; the least number of women any of his predecessors had was over forty," wrote the Spaniard Sebastian Vizcaino about the second shogun Hidetada. It is often surmised that Hidetada was given little choice by his resolute wife.[11]

Women were pawns used to further military and political ambitions. Yet the harshness of their fate on occasion tempered characters so strong that they challenged the world dominated by men. Yodogimi, who for some seventeen years upheld her son's claim as ruler against the machinations of Ieyasu, was one example. Yodogimi's younger sister, Sūgen-in, Hidetada's wife, was apparently an equally determined woman. Among all the wives of Tokugawa shoguns, she was unusual in that she gave birth to all but one of the shogun's children, permitting him no concubines. A child resulting from the shogun's only known faux pas, Hoshina Masayuki (1611–1672), was given away in adoption and only met his father and was recognized as his son after Sūgen-in's death.[12] In addition to five daughters, she bore Hidetada two sons. The eldest, later to be known as Iemitsu, was born in 1604; the second, Tadanaga, two years later. Iemitsu was a sickly child, withdrawn and handicapped in his speech. The younger Tadanaga was healthy, responsive to his mother's affection, and intelligent, so much so that his parents decided to groom him as shogunal successor.[13]

The rivalry between the two brothers is recorded in many different stories. The best known recounts how Iemitsu's later famous wet nurse, Kasuga no Tsubone, pretending to leave Edo on pilgrimage, secretly informed Ieyasu at his retirement seat at Sunpu about the plan to install the younger as successor.[14] *Tokugawa jikki*, however, simply notes that Ieyasu visited Edo and in the way he presented the boys with cakes made it clear that the elder, Iemitsu, was to be the ruler and the younger his vassal.[15] Although Iemitsu's succession as third shogun was established before Ieyasu's death in 1616, the elder found himself frequently eclipsed by the younger. Tadanaga, it appears, exceeded Iemitsu not only in intelligence, but also in military skills. At the age of twelve he managed to shoot a duck in the compound of the castle to the great joy of his mother, who had it turned into a meal. His father, however, protested, pointing out that it was an act of disrespect towards Iemitsu for the younger to shoot a duck in the compound of the castle where his elder brother, the future shogun, resided.[16] Iemitsu continued to be haunted by Tadanaga's talents after childhood. When in Kanei 3 (1626) Iemitsu proceeded to Kyoto with a great number of retainers, he ordered the daimyo along the Great Eastern Highway, the Tōkaidō, to make the necessary preparations to facilitate his journey. Tadanaga ingeniously designed and constructed a floating bridge over the wide bed of the river Ōi, a major obstacle on the journey. This, however, was greatly resented by Iemitsu, who saw the river, together with the Hakone pass, as a barrier protecting his residence at Edo.[17]

Though Tadanaga had to content himself with the role of vassal, his parents ensured that he was the shogun's most powerful. By the death of his mother in Kanei 3 (1626), Tadanaga had a domain of 550,000 *koku*, nearly one-seventh of the total domain of the *bakufu*, and had been promoted to the high court-rank of *dainagon*. His last enfeoffment was in Kanei 1 (1624), one year after Hidetada had ceded the office of shogun to his son Iemitsu, and included Ieyasu's former retirement seat of Sunpu. From then on Tadanaga was known as Suruga *dainagon*. With his domain strategically located along the main highway, the Tōkaidō, daimyo visiting Edo called on him to pay their respects and often were invited to stay several days. Moreover, some of his senior retainers were awarded castles and domains, such as Fushimi and Kai, in similarly important locations.[18]

The authority Tadanaga commanded is also evident when he met his half-brother Hoshina Masayuki to persuade Hidetada to finally recognize him as his child. Being aware that Masayuki had grown up in the countryside, Tadanaga sent away his servants so as not to embarrass the youth in case he was unskilled in the appropriate ceremonial conduct. Only when he realized that there was no need for such precautions did he call his servants to bid farewell to the visitor with due respect. During their meeting Tadanaga presented his half-brother with presents, including a garment *(kosode)* bearing the Tokugawa crest inherited from the first shogun Ieyasu. This story shows Tadanaga as a sensitive man, yet assuming some authority as he broke taboo and welcomed the half-brother to the family, bestowing on him an important heirloom.[19]

Tadanaga's fortunes abruptly changed, however, when Hidetada fell seriously ill in Kanei 8 (1631), and charged with insanity, he was placed under house arrest in Kōfu.[20] The reason given is that in spite of the warnings of his retainers, he had shot well over a thousand sacred monkeys in his domain. One could also consider this to be an enlightened act, considering the large amount of food so many sacred monkeys would have robbed from the local farmers. But there were also reports of vassals and servants brutally killed in anger. How much of this is true is difficult to determine. As the historian Tokutomi Sohō has pointed out, the sources date these acts to a period when Tadanaga was already under house arrest and could not possibly have committed them.[21] Moreover, that Tadanaga, considered reliable enough to be placed in a controlling position with a large, strategically important domain, suddenly turned insane the moment his father was approaching death and no longer able to control the affairs of state is difficult to believe. Rather it appears that Iemitsu feared the stratagems of his more talented brother once the father who had installed him and upheld his right as shogun was gone. In a letter to his uncle Mito Yorifusa, Iemitsu made no bones about the fact that Tadanaga was of "no use" to him as a brother.[22]

Tadanaga failed in his desperate attempts to gain permission to leave the castle in which he was confined in order to visit his father on his deathbed at Edo.[23] Shortly after Hidetada had died, Tadanaga's entire domain was confiscated, and he was imprisoned in Takazaki castle, where eventually he chose death by suicide.[24] Tadanaga's retainers and their families, charged with failing to prevent their lord's conduct, were punished with confiscation of property and exile, some to be pardoned only three decades later.[25]

The Sons of the Third Shogun Iemitsu

Long before the crimes of Tadanaga's retainers were atoned for, just over ten years after his tragic death, Tsunayoshi was born on 8.1.Shōhō 3 (1646) as the fourth son of Iemitsu. For a brief period during his childhood, the lively and precocious child was, like his infamous uncle had been, second in the line of succession to his sickly elder brother. The latter came to be known as Ietsuna, but at the time he was known under the same childhood name as his father Iemitsu, namely Takesendai (Thousand-Year Bamboo).

Iemitsu's third son, Kamematsu died early in childhood, and his second son, later known as Tsunashige, was given away in adoption on birth. He had the bad fortune of being born in his father's fortieth year, which meant that in his forty-second year the shogun would have a two-year-old son. Since the words for "four" and "death" are homophones in Japanese, and forty-two and two add up to forty-four, this was considered an unlucky combination, suggesting that the son might kill his father. Consequently, when one of the shogun's concubines was found to be pregnant at the crucial time, she was placed into the care of the shogun's elder sister Tenju-in, who adopted the child at birth.[26] After the death of her first husband, the young Hideyori, she had been given away in marriage to the lord of Himeji castle, Honda Tadaoki, but on his early death and that of her son, she had returned to Edo.

From birth Tsunashige was considered Tenju-in's and not the shogun's son. Thus on the celebrations held seven days after his birth *(o shichi ya)* he was not presented by the daimyo with gifts appropriate to a son of the shogun, but only with those required for a shogunal relative,[27] while Tenju-in received presents as his mother.[28] Childhood ceremonies, such as that of the dressing of the hair *(kamioki)* were performed by Tenju-in in Tsunashige's case, while Tsunayoshi had the honor of having this ceremony performed by his eldest brother, the future shogun.[29] Moreover, shortly after Tsunayoshi's birth, the construction of new buildings for both Tsunayoshi and his elder brother Kamematsu at the third enceinte *(san no maru)* of the castle were planned, but buildings for Tsunashige find no mention.[30] Only some time after the death of Kamematsu early in Keian 1 (1648) did Tsunashige and Tsunayoshi begin to be treated more or less equally with respect to retainers and enfeoffments.[31] When shortly before Iemitsu's death in Keian 4 (1651) both Tsunashige and Tsunayoshi were given a major increase in domain of 150,000 *koku* each, *Kenbyō jitsuroku* (True record of Kenbyō), the record of Tsunayoshi's government, commented that previously Tsunashige and Tsunayoshi were treated differently, presumably because

Tsunashige was "from the time he was in the womb" the adopted son of Iemitsu's sister.[32]

Apart from his being treated equally, Tsunashige's name began always to appear first, indicating that Tsunashige had been reinstalled as Iemitsu's second son and Tsunayoshi moved to third place in the line of succession. What had made Iemitsu change his mind?

One reason could be that since the inauspicious period had passed, there was no more to fear from the son born in the father's forty-second year, and thus the child was readopted into the family. Sources, however, suggest that Iemitsu had come to perceive an even greater threat to the Tokugawa leadership from a different quarter.

The Specter of the Past

Buya shokudan (Talk of soldiers around a lantern), a chronicle completed in 1709,[33] provides information that the compilers of *Tokugawa jikki* considered important and reliable enough to cite at length in their account of Tsunayoshi's life. According to this work, Iemitsu noticed at an early time that Tsunayoshi was more gifted and advanced than his brothers and frequently said to the boy's guardians: "This child exceeds other children in precocity and talent. That promises a bright future for the child. However, if as he grows up his genius is left to its own devices, and he is permitted to behave as he likes, there is no telling what horrible disasters this might bring about."

Such "horrible disasters," Iemitsu explained, might come about if Tsunayoshi were to become overbearing and fail to treat his elder brothers with the appropriate respect. To prevent this he was to be taught humbleness.[34]

Tokugawa jikki continues, citing another episode from the same work. This time Iemitsu directed himself to Tsunayoshi's mother Keishō-in. He explained that as he, Iemitsu, had been born in times of military unrest, he was from childhood trained in the military arts but not in literary studies. Having had to take over the government of the country at an early age, he had no time to read books, and even now to his great regret he was unable to find the time for literary studies. He continued: "This child exceeds others in intelligence. In his education literary studies should be first and foremost."[35]

Iemitsu's excuse that he had no time to pursue literary activities does not have much credibility since the record shows him spending a great part of his time hunting, especially during the cooler months of the year. On one occasion he was engaged for four days watching a grand spectacle of "chasing dogs" *(inu ōu)*. To cater to the shogun's taste, the daimyo Shimazu Mitsuhisa had revived this sport popular in the Kamakura and Muromachi periods, where samurai showed their archery skills by targeting dogs encircled by horsemen.[36]

Iemitsu's preference for military sports over book learning was not unusual and simply reflected the low esteem in which literary studies were held by the military aristocracy at the time. Confucian scholars like Nakae Tōju (1608–1648) attempted to win an audience among the military class by asserting that the military arts, *bu*, and literary skills, *bun*, were inseparable, but he had to concede that the actual situation was very different: "According to popular opinion, scholarship is a matter for bookish priests, or monks, and so forth, and not an occupation for samurai. People who engage in too much learning are said to be slow-moving, and of not much use in military matters. If among the samurai someone pursues scholarship, he is, to the contrary, abused."[37]

As a consequence Tōju in his youth was careful to hide his studies from his fellow samurai, confining them to the late night.[38] The second generation of scholars fared no better. The later famous scholar Arai Hakuseki (1657–1725) was first attracted to Confucianism at the age of seventeen when perchance he saw Tōju's work on the desk of a friend and resolved to engage in literary studies to be able to read the Chinese classics. He was, however, careful to conceal his studies from his father and the latter's friends.[39]

Tōju, in a separate essay, lays the blame for the disrespect for scholarly studies by the military aristocracy at the feet of the Hayashi house, the so-called official Confucian scholars of the government, who were wearing the tonsure, dressing and acting like priests. But the founder, Hayashi Razan (1583–1657), as discussed in greater detail below, had little choice if he wished to accept this tenured position in a difficult job market. The conditions imposed on Hayashi were, in turn, no more than a reflection of what the military aristocracy considered scholarship to be about.

One might, as the scholar Tsukamoto Manabu does, suggest that *Buya shokudan* is unreliable.[40] But the fact that Tsunayoshi was not given a traditional military education is readily born out by his life and government. The only person who could have made or sanctioned the decision to give him such an unusual education was his father. Even though the words cited might not have been those Iemitsu spoke at the time, they must have reflected his sentiments or those of his advisers.

After Tsunayoshi's accession as shogun, the contemporary Toda Mosui criticized Tsunayoshi as lacking the ability to function in this position.[41] Tsunayoshi was in no way inferior in intelligence to his predecessors; to the contrary, he was even by his critics described as highly intelligent. Yet, as indicated above, scholarship was considered an occupation for "bookish priests" and not appropriate for a samurai. Why would Iemitsu have ordered an education for his son so unacceptable to the military aristocracy of the time?

A key to this question is provided by another incident related in *Buya shokudan*. Here, again, Iemitsu comments on Tsunayoshi's intelligence and then continues: "When Tsurumatsu [Tsunayoshi] knows something, he ought to pretend that he does not. If he is too clever, he will be hated by Takesendai [Ietsuna]." Iemitsu continued firmly to instruct Tsunayoshi's caretakers not to praise him for his cleverness.[42]

As Tokutomi Sohō has suggested, Iemitsu could hardly have escaped noticing the parallels to his own life.[43] Here once again there was the weak and sickly firstborn, answering, like he himself had done as a child, to the name of Takesendai. The younger brother, formally the second in line, was the bright and energetic competitor. His own experience had taught Iemitsu that the younger would be hated if he were to be seen to be too clever and that "horrible disasters" might occur if the elder was not shown the appropriate deference. By ordering that Tsunayoshi be educated as a literary man, unable to command the respect of his fellow samurai in the way his younger brother Tadanaga had done, Iemitsu hoped to forestall a repetition of history.

Tsunashige's reinstallment as Iemitsu's second son must be seen in the same light. Tsunashige was unlikely to present a threat to his tacit elder brother. When his physical remains were examined at the shogunal mausoleum attached to Zōjōji as it was removed to make room for development, his bone structure showed signs of degeneration.[44] His frequent bouts of illness suggest that the degeneration visible in his bones had also affected his physical and intellectual vitality. Yet while he did not have the spirit to challenge his frail elder brother, Iemitsu must have considered Tsunashige an asset in preventing Tsunayoshi from attempting to usurp the leadership. Once Tsunashige was reinstalled as Iemitsu's rightful son, Tsunayoshi had to defer to two elder brothers and was moved to third in the line of succession.

Socialization and Identification

Early foreign visitors to Japan noted that Japanese children were not forced to learn as in the West but that instead at an early age the desire to excel over others was implanted in their minds by telling them stories of children who through their achievements brought great honor to their families. In this fashion, one writer claims, more was achieved than with beatings and rough words common in the West.[45] Modern psychologists call this part of a child's early education "socialization" and describe it as "a process by which the child acquires the dominant beliefs, values, motives, and behaviors of his culture and gradually becomes more similar to other members of a particular cultural, ethnic or religious group." During this process the child learns which traits a person should ideally possess and which should be inhibited.[46] While it is acknowledged that the content of what is socialized differs from culture to culture, psychologists maintain that the mechanisms of socialization are universal.[47]

In this process the concept of "identification" plays an important role. Perceiving that adults, especially its parents, are stronger, more powerful, and have privileges beyond those granted to the child, it strives to become like them in order to attain these privileges and powers. Psychologists believe that the attractiveness of an identification model is based "both on the model's nurturance of the child and the degree to which the model seems to posses desirable attributes, especially power over the child and over other adults." Accomplishments in skills the child values, and admiration and acceptance by others are also considered important in determining the person chosen as role model [48]

Applying these theories to the behavior of the third shogun Iemitsu, we find a sickly and delicate child who, nevertheless, makes martial sports his favorite diversion. When Shimazu Matsuhisa at great expense revived the sport of chasing dogs and staged a grand four-day spectacle outside Edo, it was in the knowledge that the shogun delighted in such traditional warrior games. Identifying himself with the grandfather who nurtured him, the man he admired beyond anybody else and whose glorification he so actively pursued, Iemitsu upheld modes of behavior that were appropriate neither to his physical condition nor to the times he lived in.

The fourth shogun Ietsuna was again of weak physical constitution and the governance of the country increasingly required complex bureaucratic strategies, rather than military solutions. We see the fourth shogun again delight in military pursuits such as fencing and horse riding, even though such pursuits are inappropriate for the times and his physical condition. Visits to the stables of the castle are recorded from not long after his accession as ten-year-old, and at times he is visiting the stables nearly daily to spend time with his horses.[49] Later the sixteen-year-old shogun, stepping into the image of his father, presents the ten-year-old Tsunayoshi and his elder brother each with a horse accompanied by the exhortation to practice riding diligently.[50] The record shows Tsunayoshi doing some riding occasionally, but he obviously preferred using his brush to paint the images of horses, a number of examples of which have remained. At the age of thirteen Tsunayoshi is given his first fencing lessons, and these lessons continue but are much less frequent than those of his sickly hump-backed brother Tsunashige, who starts fencing lessons in the same year.[51] To both Ietsuna and Tsunashige the value system of the upper samurai had been well transmitted, and the powerful, military-oriented father had become the role model with whom identification was sought.

With Tsunayoshi the case was different. Though he was the strongest and healthiest among the brothers, even as a small child displaying unusual physical and mental liveliness, and thus bodily well suited to excel in the military arts, the military values his father and those who surrounded him cherished were not transmitted. As shogun he would criticize these values of his predecessors, where "brutality was regarded as valor, high spirits were considered good conduct, and there were many actions which were not benevolent and which violated the fundamental principles of humanity."[52]

If one believes *Buya shokudan*, then Iemitsu purposefully set Tsunayoshi on a path of education where he was unable to acquire the skills and values of his father and identify with him. But even if one doubts the reliability of this work and considers the episodes relating to Tsunayoshi's education fabrications to justify later events, one cannot ignore the obvious parallels between Tsunayoshi and his uncle Tadanaga. With their physical and mental liveliness, they posed a threat to the birthright of their older brother, in both cases the child known as Takesendai. The strong emotional pain Tadanaga's rivalry had inflicted on Iemitsu is reflected in the cruel treatment meted out to his brother. There can be little doubt that, on seeing his eldest withdrawn and sickly, and the younger lively and assertive, this suffering revisited him and influenced his attitude towards the younger son. Moreover, with Tadanaga's tragic death having occurred just thirteen years before Tsunayoshi's birth and with Tadanaga's retainers still under punishment, the similarity of the situation cannot have escaped the shogun's entourage. Also the fact that some of Tadanaga's retainers, like the father of the later powerful Yanagisawa Yoshiyasu, were assigned to the young Tsunayoshi after punishment would have contributed to identification with the unfortunate uncle. Iemitsu might not have verbalized his anxiety in the words cited in *Buya shokudan*, yet the fear that history might repeat itself was likely to have been on the minds of many. The obvious answer to this anxiety was to bring up the child so it did not identify with the warrior class but saw its mission in becoming a "bookish priest."

The third shogun Iemitsu died when Tsunayoshi was a child of five. But in these first five years, considered the most important in the development of the personality, Tsunayoshi is unlikely to have received the nurturing and praise of his father. To the contrary, in the shadow of the uncle and with his precocious behavior watched with suspicion, he was not taught the skills and values of the warrior class and not encouraged to emulate his powerful father.

Not having been encouraged to acquire the value system of his ancestors, it is not surprising that Tsunayoshi would later criticize their ideals and under pain of death forbid those sports his father had cherished most. With this lack of approval on the part of his father, the love, encouragement, and expectations of his mother assumed all the greater importance. Her expectations and ideals would much influence his political philosophy and government policy. Hence her legacy requires examination.

3

When a Child's Nurse Ought to Be Male

He [the fifth shogun] was a model of filial piety in his conduct towards her ladyship, the nun of the first rank [his mother]. Every day he would send a messenger to inquire after her well-being, and on occasion he would go himself to ask after her health. He would send her utensils, patterned materials, and a variety of other things in her preferred colors, attempting to meet her taste. Or he would personally draw pictures or dance [nō] for her, and would do everything to make her happy. When her ladyship the nun visited the main enceinte [the residence of the shogun], he would always offer her a tray of food in person. He would also personally serve her tea and so forth."[1]

The woman thus honored by the shogun, his mother, was born as the daughter of a Kyoto greengrocer, a mere commoner. Tokugawa society was officially divided into four classes: samurai, farmers, artisans, and merchants.[2] In this system the barrier between samurai, as the ruling elite, and the remaining classes, the commoners, was the strongest, with many laws—most noticeably that of permitting only samurai to wear two swords—enforcing the difference between them.[3] In this strictly stratified society women, however, were permitted extraordinary mobility. Many of the laws did not apply to them.[4] More important, women of humble status not uncommonly bore the children of men belonging to the upper military aristocracy.

The official wives or consorts of the upper class were usually of equally high, if not of higher standing, and were generally chosen to cement connections between families. Yet these arranged marriages often produced no offspring, and the lord's children were born to one or several of the many other women who resided in the *oku,* literally, the back of the manor. While some of these had been officially chosen as secondary wives, it was not uncommon that a woman bearing the lord's child was a mere servant. Stories abound about the other women jealously trying to prevent the birth of such a child or even to kill the infant. The reason was that, unlike in the West, the children of such lowly women were not regarded as "bastards" but were considered the legitimate offspring of the man who fathered them, with the right to succeed to the position of head of the household.[5]

The rationale behind permitting the children of lowly women to take their place among nobles was the conviction that the bloodline went from father to son and that women were no more than carriers of the womb that made this transmission possible.[6] How little importance was attributed to the biological mother amazed the seventeenth-century Dutch traders at Nagasaki. They were permitted entry into Japan on the condition that as Protestants their faith was different from and they had no sympathy for the much-feared Catholics. When questioned by officials on the Dutch ruling family to ensure that there was no connection with a Catholic nation, the fact that the royal prince was of French descent on his mother's side was considered so unimportant as to not require translation into Japanese. The Dutch record states, "The interpreter did not consider it necessary to answer this, for it concerned a woman, who is not regarded highly in Japan."[7]

While the genetic inheritance from the mother was largely discounted, the emotional influence a mother could exert over her children was well known. The acceptance of lower-class women as the mothers of future heirs and the demands of the purely male power structure of samurai society therefore made the early separation of mother and child mandatory. Only in this way could women be prevented from becoming power brokers by establishing emotional bonds with a male child destined to occupy a leading position. Consequently upper-class children were generally taken away from their mothers as soon as they were born. An early-eighteenth-century encyclopedia states very firmly that a mother was not to nurse her own child.[8]

The early Europeans in Japan were amazed at the rough treatment small children born into samurai families received in order to harden them early in life. As soon as they had stopped nursing, one report states, they were toughened by being taken out into the wild on the hunt, far from their mothers or nursemaids, since it was believed that nothing would weaken the child more than a soft upbringing by women.[9] Japanese sources have shown that from the Kamakura period onwards even the caretaker of the child denoted as *menoto* (nurse) was frequently male. While previously the addition of the character for husband or for father in writing *menoto* was thought to denote a male family member related to the female nurse, recent research has shown that the male *menoto* was a caretaker in his own right who was assigned from the lord's entourage to look after the needs of the young child.[10]

In light of this tradition, it is surprising that the third shogun Iemitsu was permitted to establish a close bond with his wet nurse, later known as Kasuga no Tsubone.[11] Only after he was confirmed as shogunal successor through Ieyasu's intervention were three high-ranking daimyo appointed to take care of his education.[12] By this time, however, Iemitsu was eleven years old. The bond that had formed between the wet nurse and the future shogun was so strong that on his accession she came to yield considerable political authority. Eventually she was received by the emperor and given the court title of *tsubone*, an unprecedented honor for a wet nurse of the military and the cause of much criticism.[13] Iemitsu's unusual bond with his wet nurse and the authority she yielded in later years were an aberration in the system and the power structure of samurai society. The fact that she was permitted access to the child far beyond physically nursing it can only be attributed to neglect in the early upbringing of the boy. If later Iemitsu saw this neglect as having been intentionally brought about by his parents to make him less fit for the office of shogun and the choice of his younger brother a more compelling and rational one, then the close bond Tsunayoshi was permitted to form with his mother takes on new significance.

According to *Buya shokudan*, Iemitsu turned to Tsunayoshi's mother Keishō-in when he made the fateful order concerning his son's education and charged her to have him brought up as a scholar. But there is no record of men appointed to supervise this special education. Instead his mother was charged with this task, opening the way once again to a strong emotional attachment to a woman, this time to a lowly greengrocer's daughter from Kyoto. Did Iemitsu— perhaps subconsciously—reenact a stratagem that he believed was used by his parents to make him less acceptable as military hegemon? There is no historical material to answer this question unequivocally. What is certain, however, is that Tsunayoshi was permitted to form an extraordinary attachment to his mother and that this attachment not only made him less acceptable as shogun in the eyes of his contemporaries, but also came to shape his much criticized policies.

The Greengrocer's Daughter

Tsunayoshi's mother Keishō-in (1627–1705), also referred to by her earlier name, Tama, was officially the daughter of a lower Kyoto aristocrat, Honjō Munetoshi. Munetoshi belonged to a junior branch of the Kitakōji family and was a retainer of the Nijō Kanpaku Mitsuhira. He was, however, only her father by adoption. Her real father was a greengrocer by the name of Nizaemon from Horikawa Dōri, Yabutamachi, in Kyoto. After the death of her father, her mother found employment in the Honjō household and took the young Keishō-in and her elder sister along. When her mother bore a son to the head of the household, the two girls were adopted into the family. Later Keishō-in became an attendant to O Ume, the daughter of the noble Rokujō Saishō Aritsuna, and entered the shogunal castle to serve her. There she was singled out by Iemitsu's powerful nursemaid Kasuga no Tsubone to appear in the presence of the shogun, and eventually she bore the shogun's son.[14]

The above are the explanations of *Ryūei fujodensō* (Biographies of shogunal women), a work completed in Kyōhō 10 (1725) and generally considered reliable.[15] The genealogy of the Tokugawa family, however, states that Keishō-in came to Edo castle as an attendant to Iemitsu's official consort, the daughter of the high Kyoto noble Nakatsukasa Nobufusa known as Takako or Naka no Maru.[16] She entered the western enceinte of Edo castle in Genna 1 (1615), but the record states that Keishō-in became her attendant in the Kanei period (1624–1643).

Scholars favor the first explanation, also contained in *Gyokuyo ki*, (Record of the jeweled palanquin), since close ties between the Rokujō and Nijō families make the selection of Keishō-in as attendant more likely.[17] O Ume, also known as O Man, called on the shogun in Kanei 16 (1639) to be confirmed as prioress of a convent at the inner shrine of Ise.[18] Apparently the shogun, who had so far shown no interest in the heavily made-up women presented to him, was so impressed by her unadorned beauty that he ordered her to stay in Edo. She consequently left religious life and became the shogun's first mistress. Keishō-in was twelve in Kanei 16 (1639), the year O Ume went to Edo. But she could also have been sent to Edo after that date, once O Ume had left the convent and the Rokujō family wanted to supply her with attendants from her native Kyoto.

How little information concerning the women of the shogun was considered worth recording is indicated by the fact that there is no agreement on whether Keishō-in was the mother of one or two of the shogun's sons. Iemitsu's third son, Kamematsu, was born in Shōhō 2 (1645) but died only two years later. While *Tokugawa jikki* notes that his mother was said to have been a woman named Masa of the Naruse family about whom no details were known, elsewhere Keishō-in is said to have been his mother.[19]

With Keishō-in's rags-to-riches story it is not surprising that many tales were in circulation concerning her origin. In popular rhymes she was referred to as a weaver's daughter, while others even claimed that she was of Korean origin.[20] The details of Keishō-in's family background need not concern us here. What is important is that she was indeed born the daughter of a commoner and thus in her genetic make-up as well as her formative childhood experience was far removed from the shogunal family. Her humble background has been proven by an examination of her bones.

The Testimony of Bones

On her death at age seventy-eight in Hōei 2 (1705), Keishō-in's remains were interred at the shogunal mausoleum at Zōjōji. During World War II, the ornamental buildings of this large-scale mausoleum were largely destroyed, and after the war it was decided to remove the graves to make way for city development. The remains of the members of the shogunal family buried there were eventually cremated. But before this, a team of anthropologists under the leadership of Suzuki Hisashi studied the bones and recorded the measurements in detail.

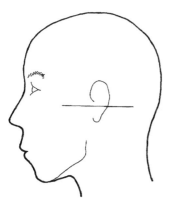

Reconstructed profile and bust by Suzuki Hisashi of Keishō-in's face as she would have looked in her seventies. Photo of the bust courtesy of Gokokuji, Tokyo.

According to these studies, Keishō-in was 146.8 centimeters tall, which meant that she was somewhat taller than the other women of the shogun's *oku*. Her head was large, compared both to today's Japanese and to those of the Edo period. Her face was round and roughly average in width compared to other commoners of the period. However, when compared to that of the other women of the *oku*, her face was extraordinarily wide. Her personal beauty lay in the fact that the lower half of her face was very much narrower than that of the average commoner. The sockets of her eyes sat much lower than those of the women of the castle but were average for commoners of the time. Again the width of her nasal root was atypical for the women of the shogun's *oku* but characteristic of the common people. It was, however, more elevated than was usual for the latter and thus gave her a distinctive profile. In short, Suzuki's study establishes that there was a significant genetic difference between the women of the shogunal *oku* and the common people, and that Keishō-in belonged to the latter.[21]

Intelligence and Determination

Yet her somewhat unconventional beauty could not have been the only factor that eventually earned her the attention of the shogun among the nearly four thousand women that lived in his *oku*.[22] She must have had intelligence and determination to match her beauty.

It required a large amount of self-assurance, courage, and independence for a young woman to leave her native Kyoto and travel for some two weeks to a distant land from which she might never return to live a life about which little was known.[23] She would secure accommodation, food, and luxury clothing, and, if she was clever, advancement for some of her family members. But she would have to part from her known environment, leave friends and family most likely forever, and face the prospect of never entering into marriage, being the mistress of her own home, or bearing children. The life she embarked on was glamorous and held the promise of great success. Yet her chances of becoming the shogun's mistress were as slim as the prospect of dancing a solo part on a world-renowned stage is for the thousands of young women practicing their pas-de-deux in ballet schools. And the dedicated training and determination required to succeed were likely to have been no less, for the women of the *oku* were—in modern terms—the production team for an elaborate show that could be called upon to perform at any time. The attendants of the lady had to be sophisticated make-up artists; well-trained hairdressers; experts on the patterns, colors, weave, and durability of fabric; skilled entertainers and scribes; and, most important, authorities on the extensive ceremonial that governed all actions.

To paint eyebrows on the whitened face required not just the production and choice of the right material and skill with the tools of application, but also the study of various prescribed styles, each differing in small but significant detail.[24] All of the many embellishments of the body and accoutrements such as jewelry, fans, umbrellas, bags, and footwear required expert knowledge,[25] and when an attendant had risen in status to no longer take care of these herself, she had to have the expertise to see that they were chosen and handled correctly by others.

The lady's attendants were not only a well-trained production team, they were also the actors, required to remember the minutiae of elaborate rituals while at the same time impressing the observer with their serene beauty, deportment, and elegance of movement.[26] One might argue that with the low position of women, it might not have been Keishō-in's choice to enter the complex and competitive world of the shogun's *oku*. Yet successful service depended on the poise, confidence, and inner contentment the individual projected, and an unwilling candidate would have been an unlikely choice for an important position as attendant from the lady's native place.

In short, Keishō-in must have been more than just an unusually beautiful young woman. She must also have possessed a great deal of courage and ambition as well as the intelligence to fulfill her ambitions by acquiring the demeanor, knowledge, and skills that ranked her above the nearly four thousand other women of the *oku* similarly intent on gaining the shogun's attention.

Her ambition did not stop at securing for herself physical comforts and an eminent position in the hierarchy of the shogun's women by bearing his child.

She was also ambitious for her son. Not satisfied that he exercised authority as shogun, she strove to ensure that he did this in the very best manner. The following episode, recorded by the scholar Toda Mosui, shows her as anything but the foolish, superstitious woman she is generally portrayed as.

On Hunger Strike

On Tsunayoshi's accession many of his earlier retainers were assigned to the entourage of his young son Tokumatsu. When the latter died prematurely in Tenna 3 (1683), the shogun ordered that Tokumatsu's retainers be released from service. This left them without means of support like the many other masterless samurai (*rōnin*) roaming the country. Keishō-in considered this to be unjust and to make her point went on a hunger strike, even refusing to drink tea. Messengers were sent by the shogun to inquire after her health and doctors called to check her pulse, but this was not a matter of health. Finally the shogun's two most senior ministers, the grand councilor Hotta Masatoshi and the grand chamberlain Makino Narisada, were dispatched to inquire about the matter. She told them that with Tsunayoshi's accession she had expected people to be extolling the times of great peace and to hear only good. Instead she was hearing that the laws were severe and the people were complaining about their suffering. The government showed a lack of compassion in dismissing and thus punishing Tokumatsu's retainers, who had committed no crime. She continued, citing a passage from the Confucian *Analects* pointing out that people governed by punishments will try to evade the law and have no shame, but those governed by virtue will have a sense of shame and become good.[27] She expressed fears that if the government were to continue in this fashion, there would soon be revolt, and she added that strange events at Ieyasu's mausoleum at Nikkō indicated that he, the avatar (*gongen*), was also troubled. Finally she made the point that a government without the right ministers was invariably doomed to fall. Nobody but Hotta Masatoshi and Makino Narisada had the ear of the shogun. However, if, trying to flatter him, they kept their mouths shut, let foolishness reign instead of wisdom, and out of greed turned into cowards, then they were not qualified to lead the country as faithful retainers and were the bane of their ruler. As "mother of the people" she did not want to live to see the country in revolt or to see bad government by strict laws. But since killing herself by the sword or with a rope would expose her to the ridicule of posterity, she was slowly ending her life by not eating.

The two ministers, Toda Mosui recounts, were so ashamed that they bowed low in their prostration on the tatami floor and, unable to answer these charges, did not dare to lift their heads. As a result the retainers were redeployed.[28]

Tsukamoto Manabu, who has edited and annotated Toda Mosui's work, believes that the quote from the *Analects* was added by Mosui to give vent to his own complaints about Tsunayoshi's government.[29] This explanation is only convincing if one postulates that Keishō-in was an unintelligent woman with little education. Yet this conclusion is not supported by the rest of the story or by other evidence.

Among the retainers of Tokumatsu was Keishō-in's stepbrother, and she could have pleaded privately for a position for her relative. Yet instead we see a woman who is politically aware and ambitious for her son. To have him live up to her expectations she is prepared to sacrifice her personal comforts, though one might assume that she would not have expected to die. With her deep concern for the reputation of her son and his government, she, no doubt, would also have had some interest in the only authoritative political writings of the times, namely, the Confucian classics. This is supported by the fact that just over a month after Ogyū Sorai had first been summoned to the castle, Keishō-in asked the scholar to lecture in front of her and rewarded him with presents. The record of the Ogyū family further records that she accompanied the shogun to the Yanagisawa mansion, where Sorai was employed, to listen to lectures there.[30] If the attention she paid to the scholar had not been considered an honor, this fact is unlikely to have been included in the house record. Moreover, the level of intelligence Keishō-in demonstrates elsewhere would have permitted her to cope with the content of these writings.

Keishō-in has been criticized for meddling in government affairs. Yet the fact that she had to resort to a hunger strike to call attention to her protest indicates that, though her influence over the shogun's weltanschauung is undeniable, the criticism that she was permitted involvement in day-to-day government affairs is unjustified. Moreover, rather than pulling strings behind the scene, she courageously attacks the problem front on by confronting the two most powerful ministers with their shortcomings.

We encounter the same frankness in another episode from a different source. In the summer of Genroku 7 (1694), Keishō-in paid a visit to Zōjōji.[31] On this occasion the abbot of the temple conveyed to her that it was inappropriate for the shogun of the country to spend his time and energy on Confucian lectures to the extent Tsunayoshi did. Keishō-in replied firmly that she did not agree. As ruler of the country, she asserted, he had the duty to study the Confucian "Way of Government" no matter how much time and effort it might cost him. Anybody who understood this correctly could not possibly encourage him to take even the slightest rest from his studies. The abbot's face, the record notes, became red with shame on hearing these words.[32]

While Keishō-in is likely to have received little education during her childhood, there is evidence that later she attempted to learn not just to read, but also to write in the Chinese *(kanbun)* style generally reserved for men of some education. A piece of writing in her hand, praising the shogun for the devoutness

When a Child's Nurse Ought to Be Male   29

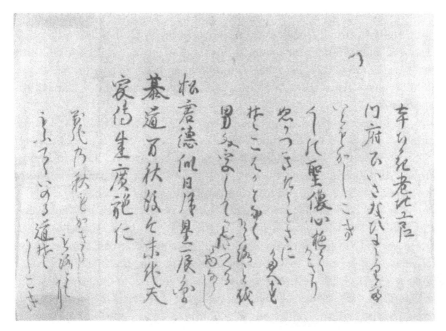

Holograph of Keishō-in. The piece of writing is not dated, but since it praises the shogun's devotion in visiting the Yushima Confucian shrine, it must have been written after 1691. Reproduced courtesy of Kunō Tōshōgu Museum, Shizuoka.

with which he paid homage and bent his head at the Yushima Confucian shrine, expresses her desire to use men's characters *(otoko myōji)*, and she follows this up with an attempt to write three lines in that style. Her reference to the shogun governing with *jin* (benevolence/perfect virtue) in this short piece further shows her endeavor to become familiar with the vocabulary of the Chinese classics. The piece of writing ends with a poem in Japanese style *(waka)*.

Given Keishō-in's determination to step up to the task of being the sole parent of Japan's ruler, the effect of mothering by this resolute woman on the personality and ultimately the government of the fifth shogun requires examination.

Mother-Child Bonding

Tsunayoshi's strong attachment to his mother has been much criticized by historians and is seen as one of the underlying causes of the so-called evils of his government, though filial piety is elsewhere praised as a Confucian virtue. Even a modern historian, trained to treat the past objectively, feels moved to remark that in Tsunayoshi's case it showed signs of madness.[33]

It was "evil" in as much as it perverted the established male hierarchical order and introduced female concerns into government policy. But rather than madness, Tsunayoshi's attachment to his mother during adulthood indicates that close bonding took place between mother and son early in life, validating the story that Keishō-in was permitted to play a significant role in Tsunayoshi's upbringing.

A further indication that no attempt was made to limit Keishō-in's influence over her son is the appointment of her stepbrother Honjō Michika as one of three senior retainers to the two-year-old Tsunayoshi.[34] Early in Keian 1 (1648) Michika had received the lower fourth court rank and had accompanied the former regent *(sesshō)* on his trip from Kyoto to the mausoleum at Nikkō. On his return he remained at Edo, became a shogunal retainer, and was given a stipend of 1,000 bales *(hyō)* of rice.[35] In that same year Makino Narinori (also Norinari) and Muroka Masatoshi were appointed as Tsunayoshi's first personal retainers when he moved to his own mansion in the third enceinte of the castle.[36] Some five months later, Keishō-in's brother was directed "to do the same work" as Masatoshi. He was the odd man out, being the only one of Tsunayoshi's early retainers who did not come from the guard units *(ban kata)* of the *bakufu*.[37] Moreover, as a recent arrival from Kyoto, he would have been unfamiliar with *bakufu* procedures.

That Keishō-in's relatives would receive emoluments and appointments on the birth of her son was only to be expected. But considering the fact that the maintenance of the *bakufu* hierarchical order depended on the elimination of the mother's influence on the shogun's sons and heirs, one would anticipate appointments of her relatives in areas where such family ties had no influence on the upbringing of the child. Assigning Keishō-in's stepbrother to a leading position in the household of the infant Tsunayoshi was tantamount to investing Keishō-in with these powers, for Michika was solely beholden to her for his rise in status. No doubt the appointment reflected Keishō-in's willpower and ambition to raise her own child, but it also indicated that education in the samurai tradition of the shogunal family was not considered a priority in the case of Tsunayoshi.

While a social system permitting women mobility on the grounds that they yield no influence on their offspring could not but condemn mother-child bonding, modern studies have shown that it plays an important part in creating a healthy and self-reliant personality in the child. The quality of mother-child interaction has been found to be a predictive indicator of cognitive development; while disturbed mother-child interaction produced retardation, a high level of positive interaction was found to result in optimal mental and behavioral advancement.[38] For a child the mother's love and adoration becomes the mirror of its own vigor, greatness, and perfection. This positive reflection permits the still fragile self to establish a firm belief in its self-worth and importance, and lay the foundations for a strong, self-assured personality.[39] Tsunayoshi received from his mother the love and approval a child seeks, and it is not surprising that later in life he would also seek her endorsement and be receptive to her wishes.

There was, however, yet another psychological force that set mother and son apart from the larger environment of Edo castle and strengthened their relationship. Through his close association with his mother, Tsunayoshi came to acquire what Pierre Bourdieu would term the *habitus* of her social class, namely, "a set of dispositions which generates practices and perceptions." "The result of a long process of inculcation, beginning in early childhood," it is largely shaped by patterns of child rearing.[40]

Patterns of Child Rearing

I have discussed the role of socialization and identification in forming the character of an individual. However, even before a child is able to recognize individuals with certain qualities and prerogatives, and to make choices, a process of inculcating the child with the *habitus* of the primary caregiver, usually the mother, begins. As the newborn infant attempts to satisfy its most basic physical and emotional needs, the mother's instinctive response will set the pattern in the subconscious mind of how the satisfaction of these needs is to be pursued later in life. This instinctive response in turn is shaped by the caregiver's own childhood experience, and ultimately finds its origin in the conditions in which members of a group must struggle to survive and assert themselves. Thus, for instance, child-rearing practices in societies where the individual is frequently faced by physical danger encourage the development of self-initiative, self-reliance, and fighting-spirit, while highly organized societies with high population density and relative physical safety emphasize group cohesion, coordination, and submission to established rules to ensure smooth functioning. Long before these values are taught to the child verbally, they are transmitted to the infant by the mother or other primary caregiver encouraging or restricting certain activity. Inasmuch as the behavior towards the infant is instinctive and is based on the individual's own experience, child-rearing practices do not immediately respond to a change of environment but undergo much slower transformation.[41]

Keishō-in had grown up in the streets of Kyoto as the daughter of a humble greengrocer. She is likely to have been carried on her mother's back until able to fend for herself, beginning her life in close physical proximity to her mother. Once she was able to stand on her own two feet, motor activity, cognitive skills, and, above all, the ability to make herself heard and to aggressively and stubbornly pursue her aims would have been fostered in an environment where the mother was too busy to give her children much attention.

The rough-and-tumble conditions in which a shopkeeper's child had to learn to assert itself were very different from the strict hierarchical order observed by the military aristocracy. The latter still valued and practiced martial skills, but in the privileged environment of the upper classes, there were few physical dangers to contend with. Paradoxically assertiveness and aggression jeopardized rather than promoted an individual's place within the military aristocracy, for such behavior posed a threat to the fixed order. Hierarchical status and subordination to the many rules appropriate to this status were more important than initiative and ability, as the conflict between Iemitsu and his younger brother Tadanaga shows. As the story of the so-called Forty-Seven Rōnin also illustrates, in late-seventeenth-century Japan honor was no longer lost or gained on the battlefield but acquired through the correct performance of intricate ceremonies. Consequently what had to be fostered in child rearing was not daring and initiative but patient and unquestioned submission to the established order.

The strong bond between Tsunayoshi and his mother in adult life supports the evidence that Keishō-in was permitted an active role in rearing her own child. In the intimate physical and emotional contact between mother and child, the specific cultural behavioral traits of the lowest class of Tokugawa society were thus surreptitiously transmitted to the child who eventually was to rule the country. But it was not only the nurturing he experienced that set Tsunayoshi apart from his environment; his genetic inheritance also differed from that of his brothers.

A Born Devil

> A devil, a born devil, on whose nature
> Nurture can never stick.
> W. Shakespeare, *The Tempest*, IV:1:189

Unlike Shakespeare, historians have generally shown little interest in what has since come to be known as the "Nature versus Nurture debate." Behavioral scientists, however, though differing on which has greater influence, agree that nature, namely, genetic inheritance, must be distinguished from nurture, or the emotional influence of a mother or primary caregiver, and that it plays an important role in shaping behavior.[42] When, as in the case of the fifth shogun, behavior out of keeping with his class and station is a major point of criticism, such research cannot be ignored.

In Tsunayoshi two very different genetic streams came together, affecting both his physical appearance and his behavior. The genetic inheritance from his mother apparently eliminated some of the physical disabilities his father, the third shogun Iemitsu, and his older half-brothers, the fourth shogun Ietsuna and the second-born Tsunashige, were subject to. All frequently suffered from ill health, which was not the case with Tsunayoshi. The latter's greater physical robustness is also reflected in a comparison of life spans: Iemitsu died at forty-nine, Ietsuna at thirty-nine, while Tsunayoshi reached a for these times respectable sixty-three. Since he died of an infectious disease, one must assume that he would have lived longer if spared infection. Both Iemitsu and his son Ietsuna were said to have been quiet, having difficulty expressing themselves in their youth. The bone structure of Tsunayoshi's elder brother Tsunashige showed signs of severe degeneration, with a large hump deforming his body and an inadequately developed lower mandible causing his upper teeth to project inordinately.[43] In Tsunayoshi the influx of altogether different genetic material produced a child that was energetic and, as the sources state, of above average intelligence. The energetic behavior that Iemitsu found so disturbing when observing Tsunayoshi as a child, especially when compared to his elder brother, the shogun designate, was later to characterize their governments. As will be discussed in greater detail below, neither was content with the daimyo serving them as ministers. But Ietsuna preferred to keep the peace and became known as *sayō-sama* (Lord So-Be-It), while Tsunayoshi energetically set about changing the power structure.[44]

While it is difficult to measure degrees of intelligence even today, let alone hypothesize about that of historical figures, even the otherwise critical comments by the compilers of *Tokugawa jikki* suggest that Tsunayoshi's intelligence was perceived as unusually high by his contemporaries.[45] It distinguished him from his environment and gave him an uncomfortable edge over his contemporaries in matters requiring mental rather than physical input. The visitor Kaempfer too was told that Tsunayoshi was a "clever" ruler.[46]

Tsunayoshi's grave at Kaneiji has remained undisturbed, and his bone structure has not undergone examination. But the skull measurements obtained by Suzuki leave not doubt that Keishō-in showed variants from the dominant pattern of the samurai class, and these are likely to have been reflected in the physical appearance of the fifth shogun. A painting preserved at the Hase temple, Yamato, in the possession of the monk Ryūkei (1647–1717) and likely to have been painted during the shogun's lifetime, shows a man with a relatively broad face and heavy bone structure of the lower jaws.[47]

Tsunayoshi, one can conclude, stood out from his environment not only by his energetic behavior and sharp mind, but also by physical features marking him as a man with the blood of the common people in his veins. This difference between him and those of his environment was pronounced enough to draw a comment from a foreigner who briefly met Tsunayoshi before he became shogun. The director of the Dutch trading settlement at Nagasaki, Albert Brevinck, singled him out as having "a stately" face.[48]

Researchers have shown that the interaction of genes and environment can have particularly strong effects. They speak of active covariance in behavior, when a child seeks out its own niche in its environment according to its particular genetic disposition. This in turn is reinforced by reactive covariance, when others adjust their treatment of the child according to its behavior. Thus a genetic disposition can become extremely powerful in the determination of a person's character when combined with an environment consonant with that disposition.[49]

In terms of Tsunayoshi's upbringing, we see an infant predisposed to physical and mental activity who, owing to his mother's cultural values, is permitted to develop such activity beyond the norm of the greater environment. On account of this development, the father orders that the high-spirited child not be subjected to the usual discipline of military education. Rather than have his inclinations curbed by the limits and restrictions customary in the education of the sons of the high-ranking military aristocracy, Tsunayoshi apparently was permitted to create his own niche in a much less supervised environment. While an education appropriate to his station as shogunal heir would likely have reduced behavioral deviations from the norm, permitting the child to follow his own inclinations favored and enhanced those deviations. Exempted from the conventional education of his class and family, Tsunayoshi learned from an early age that the rules applying to others did not necessarily apply to him. This might well have been the basis for his remark to his grand councilor Hotta Masatoshi that he had become shogun under "unusual circumstances" and hence felt no need to observe Tokugawa precedent.[50]

A Model of Filial Piety

Tsunayoshi could have chosen to confine his close relationship with his mother to the personal sphere, but he did not. He did not consider his close bonding to his mother as unusual but publicly turned it into a virtue that others were lacking. His so-called filial piety placards, erected throughout the country two years after his accession, proclaimed deep filial conduct the desirable norm, and the population was exhorted to practice it.[51] He was not ashamed to show his respect for the woman of humble background publicly, and he moved her into the limelight by taking the unprecedented step of securing for her the highest court rank.[52]

A corollary of Tsunayoshi's respect for his mother was a sympathetic view of the lower classes of Tokugawa society and the suffering they endured. Although his life within walled compounds provided no direct knowledge of this world, some of his curiosity could be satisfied by accounts from his mother. In all likelihood he would have received a detailed and sympathetic report of what it was like to grow up on the streets of a busy city, where poverty caused some

Portrait of Keishō-in painted for her one hundredth death anniversary in 1804. Reproduced courtesy of Hasedera, Nara.

parents to abandon or kill their young children, especially their daughters. He would have been able to obtain firsthand information on the overbearing and profiteering behavior of samurai officials, the misery of horses beaten to death when too weak to transport heavy loads, or the dangers of scavenging dogs abandoned by their samurai masters.

Ironically Iemitsu's order that Tsunayoshi study the Confucian classics had inadvertently placed a premium on the knowledge his mother could provide of life at the lower end of the social scale, for the ideal Confucian rulers Yao and Shun, whom Tsunayoshi would strive to emulate, did not rule over a hierarchically ordered, feudal-type samurai society, where care for the lower orders was left to the discretion of lower officials. The emperors Yao and Shun of the Confucian classics were absolute rulers, in autocratic fashion personally taking responsibility for even the lowest of their subjects.

The conditions for the development of Tsunayoshi's character at variance with the norm of his times and class were set early in childhood by the unusual influence his mother, a commoner, was permitted to have upon him. The early death of his father ensured that the filial piety demanded by Confucian ethics was solely directed towards her. But the third shogun's sudden and premature demise also meant that as a young child Tsunayoshi officially became the lord of his own retainers and manor, and as brother of the shogun he was honored with formal respect by the adult world. As he rose to this early challenge, the groundwork for his controversial government policies was laid.

4

Lord of Tatebayashi

With the beginning of Keian 4 (1651), the third shogun Iemitsu suffered increasing bouts of illness. Less than three weeks before his death in the fourth month, Tsunayoshi and Tsunashige were enfeoffed as daimyo with domains of 150,000 *koku* each, but Iemitsu was already too ill to attend the ceremonies.[1] Perhaps feeling the approach of death, he was moved by the desire to provide for his young sons.

Tsunashige, as Tenju-in's son, had resided outside the castle from an early age, but now the five-year-old Tsunayoshi also left the castle, exchanging his quarters in the castle's third enceinte for his own residence outside the castle walls. A commissioner *(bugyō)* to supervise the construction of his mansion was officially appointed in the seventh month; by the ninth month the raising of the mansion's central pole could be celebrated. By the end of the year, the buildings were completed and the young Tsunayoshi moved in with the appropriate ceremonies.[2] Both brothers received an additional 150 retainers, described as the younger brothers and sons of *bakufu* personnel, to staff their residence in addition to some eighty who had so far made up their entourage.[3] The young shogun Ietsuna also presented them with household goods, woolen cloth, and weapons, including fifty bows and two hundred muskets each.[4] Finally that same year the brothers received secondary residences, that of Tsunayoshi being located at Koishikawa.[5] Later he would request additional lands to enlarge the residence and the gardens. It was here that his wife and concubines came to reside, and we find him frequently commuting between the two residences. Today this is the site of the Koishikawa Botanical Gardens. Between Koishikawa and the temple complex at Ueno lies the Nezu valley, where the secondary residence of his brother Tsunashige was located. When in Hōei 1 (1704) Tsunayoshi made Tsunashige's son, the later Ienobu, his successor, he had the Nezu temple constructed at the site. Today the temple annually draws large crowds with its splendid display of azaleas.

In the summer of 1653 the seven-year-old Tsunayoshi celebrated *genpuku*, the coming-of-age ceremony of the male members of the aristocracy. On that occasion his childhood name of Tsurumatsu was changed to Tsunayoshi, with the character *tsuna*, the second character of the shogun's name, being bestowed upon him. He was also granted the name and title of Matsudaira *u ma no kami* (commander of the stables of the right) and the third court rank.[6] His brother Tsunashige, though two years older, celebrated his coming-of-age ceremony at the same time. Parallel to Tsunayoshi he was made Matsudaira *sa ma no kami* (commander of the stables of the left) and was bestowed the second character of the shogun's name for his adult name of Tsunashige.[7]

These titles and ranks were to remain the same until Tsunayoshi succeeded as shogun some seventeen years later. Only his domain was to be increased in Kanbun 1 (1661) by 100,000 *koku*, bringing it to a total of 250,000 *koku*, and on this occasion he was bestowed Tatebayashi castle. Tsunashige's domain was similarly increased, and he received Kōfu castle.[8]

Two years later the shogun ordered that Tsunayoshi wed Nobuko, the daughter of the Kyoto court noble Takatsukasa Norihira and younger sister of the *kanpaku* Takatsukasa Fusasuke, with the ceremonies taking place in the summer of the next year.[9] Since she was also the elder sister of Emperor Reigen's consort Fusako, Tsunayoshi herewith became the brother-in-law of the emperor.[10] Having been officially married to a woman of noble descent, Tsunayoshi was now free to have children with concubines of lesser birth. His brother Tsunashige did not observe these rules, and when his son, the later Ienobu, was born in Kanbun 2 (1662), the child was placed in the care of and given the family name of a retainer. Only eight years later, after Tsunashige's official wife had died, was Ienobu declared his son.[11]

Tsunayoshi stuck to the rules, maybe owing to homosexual preferences, and it was only in Enpō 5 (1677) that a woman by the name of Oden, said to have been a maid of his mother, gave birth to his daughter Tsuruhime.[12] Two years later, Oden gave birth once again, this time to a son, named Tokumatsu.[13]

Family Cohesion

There is little material that permits us to reconstruct in any detail Tsunayoshi's life during this period. The record of his house, *Kanda ki* (named after its location, "record of Kanda"), which furnishes some information, was partly destroyed by fire and contains a large gap between the eleventh month of Jōō 1 (1652) and the beginning of Enpō 3 (1675).[14] But even where the record exists, it is mostly concerned with matters of ceremony and does not permit us to draw a lifelike picture of Tsunayoshi's early years. What can be pieced together from various sources, including *Sakurada ki*, the diary kept at the Sakurada mansion of the elder Tsunashige, conveys a sense of family cohesion among the three brothers as well as the wider Tokugawa clan. The two younger brothers had to observe the prescribed ceremonial attendance upon the shogun, but when, for instance, Tsunashige does not attend at the castle due to illness, we find Tsunayoshi calling on him on his return home. At times he is asked to convey messages from the older brother. Besides formal presents determined by the rules of protocol, there are those that reveal the children's sentiments, like a picture book *(ezōshi)* from the eleven-year-old shogun to his six-year-old brother.[15]

On other occasions Tsunayoshi enjoys outings with the elder Tsunashige, such as a trip on the Sumida river in the heat of summer, or sends gifts with him jointly.[16] A lapse in gift-giving on the part of Tsunashige's mansion is noted in Tsunayoshi's record, perhaps with concern.[17] As uncle, Tsunayoshi receives visits and on occasion accompanies Tsunashige's son, the future Ienobu, when his father is sick.[18] There are visits and exchange of presents with his aunt, Tsunashige's adopted mother Tenju-in, the former bride of Hideyori, until her death in Kanbun 6 (1666). Similarly there are messengers and gifts from the Three Related Houses of Owari, Kii, and Mito. Especially frequent are contacts with the house of Owari, where Tsunayoshi's older sister Chiyo is married to the head of the house, Mitsutomo. When the mansions of Tsunayoshi and Tsunashige are destroyed in the great fire of Meireki 3 (1657), the brothers find shelter with the relatives of the house of Kii.[19]

The premature death of Iemitsu placed Tsunayoshi and his brothers in the limelight at an early age. In theory the ten-year-old Ietsuna as shogun, with his two younger brothers, fully fledged daimyo at the ages of five and seven, respectively, stood at the apex of the *bakufu* hierarchy. As Tsukamoto has pointed out, owing to his high position as the shogun's brother, even the most senior daimyo, regardless of his age, had to prostrate himself before the young Tsunayoshi and pay ritual respect.[20] Yet however high Tsunayoshi's position was in terms of the *bakufu* hierarchy, there is the question of who ran his household from the time he left the castle as five-year-old and represented his interests vis-à-vis the *bakufu*.

The Caretakers

Before his death Iemitsu had assigned his younger half-brother Hoshina Masayuki as guardian to the young Ietsuna.[21] Masayuki's high position as uncle of the young shogun and daimyo of Aizu, as well as his philosophical and scholarly interests, made him well suited, and historians have portrayed him as selflessly fulfilling this task. It is true that Masayuki neither used his high position to profit materially nor usurped the authority of the young ruler. Where he failed, however, was in preserving shogunal authority for the young incumbent. After Iemitsu's death, *bakufu* policies testify to a decline of shogunal authority. For the first time in Tokugawa history, it was not men personally chosen by the ruler who were running the government, but established *fudai* (hereditary) daimyo, whose loyalty lay with their own class. The succession of the ten-year-old shogun gave them the opportunity not only to establish their authority as ministers, but also to ensure that the favorable status quo was preserved once he grew up. Laws were enacted that assured the continuity of the established houses, such as the permission of deathbed adoption to ensure an heir and the prohibition of the act of *junshi*, following one's lord into death. The confiscation and transfer of domains and other such punishments showed a marked decrease, as did the building impositions the *bakufu* had previously placed on its vassals. To the contrary, when the Meireki fire destroyed a large part of Edo castle and many daimyo mansions, the *bakufu* contributed funds to the rebuilding of daimyo mansions, while the castle's famous keep, the symbol of shogunal authority, was not reconstructed.[22]

Foremost among the daimyo who exercised authority in the name of the young shogun was Sakai Tadakiyo (1624–1681). Just over six months after Iemitsu's death, Tadakiyo took over the position of *gonaisho* from his relative Sakai Tadakatsu (1587–1662), in which he was responsible for handling the shogun's correspondence with his vassals, primarily the daimyo.[23] This was a position of trust when the shogun was an adult, but it became one of authority when he was a minor. Only two years later Tadakiyo advanced to the position of senior councilor.[24] It took another thirteen years until Tadakiyo finally progressed to grand councilor, the position at the apex of the Tokugawa bureaucracy, but from the beginning of the record of Tsunayoshi's mansion, we see Tadakiyo giving orders on behalf of the *bakufu* to the shogun's younger brothers.[25]

However highly Tsunayoshi, as the shogun's brother, ranked in matters of protocol, as a five-year-old he was dependent on those assigned to guard his interests, and these men were comparatively low-ranking in terms of the *bakufu* hierarchy.

His most senior retainer was Makino Narinori (1606–1660), formerly one of five commanders of the guard of Edo castle *(goshoin no bangashira)*.[26] In this capacity, and perhaps because he had already served the second shogun Hidetada, he had reached the lower fifth court rank, but his fief was a mere 500 *koku*. Only on being assigned to the household of the two-year-old Tsunayoshi was his fief increased tenfold to 5,000 *koku*.[27]

Second in charge was Muroka Masatoshi (1609–1680), also a commander of the guard *(ko jū nin gashira)*, whose stipend was increased to 3,000 *koku* on being appointed as Tsunayoshi's retainer.[28]

The third of Tsunayoshi's triumvirate of senior retainers was Keishō-in's stepbrother, Honjō Michika (1604–1668).[29] His stipend amounted only to 1,000 bales *(hyō)* of rice.[30] He had arrived from Kyoto only in the year of his appointment to Tsunayoshi's staff, and he consequently had no experience in the workings of the *bakufu*. The relatively lowly position of these three men in the *bakufu* hierarchy makes it unlikely that they would have been effective in representing the interests of the minor in their charge vis-à-vis a power broker like Sakai

Tadakiyo. The work of Fukai Masaumi has shown, moreover, that the men who were appointed as Tsunayoshi's retainers before he became lord of Tatebayashi castle in Kanbun 1 (1661) were still considered *bakufu* officials. Only those who joined him after that event had a status comparable to that of the retainers of the Three Related Houses.[31] Although Tsunayoshi was in theory a daimyo, in practice his household was much more under the control of the *bakufu* than those of other daimyo.

Upon becoming shogun in Enpō 8 (1680), one of Tsunayoshi's first actions was to retire the powerful so-called *geba shōgun*, as Sakai Tadakiyo had become known. Since his mansion stood at the entrance of the gate to the inner castle, where a sign instructed visitors to dismount *(geba)* and proceed on foot to the castle, this name evolved, insinuating that he was the real ruler. Most likely Tsunayoshi's hostility to Tadakiyo began in these early years when the latter could impose his will upon the shogunal brothers regardless of their formally high status. The sources, however, supply no evidence of such personal sentiments, except an occasional complaint that the senior councilors requested Tsunayoshi's attendance at the castle even though the weather was bad.[32]

Again, the sources do not tell us how much Tsunayoshi was restricted in his movements. Curiously enough we see him making only one pilgrimage to the sanctuary of his grandfather Ieyasu at Nikkō, though his filial piety and respect for the spirits of his ancestors is otherwise amply documented. This short trip is also the only occasion on which he visits his castle at Tatebayashi.[33] Could it be that apart from this one trip permission to leave Edo was not forthcoming, with the specter of his uncle Tadanaga and his stronghold at Suruga still in the minds of those in power?

As shogun Tsunayoshi became infamous for his authoritative behavior and the strict punishment of his retainers. Perhaps dissatisfaction with what his relatively low-ranking senior retainers could achieve on his behalf vis-à-vis the authority of senior *bakufu* officials acted as an incentive to devise and develop leadership strategies at an early age. He certainly showed a tendency to be, in the eyes of his contemporaries, "over-scrupulous in conducting investigations"[34] even before his appointment as shogun.

Overscrupulous Investigations

At Kinkatsu temple at Shibuya in Tokyo, there is a gravestone of a woman by the name of Gyokushin-in. The inscription says: "She became the wife of the right-hand man and received the favors of his august lord."

Gyokushin-in is believed to have been the Buddhist name of the wife of Tsunayoshi's grand chamberlain Makino Narisada (1634–1712), and the inscription is interpreted to mean that she was the mistress of the shogun. It is also said that Narisada's daughter became Tsunayoshi's mistress.³⁵ These stories are based on *Sannō gaiki* and similar defamatory writings that circulated soon after Tsunayoshi's death, seeking to explain why the shogun placed his greatest trust in men of relatively lowly samurai origin, while many of much higher birth fell serving him.³⁶ The fact, however, is that Makino Narisada came to occupy this position because his elder brother had become the victim of one of the investigations for which Tsunayoshi would become infamous as shogun.

When Makino Narinori, who had been assigned by the third shogun Iemitsu to be one of Tsunayoshi's senior retainers *(karō)* at an early date, died in Manji 3 (1660), his oldest surviving son, Narinaga, succeeded to the position, as was customary. Eleven years later he was demoted and his lands were confiscated for reasons much resembling those that later, when Tsunayoshi was shogun, would cost many a senior vassal his domain. These were, in the first place, mismanagement of his lands and inflicting hardship upon his peasants. Secondary reasons were not assisting with manpower and horses as requested, a disharmonious relationship with his relatives, and generally a bad attitude.³⁷ The younger brother, Narisada, to the contrary, gained a reputation for not being "ambitious, revengeful, unjust or selfish" and consequently managed to serve Tsunayoshi to his satisfaction.³⁸

Makino Narinaga had grown up in Tsunayoshi's entourage, and his dismissal appears not to have raised concerns on the part of the *bakufu*. However, when Tsunayoshi some years later dismissed another senior retainer who had only seven years previously been assigned to him by the *bakufu*, a man who had served successfully under the second and third shoguns, there was opposition.

Ōkubo Masatomo Izumi no Kami, whose dates are unknown, had his first audience with the second shogun Hidetada in Genna 5 (1619), fulfilled guard duties in the shogun's personal entourage, and accompanied the third shogun Iemitsu on a journey to Ieyasu's mausoleum at Nikkō in Kanei 9 (1632).³⁹ In Kanbun 1 (1661), when he was most probably in his late fifties, he was appointed as senior retainer to Tsunayoshi's entourage, and three years later he had the honor of travelling to Kyoto in the matter of Tsunayoshi's marriage. Fourteen years afterwards, however, in the ninth month of Enpō 6 (1678), Tsunayoshi dismissed him on the charge of inappropriate behavior and lack of discretion. The dismissal of this senior man of long-standing service, selected to assist Tsunayoshi, was apparently unacceptable to the *bakufu*, and it took various discussions with senior government ministers until it was officially confirmed in the tenth month.⁴⁰

It was on this occasion that Ogyū Sorai's father, the physician Ogyū Hōan, was sent away into exile because he had been close to Ōkubo Masatomo. As the record of his mansion states, Tsunayoshi was uncomfortable having someone serve him in the intimate position of physician who was a friend of a punished man.[41] This act of precaution well conveys the spirit of the times, where revenge and revolt were more frequent than our records spell out.[42] But the incident also sheds light on the limits of Tsunayoshi's authority to handle the affairs of his house as he pleased as well as his unwillingness to observe these limits.

Resistance to established rules of a much more foreboding nature had, however, become apparent earlier. In the year Tsunayoshi decided to assert his authority by dismissing the eldest son of his late senior retainer Makino Narinori, he also took the bold step of discontinuing the traditional samurai sport of hawking. From then on there is no further record of him complying with the ritual of offering the shogun the first kill of the chase.

The Importance of Ceremony

The importance of established ritual behavior in the Tokugawa world order is attested to by the fact that the greater part of our main source of the workings of the *bakufu*, *Tokugawa jikki*, consists overwhelmingly of lists and details of ceremonies performed. Care is taken to note who performed which role, what presents were exchanged, and what food was offered at formal entertainment. The manuscript on which *Tokugawa jikki* is mostly based, the as yet unpublished *Ryūei hinami nikki* or *Edo bakufu nikki*, the daily record of the *bakufu*, contains an even more detailed description of such matters. So does the record of Tsunayoshi's house before he became shogun, *Kanda ki*, and that of his brother Tsunashige, *Sakurada ki*. Details include who was wearing what ceremonial dress and who was welcomed by whom at what location of the house, matters that were obviously considered significant. Visits and presents were a matter of ritual, and a messenger had to be dispatched to offer thanks, and then the call by this messenger in turn had to be acknowledged, so that life consisted of an endless stream of ceremonial events. It was a point of honor that these were executed correctly, and for this purpose manuals with drawings and charts were composed and personal records kept, where, for example, how to receive sweet cakes at court was a major item to be studied.[43] It is no accident that one of the most famous stories of the Tokugawa period, the revenge of the Forty-Seven Rōnin, began with a daimyo's frustration about insufficient instructions on difficult-to-remember ceremonies he was expected to perform. Yet these ceremonies cannot be termed useless or empty, for they played an important role in *bakufu* dominance.

The Tokugawa had established their hegemony on the battlefield but maintained it for some two and a half centuries by force of the law. As the French philosopher Michel Foucault argues, war does not exhaust itself in its own contradictions and does not end "by renouncing violence and submitting to civil laws." He explains: "On the contrary, the law is the calculated pleasure of relentlessness. It is the promised blood, which permits the perpetual instigation of new dominations and the staging of meticulously repeated scenes of violence."[44] The elaborate rituals the *bakufu* upheld were such "meticulously repeated scenes of violence," continually confirming each individual's place in the hierarchical order of submission.

"Humanity installs each of its violences in a system of rules," Foucault maintains and continues: "The successes of history belong to those who are capable of seizing these rules, to replace those who had used them, to disguise themselves so as to pervert them, invert their meaning, and redirect them against those who had initially imposed them; introducing themselves into this complex mechanism, they will make it function in such a way that the dominators find themselves dominated by their own rules."[45]

The universal validity of Foucault's words is attested to by the fact that they not only describe political developments in Europe—his primary concern—but also those in Japan. Already Hideyoshi had "seized" the rules of the imperial house and, "disguised" as *kanpaku* (senior regent to the emperor), attempted to clad the band of country warriors that had submitted to him with the mantle of respectability by seeking court ranks for them from the emperor. Thus he "perverted" the system, whose proper function was to distinguish the Kyoto nobility from upstarts such as himself, and inverted its meaning. By this process Hideyoshi not only elevated those who served him, but also bound them in their conduct to the rules of a hierarchical order of which he had usurped the top position. Ieyasu in turn showed himself "capable of seizing these rules." He continued the practice of turning country warriors into nobility by awarding court titles and, moreover, he permitted them to adopt names akin to those of the nobility that indicated an illustrious, albeit mostly fictional, ancestry.[46] He introduced himself "into this complex mechanism" by claiming descent from the imperial Seiwa Genji clan, a claim that provided him with some legitimacy to rule the country.[47] As a result the Kyoto aristocracy, who had established the system of imperial rule based on an elaborate structure of court ranks as "the dominators," found themselves "dominated by their own rules."

The court noble Konoe Sakihisa (1536-1612), a witness to these events, described in a letter to his son of Keichō 7 (1602) the difficulties Ieyasu had originally encountered in even obtaining the title of Mikawa no Kami, lacking, as he was, suitable pedigree. He then lamented that "in these days people with no lineage are all turned into nobility by those in power."[48]

Since the illegality of Ieyasu "seizing the rules" was so well recognized— some nine decades later he was still described as a usurper to the visiting Engelbert Kaempfer[49]—the laws, ordinances and rites that reenacted and perpetuated submission were of utmost importance. Even as military preparations were under way for the final defeat of Toyotomi Hideyori with the battle at Osaka castle, Ieyasu's adviser and scribe, the monk Sūden (1569-1633), supervised the drafting of formal legislation to prescribe the conduct of the military and the court. The so-called *Regulations for the Military Houses* and *Regulations for the Court* were proclaimed just two months after the fall of Osaka castle, in the seventh month of Genna 1 (1615).[50]

Foucault noted that the "relationship of domination . . . is fixed, throughout its history, in rituals, in meticulous procedures that impose rights and obligations." These engrave "memories on things and even within bodies."[51] Ieyasu, apparently, was well aware of this fact. Soon after his decisive victory at Sekigahara, he began to seek out men with expertise in ceremonies of the Ashikaga shogunate, such as Hosokawa Yūsai (1534-1610), and ordered his trusted vassal Nagai Naokatsu (1563-1625) to design Tokugawa ritual by studying that of the Ashikaga rulers and their Muromachi *bakufu*. Naokatsu did this, further enlisting the help of Soga Naosuke (1558-1626), who similarly had served the shogun Ashikaga Yoshiaki. Later Naosuke was in the employ of the second shogun Hidetada. Both Yūsai and Naosuke wrote several books on ritual for the *bakufu*. They also ensured that Ieyasu's proclamation as shogun in Keichō 8 (1603) and that of his son two years later took place with the appropriate solemnity and pomp.[52]

Ieyasu considered matters of ceremony so important that, just months before his death, he was occupying himself with its details. Already in Keichō 14 (1609) he had instituted the attendance of his daimyo at elaborate New Year celebrations, with various changes being decreed over the following years. On the eve of his last New Year celebration, he was still concerned with the dress code to be observed by the daimyo on this occasion and issued his personal instructions.[53] Ieyasu's successors showed no less concern in this respect. *Bakufu* ritual continued to be elaborated and refined, and new rituals were instituted as new laws, such as those regulating compulsory alternate attendance at Edo *(sankin kōtai)* were proclaimed.[54]

With Ieyasu's death, a body of elaborate death rituals was added. If he had demanded ceremonial respect as ruler, then he required even more as the Great Avatar *(daigongen)* he became. Ieyasu might well have made plans for his own deification, and his successors might well have furthered them for political reasons.[55] Yet, as Cassirer observes, the denial of the reality of death is an integral part of all religions, as is the belief that the deceased continue to exercise their authority and protection.[56] In Tokugawa Japan not only did the spirit of the powerful Ieyasu require worship by his descendants, but also those of other ancestors, including women.[57] With the unavoidable increase in the number of Tokugawa worthies came an increase in the number of ceremonies to be observed.

This ritual punctuated the rhythm of Tsunayoshi's life and household.[58] *Tokugawa jikki* notes that Tsunayoshi assiduously observed the many abstentions and taboos required in religious ceremonies and the reception of imperial messengers.[59] Yet apparently when it came to lesser mortals, Tsunayoshi was less fastidious, as the Dutch record testifies.

The resident director of the Dutch trading settlement at Nagasaki had to travel annually to Edo to pay his respects in a short formal audience and to present his gifts much as the daimyo were required to do. Two of these directors had the experience of suddenly and unceremoniously being inspected by Tsunayoshi while waiting for their formal audience at Edo castle. The first of these incidents is recorded by Daniel Six in 1669 and the second by Albert Brevinck early in 1680, before Tsunayoshi succeeded as shogun later in the year. Brevinck described how all of a sudden there was loud shouting with attendants fleeing the room. Without further warning Tsunayoshi appeared, placed himself in front of the foreigners, and, regarding them intently, asked their names and ages, disappearing as unceremoniously as he had come.[60]

There was no place in Japanese records for such inordinate behavior, and we have no way of assessing whether Tsunayoshi championed such conduct on other occasions and once he became shogun. Similarly the sources do not call attention to the fact that, in Kanbun 11 (1671), the twenty-five-year-old Tsunayoshi boldly discontinued the hallowed tradition of hawking and presenting the shogun with the first kill of the chase. As the scholar Nesaki Mitsuo has pointed out, after that date there is simply no further record of Tsunayoshi hawking or offering the prey of his hawks to the shogun.[61]

The Sport of Falconry

As in the West, in Japan falconry had been "the sport of kings," the privilege of the rulers. Utensils for falconry are found in Japanese tombs from the fifth century on, and *Nihon shoki* claims that Emperor Nintoku (313?–399) enjoyed this sport. It demonstrated the ruler's claim to ownership over the beasts of the land and displayed his authority over those who ferociously killed in his name and submissively laid the booty at his feet.[62] In Keichō 17 (1612), however, Ieyasu forbade the Kyoto aristocracy to hawk and commanded them to turn their minds to the traditional learning of their houses—mostly of artistic and philosophical nature—instead.[63] From then on it was the privilege of the Tokugawa shogun to grant permission for the keeping and breeding of hawks, and the use of them for hunting.[64] The ritual of the shogun presenting the emperor with the first booty of the chase, such as cranes, ducks, and other fowl, was preserved in line with other ritual vestiges of imperial authority. But those granted the right to hawk by the shogun were now obliged to present him with the first animals they killed.

There was in these actions deep symbolic significance, as the first hunt and harvest was traditionally offered to the gods. These gifts to the shogun were therefore interpreted as ritual confirmation of his absolute power over the daimyo.[65] This tradition was so significant that, as discussed later, even Tsunayoshi could not afford to refuse enactment of this ritual submission to the emperor, and on becoming shogun he continued the practice of offering the fowl even though hunting was largely abolished.

Hawking played an import part in the lives of the shogun and the daimyo. The third shogun Iemitsu, especially, was a keen falconer, hunting on the outskirts of Edo, for example, at Shinagawa, Takada, Azabu, and Meguro.[66] The raising, training, and feeding of hawks became the preserve of a body of experts on ranked *bakufu* appointments. With their warlike occupation of teaching fledgling hawks to chase prey as well as daily slaughtering dogs and birds to provide nourishment for their charges, they themselves were not infrequently involved in brawls.

Konrad Lorenz argues that aggression and cruelty are an essential element of the primitive human psyche and are rationalized as acts justified by a higher purpose or cause as societies become "civilized" and come to frown on the use of brutal force.[67] This might explain why blood sports could be eulogized by Europe's very Christian nobility; it was proverbial in Tudor England that "he cannot be a gentleman which loveth not hawking and hunting."[68] Just as man's barbaric instincts were masked as noble in Christian Europe, so they were in Buddhist Tokugawa Japan. The kill of the chase provided at least the privileged samurai with a surrogate for the cruelty of battles no longer fought. For Tudor England we have on record a few timid voices from the clergy pointing out to their patrons the contradictions between Christian worship and the delight in senseless killing.[69] In Tokugawa Japan it was the young Tsunayoshi, a member of the military nobility, who dared to make the point by calling to a halt these very un-Buddhist practices that had become ritualized and were conducted in his name.

When the ten-year-old Ietsuna succeeded to the position of shogun, he and his brothers were too young to carry out the physically taxing sport of hawking. The presentation of fowl caught by the shogunal hawks to the imperial house, however, continued, as did the exchange of hawks as formal gifts between the shogun and his young brothers. In Jōō 1 (1652) six-year-old Tsunayoshi and eight-year-old Tsunashige were both presented with a hawk by their eleven-year-old brother, the shogun.[70] From then on cranes, wild geese, ducks, skylarks, and other birds would regularly be presented to the shogun in Tsunayoshi's name. Moreover, between Meireki 2 (1656) and Kanbun 3 (1663), fledgling hawks were annually presented to the shogun in Tsunayoshi's name. When the shogun awarded an increase in domain lands to his now teenage brothers in Kanbun 1 (1661), he also granted them permission to establish hawking grounds in their domains. The establishment of an additional hawking ground was granted to the elder Tsunashige in Kanbun 3 (1663) and to Tsunayoshi in Kanbun 4 (1664).[71] In view of the purely ritual presentation of birds when Tsunayoshi was too young to hunt himself, there remains the question of whether he ever practiced the sport, even though until Kanbun 11 (1671) *Tokugawa jikki* has entries of him and his brother receiving permission to set out to hawk and presenting the fowl on return.[72] By the time of the accession of the fourth shogun, hawking had become institutionalized and ritualized to the point where the physical act of hawking was deemed no longer necessary to support the ceremonial. One must conclude that those men in the *bakufu* administration who decided that the empty ritual must continue had a stake in it. Indeed, scholars have noticed that *bakufu* ritual increased rather than decreased during the government of the fourth shogun, when the authority of the shogun was exercised by his ministers. The latter had a vested interest in maintaining what the French sociologist Pierre Bourdieu has termed "the field of cultural production."

Destroying the Field of Cultural Production

Law and ritual have been discussed above as "promised blood" permitting "the perpetual instigation of new dominations." There is, however, another side to this process. Laws and rituals also serve to distinguish and elevate certain members of a community and thus make their continuance desirable not only for the "dominator" but also for the "dominated" benefiting in this process.[73] In our case, the shogun's restrictions on hawking made it possible to distinguish and honor a select group of people, namely, those whom the shogun granted permission to hawk. The abolition of hawking robbed the beneficiaries not only of their ability to enjoy the sport of hawking, but also of the distinction and social elevation accompanying the grant. To elucidate the significance perceived by contemporaries in Tsunayoshi's early refusal to conform to the ritual established by his ancestors, aspects of Bourdieu's theory of the field of cultural production, based on a number of concepts in the writings of Max Weber, are useful.

Weber's separate discussions of "status privileges," the monopolization of "ideal goods," and his nascent concept of *Kulturgüter* (translated as "culture goods")[74] have been combined and developed by Bourdieu to explain the process by which goods—mainly artistic works such as paintings, sculpture, or pieces of literature—attain value far beyond the cost of the material and labor involved in their production. Weber's social *Umwelt* (environment) becomes Bourdieu's "field," where the artists sharing the field, the "actors," compete for positions *(prise de position)* akin to Weber's quest for *ständische Ehre* (status honor) within a certain social environment.[75]

While in Bourdieu's case the "cultural goods" are produced by a variety of competing artists, in our case they are produced by a single agency: the shogun or his representatives. Moreover, what I would like to designate here as "social goods" are "ideal," abstract goods, like Weber's "status honor," rather than the artistic goods Bourdieu refers to. But the idea that these goods are "produced" for a purpose, that their value is dependent on the mind-set or value system of a social group, and that the maintenance of their value is of interest to all sharing the field are useful concepts to explain the impact of Tsunayoshi's actions.

Ieyasu, by establishing a large body of laws restricting the conduct of his vassals and ceremonies requiring their participation, produced a large pool of "cultural goods." These ranged from the permission to enter and prostrate in his presence, carrying his sword during a procession, or representing him at lengthy ceremonials for the dead, to the above-discussed permission to hawk with the obligation to offer the first prey. Though these goods cost the shogun nothing, they were cherished and competed for by his vassals for the honorific distinctions they conferred. The promise of the disbursement of such goods was part of the compensation the daimyo received upon submitting to the Tokugawa hegemony, when they exchanged their status as independent lords for their subordination to a larger political unit. As indications of their lofty status, these symbolic goods conferring ritual preeminence increased in importance relative to the decline of the daimyo's material goods and financial preeminence. Especially after the Edo Meireki fire caused great material loss and even the greatest of them came to live on borrowed money, such symbolic goods were important in confirming the daimyo's lofty status. It was in such an environment that Tsunayoshi dealt a blow to the value system of these symbolic goods by his refusal to consider the permission to hawk an honor and by refusing to play his part in the established ritual. It was a public rejection of the world of his father in favor of the values of his mother, an ardent Buddhist.

It would have been clear to contemporaries that there was more at stake here than the pleasures of hawking. Tsunayoshi's disregard for privileges established by his ancestors and his authoritarian behavior towards his retainers, combined with a value system not shared by the present powerholders, augured ill for the eventuality that one day he might outlive his sickly brothers and be a candidate for the position of shogun.

Whether they had been designed to stop Tsunayoshi from threatening the established order by exposing him to his mother's influence or simply neglected his education to the point of permitting this to happen, the arrangements for his upbringing were showing disastrous consequences. The strategy to direct Tsunayoshi's energies towards Confucian book learning rather than the military arts produced similar unwelcome results.

5

Confucian Governance

"Ieyasu had conquered the nation on horseback, but being an enlightened and wise man, realized early that the land could not be governed from a horse. He had always respected and believed in the way of the sages. He wisely decided that in order to govern the land and follow the path proper to man, he must pursue the path of learning. Therefore, from the beginning he encouraged learning."[1] These often-cited words from the first volume of *Tokugawa jikki* have traditionally been interpreted to mean that the Tokugawa regime sponsored Confucianism from its inception. This raises the question of why the fifth shogun's support of Confucianism was deemed unusual and much criticized. The explanation is generally that it was dilettante, insincere, and ardent to the point of madness. This contention, however, rests on a rather shaky interpretation of the sources, as will be argued in detail later.

Ieyasu and Confucianism

Ieyasu's declaration that the empire could not be ruled from the back of a horse was a well-known Chinese saying and suggests that the authors of *Tokugawa jikki* were more intent on providing an ideologically potent image than on relating historical facts. In the Chinese classics the saying is attributed to a scholar counseling Genghis Khan, who in turn is citing an official admonishing Emperor Kao-tsu (r. 202–195 BC), founder of the Han dynasty.[2] Ieyasu is portrayed as superior to these two powerful rulers inasmuch as he hit upon this point himself.

In the last two decades a number of scholars, most notably Watanabe Hiroshi and Hori Isao in Japanese and Herman Ooms in English, have shown in some detail that Confucianism did not play the role in early Tokugawa Japan traditionally assigned to it. It could even be argued that Confucian studies were more widespread before their separation from and opposition to Buddhism, when Confucianism enjoyed the institutional support of the Buddhist monastic system, than during the early Tokugawa period, when comparable support was lacking. The German scholar Engelbert Kaempfer likened the study of Confucianism before the Tokugawa period to that of the Greek and Roman philosophical texts in the monasteries of Europe.[3]

By the end of the sixteenth century, dissatisfaction with their Buddhist environment and the encounter with Korean Confucians after Hideyoshi's campaigns in that country persuaded some monks to leave their monasteries, renouncing Buddhism, and to style themselves independent Confucian scholars. The most famous of these was Fujiwara Seika (1561–1619), often referred to as the father of Tokugawa Confucianism. Seika was summoned by Ieyasu as early as Bunroku 2 (1593) to be probed, much like Hayashi Razan later, on a Chinese emperor who had overthrown his erstwhile lord to establish his own dynasty.[4] But Seika subsequently insisted on appearing before Ieyasu in *shin'i dōfuku*, the traditional garment of the Confucian scholar, and Ieyasu employed his student Hayashi Razan, who agreed to shave his head in Buddhist fashion, wear Buddhist robes, and adopt the Buddhist name of Dōshun. Later, in Kanei 6 (1629), the title *hō-in*, used for high-ranking Buddhist priests, was bestowed on him and his brother.[5] Contemporaries sympathetic to Confucianism, like Ieyasu's son Yoshinao, thought this regrettable, lamenting that scholars such as Razan who dressed like monks could hardly be called Confucians.[6]

Ieyasu was unwilling to accord Confucians the independence from Buddhism they were now championing. He was interested in the Confucian classics to justify his own conduct and the establishment of his regime. Razan's expertise in classical Chinese was also usefully employed in the translation and exposition of Chinese military and medical texts and other clerical and administrative duties.[7] Literary education was accorded some importance, and as early as Keichō 6 (1601), Ieyasu established a school at Fushimi. But it was a temple school, where the Confucian classics were studied under the supervision of monks.[8] Razan's request in Keichō 19 (1614) to open a Confucian school in Kyoto with Fujiwara Seika as instructor came to nothing.[9] It was not until Kansei 5 (1793) that the government finally decided to repair and restore to some importance the Ashikaga academy in Kyoto.[10] Ieyasu patronized the collection, copying, printing, and distribution of books, but again those dealing with Confucianism were in the minority. None treated Neo-Confucianism, the philosophical system Ieyasu is supposed to have made the basis of his government.[11] Ieyasu's meetings with Seika and Razan have been much made of by the Hayashi house, but Ieyasu had many more meetings with Buddhist monks.[12] As Hori Isao has pointed out, Ieyasu was a convinced Buddhist and felt no sympathies for a Confucianism that did not respect the religious teachings of Buddhism as superior.[13]

Japan's own history as well as the examples of China and Korea provided Ieyasu with models he could have followed had he wanted to promote Confucianism. But Ieyasu established no Confucian schools or Confucian public service examinations, nor did he delegate important administrative functions to Confucian scholars. These matters, such as the drafting of diplomatic correspondence and of laws, like the three ordinances *(shohatto)* for the military (buke), the nobles (kuge), and the temples and shrines (jiin), were entrusted to the monks Sūden and Tenkai (1536-1643).[14] As for Razan, the early-nineteenth-century work *Sentetsu sōdan* (Collected tales of sagacious precursors) by the Confucian scholar Hara Nensai (1774-1820) claims that "all important government documents passed through his hands."[15] This claim could also be made for the filing clerk.

Sūden proclaimed: "Again Confucius said: to give oneself completely to one's parents and to do no injury is the first principle of filial piety. But in order to perfect oneself one must venerate the gods."[16] Like their predecessors who advised the Ashikaga shogunate, the monks in Ieyasu's employ were well versed in the Confucian classics and respected them as the only available texts that provided pertinent information on statecraft. If the concepts of filial piety and subordination were required to strengthen social structures and justify the authority of the state, then Sūden knew which part of the Chinese classics to cite. The reason the orders of the early *bakufu* show a Confucian or Legalist flavor is not that there were influential Confucians in the *bakufu*'s employ, but that the powerful Buddhist clergy was familiar with the traditional works of Chinese scholarship and made eclectic use of those elements that were politically expedient. There was nothing new about this. Already Takeda Shingen (1521-1573) had cited the Confucian classics in his house rules to lend greater authority to his commands.[17]

No Tokugawa ruler saw the need to change the status quo of Confucianism's subordination to Buddhism. To the contrary, the government made the conscious choice of making Buddhism its "state religion." It would have been foolish not to. Buddhism was not only the native religion of the warrior class and the greater part of the country, it was also the only system that could provide the Tokugawa hegemony with the kind of ideological and administrative support Shinto afforded to the imperial institution. This is most apparent in two government policies: the veneration of past rulers as Buddhist avatars and the proclamation of the so-called Laws for the Examination of Sects (*shūmon aratame no jō*) that tied every citizen to a Buddhist temple.

Confucianism provides ample ritual for ancestor worship. Yet in practical political as well as personal emotional terms, this was not a useful alternative for the Tokugawa hegemony. Confucianism was the preserve of an intellectual elite. Neither the military aristocracy nor the population at large had knowledge of or attachment to its philosophy and practices beyond such matters as using the *Book of Changes* in an oracle-like fashion. Ancestor worship in Confucian terms would have had to be accompanied by a broad educational campaign. Buddhism, in contrast, offered itself, in modern terms, as a well-established expert, a public relations operator with a countrywide network of offices and an excellent success rate. As a seasoned politician Ieyasu could not possibly overlook the advantages of leaving the establishment of a new cult in the experienced hands of the Tendai monk Tenkai rather than some individual with no infrastructure to back him. Tenkai took care of Ieyasu's first burial on mount Kunō in Sunpu, the subsequent building of the mausoleum at Nikkō, and the mortuary temple complex at Ueno with Kaneiji at its center. Scholars estimate that the construction of Ieyasu's mausoleum at Nikkō alone consumed one-seventh of Iemitsu's treasury. A comparison with the small plot of land Hayashi Razan was eventually given in Edo to establish a school, without government funds for the buildings, can leave no doubt about what the *bakufu* was sponsoring.[18]

The Laws for the Examination of Sects

The government's use of the countrywide network of Buddhist temples and, at the same time, total neglect of Confucianism as an independent discipline is well demonstrated by the so-called Laws for the Examination of Sects first promulgated in Keichō 8 (1613). The main purpose of the laws was to stamp out Christianity, but they were also directed against rebellious Buddhist sects such as the *fuju fuse* (no giving, no receiving) sect that refused contact with mainstream Buddhism. The eighteen articles detailed mandatory worship at Buddhist temples to prove adherence to mainstream Buddhism. The regulations included being registered at a temple, supporting this temple financially, attending Buddhist festivals, and receiving Buddhist rites, especially on death. Anyone not complying with these regulations, the law stated, was considered suspect and had to be investigated.[19] Beyond enforcing religious orthodoxy, the laws provided the government with a countrywide free census and policing system.[20]

Although the correctness of the figures are doubted by some historians, thousands of students are said to have studied at the Confucian schools of Itō Jinsai and Yamazaki Ansai in Kyoto. Yet the *Kyōto aratame*, the official record of the capital's population compiled in accordance with the Laws for the Examination of Sects, even at the time of the fifth shogun, does not list a single Confucian.[21] All, including the most prominent Confucian teacher and his disciples, had to register at and patronize a Buddhist temple.

The law was not directed against Confucianism; it simply made no allowance for the new breed of Confucian scholars that detested Buddhism. The vehemence with which these laws were resented and considered oppressive by them is documented in the writings of the Confucian scholar Arai Hakuseki (1657–1725). Hakuseki was careful not to express his criticism of the government's laws publicly. But he airs his frustration in a private communication known as *Honsaroku kō* (Observations on The record of Honsa)—since it was in reply to questions concerning a work known as *Honsaroku*—written in Kyōhō 12 (1727) towards the end of his life, when he had little to lose.[22]

He first discusses "the evil" of Christianity, attributing the religion's success in Japan to its novelty. "Christianity is, like Buddhism, based on Western customs, and people everywhere are generally attracted to new things," he argued, and he explained how Buddhists and Christians began to fight over which teaching was correct. Yet, while there was no question that Christianity was evil, as a Confucian he was also unable to accept the Buddhist rites and beliefs the government was enforcing. He states emphatically:

> Yet from the point of view of our Way, what the Buddhists claim to be right cannot be right for us. Still, it was decided to ban Christianity on account of what the Dutch alleged in an effort to improve their trade. Since at that time there was no other teaching that could be relied on, it was rather like the ancient strategy of using the barbarians to expel the barbarians. From that time it became the official law of the land that in all the sixty provinces everyone from infancy on had to be a follower of Buddhism. If at this time someone desires, for example, to practice our Confucian Way, he violates the country's official prohibition and he is obliged to worship the Buddha.[23]

With Confucians forced to follow much despised Buddhist practices to stay within the law, it was impossible to live the life of a "gentleman of honor" or "attain the utmost truthfulness of the sage," Hakuseki laments. He believes that more than 250,000 Christians were killed during the persecution but points out that for Confucians as well it was the beginning "of the great suffering and ordeal of not being able to live in our country in accordance with the writings and laws of the ancient sages."

On various occasions Hakuseki was extremely critical of the policies of the fifth shogun. Yet, in his discussion of Confucianism, he admits that there was some merit in his government:

> I am reluctant to speak about such matters, but between ourselves I believe that the government of the fifth shogun benefited our Way. From the time of his government the teaching known as Confucianism was officially established and even the lower classes in the neighboring provinces came to know of it. Under the previous shoguns even superior persons mistook those who spoke about Confucianism for followers of Christianity. This was the situation when I first began to study. Such explanations were perhaps part of a plan by the Buddhists, who, having gained the upper hand, wanted to get rid of us Confucians as well. But my greatest doubt for a long time was that a teaching such as our Confucianism could resemble Christianity, and when under the previous shogun I was ordered to meet a man from the West, I inquired about this matter and my doubts were cleared up.[24]

This document has been cited at length because it is frequently ignored by historians or dismissed as hyperbole, for it does not fit with the assertion that Confucianism was the official ideology of the *bakufu*. Nor does it support the portrayal of the Hayashi family and Arai Hakuseki, the Confucian scholar employed by the sixth shogun Ienobu, as government officials influential enough to effect change in any government policy they detested. It indicates that so little was known about Confucianism before the government of the fifth shogun that even Hakuseki, who styled himself a Confucian scholar, took pains to convince himself of the difference between Confucianism and Christianity.

The Laws for the Examination of Sects were not repealed under the fifth shogun, who considered both Buddhism and Confucianism essential, like the two wheels of a cart, and himself practiced both. Scholars like Hakuseki, for whom the association with Buddhism was unacceptable, did not dare to criticize *bakufu* policy openly. Hence it is not surprising that corroborating evidence comes mainly from a foreigner who was not subject to such constraints in his writing.

According to Engelbert Kaempfer, Confucians became suspect because they were seen harboring sympathies for Christianity. These, he explains, arose from similarities between the Confucian ethical code and the Ten Commandments. He continues: "According to the new laws, which came into effect with the banishment of the Christians, they must, against their will, keep in their houses the image of a god or mount, or paste up, the characters of a name of a god, with a pot of flowers and an incense burner placed in front of it." After describing how Confucians usually had a picture of Kannon or Amida in their houses to satisfy the authorities, he writes of Confucianism: "In the past this now-suspicious sect comprised the greater part of the population and practically held a monopoly on the sciences and liberal arts. But after the martyrdom of the Christians, their numbers decreased yearly and their books were brought into disrepute, even though those books had been valued by all other believers no less than we do the instructive works of Seneca, Plato, and other heathens."[25]

Kaempfer wrote that he had discussed the subject of Confucianism with a number of different people. This is likely, for the Japanese doctors who came to consult him on medicine were known as *jui* (Confucian and doctor) to indicate their expertise in both subjects.[26] Scholars Kaempfer instructed in astronomy and mathematics were also Confucians.[27] His own student in medicine, who later excelled as an interpreter, Kaempfer described as "learned in Japanese and Chinese writing and scholarship."[28] Similarly other interpreters attending upon the Dutch, like Motoki Ryōi,[29] were well grounded in the Confucian classics and often scholars in their own right.

Kaempfer's report consequently can be deemed to reflect the feelings of Confucian scholars of the period, Hakuseki's contemporaries. Today many might term the statement that in previous ages adherents of Confucianism "comprised the greater part of the population and practically had a monopoly on the sciences and liberal arts" a gross exaggeration, but similar sentiments were expressed elsewhere. Honda Masanobu (1538-1616) in his *Honsaroku*, for instance, maintained that Japan had been ruled according to Confucian precepts for some two thousand years.[30] The decline started, according to both Kaempfer and Hakuseki, with the Laws for the Examination of Sects, which Hakuseki regards as a Buddhist plot. As the laws were the work of the monk Sūden, Hakuseki might not have been far off the mark. Neither of them mentions, however, that the Buddhists had reasons to be on the defensive.

The early independent Confucian scholars, including Fujiwara Seika, Hayashi Razan, Hori Kyōan (1585-1642), Yamaga Sokō, and Yamazaki Ansai (1618-1682), were apostate Buddhist monks. They had received training in the Confucian classics in Buddhist monasteries and then abandoned their faith. Armed with inside knowledge and reformatory zeal, they began to accuse their erstwhile brethren publicly of crimes such as rapacious conduct and misleading the populace.[31] Not much documentation has remained of the fierce personal battles that must have resulted when disciples turned into accusers. That these battles did not always take place behind closed doors is documented by the sharp polemic displayed in *kana zōshi*, works published in simple phonetic script to assure wider public distribution.[32]

The split between Buddhists and Confucians was not limited to debates of religious and philosophical nature. It also had important political implications. Assisting the ruler, Buddhist monks performed political duties, but ultimately their ambitions lay with the intangible, spiritual world, as the career of the priest Tenkai crowned by establishing the worship of Ieyasu well illustrates.[33] Confucians, however, saw their field of action in the tangible, present world, and in Japan conditions differed greatly from the Confucian ideal. While in the perfect Confucian world order, status was commensurate with learning, and learning was available to all, in Japan status depended on the birthright of the warrior elite. In the Chinese model authority was centralized in the hands of a benign autocrat, appointing officials in accordance with their ability, while in Japan authority was inherited and divided on a feudal pattern. The split of political leadership between emperor and shogun was also alien to the Confucian model. The practical effects of the application of Confucian principles in government were seen in a number of domains in which the lord felt bold enough to challenge the status quo.

The Government of Tokugawa Yoshinao

It is perhaps ironic that one of the first to challenge the system by putting Confucian theory into practice was Tokugawa Yoshinao (1600-1650), the ninth son of Ieyasu and, as Lord of Owari, a member of the so-called Three Related

Houses. He invited a number of Confucian scholars to his domain, including Fujiwara Seika's student Hori Kyōan and the Chinese refugee scholar Ch'en Yüan-pin (Jap.: Chin Genpin, d. 1671), and was also visited by Kumazawa Banzan. He is credited with having built the first Confucian hall *(senseiden)* in the Tokugawa period. In the last month of Kanei 6 (1629), Hayashi Razan visited Nagoya on this return to Edo and was shown the hall well supplied with golden statues of Confucius, the sage kings Yao and Shun, and other Confucian luminaries. When finally Razan persuaded the *bakufu* in the following year to give him his own plot of land, it was Yoshinao who financed the Confucian hall for the Hayashi family in Edo and personally wrote the characters on the tablet over the entrance. At both locations the celebration of the Confucian ceremony of *sekiten* was revived.[34]

But the government of this patron of Confucianism had uncomfortable consequences for the population as a whole and the samurai in particular. Like other Confucians, such as Yamaga Sokō, Kumazawa Banzan, and later Tsunayoshi, he believed that the samurai should justify their existence by serving as a model of morality to the people. He insisted strictly on frugality and banned courtesans and theater troupes from his domain. Since he believed that it was his duty as ruler to lift the moral standard of his subjects, he appointed inspectors and investigators to see that good conduct was maintained and the laws strictly enforced. He much disliked Buddhism and patronized Shinto instead, visiting the Ise shrine and ordering important Shinto works to be copied for his domain. In spite of his dislike of Buddhism, he, like the fifth shogun later, nevertheless held scholarly debates pitting Buddhist monks and Confucian scholars against each other to defend their beliefs.[35]

Of much greater concern for the *bakufu*, however, was his reverence for the imperial institution. Although he was Ieyasu's son, he believed that the daimyo and the Three Related Houses were not the shogun's retainers but those of the emperor. The shogun was no more than the "head of the troops" *(hatagashira)*. Consequently Yoshinao instructed his descendants that if the *bakufu* were to take military action against the emperor, as the Kamakura *bakufu* did in the Jōkyū (1221) and Genkō (1331) wars, they were not to fight against the imperial house.[36] Fortunately for Yoshinao, his loyalty was not put to the test, and it was only two hundred years later that the fourteenth domain lord, Yoshikatsu, acted on these instructions and refused to obey the commands of the shogunate.[37]

With Yoshinao holding such convictions, it is not surprising that rumor spread that he was planning rebellion. Iemitsu consequently found it necessary to send his trusted uncle Mito Yorifusa to Nagoya to check out the situation before he himself decided to visit there on his way to Kyoto in Kanei 11 (1634).[38]

While Yoshinao was successful in establishing the first Tokugawa Confucian hall in his domain, he was less so in establishing a school. His plans met with strong resistance from the *bakufu*. One of the reasons given was that, since the government had not yet established its own school, it was not appropriate for Yoshinao to do so. The school of the Hayashi house was considered a private establishment. Since Yoshinao had been able to establish his own Confucian hall long before an official one was built at Edo, this explanation is suspect. Official records contain no information on whether Yoshinao accomplished his ambition. Some sources suggest that he built a school secretly in the southern part of Ōtsu Machi and asked the Kyoto scholar Fukata Seishitsu to teach. Later the school apparently came under the direction of the monk Reihō, but it was abolished on Yoshinao's death. At times the school is referred to as the forerunner of the many domain schools that appeared in the latter part of the Tokugawa period.[39]

Tokugawa Mitsukuni of Mito

Yoshinao's respect for the imperial house was not only handed down to his own descendants, but also deeply impressed his nephew, Tokugawa Mitsukuni (1628–1700), lord of Mito.[40] The latter's regular ceremonial obeisance in the direction of the imperial palace and his personal relationship with the imperial house left no doubt where his loyalties were placed.[41] As in the case of Yoshinao, his studies of the Confucian classics had convinced him that political authority in Japan rightfully belonged to the emperor. Mitsukuni demonstrated where his sympathies would lie if a confrontation between the imperial house and the *bakufu* were to occur by repairing the grave and erecting a memorial for the warrior Kusunoki Masashige (1294–1336). This brilliant military strategist had fought with inferior numbers of forces for the emperor Godaigo (1288–1339) against the shogun Ashikaga Takauji (1305–1358) and was therefore branded a traitor during the Muromachi period. Mitsukuni had the epitaph praising Masashige for his unselfish loyalty to the imperial house written by the Chinese refugee scholar Chu Shun-shui (Jap.: Shu Shunsui, 1600–1682). By enlisting this Chinese Confucian authority for the task of praising the Japanese hero, Mitsukuni pointed out that however much scholars might argue that in Japan the position of Son of Heaven *(tenshi)* was occupied by the shogun, there was in orthodox Confucian terms no question that political authority ought to rest with the emperor. Yet while Chu Shun-shui wrote the epitaph in Kanbun 10 (1670), it was installed on Masashige's grave only in Genroku 5 (1692). No doubt Mitsukuni considered it wise to publicize such a politically subversive statement only on his retirement and, moreover, at a time when the government was headed by a shogun who, patronizing Confucianism, showed unprecedented respect for the imperial institution.[42]

Mitsukuni's respect for the imperial family also finds expression in his monumental history of Japan. The Confucian scholars employed for this compilation were permitted to shed their Buddhist robes and grow their hair in samurai fashion as early as Enpō 4 (1676), long before the *bakufu* under Tsunayoshi granted them this right.[43] Yet Mitsukuni, no less than his uncle Yoshinao, was again unable to officially establish the school he had planned, for which he apparently had brought the Chinese refugee scholar to Edo.[44]

Bakufu Policy Opposed

Though restrained in the establishment of domain schools, it was possible for these daimyo to sponsor Confucianism in their domains to the extent that they did because the Laws for the Examination of Sects were initially enforced only in *bakufu* lands. Definite source material is lacking, but scholars believe that enforcement on a national basis began around 1635.[45] What is certain is that in Kanbun 4 (1664) the *bakufu* made a renewed effort to have formal and detailed temple registers *(shūmon ninbetsu aratame chō)* kept for samurai and commoners alike, not just in areas under direct government control, but also in daimyo domains. The daimyo were ordered to appoint comptrollers of temples and shrines, and registers were to be submitted from Kanbun 5 (1665).[46]

This has been seen as a countermeasure against rebellious Buddhist sects.[47] Had this been so, the problem could have been left up to the domains where it occurred, without requesting reports to Edo. Requiring the maintenance of temple registers countrywide gave the central administration a complete record of the movement of all individuals and their religious affiliation, a policy apparently out of tune with the strengthening of daimyo independence otherwise characteristic of this period. Here, however, a far more fundamental issue was at stake. Confucian principles applied to domain administration threatened the birthright of the samurai as the ruling class and could not be condoned. That the demand for countrywide temple registers was considered a critique of the patronage of Confucianism is indicated by the measures three powerful daimyo embarked upon in open defiance of the *bakufu*'s decree.

It can hardly be considered a coincidence that Mitsukuni chose precisely the year Kanbun 4 (1664) to send the scholar Koyake Seijun to Nagasaki to look for "men of talent," in other words, to increase the number of Confucians in his employ. As a result Mitsukuni invited the Chinese Confucian Chu Shunshui to become his retainer in the following year. The latter had already eked out a meager existence in Nagasaki for half a decade.[48]

In Kanbun 6 (1666) Mitsukuni embarked upon a program of eliminating 3,088 Buddhist temples and restoring Shinto shrines.[49] An order issued in his fief at the time carried a scathing attack on the Buddhist clergy, describing them, among other things, as being too old, too sick, too ignorant, and too uneducated to carry out their work. The clergy were also accused of spiritually misleading the people and oppressing them with unreasonable demands for temple construction. Like Hakuseki later, Mitsukuni regretted that people were not allowed to carry out their filial duty of returning their parents' bodies to the soil, a reference to mandatory Buddhist cremation in place of Confucian burial in the ground.[50]

In the eighth month of that year, Mitsukuni paid a secret visit to Hoshina Masayuki to listen to an exposition of *The Doctrine of the Mean* by the Confucian scholar Yamazaki Ansai. Masayuki, son of the second shogun Hidetada and former regent for the young Ietsuna, had, like Mitsukuni, chosen the year Kanbun 5 (1665) to summon into his presence for the first time and then employ this prominent scholar, ranking Ansai above even his senior retainers. In the following year Masayuki not only drastically reduced the number of temples and clergy in his fief, but also decreed, in opposition to *bakufu* orders, that registration could also be carried out at Shinto shrines.[51]

These two powerful daimyo, both grandsons of Ieyasu, appear to have been able to ignore the *bakufu*'s orders with impunity. But the third daimyo to take such measures, Ikeda Mitsumasa (1609–1682), lord of Okayama, even though he was the son of an adopted daughter of the second shogun Hidetada and the son-in-law of Iemitsu's sister Tenju-in, apparently could not.

Ikeda Mitsumasa

Ikeda Mitsumasa, lord of the Okayama domain, was at first well disposed towards Buddhism, as the still extant copies he made of Buddhist scriptures show. His search for guidance in government, however, led him to Confucianism, and he is said to have called upon the Confucian scholar Nakae Tōju (1608–1648) and later to have tried to invite him to his domain.[52] Instead, however, he employed Tōju's student Kumazawa Banzan (1619–1691). Banzan was of samurai origin, had ambitiously and wholeheartedly trained himself in the martial arts in his youth, and had previously served Mitsumasa as a page for four years on the recommendation of the Kyoto deputy *(Kyōto shoshidai)* Itakura Shigemune (1586–1656).[53] Sources do not agree on the year of employment, but in Shōhō 4 (1647) he was promoted to chamberlain *(soba yaku)* at a salary of 300 *koku*.

Banzan became known for his Confucian learning and its practical application in domain management. He accompanied Mitsumasa on his visits to Edo, where he came to be consulted by other daimyo and officials. His scholarly impact must have been considerable, for only three years later he was promoted to the position of officer of the guard *(ban gashira)*, which increased his stipend tenfold to 3,000 *koku*.

Banzan enjoyed his greatest officially sanctioned acclaim when he accompanied Mitsumasa in the following year. His advice was sought by the highest-ranking officials and daimyo including the senior councilor Matsudaira Nobutsuna (1596–1662), Ieyasu's son Yorinobu, the founder of the house of Kii (1602–1671), and the Kyoto deputy Itakura Shigemune. An audience with the third shogun was apparently under consideration, but the latter died before such plans materialized.[54]

As early as Kanei 18 (1641), Mitsumasa had established a place of learning for the literary and military arts at Okayama, which historians later came to refer to as the Hanabatake School. With Banzan's presence and fame, this establishment expanded greatly in scope and attracted various scholars. Especially after Nakae Tōju's death in Keian 1 (1648), a number of Tōju's disciples, including Banzan's younger brother and one of Tōju's sons, gathered at Hanabatake to study under the leadership of Banzan.[55]

The steep promotion of the outsider Banzan caused considerable resentment among Mitsumasa's retainers, but Mitsumasa explained that the appointment was necessary since his own men had become lax and lazy in the performance of their duties.[56] Together with Banzan's appointment, his teaching, known as Shingaku (Learning of The Mind), was resented and declared incomprehensible and useless by some of Mitsumasa's retainers. The real reason for complaint, however, was no doubt that Banzan's teaching had uncomfortable consequences for the samurai. Like other Confucians he believed that the existence of the military aristocracy could only be justified if they became paragons of virtue and served as models for the commoners to emulate. Samurai, who considered it to be their birthright to live off and subjugate the commoners to their will, were to be turned into upright civil servants, untiringly succoring the people under their control. Unemployed samurai were to be returned to the land to earn their keep farming.[57] Although Banzan discussed this policy in detail in writing only much later, he put it into practice on a small scale during his employment in the Ikeda domain.

A similar policy of returning unemployed samurai to the land was implemented in the Tosa domain by the Confucian Nonaka Kenzan (1615–1663). By Kanbun 3 (1663), however, the otherwise highly connected Kenzan had come to fall. Similar to Banzan, his exceptional advance in the administration had created resentment. The illegal Confucian burial of his mother was interpreted as defiance of *bakufu* policy.[58] Both were challenging the preeminent position of the samurai, with the policy of returning the samurai to the land being the most visual and obvious challenge to the class system. In the eyes of the scholar Kinugasa Yasuki, the revolutionary character of this challenge has been much underestimated.[59]

However much official approval Banzan's teaching had enjoyed before Iemitsu's death, with the succession of the ten-year-old Ietsuna and the discovery of abortive anti-*bakufu* plots by discontented samurai, the political situation became tense. New theories of government elicited fear rather than curiosity.

When Mitsumasa visited Edo the next year, he was told by the senior councilor Sakai Tadakatsu that the gathering of Confucians at his domain was unacceptable. The reason given was that "since a place where crowds assemble is bad, it should be closed."[60] Tadakatsu was obviously referring to groups of intellectuals rather than common crowds, because the latter were present at religious festivals in much greater numbers.

Banzan's teaching of Shingaku, moreover, was said to have inspired the most notorious plotters, the followers of Yui Shōsetsu. In one instance Banzan's younger brother, and even Banzan himself, was said to have been connected to one of the plotters. On his return from Edo that year, Ikeda Mitsumasa was informed by the senior councilors that he, together with other daimyo, including the lords of the related houses of Owari and Kii, had been implicated in the confessions of the plotters. The daimyo were said to have fallen under the spell of Banzan's teaching, which was "Confucian in appearance, but covertly inciting rebellion."[61]

Ikeda Mitsumasa was, however, not easily dissuaded. In the very same year he employed one of Banzan's younger brothers as a page with an income of 500 *koku*, and he promoted him to head page the next year.[62]

Although warned even by Itakura Shigemune not to spread Banzan's philosophy of Shingaku, when the Okayama domain shortly afterwards was devastated by floods followed by large-scale famine, Mitsumasa undertook far-reaching reforms based on Banzan's teaching.[63] Their resemblance to those instituted by Tsunayoshi later, on succeeding to the shogunate, is difficult to ignore.[64] Administration of the farmers was centralized, and officials were sent out, paid and strictly controlled by the domain government. They were firmly instructed to acquaint themselves with local conditions, to administer the populace with compassion, and to ensure that there were no further cases of starvation. Relief funds obtained from Edo through the good offices of Mitsumasa's mother-in-law, Iemitsu's sister Tenju-in, were distributed to relieve suffering in the countryside as necessary. Finally Banzan was sent to tour the country as Mitsumasa's personal representative *(myōdai)* to ensure that the orders of the domain government were followed.

While these measures were in line with the benevolent government *(jinsei)* of the Confucian sage ruler, they violated the established prerogatives of the military aristocracy, reducing their privileges vis-à-vis the peasants of their landholdings. Banzan came to be criticized for favoring the commoners and treating the samurai "as though their life or death did not matter." A proposal to drastically reduce the tax samurai were permitted to levy apparently resulted in threats to his life.[65] The tax was cut, though not as drastically as Banzan had proposed. This measure again had much in common with Tsunayoshi's financial imposition on the daimyo to relieve famine after the eruption of Mount Fuji, a topic discussed below.

Historians generally maintain that Mitsumasa finally felt compelled to distance himself from Banzan. In the year before his retirement, however, Banzan was permitted to adopt Mitsumasa's third son and transferred his stipend to the latter. Moreover, another younger brother of Banzan was employed by Mitsumasa in the next year at a stipend of 500 *koku*. Sources show that Banzan actively pleaded for his retirement. In line with his own philosophy he declared that since he had become too ill to shoot an arrow or drive a spirited horse through a river, he did not deserve a samurai's stipend. He asserted: "Those who turn the study of books into a trade are Confucians of low stature." They were no more than "book-reading monks."[66] Banzan's words indicate why a Confucian such as Hayashi Razan was employed by the *bakufu*, but the teaching of Banzan was condemned. When practiced by "book-reading monks," Confucianism presented no threat to the political status quo. But championed by members of the military aristocracy, it did, as the government of the fifth shogun was to demonstrate amply later.

A year after Banzan's retirement, Mitsumasa, too, apparently realized the political dangers inherent in Banzan's Shingaku, and he decided to switch to orthodox Confucianism. As Mitsumasa put it, Shingaku was beneficial to the individual "but, it is said, not good for government."[67] Mitsumasa does not spell out whether the concepts of Shingaku were not relevant or useful for government, or whether to pursue Shingaku in the political climate was not beneficial for the domain's relations with the *bakufu*. The latter might well have been the case.

With Sakai Tadakatsu's retirement in Meireki 2 (1656), his entering the priesthood in Manji 3 (1660), and his death in Kanbun 2 (1662), the confrontation between Ikeda Mitsumasa and the central government eased temporarily. But in the same year Banzan's and Mitsumasa's erstwhile supporter, the senior councilor Matsudaira Nobutsuna, also died. Already in the previous year Hoshina Masayuki had begun to limit his participation in government affairs owing to a serious eye ailment.[68] In the meantime another member of the Sakai clan, Sakai Tadakiyo, had consolidated his position and in Kanbun 6 (1666) had risen to grand councilor. It was with Tadakiyo that Ikeda Mitsumasa was to fight his next round, yet perhaps on account of the death of Mitsumasa's mother-in-law, Iemitsu's sister Tenju-in, in that same year, the result would be far less favorable for Mitsumasa.[69]

When Engelbert Kaempfer visited Japan in 1690–1692, some ten years after Mitsumasa's death, he heard the following story:

> Some thirty years ago it came to pass that the Lord of Bizen, Inaba [Ikeda Mitsumasa], an excellent *judōshi* [Confucian] and patron of the liberal arts, attempted to popularize once again in his fief this sect [Confucianism] and its stoic manner of living. He founded an academy, appointed learned men

and teachers from all parts of the country, and paid them handsomely. Gaining greater understanding and prompted by the example of their superiors, the people no longer wanted to believe in the incomprehensible revelations and fantastic tales or to continue supporting the ignorant rabble of priests, who mostly depended for their living on alms. Consequently these gangs (with which the whole country is packed) nearly died of starvation in this fief. But both the emperor and the shogun were so angered about this matter that they were about to deprive this honest patriot of his inherited fief and would have done so had he not taken the precaution of retiring in favor of his son to prevent his family from falling out of favor. His son, who has governed ever since, demonstrates with his stoic conduct that he is still following his father's path."[70]

Mitsumasa, together with Mito Mitsukuni and Hoshina Masayuki, later became reverently known as one of the Three Wise Lords *(san kenkō)*, owing to their early sponsorship of Confucianism, and the fact that at the time he stood in open opposition to the government was conveniently forgotten.[71] Yet there is evidence that what Kaempfer heard is historically correct.

Like Mito Mitsukuni and Hoshina Masayuki, Ikeda Mitsumasa chose precisely the year of Sakai Tadakiyo's accession to the position of grand councilor (Kanbun 6, 1666) for what historians generally describe as the "weeding out" *(tōta)* of Buddhist clergy and temples. Of the existing 1,044 temples in his domain, 583 were closed, while the number of clergy was reduced to less than half from 1,957 to 847.[72] At the same time he permitted, in defiance of the central government's orders, that the registration required under the Laws for the Examination of Sects take place either at Shinto shrines or at Buddhist temples, and that burials could also take place according to Shinto rites. Mitsumasa personally showed his opposition to the *bakufu*'s order limiting burials to Buddhist temples by removing the remains of his father and grandfather in that year from the temple Myōshinji in Kyoto. Instead they were laid to rest in a Confucian burial place Mitsumasa constructed at Wa'itani, Wakigun, on a remote hillside in the country.[73]

Mitsumasa was careful to explain to his retainers that he did not stand in opposition to the Tokugawa regime, but only to the orders of the present government leaders. Ieyasu had intended to have Shinto, Confucianism, and Buddhism equally revered, he explained, and his measures were necessary since Buddhism had become too powerful and had declined morally.[74]

Mitsumasa sought to rectify this by establishing Confucian schools open equally to samurai and commoners, including primary schools *(tenarai)* to replace the Buddhist *tera koya*.[75] Protest from the Buddhist clergy of the domain to the *bakufu* led to several confrontations between Mitsumasa and the grand councilor Sakai Tadakiyo. A letter containing a scathing attack on the *bakufu* and particularly on Sakai Tadakiyo, the addressee, belies the traditional image of Mitsumasa as the wise Confucian, ruling in harmony with his world. Mitsumasa cautioned Tadakiyo to cast aside his arrogance and take advice from others. Impoverishment had already resulted in a number of uprisings, and if matters did not improve, even the daimyo might rebel.[76]

Historians often suggest that Mitsumasa was sufficiently powerful to carry out his unlawful policies and address such strong words to the *bakufu* without retribution.[77] Only Kaempfer records that he would have lost his fief had he not retired in favor of his son. Moreover, while the changes that took place in the domain after Mitsumasa's retirement are usually interpreted as reflecting his son's dislike of Confucianism,[78] Kaempfer states that Tsunamasa too was a staunch Confucian and carried on his father's work.

Mitsumasa retired in Kanbun 12 (1672), three years after admonishing the *bakufu* and Tadakiyo, and some six years after instituting registration at shrines. Perhaps because he was related to the Tokugawa house and also a senior relative of Sakai Tadakiyo, and because Mito Mitsukuni and Hoshina Masayuki had issued similar orders, the *bakufu* felt restrained from taking immediate action. Curiously enough, Mitsumasa's diary, which could have shed light on this period, stops at the second month of Kanbun 9 (1669), and other primary sources are scarce. Since the recasting of history later demanded that the three early supporters of Confucianism, namely, Mitsumasa, Mitsukuni, and Hoshina Masayuki, be praised as sagacious Confucian rulers, the elimination of material attesting to the conflict between one of them and the *bakufu* is perhaps not surprising.

Under Mitsumasa's son Tsunamasa the local *tenarai* Confucian schools were closed. Correspondence between father and son indicates that this was requested by Sakai Tadakiyo, who argued that at a time when the domain experienced economic problems, expenditure on services supporting the central administration of the *bakufu* (*hōkō*), such as military and public duties (*gun'yō, kōyō*), must take priority over the domain's local expenditures. In a long reply Mitsumasa cautioned his son that Tadakiyo's advice was motivated by his distaste for learning and that "right-minded" people (*kokoro aru mono*) would not look favorably at such measures. Mitsumasa himself offered to contribute 500 *koku* from his retirement stipend to meet part of the total annual cost of 2,000 *koku*, but the *tenarai* schools were nevertheless closed down.[79]

Yet Mitsumasa had taken precautions while still in office to realize at least part of his project of furthering the education of both samurai and commoners in his domain. Searching for a quiet valley in which to bury his ancestors in Confucian style, Mitsumasa had come across a secluded little valley with a good water supply and decided that a school should be built there. The later famous establishment, the Shizutani school, was, apparently, "the lord's secret [project]" *(go nainai nite)* and entrusted to the personal supervision of the senior retainer Tsuda Eichū. Moreover, the fact that, in the domain's official record of educational institutions, the information that the school received special attention on the orders of the domain lord was only later stuck in on a separate piece of paper seems to confirm this secrecy.[80] During the next few years a number of new school buildings and dormitories as well as a Confucian shrine were added. In Enpō 1 (1673) the school was given its own income of some 280 *koku,* making it financially independent from the budgetary considerations of the domain government. Moreover, it received all school equipment from the domain's primary *tenarai* on their closure.

After Mitsumasa's retirement various changes took place in the government of the domain, including the creation of an additional council of officials, reducing the daimyo's direct involvement in the administration.[81] In a letter addressed to Mitsumasa's successor Tsunamasa, a senior retainer complained that the domain was now run entirely according to Edo's directives.[82] Scholars attribute the changes in government at least partly to the personality of Tsunamasa, "who had been brought up to enjoy life too much" or who alternatively is portrayed as a convinced Buddhist.[83]

Yet with the onset of Tsunayoshi's government, Kaempfer's statement that the son was "following the path of his father" is validated. After his father's death in Tenna 2 (1682), Tsunamasa invested considerable sums to surround the school with a wide Chinese-style stone wall and erect expensively tiled buildings so well constructed that they have lasted until today. These include a large lecture hall and a Confucian shrine where from Jōkyō 3 (1686) Confucian ceremonies were performed. Bronze statues of both Confucius and his father as well as a Confucian burial mound containing the nails, hair, and beard of the latter further demonstrate Tsunamasa's filial piety.[84]

Diverging Political Ideologies

Ikeda Mitsumasa's policies and the opposition they engendered have been discussed in some detail because these events foreshadow developments under the fifth shogun. The similarities with regard to the promotion of learning, concern for the plight of the farmers, together with orders reducing samurai privileges in favor of the former cannot be overlooked. Both men are in conflict with the grand councilor Sakai Tadakiyo, for whom military expenditure takes precedence. Tokugawa sources attempt to convey the image of leadership united in its political aims and philosophy. Yet here we have clear indication of a confrontation between two divergent streams of political ideology with regard to the governance of the country.

Japan's leadership was confronted with serious questions. Northern China had more or less peacefully capitulated to the invading Manchu forces, abruptly ending the supremacy of the nearly three-hundred-year-old Ming dynasty. From Shōhō 3 (1646) onwards over some forty years the *bakufu* received requests for military assistance from the supporters of the beleaguered Ming holding out in South China.[85] These served as a constant reminder of the fallen giant. Chinese scholars seeking refuge in Japan readily pointed out that the Chinese imperial house in no small way had been brought down by misgovernment and the discontent of the commoners.[86] The question of how Japan would stand up to a Manchu threat could not be ignored. We know that the senior councilor Matsudaira Nobutsuna probed Kumazawa Banzan on this topic. The latter feared that last-minute preparations for battle would create enormous logistical problems with regard to food supplies. Shortage of rice would cause mutiny and riots, making it easy for the invaders to conquer Japan. Even if the invaders were repelled, the social and economic havoc resulting from the attempted invasion would leave Japan in a state of anarchy and civil war.[87]

A solution in accord with Confucian concepts was to better the lot of the commoners so that they would rally behind their government. This was to be achieved by Confucian-style benevolent government *(jinsei)*, where the commoners were administered with increased expertise, efficiency, and dedication on the part of samurai officials. Education brought enlightenment and reduced violence. Yet education and appointment commensurate with performance challenged the inherited birthright of the samurai. Moreover such benevolent government often required financial sacrifice. Especially at times of natural calamities, the military was expected to forgo tax collection and contribute to relief funds.

In opposition stood the resolve to maintain the political status quo by consolidating the privileges of the ruling class. This strategy meant adherence to Ieyasu's maxim that farmers were to be taxed so that they barely retained enough grain for seeding and burdened with corvée leaving just enough energy to produce good crops.[88] Education encouraged insubordination.[89] As Sakai Tadakiyo had advised Ikeda Mitsumasa, in these troubled times expenditures on military and public duties were more appropriate.

This opposition showed complex variations according to circumstance and the personal ambitions of the players. Confucians were divided among themselves, with, for instance, Kumpazawa Banzan denigrating the Hayashi family as clerics and the latter accusing Banzan of unorthodoxy and rebellion. Sakai Tadakiyo patronized the Hayashi family, frequently calling the head of the house to his mansion.[90] Yet in spite of this patronage, Tadakiyo was not prepared to accord Confucians a political role beyond that of watchdog over ideologically dangerous thought and editors of historical records.[91] For their part, those rulers subscribing to the classical Chinese pattern of benevolent government were, nevertheless, generally not prepared to accord their Confucian advisers the respect and emoluments due them in the perfect Confucian world order. They also differed from the ideal in their unwillingness to be admonished by their Confucian tutors. Such discrepancies created criticism and friction. In turn samurai Confucians were reluctant to give up their traditional warrior prerogatives. The Confucian scholars Arai Hakuseki and Ogyū Sorai were at variance on what constituted good Confucian government but were in agreement in counting the life of a commoner for little, lacking the essential Confucian compassion for their fellow men.[92]

In spite of these variations, we can see two distinctive political patterns of governance, with the Confucian pattern being followed by men such as Tokugawa Yoshinao, Mito Mitsukuni, and Ikeda Mitsumasa, while opposition to their policies is voiced by Sakai Tadakatsu and Tadakiyo on behalf of the *bakufu*. An appreciation of this confrontation in political ideology is essential for understanding the administration of the fifth shogun and the opposition it encountered. Evidence of this split in political ideology well over a decade before Tsunayoshi's government explains the disagreement over his succession.

A Great and Excellent Lord

"The presently reigning monarch Tsunayoshi . . . is a great and excellent lord. Having inherited the virtues of his father, he is both a strict custodian of the law and very compassionate. From early in life he has been imbued with Confucianism, and governs his land and people how they ought to be. Under his government all citizens live in complete harmony, honor their gods, observe the law, obey their superiors, and treat their equals with politeness and affection."[1] Thus wrote Engelbert Kaempfer in his *Amoenitates exoticae*, the voluminous Latin account of his travels that brought him fame in Europe. The years of his visit to Edo, 1691–1692, coincided with the high point of Tsunayoshi's patronage of learning and Confucianism. The *bakufu*'s Confucian scholars were permitted to shed the garb of Buddhist monks, the grand new Confucian temple and lecture hall were built at Yushima, and the shogun proceeded with his entourage to the new buildings to lecture on the Confucian classics.[2] For Kaempfer and scholars in Europe he became the ideal ruler at whose feet, later writers jokingly suggested, even the German popular playwright Gotthold Ephraim Lessing (1729–1781), famous for advocating religious tolerance in his works, might sit.[3]

Perhaps not to distract from this ideal—which Kaempfer might well have wished his own ruler to emulate—what he heard about the more Machiavellian aspects of shogunal politics remained buried in his unpublished notes, in a mix of languages and minute writing, extremely difficult to decipher. Here he wrote:

> The two councilors [the grand councilor Sakai Tadakiyo Uta no Kami and the senior councilor Inaba Masanori Mino no Kami] were so puffed up with conceit that they respected nobody. Yes, indeed, they did not even respect the shogun's brothers, the princes. For when the middle brother in the year 1679 *[sic]* asked repeatedly that a grant of additional revenue be approved by the shogun, he, as the shogun's brother and successor, was unable to stand up for himself, and was continually sent away. He had to approach his majesty personally, even though this is against the custom, and solely the duty of the councilors, especially at that time when the shogun was under their thumb. Finally, even though it was against the law of the land, he personally put his request to his brother. The shogun got so angry about this (especially

on account of the reaction of the councilors) that he commanded him to leave his presence, and said that because of this offense he no longer considered him worthy to be his brother. Thereupon the disgruntled prince returned home and cut his stomach, leaving behind a little son of some ten or twelve years. This event embittered the youngest prince [Tsunayoshi] and especially their sister, the wife of the daimyo of Owari. A year later they found occasion to revenge themselves, because the shogun, having been ill for a long time, died.

The two above-mentioned councilors, Uta and Mino, feared the revenge of the successor Tsunayoshi . . . and with the workings and help of the grandees of the country attempted to impose a nephew of the emperor on the shogunal line of succession, for whom they had already sent. But since the daimyo of Kii no Kuni and Mito, as well as the son-in-law of Mino called Bichū [Hotta Masatoshi Bichū no Kami] remained on Tsunayoshi's side, he was, in spite of his enemies, installed as successor at the age of thirty-four.[4]

Does this cloak and dagger story shedding light on the events of Tsunayoshi's succession find support in Japanese sources?

Did Tsunashige Commit Suicide?

There is no reliable Japanese documentation that Tsunashige, Tsunayoshi's elder brother and second in line to the shogunate, committed suicide or died in anger. It is suspicious, however, that the official sources *Tokugawa jikki* and *Edo bakufu nikki* have unusually brief entries for the death of a person of Tsunashige's rank. Under the date of 15.9.Enpō 6 (1678), they state without further explanation that Tsunashige died on the previous day, adding only that after the event two high officials were sent to Tsunashige's son and Tsunayoshi respectively to convey the condolences of the shogun.[5]

The story of Tsunashige's suicide is, however, contained in *Sannō gaiki*, the anonymous send-up of the governments of the fourth, fifth, and sixth shoguns attributed to Dazai Shundai. This work relates that Tsunashige asked his elder brother, the fourth shogun, for money. The shogun consented and asked Sakai Tadakiyo to handle the matter. Yet Tadakiyo refused, and Tsunashige thereupon committed suicide.[6] *Sannō gaiki* appeared after the death of the fifth shogun and consequently could not have been the source of Kaempfer's information. Yet since its narrative of other events is quite clearly spurious and unreliable, it cannot be cited as supporting evidence.

Kaempfer's information seems to have come from a Dutch source, one that also provided the material for a report of this incident from the Dutch East India Company offices at Batavia to the directors in Holland dated December

1679. This hypothesis is strengthened by the fact that Kaempfer often uses Dutch words and spelling in his notes describing the event, and that he mistakenly places the death of Tsunashige in the year 1679, the date of the report. Tsunashige had died in the previous year. The report to Holland states:

> The brother of his majesty [the shogun] lord Kōfu Saishō [Tsunashige] required money but was unable to persuade the above-mentioned Minosama [the senior councilor Inaba Mino no Kami Masanori] to approach the shogun on his behalf in accordance with the duty of his office. Consequently he had no choice but to approach his brother himself, whereupon his majesty was upset and had a vehement outburst saying that he did not like that sort of thing and so on. Consequently the above lord Kōfu Saishō cut his stomach and made an end to his life, either out of spite or because he was disgruntled.[7]

For this news to be contained in a report to Holland of December 1679, it must have been current before the Dutch fleet left Nagasaki for Batavia in the autumn of that year, within a year of Tsunashige's death. It was not a story made up later but a current rumor. No doubt contemporaries were as astonished as historians are today at the lack of explanation on the part of the *bakufu* at the sudden death of the shogun's brother and drew their conclusions from the circumstantial evidence.

Circumstantial Evidence

The record leaves no doubt that both Tsunashige's and Tsunayoshi's households suffered from financial difficulties. Salaries had been reduced to the lowest possible level, so that Tsunayoshi felt the need to assure his retainers that even if their clothes were in a wretched state, they need not worry and could still conduct official business.[8] Tsukamoto Manabu makes the point that whatever economic measures their households might take, they still had to provide entertainment for the men in power and expensive gifts to the order of over one hundred carp and twenty pheasants shortly before the New Year, when such animals sold at premium prices.[9] Cash was required on other occasions, such as the coming-of-age ceremony (*genpuku*) of Tsunashige's son Tsunatoyo late in Enpō 4 (1676), when a large number of senior *bakufu* officials had to be rewarded.[10]

The destruction caused by Edo's frequent fires added to the financial burden. In the first month of Enpō 6 (1678), a fire broke out in Aoyama Gondahara and reached both Tsunashige's main mansion (*yashiki*) and his suburban villa (*shimoyashiki*).[11] In the fifth month of that year, Tsunashige sent an urgent request for funds to the grand councilor Sakai Tadakiyo. He stated that, from the beginning of the Enpō period (1672) his revenue had been insufficient, tax from previous years had not been received, and Tsunayoshi's household was in similar financial straits.[12]

The deterioration of Tsunashige's financial affairs was accompanied by the deterioration of his health. Tsunashige was not a robust man, as an examination of his bones has revealed. From early 1674 Tsunashige suffered long bouts of illness. The shogun showed his concern by instructing that good care be taken of him or by asking Tsunayoshi to pass on messages.[13] At times Tsunayoshi would call on his elder brother on his way home from the castle when the latter had not attended.[14]

When in Enpō 6 (1678) Tsunashige did not attend the New Year's celebrations at the castle, it was already the third year running he had to excuse himself on account of illness. Even at his own mansion the passing around of the traditional sake cup was cancelled.[15] In the middle of the second month, Tsunashige managed an outing to the banks of the Sumida river, but again on the third day of the third month, he was too ill to attend the ceremonies in the grand hall *(ōhiroma)* of the castle marking one of the five *sekku*, or important seasonal festivals.[16] Early in the fifth month Tsunashige sent an urgent plea to the *bakufu* for financial help, as noted above.

On 25.7 Tsunashige's health seems to have finally been restored, for the record notes that after a long illness he paid his first visit to the shogun.[17] He also attended ceremonies at the castle marking the first day of the eighth and ninth months respectively.[18] However, on the ceremonies of 9.9 he was absent, presumably again for reasons of health.

Three days later, on 12.9, Tsunashige's retainers sent letters to the doctors Iseki Gensetsu (1617-1699) and Sugiyama Wa'ichi (1610-1694) requesting their urgent attendance.[19] Both doctors called on Tsunashige on 13.9. The blind acupuncturist Sugiyama Wa'ichi later became famous for healing Tsunayoshi, but on this occasion he was not successful.[20] Both doctors were summoned again in the early hours of 14.9, but Tsunashige died that same day.[21]

In the manuscript of *Sakurada ki* preserved in the National Archives (Naikaku Bunko), the following words have been inserted in the margin of the entry for that day in red ink: "It is said that he committed suicide because of insanity, but since this matter is taboo, it is not recorded." Although the language and writing are not out of tune with the rest of the manuscript, it is impossible to say when this addition was made. The date and importance of this addition is made even more elusive by the fact that the manuscript is a copy of the original.

We know that Tsunashige was suffering from a long-standing illness, and it is not difficult to imagine that the rejection of his plea for financial assistance resulted in considerable mental anguish and frustration. The chances are that the combination of these negative circumstances led to stress so intense that it either caused a natural death, such as a stroke, or resulted in depression so deep that Tsunashige decided to end his own life. In either case the symptoms of stress and deepening depression would have been foreboding enough to have his retainers summon the two physicians. And in either case the circumstances of Tsunashige's sudden death were ignominious enough not to make them public. Any details that might have been recorded at the time are likely to have been eliminated when his son was installed as the sixth shogun Ienobu. At this time Tsunashige's body, in keeping with the honor he deserved as the shogun's father, was moved to the official shogunal cemetery at Zōjōji.

We also know that barely two months after Tsunashige's death, his son, as successor to the domain, as well as Tsunayoshi were granted 50,000 *hyō (tawara)* of rice each, "it having been noted that the finances of the two mansions of Tatebayashi and Kai were destitute."[22] Moreover, less than a month after Tsunayoshi's succession as shogun, he granted his nephew a sizable increase in domain lands, raising his holding from 250,000 *koku* to 350,000 *koku*.[23]

The first part of Kaempfer's story thus finds support in reliable sources. Is there also support for the claim that Sakai Tadakiyo wanted to install an imperial prince as shogun?

Tsunayoshi's Succession

Three months after his succession, Tsunayoshi used his new powers as shogun to retire the grand councilor Sakai Tadakiyo, ostensibly for reasons of ill health.[24] Less than half a year later, Tadakiyo died suddenly and mysteriously. The death of the former leader of the *bakufu* found no notice in the official records on the day in question. Relating the events of Tsunayoshi's succession, *Tokugawa jikki* merely reports a rumor that Tadakiyo had attempted to install an imperial prince as a puppet ruler but had been unsuccessful owing to the opposition of the Three Related Houses.[25] Similarly the contemporary diarist Toda Mosui notes Tadakiyo's opposition to Tsunayoshi's succession and his plan to install a nephew of the emperor simply as "one explanation" used to explain the unusual dismissal of the former grand councilor.[26] It has been suggested therefore that the rumor was a mere rationalization to explain the unprecedented dismissal of the former grand councilor.[27]

After describing the rumor, Toda Mosui adds words of some significance: While nobody disputed that Tsunayoshi as the only remaining brother had the right to succeed, he did not qualify for the position *(go kiryō nashi)*. If he became shogun, many people would suffer, he would act in violation of established customs, and uprisings were likely to occur.[28] Mosui's statement supports what has been outlined in the previous chapter, namely, that even before his accession, Tsunayoshi's support of policies auguring a loss of privilege for members of the military aristocracy had become apparent. There was a fundamental split in political orientation, and one does not need to charge Sakai Tadakiyo with self-aggrandizement or the desire to usurp authority to explain his desire to replace Tsunayoshi with a neutral candidate from Kyoto. To him the political convictions of Tsunayoshi are likely to have seemed as threatening as communism to a capitalist society, and a revolt by the military in defense of their privileges, resulting in civil war, would have seemed a distinct possibility.

Bloody Murder

While the Japanese sources offer little information about the power struggle surrounding the succession of the fifth shogun, the Dutch are more explicit. Already in the autumn of 1679, before the Dutch fleet left Nagasaki that year, they had heard of the senior councilors' opposition to Tsunayoshi's succession. The report from Batavia to Holland of 1679 mentions "two pregnant wives" of the "emperor," presumably the shogun, whose children ought to succeed, though some believed that these pregnancies were a plot of the councilors to prevent Tsunayoshi's succession. There was general consent, however, that if a successor was not named soon, there would be "bloody murder" *(moorden en dootslaan)*, and "many will die more easily and with less pain as if they were dying of hunger, as thousands have done recently."[29]

As the Dutch were indicating, the year 1679 was one of natural and man-made disasters. Fires destroyed various cities, and unusual rainfall and violent storms devastated the countryside and sank ships in the harbors. Masterless samurai and farmers alike were petitioning the *bakufu* for relief.[30] Natural disasters were seen as an indication of the anger of the gods and heightened the political unease.

By the beginning of Enpō 8 (1680), Sakai Tadakiyo and his senior councilors seemed apprehensive of a leadership change, for they saw to it that with the New Year's celebration they were given sizable salary increases.[31] That contemporaries saw this not as a shogunal gift but as rapacity on the part of the senior councilors is reflected in satirical verses that were circulating in Edo at the time.[32] On 4.3 the fourteen-year-old nephew of the emperor, Arisugawa no Miya Yukihito, paid his first visit to Edo and was greeted by Sakai Tadakiyo. Yukihito came along with the imperial messenger and temple envoys in order to thank the shogun for being permitted to succeed to the Arisugawa house shortly after he was born—the position being vacant since the previous incumbent succeeded as Emperor Gosai—an event that had taken place some thirteen years earlier.[33] On the tenth day the visitors were entertained with *nō* performances at the castle, but the shogun was too sick to attend. As the young imperial prince was watching the plays, a thunderstorm accompanied by an unusually heavy downpour turned the daytime sky dark. It was a phenomenon that did not go unnoticed. More than a decade later Mosui noted in his diary that when the sky turned dark in this fashion, people were still recalling the visit of Arisugawa Yukihito, wondering whether it meant "that the world was entering into darkness."[34]

There is no material to substantiate that Tadakiyo intended to install Yukihito as shogun. Yet the above remark indicates that for contemporaries these were troubled times. It ought to alert historians to the possibility that as records were copied over and over again before they finally reached the version available to us today, material considered "unsuitable" for posterity was eliminated. From the Dutch we know that rumors were rife in Edo. As they were waiting for their audience at Edo, they heard different ones each day. On one occasion they heard that the shogun was already dead but his death was to be kept secret for two or three months to await the outcome of the pregnancy of a consort. Civil war seemed a distinct possibility.[35]

From the beginning of the fourth month, the rays of the sun had an extraordinary red tinge, the color of cinnabar.[36] No doubt this unusual natural phenomenon, interpreted as a message from the gods, added to the political tension.

On 6.4 the daimyo Matsudaira Yamato no Kami Naonori visited Sakai Tadakiyo and noted in his diary that Tadakiyo had sent a secret letter to the imperial messenger Kawahara Sansaemon. Unfortunately the content of the letter is not specified. On this occasion Naonori heard from Tadakiyo about the extremely bad state of health and melancholic state of mind of the shogun. The shogun's face was colorless, he was told, but according to his attendants the emaciated state of his body was of even greater concern. His doctors were wondering how his weakened body would stand up to the humidity of the rainy season due to start in the following month.[37]

Despite these serious concerns about the shogun's health, which the record states was not improving, no action was taken to have him adopt a successor. What followed instead was an extraordinary round of entertainment staged in the second enceinte of Edo castle by the most powerful men in the government, ostensibly to cheer up the shogun. On 10.4 Sakai Tadakiyo played the host. Records list the personal rare art treasures he put on display. A stage was built in the garden, famous puppeteers were invited, and some eight hundred guests were entertained at a banquet at a time when the shogun was too sick to attend audiences. The members of the Sakai family in turn were rewarded generously by the shogun with presents, presumably in his absence.[38] Eight days later Inaba Masanori put on a similar display of his art treasures and largesse, entertaining his guests with *nō* performances. Again the close members of the Inaba family were lavishly rewarded.[39] Next the senior councilor Ōkubo Tadatomo hosted a similar event on the twenty-seventh day of the month, and then it was to be the turn of the senior councilor Doi Toshinobu.[40] However, before the next "lucky day" of the calendar suitable for such an event—the seventh and eighth days of the fifth month—approached, the shogun lay on his deathbed.[41]

Nocturnal Adoption

On the sixth day of the fifth month, Tsunayoshi was celebrating the first birthday of his son, when in the late afternoon—the seventh hour, roughly 5:00 p.m.—the news came that the shogun's condition had worsened and he was to proceed to the castle with the greatest haste. He did so, and the official record states that he was then adopted by the shogun as his heir. There are some discrepancies in various records as to the time when the urgent call for assembly was issued. Historians have taken this to indicate that the lords of the Three Related Houses and the senior daimyo met to deliberate before Tsunayoshi was called in. The official record, *Edo bakufu nikki*, has only a very brief entry for this important event.[42]

Buya shokudan, however, relates that Tsunayoshi's adoption as Ietsuna's heir and successor had already taken place the previous night, secretly at the instigation of Hotta Masatoshi (1634-1684), who that month happened to be the senior councilor in charge *(tsukiban rōjū)*. After all senior officials had gone home, at around seven o'clock in the evening, Masatoshi secretly summoned Tsunayoshi, who arrived in haste accompanied by a fearful Makino Narisada. When Narisada was told to let Tsunayoshi proceed by himself, he protested that such a nightly summons had never occurred before and expressed his concerns that something of dubious nature was about to happen. Masatoshi tried to persuade Narisada that, if only he let Tsunayoshi proceed out of his sight, something of great merit and importance was going to occur. But Narisada, grasping Masatoshi by the sleeve, would not consent until the latter had sworn that nothing untoward would happen to his lord. Tsunayoshi proceeded by himself to meet the shogun and was promptly adopted by him as his heir. According to *Buya shokudan* nobody knew the words exchanged between the two brothers on this occasion.[43]

One might well ask why no witnesses were present at the politically decisive occasion of the shogun adopting his younger brother. Why did Masatoshi insist that only if Tsunayoshi were to proceed alone, would something of great significance happen? Perhaps we can rule out the possibility that Ietsuna was already dead. A note next to the official entry in *Edo bakufu nikki* speaks of a brief improvement of the shogun's health on the sixth day as well as visits by priests, daimyo, and family members, and his demise is recorded to have occurred two days later.[44] But what cannot be ruled out is that Ietsuna was already in a coma or at least in a state where he would have been unable to enunciate the wish of adopting his younger brother. Hence it was imperative that Tsunayoshi proceed by himself and some kind of communication, inaudible to others, take place between the two brothers.

After this secret communication with the shogun, Tsunayoshi immediately returned to his own mansion, and when Sakai Tadakiyo and others arrived at the castle on the following day, they were faced with the fait accompli of the adoption. As a precaution, however, the roads were secured in a manner appropriate for a shogunal procession, and only the Hirakawa gate was open for entry into the castle.[45] Special troops were stationed at the Ōte and Sakurada gates.[46] Such military precautions serve to indicate the political danger perceived at the time.

In the Hotta family a document believed to be in Ietsuna's hand is preserved, which is addressed to Masatoshi and approves a certain proposal. The document is claimed to be of 5.5.Enpō 8, the date of the secret adoption, and the proposal referred to is supposedly a list of thirteen articles that Tsunayoshi would observe on his adoption.[47] One of these articles stated that Tsunayoshi would cede the position of shogun to any son of Ietsuna born to a concubine after his death. The acceptance of this condition by Tsunayoshi is confirmed in *Kenbyō jitsuroku*.[48] Also the daimyo Matsudaira Naonori recorded a rumor about a document of thirteen articles being presented to Tsunayoshi containing the stipulation of installing as heir any son of Ietsuna's born in the future.[49]

The question remains whether such clauses were indeed approved by Ietsuna or were simply the outcome of negotiations between the opposing parties of senior daimyo. If Ietsuna was not in a state to take part in an official ceremony of adoption, it is doubtful whether he could have perused and approved the document in question. Akin to what Kaempfer had heard, *Buya shokudan* reports that Mito Mitsukuni played a leading role in supporting Tsunayoshi's succession. It is interesting that *Buya shokudan* questions whether Sakai Tadakiyo and others were aware of the nocturnal adoption, but does not categorically rule out the possibility that they were. An added note in *Edo bakufu nikki* for the sixth day suggests that Sakai Tadakiyo had come to agree to Tsunayoshi's succession as long as Tsunayoshi's son remained in the Tatebayashi mansion. This indicated that the succession was a temporary measure (since the line of succession had not permanently moved to Tsunayoshi's branch of the family) and accords well with the clause that any child born after Ietsuna's death should have precedence. Thus it is plausible that negotiations were conducted beforehand, the conditions of Tsunayoshi's succession laid down in the thirteen articles mentioned, and it was then decided to stage the "secret adoption" to have the outcome of the negotiations validated by the authority of the shogun. In this scenario Sakai Tadakiyo, in order to preserve the peace, would be seen as having reluctantly given in to the pressure of the Three Related Houses and agreed to Tsunayoshi's succession. Consequently he was able to continue in his position of grand councilor only to resign when it became apparent that Tsunayoshi was not inclined to let the past be forgotten, as discussed in the next chapter.

Historians might not be able to fathom the details of Tsunayoshi's succession, but one can say with some certainty that the circumstances surrounding it were extraordinary. The scant attention official sources pay to this important event must be seen as evidence that embarrassing and potentially explosive conflicts were not recorded and alert us to the fact that the workings of the *bakufu* were not quite so tranquil as the record suggests.

When the political commotion surrounding Tsunayoshi's succession is taken into account, the turbulent events of his government need not come as a surprise.

The First Year of Government

"Before Tsunayoshi became shogun[1] he would go daily to inquire after the health of the shogunal family. While making these visits [to the castle], he would wear the formal dress of the linen *kamishimo* and behave ceremoniously. Sitting on an elevated seat, he would question any messenger returning from an errand, thrusting his hand towards his inferior. This went on daily without fail." *Buya shokudan*, the source of this passage, continues to describe how Tsunayoshi would also inspect all gifts being presented, presumably to establish who was currying favor. In the afternoon, once the senior councilors and other officials had left the castle, he would enter their offices and peruse the records of daimyo and housemen *(hatamoto)*. The author surmises that Tsunayoshi's early interest in these records was responsible for the fall of many a *fudai* daimyo later.[2]

Great Changes in Government

Buya shokudan is believed to have been completed in 1709, and its content is unlikely to have been known to Kaempfer or his informants in the early 1690s. Yet the foreign visitor writes in somewhat similar terms:

> With this new shogun great changes occurred in government, [the workings of which] he had observed from afar at a time when nobody had been paying attention to him. Consequently he knew how to arrange things so that the councilors were doing nothing more than their common duty and daily service, and that nobody except him had any authority. . . . He punished the slightest misdemeanor as severely as he thought fit, and condemned people to death or banishment as he wished.[3]

According to the official record, Tsunayoshi had little time to prepare for the weighty duties of ruler of the country, for between his adoption as Ietsuna's son and heir, and his proclamation as shogun lay only days. Yet not only the above-cited documentation, but also the record of Tsunayoshi's early government makes it clear that he had prepared himself well for the task. Even though he was not designated as successor after the death of his elder brother Tsunashige or during the months of rapidly declining health of the shogun, it is likely that for Tsunayoshi himself there was no question of who was going to be the next ruler. Although Japanese sources give little indication of conflict, the prediction of the Dutch that "bloody" military strife was imminent should the question of succession not be settled quickly could well indicate that Tsunayoshi was prepared to do what his father had feared when he saw the unusually lively and intelligent child: namely, use force to claim what he believed was rightfully his.

Tsunayoshi finally succeeded by peaceful means, but he was well aware that with his accession, opposition to his authority did not disappear. According to Kaempfer, Tsunayoshi coped ingeniously with the situation. The German doctor noted: "At the beginning of his government he retired sixty of his most senior servants as a pretense, for in reality they were his trusted nobles. They went to the East and West as if forced to, and each took his predetermined place in the service of a daimyo whom the shogun was suspecting, so that the shogun would be able to find out all the better what went on under their direction. For he knew that many nobles begrudged him his position."[4]

Toda Mosui's record of the fifth shogun's government opens with a list of Tsunayoshi's retainers dismissed by him for various reasons as soon as he was named shogun.[5] Mosui voices no doubt about the genuineness of these dismissals. Yet the action of sending away longtime retainers at the very moment when their support would have been most needed and at a time of his career when Tsunayoshi's predecessors had done the opposite, namely, surround themselves by the men they knew, sounds suspicious and gives support to Kaempfer's theory. Later, when Tsunayoshi had established his authority, he could afford to be less secretive about the placement of his spies. By the time the German doctor arrived in Japan, some ten years after the event, it was apparently an open secret, for he noted when describing the procession of the daimyo of Owari on the Tōkaidō highway: "These stewards or chancellors appointed to a fief by the shogun must be regarded as informers rather than stewards, because they are selected from among the shogun's courtiers and companions."[6]

The importance Tsunayoshi placed on clandestine information about his senior subjects is also reflected in a work with the interesting title *Dokai kōshūki*. The title alludes to a passage in Mencius that Legge renders as "When he [the prince] regards them [his ministers] as the ground or as grass, they regard him as a robber and an enemy." An alternative translation of "ground" and "grass" (*dokai*) is "rubbish." The title of this detailed and candid government record about the character and habits of the daimyo and their senior retainers is likely to have been added at a later date, when after the death of the fifth shogun the daimyo discovered the often unflattering remarks about their families in the *bakufu* record. The provocative title says much about the relationship between the ruler and his vassals, and the source of the document was no doubt the many informers placed in the above fashion.[7]

Tsunayoshi's well-planned and prompt action upon becoming shogun contradicts the writings of historians who see him as a dilettante and a political lightweight. Traditionally Tsunayoshi's administration is divided into a period of beneficial reforms under the leadership of Hotta Masatoshi, and corrupt and incompetent government after Masatoshi's death in 1684. A closer examination of the record reveals, however, that Tsunayoshi himself consistently held the reins from the beginning of his government, at a time when the grand councilor Sakai Tadakiyo was still in office and before Masatoshi was appointed to a leading position.

Setting the Tone

Only twenty days after Ietsuna's death, and just two days after his funeral, Tsunayoshi issued his first directive to the administration. The order of 28.5.Enpō 8 (1680) notes that, until then, senior officials had returned to their homes at the hour of the sheep. Depending on the season, this was sometime between two and four o'clock in the afternoon. From now on, the order decrees, if there is work to be done, officials are to stay until late into the night.[8] This early directive encapsulates the spirit of the next thirty years of Tsunayoshi's government. It is likely to have been conceived even before he became shogun, when the early departure of officials permitted him perusal of their records; it clearly bears the imprint of his personal style and is unlikely to have been initiated by anybody but the new shogun himself.

Tsunayoshi was soon able to put into force his policy of strict punishment of *fudai* daimyo, a hallmark of his government. On 24.5 the daimyo Naitō Tadakatsu, while on duty at Zōjōji, unsheathed his sword and killed the daimyo Nagai Hisanaga. Within the same day, the record notes, Tadakatsu was condemned to death and his castle confiscated. But Hisanaga's castle and domain were also confiscated rather than passed on to a candidate within his family since the former, it was argued, had failed to appoint a successor.[9] Thus even before his official installation as shogun, Tsunayoshi had added over 100,000 *koku* to *bakufu* coffers.

Tsunayoshi moved from the second enceinte, where he came to reside on being proclaimed shogunal successor shortly before Ietsuna's death, to the main castle on 10.7.Enpō 8 (1680). Even though the grand ceremony of installment took place only in the eighth month, the official record considered 27.7 as the first day of his government.[10] But already on the ninth day of that month, he appointed Makino Narisada as his chamberlain *(go soba)* to serve him at the main castle.[11] This was not the action of a dilettante promoting his favorites, as traditional historians are wont to portray it; the speed with which Tsunayoshi singled out and appointed Narisada accurately reflects the priorities and power structure of his future government. In his position of chamberlain, Narisada rose to become one of the most powerful men in the country, gradually taking on many functions and prerogatives of the senior councilors, and his appointment predates that of Hotta Masatoshi by nearly a month.

Next, only four days after succeeding to the position of shogun, Tsunayoshi took the unusual step of personally charging his senior inspectors *(ōmetsuke)* and inspectors *(metsuke)* with their duties.[12] These officials are often described as the eyes and ears of the senior councilors and junior councilors respectively, with the senior inspectors reporting the actions of the daimyo, while the inspectors supervised the Tokugawa housemen, the *hatamoto*, and all duties performed at Edo castle. Yet having the prerogative of directly reporting to the shogun, the inspectors were much feared even by those whom in theory they served and represented one of the shogun's most important tools in gaining control over officialdom.[13]

On the following day, 26.7, the shogun personally appointed new men to the important offices of magistrate of temples and shrines *(jisha bugyō)*, Edo city magistrate *(Edo machi bugyō)*, and director of finance *(kanjō gashira)*.[14] In these three offices was vested the major responsibility for the government of the people and the country's finances, and the immediate change of officials on the accession of a new shogun was, again, highly unusual.[15]

The above orders and appointments systematically prepared the ground for the shogun's personal involvement in the administration of the country within a short time frame. In view of their nature and timing, they are unlikely to have been initiated by anybody but the new shogun himself.

The special appointment of the senior councilor Hotta Masatoshi to be responsible for the "administration of the farmers" took place early in the following month of that year. But before Masatoshi's role in Tsunayoshi's government is examined in greater detail, another incident that clearly set the tone of the new administration must be discussed. This is the punishment of a close, senior relative, the daimyo Matsudaira Mitsunaga, in what is known as the Echigo *sōdō*: the succession dispute of the Echigo domain.

The Echigo Dispute

The large and strategic Echigo domain facing the Japan Sea and Korea was assigned by the first shogun Ieyasu to his sixth son, Tadateru, in 1614. The surrounding *tozama* daimyo, lords that supported Ieyasu only after the battle of Sekigahara, were ordered to assist with the building of a fortress worthy of the owner, Takada castle, and the domain with its considerable lands of 750,000 *koku* became the Tokugawa stronghold in northeastern Japan. Yet Tadateru's fortunes did not last long. On account of misconduct during the Osaka campaigns, the domain was confiscated three years later and after several owners was eventually assigned in much reduced form to Matsudaira Mitsunaga (1615–1707), the daimyo involved in this succession dispute.

Mitsunaga was the grandson of Ieyasu's second son, Yūki Hideyasu.[16] It will be recalled that Hideyasu was originally adopted by Hideyoshi and, when an heir was born to Hideyoshi, given to the Yūki family of Echizen in adoption. Hideyasu's son, Matsudaira Tadanao (1595–1650), inherited his father's domain of 650,000 *koku* in Echizen but on account of mismanagement was later stripped of it and sent into exile in Bungo.

Mitsunaga's mother Katsuko was the third daughter of the second shogun Hidetada and was also known as Takada *hime*, the Princess of Takada.[17] Presumably on account of being the third shogun's nephew, the young Mitsunaga in spite of his father's downfall eventually received Takada castle and a domain of 250 *koku* in Echigo.[18] At his coming-of-age ceremony the third shogun Iemitsu awarded him the second character of his own name, he was promoted to the third court rank, and his status was similar to that of the Three Related Houses of Owari, Kii, and Mito.[19] Born in the year of the battle of Osaka, he was some thirty years Tsunayoshi's senior, and throughout the latter's early life he had occupied a prominent and favored position at Edo castle. The third shogun Iemitsu had even requested his special support for his young son, the future fourth shogun.[20] Mitsunaga's father and mother were both grandchildren of the first shogun Ieyasu, and he could thus boast of more Tokugawa blood in his veins than Tsunayoshi himself. Ranking right after the Three Related Houses, he was also received by Tsunayoshi in that order when he became shogun.[21] Yet this senior scion of the Tokugawa house was to be stripped of his domain and placed in detention by the judgment of a court presided over by the shogun in person before the first year of the new administration had ended.

Scholars are divided on who was responsible for the incident that caused Mitsunaga to fall. *Tokugawa jikki* places the blame firmly on the "villain" *(kanjin)* Oguri Masanori,[22] but the scholar Momose Meiji believes that Masanori was dealt with unjustly and presents a more nuanced account.

He points out that in Kanbun 5 (1665) the Echigo domain was struck by a devastating earthquake, destroying a large number of dwellings as well as part of the castle, killing some 150 samurai and ten times as many commoners. Among those killed were the domain's two senior and most capable administrators. On their death their respective sons, Oguri Mimasaka no Kami Masanori and Ogita Shume were appointed, and this inaugurated a period of misadministration and rivalry between the two houses. Momose argues that Oguri Masanori had progressively undertaken successful reforms, while Ogita Shume stood for the conservative party resenting the change.[23] The latter, however enjoyed greater support, being backed by some 850 retainers of the domain, while Oguri

Masanori's supporters amounted only to 135.[24] When in Enpō 2 (1674) Mitsunaga's only son, Tsunakata, died at the age of forty-one without an heir, the division deepened, with rumors circulating that Tsunakata had been poisoned by Oguri Masanori. Not expecting to father more children, Mitsunaga decided to appoint an heir from among his relatives, but there were several contenders.

During his exile in Bungo, Mitsunaga's father had started a second family into which two sons and one daughter were born, and Mitsunaga took care of them on his father's death. These stepbrothers and their sons were now contenders for the position. Mitsunaga's stepsister was married to Oguri Masanori, and the son of this union was a further contender. In addition, a younger son of the Owari house was being considered for adoption into the Echigo branch. The council of retainers finally settled on the fourteen-year-old Mantoku, the son and successor of the eldest, already deceased, stepbrother of Mitsunaga, Nagami Shisei. In Enpō 3 (1675) the *bakufu* confirmed Mantoku's succession, and the fourth shogun Ietsuna bestowed upon him a character of his own name, calling him Tsunakoku.[25]

Oguri Masanori had supported the candidacy of Tsunakoku rather than that of his own son. As a reward Mitsunaga intended to adopt Masanori's son, his nephew, so that he might eventually succeed to the 50,000 *koku* domain left to Mitsunaga on his retirement. When this became known in the first month of Enpō 7 (1679), it led to a riotous gathering of several hundred samurai around the Oguri mansion. At this point Sakai Tadakiyo stepped in on behalf of the *bakufu*. He sent a letter of sympathy to Oguri Masanori and, on the basis of a judgment of the *hyōjōsho*, the *bakufu*'s highest judicial organ, had the leaders of the protest, Ogita Shume and Mitsunaga's younger stepbrother, Nagami Ōkura, exiled to Chōshū and Matsue respectively.[26]

Toda Mosui, however, heard that this judgment went against the wishes of the fourth shogun Ietsuna, who accused Tadakiyo of favoritism towards Oguri Masanori and of dealing with the affair as a private rather than a public matter. Further, according to Mosui, the shogun considered also the domain lord Matsudaira Mitsunaga guilty and wanted him punished. But apparently Tadakiyo pointed to the illustrious ancestry of Mitsunaga, emphasized that his house was the most important among the Tokugawa relatives, and would not consider confiscation of the domain.[27]

Mosui's account relies on hearsay. However, similar information is contained in *Buya shokudan*, though here the story goes that with Ietsuna being ill, Tadakiyo did not wish to take on the responsibility of punishing a Tokugawa scion.[28] A reliable source spells out that Tsunayoshi was given similar advice when, after becoming shogun, he consulted his brother-in-law, the lord of Owari, Tokugawa Mitsutomo, on whether Mitsunaga's domain should be confiscated. According to *Yamato no kami nikki*, the diary of Matsudaira Naonori, a relative acting as intermediary in the affair, Mitsutomo also reminded Tsunayoshi of Mitsunaga's illustrious ancestry. Mitsunaga's father had fought in the battle of Osaka, and thus this branch of the family was even more important than the Three Related Houses. Mitsutomo further pointed out that punishment of Mitsunaga would act as a precedent: should similar trouble arise among the retainers of one of the Three Related Houses, their domains would also have to be confiscated. This, he argued, would seriously weaken Tokugawa supremacy.[29]

Tsunayoshi, however, did not take the advice of his brother-in-law. Mitsunaga's domain was confiscated, and he and his successor designate were placed under house arrest.[30] Among his retainers all the parties were punished, with the severest punishment, the order to commit *seppuku*, being handed to Oguri Masanori and his son, who previously had Sakai Tadakiyo's support. Yet punishment did not end here. The senior daimyo and officials who had dealt with the case before Tsunayoshi's accession were also punished.[31] Even the two related daimyo who had acted as intermediaries in an attempt to solve the problem, Matsudaira Naonori, the author of *Yamato no kami nikki*, and Matsudaira Chikayoshi, lord of the neighboring Echizen domain, were transferred to smaller domains and placed under house arrest.[32]

Sakai Tadakiyo and the Echigo Dispute

A further casualty of the Echigo succession dispute was, according to Toda Mosui, the former grand councilor Sakai Tadakiyo. A month before the judgment was pronounced in the sixth month of Tenna 1 (1681), he had died a mysterious death in his secondary villa at Ōtsuka, away from the hub of government. What Toda Mosui described as an unconfirmed rumor, namely, that Tadakiyo's handling of the affair was contrary to the wishes of the fourth shogun, finds support in other sources.

If the fourth shogun had criticized Tadakiyo for handling the Echigo dispute as a "private matter,"[33] then certainly Tsunayoshi saw to it that it was dealt with in the most public fashion possible. The *bakufu*'s highest judicial organ, the *hyōjōsho*, was assembled in the grand hall of Edo castle. It normally was presided over by the senior councilors,[34] but on this occasion the shogun headed the assembly in person, and a large number of people, from the shogun's nephew and the Three Related Houses down to inspectors of various ranks, Confucian scholars, and the shogun's pages were assembled. In front of this large audience, senior officials of the Echigo domain were questioned by Hotta Masatoshi. After this had continued for some time, the shogun droned in a loud voice: "Reach a decision now! Finish quickly!" "There was nobody among the assembled who did not tremble in fear," the record notes.[35]

Historians have criticized the shogun for having made up his mind earlier and having staged the official hearing merely as a display.[36] This criticism, I believe, is justified. The main purpose apparently was to show that—contrary to the previous government's handling of the affair—the matter ought to be dealt with publicly. But it must not be forgotten that, as outlined above, the shogun had previously given thought to the judgment, and we know that he was troubled enough to consult a relative on how to deal with it. The questioning of the parties, moreover, was not confined to the court hearing. Some six months earlier a detailed investigation into the affair had begun, with a continuing stream of people requested by the senior councilors to come to Edo for questioning. It is here that we can see an interesting correlation with the withdrawal from politics of Sakai Tadakiyo.[37]

The new inquiry began with the senior councilors requesting Matsudaira Mitsunaga to send Oguri Masanori as well as two other senior retainers to Edo for questioning on 3.12.Enpō 8.[38] Six days later Sakai Tadakiyo was granted retirement, ostensibly on account of frequent illness during "recent years."[39] Illness was a standard excuse for retirement when it was preferable not to mention the real cause, and it is consequently not surprising that we do not find any reference to Tadakiyo's bad health in records for earlier years. It is true that, by the tenth month of Tenna 8, there are reports that Tadakiyo was not altogether well, but the incidents are minor. On climbing a slope to the entrance of a mansion, he was troubled by phlegm, and he was given hot water to drink to overcome the trouble. His face, hands, and feet were reported to be swollen; another source describes him as a little bloated. Tadakiyo had continued to perform his duties as grand councilor after Tsunayoshi's accession, but there must have been a host of obvious and less obvious signs that the new shogun's policy made him vulnerable to attack. The health problems recorded in the tenth month might well have reflected the continuing stress caused by the uncertainty of his position.[40]

Tadakiyo was not content with the shogun's official permission to retire and the obvious consequences with regard to his involvement in government affairs. To emphasize the point that he had totally distanced himself from politics, two days after his official retirement he sent messengers to the Three Related Houses and other daimyo to inform them that from now on he would refuse any requests concerning government business. And to demonstrate that he was no longer accessible in any way, he took the drastic step of closing the wooden doors at the entrance of his villa, forbidding the passing of all traffic.[41] Since one form of punishment current in Tokugawa Japan was the confinement in one's residence with doors and windows barred and outside access denied,[42] this might well have been the origin of the rumor Kaempfer heard that the shogun had put Tadakiyo under house arrest and had forbidden that provisions enter his residence.

Early in the next year, on 12.1.Tenna 1, the *bakufu* revised the rules governing the workings of the *hyōjōsho*. The days and time of the court's sitting were determined, and the behavior of officials and regulations for speedy and thorough questioning were detailed. As these revisions were being promulgated, Tadakiyo's official residence at the Ōte gate was confiscated and reallocated to Hotta Masatoshi.⁴³

It was well known to contemporaries that the new shogun was displeased with the performance of government duties under his predecessor; the shogun's complaint that public procedures had been corrupted by private interests was discussed in daimyo correspondence. The scholar Fukuda Chizuru, the author of the most recent and most detailed study of the Echigo succession quarrel, therefore concluded that this new emphasis on correct official procedure would have prompted Sakai Tadakiyo to distance himself from the Echigo affair.⁴⁴ When the shogun instructed the senior councilors to undertake a detailed examination of the matter, the only possible way Tadakiyo, as one of the councilors, could distance himself was by resignation. When the rules of the *hyōjōsho* were redefined and tightened, the implication was that Sakai Tadakiyo as grand councilor had been negligent in his duties of supervising this, the *bakufu*'s highest judicial organ.

The first three Tokugawa rulers had not hesitated to confiscate the domains of related houses on account of internal dispute as a display of their supreme authority. After the weak government of the fourth shogun, the Echigo quarrel provided Tsunayoshi with an opportunity to reestablish such earlier shogunal authority. But, as Fukuda has pointed out, Tsunayoshi's action was unprecedented inasmuch as he not only confiscated the domain and punished domain officials, but also punished those in the central government in charge of the affair.⁴⁵ Moreover, punishment was not confined here to officials handling the affair. As mentioned above, even the *fudai* daimyo acting as intermediaries were disciplined. The grand councilor Sakai Tadakiyo and the senior councilor Kuze Hiroyuki (1609-1679), both involved in the handling of the affair, had died in the meantime. But they were nevertheless pronounced guilty, and in their stead their descendants and relatives were punished.⁴⁶ Matsudaira Naonori, himself a victim of this new policy, notes expressly in his diary that the punishment was given because the shogun believed that Tadakiyo and Hiroyuki had handled the Echigo quarrel badly.⁴⁷

Tsunayoshi's judgment of Tadakiyo's performance only appears in the records some twelve months after his accession as shogun and after Tadakiyo's death. Yet contemporaries would have noticed the winds of change in government on Tsunayoshi's accession, and Tadakiyo at the center of the administration would soon have come to anticipate the punishment he received post mortem. In the past, the practice of *junshi*, following one's lord into death, had prevented such conflicts between the new shogun and those who had risen to power under his predecessor. When under Ietsuna the seat of authority shifted from the shogun to his ministers and government positions were linked to hereditary rights, continuity in government offices on the appointment of a new shogun seemed assured, and the practice of *junshi* was forbidden. Tsunayoshi, however, was determined to turn back the clock, and the Echigo quarrel provided him with an excellent occasion. It not only permitted him to establish his authority over the Related Houses by punishing a senior relative with illustrious credentials, but also afforded him an opportunity to rid himself of a strongman whose political philosophy was incompatible with his own.[48] An addition of several hundred thousand *koku* to government coffers and the chance to conduct the first of many land surveys to match the nominal income from lands with their actual yield were further benefits.[49]

Did the Echigo judgment also provide Tsunayoshi with the occasion to revenge himself for the attempt to install an imperial prince as shogun in his stead? As some historians have pointed out, the lord of Echizen, Matsudaira Mitsunaga, was the uncle of Arisugawa Yukihito, the imperial prince Sakai Tadakiyo was rumored to have favored as successor.[50] Yet Mitsunaga was no blood relative of Yukihito. After having been adopted by the second shogun Hidetada, Mitsunaga's sister Kameko was betrothed to Takamatsu Miya Yoshihito, who later succeeded as Emperor Gosai. Yukihito was a son of the latter but by a different woman.[51] Yet even though Mitsunaga and Yukihito were not blood relatives, Mitsunaga might well have used his family connections to assist with Tadakiyo's plans.

Our sources do not permit us any insights into the personal sentiments of the new shogun or to determine with any certainty whether Tadakiyo had indeed contemplated installing the imperial prince as successor. What can be established is that Tsunayoshi failed to send the usual gifts and messages of sympathy on the illness of his former grand councilor and even forbade one of his physicians to visit Tadakiyo on the excuse that he was needed elsewhere.[52] After Tadakiyo's death, his son experienced great difficulty in getting permission to send the body back to the family temple in the domain at Maebashi, and the procession finally left secretly in the dark of night.[53] The nineteenth-century *Kasshi yawa* contains the rumor that Tsunayoshi, still in fear of Tadakiyo even after he heard of his death, sent messengers on two occasions to ascertain that the former grand councilor had indeed passed away. This seems an unlikely story, since Tsunayoshi could much more easily have questioned the attending physicians, but the fact that Tsunayoshi resented his daimyo visiting the ailing Tadakiyo is well documented.[54]

In turn the man who had supported Tsunayoshi's succession, the senior councilor Hotta Masatoshi, was favored by the new shogun. He inherited Sakai Tadakiyo's mansion, strategically located at the Ōte gate of the inner castle compound, and conducted procedures at the grand court hearing of the Echigo affair. Earlier, on 5.8.Enpō 8, soon after the shogun's accession, he had been made solely responsible for the farmers of the shogunal domain. Domain increases and the promotion to grand councilor were to follow. Consequently some historians see in Hotta Masatoshi a successor to Sakai Tadakiyo.[55] Whether Masatoshi was merely an initially more pliable replacement for Tadakiyo will be taken up in the next chapter.

8

The Rise and Fall of Hotta Masatoshi

As the preparations for the official installation of the new shogun were under way in the summer of 1680, typhoons were battering northeastern Japan, causing high seas and flooding. Fields were devastated, and the lack of sun prevented the crop from ripening. In anticipation of the festivities and a shortfall in the harvest, rice was being hoarded, and the price skyrocketed. People were starving, and Edo and its surrounds were on the brink of a major famine.[1]

To contemporaries the havoc caused by the natural elements signified the discontent of the gods with the government. Action was needed to placate the gods and help the people. Tsunayoshi responded to the challenge by taking the unprecedented step of appointing one of his senior councilors, Hotta Masatoshi, to be solely responsible for the administration of the farmers.

The *bakufu* domain was traditionally administered by intendants *(daikan)* under the supervision of the directors of finance *(kanjō gashira)*. These in turn were administered by the senior councilors in monthly rotation, a procedure that encouraged neither the acquisition of specialized technical expertise nor close supervision. On 5.8.Enpō 8 (1680), the shogun broke with tradition and charged Hotta Masatoshi solely and permanently to oversee this important sector of government.

Yet Tsunayoshi was not content simply to delegate these important duties. Only two days later Masatoshi was again called into the presence of the shogun to receive instructions on the subject, but this time Masatoshi's new subordinates, the four directors of finance, were also summoned directly to receive the shogun's orders. The shogun had heard that in recent years the farmers of the *bakufu* domains had been worked to exhaustion, and he ordered that they be administered with benevolence *(jinsei)* so that they would not be debilitated.[2] For all intents and purposes, Masatoshi's role of instructing the directors of finance had been taken over by the shogun.

Nine days later the shogun went one step further. Even though he had charged Masatoshi to supervise the farmers, he personally and publicly issued a stern warning to the intendants that their work was unsatisfactory and that in the future any misadministration would be strictly punished. Since the *bakufu*'s income was largely generated by its farmers, their supervision was synonymous with the supervision of "national finance" *(kokuyō)*. But these duties of supervision by just one senior councilor were now being redefined by placing an additional six high-ranking officials at Masatoshi's side. Two of these were Kyoto magistrates, three were directors of finance, while one occupied the position of inspector *(metsuke)*.[3]

For the first time in Tokugawa *bakufu* history, one senior councilor had been made solely responsible for the collection of tax rice and for the farmers who produced it and, moreover, had been personally given by the shogun a team of officials to assist him in these duties.[4] All this had been accomplished in less than a month, even before the official grand ceremonies *(tairei)* of shogunal succession had taken place on 20.8.[5] But the question remains whether Tsunayoshi saw in Hotta Masatoshi someone with the capability and willingness to execute his wishes or simply the best of a bad lot, whose unusual appointment was necessary to wrest the country's administration of financial affairs from the remaining senior councilors. Had the transfer of duties to Masatoshi and his team of officials been in fact no more than a clever maneuver to strip the senior councilors of part of their authority and place it in the shogun's hands?

Hotta Masatoshi's Role

Related to the question of Hotta Masatoshi's role is the timing of a comprehensive order detailing the responsibilities and duties of the intendants of the *bakufu* domain and regulating their work as tax collectors and administrators of the farming population. The order stated:

> The intendants are given the following orders.
>
> The people are the foundation of the state. All intendants must always bear in mind the hardships of the people and must govern them so that they do not suffer from hunger, cold, and so forth.
>
> When the administration is slack, people take to luxuries, and where there is luxury, work is neglected. There must be no luxury in the clothing, food, and housing of the people.
>
> Where there is a great distance between the people and their superiors, there is much distrust. Again, superiors also frequently do not trust their inferiors. You must be diligent to govern all matters so that there is no distrust between superiors and inferiors.
>
> All intendants and others must always be circumspect, frugal, well informed about the details of farming, and diligent in the collection of tax. They

must not leave matters to assistants; it is essential that they perform them themselves. Then the assistants cannot enrich themselves. Needless to say, the intendants, but also their assistants and others, are under strict orders not to use the people under their administration for private purposes and not to permit any borrowing of gold, silver, rice, or copper coins.

Attention must always be paid to dikes, bridges and similar structures, and they must be repaired before major damage occurs. If there is strife among the peasants, it should be arbitrated privately while it is still a minor matter and not be permitted to become a major issue with parties taking sides.

When there is a change of personnel at the intendancy or when people are transferred to other locations, there should be no outstanding taxes. There should be no negligence in any matter. Orders must always be executed promptly.[6]

Based on the original *bakufu* record, *Tokugawa jikki* cites the order under 3.8, two days before Hotta Masatoshi was appointed by Tsunayoshi to singly supervise the administration of the farmers. In official compilations of laws, such as *Gotōke reijō* and *Ofuregaki kanpō shūsei*, however, the order is listed in a slightly different version a month later, namely, under the third day of the eighth intercalary month *(urū hachigatsu)*. The historian Tsuji Tatsuya admits that the *Tokugawa jikki* date, based on the actual *bakufu* record, must be considered more reliable than that of later compilations such as *Gotōke reijō* and *Ofuregaki kanpō shūsei*. But since the order as listed in the latter is signed by Hotta Masatoshi, he prefers the later date. Tsuji argues that while Masatoshi could have been the senior councilor in charge for that month *(tsuki ban)*, the order would have been too important to have been signed merely by one senior councilor under the old system of rotation.[7]

There is also the possibility that Tsunayoshi had personally and directly issued this comprehensive order to the intendants before Masatoshi's appointment, just as he had previously taken the unusual liberty of personally appointing and instructing the inspectors and magistrates. At the protest of the senior councilors that this was in violation of bureaucratic custom, Tsunayoshi could then have used the stratagem of making the senior councilor who had shown him the greatest support, namely, Hotta Masatoshi, solely responsible for this area of the administration to prevent the interference of the remaining senior councilors in the future. The fact that even after Masatoshi's appointment the shogun did not simply let the matter rest in his hands, but repeatedly issued directives and called Masatoshi's subordinates into his presence, supports the theory that Masatoshi's appointment was made to permit the shogun more interference in government affairs rather than less. In his own writing Masatoshi refers to the order as having come from the shogun.[8] Finally, Tsunayoshi used the same kind of persistent bureaucratic maneuvering when he tried to enforce his so-called Laws of Compassion discussed later.

The order to the intendants is conceptually very much in line with what we know of Tsunayoshi's political philosophy. The saying from Mencius that the people are the most important element of a nation[9] was not new in Japan. Similar words were put into the mouth of Ieyasu in *Honsaroku*, a work attributed to Honda Masanobu. But here little consideration is given to the welfare of the farmers. To the contrary, Ieyasu ordered the intendants to pitch tax levels so that the farmers barely retained enough grain to continue, and to demand corvée to the extent that they had just enough energy to produce good crops.[10] The effect of this policy on the farmers is described by the Korean Confucian Kang Hang (Kyōkō, 1567–1618), famous as teacher and associate of Fujiwara Seika, who was appalled by the conditions under which Japanese farmers eked out a living.[11] While Tsunayoshi does not permit the farmers any luxuries, neither are they to be squeezed to the last: hardship must be avoided. But the greatest difference is that attention has shifted from the duties of the farmers to that of the intendants. The intendants are to deal in person with the farmers and not to delegate, to earn the trust of the farmers by not emphasizing differences in status, and to become knowledgeable about the details of farm work. In other words, the intendants were not just to command and collect taxes but were to take a hands-on approach and personally interact with the people they governed.

The matter of the intendants is discussed in greater detail in a later chapter. As for Hotta Masatoshi, the question of whether, apart from welcoming an enhancement of his own position, he equally welcomed and understood the fundamental changes that were taking place in government policy requires investigation. His *Yōgen roku*, a document he began to compose in Tenna 3 (1683), throws doubt on whether he did.

The *Yōgen roku* of Hotta Masatoshi

Hotta Masatoshi began his *Yōgen roku* in the eleventh month of Tenna 3 (1683), but with his assassination only nine months later, it remained a short document, the printed version barely covering nine pages. Tokutomi Sohō has suggested that the style and writing are rather too polished for Masatoshi, and the final copy might well have been edited by a Confucian scholar like Hitomi Yūgen, accustomed to producing such records. He has no doubt, however, that the content owes its existence to Masatoshi. While Tokutomi refers to *Yōgen roku* in his detailed history of the premodern period, modern historians rarely give it a mention.[12] The title itself, alluding to a passage in *The Book of History* about a faithful minister recording the words of the mythical Chinese sage emperor Shun,[13] suggests that this is a piece of hagiographic, and hence unreliable, writing. The short introduction certainly follows the classic pattern of praising the shogun for his virtue and untiring efforts. Yet an examination of the content shows that the document describes a host of untraditional and highly unpopular shogunal measures that often seem to elicit doubt and surprise rather than praise from the author.

Tsunayoshi has traditionally been described as spendthrift and pleasure-loving, and the rather puritan measures of his early government are usually attributed to Hotta Masatoshi. Details cited in *Yōgen roku*, however, firmly point out that these were the shogun's initiatives and convey the impression that the author was at pains to record for posterity that he was not responsible for these often highly unpopular measures.

One such unpopular policy was the scrapping of the large vessel *Atake maru*. The ship had been built with great expense by the third shogun Iemitsu and was said to have been an impressive sight with its mast of over fifty meters and a two-story donjonlike construction on its deck. As the name implied, the vessel's primary purpose was to provide the shogun with a safe haven in case of danger.[14] But it was also used by Iemitsu to entertain his daimyo and officials, who were instructed to dress in particularly colorful clothes for such grand occasions, where sake flowed freely. When the fifth shogun heard about expensive repairs required to maintain the large vessel, he asked for an inquiry into the ship's military capabilities. Hearing that it had in fact very few and mainly a decorative function, he decided that the expense was not justified and ordered the vessel to be scrapped. The contemporary observer Toda Mosui recalls nostalgically the grand festivities on the vessel and leaves no doubt that scrapping it was a bad and unpopular decision.[15]

No doubt even more unpopular among *bakufu* officials was the shogun's order of sweeping dismissals and replacement of officials to combat corruption. One casualty in this general cleanup was the northern and southern offices of the Edo city magistrates, which Tsunayoshi considered overstaffed, and he ordered that each reduce its contingent of one hundred lower officials by forty people to sixty men.[16]

Yōgen roku relates how the shogun's exemplary behavior was causing people to change their lifestyle for the better, abandoning bad habits. Officials were no longer selling the residences granted to them by the *bakufu*, the use of pleasure boats had stopped, and so had feasting and elaborate tea parties. People were no longer calling on powerful officials for their own gain.[17] It is difficult to believe that the enforcement of such virtues was popular with Masatoshi. Considering the charges of opulent living made against him on his assassination, he might well have counted on the usual rewards of lavish entertainment and presents from his new powerful position. Toda Mosui certainly vents his anger over such austerity measures, the enforcement of which he claims resulted in the destruction of fine gardens by their owners and shogunal spies roaming the city to ferret out entertainment that exceeded the stipulated limits.[18]

One reason the Japanese government tolerated the Dutch at Nagasaki was the establishment's desire for imported luxury items. Tsunayoshi, however, declared foreign luxury goods to be unnecessary and forbade the import of rare animals that could not be turned into medicine. Insisting that a padded cotton garment was sufficient to keep warm, he also stopped the import of silk gauze and cloth with gold threads.[19] Thereupon the mother of his son decided to pull out the gold threads from the child's garments, and the servants had no choice but to do likewise. *Yōgen roku* explains that the virtue displayed by the shogun resulted in the military aristocracy and officials, the samurai as well as the commoners, willingly following suit. This must have been as hard to believe then as it is now, and Tokugawa readers might well have understood the word "willingly" to be a euphemism for "had no option but." While modern historians often assert that such economy measures were initiated by Masatoshi, *Yōgen roku*, by carefully detailing how such stringent economy measures came about, leaves no doubt that Masatoshi did not want to be seen as the originator of such unpopular policies.[20]

Yet worse was to come. To further set an example to his subjects, the shogun one day ordered not only that from now on his garments were no longer to be made of fine material, but also that his clothes were not to be replaced even when old and soiled. Masatoshi's record states laconically that officials serving him had no choice but to do likewise.[21] In a country where personal cleanliness was sacrosanct and the luxury of replacing soiled items a much cherished privilege by those who could afford it, the shogun's unwillingness to part with his soiled garments must have been considered eccentric rather than virtuous. Surely, any author intent on embellishing the shogun's reputation would have omitted such onerous detail. Masatoshi and his colleagues, forced to join the shogun in his eccentricities, no doubt were highly irritated, and here again the likely purpose of the record was to set down for posterity that Masatoshi had to suffer and did not initiate such directives. That these directives and practices were not limited to the life span of Hotta Masatoshi is documented by Ogyū Sorai's evidence for the later part of Tsunayoshi's government.

Tsunayoshi was fond of citing the Chinese classics he had studied during his youth to legitimize his policies. But he was quick to reject any admonition from his ministers that no "previous example" for his actions existed in *bakufu* history. He argued that his predecessors had followed in direct succession but that he had succeeded "in unusual circumstances" and therefore felt no need to observe Tokugawa precedent.[22] Did this statement refer to the fact that he had not been groomed for the position of shogun like his predecessors and with his very different education could not be expected to follow their example? Masatoshi was soon to find out that his lord not only refused to respect the standards of cleanliness adopted by the privileged elite, but also expected his minister to care for those people who had never known anything but old, soiled clothing.

The Rays of the Sun and the Moon

Yōgen roku relates how one day Masatoshi reported to the shogun seeing two wretched street urchins. Moved by the abject poverty of the two children, he had felt a strong inner compulsion to help the children immediately. But then he rejected this urge, it not being the duty of the shogun's highest minister to attend to such a trifling matter. The shogun, however, corrected him saying: "Why should a truly benevolent man ask whether a matter is great or small? The rays of the sun and the moon light up even the smallest object. Actually your mistake was in thinking that it was wrong to agonize over such a small matter. Masatoshi went red with embarrassment and engraved this in his heart as perspiration was streaming down his back."[23]

Like his famous contemporary in France, the Roi de Soleil Louis XIV, Tsunayoshi saw himself as absolute ruler of his empire. This paradigm of autocratic authority was fundamental to the Confucian classics, where the sage rulers Yao and Shun governed their peasant population with the help of devoted ministers. It was, however, not a paradigm applying to Japan, where Ieyasu initially had established Tokugawa supremacy as primus inter pares among a military elite. Even though the third shogun Iemitsu succeeded in strengthening central authority, these gains were more than lost during the thirty-year government of the fourth shogun. Men who in their capacity of territorial lords had divided loyalties had come to take charge of the central government, and had instituted policies and reforms to preserve their gains in authority. These covered every aspect of government, ranging from restricting *bakufu* posts to certain families and channeling funds to the daimyo after the Meireki fire— rather than restoring Edo castle to its former glory—to abolishing the practice of *junshi*, thus compelling a new shogun to accommodate the strongman of his predecessor.[24] The Confucianism Tsunayoshi had adopted as his guiding principle, however, knew no other political system than the autocratic one, and this could not but lead to conflict with any minister whose loyalties were divided between a strong central government and daimyo autonomy.

Yōgen roku indicates that the shogun's very simple and graphic explanation of his principles of autocratic government came as a shock to Masatoshi. One must question here why Masatoshi would provide a detailed description of his personal embarrassment in a record that was not a private diary but clearly a document to be made public and handed down to future generations. What was the purpose of showing himself so little attuned to the shogun's compassionate concern for the poor?

Accustomed to the ideals of the welfare state, where the central government is held responsible for the weaker members of society, today's reader has no doubt that the shogun's pronouncement was humane and appropriate. Within the framework of decentralized, delegated authority of seventeenth-century *bakufu* government, however, Masatoshi's personal restraint from helping the two street urchins would have been correct. The direct help the shogun demanded from his most senior minister was a gross interference with the duties of the Edo city magistrates and those below them who held the responsibility for the poor of the district in question.[25] As becoming a faithful minister, Masatoshi took the shogun's words of admonishment to heart. But this does not necessarily mean that he agreed with them. The realistic, detailed description of the effect the shogun's reprimand had on him indicates that it challenged his most cherished and fundamental convictions. Instead of keeping his embarrassment to himself, it was described in detail to elicit the sympathies of the reader for Masatoshi in his predicament of having to bow to the wishes of such an unreasonable ruler.

Masatoshi had supported Tsunayoshi's claim for the position of shogun, but this does not indicate that he wanted to change the status quo. Quite to the contrary, his support might well have been motivated by a desire to maintain the established order by ensuring the succession of a son of the third shogun, for his family had come to prosper under this ruler. Hotta Masatoshi was the third son of Iemitsu's senior councilor Hotta Masamori (1608–1651) and the daughter of his grand councilor Sakai Tadakatsu. While the Sakai family had already risen to prominence under the second shogun, Hotta Masamori's fortunes were due to the ardent patronage of the third shogun. Iemitsu's estimation of Masamori was indicated by the latter's rise in domain lands from a mere 700 *koku* to 110,000 *koku* in less than twenty years.[26] How close the ties were between ruler and minister is also indicated by Masamori's suicide on the shogun's death. While Masatoshi was only the third son, Iemitsu provided for him by having him adopted by his much-honored wet nurse Kasuga no Tsubone.[27] On the birth of Iemitsu's own son, the later Ietsuna, the then seven-year-old Masatoshi was appointed the infant's page, opening the door for an illustrious career. Succeeding to the position of junior councilor in Kanbun 10 (1670), Masatoshi was appointed senior councilor nine years later, in Enpō 7 (1679).[28] Marriage ties also allied him to those in authority: his wife was the daughter of the senior councilor Inaba Masanori, the son of the senior councilor Inaba Masakatsu, and grandson of Kasuga no Tsubone's husband Inaba Masanari.[29]

Hotta Masatoshi was a rival of the grand councilor Sakai Tadakiyo, but while his aim was to replace Tadakiyo in his position of authority, it was not to change the pattern of authority Tadakiyo had established. *Yōgen roku* shows that Masatoshi had little understanding of the shogun's vision of autocratic government, and contemporary sources indicate that he was attempting to step right into Tadakiyo's shoes, striving to assume the political power his predecessor had held.[30]

The Assassination

Fortunately for Tsunayoshi, Hotta Masatoshi was assassinated before such differences became a major political issue. Why he was assassinated by a distant cousin, the junior councilor Inaba Masayasu (1640–1684), has remained a mystery, for Masayasu was struck down immediately afterwards. The official *bakufu* record states that Masayasu had acted in a fit of insanity.[31] This is contradicted, however, by the fact that before the incident Masayasu made preparations for the move of his aged mother from his official villa, which would quickly be confiscated, and he had parted from her with due ceremony on the morning in question. Moreover, the previous night he had prepared a letter, and before climbing into his palanquin on the fatal morning, he instructed his retainers to send the letter he had left in his study to the castle should unexpected news arrive from there. He further carried a letter on him stating that the assassination was performed out of deep gratitude to the shogun for favors received.[32]

The contemporary Toda Mosui believed that Masayasu indeed had killed Hotta Masatoshi in good faith to rid the shogun and the country of an evil minister. He explains in some detail how Masatoshi had recently taken to extreme extravagance and had become self-seeking and ill-mannered to the point of ignoring the law. He had assumed authority to an extent that even his inferiors, the inspectors, fearing the consequences, had taken to counseling him gently. Mosui dwells at some length on Masatoshi's vices, which included ignoring the days of mourning for the previous shoguns and instead spending his time at unruly entertainment at his Hamachō villa near the water or at the mansions of his friends. Mosui even heard rumors that he was plotting against the shogun.[33]

Like Hotta Masatoshi's father, the Inaba family had come to prominence under the third shogun. Masayasu was the grandson of Kasuga no Tsubone's husband, Inaba Masanari, and first cousin of Ietsuna's and Tsunayoshi's senior councilor Inaba Masanori. In his capacity of chamberlain, Masayasu had been close to the fourth shogun, and the fifth shogun had personally picked him as his junior councilor. Unlike Hotta Masatoshi, Masayasu had come to share the shogun's enthusiasm for Confucianism and as such embraced his ideal of the autocratic sage rulers Yao and Shun. When dispatched to the Kinai region, Masayasu had personally visited the Confucian scholar Itō Jinsai and had received copies of his two major works, *Rongo kogi* (The ancient meaning of the Analects) and *Gomō jigi* (The meaning of terms in the Analects and Mencius), a fact noted in Jinsai's own record. Like the shogun himself, Masayasu had begun to assemble Confucian scholars around him, and it was said that on the fateful day he had on him Jinsai's *Gomō jigi*. There was no question for Mosui that the assassin Masayasu was the faithful minister who freed the ruler from a treacherous vassal.[34] His sentiments of commiserating with the assassin rather than the assassinated were shared by many at the time. Mito Mitsukuni felt that Masayasu should have been permitted to argue his case and criticized the senior councilors for not allowing him to remain alive. Mitsukuni publicly expressed his sympathy for Masayasu by calling at his mansion to express his condolences to the bereaved family.[35]

It was known, however, that Masayasu and Masatoshi were in disagreement over river works in the Kinai area. Masayasu had been placed in charge and only two months previously had returned from an inspection tour of the area to make his recommendations. Hotta Masatoshi, however, relied on the opinion of a man known as one of his fellow revelers, the entrepreneur Kawamura Zuiken (1618–1699), who had been assigned to the team. Masayasu not only resented the interference, but, it was said, also feared the report of the more knowledgeable entrepreneur, and it was believed to be no mere coincidence that he assassinated Masatoshi on the very day Zuiken was expected in Edo to make his report. The previous night Masayasu had visited Masatoshi, apparently in the hope of sorting out their differences, but when this proved impossible, he calmly prepared himself for the assassination the next day.[36]

Soon after the incident, the debate began on whether Masayasu had killed the grand councilor out of a personal grudge or for the greater good of the country. Arai Hakuseki, who was in the employ of Hotta Masatoshi, discussed this point with his fellow scholar Muro Kyūsō (1658–1734) and predictably came down firmly in favor of his slain master. Kyūsō noted that his opinion differed from that of most other people.[37] Masayasu's motive for killing his cousin could well have been a mixture of both factors.

Hotta Masatoshi is consistently described as honest, straightforward, quick-tempered, and arrogant.[38] Early in his life, his father had admonished him for his excessive pride by presenting him with two characters meaning "no arrogance" *(fukyō)*.[39] The quality of being honest and outspoken in his criticism he shared with his elder brother Hotta Masanobu (1631–1680). The latter became famous for returning his domain to the *bakufu* so that it might be used to alleviate the financial plight of the lower samurai. This action was accompanied by a document sharply criticizing the ministers conducting Ietsuna's government. It was only because of the esteem in which his father had been held by the third shogun that this was not taken as a punishable critique but as the action of a madman, and Masanobu was placed under house arrest. Masanobu again demonstrated the strength of his convictions when he committed suicide on the death of the fourth shogun, although the practice of *junshi*, following one's lord into death, had by that time become illegal.[40]

Hotta Masatoshi's support for the succession of the fifth shogun in the face of opposition from the influential grand councilor Sakai Tadakiyo showed a similar strength of conviction.[41] His forthright manner and honesty might well have endeared him to the fifth shogun—known to have been similarly outspoken—when both were united in their goal of establishing a new hierarchy of authority on the death of the fourth shogun. However, once opponents had been eliminated and the most urgent matters settled, their differences began to appear. This development could well have prompted Masatoshi to record for later generations his dutiful service but also his differences of opinion with the shogun in *Yōgen roku*. This would explain why Masatoshi began to compose the record only in the second half of 1683, some three years after he had begun service under the fifth shogun.

In Tenna 1 (1681) Masatoshi had been promoted to the high office of grand councilor, and his domain had steadily increased, demonstrating the shogun's favors. If he was arrogant in his youth, then succession to the highest ministerial office and the shogun's patronage could only have encouraged such tendencies. Although promoted by the fifth shogun, his temperament did not permit him to acquiesce to policies he believed to be wrong. Akin to his elder brother, he frankly expressed his criticism and took it upon himself not just to correct his colleagues, but also to council the shogun.[42] Tsunayoshi, however, was no less convinced of the correctness of his views and is unlikely to have appreciated the admonishments of his grand councilor. Those in government could not fail to notice that the shogun and his highest minister were set on a collision course and, as Mosui reported, even lower officials attempted to warn Masatoshi. For the junior councilor Inaba Masuyasu, who shared the shogun's Confucian ideals, there could be no question of who was right. His personal disagreements with Hotta Masatoshi could only have confirmed to him the importance of ridding his lord of his powerful grand councilor.

Some six years later Engelbert Kaempfer was told of the incident as well as of Masatoshi's unruly behavior. He heard of Masayasu's careful preparations, including the letter for the shogun with the explanation that he had sacrificed his life to remove a minister harboring evil designs. But the foreigner also heard a rumor that the assassination had been secretly ordered by the shogun.[43]

This rumor also appears in Japanese sources.[44] The fact that, while Masayasu was disabled by two senior councilors, the final death blow was delivered by Tsunayoshi's longtime retainer and chamberlain Kaneda Masakatsu could support this theory.[45] Further, Tsunayoshi was said to have been afraid of the spirit of the slain Masatoshi. According to Toda Mosui, when the shogun visited the graves of his predecessors at Kaneiji in Ueno at the end of the next year and heard that the temple Enkaku-in with Masatoshi's grave was close by, he had two screens set up in the direction of the temple to shield him during his visit. Later he apparently ordered that Masatoshi's stone coffin be dug up and interred deeper in the ground.[46] It was also noticeable that Masatoshi's heir, Hotta Masanaka, did not receive the treatment expected for a son of the shogun's highest minister slain in the course of duty. Over the years Masanaka's domain was repeatedly reduced in size, plummeting the house into poverty.[47]

More significant, however, is the fact that Hotta Masatoshi's assassination initiated what is generally referred to as "chamberlain government." It permitted the shogun to rid himself of his senior councilors in a very direct, physical fashion. Masatoshi's assassination had taken place outside the *goyōnin beya*, the room where the senior councilors habitually assembled, next to the shogun's own quarters. This justified the order that the ministers' chamber be moved to a more distant location within the castle. The now necessary work of go-between was assigned to the shogun's chamberlains, much increasing their authority and detailed knowledge of government affairs. It also opened the door for the shogun to bypass the senior councilors and use his chamberlains to deal directly with officials.[48]

The Imperfect Vessel

We will never know whether and how far the shogun or his chamberlains encouraged the assassination that brought about these political developments. We know, however, that the shogun had already explained to Hotta Masatoshi how at times good government required the use of violence. No doubt in an effort to counsel the shogun with due propriety, Hotta Masatoshi one day questioned him about the violence committed by King Wu of ancient China to pacify the country. Tsunayoshi defended the sacrifice of morality to political expediency with the following words: "We all want everything to be perfect, but this is impossible to achieve. For instance, when we order a small vessel to be made, we at first consider the product to be pleasing. Yet when it is completed, we realize that it has defects and we are not altogether pleased with it. This applies to everything we do. The ancients said that in the purest water, fish cannot exist. Those ruling the country should ponder deeply about this matter."[49] The saying that fish need some mud and weeds to hide under in order to thrive appears in a number of classical Chinese texts and also in *Hagakure* (Hidden leaves). There are two slightly differing interpretations. One is that an overly exacting ruler does not attract men of talent. The other is that certain matters of government need to remain unexamined for the lower classes to live in tranquility, an explanation adopted by the contemporary *Hagakure*.[50] It appears that Tsunayoshi also subscribed to the latter interpretation, for the concept of relative morality in the conduct of government well applied to the enforcement of his Laws of Compassion. In the supervision of his daimyo and officials, however, Tsunayoshi was exacting and unwilling to tolerate any muddy waters, as will be discussed in the next chapter.

9

The Shogun's New Men

It is said that the French nobility—as represented by its famous diarist Louis de Rouvroy, second duke of Saint Simon—never forgave Louis XIV "for his prudent habit of entrusting the affairs of the realm to men who had risen from the professional classes by their proven ability, rather than to those who were descended from the great families of France."[1]

The Japanese establishment reacted no differently to Tsunayoshi's policy of promoting men regardless of their station. Those who profited from such measures, such as the philosopher Ogyū Sorai, however, concurred with the policy and pointed out that many members of the upper military aristocracy had failed to acquire the skills required for peacetime administration of a rapidly increasing population. Around 1720, under the eighth shogun Yoshimune, Sorai noted that "the daimyo especially are in every respect ignorant of the actual situation of the lower classes. Their learning is not even equivalent to that of ordinary people." He observed that, since government appointments were made in accordance with the level of an individual's inherited stipend, it was difficult to appoint "ordinary" people, and he continued to praise the fifth shogun for ignoring such constraints and employing his pages and castle servants in the shogunal secretariat. In this fashion Tsunayoshi bypassed the daimyo in their traditional high government positions, and Sorai noted that, since the fifth shogun's appointees were well-trained and experienced men, many were even now, under the eighth shogun, holding important posts.[2]

The Tenna Government

The majority of historians, however, see Tsunayoshi's attempt to minimize the influence of the daimyo in a different light. For them Hotta Masatoshi's assassination in Tenna 4 (1684) ended what is referred to as the Tenna Government *(Tenna no chi/ji)*, described as a period of positive reforms under his stern leadership. The years that followed are judged to have been the corrupt years of chamberlain government, where the daimyo in charge of the administration under the fourth shogun lost their restraining power over Tsunayoshi. The assertion of Ōishi Shinzaburō that, to the contrary, the early period of Tsunayoshi's government was reactionary, while the later part was progressive, preparing the ground for the modern state, has found little favor.³

As explained in the previous chapter, Masatoshi's assassination close to the shogun's quarters justified the order that the senior councilors' office be moved to a more distant part of the castle. The now necessary task of go-between was performed by the chamberlains, increasing their authority and giving them detailed knowledge of government affairs. It also opened the door for the shogun to bypass the senior councilors and use his chamberlains to deal directly with the appropriate officials.⁴ Four years after Masatoshi's assassination, the grand chamberlains had acquired such status that they were performing ceremonial functions on behalf of the shogun at the ancestral sanctuaries of Momijiyama, Kaneiji, and Zōzōji, which formerly had been the preserve of the senior councilors.⁵

Their unusual rise in status soon attracted the attention of contemporaries. Just one year after Masatoshi's assassination, Toda Mosui noted in his diary:

> On the twenty-first Matsudaira Iga no kami [Tadachika] entered the shogun's inner chambers, having been commanded to observe and learn the duties of Makino [Narisada] Bingo no Kami. He is neither a junior councilor nor a chamberlain. The three men, Makino Bingo Kami, Matsudaira Iga no Kami and Kitami Wakasa no Kami, serve the shogun in a manner unheard of in previous reigns. They are below the senior councilors but above the junior councilors. The authority of Makino Bingo no Kami, however, is greater than that of a senior councilor.⁶

Makino Narisada

Makino Narisada's authority was also evident to the Dutch, who on their annual visit to Edo had to negotiate the ladders of authority to be granted an audience with the shogun without too much delay after their arrival in Edo. Engelbert Kaempfer, as a member of the Dutch delegations of 1691 and 1692, described Narisada as the shogun's "most intimate councilor and the only one whom the shogun trusts." His privileged position became obvious when Kaempfer noted that "he enjoys the singular honor of receiving the shogun's words directly from his mouth during the audience and passing them on to us." The somewhat tall, thin man, who at the age of fifty-seven was judged by Kaempfer to be "almost seventy," obviously gained his sympathy, for he described him as having "a long, ordinary, nearly German face," "slow gestures," and "a friendly disposition." Although in popular history Tsunayoshi's chamberlains were to go down as greedy sycophants, at the time Narisada's reputation was very different. Kaempfer noted: "He is said not to be ambitious, revengeful, unjust, or selfish and consequently deserves to be favored by His Majesty."⁷

With these attributes Makino Narisada was the right man to administer the shogun's unconventional policies, but to find men to "observe and learn his duties" and to provide the infrastructure to his demanding office proved to be a difficult task.

Tsunayoshi's chamberlains are traditionally seen as the shogun's homosexual partners, or at least his favorites, appointed and dismissed at whim. Consequently this office is pictured as one where talent in flattering and amusing the shogun, rather than political expertise, was considered essential. Homosexual relationships Tsunayoshi might well have had, but it is doubtful whether these determined the employment of those who were to assist him in the government of the country. Some scrutiny of the office of grand chamberlain as well as the background of those entrusted with its duties reveals the exacting nature of this work and the arduous path men had to tread before they were eligible for appointment.

The Office of Grand Chamberlain

One problem in mapping out the career of the incumbents of this office is the discrepancy in information contained in various so-called reliable sources. Discrepancies about the length of service and reason for termination also exist with regard to other appointments, but nowhere are they so marked as here, an indication, perhaps, of the fluidity and experimental character of the office.

Thus according to two records, Makino Narisada was first appointed as chamberlain *(sobashū)* on Tsunayoshi's accession and only later was given the title of grand chamberlain, while a third one records him as becoming grand chamberlain soon after Tsunayoshi succeeded as shogun.[8]

There is also some difference of opinion as to whether Makino Narisada was the first grand chamberlain. He was the first man to carry this title, but Arai Hakuseki maintained that the first grand chamberlain was in fact Hotta Masamori, who under the third shogun had risen from page *(koshō)* to senior councilor, displaying his ultimate devotion to his lord by following him in death.[9] Scholars such as Tsuji Tatsuya argue that Hakuseki's theory was no more than an attempt to furnish the much-criticized office of grand chamberlain with a respectable past. Hakuseki did not look kindly on Tsunayoshi and his government, and it would have been painful for him to admit that his mentor, Manabe Akifusa, was occupying his influential position thanks to the fifth shogun. Tsuji points out that the term *kinju shuttōnin*—often said to denote the forerunners of the chamberlains—had been used for all officials in direct contact with the shogun before the *bakufu* was structured along more rigid lines. Once a system of separate offices had been imposed, the *kinju shuttōnin* filled offices such as those of senior and junior councilors. Thus they were not the forerunners of the grand chamberlains but those of various other *bakufu* offices.[10]

The question of whether the office of grand chamberlain had existed previously is merely theoretical. The first three shoguns all had personal advisers who acted as important ministers. Owing to the still fluid structure of the *bakufu*, they encountered no opposition in creating new offices for their new men, and in this sense the *kinju shuttōnin* as well as Iemitsu's junior and senior councilors were all forerunners of Tsunayoshi's grand chamberlains. Under the fourth shogun, however, these offices had become the preserve of the descendents of the men for whom they had originally been created, families who on the succession of the fifth shogun some three decades later had become strong enough to oppose the admission of newcomers to their ranks and the creation of new offices. Tsunayoshi, consequently, was unable to promote his own men freely to high government positions as the first three shoguns had done. Skillfully he used an existing office to eventually bypass the increasingly rigid structure of *bakufu* officialdom.

The office of chamberlain *(sobashū)*, of which Toda Mosui spoke with familiarity, had been created some thirty years before to take care of the young fourth shogun Ietsuna. Tsunayoshi used this office, which apparently had not yet assumed the rigidity of other *bakufu* appointments, in two ways. First, he upgraded it. With widened duties and powers, it gave rise to the office of grand chamberlain, the base of operation for the shogun's righthand man. Second, it served as a testing ground for men in whom the shogun saw some talent.

Also under the fourth shogun, successful performance in the position of chamberlain had led to higher appointments. Of the first twelve appointees, four men resigned and one was put under house arrest. The remainder, however, all proceeded to relatively important positions, including one appointee as Kyoto deputy *(Kyōto shoshidai)* and three promotions to junior councilor.[11]

What differed under Tsunayoshi was the background of men appointed as chamberlains. In Ietsuna's case they had with one exception held positions in the shogunal entourage such as senior head page *(koshō kumi gashira)* or performed various guard duties *(goshoin ban gashira, ōban gashira)*. Under Tsunayoshi the majority of appointees came from a much wider background of offices outside the shogunal entourage ranging from inspector general *(ōmetsuke)* to superintendent of finance *(kanjō bugyō)*. This change of background in appointees reflected Tsunayoshi's much wider interest in government affairs. His chamberlains were all men with specialized experience in various fields of *bakufu* administration, well qualified to put their technical skills at the disposal of the ruler.

Another difference between the appointees of the fourth and fifth shoguns was that the selection process was much more rigorous in the case of the latter, with a much smaller percentage of men proceeding to higher offices. In Ietsuna's case 83 percent of all chamberlains were promoted, while under Tsunayoshi only 42 percent were. Of the nineteen men who had been appointed as chamberlain during the initial decade of Tsunayoshi's government, nine were either dismissed or resigned, two died, and only four were promoted to the post of grand chamberlain. Three others became junior councilors, and one man was promoted to master of shogunal ceremony (sōshaban).

In Genroku 2 (1689) Tsunayoshi created the office of personal adviser (okuzume), and from that time on it was largely in this office that future grand chamberlains had to prove themselves. Relatively little is known about this position, which was abolished at Tsunayoshi's death. Its functions are described as "answering the shogun's questions," and it appears that initially they largely overlapped with those of the chamberlains. The nineteenth-century bakufu record of appointments Ryūei bunin gives only sparse information on the termination of service and future career of the occupants of this office,[12] but the turnover of men appears to have been similar to that of the chamberlains. At times sources such as Tokugawa jikki and the Kansei period (1789–1801) bakufu genealogy of its retainers Kansei chōshū shokafu do not differentiate between the two offices, indicating the close connection existing between them.

A third office on which Tsunayoshi initially drew for his grand chamberlains was that of junior councilor (wakadoshiyori). This office, like that of senior councilor (rōjū), was traditionally limited to men of fudai status, but Tsunayoshi did not observe these restrictions. The office was less prestigious than that of senior councilor, and the fact that it did not deal with the affairs of the daimyo and consequently was not involved in the power struggle between the latter and the shogun might have lessened the opposition of the established families. Nearly half of Tsunayoshi's junior councilors had proved themselves under the shogun's watchful eye as either chamberlain or personal adviser, while another third had served successfully in the position of magistrate of temples and shrines.

The above analysis of the careers of Tsunayoshi's junior councilors demonstrates the close connection between occupants of offices well established before Tsunayoshi's accession and those created for his new men. It refutes the general assumption that the shogun's entourage consisted of his personal favorites, who were professional lightweights, while those staffing the traditional positions were altogether different: hard-working and sober men trying to cope with the shogun's erratic policies.

The three above-mentioned offices—those of chamberlain, personal adviser, and junior councilor—account for the background of all but one of Tsunayoshi's grand chamberlains. It was an elite the shogun had personally chosen: all men who had proven themselves both in senior offices in the *bakufu* and under the shogun's personal supervision. Yet in most cases the careers of Tsunayoshi's grand chamberlains were short. In several instances the reason for termination of appointment cannot be traced, making it difficult to define a pattern. Conspicuous, however, is the fact that a relatively large number of resignations are owing to ill health. Omitting those cases where the reason for termination is unknown or where it occurred on Tsunayoshi's death, six out of ten resignations were for this reason. Of the rest, three were terminated owing to "unsuitability," which at least in one case was on account of insufficient devotion to duties. Only one man was dismissed and his domain confiscated for going against the shogun's will.

Traditionally resignation owing to poor health was a way of politely shedding unpleasant duties, but not so under Tsunayoshi. The point is well made by the case of two men who were appointed as Tsunayoshi's pages *(koshō)* but feigning illness declined to serve, fearing that they would soon displease the shogun. The shogun's displeasure, however, was incurred all the same when investigations revealed the true state of their health.[13]

It is unlikely after this incident that anybody serving in Tsunayoshi's proximity would have attempted to resign with a similar false excuse. Unless one makes the rather absurd assumption that the shogun preferred men of delicate health as his officials, the high percentage of resignations owing to illness can only suggest that the duties of grand chamberlain were so demanding that few men had the stamina to withstand the pace of work. Those who did not exert themselves were presumably considered "unsuitable."

Tsunayoshi's interest in government affairs is well documented in Ogyū Sorai's writing, and his untiring devotion also finds elaboration in the pages of *Matsukage nikki*. The latter describes how Tsunayoshi's interest in government affairs dominated his life, driving him to rise early "even on mornings of fog and deep snow" and to work late into the night.[14] One can dismiss such statements as hagiography, but they accord well with the facts furnished by the careers of his grand chamberlains. Even the aging Makino Narisada was not spared. Being twelve years the shogun's senior, he could not keep up with the pace of work demanded of him, and in his later years in office he was progressively hampered by bouts of illness. Finally, in his sixtieth year, after a particularly bad spell of ill health, he petitioned the shogun for permission to retire. But his request was refused, and it took another two years before the ailing Narisada was permitted to resign.[15] It is perhaps telling that Kaempfer considered him to be more than a decade older than in fact he was. Rare was the official who had both the devotion and the stamina to satisfy the shogun's relentless demands. Among Tsunayoshi's fourteen grand chamberlains there was only one man who could successfully bear the heavy load of work over many years. That was the later to be much reviled Yanagisawa Yoshiyasu.

The Grand Chamberlains of the Fifth Shogun

Name	Appointment Tokugawa jikki	Kansei chōshū shokafu	Ryūei bunin	Resignation Tokugawa jikki	Kansei chōshū shokafu	Ryūei bumin	Previous Position	Reason for Resignation
Makino Narisada	11.12. Tenna 1	12.12. Tenna 1	9.10. Enpō 8	29.11.Genroku 8	ibid.	ibid.	gosoba	ill health (old age)
Matsudaira Tadachika (Tadayasu)	21.7. Jōkyō 2	ibid.	22.7.Jōkyō 2	22.3.Genroku 2	ibid.	ibid.	wakadoshiyori	sickness
	21.9.Hōei 2	ibid.	ibid.	17.1.Hōei 6	ibid.	ibid.	okuzume	shogun's death
Kitama Shigemasa	6.9.Tenna 2* 26.7.Jōkyō 2**		6.9.Tenna 2* 26.7.Jōkyō 2**	2.2.Genroku 2		2.2.Genroku 2	koshō/gosoba	disopedience
Ōta Sukenao	11.1.Jōkyō 3	ibid.	ibid.	26.6.Jōkyō 3	ibid.	ibid.	wakadoshiyori	sickness
Makino Tadataka	12.9.Genroku 1	ibid.	ibid.	13.10.Genroku 1	ibid.	13.11.Genroku 1	gosoba	insufficient devotion
Yanagisawa Yoshiyasu	12.11.Genroku 1	ibid.	ibid.	3.6.Hōei 6	ibid.	ibid.	konando jōza	requested retirement***
Nanbu Naomasa	12.11.Genroku 1	ibid.	ibid.	26.1.Genroku 2	ibid.	ibid.	gosoba	sickness
Kanamori Yoritoki	11.5.Genroku 2	ibid.	ibid.	14.4.Genroku 3	ibid.	28.7.Genroku 5	okuzume	unsuitable
Soma Masatane			4.6.Genroku 2			14.4.Genroku 3	okuzume	illness
Hatakeyama Motoharu	6.12.Genroku 2	14.11. Genroku 1	1.12.Genroku 2	28.5.Genroku 4	17.12. Genroku 2	5.2.Genroku 4	okuzume/gosoba	too old: made sōshaban
Sakai Tadazane	11.2.Genroku 6	ibid.	21.2.Genroku 6	1.3.Genroku 6	ibid.	2.3.Genroku 6	okuzume	reason not given
Matsudaira Terusada	7.1.Genroku 6	ibid.	27.8.Genroku 7	17.1.Hōei 6	ibid.	ibid.	gosoba	shogun's death
Toda Tadatoshi (Tadatoki)			5.12.Hōei 1			15.10.Hōei 3	gosoba	reason not given
Matsudaira Nobutsune			1.10.Genroku 9			19.4.Genroku 10	okuzume	promoted to shoshidai

Note: Enpō 1 = 1673; Tenna 1 = 1681; Jōkyō 1 = 1684; Genroku 1 = 1688; Hōei 1 = 1704
Konando jōza = senior attendant; wakadoshiyori = junior councilor; gosoba = chamberlain; koshō = page; okuzume = personal adviser; shoshidai = Kyōto shoshidai (deputy)
*apprenticed as grand chamberlain
**appointed as grand chamberlain
***after shogun's death

Yanagisawa Yoshiyasu's Political Career

Yanagisawa Yoshiyasu was, like Tsunayoshi, born in the Year of the Dog, but twelve years later, in Manji 1 (1658). His family was of lower bannerman *(hatamoto)* status but, like many samurai, prided itself on its descent from the Seiwa Genji branch of the imperial house. At the age of only thirteen, Yoshiyasu's father took part in the battle of Osaka in place of his older, sick brother. He was consequently granted an audience with the second shogun Hidetada and received his brother's stipend of 160 *koku*. Afterwards both brothers came into the employ of Iemitsu's unfortunate younger brother Tadanaga, and their service came to an end when Tadanaga was forced to commit suicide in Kanei 10 (1633).

In Keian 1 (1648) Yoshiyasu's father finally became part of the retinue of then two-year-old Tsunayoshi. When Yoshiyasu was born ten years later, his father had reached the position of director of finance with a stipend of 530 *koku*.

At age seven Yoshiyasu had his first audience with the nineteen-year-old Tsunayoshi. Stories that Tsunayoshi took a strong liking to the boy at their first meeting[16] are not substantiated by *Rakushidō nenroku*, which, as Yoshiyasu's own record, would have made much of any early signs of favor from the future shogun.

In Enpō 3 (1675) Yoshiyasu's father retired at the age of seventy-four, and Yoshiyasu, then eighteen, succeeded as head of the house and was granted his father's stipend of 530 *koku*. At the same time he was employed as page *(koshō)* in Tsunayoshi's residence at Kanda. When Tsunayoshi succeeded as shogun five years later, Yoshiyasu was made an attendant *(konando)*, one of the lowest official positions in the shogunal entourage. This rank was below that of page, and his new appointment was only a promotion inasmuch as he was now serving the shogun and not merely a relative of the ruler. But it did entail a salary increase of 300 *koku*,[17] the first of many that later were to arouse the envy and anger of his contemporaries.

In the sixth month of Tenna 1 (1681), the shogun officially made Yoshiyasu his disciple in Confucian learning, and during the following New Year's celebrations Yoshiyasu was given the honor of delivering the first reading of the Confucian classics, a ceremony he was to perform yearly until Tsunayoshi's death.[18] Shortly afterwards Tsunayoshi presented Yoshiyasu with handwritten advice that was to map out his future. Appropriately titled "Loyalty to One's Lord," the poem read: "If, indeed, a man were not to forget the two characters that spell the word sincerity *(makoto)*, he would prosper for generations to come."[19]

Yet however much Yoshiyasu strove to please his lord, in Tenna 3 (1683) an incident occurred that could well have jeopardized his career. His father's adopted son, Nobuhana, became involved in a quarrel within the precincts of Edo castle and died of his wounds. Bloodshed within the castle walls was a serious crime, and Nobuhana's stipend was confiscated, leaving his heir without in-

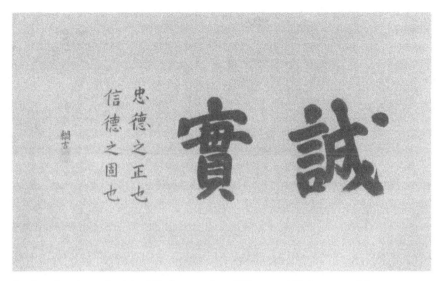

"Makoto." Holograph of the fifth shogun, signed "Tsunayoshi." Courtesy of the Kunō Tōshōgu Museum, Shizuoka.

heritance. Customarily Yoshiyasu, as his stepbrother, would have been similarly liable to punishment, but he was pardoned by the shogun. Several months later Tsunayoshi personally praised Yoshiyasu for his services, showing his appreciation with a gift of gold coins and ceremonial garments.[20] Apparently Yoshiyasu's untiring work had well compensated for the misbehavior of his stepbrother. Moreover, from this time on Yoshiyasu was given additional duties as *jikkin*, which might be termed "aide" in English. The appointment was apparently a semi-official one, for it appears only in *Ryūei bunin* and finds no mention in otherwise detailed records such as *Rakushidō nenroku* or *Tokugawa jikki*.

The office of *jikkin* had been in use since Ieyasu, but appointments had been few, the position apparently being reserved for men in whom the shogun placed his special trust. It was commonly held concurrently with other duties, and all those who had occupied this position were of higher rank than Yoshiyasu.[21]

At the end of Jōkyō 2 (1685), Yoshiyasu was honored with the lower fifth court rank and became Dewa no Kami. Shortly afterwards his stipend was nearly doubled to reach 2,030 *koku*. His new wealth and standing was enhanced when he received a concubine from one of Kyoto's noble families. She was Tanaka Machiko, the daughter of the high-ranking courtier Ōgimachi Dainagon Sanetoyo, but her mother was probably not of noble descent, and it is likely that therefore her name does not appear in the Ōgimachi genealogy.[22] Yet her erudite and elegant style of writing gives credence to her claim that she was brought up close to her father's side, permitted to mix his ink and dip his brush.[23] Later she was to use her connections in Yoshiyasu's various dealings with the court, especially in obtaining the first court rank for the shogun's mother. One cannot rule out that this woman with an aristocratic education and connections but not quite of aristocratic status was deliberately chosen to match the background of the humbly born Yoshiyasu and to open for him an avenue to the court.[24] But beyond mediating between the Edo warriors and the Kyoto nobility, she was also to use her education and literary skills to furnish a permanent record of Yoshiyasu's achievements in the pages of her *Matsukage nikki*.

The Birth of Yoshisato: The Shogun's Son?

Before Yoshiyasu's father died at the venerable age of eighty-six, he was able to witness the birth of a grandson and proudly to hand to the infant the sword with which he had fought for the Tokugawa at the battle of Osaka.[25] The boy, who was later granted the name of Yoshisato by the shogun, became infamous for being at the center of what is known as the Yanagisawa dispute *(Yanagisawa sōdō)*. He was the child of Yoshiyasu's concubine, Someko, but *Sannō gaiki* and later works that relied on it, such as *Gokoku onna taiheiki,* claimed that he was not Yoshiyasu's son but the son of the shogun. This well-kept secret, it was argued, was ultimately responsible for Yoshiyasu's rise to influence and prosperity. In Hōei 6 (1709), so it is claimed, the shogun and Yoshiyasu were planning to reveal the true identity of the child and have him proclaimed shogunal successor. Official chronicles maintain that the fifth shogun died in the first month of that year from measles, an illness that had already afflicted various members of his family and entourage for several months.[26] Yet according to *Sannō gaiki* and *Gokoku onna taiheiki*—the latter work taking its name from this very episode—he died by the hand of his own wife. Allegedly more devoted to the future of the country than to her husband, she prevented the impending disaster of having his "bastard" son rule over the Japanese isles by stabbing first the shogun and then herself.[27]

There are obvious flaws in this story. To begin with, as a number of historians have pointed out, Tsunayoshi's first visit to the Yanagisawa mansion took place only in Genroku 4 (1691), five years after Yoshisato was born, and consequently he could not have fathered the child on such an occasion.[28] There is no way to prove that Someko did not, before this event, secretly meet the shogun. However, if a boy had been born of such a union, it seems likely that he would have been proclaimed the shogun's son upon birth. Curiously the authors who claim that Tsunayoshi carefully kept the existence of a son secret for some twenty years also maintain that his overwhelming anxiety for a successor drove him to proclaim the infamous Laws of Compassion.[29] Surely if Someko had been found pregnant with the shogun's child, she would have been moved to Edo castle as his concubine to give birth there to his longed-for heir.

Another source of contradiction to established fact is that Tsunayoshi's nephew Ienobu had officially been adopted as Tsunayoshi's son and installed in the western enceinte as his successor in Hōei 1 (1704), some five years before the alleged intended proclamation of Yoshisato as shogunal heir. Curiously the circumstances of Ienobu's birth and childhood somewhat resemble those attributed to Yoshiyasu's son. Ienobu was born the son of a chambermaid when his father, Tsunayoshi's older brother Tsunashige, was only nineteen. So that this early offspring might not preclude Tsunashige's marriage to a girl of suitably high status, the birth was kept secret and the child brought up by a retainer. Only after Tsunashige's aristocratic wife died and no other son was born was Ienobu's true identity revealed and was he installed as his father's heir.[30] It is therefore difficult to argue that Tsunayoshi would have installed the "illegitimate" child of his brother as heir if he himself had a son born under similar circumstances.

It might even have been the story of Ienobu's birth and childhood that inspired the story that Tsunayoshi had similarly asked his loyal retainer Yoshiyasu to bring up his illegitimate child when explanations were sought for Yoshiyasu's rise to high position. Moreover, Tsunayoshi is recorded as having once expressed his regret at not having made Yoshisato his son-in-law.[31] Such statements, together with the fact that Yoshisato was generously treated by both Tsunayoshi and his successor Ienobu, must have inspired people to speculate about his true identity.

There can be little doubt that the claims made by *Sannō gaiki* and *Gokoku onna taiheiki* are spurious, but the story is apparently too colorful to be ignored. Even historians writing in modern times on occasion defend it with intriguing arguments, such as the argument that Yoshiyasu would have been too busy to beget his own child.[32]

The Rise to Grand Chamberlain

After Yoshisato's birth the fortunes of the Yanagisawa family continued to rise, but *Matsukage nikki* points out that Yoshiyasu's success was due to other reasons: "As the fleeting days and months passed, we came to the year called Genroku 1 [1688]. As his lordship was working steadily without a single break, his stipend was increased this winter. From the shogun's own hand he received the sword named Aoe."[33]

Initially Yoshiyasu's promotion was not overtly fast. Eight years after Tsunayoshi's succession, he was still an attendant, albeit a senior one *(konando jōza)*. But the increase of stipend Machiko referred to was a substantial one of 10,000 *koku*, with a total of 12,030 *koku*, elevating Yoshiyasu from *hatamoto* status to that of daimyo. At the same time he was commanded to work alongside the shogun's grand chamberlains, an order generally taken to indicate that from then on he too had acquired this status.[34]

Yanagisawa Yoshiyasu was the only one of Tsunayoshi's fourteen grand chamberlains who did not gather experience in one of the three offices qualifying other officials for appointment. It is something of a mystery why during the first thirteen years he served Tsunayoshi—including eight at Edo castle—he never proceeded beyond the rank of attendant; previously officials performing duties as *jikkin* all had held more senior ranks. As attendant Yoshiyasu was merely one of around hundred men serving in a variety of relatively menial jobs, such as dressing the shogun's hair and serving his food.[35] Perhaps Tsunayoshi wanted to keep him close at his side as his disciple sharing his interest in the Confucian classics, or perhaps he did have a homosexual relationship with Yoshiyasu, or both. One could even suspect that initially the shogun did not consider him clever enough to deal with the intricacies of government business in competition with the experienced officials employed as chamberlains. *Genkō jitsuroku*, a record written by one of his retainers, quoting Yoshiyasu's account of his appointment as grand chamberlain, makes much of the intellectual abilities of his colleagues.

> When Nanbu Tōtōmi no Kami and I were appointed together, the order of seniority was first Tōtōmi no Kami and then myself. When we offered our expressions of gratitude for this appointment in the shogunal chambers, Tōtōmi no Kami rose to proceed first, according to the order of seating. The shogun, however, commanded, "Dewa [Yoshiyasu] first," and I proceeded first and offered my gratitude. From then on we sat in this new order. Although Tōtōmi no Kami was exceedingly intelligent, after some time he did not measure up to the shogun's expectations and was dismissed. The master of court ceremony *(kōke)* Hatakeyama Mimbu no Taifu was ordered to serve at the shogun's side.[36] But again, he was old anyway and was soon suspended from office. Kitami Wakasa no Kami and Saitō Hida no Kami were both employed before me at the shogun's side, and although both were of outstanding intelligence, they disobeyed the shogun's commands. Hida no Kami was suspended from office in disgrace, and Wakasa no Kami was ordered under house arrest in the care of Matsudaira Etchū no Kami Sadashige, lord of Kuwana castle. It is the shogun's intention that men, whether of high or low rank, will not succeed unless they apply themselves with sincerity to their work.[37]

Yoshiyasu took up his appointment as grand chamberlain together with Nanbu Naomasa, who had successfully served as Tsunayoshi's chamberlain and was thus his senior. Yet the shogun placed Yoshiyasu ahead of Naomasa, and one can only guess whether it was because of Yoshiyasu's long years of service, better performance, or some personal reason. Barely three months later, Nanbu Naomasa was suspended from duties. The above passage claims that it was owing to disobedience, but other sources state that it was on account of illness. Toda Mosui specifies a small boil on Naomasa's hand, adding that he would be permitted to return to his office as soon as he was cured. But although Naomasa lived for another ten years, he never returned to his office or was appointed to any other post.[38]

It was, consequently, neither high birth nor superior intellect that qualified men for the position of grand chamberlain but untiring devotion to duty. And that Yoshiyasu had. "He diligently worked night and day without a break," "served without a minute's rest," and "generally came home only every second night." He was too busy to visit his father's grave and could not afford the time to finish the latter's temple. Even to arrange his daughter's wedding he could not take time off from work. Yoshiyasu's pace never slackened until finally he too succumbed and fell sick in the heat of summer.[39] If *Matsukage nikki* is given any credence at all, then this constantly recurring theme, echoed also in other sources, cannot be ignored.[40] Yoshiyasu, one can assume, was an official whom the shogun never had occasion to reprimand for lack of devotion to his duties.

The picture of Yoshiyasu that emerges is that of a man not particularly brilliant but devoted and hard-working. And although he himself was perhaps not overly gifted, he had a talent for recognizing superior intellect in others. It can hardly be a coincidence that Yoshiyasu employed not only Ogyū Sorai, long before he had produced the works that were to earn him fame, but also scholars such as Hosoi Kōtaku (also Shinzuke, 1658-1735) and Hattori Nankaku (1683-1759); both spent their early years in the Yanagisawa mansion.

Other men employed by Yoshiyasu are not so well remembered by posterity but in their day must have been just as remarkable scholars. The mathematician Kaneko Gonshichi was the only man in Japan besides Shibukawa Shunkai (1639-1715) able to calculate the new calendar adopted by Tsunayoshi in Jōkyō 1 (1684).[41]

Taking his cue from his master, Yoshiyasu followed the policy of advancing men according to talent and not status, for example, promoting the young Ogyū Sorai shortly after he had entered the mansion.[42] Sorai later described how under Tsunayoshi "ostentatious clothes and swords, and even conspicuous hairstyles were disliked, and it was considered proper to attune oneself with what was usual in society and take a moderate stance."[43] Yoshiyasu took care to observe such maxims and did not fall into the temptation of publicly taking advantage of his new status or permitting his retainers the boisterous behavior the servants of other powerful men would frequently adopt.[44] The fact that he outlasted all others in his service to the shogun lends credence to Machiko when she notes:

My lord did not boast. He was very reticent. No matter how much power he held in his hands, his constant and profound concern was only that he not err in the discharge of the affairs of state. Therefore he thought it most inappropriate if his retainers were excessively boastful like Yan Ying's stupid charioteer.[45] "Under no circumstances are you to take advantage of your influence, ridicule people, or behave impolitely. It should be repugnant to you to think that merely because you are a member of an influential house you can always behave as you please," he frequently cautioned his retainers.[46]

Yoshiyasu was careful to nip all gossip in the bud, and when two guards of his residence were rumored to have accepted bribes, he promptly dispatched them to his castle at Kawagoe.[47]

The Charge of Corruption

Yoshiyasu was well aware that his sudden rise to fame and fortune would make him the subject of slander and public criticism. It was inevitable with a career considered unparalleled in the peacetime history of Japan.[48] As his authority increased, so did the number of supplicants lining up in front of his mansion. *Matsukage nikki* describes how everyone, from the lowest to the highest—even "the puffed-up daimyo"—came to his gate. Yet, Machiko noted, her lord tried to avoid seeing people with personal requests, which invariably were accompanied by gifts. Yoshiyasu has been much criticized by historians for his greed and depravity, but the sources do not support such accusations.

Gifts were a normal part of social intercourse, and even the Dutch were instructed in detail what presents were to be delivered to whom on their visits to Edo. In return they received gifts, much regulated by the status of the donor.[49] Today's Japan has not completely shed this practice, as the much-advertised service by department stores delivering gifts at the onset of summer and the New Year demonstrates. Under these circumstances it seems arbitrary to criticize such practices in the past, especially when this is done with regard to selected individuals only.[50]

Toda Mosui lists the presents Yoshiyasu received when his house burned down, but there is no suggestion that this was unusual. When Yoshiyasu showed interest in landscaping his gardens at Rikugien, still famous today, large amounts of rare stones and plants arrived from all over the country. Machiko mentions this to illustrate his rise to authority, and there is no indication that at the time this was considered anything but the justly earned perks of high office.

The philosopher Arai Hakuseki was deeply critical of the fifth shogun's government and noted of Yoshiyasu that "affairs of state were conducted as he wished, and all the senior counselors did was to relay what he told them."[51] Yet he had nothing to say about corruption. Hakuseki's friend and colleague Muro Kyūsō could do nothing more than to accuse Yoshiyasu of amorous liaisons with some twenty concubines, criticizing this as the "height of profligacy" and claiming that three of Yoshiyasu's retainers had resigned because their admonitions had been ignored.[52] Such rumors surely contradict claims that Yoshiyasu owed his rise to a sexual liaison with the shogun or had no time to father a child, and perhaps indicate that more substantial accusations could not be found.

Kyūsō's rival, Ogyū Sorai, for his part, described the much-maligned Genroku period as one when officials behaved in a modest fashion, and their speech and behavior "were excellent." For him the rot set in with the Shōtoku period (1711–1716), when Hakuseki, and thanks to him also Kyūsō, were employed by the government.[53]

Yet the fear of being accused of improprieties by those jealous of Yoshiyasu's unprecedented rise to power and fame was always there. By paying great attention to people's opinion and "common talk," Machiko subtly conveys the family's constant concern about being the subject of malicious gossip. In the final pages of her work, she admits frankly that it was composed to counteract the "nasty slander" circulating about Yoshiyasu.[54]

The Shogun's Visits

The most fertile subject for such "nasty slander" was Tsunayoshi's many visits—fifty-eight in all—to the Yanagisawa mansion. The rumor that on one of these occasions Yoshiyasu's eldest son Yoshisato was conceived by the shogun has been mentioned. Other writers suggest that Yoshiyasu raised boys and/or girls for the shogun's sexual pleasures on such visits. There is, however, no evidence of the sexual mores Tsunayoshi is accused of, or indeed sexual conduct of any form, beyond that contained in the obviously spurious *Sannō gaiki*. Yet even Kurita Mototsugu in his otherwise solid work *Edo jidai shi* suggests that Tsunayoshi inspected the young sons of retainers to select some for his sexual pleasure. His sources are Toda Mosui's contemporary record *Go tōdaiki* and *Sannō gaiki*. Mosui indeed has an entry describing the selection of children *(kodomo mitate)* as pages for the shogun, but there is no suggestion that this was for sexual purposes. As in other premodern societies, children were used as servants but not with the intent to misuse them for sexual purposes. To the contrary, Ogyū Sorai, for instance, liked to be served by pretty young girls but after one incident assured himself that they were young enough not to develop any sexual feelings towards their master.

Based on *Go tōdaiki*, Kurita then implies that fear of sexual exploitation was the reason for the refusal of Yamana Shinano no Kami to be adopted by the grand chamberlain according to shogunal orders. Yet he fails to mention that the former was not a child but a man of twenty-eight. As another source explains, his refusal was based on the fact that he had already been adopted and considered accepting a further adoption to be unfilial conduct towards his present father. Only when interpreted in conjunction with the spurious claims of *Sannō gaiki* can such passages from *Go tōdaiki* be interpreted to suggest that the shogun had pederast tendencies.[55]

While there is no evidence to suggest that the shogun's visits to the Yanagisawa mansion were motivated by the desire to satisfy carnal pleasures, there is, however, plenty of material to document the intellectual debates taking place on such occasions. As discussed in more detail below, Yoshiyasu assembled in his mansion the brightest scholars of his day, men with an unusual knowledge of Chinese and the ability to read the Confucian classics in the original, and men such as Ogyū Sorai, with sharply penetrating minds. On the shogun's visits they were pitted against the Buddhist clergy in their philosophical debates. The occasions were usually rounded off by the performance of *nō* plays, classical theater created some three hundred years earlier, with acting conforming to exacting, equally archaic rules.

When these events are not viewed through the distorting lens of *Sannō gaiki* or works that follow its spurious claims, then they must surely be evaluated as important intellectual and cultural events. So they were by a contemporary foreign visitor, the physician Engelbert Kaempfer. For him the fifth shogun presented the ideal of the enlightened ruler, patron of scholars and artists, the likes of whom was not found in Europe.

Kaempfer heard that on his visits to the Yanagisawa mansion the shogun was always "served by young women."[56] But this did not distract from the admiration Kaempfer felt for the ruler. He was much shocked by young male prostitutes along the highways and perhaps considered the use of young women as servants—as was generally done in Europe—a healthier phenomenon. Indeed, the reason it was mentioned to the foreigner in the first place that the shogun was served by young women might well have been that normally young boys were used for such tasks, as Kaempfer observed on a number of occasions.[57]

The performance of *nō* plays had equally been a pastime of Tsunayoshi's predecessors, but learned debates were unprecedented. They strained the brainpower of many daimyo, revealing their inferiority to men of much lower status with respect to their learning. Ultimately such scholarly testing activity exposed the flaws of the firmly established social hierarchy and justified Tsunayoshi's policy of appointing men of talent without regard to status. He openly made this point when on occasion he would greatly praise one of Yoshiyasu's industrious retainers, accompanying his praise with the rhetorical and much-loaded question "Should we make a difference between low and high rank when it comes to the way of the officials?" only to conclude: "Everyone ought to serve like this man."[58]

No wonder the shogun's visits to the houses of his favorite retainers were unpopular with the greater part of the military aristocracy. They signified exclusion from the shogun's inner circle for many who considered such privilege to be rightfully theirs and created a sense of intellectual inferiority in many permitted to attend. Fostering rumors of immoral conduct on such occasions was but one strategy of revenge.

That these debates were serious scholarly events is testified by Ogyū Sorai. As a beneficiary of the shogun's attention on these occasions, he was naturally well disposed towards such activity. But since—as will be argued below—such scholarly activity provided the training ground for one of Japan's greatest political philosophers, it can hardly be said to have been without value.

The Yanagisawa Confucian School

There is, moreover, good reason to believe that beyond ad hoc debates on the Chinese classics being held at the Yanagisawa mansion, something akin to a private academy for the education of Tsunayoshi's personal disciples in the study of Confucianism was established. The scholar Hiraishi Naoaki suggests that Yoshiyasu employed a large number of Confucian scholars at his mansion not based on his own interests, but for the sake of educating those who were to serve the shogun. Although the date of establishment of this school cannot be determined, there is evidence of its closure in the months after the shogun's death and the redeployment of the scholars who had acted as instructors, including Ogyū Sorai. Similarly the land on which the school was apparently located was returned to the *bakufu* at that time. There is evidence that Tsunayoshi ordered some of his pages to live at Yoshiyasu's Kandabashi mansion and on his visits listened to their expositions on the Confucian classics.

Being granted leave from service at the castle to pursue a Confucian education was, no doubt, an expression of the shogun's trust that the incumbent had potential for intellectual development. Those who failed to live up to his expectations were sent away from the distractions of the city to the more austere environment of Yoshiyasu's domain, first at Kawagoe and then at Kōfu, to devote themselves with greater intensity to their studies. After Tsunayoshi's death some twelve men are listed as being released from such temporary exile.[59]

Under the third shogun Iemitsu, Kawagoe castle—rather than house recalcitrant students of Confucianism—had served to host the ruler's hunting parties as he roamed the environments of Edo. The castle had then belonged to Iemitsu's favorite Sakai Tadakatsu, who, like Yanagisawa Yoshiyasu, had risen from lowly samurai origins to high position. Iemitsu not only frequented the castle of his favorite for hunting parties, but also regularly proceeded to Tadakatsu's Ushigome mansion in Edo: over 150 visits are recorded. Further opportunities to escape the confines of Edo castle were provided by boating parties on the grandiose vessel *Atake maru* that Iemitsu had constructed.[60] Tsunayoshi's fifty-eight visits to the Yanagisawa mansion have been the subject of much criticism, but no similar censure has gone down in history regarding the much more frequent outings of his father.

The difference was that in Iemitsu's case the emphasis was on amusement, as, for instance, his order that for boating parties daimyo and courtiers were to dress in outlandish clothes indicates.[61] They provided welcome distraction for the military aristocracy, which Tsunayoshi's outings were unlikely to have done.

For Tsunayoshi, whose strong Buddhist beliefs ruled out hunting parties, visits to the mansions of his daimyo were some of the few occasions he could leave behind the cloistered confines of Edo castle and catch a glimpse of life outside. Such outings also provided an escape from the restrictions traditionally governing the life of the shogun and permitted new initiatives outside the established pattern, such as, for instance, the Confucian instruction at the Yanagisawa mansion.

The creation of the private academy at the Yanagisawa mansion must have taken place after Genroku 4 (1691), the year of the shogun's first visit, when the large Confucian temple at Yushima had been completed and the educational facilities there had been extended. In Genroku 5 (1692) Kaempfer heard of the shogun's visit to Yushima and a lecture he had given that was so excellent "that those prostrated in his presence were overwhelmed with emotion."[62] Despite the favorable assessment of the shogun's lecture reported to Kaempfer, it must soon have become evident that the ruler's personal brand of hands-on Confucianism was incompatible with the traditional and much more learned and theoretical teachings of the Hayashi family. Questioning the Hayashi family's expertise and encroaching upon their generations-old prerogatives would have met with considerable resistance. Akin to bypassing the established ministers by charging his erstwhile page Yanagisawa Yoshiyasu as grand chamberlain with the highest political duties, the school established at the Yanagisawa mansion permitted the shogun to bypass the Hayashi scholars and educate his courtiers in the practical brand of Confucianism he favored. As will be discussed in more detail later, when political problems were to be solved on the basis of Confucian doctrine, the shogun favored the interpretations championed by the scholars of the Yanagisawa mansion rather than those of the Hayashi house. No doubt this is one of the reasons why the Hayashi tradition never considered Tsunayoshi a Confucian scholar and has given relatively little praise to the ruler who raised the family from obscurity.

Court of Justice

Visits to the Yanagisawa mansion not only permitted Tsunayoshi to imprint his personal stamp on the education of future officials, they also provided occasion to observe senior officials in their administration of the commoners. For this purpose a public court of justice was staged in the gardens of the mansion, where fifteen cases of disputes among commoners were heard. In a building overlooking the proceedings, the shogun sat concealed behind bamboo blinds with his attendants. A group comprising two city magistrates, four magistrates of temples and shrines, and four superintendents of finance acted as judges. The shogun proclaimed to his courtiers that with such procedures the true nature of government was revealed and carefully listened to the proceedings, asking detailed questions. The senior and junior councilors were also in attendance, suggesting that the shogun did not simply intend to satisfy his own curiosity, but also wanted his ministers to become familiar with some of the problems of the commoners. As *Matsukage nikki* notes, normally people of such rank would not lend an ear to the voices of the commoners, and these procedures were considered highly unusual. Yet although the audience present at the trials was unusual, the author's detailed description suggests that those pleading their cases did not feel overawed by it. As the parties argued, one party would shout "Be quiet, you fool!" completely ignoring the point of contention, and Machiko, the highborn author of *Matsukage nikki*, had to admit that there were many things she could not grasp. The lawsuits covered a wide area, ranging from thefts, outstanding debts, and land disputes, to adultery and other complaints about marriage partners.[63]

After the court procedures ended in the pronouncement of the judgments, the usual Confucian lectures by Yanagisawa Yoshiyasu and his scholars took place. One could interpret the procedures staged at the Yanagisawa mansion as nothing but a novel form of entertainment. Machiko does not fail to hide some of the comic aspects in watching people so drastically different from herself. But Ogyū Sorai, one of the scholars present, recorded no complaints. To the contrary, as the shogun did here and on a number of other occasions, he would later greatly emphasize in his writings the importance of those governing the country being familiar with the affairs of the common people.[64]

In Makino Narisada's Footsteps

When Kaempfer visited Edo in 1691–1692, he heard that the sole person the shogun trusted was his grand chamberlain Makino Narisada. On Narisada's retirement in Genroku 8 (1695), this trust became vested in Yanagisawa Yoshiyasu. Already in the previous year Yoshiyasu had been assigned to attend the sessions of the supreme court *(hyōjōsho)*. Traditionally members of the shogun's entourage did not attend the sessions of this highest organ of justice, but Tsunayoshi had ordered Narisada to do so soon after his accession. Now Yoshiyasu was following in Narisada's footsteps.[65] In addition to attending to the everyday affairs of government on behalf of the shogun, a great number of other special tasks and projects were placed on his shoulders.

Some months after Narisada's retirement a shogunal order stipulated that henceforth presents to the great interior of Edo castle (ō oku), the residence of the shogun's wives and daughters, had to be channeled through either Yoshiyasu or his assistant Matsudaira Terusada, increasing Yoshiyasu's control over access to the shogunal family.[66] Yoshiyasu was also placed in charge of supervising the construction of the Konpon Chūdō hall at the ancestral temple Kaneiji at Ueno. Daimyo were requested to assist with the project, and Machiko speaks of tens of thousands of laborers toiling on it. The authority to arbitrate among the many requests for government-supported temple restoration also brought long lines of supplicants to his door.[67] Moreover, Yoshiyasu took control and became expert at handling the shogun's relationship with the imperial court.

The Imperial Court

The shogun—although angering some nobles, as mentioned in chapter 1—showed greater respect than any of his predecessors for the imperial institution. He expressed his reverence by carefully performing the appropriate purification ceremonies before receiving imperial messengers as well as by increasing financial support for the impoverished imperial house and nobility. The court was given permission to revive the ancient ceremonial of Daijō-e on the accession of Emperor Higashiyama in Jōkyō 4 (1687), elaborate rites that had not been performed since the accession of Emperor Gotsuchimikado in the middle of the fifteenth century. A shogunal donation of 700 koku also made it possible to revive the Kamo or Aoi festival. This festival had been celebrated by the nobility since the early ninth century, but, again, owing to lack of funds had not taken place for several hundred years.[68] That these tradition-steeped events are still enacted today is in no small measure owing to the fifth shogun's generosity.

Yoshiyasu's door to court circles was opened when Machiko entered his household sometime around 1690.[69] He shared the shogun's reverence for the imperial family and, perhaps as a result, strove to excel in the aristocratic pastime of poetry composition. By Genroku 14 (1701) poetry meetings were held at the Yanagisawa mansion under the direction of the eminent poet Kitamura Kigin (1624–1705).[70] Kigin, in the employ of the shogun, was permitted to become Yoshiyasu's private teacher and, it appears, was not disappointed by the zeal of his student. In Genroku 15 (1702) he presented Yoshiyasu with a manuscript on the secret tradition of the *Kokin waka shū* (Collection of ancient and modern poetry), an indication that his student had mastered the subject to his entire satisfaction.[71] Around that time a fire in the Yanagisawa mansion destroyed many valuable books. Learning of this loss through Machiko's relatives, the emperor showed his recognition of Yoshiyasu's talent and position by sending him a manuscript of the *Three Imperial Anthologies* of poetry, carefully copied out by the highest-ranking court nobles. As a mark of distinction it contained a preface of the emperor's own composition.[72]

Through the Confucian scholar Hosoi Kōtaku, Yoshiyasu's attention was directed to the need for surveying and marking the imperial tombs, which were becoming obliterated by herding and farming. For the local population the tombs were merely inconvenient structures, occupying valuable land, and a report under Iemitsu stated that there were none to be found in the province of Yamato. After a team was dispatched to conduct an extensive survey, twelve sites were newly fenced in and sixty-eight tombs were marked and honored. In the twentieth century Emperor Taishō finally awarded Yoshiyasu the third court rank posthumously for preserving the imperial tombs.[73] But the gratitude felt by the court at the time no doubt helped Yoshiyasu with the difficult task of obtaining the highest imperial order, the first rank, for the shogun's mother.

Keishō-in's humble origins were well known in Kyoto, her hometown, and receiving the third court rank some four years after Tsunayoshi's accession as shogun was already a great concession. Generally it was the highest rank samurai women were awarded during their lifetime; only after her death was the mother of the fourth shogun Ietsuna awarded the second court rank.[74] For the mother of the fifth shogun to skip the second rank and be raised to the highest court rank before her death was hence an extraordinary request on the part of Tsunayoshi, though Hideyoshi had obtained the same honor for his mother on being made *kanpaku*. When the degree was finally awarded in the ninth month of Genroku 15 (1702), the shogun in his speech of gratitude stressed how obtaining this great honor for his aged mother had relied entirely on Yoshiyasu's efforts.[75] Yoshiyasu had developed all the abilities the shogun required of a retainer.

Although the difficult task was completed, Yoshiyasu continued with what might be termed "poetry diplomacy." Perhaps he was also motivated by a desire to obtain the recognition in Kyoto that was accorded to him only grudgingly by his rivals at Edo.

The next year Yoshiyasu was given to understand that the retired emperor would gladly judge a collection of his poetry, and he composed one hundred verses for this purpose. Machiko proudly noted that even among the important nobility it was considered a rare honor if the retired emperor consented to look at just one or two verses. A month had barely passed when high praise of Yoshiyasu's poetry was received from Kyoto; it was accompanied by a detailed list of which court nobles should be thanked with gifts for acting as go-betweens.[76]

Even as these presents were hastily forwarded, Yoshiyasu was embarking on a more ambitious project; this time he hoped to submit one thousand verses for imperial judgment. And as if such effort would not suffice for the glory of the family, Yoshiyasu exhorted his eldest son similarly to present one thousand poems to the court. After suitable encouragement had been received from Kyoto, both collections were ceremoniously dispatched, naturally accompanied by an appropriately rich collection of gifts. In reply there was abundant praise of this unparalleled devotion to poetry by father and son. The poems were to be preserved in the imperial archives and would be handed down to future generations. As a sign of great recognition, an imperial fan and hat cord arrived at Edo. Machiko eulogized: "It is an honor unheard of in this world that a man from the distant eastern provinces receives such attention from the imperial heights."[77]

Signs of Protest

Imperial presents of poetry manuscripts, fans, and hat cords might sound innocuous enough, but the emperor's patronage had greater political implications. With the rigidity the *bakufu* hierarchy had acquired after the death of the third shogun, Tsunayoshi was unable to appoint his own "new man" to the senior government positions his father had created for his. But the emperor's goodwill enabled the shogun to obtain for his grand chamberlain imperial ranks and in this fashion raise his standing in the *bakufu* hierarchy. In Genroku 11 (1698) Yoshiyasu was granted the imperial title of Lesser Commander of the Guards *(sakon'e no shōshō)* for his successful supervision of the construction of Konpon Chūdo hall at Kaneiji.[78] A year later he was given for the first time the task of herald *(sendō)* of the shogun's procession to the ancestral temples at Momijiyama.[79] This function had previously been carried out by men such as Sakai Tadakiyo and Hotta Masatoshi, and after their deaths had been shared by the families of Hoshina and Ii.[80] For one of the shogun's new men, such as Yoshiyasu, to be assigned this solemn and prestigious duty was an unheard of break with tradition. It demonstrated publicly the neglect with which Tsunayoshi treated the old established families.

Signs of protest against shogunal decisions are not easy to detect in contemporaneous sources. The shogun's pronouncements were infallible, and to express doubt on this point would have amounted to treason. It would be especially unbecoming to the *fudai* daimyo, whose claim to privileges rested on their display of loyalty. Consequently disagreement with Tsunayoshi's policy of advancing men of talent and permitting a newcomer to usurp a position of influence traditionally occupied by the *fudai* finds no direct expression in the official sources. That such protest did exist, however, is indicated at times by less official chronicles or subtly suggested by a somewhat puzzling progression of events, inviting historians to draw their own conclusions.

One such event is the resignation of Tsunayoshi's grand councilor *(tairō)* Ii Kamon no Kami Naomori. According to *Tokugawa jikki*, Naomori terminated his duties on account of illness.[81] Yet Toda Mosui noted:

The grand councilor Ii Kamon no Kami has been granted permission to resign. Apparently he made a submission to the shogun stating that according to Iemitsu's code the court rank appropriate for a senior councilor is gentleman-in-waiting *(jijū)* and the fief should be no more than 100,000 *koku*. Therefore the appointment last year of Yanagisawa Dewa no Kami to lesser commander *(shōshō)* was against the code. It is rumored that this is the reason [for his resignation]. I heard this from an unreliable source.[82]

Yoshiyasu's stipend at this time did not exceed the limit specified.[83] Yet his rank did, a breach of tradition all the more serious since as grand chamberlain he was officially placed below the senior councilors. Toda Mosui's statement, however, is incorrect insofar as Yoshiyasu had not received his new rank in the previous year but two years earlier. Yet in the previous year he had been ordered to act as the shogun's herald to Momijiyama, an honor that should have gone to the grand councilor. Ii Naomori would no doubt have been unhappy about a newcomer decorated with the same court rank as himself. Yet the timing suggests that Yoshiyasu's encroachment upon the office of herald to the sacred ancestral temples of the Tokugawa family was the final impetus for Naomori's protest and resignation.

Any differences that might have existed between the shogun and his departing grand councilor were handled with discretion, and none appear in the record. But it is perhaps no coincidence that Naomori was reinstated as grand councilor when the sixth shogun Ienobu lay on his deathbed, at a time when one of the few men of influence from Tsunayoshi's days still in government, the superintendent of finance, Ogiwara Shigehide, was finally discredited.[84]

With Ii Naomori as guardian of tradition having vacated the highest government post, Tsunayoshi felt free to cement the position of his grand chamberlain further. Conferring the shogunal family name of Matsudaira on Yoshiyasu and his sons, the shogun lauded his grand chamberlain as "a model for all officials" and stated that henceforth he considered him a member of his family.[85] When four months later the first court rank was conferred upon the shogun's mother, Tsunayoshi again had occasion to sing Yoshiyasu's praises publicly. During recent years Yoshiyasu had handled internal and external matters single-handedly without the slightest mistake. His talent, Machiko recalled the shogun as stating, was beyond compare.[86]

After such great honors, misfortune befell the Yanagisawa house. Only weeks later a fire broke out at night and razed the whole property to the ground.[87] Was it an accident coinciding with Yoshiyasu's new honors, or did some human hand help to make known the disapproval of the gods? If Yoshiyasu suspected arson, it found no mention in the records. He had, moreover, little time to reflect on such matters, for with the departure of the grand councilor he was acting in this position even though the shogun could not confer that title on him. Yet while the burden of public administration rested on his shoulders, the shogun also used him for work behind the scenes. The most important assignment was installing the shogun's heir.

The Limits of Shogunal Authority

Tsunayoshi's only son had died early in childhood. But there was hope that his daughter Tsuruhime, married to Kii Tsunanori, a member of the Three Related Houses, might produce a successor. When Tsuruhime died childless in Genroku 17 (1704), Tsunayoshi decided that his nephew, the son of his older brother Tsunashige, should be installed in the western enceinte as his heir. This task brought Yoshiyasu not only once again unparalleled shogunal praise, but also a domain of great prestige, namely, one including Kai and parts of Suruga, vacated by Ienobu on this occasion. The domain had an official value of just over 150,000 *koku*, but the actual yield well exceeded 200,000 *koku*, giving Yoshiyasu one of the largest *fudai* domains in the country.[88]

In his speech the shogun stressed that the task Yoshiyasu had just performed was of the greatest political importance. "From the time of our initial secret decision, you have handled all matters, completely freeing us from anxiety. We are quite unable to express even one hundredth part of the gratitude we feel," he is reported as having stated.[89]

We do not know what tasks were involved in installing Ienobu as successor, but we do know that neither the senior councilors nor the members of the Three Related Houses were party to the secret preparations. Earlier than they, the monk Ryūkō and the shogun's mother were secretly informed.[90] Tsunayoshi had successfully established a power structure largely eliminating the traditional holders of authority. Little wonder that those who held the shogun's confidence—the grand chamberlain, the mother, and the monk—were later to become the targets of the greatest criticism.

Yet the shogun's autocratic powers were not complete, as is shown by the following episode, which is said to have taken place after the announcement of Yoshiyasu's new domain had been made. *Genkō jitsuroku,* the record of Yoshiyasu's retainer Yabuta Shigemori, recounts:

> The shogun went to call on her ladyship his mother.... Lord Eikeiji [Yoshiyasu] was also in attendance. On this occasion her ladyship the shogun's mother voiced her thoughts, saying: "Why was Mino no Kami [Yoshiyasu] not enfeoffed with the whole province of Kai? During your august reign, matters ought to be handled according to your wish." When the shogun heard this, he was troubled. Apparently he sat there and laughed. Lord

Eikeiji thought the situation to be extremely awkward. I believe his hands trembled and perspiration ran down him in streams. "There are many occasions on which even the shogun cannot act according to the dictates of his heart," the shogun exclaimed. "Lord Gyōbu Shō and Lord Shikibu Shō [Yoshiyasu's second and third sons] were given 20,000 *koku* in the east of Kai, and at that time even the keepers of castles heard that there was public protest."[91]

This animated event finds no mention in other records. Yet this need not detract from its credibility. It took place in the apartments of the shogun's mother, and except for the privileged grand chamberlain, no other officials were present. The shogun would hardly admit so frankly to the limits of his powers except in the most intimate company, nor presumably would his mother have questioned his decision if a wider audience had been present. Consequently there would have been no one to report this event except Yoshiyasu, who, it appears, later described it to his senior retainer Yabuta Shigemori. Quite understandably this emotionally charged scene, testifying to the limits of the shogun's authority, finds no place in the terse, semi-official record *Rakushidō nenroku* of the Yanagisawa mansion. Nearly half a century later, however, when all the participants were dead, it made sense to include the event in a work that tried to correct some of the gossip current at the time. In fact, if the author had been more concerned with appearance, he could have restyled the story as Machiko appears to have done. She merely noted the shogun's mother as saying that however large a fief Yoshiyasu had received, it would be insufficient to reward his services.[92] Under her skilled brush the awkward scene was pruned to suit her poetic description of the harmonious world she painted for her readers.

Official sources concur with *Matsukage nikki* inasmuch as neither openly discusses the struggle that existed between the shogun and the families that had established political authority in the thirty years of the fourth shogun's government and were now claiming the right to govern the country. The fact that a man such as Yanagisawa Yoshiyasu, whose father fought for the Tokugawa in the battle of Osaka, was not very different from, for instance, Iemitsu's Hotta Masamori, whose descendants were now seen as rightful holders of political authority, has traditionally been given little attention. Since the shogun's need for "new men" to establish his authority was not recognized as a legitimate cause, it was easy for popular history to stamp them as predators, power-hungry sycophants, usurping the shogun's power while pandering to his vices. The sources, however, show them as hard-working officials, used by the shogun as tools in his continuous struggle to regain the authority lost since the death of his father, the third shogun. This process is well demonstrated by and fundamental to the understanding of Tsunayoshi's much-criticized Laws of Compassion.

10

The Laws of Compassion

The Laws of Compassion have been called "the worst laws in Tokugawa history" and even "the worst laws in the feudal history of mankind."[1] They secured Tsunayoshi a prominent position among the fifteen Tokugawa shoguns as the ruler who killed men for the sake of dogs and earned him the irreverent nickname of *inu kubō* or Dog Shogun. Since their inception they have spurred the imagination of writers and given rise to a large body of colorful, but frequently misleading, material. The fact that they also comprised laws much advanced for their times, such as those protecting the weakest members of society, down to the unborn child, has often been overlooked. Nor has the sociopolitical environment that formed the backdrop for the laws been given due attention. All too frequently they are represented as the crazed love for dogs of a superstitious ruler or even the result of a mental disorder.[2] There has also been an unusual degree of uncritical acceptance of doubtful sources, with even respectable academic journals publishing articles stating that several hundred people were executed every day for offenses against dogs.[3]

As early as 1920 the historian Kurita Mototsugu examined the Laws of Compassion and came to the conclusion that Tsunayoshi was not the cruelest of the Tokugawa rulers, as commonly asserted, but the one who most cared for the life of his subjects.[4] Unlike the remainder of Kurita's work, however, this assertion has had little impact on subsequent historical writing.

Over the last two decades the scholar Tsukamoto Manabu has thoroughly researched the Laws of Compassion and their historical background, and has published a large number of articles and books reappraising the subject.[5] Yet how slowly the myth of the crazed ruler is dying is demonstrated in the pages of the standard history textbooks of Japanese high schools. Despite Tsukamoto's many publications there is generally no mention here of the socially advanced and humane aspects of the Laws of Compassion. Students still learn that the fifth shogun protected birds and beasts because of his religious beliefs and with his extreme love for dogs inflicted suffering upon the populace. A footnote adds that his love for dogs was due to his birth in the astral Year of the Dog.[6]

The Shogun's Birth in the Year of the Dog

What prospective Japanese university students have to memorize for their entrance exams is basically the contents of *Sannō gaiki*, the anonymous essay of mischievous gossip about the fifth, sixth, and seventh shoguns that came to circulate among scholars in the early eighteenth century. Imitating the style of the Chinese classics, the shogun is referred to as "king" and his heir as "crown prince." On the origin of the Laws of Compassion, the work states:

> After the death of the crown prince, no further children were born to the king's consorts. But an heir was desperately wanted. The monk Ryūkō memorialized: "When people lack an heir, it is always due to the fact that they have done much killing in their previous lives. Therefore the best thing to do for those who desire an heir is to show great love for all animate creation and not to kill. If Your Highness truly desires an heir, why not stop all taking of life? Moreover, as Your Highness was born in the Year of the Dog and this astral sign is related to the common dog, it would be good if dogs were to be cherished most." The royal mother also heeded Ryūkō and, for the sake of the king, said the same. The king said: "I consent." Then the prohibition against killing was promulgated and laws that dogs must be cherished were issued to the cities and the countryside.[7]

The birth of the fifth shogun in the Year of the Dog, the death of his only son in childhood, and the close relationship of the monk Ryūkō with the shogun and his mother are well-documented facts. Thus the above explanation of the origin of the Laws of Compassion appeared reasonable to later historians, and the account in *Sannō gaiki* became the basis for most subsequent historical writing on the subject. Authors ignored that with its many other wild claims, *Sannō gaiki* was obviously a scholar's hoax and learned send-up of previous rulers, to be savored by those familiar with the Chinese classics, condemned already in the eighteenth century for its distortion of facts.[8]

Moreover, there is no evidence to support this story. The monk Ryūkō left a detailed personal diary, but as early as 1917 Miyazaki Eiga pointed out that there was not a single reference to the Laws of Compassion or the laws protecting dogs in this record.[9] If Ryūkō had believed in the religious efficacy of such laws, then surely his concern with this matter and his success in persuading the shogun to adopt such measures to improve his karma would have found expression in the pages of his diary. What did find expression in the diary was, for instance, that the shogun had entrusted him with the important political information that his nephew would be installed as his successor even before the senior councilors and the heads of the Three Related Houses were informed. As has been elaborated above, those who received the shogun's trust as he was usurping the rights of the traditional holders of government authority—the priest, the mother, and the chamberlains—later became the subjects of the greatest criticism.

Tsunayoshi's predecessors had similarly relied in matters of administration on the Buddhist clergy. But none of them had permitted Buddhist principles of nonviolence to infringe upon the samurai's traditional right to kill. *Sannō gaiki* reflected the outrage at the fundamental change in ethical values forced upon the samurai population by the fifth shogun. Tsunayoshi's age was still a time when even a Confucian scholar would recommend that servants who had committed theft or absconded be killed by their samurai masters without further ado, and one such scholar expressed regret that "killing on sight" had virtually become unheard of under the fifth shogun.[10] To such men the shogun's repeated public admonitions to practice love and benevolence may have sounded like the sermons of priests or the babbling of a woman rather than the pronouncements of a military hegemon.

This impression was not altogether wrong. The Laws of Compassion bear the imprint of the shogun's pious mother. Permitted close personal ties with her son in early childhood, her personality and experience greatly shaped his weltanschauung and value system. She implanted in him the ideal of a ruler who would free the world from the evils she herself had experienced as the child of a commoner. The magnitude of the paradigm change required to attain this ideal becomes apparent when the idealized world of the samurai and the lot of a commoner's daughter are examined.

The Life of the Samurai

When the realities of the much-glorified life of the samurai are examined, the promulgation of the Laws of Compassion takes on a different aspect. A good source is *Hagakure*, the jottings of Yamamoto Tsunetomo, a samurai who had chosen to retire as a Buddhist hermit. On the death of his lord, Nabeshima Mitsushige, in 1700, Tsunetomo had been edged out by a new brand of retainers whose emphasis on "civil service" rather than traditional samurai values reflected the changes that were occurring under the government of the fifth shogun. In *Hagakure* Tsunetomo nostalgically remembers what had been and what—in his opinion—society ought to be like.

Killing was an important part of the young samurai's education. Tsunetomo lauded the father who had his son cut down a dog at the tender age of five. When a boy reached the age of thirteen or fourteen, it was usual to have this practice extended to killing criminals. Praise goes to the young man who cuts down more than ten men in one session. Excuses not to kill are regarded as cowardice, and speaking from experience the author vouched that "beheading" a fellow human being produced a pleasant feeling.[11]

The famous swordsman Miyamoto Musashi (1584-1645) elevated killing to a fine art, boasted that he had never lost a fight, and exhorted his followers to dedicate their lives to the practice of the sword. His famous *Book of Five Rings (Gorin sho)* consists of detailed instructions on how to kill quickly and effectively.[12] Yet Tsunayoshi's government condemned such violence, and by the time Kaempfer visited Japan in the early 1690s young samurai had to be content to test the effectiveness of their swords on the corpses of the execution grounds. They did so "until they [the corpses] have been cut into pieces half the length of a finger," Kaempfer noted.[13]

What constituted a crime requiring execution on the spot had traditionally been left for individual samurai to decide. According to Tsunetomo, it could be a child stepping accidentally on one's foot or a fellow passenger disturbing the aesthetics of a riverboat ride in summer by relieving himself overboard. In the latter instance, the offender's head was quickly cut off and fell in the river, and the boatman was ordered to bury the corpse. To ensure secrecy, the life of the boatman was taken too. A young male prostitute present was cowered into silence by the samurai cutting up the boatman's corpse and musing on how it was best to learn how to kill when still young.[14]

It was considered a virtue for a samurai to guard his image in narcissistic fashion. Tsunetomo recommends always carrying some powdered rouge in one's sleeve to be applied to the face when a little pale.[15] But frequently keeping face required more drastic action, as in the case of the samurai who found his wife committing adultery with a retainer. The latter fled, but the wife was killed on the spot. So the shame would not have to be admitted to the world, the maid was told to make it appear like death by illness. Had she refused to play her part in the charade, she too would have lost her life.[16]

For the samurai's honor no price was too high, and no pangs of conscience were felt when the lives of innocent people were sacrificed in the process. That was not only the opinion of the country samurai Tsunetomo, but also of the very righteous philosopher and adviser to the sixth shogun Arai Hakuseki at Edo. On one occasion during his youth he had made up his mind to support a friend in a fight between hostile samurai groups even though he himself was in detention. If necessary he would have killed the old couple guarding the side gate obstructing his route of escape. The death of these insignificant commoners would have counted for little, since it was a matter of defending his honor, he later explained with pride. Fortunately for Hakuseki, the fight was called off, but the memory of such noble resolve he considered important enough to record for posterity.[17]

Similar levels of violence are found in the pages of the diary of Asahi Shigeaki, a lower samurai in the domain of Owari. Murder was a common occurrence, the victims including officials and commoners, wives, lovers, mothers, and even children.[18] For groups of young, unemployed samurai, killing was a sport and often a means of support. In what was known as street murders *(tsuji kiri)*, groups of young men attacked and killed passersby and robbed them of their possessions. Certain sections of the highway were famous for such attacks, like the lonely mountainous stretch of the Tōkaidō between Mishima and Hakone,[19] but they also took place in cities. Those held responsible were said to have been lower-class and masterless samurai, but on occasion the sons of daimyo also attempted to exercise their martial skills in this fashion. Even the head of the house of Mito, Tokugawa Mitsukuni, later much praised as a wise Confucian ruler, is said to have engaged in such activities in his youth.[20]

In this ideal world of the samurai, compassion was frowned upon. The woman who opened her door to a sick stranger in urgent need of a toilet should be killed for her depravity, the author of *Hagakure* moralized. Buddhism was bad for young warriors, because it stirred feelings of compassion and inhibited ruthless killing. Only in old age, after having retired from active service, was the samurai permitted to console his soul with religion.[21]

An expression that frequently occurs in Tsunetomo's moralizing tract is *inu jini*, the death of a dog. It was a wretched end, a death without honor, the worst that could happen to a samurai.

A Dog's Life

Dogs were closely associated with the life of the samurai. As in the West, they were bred for hunting, and large, fierce dogs were particularly in demand. The first shogun Ieyasu requested 670 large dogs in addition to five to six thousand archers and riflemen for a deer hunt in Keichō 17 (1612).[22] A seventeenth-century screen depicting life in and around Edo shows not only the use of falcons to chase and kill prey, but also that of large fierce dogs. One scene shows a big dog chasing a fully-grown wild boar. For the third shogun Iemitsu these dogs were so important that his senior minister Hotta Masamori engaged in breeding them for the shogun's hunt, and the exploits of his canines were important enough to find mention as one of Masamori's achievements in the otherwise terse official write-up of his life.[23] The Dutch were well aware how sought after dogs were and tried to curry favor by importing such animals for the daimyo.[24] Tsukamoto suggests that these large fierce dogs, often referred to as Southern Barbarian dogs or Chinese dogs, were a type of greyhound and were used by the daimyo to threaten and impress their authority upon the commoners as well as to project their power in rivalries among themselves.[25]

The dogs were fed on raw meat, increasing their fierceness, and pigs were specially raised for this purpose.[26] Daimyo mansions in Edo kept several hun-

Dogs used for hunting. From *Edo zu byōbu* (View of Edo, pair of six-panel folding screens), seventeenth century. Courtesy of the National Museum of Japanese History, Sakura, Chiba.

dred dogs at a time, and with dogs being prolific breeders, the expense could become overwhelming.[27] Unwanted litters were frequently drowned. One archaeological site revealed dogs disposed of in a lake being of an unusually large breed, with adult dogs having their teeth cut, presumably to reduce the risk of harming people.[28] An easier way to get rid of unwanted litters was by setting them free beyond the walls of samurai mansions, and this is likely also to have happened by accident.[29] Stray dogs roamed the city in search of food, the open shop fronts of merchants, the ware of itinerant food vendors, and the supplies kept behind flimsy paper-screened doors in the houses of commoners being easy targets for hungry animals. Children were attacked and killed by hungry strays. One source records a sick maid thrown out by her employer falling victim to such ravenous animals.[30] Samurai, for their part, had little to fear from dogs, being protected by the walls of their mansions and the weapons they habitually carried. To the contrary, stray dogs offered occasion for the practice of sword skills.

That commoners lived in fear not only of falling victim to samurai swords but also to attack by dogs is well portrayed in contemporary art. A seventeenth-century screen of Edo shows two samurai each with a very large dog on a leash. One of the dogs is straining towards a child, fearfully pulled back by its mother. A similar screen shows two somewhat smaller dogs barking at passersby while being fought off by men with sticks. One of them seems to be protecting a woman from the dogs.[31] The screens were painted to decorate and please, and only hint symbolically at the dangers the dogs posed to the unarmed populace.

While dogs were displayed as symbols of the samurai's fierceness, they also had to suffer the role of imaginary enemy to be vanquished. The custom of having children practice on dogs before graduating to killing humans has been mentioned above. A similar role as proxy was assigned to dogs in the sport of *inu oi*, literally, "chasing dogs." Some forty years before Tsunayoshi's laws forbidding the killing of dogs, his father, the third shogun Iemitsu, had revived this samurai pastime popular in the Kamakura and Muromachi periods.[32] A bamboo fence of some hundred meters was erected around a horse training ground, and thirty-six mounted riders wearing ceremonial dress aimed their arrows at dogs released into the center. In the autumn of 1646 the daimyo Shimazu Mitsuhisa staged such an event with great splendor at the village of Hachiōji outside Edo to the great pleasure of the shogun. The record notes that one of the riders succeeded in piercing eight animals out of ten with his arrows. It was a grand affair with buildings specially erected for the occasion and was considered so important that not only details of the participants and clothes worn but even the color of the cakes made for the occasion are handed down in detail.[33] The event of shooting the hapless dogs had the full endorsement of the shogun and his ministers who all attended and like the shogun's great love of falconry presented the public face and nature of Iemitsu's government.

Paradigm Change

In the face of such violence, both institutional and private, the reasons given by the compilers of the record of Tsunayoshi's government for the Laws of Compassion ring true: "The traditions of the Warring States period became the way of the samurai and senior officials. Brutality was permitted and considered to be *bu* (military [virtue]). Spirited behavior was considered righteous, and there was much conduct lacking benevolence, violating the principles of humanity."[34]

The samurai's use of the sword, be it to punish, to solve interpersonal problems, or for amusement became increasingly problematic with rapid

Two large dogs held on a leash by a samurai with fearful commoner mother and child. From *Edo zu byōbu* (View of Edo, pair of six-panel folding screens), seventeenth century. Courtesy of the National Museum of Japanese History, Sakura, Chiba.

Dogs are fought off with sticks by passersby. From *Edo meisho zu byōbu* (Famous views in Edo), believed to be the oldest depiction of Edo dating from the Kanei era (1624–1643). Reproduced courtesy of the Idemitsu Museum of Arts, Tokyo.

urbanization. The population of the city of Edo is believed to have reached the million mark during Tsunayoshi's government, and roughly half are estimated to have been of samurai status, overwhelmingly male, constantly girded by two lethal weapons.[35] Many samurai had few duties to keep them occupied and little financial means to purchase amusement. Urban violence, illegal hunting and fishing—even in the castle moat—and related issues, such as the rotting corpses of animals killed or abandoned, were threatening the peace and welfare of the city.

Laws against violence—such as orders against street gangs—had been issued before Tsunayoshi's government, but with both legislators and executors sharing the value system that lay at the root of such violence, little change occurred. It took a ruler with a fundamentally different value system and the determination to enforce nonviolence to break the established pattern.

For Tsunayoshi's father Iemitsu and his elder brother Ietsuna, hunting, with the thrill of the chase and kill, provided an outlet for the violence that formed part of the ethos of their education as samurai. The story that the third shogun ordered Tsunayoshi to be educated as a scholar and entrusted his education to his mother can be challenged on the basis of insufficient reliable primary material, but the fact that he did not share the samurai's love of violence for violence's sake and the belief in the preeminent right of the samurai to exercise it cannot. As he so graphically explained to his grand councilor Hotta Masatoshi, his concern was less the rights of the samurai than those of the street urchin. Inspired by the ideal of the Confucian sage rulers Yao and Shun who governed as benevolent autocrats, he compared himself to the sun that sent its light to even the most wretched corner of his realm.

But beyond striving for Confucian ideals, there were also more concrete reasons for his concern. Refugee scholars from the continent such as Chu Shun-shui described authoritatively how it was not the invaders but the protests of the peasants at the cruelty and mismanagement of the ruling class that had ultimately brought the imperial Chinese government to fall. As son of the shogun and later as ruler, Tsunayoshi was unable to experience the sufferings of the Japanese commoners, but in his mother Keishō-in he had an experienced informant. I do not believe it to be coincidental that Tsunayoshi's Laws of Compassion attempted to remove from everyday life the cruelty that would have been witnessed by and would have traumatized the child of a city shopkeeper like his mother.

Threats to the commoners' welfare included the arbitrary power of the samurai to kill instantly, the threat of marauding dogs, and the ugliness and dangers to health of rotting corpses of animals cruelly butchered. But for a young child there was also the trauma of being abandoned to die, or, even worse, to become the victim of infanticide.

Abandoned Children

Sutego, literally "children thrown away," were not an uncommon sight. When the poet Matsuo Bashō set out on his journey in 1684, he came across a two-year-old child abandoned on the bank of the river Fuji. He gave the child some food, but though he knew it would not survive the frost of the night, he went on his way without further ado, blaming the child's imminent death on the gods: "How can this happen? Did his father despise him? Did his mother neglect him? I think not. This must be the will of heaven."[36]

Bashō spells out the attitude of his society towards those who were of no immediate use and too weak to fend for themselves. Even the sensitive poet felt no twinge of conscience at passing, leaving the child to die. The same sentiments can be found in the novels of the contemporary Ihara Saikaku, although Tsukamoto points out that in Saikaku's later novels there is greater social awareness of the evil of such conduct. Surprise is expressed to find that an abandoned child somehow had not been attacked by dogs and had survived, an indication that the opposite was normally the case.[37]

The problem was not a new one. Although admitting that abortion and infanticide were not unknown in Europe, the Jesuits writing at the end of the sixteenth century were amazed at the ease and frequency with which mothers killed their infants in Japan. Especially if the newborn was a girl, the method was simply to kill the infant by placing a foot on its throat. Abortion was equally frequent: there were women who had aborted some twenty children. At times the Jesuits attributed this conduct to extreme poverty, making it impossible for a couple to raise more than one or two children. At other times, however, they simply ascribed it to the ease with which life was taken, especially that of people below one's own station.[38]

The Jesuits witnessed the Warring States period, the very period Tsunayoshi referred to when he lamented the continuation of the brutal traditions of the past. The pax Tokugawa had brought an end to military fighting, yet the ensuing rapid increase in population and urbanization exacerbated the problem of disregard for the sanctity of life. This was so especially with respect to children. Single women went to the city in search of employment, and when they became pregnant, they lacked an extended family to care for the child.

In Kyoto unwanted children were often left at Rokkakudō temple. Since wet nurses gathered here in search of work, it was hoped that one of them would feel pity and take care of such a child. In practice, however, the opposite was known to occur. Wet nurses were now selling their services to the less well to do, to women in employment unable to feed and care for their babies. On giving birth they had little choice but to entrust the child to a commercial wet nurse for a fee. Yet having received payment, it happened that the wet nurse would either abandon the child or feed it insufficiently and let it die. Of seventeen recorded punishments for child abandonment from 1683 on, over half were of women who had abandoned infants entrusted to them for nursing on such a commercial basis.[39] Abandoning children had always been illegal, but it is only from the early years of the government of the fifth shogun that we have a record of prosecution for such offenses. Earlier such conduct was apparently tolerated as an unavoidable evil.

The influx of large numbers of single people seeking work in the growing cities led to an increase not only in abandoned children but also in abortions. By the middle of the seventeenth century, doctors specializing in the termination of pregnancies appear in the records. In Kanbun 7 (1667) an ordinance forbade abortionists in Edo to erect signs advertising their services, indicating that this had become the practice and that the authorities were beginning to consider the trade to be reaching unacceptable levels.[40] Shortly after Tsunayoshi's accession we find for the first time a prosecution for killing a woman while performing an abortion. Previously such deaths went unpunished; indeed this first prosecution appears to have been intended as a warning only, since the offender was pardoned not long afterwards.[41]

The Exorcist

At about this time an exorcist became famous in Edo who would soon enjoy the patronage of the shogun's mother and would later rise to high clerical position. The Jōdo monk Yūten (1637–1718) succeeded where others failed in freeing women from demoniacal possession by his gift of hearing the voices of the vengeful spirits of the dead, even if the deceased had merely been a child or an aborted fetus.

His first spectacular success occurred in Kanbun 12 (1672) while attached as *gakusō*, an acolyte studying the scriptures, to Iinuma Gukyōji, a temple in Shimoosa (present-day Chiba). After protracted ceremonies, Yūten was able to establish that a young married woman was possessed by the spirit of a former wife of her father by the name of Kasane, whom her father had murdered together with five other previous wives. Yet the young woman was not cured until finally the spirit voice of a young boy made itself heard. It was Kasane's stepbrother who had been murdered by his parents when Kasane was born. Later, in the eighteenth and nineteenth centuries, the story of the vengeful spirit Kasane, who, though unwittingly, had herself caused the death of a child, was repeatedly used in plots for kabuki plays. But by Tenna 2 (1682) the story had already appeared in print.[42]

Yūten subsequently moved to Zōjōji at Edo, and it was here that even the voices of aborted fetuses revealed themselves to him. The following story greatly increased Yūten's fame and was recorded in writing during his lifetime.

A merchant of some standing by the name of Takano Shinemon had a secret affair with his maid. When the maid became pregnant, Shinemon, in an attempt to hide his liaison, sent her back to her parents under the pretense that she was ill, giving her medicine to abort the child. Yet the maid died under great pain from the effects of the drug in the third month of Tenna 2 (1682). Shinemon had a married daughter who subsequently was divorced and returned to her parents' house. Exactly three years after the maid's death, the daughter fell sick. As her illness worsened she began to speak with the voice of the dead maid, accusing Shinemon of the pain and death he had caused and lamenting her fate as undelivered spirit in hell. The usual prayers failed to exorcise the spirit of the maid until finally Yūten was called. But as Yūten conducted the rituals and prayers to appease what he believed was one tortured soul, he heard that there was not just one but an additional fifteen vengeful spirits. These were those of other children Shinemon had caused to be aborted, and the spirit voice listed the names and locations of the mothers in detail. Only when the spirits of the aborted children were also led to salvation through rituals and prayers did the daughter recover, though she died a year later of other causes. Shinemon renounced the world and entered the priesthood to atone for his crimes for the rest of his life.[43]

One could question how a deeply Buddhist society holding parting rituals even for discarded sewing needles could tolerate abortion and infanticide on the scale seen in these stories. As justification it was held that children under seven were not totally human and had no soul that could enter hell or experience salvation. Seen as beings from a different world, they, like an unwanted gift, could be returned to where they came from, a view well reflected by euphemisms for infanticide, generally containing the verbs *kaesu* or *modosu,* giving or sending back.[44] Children were not accorded the usual funeral rites but were often buried under the earthen floor of a house or in the corner of a cemetery, if the body was not simply disposed of like normal refuse. Unlike the spirits of older people, those of young children were not believed to have the power to haunt or cause mischief in the world of the living after death. Contemporary Buddhist teaching had them gathering at the feet of the god Jizō or living in dry riverbeds and at the shore of lakes, where the faithful on passing even today pile up stones in the shape of little pagodas for their comfort.[45]

This thought pattern dehumanizing the fetus and young child permitted the natural consequences of sexual intercourse to be obliterated without feelings of guilt. Tailored to suit a warrior society as idealized in the pages of *Hagakure,* it pandered to the dominance of the physically strong male, permitting indulgence in sex without regard for the consequences. Beyond sex, in their capacity as daughters, women were considered merely a burden, and *Hagakure* recommends that all but the eldest be abandoned.[46] Yūten challenged this thought pattern by listening to the voices of aborted fetuses and murdered children, declaring that, contrary to popular belief, they had the power to possess people and cause havoc in the world of the living. He insisted that penance be done for harming them and religious ceremonies performed for the salvation of their souls, just as they were for older people.

As Carmen Blacker has well described in her work *The Catalpa Bow*, exorcism is still practiced in modern Japan. The exorcism of the Nichiren sect she investigated used the same method employed by Yūten, namely, that of challenging the vengeful spirit directly in the body of the sufferer without resorting to a medium. In her research conducted in the late 1960s, the possessed were mainly young housewives between the ages of twenty-five and thirty-five, at the time "among the most oppressed people in Japanese society." Blacker postulates that the psyche can "split into multiple autonomous parts, each with its own personality." She suggests that "when one of these parts is too much repressed by the conventions of family and society . . . it is apt to force its way to the surface of the mind, upsetting the normal balance of the personality and behaving in exactly the manner most calculated to offend convention. But once this suppressed and neglected side is accepted and acknowledged, the mind may once more return to its former balance."[47]

Blacker's explanations shed light on Yūten's exorcism. In his most famous cases young women are haunted by the women and children their fathers had murdered or caused to be aborted, crimes that went unacknowledged, let alone unpunished. The women fall ill and are deemed possessed on reaching the age where they might well experience the same cruelties their fathers had inflicted upon other women. Religion with its male-oriented constructs offered little solace, and the prayers and rites of other priests were consequently without effect. The priest Yūten was exceptional in going beyond the religious conventions of his times, recognizing the trauma caused to women by the violence inflicted on their bodies and their children. Like the cases described by Blacker, the person deemed possessed returns to normal health once the crime is acknowledged and atoned for.

Yūten's dissatisfaction with contemporary religious dogma shaped by the demands of an exclusively male-oriented society might well have been the cause for his departure from Zōjōji and the religious establishment in Jōkyō 3 (1686). Aged nearly fifty, he crossed his name off the temple register and spent the next thirteen years as a wandering monk. Yet even though he shunned religious status and affiliation, his impact on society was significant, and as he attended the afflicted, the stories of his exorcism began to circulate in print.[48]

Yūten's work seems to have inspired Ihara Saikaku when he wrote his novel *The Life of an Amorous Woman (Kōshoku ichidai onna)*. In this work, published one year after Yūten had exorcised the vengeful spirits of the fetuses haunting Shinemon's daughter, the heroine, a courtesan, is possessed by a vision of over ninety aborted children. Their faces covered by large lotus leaves like hats and blood dripping down from their waists, the children lament the cruelty of their mother. The scene is not only graphically described in the text but also appears in an illustration.[49]

Yūten was patronized by the shogun's mother, Keishō-in, who is said to have called on him in his hermit's hut on the outskirts of Edo. The evidence of Keishō-in calling on Yūten in person has been questioned, but *Tokugawa jikki* notes that in Genroku 12 (1699) he was at Keishō-in's request summoned to Edo castle in an unprecedented fashion and promoted from being a lowly wandering monk to the position of head priest of one of the Jōdo sect's eighteen major temples in the Kantō area. In samurai terms, his status has been likened to a daimyo with a fief of 100,000 *koku*.[50] In the following year he was further promoted by appointment as head priest at Iinuma Gukyōji in Shimoosa, the very temple where he had performed his first famous act of exorcism. Finally in Hōei 1 (1704) he was placed in charge of Koishikawa Denzū-in in Edo, a temple next in rank only to Zōjōji, the ancestral temple at Shiba. At this temple were the graves of the first shogun's mother and other high-ranking women of the Tokugawa clan, and Keishō-in, already over eighty, was perhaps preparing for her own death.[51] Unlike other priests who had risen under the fifth shogun and his mother, Yūten was not retired on the death of the fifth shogun. To the contrary, under the sixth shogun Ienobu, Yūten was promoted to one of the highest posts in the religious hierarchy, namely to the headship of Zōjōji.[52] Even when at the age of seventy-six Yūten asked to retire, he was refused on the grounds that his brain was still in perfect working order.[53]

Yūten's patronage by the sixth shogun must have irked the scholar Arai Hakuseki, who came to participate in government affairs under this ruler. Hakuseki is said to have written his Genroku period *Kishin ron,* a treatise on the manifestation of spirits, as criticism of the trust that was placed in Yūten's exorcism.[54] Hakuseki's criticism of the foolishly credulous in his treatise—only published some hundred years later—implied criticism of the shogun's mother and her entourage for patronizing Yūten. That the shogun saw the matter in a different light is suggested by government orders that followed, supporting the efforts of the priest to stop abortions and infanticide.

In Jōkyō 4 (1687) a law decreed that abandoned children should be cared for locally and placed in foster families.[55] Bashō's conduct of doing no more than sharing his provisions with a deserted child and recommending it to the gods was now a criminal offense. Three years later, in the tenth month of Genroku 3 (1690), a decree was issued stipulating that if people found it difficult to raise their children, it was the responsibility of the employer or local official to provide for the child's upkeep. Merely a month later this law was recast to order in an unprecedented fashion the registration of pregnant women and children under seven. The authorities were similarly to be notified if children entered employment or their domicile changed for any other reason.[56] The laws protected the children to whom current Buddhist beliefs did not assign a soul, who people felt free to return to the other world, and whose voices the monk Yūten was bringing to the attention of society. The short interval between these two decrees on the same subject suggests that there was protest from some quarters at the inadequacy of the first order. Was it the shogun or the shogun's mother who failed to agree with the wording of the first decree? Whatever the case, the officials who had worded the initial order were no doubt reprimanded for their ineffectiveness in preventing infanticide.

Later laws brought the age of children to be registered down to three years but admonished landlords to pay close attention to any pregnancies among their tenants. Natural abortions had to be recorded. The fact that the laws were repeated at intervals of four to five years indicates that existing customs of abortions and infanticide were deeply ingrained and resisted change.[57] After Tsunayoshi's death the next decree on this subject did not appear until Kyōhō 19 (1734).[58] When the philosopher Ogyū Sorai wrote his *Seidan* (Discourse on government) around 1720, he felt cause to lament the great number of abandoned children.[59]

Travelers and Prison Inmates

As Engelbert Kaempfer and his party were approaching the city of Hamamatsu on their return from Edo in 1691, they saw the pitiful sight of a priest dying next to the road. He "was lying face down in the open field, completely drenched by a downpour" making "noises to indicate that he was still alive, because he assumed he would be handled roughly as a corpse. The sight would have moved stones but not the heart of a Japanese."[60]

The sight of unattended corpses along the road, both human and those of animals, was not altogether rare. Sick and hence useless beasts of burden were abandoned, while sick travelers were turned out of inns for fear they could infect others and were left to die along the road. Tsunayoshi charged his magistrate of roads and highways to ensure that at rest stations and inns all living beings were treated with benevolence. Sick people were to be reported to the authorities, and efforts were to be made to nurse them back to health. Their place of origin and next of kin were to be established, and on their death Buddhist funeral rites were to be held.[61] When C. N. Vaporis in his detailed work on Japan's highways states that travelers would not be left to die on the road "alone and unaided" and that authorities immediately dispatched a local doctor to treat sick travelers, this applies to the later Edo period and was in no small way thanks to the unprecedented orders of the fifth shogun.[62] The shogun's very personal involvement with the hardships endured by the lower orders is documented by Ogyū Sorai when he notes that, since Tsunayoshi was concerned about travelers having their heads scorched by the blazing sun, even those in daimyo retinues came to be permitted to wear sun hats.[63]

Another danger to travelers were the above-mentioned highway robbers and street gangs, often referred to as *taishō jingi gumi*. After some two hundred were rounded up and eleven men were executed in Jōkyō 3 (1686), the problem was greatly reduced.[64]

Although strictly disciplinarian, the shogun nevertheless was concerned that people ending up in prison were treated humanely. An order of Genroku 1 (1688) stated that it had become known that many were lately dying in prison, and hence ventilation in jails was to be improved and prisoners were to be given baths five times monthly and an additional garment for the winter months.[65] Four years later, when it came to Tsunayoshi's notice that many of his subjects were living in poverty, the newly appointed senior councilor Inaba Tango no Kami Masayuki (1640–1716) was personally charged by the shogun to devise ways and means of dealing with this matter.[66]

This unprecedented concern on the part of the ruler with the weakest and most insignificant members of society was difficult to understand for samurai, who considered it their moral right to cut down offending commoners. Such policies were seen as the root of an increasing feminization and weakening of the samurai, viewed by some with great concern.[67] Yet most of the laws discussed above could generally be ignored by the greater part of the samurai population. Only those charged with their enforcement had to accept the onerous burden of rendering service to the less privileged. There were, however, other orders the samurai could not ignore, since they directly affected their everyday life, greatly infringing upon their traditional privileges. These were Tsunayoshi's laws concerning the protection of animals, particularly dogs.

The Dog Shogun

> We should also count the dogs among the inhabitants, as they are maintained like citizens, but here [in Nagasaki] not as carefully as in other cities. . . . The streets are full of these rascals, which move neither for horses nor for people. If they harm people or deserve to die, only the executioner may kill them on command from high authority. Sick dogs, or those incapacitated by age, are maintained by each street in cages or huts. When the dogs die, they are carried up the mountains and buried no less carefully than people. This is done on the superstitious command of the shogun, who was born under the symbol of the dog, or the year of the dog, and consequently esteems them no less than Emperor Augustus did the ibex. A certain farmer laboriously carrying his dead dog up the hill complained to his neighbor about the year of birth of the shogun, which was responsible for his pains. The other replied: "Oh my friend, don't let's complain. If he were born in the year of the horse, our load would be much heavier!"[1]

This is how the German visitor Engelbert Kaempfer explains to his readers the infamous laws for the protection of dogs. The first decrees had been issued some five years before his arrival, and he witnessed the full effects of these laws upon the population. While at Edo, Kaempfer treated a man from Nagasaki for a dog bite. Asked whether he had revenged himself on the animal, the patient retorted: "Do you think that I am also going to risk my life?" a reply Kaempfer explains in terms of the laws that forbid the killing of animals. When passing through the city of Kurume on his return from Edo, Kaempfer observed, "next to a new notice twenty *shu* had been nailed down as a reward for anyone who would hand over the murderer of a dog. It must be noted that frequently here and there some people get their pelt beaten because of dogs."[2] Kaempfer uses difficult-to-translate humor to describe the effects of the laws, suggesting that he did not take the matter all too seriously. Considering the attention he paid to other features of seventeenth-century Japan, the space allotted to what historians have described as the worst laws in Tokugawa history is small. Moreover, he uses virtually identical wording when he refers to dogs first in his description of Japanese animals and later in that of Nagasaki, as if he had nothing more to say on the subject.³ Kaempfer has a lengthy section on taxes and civil duties, and he dwells on how people are so entangled in the tight net of mutual responsibility and "punishment is incurred so easily without one's own fault or knowledge that almost nobody can live assured that he will be spared." Yet it is "drunkenness and a tendency to brawl" Kaempfer cites as the cause. Many lives were also forfeited for smuggling. At Nagasaki alone more than three hundred people received the death sentence in the previous six to seven years, Kaempfer claims. Even during his two-year stay, "more than fifty died wretched deaths" on account of this crime. Punishments for offenses against animals find no mention.⁴ Beyond the inconvenience of dogs cluttering up roads and having to be fed, Kaempfer has nothing to say about the alleged tyranny and suffering caused by the laws protecting these animals. To the contrary, elsewhere Kaempfer praises the fifth shogun as "a great and excellent lord," "very compassionate" toward his subjects.⁵

The difference in perception from Japanese sources results from the fact that Kaempfer did not identify with the samurai class. To samurai, who thought nothing of killing a commoner to maintain their honor, the punishment of these same commoners for going against the laws of the shogun and harming a dog could have counted for little. What did count, however, was when samurai who had previously held the lives of their inferiors in their hands were now not even permitted to kill a dog. The records historians rely on are almost exclusively written by samurai, and little allowance has been made for the fact that when these men wrote about "the people" suffering greatly, they meant those that counted in their eyes, namely, their fellow samurai.

To Let the Punishment Fit the Crime

A visitor such as Kaempfer was amazed about the samurai's power to arbitrate on the spot over the life and death of their inferiors. In Nagasaki this practice was reflected in the conduct of the governor *(Nagasaki bugyō)*, Yamaoka Tsushima no Kami. He was a "very humble, righteous, and benevolent" gentleman but in the habit of executing "the servants of his mansion without much ado for the slightest act of dishonesty," Kaempfer explained.⁶ Such conduct was considered so absurd and outlandish by Kaempfer's European readership that it came to furnish the plot for Gilbert and Sullivan's comic opera *The Mikado,* though in this work of 1885 the conduct of the governor is ascribed to the ruler of Japan.

Even a samurai philosopher such as Ogyū Sorai regretted that Tsunayoshi's government discouraged the practice of killing guilty servants on the spot and bemoaned the fact that it had become "fashionable to quibble that killing people is inhumane."⁷ In contrast the foreigner Kaempfer apparently considered the limitations the fifth shogun imposed on the samurai's use of the sword fully justified, even though it resulted in an occasional dog bite and the inconvenience of dogs hindering the traffic.

Kaempfer did record the rumor contained in *Sannō gaiki* that the protection of dogs was due to the shogun's year of birth; this was undeniably part of the gossip of the times. With the shogun's most powerful chamberlains Makino Narisada and Yanagisawa Yoshiyasu similarly born in the Year of the Dog, one being his senior and one his junior by twelve years, they were ridiculed as the "Three Dogs."[8] Yet Hotta Masatoshi, Tsunayoshi's early grand councilor with impeccable traditional credentials, was born in the same Year of the Dog as Narisada. The fact that this finds no mention and no significance was attached to it in the case of Masatoshi must surely indicate that the year of birth was conveniently used to poke fun and mock rather than regarded with any seriousness. What Kaempfer heard was apparently one of the many satiric tirades against the government habitually making the rounds, since the ensuing story of the man considering it a blessing that the shogun protected dogs and not horses was clearly a joke. Kaempfer's informants were limited to men of some education, such as interpreters and other officials, who would have been aware that before the burial of deceased dogs was made mandatory, the abandonment of sick and dead horses had become a crime.[9] Either Kaempfer failed to recognize the joke, or he decided to pass it on for the amusement of his readers.

Unlike British royalty past and present, the fifth shogun showed no predilection for dogs. There is no record of any pet dogs at Edo castle. Over one hundred paintings of his have remained, but none of those are of dogs. They cover a variety of traditional Chinese subjects, but the majority are of horses and a number are of cranes. A little hot-water foot warmer in the shape of a Chinese dog, which is merely "purported" to have been in the possession of the shogun, is the best historians have been able to come up with.[10] Moreover, no serious contemporary observer made the connection between the protection of dogs and the year of birth of the shogun. Even the Confucian scholar Arai Hakuseki, outspoken in his criticism of the Laws of Compassion, and carefully noting a rumor concerning their cancellation on the death of the fifth shogun, had nothing to say about their origins.[11] In the domain of Owari, the lower-ranking samurai Asahi Shigeaki kept a diary about all noteworthy events. He heard from time to time how samurai at Edo were punished in unprecedented fashion for maltreating animals and noted down popular verses mocking the shogunate. Yet he does not offer an explanation for the origins of these laws that inflicted the punishment.[12]

The scholar Toda Mosui, also highly critical of the Laws of Compassion, gave his imagination free rein on what might befall people in the future if dogs were no longer killed. Noting that a male and female dog produce four puppies each autumn and spring, which then each in turn produce litters of that size, he calculated that within two years the original two would have multiplied to 152 animals. With his imagination more developed than his mathematical skills, he continued:

Horses under Pine, painted and signed by the fifth shogun. Reproduced courtesy of Hasedera, Nara.

People say if this is so, then they ought to be killed so that this age of moral decay will not continue indefinitely. The opposing view says that this is an evil way of thinking—should there be an order to kill dogs? If on account of these measures there will be a great number of dogs, then houses ought to be handed over to dogs so that they will not be drenched by dew or rain. Anyone opposing this should be made into dog food![13]

Mosui both pokes fun at and complains about the hardship resulting from the protection of dogs, but he offers no information or criticism about the cause of the law's inception. The reason is that the shogun's aim of making his society a more compassionate one was well known and that the laws for the protection of dogs were simply the most troubling aspect for the samurai of this political paradigm change. For the commoners, in contrast, matters looked different. Not only did protection from the sword of the samurai prove to be a blessing, but the abolition of hunting did as well.

The Shogun's Pleasure of Hawking

"The shogun's pleasure of hawking—the suffering of the commoners" was a complaint heard when, after a respite of some thirty-five years, the eighth shogun Yoshimune resumed hawking and again burdened the government and people with the considerable cost the "sport of kings" incurred. "Under the government of the fifth shogun, compassion for living creatures caused hardship for the people; now I am inclined to think that killing creatures spells hardship for the people," wrote the Confucian Muro Kyūsō around that time.[14] This criticism comes from an unexpected source, for Kyūsō was employed as a lecturer by Yoshimune's government. He had, moreover, initially been sponsored by Arai Hakuseki and like the latter was otherwise critical of the government of the fifth shogun.

The shogun's right to arbitrate over the sport of kings had been established by Ieyasu, and the ruler's annual dispatch of his hawks' first prey to the emperor and the highest imperial officials was an important political ritual, symbolizing his sovereignty. The granting of hawking grounds to the daimyo, but never to the imperial aristocracy who had enjoyed this sport in an earlier age, reinforced the samurai's image of an invincible predator above, able to strike swiftly at the world below. But the food and care the hawks demanded was considerable.

Hawks were fed largely on dog meat, and the necessary animals had to be supplied by the local farmers. For this purpose detailed registers of dogs were established long before the fifth shogun demanded such records. For instance, a register of Keian 4 (1651) of the domain of Aizu lists a total of 2,687 dogs and noted that less than half, namely, 1,166, were of a breed suitable to feed the hawks. Whether to kill the remainder was debated, but finally the matter was left up to the owners. Dog meat was widely eaten and thus a valuable commodity. There was even the case of a man claiming to survey the number of dogs suitable as feed for the lord's hawks and confiscating all others, as it turned out for his personal trade in dog meat.

In the Aizu domain there was a levy on every village of one dog per 1,000 *koku* of rice harvest. If appropriate animals were not available, a fee of 1 *bu* 10 *momme* was levied instead.[15] At other times such levies were paid in rice. In the Owari domain in Kanbun 13 (1673), land worth some 483 *koku* paid the equivalent of 0.245 *koku* in rice as contribution to feeding the lord's hawks.[16] Records of the Mito domain reveal that two average-sized dogs per day were required in feed for the birds; the farmers were returned the pelts, as only the meat was required.[17] No doubt the pelts were used to ward off the cold, and such practices might have given rise to the most likely fictitious story that the lord of this domain, Mitsukuni, presented the fifth shogun with a blanket of dog pelts to express his displeasure at the Laws of Compassion.

But the farmers' forced contribution of dogs, or at times fish, to feed the hawks was not all. The hawks had to be trained to catch their prey, and when the lord set out to hunt, he wanted the area to be well stocked with wild animals. Hence farmers were not allowed to chase away the flocks of birds that settled on their fields to feed or other wild animals devastating their crops, and so they lost their harvest. "Chasing away birds and beasts that destroy the five crops has been made into a crime, punishable by banishment and imprisonment or, as the case may be, by death. In this way people are irreverently given the treatment appropriate for lowly beasts. Among all living creatures, humans are to be respected most. To pay to lowly birds and beasts the respect due to men is evil government."[18]

These words of the itinerant monk Asai Ryōi (d. 1691), written in the 1660s when the fourth shogun Ietsuna much valued the sport of hawking, cast Tsunayoshi's endeavors to abolish this sport in a different light. Ryōi explains that in ancient China the rulers used their outings to hawk to ascertain personally the well-being of the rural population and to amend government if they discovered wrongs. In his day, he laments, it was carried out for the pleasure of the lord only, causing great hardship to the farmers. Hunting parties trampled the fields, and a flock of wild geese or ducks descending to feed often destroyed the year's harvest in an instant. "Still drenched in the sweat of their labor, shedding tears of blood," the farmers stood helpless, restrained by the fear of punishment from patrolling officials. They ended up with no choice but to support themselves by performing the labor of oxen, treading water mills, and selling their wives and daughters.[19]

Acknowledging the heavy cost of hawking, some domains, long before the government of the fifth shogun, had abolished the sport when failed harvests caused economic hardship. Even before becoming shogun, Tsunayoshi had punished retainers for mismanagement of the land entrusted to them, and economic problems were constant. Thus when Tsunayoshi, like his older brother Tsunashige, stopped hawking in his own domain, there is no reason not to see this as first a measure protecting the farmers and their harvest, rather than animals.[20] Tsunayoshi's early concern with the devastation of fields and their produce caused by hawking is also described in *Buya shokudan*, where the abolition of this sport is described as the beginning and origin of the Laws of Compassion. The work discusses the limits set on other forms of hunting and fishing, and explains that there was no restriction on shooting animals devastating fields, though the shogun considered it uncompassionate to eat their meat and ordered that they be buried where they had died.[21]

That the farmers were the first object of the shogun's policy of compassion is confirmed by the course of political events. As outlined earlier, shortly after his installation, Tsunayoshi appointed Hotta Masatoshi to oversee and improve the administration of the farmers. Tsunayoshi's concern about the harm caused by the laws regulating the areas around hunting grounds is reflected by an order issued a month later to the administrator of the Kantō region *(Kantō gundai)* that these laws should not be enforced severely as traditional customs involving hawks would be abolished.[22] The order was premature. The ceremonial surrounding hawking and the presentation of the hawk's prey carried too much weight to be simply abolished by an order of the new shogun. Over the years of Tsunayoshi's government such rituals were greatly simplified and reduced, especially with regard to the exchange of young hawks and the hawk's prey between the shogun and the daimyo. No further hunting grounds were awarded, and daimyo began to return to the government those that had been bestowed upon them by Tsunayoshi's predecessors. Officials in charge of hawking were redeployed, often to man kennels in which stray dogs were collected. Yet the shogun had the authority neither to force daimyo to return their hunting grounds bestowed by his predecessors nor totally to stop the ritual gifts to the imperial house resulting from the hunt.[23]

Dogs

Unlike hawking, there were no ceremonial restrictions concerning the treatment of dogs. Yet the first order mentioning them appears only in Jōkyō 2 (1685), five years after Tsunayoshi's accession. It stipulates that dogs and cats need not be tied up when a shogunal procession was passing.[24] As Tsukamoto Manabu suggests, this law might well have been the result of an incident that occurred at Asakusa earlier that year. On the announcement that the shogunal procession would be passing, the priest of one of the temples and the local magistrate, fearing that the stray dogs of the area might attack members of the procession, put them into bags and drowned them in the river.[25] The first prohibition to harm dogs and exhortation to practice compassion to all living creatures appears early in the following year.

By then the shogun's only son and heir Tokumatsu had been dead for three years, and the grand councilor Hotta Masatoshi had been assassinated two years earlier. Historians have therefore upheld *Sannō gaiki*'s explanation that the shogun's protection of dogs was caused by the pious belief that caring for this animal would cause the gods to bless him with a successor but that the laws had not been possible under the restraining influence of Hotta Masatoshi.[26]

One could also look at the matter from a different angle, namely, that the protection of dogs had not been a priority for the shogun, and that his attention turned to the matter only when major problems facing the society he had inherited had been dealt with.

The shogun's first priority had been the plight of the farmers, about which samurai sources tell us little. But the farmer's suffering could not be ignored by the monk Asai Ryōi. Surveying the scene at the time of Tsunayoshi's predecessor, he described those governing the land and collecting the taxes as men with the hearts of brutes.[27] Tsunayoshi replaced local officials and restructured the supervision of farmers and the collection of taxes, a process that, as explained above, lasted well beyond Hotta Masatoshi's death. River works were undertaken to prevent floods, and land was returned to farmers where houses of entertainment had been built. The bureaucracy was reduced, the conduct of officials regulated, and registration of all lower samurai enforced.[28] Economy measures taken included the scrapping of the costly pleasure boat *Atake maru*, regulating the use of houseboats, and the reduction of hawking to the limits possible, as explained above. Even the now superfluous tools of the falconers were put up for sale.[29] Habits such as gambling and the problem of the daimyo's excessive luggage when traveling were addressed. Orders to ensure that money was not wasted on foods out of season and costly clothes or large palanquins, as well as that mourning rites were observed in the correct fashion, all preceded the first exhortation not to harm dogs.[30] A detailed study of the measures that were taken during the first six years of Tsunayoshi's government would fill the pages of several volumes. Historians have attributed the thoroughgoing reforms of the early years of Tsunayoshi's administration to the good government of the grand councilor Hotta Masatoshi. Yet since the grand councilor himself described many of these measures as being the shogun's initiatives, while others continued after the death of Masatoshi, this conclusion is not tenable.[31]

With regard to the protection of animals, orders ensuring the welfare of horses long preceded those concerning dogs. Only weeks after becoming shogun, Tsunayoshi issued an order that, in the stables that had been the pride of his predecessor, the practice of slitting horses' sinews to make their gait more sprightly be discontinued. Later this order became effective also for other horses, including those of daimyo.[32] People were being punished for overloading horses before penalties for offenses against dogs were incurred. The use of guns was regulated, and only those with hunters' licenses were permitted to shoot animals. In the shogunal kitchens, birds, shellfish, shrimps, and prawns were no longer to be used except for the entertainment of aristocratic visitors from Kyoto, an order that could either be interpreted as an economy measure or compassion for animals.[33]

Yet it appears that after all this had been achieved, the shogun suddenly and single-mindedly set his heart on the protection of dogs, to the point of eventually punishing any violation by death.[34]

The incident at Asakusa indicates why the government's attention was turned to dogs. On this occasion dogs had been drowned since it was feared that, even if the strays of the area were tied up, they might free themselves and bite members of the shogunal procession. Stray dogs had become a menace to those who could not fight them off, including men marching in a procession, and were so fierce that tying them up proved insufficient restraint. This state of affairs also posed a threat to others unable to defend themselves: old people, women, and children. Drowning the animals was not a solution, not only because it went against the shogun's policy of creating a more compassionate society, but also because rotting corpses in Edo's waterways posed a health threat. The incident called attention to the fact that the government urgently had to deal with this urban problem and to find a solution within the framework of the shogun's overall political aim of reducing violence. That solution was first ordering the feeding of stray dogs so they would no longer attack people and, second, stopping people from harming dogs to free the city of dying animals and rotting corpses. Finally, proper burial of animals was decreed, a directive that had not only religious but also hygienic implications.

Yet this nonviolent solution to the problem was difficult to accept for samurai administrators, who having been raised in a society where boys were urged to practice their sword skills on dogs, now had to pronounce and enforce these orders. The problem of being molested by stray dogs affected mainly the commoners, and among those the weakest and poorest, who could not defend themselves against marauding animals, and they counted for little in the society of the day. Requiring officials to shoulder additional, onerous duties to create a safe environment for those at the bottom of the social scale was an abrupt reversal of the value system. It is hence not surprising that the correct transmission and enforcement of these orders became a problem from their very inception.

The first prohibition against harming dogs of Jōkyō 3 (1686) decreed that it was a punishable offense to have carts running over and injuring dogs, and continued: "Although previously there have been detailed instructions, now, when a masterless dog comes along, people do not feed it. We have also heard that people no longer give and receive dogs and other animals. It appears that what has been ordered concerning compassion towards living beings has been misunderstood. It is vital that the aspiration to be compassionate towards living beings permeate everything."[35]

The shogun's attempt to solve the problem of marauding dogs by ordering that they be fed turned out to be counterproductive. People disowned their dogs and did not feed strays for fear of being held responsible for the animal in question. To remedy this situation, the government ordered owners to register their dogs. The order made the rather surprising concession that people not able to find their dogs need not take undue trouble searching for them. Any other dog could be presented for registration.[36]

Ten days later the shogun's censure of his highest ministers, the senior councilors, was made public in an unprecedented fashion with the following decree:

> The recent order dealing with dogs is reissued because of a misunderstanding by the senior councilors.
>
> Rumor has it that the color of the fur and other details of each pet dog have been recorded but that if a dog cannot be found, any odd dog is

brought along just to make up numbers. The order was issued because it is the shogun's august wish that people become compassionate, but instead, falsehood is practiced. Henceforth, if a pet dog cannot be found, thorough inquiries must be made to locate it. If any cruelty is practiced towards dogs, the deputy magistrate *(shihai)* must be informed. Stray dogs are not to be treated unkindly and must be returned as soon as the owner is known.[37]

Caring for strays had placed a burden on the lower officialdom. But the registration of dogs also affected the daimyo, whose mansions frequently housed several hundred animals.[38] The shogun demanded that they accept responsibility for animals that had escaped and have their staff find them. As daimyo, the senior councilors attempted to lighten this burden by permitting any other stray to be taken in to make up numbers.

The shogun was willing neither to let the samurai shirk their responsibility for the animals they were raising nor to tolerate alteration of his orders by the senior councilors. He showed his resentment not only by making his censure of the senior councilors' "misunderstanding" public, but also by dismissing them temporarily from their duties. Their next official engagement, a ceremonial visit to the tomb of the second shogun Hidetada, was delegated to the grand chamberlain Makino Narisada. Again the reason for this unusual change was not kept secret. The official record is explicit that it was ordered on account of the senior councilors' "error" *(ayamari)*.[39]

The Enforcement of the Laws as Power Struggle

This incident turned the protection of dogs into a power struggle between the shogun and his officialdom. The issue at stake was not the protection of dogs. Like all other policies differentiating Tsunayoshi's government from those before and after him, the issue was the prerogatives of the samurai. Did the samurai have the right to set free unwanted dogs outside their walled compounds and let them hunt for food in areas of the city where commoners lived in cramped quarters, without the protection of such walls? The early *bakufu* had upheld the military's right to impose upon the commoners according to their convenience. Within this pattern of thought, the consequences of the samurai's strays for the commoners within the increasingly densely populated city was not an issue. Tsunayoshi's reversal of such traditional premises, as apparent in the order that the samurai account and assume responsibility for every animal born in their compounds, could not but have sent shock waves through the samurai community. The registration of dogs affected all levels of the military community, whether as owners of animals or as officials with the onerous task of enforcing laws curbing the prerogatives of their class. Resistance to the correct execution of the laws was commensurate with the pain it inflicted. The orders issued by the government, the criticism of opponents, and the recollections of supporters of the shogun's policy all document this ongoing power struggle.

In a lengthy order issued to the Edo city magistrates for oral transmission to their subordinates, the shogun is seen pleading, coaxing, and threatening:

> We have issued orders concerning compassion toward living beings, but you have not understood them well and are acting in a way that apparently makes the exchange of animals difficult. Generally when a healthy dog comes along you have it fed, but when a sick dog appears, it is not fed at all. Both the above ways of acting are due to misunderstandings. The shogun issued these orders because he wished to promote feelings of benevolence in people. To all appearances you have made people follow the orders, but deep in your hearts there is very little trace of compassion—a deplorable situation. We have heard that, according to some people, anyone really compassionate towards living beings is likely in the end to be considered a nuisance by local officials. You must observe the instructions issued from time to time and administer them so that feelings of charity arise in people's hearts.[40]

Scholars have interpreted the great number of orders issued for the protection of dogs during the government of the fifth shogun as a sign of the ruler's mental instability.[41] Yet closer examination of these orders indicates that they resulted from the officials' unwillingness to accept the task of ensuring the well-being of those below their station, be they humans or animals. Unwanted puppies were still thrown out on the street and trampled on by horses and animals. Fierce dogs still were not tied up but permitted to roam the streets, attacking people. The practice of selling animals that had died a natural death, rather than burying them, was also continuing.[42] The shogun continued to plead with officials:

> You should keep in mind that [the laws of] compassion for living things are only due to the mercy of the shogun. But beyond this mercy, the shogun has a more profound intention. Even if he were not to issue orders concerning compassion, you officials should have in mind that people should become benevolent and that their intentions should become gentle. You should tell this to those under your command and those in your units, and you should pass it on so that it will be known by everyone down to the servants.[43]

The shogun's efforts to turn officials at large into caring administrators was not crowned with success. To the contrary, their anger at the laws found expression in increased cruelty to the population. When, under the sixth shogun, Arai

Hakuseki pleaded for a general amnesty of prisoners, he wrote with regard to the enforcement of the Laws of Compassion: "If one looks at what happened recently under the previous shogun, one finds that those enforcing the law spared no efforts to use unwanted cruelty."[44] Hakuseki's statement finds support in a number of orders under Tsunayoshi's government correcting extreme interpretations of the laws by local officials.[45] The case that officials enforced the laws more cruelly than was intended by the government was also made by Tsunayoshi's grand chamberlain Yanagisawa Yoshiyasu in a record of the fifth shogun's government later drafted in his name. He stated: "The policy of the Laws of Compassion initially arose solely out of the shogun's desire to admonish even the slightest lack of benevolence and to perfect the spirit of the common people. It was not supposed to be such a severe law, but—possibly because Yoshiyasu, Terusada, and others failed to administer it correctly—when it came to the rank and file there were, I believe, many instances completely against the shogun's intentions."[46]

On presentation of the document to the government, the eighth shogun Yoshimune corrected this passage, maintaining that the laws were based on the deep convictions of his predecessor and that the grand chamberlains could not be blamed.[47] This correction of the historical record by the eighth shogun might well have been influenced by the fact that Yoshimune reemployed many of Tsunayoshi's officials who had been dismissed under the sixth shogun. The above-mentioned Matsudaira Terusada, Yanagisawa's son-in-law and assistant, was again entrusted with the functions of senior councilor, and it would have been politically unwise to have him seen as shouldering any responsibility for the unpopular laws. But, reading the continuation of the above passage, one may doubt whether Yoshiyasu indeed intended to shift the blame onto himself and his assistant. He wrote:

> When I think back reverently, I remember how I, Yoshiyasu, received the shogun's great favor and was entrusted with duties of great importance. Although I worked diligently day and night and illustrious virtue was promulgated throughout the country, there was obstruction on all levels, and it was impossible to succeed. Old evils were not corrected and new evils arose. During his thirty years of governing the people, the shogun wanted to make the world like that of Yao and Shun. But the intentions of his early government were not fulfilled. Now who is to blame for this? The ancients [of China] lamented, "There was a lord worthy to be called a lord, but he had no ministers worthy of the name." Indeed, although the country is different, the saying remains true.[48]

Just as in the case of Hakuseki, Yoshiyasu's complaints about officialdom and "new evils" seem to refer to the unintended severity with which the laws were enforced. Citing an old Chinese saying, Yoshiyasu apparently shoulders the blame. Yet since he has already assured the reader of his diligent work, it is much more likely that the "ministers" he blames were the senior councilors and other high-ranking administrators who attempted to block the shogun's efforts. At the order of the eighth shogun, this passage too was eliminated in the official version of the text, the one published in facsimile by the National Archives in 1982. As he was chosen as ruler by the very daimyo who were being blamed, these statements were unacceptable to Yoshimune.

This incident should alert the historian that political aspects must also be taken into consideration when looking at the most controversial aspect of the Laws of Compassion, namely, the infliction of the death sentence for killing an animal.

Population Afflicted?

The most widely cited evidence for a hapless population suffering under the cruelty of the Laws of Compassion is the continuation of Arai Hakuseki's tract pleading for a general pardon under the sixth shogun.

> For the sake of a single bird or beast, the death penalty was inflicted. Even relatives were given capital punishment or deported and exiled. People's lives were in danger. Their fathers and mothers, sisters and brothers, wives and children were separated from them, dispersed, and died. Nobody knows even roughly to how many hundreds of thousands of people this happened. If a nationwide amnesty is not declared at this point, how can we meet people's hopes that life is returning to normal?[49]

As has been argued in greater detail elsewhere, Hakuseki's expression "how many hundreds of thousands of people" *(nan jūman nin)* must be taken as a figure of speech rather than denoting real numbers. There is no record of prison extensions that would have been necessary to accommodate such numbers, and only nine bodies of people who had died in prison before trial were preserved in brine. Moreover, the grand total of people pardoned to mark various occasions such as the death of the fifth shogun and his consort, and the accession of the sixth shogun, amounted to a total of 8,831. However, the greater part, namely, 5,599 of these, were pardoned by daimyo and houses in their employ.[50] Since most daimyo made only token gestures in enforcing the Laws of Compassion in their domains, it is impossible to argue that the greater part of pardons were for offenses against animals.[51]

In judging the reliability of a document, the purpose for which it was written must be taken into account. Hakuseki's *Told Round a Brushwood Fire (Oritaku shiba no ki)* was clearly composed to inform posterity of the author's influential and for the country beneficial role in the brief governments of the sixth and seventh shoguns. To do this effectively the sad state of affairs awaiting Hakuseki's intervention had to be graphically described. While I do not suggest that facts and figures were purposely altered, it is only natural that the vocabulary chosen was appropriately dramatic to convey the point. That Hakuseki somewhat overstated the case becomes apparent when his friend and colleague Muro Kyūsō compares the harm done by the fifth shogun's protection of animals with that inflicted upon the population by the eighth shogun's resumption of hawking, mentioned above. There is no doubt that in both cases large numbers of people suffered. The question is merely to what extent this was unusual for the times.

The foreign observer Kaempfer was not the only one who failed to notice the cruel oppression under the Laws of Compassion that historians refer to. Whether one reads the diaries of Arai Hakuseki, Toda Mosui, or Asahi Shigeaki in Owari, the space allotted to this evil generally described as dominating the lives of people is extremely small. These sources mention with disapproval convictions for offenses against animals, but cases of heavy punishment were rare enough to be cited one by one. For the year Jōkyō 4 (1687) Mosui mentions that "many" were reprimanded by officials and sent to prison for offenses against dogs. From another source we know that including the three cases he discusses in greater detail, these amounted to a total of sixteen.[52] The majority of cases concerned large carts running over dogs, and the offenders were mostly pardoned. In the three cases detailed, his description does not always match the official record. For instance Mosui mentions that a retainer of Tsuchiya Masanao was banished from Edo, while his lord was put under house arrest. The official record of punishments describes how the retainer was assailed by eight to nine dogs, had his clothes torn, and therefore resorted to using his sword. He was detained for two months but then pardoned by the senior councilors. There is no record of Tsuchiya Masanao being placed under house arrest, and the fact that Masanao was promoted to the position of senior councilor some four months later throws doubt on the accuracy of Mosui's statement. The reason for this inaccuracy might have been that Mosui was recollecting events that had taken place some months previously. For referring to Tsuchiya Masanao, Mosui uses the title of "Yamato no Kami," which the daimyo received only on 21.10.Jōkyō 4 (1687), indicating that the passage must have been recorded after this date. The incident, however, had taken place in the fourth month, and the retainer was pardoned early in the sixth month of that year.[53]

This and other inconsistencies in the punishment of samurai reflect the alarm the military felt over laws that could bring the greatest of them to fall on account of a mere dog. Such "'equalization' of subjects under a Tokugawa absolutism," to use Maruyama Masao's terminology, was even more clearly expressed in the much-publicized punishment of the shogunal veterinarian.[54]

Having had his duck killed by his neighbor's dog, the veterinarian crucified the dog and posted it on his neighbor's fence. The supreme court *(hyōjōsho)* investigated the case and ordered the veterinarian to commit *seppuku*. The proclamation announcing the sentence declared that the high and the lowly equally had to observe the shogun's orders concerning compassion.[55]

For the shogun such public disregard of his orders and personal wishes was an act of treason, and a senior retainer of Yanagisawa Yoshiyasu observed: "When someone disobeys the Laws of Compassion, regardless whether they are of high or low birth, it is equal to harboring revolt in their hearts against the shogun's orders."[56] The point is an important one. Just as today publicly burning a national flag is not merely considered an act of illegally lighting a fire but one of political subversion, so was killing a dog under the fifth shogun. The crime was not the harm done to an animal but that of publicly flouting the command of the ruler and laws of the country, an offense punished severely in all authoritarian states. The claim of many historians that the fifth shogun killed people for the sake of dogs pulls at the heartstrings of readers but is historically incorrect.

Violation of any shogunal law was invariably punished by death, the visitor Kaempfer observed, and hence the execution ground at Nagasaki was kept busy. Yet the shogunal laws violated were not those concerning compassion but the prohibition against secretly trading with foreigners. On one occasion the Dutch were forced to be present at the execution of two men, one for secretly trading a pound of camphor, the second for lending him the money. They were warned that in the future Dutch collaborators would receive similar punishment.[57] Death was incurred for a great many offenses now considered trivial, ranging from having an affair with the wife of one's master to petty thieving. Consequently the prison population was high and mass executions not unusual. Asahi Shigeaki heard that two hundred people were executed at one time in Edo. He comments on the nauseating stench at the execution site but does not appear to think that any injustice had been done or that an extraordinarily cruel event had taken place.[58]

Such disregard for human life was, however, not unique to Japan. Taken aback at how easily the death sentence was incurred, Kaempfer was, nevertheless, moved to state: "But in spite of this, the judges of this heavily populated, heathen country have fewer deaths to account for and less blood on their hands than those in our Christian countries. This shows how fear of an immutable death sentence can keep these obstinate Tartars in order."[59]

The Dog Pounds

The threat of death reduced the killing of dogs but could not persuade the population to engage actively in compassionate behavior towards animals. To the contrary. When on occasion someone was moved to feed a hungry stray dog, it would persistently stay at the side of its benefactor, and the person was faced with the problem of being considered the animal's owner by the officials. When in the past food left over from religious ceremonies was given to strays, it was now thrown away so dogs would not gather around temples and priests be considered their owners. As a result, Toda Mosui observed, starving dogs tried to get through the smallest cracks or dig holes to steal food and frequently attacked people, in particular killing abandoned children.[60] Attacks by packs of dogs were impossible to fend off without harming the animals, as the above case of Tsuchiya Masanao's retainer illustrates.

The government had to think of a solution within the framework of the shogun's policy of nonviolence. Like governments today that feel the need to respect animal rights, it came up with the idea of housing abandoned animals in dog pounds. The difference from the situation today is that the pounds had to cater to far greater numbers of strays and were not only constructed but also to a large extent maintained at the expense of the highest-ranking members of society, such as the daimyo. The ongoing expense was covered by a levy calculated according to house frontage, placing the greatest financial burden on those maintaining large mansions. By Genroku 10 (1697) just over 40,000 dogs were maintained in enclosures at Yotsuya, Nakano, and Ōkubo at the edge of the city.[61] It was perhaps ironic that these were the same locations at which the third shogun had enjoyed the hunt.

The heavy financial burden placed on the upper samurai correctly reflected their overwhelming responsibility for the situation that necessitated the dog pounds. Toda Mosui had eloquently warned of the rapid increase of dogs if new litters were no longer permitted to be killed. Yet in accord with prevailing patterns of thought, he gave no consideration to the fact that if owners had not let their dogs escape and had restrained them from mating, Edo would not have been plagued by rapidly increasing numbers of stray dogs.

Dog pounds were not new in Japan. As mentioned above, they were part of the business of hawking, where dogs were used both as food for the hawks and to catch their prey. The establishment of dog pounds inside and outside of the city coincided with the government's nearly total curtailment of hawking, and officials in charge of hawking grounds were redeployed to run the dog pounds. It is likely that, similarly, kennels originally built for dogs used as feed for the falcons were now used to house strays. There is surprisingly little reliable material on the government's kennels, and facts have to be gleaned from a variety of sources. While *Tokugawa jikki* mentions the city kennels built with the assistance of daimyo only from Genroku 8 (1695), a government account indicates that two years earlier some forty animals were already maintained in a dog pound in the village of Kitami in Musashi.[62] At the same time the government was encouraging samurai to send dogs back to their domains, and those who on account of their low status had no lands to send them to were permitted to transfer their dogs to the government's kennels. Daimyo were beginning to take note of the problem, and records show that animals were sent back to the countryside and males and females separated to prevent further increases in numbers.[63] Yet when the lord of Owari shipped an unwanted forty dogs from his Edo mansion to be released in the streets of the city of Nagoya, one might wonder whether this was in accord with the shogun's intention. Asahi Shigeaki in reporting this event makes no mention of how the citizens of Nagoya coped with the influx of forty stray animals, reminding us that our documentation on the subject is largely one-sided.[64]

Only occasionally a document surfaces indicating that the dog pounds were in fact welcomed by some sections of the community, such as a request from the citizens in the vicinity of Dentzū temple (Dentzū-in Monzen Machi) that the great number of dogs in their area be removed to the kennels.[65]

There is no question that Tsunayoshi's attempt to reduce violence in the society he inherited backfired with regard to the protection of dogs and produced suffering in turn. But it is also evident that the source of the problem was the samurai's disregard for the welfare of the commoners. Unwilling to take responsibility for the animals they were breeding, they let loose excessive numbers beyond the walls of their mansions for the commoners to cope with as best as they could. When strays affected the community to the extent that even a shogunal procession was not safe, Tsunayoshi took action that was to cost the samurai dearly both in financial and emotional terms. An order forbidding crowds to jeer at samurai officials chasing dogs for the kennels may serve as final example of the pain the orders inflicted on proud samurai.[66] No wonder that those responsible for the record we chiefly rely on painted this attack on the prestige and prerogatives of their class in the darkest colors.

A similar tendency to leave for posterity a rather one-sided record of events can be noted in what is arguably the most famous event in Japanese history: the revenge of the Forty-seven Rōnin, or masterless samurai, to be discussed next.

The Forty-Seven Loyal Samurai

There is one event in Japanese history that most, if not all, Japanese will have heard of. This is the story of how, on a snowy winter's night, forty-seven loyal samurai avenged their dead lord by killing his enemy in an attack on his mansion and in turn were ordered by the authorities to commit suicide. But rather than from history books, this knowledge is frequently gleaned from theater or film performances or one of the many novels that retell this story.

A Never-Ending Story

The world of the theater was quick to realize the potential of this dramatic event, and the first stage performance took place only sixteen days after the loyal samurai disemboweled themselves on the order of the government in the spring of 1703. Although the stage plot was set in a different age, the authorities soon realized that the play referred to recent events and after a run of only three days shut down the performance. This, however, did not deter the theatrical world, and in the remaining century and a half of the Tokugawa period over 120 plays on the theme were written and performed.

The most notable among these was then, and is still today, a play that made its debut in the summer of 1748 under the name of *Kanadehon chūshingura* (The kana copy Book of the treasury of loyal retainers) by Takeda Izumo (1691–1756), Miyoshi Shōraku (1696–?), and Namiki Sōsuke (1695–1751). First performed as a puppet play in Osaka, it quickly moved to Edo and entered the repertoire of the kabuki theater.[1] Embroidering the story with various subplots dramatizing the conflicting demands of the culture's most cherished values, such as duty and humanity or warm-heartedness *(giri/ninjō)*, and pulling at the heartstrings by a skillful staging of the powerful themes of love and death, it has succeeded in spellbinding audiences for over two centuries. As the English section of the program of the 231st annual kabuki performance in 2002 states, "the play has been performed constantly and is considered a sure recipe for full-houses."[2]

The impact of the play has been such that the historical event has since been referred to by a word from the title of the play, namely, Chūshingura. With the introduction of the silver screen in Japan, film producers were attracted by the popular plot, and since 1910 over forty films have been shown on the subject. Since television became popular in Japan in the sixties, some fifteen productions have been broadcast. Further, some eighty-three novels have been published on the subject in the last hundred years, many of them first serialized in newspapers.[3] The above figures do not include less traditional, but no less popular, stage productions of the story, such as that of the all-female Takarazuka revue, which in turn have become the subject of television programs and other publicity. Nor must one forget the early boom in Ukiyo-e prints and other visual presentations, down to today's advertisements in public transportation that catch the eye of the weary commuter and continually rekindle memories of the exploits of the loyal retainers. Occasionally there has been some mocking directed at the subject, such as in the so-called parody Ukiyo-e prints *(mitate e)*, where the best-known scenes of the play are set in the Yoshiwara entertainment quarter, and the key roles are portrayed not by staunch samurai but stylish courtesans.[4] Yet while these scenes make light of the most tragic moments of the play, they also attest to their endurance. Even the fashionable world of late Tokugawa was still interpreted in terms of an event that had happened some hundred years earlier, constantly reviving the memory of these much-lauded exploits.

Historical Research and Commemoration

Historians have been no less active in searching out documents connected with the event, and anybody wishing to make an in-depth study of the subject has well over three hundred "sources" to consult. These range from letters written by the loyal samurai themselves and contemporaneous observations to discussions of the event later in the Tokugawa period, when opinions and theories were increasingly colored by the lore that was growing up around the incident. A good example of the blurring of fact and fiction—or rather fiction taken as fact—is Motoori Norinaga's description of the event, based on the story of a wandering priest he met in his youth. Such oral presentations claimed to be based on primary documents as, for instance, the letters of Ōishi Kuranosuke, but, as Federico Marcon and Henry D. Smith have explained, contained a great variety of original and less original lore.[5]

Today most primary sources are available in eleven separate multivolume publications of collected material. But material is still coming to light in the form of writings handed down in families that had some connection with the event, documents claimed to have been written at the time.[6] Historians' output on the subject has been correspondingly prolific, with a considerable number of volumes also produced by people "who have had a lifelong interest in the subject" but are not historians by profession.[7] The unabated Chūshingura boom in light of Japan's great political and social paradigm changes is indeed a curious phenomenon, which in itself has recently become the subject of a book-length study.[8]

In English the emphasis has been for many years on the stage performance rather than on the historical event. This was remedied on the occasion of the three hundredth anniversary of the incident when the journal *Monumenta Nipponica* published a series of articles by leading scholars. Together with some other publications of recent date, they provide thorough treatment of both the event itself and the historical literature it generated.[9] I will therefore limit myself mainly to those aspects that are relevant for an understanding of the fifth shogun's government.

The event is annually commemorated both at the castle of Akō, present-day Hyōgo prefecture, the original seat of the loyal samurai and their unfortunate lord, and in Tokyo, where the revenge took place. In the latter city, members of the Central Loyal Retainers' Association (Chūō Gishi Kai) meet before dawn at the spot where the mansion in which the samurai enacted their revenge once stood (present-day Matsusaka Kōen, near Japan Railway Ryōgoku Station) and march the 10-kilometer route, as the samurai did at the time, to Sengakuji, the temple at Shinagawa where they placed the head of the enemy on their lord's grave, which also became the resting place of their ashes. At the temple, commemoration begins on the day before the actual event. The graveyard is thick with the smoke of incense sold with much noise at the gate, and at the most popular times, visitors must accept a wait of over an hour before they can file past the graves of the loyal retainers and their lord, and pay their respects. On such occasions the descendants of the loyal samurai are much in demand to attend one of the commemorations, including the descendants of the forty-eighth, who committed suicide some time before the event when pressed to take up an offer of adoption, thus making his participation in the revenge impossible. Though the actual event took place on February 1, 1703, in the Western calendar—corresponding to the fifteenth day of the twelfth month of the Japanese calendar in use at the time—the event is now celebrated on December 15, a fact that does not seem to disturb those who annually attempt to re-create the scene with some authenticity.

The enduring importance attached to the event is perhaps best illustrated by a major public standoff that broke out in the 1990s in Akō between the mayor of that city and the chief priest of the shrine dedicated to the memory of the leader of the loyal samurai, Ōishi Kuranosuke. The historian Yagi Akihiro, in a publication for the city, had questioned whether the forty-seventh retainer, who did not give himself up to the authorities, should be included in the list of loyal samurai, a suggestion fiercely rejected by the temple and its supporters. The stalemate, apparently, is continuing into the twenty-first century.[10]

With the conduct of the forty-seven samurai being celebrated even today as reflecting the best of Japanese culture and the spirit of a much-cherished samurai tradition, any writing contesting this image can cause protest of public proportions, and historians have preferred not to emphasize documented factors that run counter to this idealized image.[11] If these are given due consideration, one could be tempted to conclude—as some observers did at the time—that the incident, rather than glorifying the samurai, speaks much more eloquently of the decline of the warrior tradition. At the risk of being the devil's advocate, I need to mention some of these factors below.

The Historical Incident

On 14.3.Genroku 14 (1701) imperial envoys were being entertained for the third day at Edo castle after their arrival from Kyoto. Kajikawa Yoriteru (Yosobei), a keeper of the castle, was charged with conveying the presents of the shogun's wife (*midaidokoro*) to the envoys, and his record informs us of the events. Supervising the ceremonies was the sixty-year-old Kira no Suke Yoshinaka (also Yoshihisa, 1641-1702), who had sent a message to Yoriteru that the presentation of the gifts would take place earlier than scheduled. To confirm these arrangements, Yoriteru proceeded along the main corridor, known as the Corridor of Pines on account of its paintings, in search of Kira.[12] Unable to find him, he asked that Asano Naganori (1667-1701), the daimyo charged with entertaining the envoys, be summoned. Having exchanged the usual greetings, assuring each other of their cooperation, Asano returned to his seat. Then Kira appeared, and Yoriteru approached him to confirm the timing of the ceremonies. As the men were standing in discussion, Asano suddenly struck Kira with his sword from behind, shouting: "Did you forget my recent grievance?" Taken by surprise, Kira turned around and attempted to flee, but Asano struck him again, causing him to fall. At this point Yoriteru managed to restrain Asano, who was then led away shouting loudly that though the time and place were inappropriate, for some days he had nursed a grievance against Kira and thus had to strike him.[13] That same evening Asano was ordered by the authorities to disembowel himself. Because the area had been defiled by the shedding of blood, the ceremonies for the envoys were moved to different rooms of the castle.[14]

This is as much as contemporaneous records tell us about the event that eighteen months later caused forty-seven of Asano Naganori's retainers to attack Kira Yoshinaka's mansion in the dead of the night, cut off his head, and place it on Asano's grave at Sengakuji. Forty-six of the retainers gave themselves up to the authorities and were ordered to commit suicide some two months later.[15]

The Response

Apparently Emperor Higashiyama gained some satisfaction from Asano's attack on Kira inasmuch as it confirmed his view of the Edo warriors as a boorish lot.

But the court also lauded the shogun's quick punishment of Asano, since the incident was a mark of disrespect toward the imperial house. For the shogun, punctilious in his purification rituals before receiving the imperial messengers, this aspect of the incident must have been a major source of anguish.[16] For the *bakufu*, Asano's crime was defilement by blood of ritual space rather than simply an attack on a courtier.[17]

It is generally asserted that among "the public" the response, at least to the final act of revenge, was very different, with frenzied public discussions and much support for the loyal retainers among the population of Edo. Yet it has been pointed out that, within the political system of the times, such public discussions would have been impossible and that, moreover, contemporaneous sources do not warrant this interpretation. The diary of the samurai Asahi Shigeaki, *Ōmurō chūki* (Diary of a parrot in a cage), records without further comment, Asano Naganori's attack and ensuing death, the confiscation of Akō castle, the retainers' protest that Kira was permitted to remain alive, as well as the attack on the latter's house some eighteen months later. But there is no mention of the death of the forty-six retainers or any discussion of the issues at hand. *Shiojiri* (Salt fields), the work of Shigeaki's friend and teacher Amano Sadakage (1663–1733), does not even mention the revenge of the retainers, let alone their death. Both these men were resident at Nagoya, but the news of events and gossip from Edo is otherwise faithfully reflected in their work.[18]

Arai Hakuseki, who considered the vendettas fought in his youth worth recording for posterity, notes only briefly in his diary Asano's attack and death, and also the retainers' revenge, but not even as the most important event of the day. While debate over the fate of the forty-six samurai is supposed to have raged among the public and scholars, Hakuseki fails to mention the subject yet takes the time to describe in detail the bureaucratic wrangling over the payment of an increase in his salary. Again, the death of the samurai gets only a brief, laconic mention in his diary.

Equally matter-of-fact is the report of these events in Toda Mosui's diary. The work ends before the act of revenge took place but covers the period of Asano's attack. What is noteworthy is that, though Mosui had much to say about the vices of Hotta Masatoshi, justifying his slaying at the castle by the junior councilor Inaba Masayasu in 1684, there is no mention whatsoever of those later attributed to Kira.[19] Nor do the other diarists mentioned above make critical remarks about Kira. His vilification, it appears, was to a large degree the addition of sympathetic writers, for his greed and depravity are essential to turn the story of illegal violence into one of samurai virtue. To invest the story with the moral force that would turn the play into a perpetual money spinner and even a national myth, Kira had to be evil. For good measure the excessive preoccupation with the opposite sex documented for Asano Naganori was attributed to this villain of the story.

Asano Naganori

Asano Naganori's extreme fondness for women is recorded in *Dokai kōshūki*, an inquiry conducted under the fifth shogun on the conduct and lives of the daimyo sometime before the above incident. Although the report acknowledges his intelligence and notes with approval the strict punishment of offenses in his domain, it bemoans his sexual profligacy. Evil retainers flattering him and catering to his vices by finding attractive women for him are promoted and richly rewarded. Only concerned with his personal amusement he, from his youth on, was content to leave the government of his domain in the hands of his retainers.[20]

Asano Naganori had succeeded to the 53,500 *koku* domain of Harima and Akō castle at the age of eight on the early death of his father in Enpō 3 (1675).[21] The family had strong links with the Confucian scholar Yamaga Sokō (1622–1685), who had been employed by the domain from 1652 to 1660. One year before Asano's birth, Sokō returned to Akō, this time as an exile, but by 1675 he was pardoned and went back to Edo. Nevertheless the contact did not cease. In Jōkyō 1 (1684), one year before Sokō's death, the seventeen-year-old Naganori and his fourteen-year-old brother Nagahiro took the oath as Sokō's disciples in the military arts.[22]

Sokō's principal teaching was that in peacetime the samurai "should set a high example of devotion to duty" and in all his conduct provide a model of virtuous living for the other classes to follow.[23] These high moral principles are said to have had a pervading influence on the samurai of Akō and are believed to have been instrumental in persuading the forty-seven samurai to sacrifice their lives for the sake of their lord. However, these principles apparently had little effect on Asano Naganori, who showed concern neither for the reputation of his house nor for the fate of his family and retainers when he attacked Kira near the reception rooms where an important ceremony of state was under way.

Asano could not have been ignorant of the *bakufu*'s heavy punishment for spilling blood on a ritual occasion. His own uncle, Naitō Izumi no Kami Tadakatsu, had forfeited his life and domain when he killed a fellow daimyo in the precincts of Zōjōji during the funeral rites for the fourth shogun some twenty years previously, similarly shouting that the attack was in revenge for an earlier incident.[24] Asano must also have personally witnessed the hardship of retainers losing their homes and employment when he, acting as the *bakufu*'s representative, confiscated the castle of Matsuyama in Bichū less than a decade previously.[25] Finally, although apprenticed to Sokō in the military arts, he showed a marked lack of samurai spirit as well as sword skills in his attack on Kira. As the contemporaneous scholar Satō Naokata (1650–1719) pointed out, attacking a man engaged in discussion from behind and not succeeding in killing him showed "neither courage nor ability." If he wanted to kill Kira, at least he should have done so after the completion of official duties.[26] Asano's lack of sword skills was also made fun of in a contemporaneous ditty, which mocked that Asano should have learned from Hotta Masatoshi's assassin, Inaba Masayasu, how to cut a man down.[27]

The nature of Asano's attack on Kira became an issue as soon as it was known that the former had been ordered to commit suicide but the latter was to go unpunished. It indicated that the *bakufu* did not consider the incident as a quarrel between samurai, in which case traditionally both parties were punished, but as unilateral misconduct on the part of the daimyo. This was tantamount to the loss of Asano's honor as daimyo and samurai. His retainers protested immediately and even indicated that they would not be willing to hand over Akō castle to the authorities if Kira were not punished.[28] While they finally did yield the castle peacefully, this issue became the cause for the final act of revenge. Although the Akō samurai are lauded for forfeiting their lives to regain their master's honor, documentation throws doubt on whether their act was as selfless as it is generally made out to be.

Dokai kōshūki notes that Asano possessed neither literary nor military skills and brands his retainers as disloyal for not having admonished their lord in his young years. The chief retainer listed is Ōishi Kuranosuke, the later much-idolized leader of the band of loyal samurai.[29] There can be little doubt that the uncontrolled behavior of Asano and his lack of civil and military accomplishments were to a large extent the responsibility of his retainers. Though Asano had been left fatherless at the age of eight, they failed to school their young lord in the military arts and educate him as a responsible leader, perhaps out of a desire not to relinquish their own authority as he reached maturity. Moreover, they had lacked the circumspection to ensure that their lord received the proper instruction in his duties on this important occasion of state, whatever the price. When the letters of the Akō retainers point out that revenge on Kira was necessary to regain their own honor,[30] this claim needs to be interpreted in terms of the responsibility they themselves had for their daimyo's uncontrolled behavior. Since Kira denied that there was any point of contention between the two men, Asano's behavior became an act of one-sided violence.[31] Unless his attack could be construed as falling within acceptable samurai behavior, their own neglect of duties was apparent.

Samurai revenge was traditionally carried out by a representative of the injured party, not by that of the assailant.[32] Here the case is reversed. Asano had to become the injured party and Kira the villain who deserved punishment to absolve first Asano and later the Akō retainers from their guilt. Yet historical documentation does not support this image of Kira.

Kira Kōsuke Yoshinaka

Though perhaps not unblemished, Kira Yoshinaka had successfully served the *bakufu* in matters of ceremonies for some forty years. There is a marked lack of contemporaneous evidence to show that Kira was villain enough to justify an attack on him during the performance of his duties and his eventual murder together with sixteen of his retainers who were attempting to defend him.

The Kira house belonged to a group of families known as *kōke,* literally, high families, who from the beginning of the Tokugawa period had been responsible for ceremonial matters. With an illustrious ancestry going back to the Ashikaga branch of the Seiwa Genji clan and a distant relationship to the early Mikawa Tokugawa house, the ceremonial standing of the Kira family was high, and its members acted as the shogun's representative at court and important temples and shrines.[33] Their income was low, however, that of Kira being a mere 4,200 *koku.*

Kira showed promise from an early age and at only twenty-two, even before he succeeded to his father's position, was entrusted with the important task, as the representative of the fourth shogun Ietsuna, of congratulating Emperor Reigen on his succession. On the successful completion of this mission, he received the shogun's warm praise and was promoted to the lower fourth rank.[34] The favors of the fourth shogun were also demonstrated when in the following year Kira's one-year-old son was installed as the successor of Kira's brother-in-law, the daimyo Uesugi Tsunakatsu, who had died early and childless.[35] The story that Kira poisoned his brother-in-law to install his own infant son is not only unlikely considering the high infant mortality of the times (which would have made waiting until the child had become older a more reasonable course of action), but also lacks documentation and must be added to those accounts that were later constructed to vilify him. The *bakufu* certainly thought highly of Kira, for in Enpō 6 (1678) his son, Uesugi Tsunanori, was permitted to marry the sister of Tsunayoshi's son-in-law, the successor to the house of Kii.[36] Family ties with the shogunal house would not have been permitted had Kira been the corrupt rogue later sources make him out to be. Shortly after the succession of the fifth shogun, Kira was promoted,[37] and where many others failed, he also managed to serve this demanding ruler to his full satisfaction over the next twenty years.

Perhaps because Kira's vilification as insatiably greedy and corrupt is essential to establish a just reason for Asano's violence, historians have not questioned it, and even the otherwise detailed Tokutomi Sohō feels he can pronounce Kira corrupt, "without further investigation."[38] Tokutomi points out that graft was the order of the day and had been systematized but still considers it evil that Kira should expect such emoluments.[39]

Gift-giving was an important part of Tokugawa ritual and was conducted at all levels of society. It ranged from the shogun and his family sending gifts to the emperor to facilitate the granting of court titles and the Dutch offering outlandish presents in the hope of gaining better terms of trade to an apprentice interpreter supplying the essential *sode no shita* (lit.: under the sleeve) to gain promotion.[40] Then as now in Japanese culture it is a form of payment for services rendered or hoped for where no formal system of remuneration exists, and the line between gift and graft is a fine one. As also the record of Tsunayoshi's Kanda household attests, even though the expense might have been resented, in late-seventeenth-century Japan gift-giving was an essential element of social intercourse, and it seems arbitrary to label the gifts one official expected within this framework as graft.[41] In line with these customs it could only be expected that the daimyo Asano Naganori, requiring instruction in important ceremonies, would send gifts to Kira Yoshinaka, a man whose income was just over one-tenth of his own. No doubt Kira well knew how to use his monopoly on essential ceremonial knowledge to boost his meager income, and he might well have been unpopular and considered greedy by some. The contemporary Satō Naokata pointed out early on that while Asano's conduct was justified on account of evil-doing that people attributed to Kira, it still left open the question of whether this view of Kira was indeed supported by fact.[42] The charge of Kira insisting on bribes is first mentioned in a work that by its very title *Gijin roku* (Record of the faithful/dutiful men) suggests that the author, the philosopher Muro Kyūsō, supported the revenge of the Akō retainers. Moreover, to strengthen the justification of Asano's attack on Kira, a fictional episode of Kira insulting Asano as "country bumpkin" appears in the work. As Bitō Masahide has pointed out, Kyūsō's work "is filled with inaccuracies," perhaps because the information he was able to obtain already contained such fictional elements.[43]

Lauding the slaying of Kira meant praising an act of breaking the law. Hence Kira's vilification was necessary to justify such illegal behavior as being provoked by an even worse state of affairs. If Kira had been extracting financial gains beyond the accepted norm, it is improbable that he would have been entrusted continually with the important task of acting as the shogun's representative. Instead he would have been censured and dismissed as so many other government officials were under the fifth shogun.

Much of the source material on Kira's vices is of doubtful origin. Even Tokutomi, generally searching out primary source material, finds no better source than *Tokugawa jikki* to describe Kira's vices.[44] As another scholar has pointed out, these explanations are simply those of the compiler of *Tokugawa jikki* well over a century after the event and lack historical foundation.[45]

The Debate

The historian Tahara Tsuguo has made a list of scholars arguing for and against the propriety of the forty-seven samurai's revenge between the years 1703 and 1839. Of the twenty-two mentioned, the majority, namely, fifteen, were in praise of the Akō samurai.[46] However, when one learns that the critical essays of Ogyū Sorai and Dazai Shundai were at one time removed from their collected works,[47] one must wonder how much other critical writing failed to survive.

A strong critic of the Akō samurai was the contemporary Confucian scholar Satō Naokata, a disciple of Yamazaki Anzai's Kimon School. Appalled by some Confucians' sanction of the event, he voiced his criticism in an essay titled *Yonjūroku nin no hikki* (Notes on the forty-six men) as early as 1705. When after his death his disciple Inaba Mokuzai published his writings as *Unzōroku* (Record of a treasure trove), the essay was not included. Yet Naotaka expressed similar sentiments in a debate he held with two other luminaries of this school, Miyake Shōsai (1662–1741) and Asami Keisai (1652–1711). Here Naokata's criticism of the Akō retainers is matched and contradicted by the high praise for the samurai of the others, and perhaps for this reason publication did not present a problem.[48]

For Satō Naokata, Asano's attack on Kira was a grave violation of the law, and for this he was punished accordingly by the *bakufu*. There was nothing to be revenged, since Asano had been sent to his death by the *bakufu* and not by any private opponent. Again, the forty-seven samurais' night attack on Kira's mansion was a criminal act of gang violence and a violation of the *bakufu*'s orders. Since they had knowingly violated the law, Satō Naokata argues, it was absurd for the samurai to notify the authorities on completion of their crime with the message that they were now awaiting their orders. This leads the scholar to suspect that the driving force was not the revenge of their dead lord but the hope that praise and admiration for this act of loyalty would secure them a pardon and reemployment elsewhere. If they had not expected to live, why did they not disembowel themselves immediately on completion of their revenge?[49] Historians have been unable to answer this question, and it is usually suggested that there was some deeper, unfathomable meaning in this act.

Naotaka's opinion has not been popular. Though there can be little question that the prevention of indiscriminate violence by force of law was essential in one of the most densely populated and largest cities of its time, Naotaka is criticized as legalist, narrow-mindedly supporting the authorities by upholding such principles. Even today his appeal, as a contemporaneous witness, to judge the case on "objective evidence" rather than alleged abstract moral principles is criticized as "pragmatic and amoral rationality," "chimerical, divorced from everyday life."[50] Much like judgments pronounced on the fifth shogun, the actors in this human drama have been divided, not just by the literary world but also by historians, into villains and saints. Any material running counter to this division is considered unreliable and discarded, or, if this is impossible, the action is justified as motivated by higher, often enigmatic, moral principle.

Thus the report of Asano's prior dissolute conduct and criticism of his retainers to supervise his education contained in *Dokai kōshūki* is discounted as spurious. Yet the figures of daimyo holdings in this *bakufu* document that accompany the reports on the character and administration of daimyo are considered reliable and have been used extensively by historians.[51] An important point is that *Dokai kōshūki* was written before the incident, with no intention to single out Asano. In contrast, Kira's well-documented forty-year service in responsible government position is given no weight in the discussion. For *bakufu* officials who had to decide whether this was a one-sided unprovoked attack, as Kira assured them, or a "quarrel" in which traditionally both parties were punished, such information must have been of some importance and hence ought not to be neglected by historians.

The judgment of a contemporary such as Satō Naotaka would also have been informed by the fact that Ōishi Kuranosuke's priority was initially not the attack but the restoration of the Asano house by having Naganori's younger brother, Daigaku no Kami Nagahiro, succeed to the domain. For this purpose Ōishi repeatedly sent petitions to various members of the government, even using the good offices of the resident priest of the domain's chief temple to intercede with the monk Ryūkō, known to be close to the shogun.[52]

The younger brother, Asano Nagahiro, was placed under house arrest in Edo on the punishment of his brother. Well over a year later, on 18.7.Genroku 15 (1702), this order was finally lifted, but instead Nagahiro was ordered into exile at Hiroshima with Matsudaira Tsunanaga, head of the main branch of the Asano family.[53] This indicated that the government had no intention of permitting him to succeed to the domain of his elder brother. It was ten days after this new order, on 28.7.Genroku 15, that Ōishi called together the nineteen samurai who were in the Kansai area for the much-celebrated meeting at Maruyama in Kyoto at which he announced his decision to organize the revenge.[54] A successful revival of the house under Asano Nagahiro would have provided employment for the retainers but would have precluded a revenge on Kira. Ōishi is said to have accounted for this discrepancy by declaring the restoration of the house an alternative form of preserving the retainer's honor.[55]

With a year and a half having elapsed between Asano Naganori's death and the slaying of Kira, a contemporaneous observer such as Satō Naokata would also have wondered whether the revenge had indeed been such a priority for the retainers. He would have noted that after the termination of their service on the confiscation of the domain, the Akō samurai became known for their dissolute lifestyle, with their leader, Ōishi Kuranosuke, leaving his wife and children to live with a young mistress. Later this conduct was explained as a valiant attempt to mislead the intended victim, necessary to trick Kira into believing that the Akō samurai had given up any thought of revenge so that he might lower his defenses. Much is made of the elaborate preparations for the attack in the dead of the night, after Kira's staff was tired out by entertaining guests and when snow muffled the footsteps of the approaching band. Yet no doubt there were some contemporaries who, like Satō Naotaka and later also Dazai Shundai, thought such trickery was unworthy of a samurai.[56]

Kira was, after all, with regard to his income and his mansion, a man of lowly *hatamoto* status. The fact that sixteen of his retainers were killed in the attack, while only four of the attackers received wounds, which were light enough to permit them to march some ten kilometers to Sengaku temple afterwards, indicated that this was an unequal battle. The large loss of innocent lives among retainers and servants of the mansion could have been avoided in a spirited daytime attack on Kira on the open road by just a few men in traditional samurai fashion. In such an assault the attackers would, however, have been cut down immediately afterwards and the chance of a pardon lost.

Such an attack might also have been ruled out since it appears that the retainers' sword skills did not reach the ideal of the samurai. The *bakufu*'s charge against the samurai explicitly mentions their use of "projectile weapons" *(tobi dōgu)*. The term encompasses a wide range of meaning, from arrows and catapults to firearms.[57] It has also been suggested that the character used in the sources for *tobi* is wrong and should be that for the bird kite, in which case *tobi dōgu* refers to the tools of the fire brigade, including the ladders seen on many illustrations. However, it might well refer to the spears *(naginata)* with which the samurai are usually portrayed. They were an unusual weapon for samurai of that age, being used mainly by women to defend themselves during the Edo period.[58] In the Akō castle museum the spears of the attackers are displayed with the explanation that these weapons were chosen by the loyal samurai because they were unable to use the traditional two swords of the Japanese warrior effectively. Some sixty years had passed since Miyamoto Musashi in his *Book of Five Rings* had demanded that samurai practice until able to wield a heavy sword with each hand. The spear and halberd, he contended, were weapons to be used in battle and inappropriate for confined spaces.[59] It is doubtful whether the action of the Akō retainers would have met with his approval.

Finally consideration must be given to the fact that the Confucian Naotaka had experienced for some twenty years the government of the fifth shogun with its public emphasis on loyalty and filial piety. Like his contemporaries, he was well aware that at times the shogun would overturn the decisions of his officials to heap extravagant praise and rewards on people who in his opinion had lived up to these ideals particularly well. The suggestion that the Akō samurai did not commit suicide but gave themselves up to the authorities in the hope of being singled out for such shogunal praise was not altogether unlikely at the time.[60]

With these considerations in mind it seems unreasonable for scholars today to censure the opinion of an astute and educated observer such as Naotaka as "chimerical, divorced from everyday life" simply because he was guided by what he perceived at the time rather than the heroic thought attributed to the participants later.

The Judgment

If the forty-six retainers on giving themselves up to the authorities had, as Satō Naotaka suggests, some expectation that the shogun would give them credit for their loyal behavior, then this was not altogether misplaced. While the order for Asano Naganori's punishment had come within hours, no such swift decision was forthcoming in the case of his retainers. The attack had taken place in the early hours of 15.12.Genroku 15, and the New Year celebrations and their preparations further delayed the process of consultation that the shogun apparently considered necessary to come to a decision in this case.

According to one source, the senior councilors were divided among themselves between condemning the Akō retainers and praising their display of loyalty.[61] As a consequence an extraordinary meeting of the supreme court was convened to advise on this matter. The views expressed at the end of this meeting were represented as those of fourteen men with positions of magistrate of temples and shrines, Edo city magistrate, superintendent of finance, and inspector general.[62] The somewhat unusual absence of senior men such as the shogun's grand chamberlain Yanagisawa Yoshiyasu and the senior councilors on this occasion can be explained by the fact that these men were already deeply divided on the issue and that the genuine opinion of other officials was now being sought.

The committee of the supreme court, however, either could not agree on a judgment or did not want to commit itself on this delicate issue. The fourteen members were unanimous in condemning Kira's adopted son and retainers for not making greater efforts in saving their lord. Yet when it came to the crucial point of judging the behavior of the Akō samurai, they both condemned the secret attack on Kira's mansion and praised their loyal behavior. Finally they suggested that judgment be postponed, a proposal readily accepted by the *bakufu*, especially since the elaborate New Year's rites and celebrations were about to begin.

The opinion of the head of the Confucian school, Hayashi Nobuatsu, was also sought. For him Confucian virtues constituted the ideal way of government, and the practical demands of centralized administration counted for little. As long as loyalty such as that displayed by the samurai prevailed, the government had nothing to fear, he contended. Nobuatsu suggested that if the samurai could not be set free immediately having violated the laws of the *bakufu*, they should be kept under house arrest until an occasion for pardon arose.[63]

When Nobuatsu spoke of loyalty, he referred to loyalty toward a samurai's personal lord and not toward the ruler of the country, for Asano's retainers had disobeyed the laws of the *bakufu* in order to discharge their duties towards their lord. The scholar's view confirmed the priorities of feudal society, where a samurai's responsibilities were first to his immediate superior. It was a view that a ruler who likened himself to the sun illuminating every corner of his realm could not share. Some works maintain that Tsunayoshi sympathized greatly with the forty-six samurai and was seeking a way to acquit them without giving the appearance that the *bakufu* condoned their disobedience to the initial ruling that Kira was to go unharmed.[64] It was said that in the secret hope of obtaining a pardon for them, he asked the imperial abbot, Kōben Shinnō, for a judgment. The latter, however, remained silent.

If Tsunayoshi had really wanted to let the forty-six samurai off lightly, he would have followed the advice given by Hayashi Nobuatsu. A judgment along these lines could be justified by a precedent in the fourth shogun's government. Here the quarrel between two samurai had also resulted in punishment by disembowelment for one of the parties. On that occasion the dead man's son had similarly revenged his father by attacking his foe's mansion in the dead of the night. The grand councilor, Ii Naozumi, whose task it had been to pronounce the judgment, had decided on a compromise much in favor of the loyal son. The latter was exiled as punishment for the night attack, but the fact that the sentence was only pronounced to do formal justice to the laws of the *bakufu* became apparent when six years later the loyal son was pardoned and found employment with the grand councilor's family.[65]

Tsunayoshi, consequently, had the opportunity to let the forty-six samurai off lightly and eventually pardon them, yet he did not choose to do so. The judgment he adopted was, like that pronounced by Ii Naozumi, also a compromise, but unlike Naozumi's verdict, it well reflected the gravity with which the shogunate viewed the samurai's transgression against the law of the state. Asano's retainers were to die. To do justice to their display of loyalty, they were permitted to disembowel themselves. It was not a great concession. The forty-six were of samurai status, and it was the practice that samurai committing such offenses be punished in this way.[66] A judgment that the forty-six die as common criminals would have implied that they were not even worthy of their samurai status. This would scarcely have been feasible: in view of the shogun's great emphasis on loyalty, some degree of credit needed to be given for such conduct. The judgment, however, made relatively little of the retainers' display of loyalty towards their lord and clearly placed the demands of the central government above traditional samurai virtue.

Ogyū Sorai's Input

Controversy exists on how this decision was reached. A document known as *Yanagisawa ke hizō jikki* (The treasured, true record of the Yanagisawa family), written in the house of the grand chamberlain, Yanagisawa Yoshiyasu, describes how the latter consulted in secret two of his Confucian scholars—Shimura Sanzaemon and Ogyū Sorai—about the implications of this incident. The former could only confirm that no precedent for such an event was to be found in the classics, but Sorai was ready to elaborate on the subject. He criticized the supreme court for preoccupying itself with the details of the case while forgetting the overall issue and then continued to interpret the case in the context of the shogun's policies:

> Since at the present time those on high consider loyalty and filial piety the first virtues of government, it would be lacking in compassion to judge this case, in which the plotters acted in accordance with these virtues, as a case of burglary. If cases in which people have loyalty and filial piety in mind and act accordingly are considered as burglary, how then shall cases be judged which are committed with disloyal and unfilial intentions. Therefore, leaving Chinese matters aside, if the decision orders that *seppuku* be carried out on the basis of precedents of our present rule, it would also be in accordance with the wishes of those plotters, and how would it not set an example for the world?

Apparently Yangisawa Yoshiyasu was exceedingly pleased with this opinion. On the following morning he appeared earlier than usual before the shogun to inform him of the wise judgment pronounced by his retainer, and the shogun accepted it happily.[67]

Further evidence that the judgment of the Akō samurai came from Sorai is furnished by a document found in the possession of the Hosokawa family. It is a more detailed exposition of the reasons behind the judgment, and here the argument already foreshadows Sorai's thoughts in his mature works.

> Devotion to duty *(gi)* is the means to purify the self, while laws rule the world. Rituals govern the heart; devotion to duty *(gi)* governs action. The fact that the forty-six have now revenged their lord shows that they know what is shameful for a samurai. They decided to purify the self, and that is devotion to duty *(gi)*, but since it concerns only these men it is, in the final analysis, done out of personal considerations. The cause of their action was that upon Naganori's punishment for improper behavior in the palace they considered Lord Kira their enemy and without the government's permission created a disturbance. This is something the law cannot permit. If now the forty-six are judged guilty and if they are punished with *seppuku* in line with samurai ritual, then Uesugi's[68] wish would not be ignored, their loyalty would be given due weight, and it would be entirely in line with government

considerations. If private considerations are given priority over government considerations, then public law will have no force in the future.[69]

The document masterfully argues for the central government's right unilaterally to impose its law upon the whole country while diplomatically showing respect for the traditional feudal value of personal loyalty. It leaves open the question of whether Asano Naganori's retainers were right in considering Kira their lord's enemy but weighs in on the side of Kira by giving him the courtesy of a title that is not accorded to Asano. Finally it makes the point that the punishment of *seppuku* will permit the retainers to complete their loyal deed in due samurai fashion. Considering that by not committing *seppuku* immediately after completing their revenge the forty-six samurai demonstrated that they preferred to live rather than take the consequences of their loyal action, one might even detect some sarcasm on the part of the author.

Though the piece well displays the verbal dexterity of a scholar with Ogyū Sorai's talents, there are, nevertheless, several aspects that have prompted historians to question whether he was indeed the author of this famous judgment. First, there is the fact that no mention of the scholar's part appears in Sorai's own writings.[70] When, for instance, Sorai received Yanagisawa Yoshiyasu's praise for correctly judging the case of a peasant who had abandoned his aged mother, the event was recorded in the philosopher's papers in detail.[71] One would assume, therefore, that if Sorai had won the shogun's admiration for finding a solution where his senior ministers had failed, the matter surely would have found mention in a later work.

Second, the preamble to the above-quoted comment from *Yanagisawa ke hizō jikki* states that the supreme court had condemned the Akō samurai to die as common criminals. Although this argument formed part of the deliberations, it was not the final judgment, and it appears that here *Yanagisawa ke hizō jikki* is wrong. Even weightier is the fact that this passage does not appear in *Genkō jitsuroku*, a document on which the rest of *Yanagisawa ke hizō jikki* is based.

Another difficulty concerns the authenticity of the document. Tahara Tsuguo questions how Sorai's deliberations for the *bakufu* could have come into the possession of the Hosokawa family. As the document is not dated, he suggests that it could easily have been written as part of the debate that was to continue for decades and even centuries, and in which especially Sorai's disciple Dazai Shundai had great interest.[72] After the government's judgment had been made public, Hayashi Nobuatsu similarly philosophized about the reasons behind the decision,[73] and since this later statement differs from his original views, it appears likely that it was written as justification of the *bakufu*'s verdict.

Since the argument cannot be decided on the basis of the available sources, some historical speculation may be warranted. *Yanagisawa ke hizō jikki* states that Yoshiyasu had a secret consultation with his Confucian scholars about the incident. This is more than likely, for as the shogun's most powerful minister he would hardly have found the time to search the classics for a precedent. Yet whatever advice Sorai might have given to Yoshiyasu in this confidential meeting, the final judgment did not contain any new and original thought, and was no more than an exact application of the *bakufu*'s publicized policies. Naturally Yoshiyasu would have attempted to find a solution within this framework. If Sorai indeed formulated the judgment, he did no more than bureaucrats do today, namely, the technical work of accurately applying the government's policy to a question handed to them by their superiors.

The process that can be reconstructed is a relatively simple one. Yoshiyasu asked his personal staff to look into the technical side of the problem, and they came up with a solution that he, as head of Tsunayoshi's government, considered to correctly reflect the shogun's political aims. It was a compromise Tsunayoshi could accept. The reason previous advice had been rejected was simply that it did not reflect government policy. Sorai might have formulated the judgment, but I believe it would be incorrect to state that he influenced it, as has been suggested.[74] The shogun, therefore, saw no need to praise Sorai— for he had made no particular contribution—nor did the scholar consider the part he had played a significant one.

Having had discussions with Yoshiyasu about the incident, Sorai was later well qualified to write a detailed exposition of the argument for the Hosokawa house. The Hosokawa mansion being located close to Sengaku temple, where the Akō samurai had gathered after the incident, the family was charged with taking seventeen of the men, including the leader Ōishi Kuranosuke, into their custody. It was in the Hosokawa mansion that these men were ordered to disembowel themselves after ties of sympathy with their custodians had formed during the two-months wait.[75] It is not surprising, therefore, that the Hosokawa house asked for a detailed explanation of the judgment or that Sorai was charged by Yoshiyasu with writing this document.

Further, one must take into consideration that the popularity of the Akō samurai was in the ascendancy and that Sorai's disciples who edited and published his work might well have considered it wise not to identify their teacher with the increasingly unpopular judgment.

Hidden Sentiments

Less than one year before Asano Naganori unsheathed his sword at Edo castle, setting in motion events still celebrated today, the samurai Yamamoto Tsunetomo had shaven his head to lead the life of a hermit. Though taking Buddhist vows affirming the sanctity of life, over the next sixteen years he conceived a philosophy advocating the swift taking of life without lengthy deliberations on the right or wrong of the matter as recorded in the work *Hagakure* introduced above. Though praising the Akō samurai for taking revenge, the work regrets the lack of spontaneity. Like other contemporaries, it censures the samurai for their long delay in attacking Kira and subsequent unwillingness to follow this up by immediate suicide.

Hagakure and the Akō samurai hold in common the view that to satisfy his sentiments of personal pride and honor, the samurai is entitled to ignore the laws of the country, use deception, and count the lives of innocent people for little. In *Hagakure,* the man who joins the street brawl in which his friend has already been killed, even though he will incur the death sentence for violating the law, becomes the superior individual, morally towering over the official whose duty it is to enforce this law.[76] So also does the samurai who, when his wife complains about the lack of rice, forces farmers at the point of his sword to deliver their tax rice to his home, knowing that the punishment is likely to be death.[77]

The aspect where the two differ, namely, the lack of spontaneity to strike and die censured by *Hagakure,* is indicative of the paradigm changes that were taking place. Though their criticism is motivated by very different philosophical positions, *Hagakure* is in accord with the Confucian Satō Noakata when censuring the Akō samurai for being "intelligent and shrewd when it comes to plotting a strategy to get praise."[78]

The Akō samurai were caught in an age of rapidly changing values. The traditional concept of violence to maintain samurai honor was still cherished by part of the community. Yet the government proclaimed the very opposite, namely, a policy of nonviolence. It demanded loyalty and filial piety but essentially viewed these in Confucian terms, which entailed forbearance and sacrifice of the person's own aspirations for the benefit of the lord or the parents. The Akō samurai, however, interpreted these terms in line with *Hagakure*, where the samurai's personal concerns took precedent. As the judgment attributed to Ogyū Sorai argued, the samurai had been primarily concerned with clearing their own name as samurai. Henry Smith also points out that the question of upholding "name" and "face" were important aspects for the Akō samurai.[79]

The actions of the samurai reflect these confusions within the value system of the day. When the *bakufu* fails to show respect for their noble resolve not to hand over Akō castle unless Kira is punished, they decide to find another avenue, namely, that of bureaucratic lobbying for the domain to go to the younger brother. To suggest that the Akō samurai never believed in this possibility begs the question of why they wasted time pleading when they could have prepared the revenge. When such measures also prove unsuccessful, they appear to revert to traditional samurai values of sacrificing their lives to avenge their lord. Yet they are not prepared to go all the way in *Hagakure* fashion. The solution chosen is a hybrid. There is the effort to gain praise for upholding the traditional samurai concept of loyalty by taking the life of their lord's opponent. But traditional samurai daring is replaced by long and careful preparations to accomplish the feat without loss of life, making possible a final appeal to the authorities by submission.

The picture that emerges is that of desperate men trying to survive in the maelstrom of change. With an abrupt discrediting of traditional values, the fifth shogun attempted a major paradigm change. This must have produced feelings of helplessness and confusion in the minds of many samurai as they attempted to make their way in this changed environment with its fundamental revision of the traditional value system. The Akō samurai came to symbolize this suffering as men from a nostalgic past, as battlers against the harsh government of the day that was intent on destroying their cherished values. Their summary death ordered by an unpopular shogun permitted quick deification. To complete the process of creating larger-than-life-size images, any human foibles had to be shed. Every part of their action came to be uncritically accepted as serving a greater public good, and those that appealed to an examination of the facts were in turn accused of delusion.

The Enduring Popularity of the Akō Samurai

It has been suggested that "the usefulness" of *Hagakure* "to prewar Japanese militarism" lay in its "combination of the cult of death with the ideal of faithful and efficacious devotion to the public good." The question though arises, who is this "public" to whom the samurai is so faithfully and efficaciously devoted? It is certainly not the farmer whose rice the samurai commandeers at sword point or the innocent people murdered as they happen to stand in the way of the samurai defending his honor. There needs to be a large, emotional leap of the imagination to forget the injury to what we normally call "the public" and make the term apply to those individuals who by their search for death in *Hagakure* fashion find "a deeper meaning to their everyday activities."[80] Only when this leap has been accomplished and endorsed by people of influence can the wider public identify itself with those who in actual life would discard their rights. Only after this refashioning of reality does it become possible to use the work for political purposes.

In the same manner a certain amount of mental acrobatics is necessary to continue to celebrate today the exploits of the Akō samurai. Quite apart from the question of whether the welfare of aged parents, wives, and small children should have been sacrificed for their personal craving for honor, one needs to question whether the various forms of trickery employed in plotting the attack on Kira's mansion lived up to samurai ideals. Only when questions about the suffering of innocent people are glossed over can the public enjoy the exploits of the samurai, though the latter would have thought little of ignoring this same public's rights should their personal honor thus demand.

Japan is not singular in this respect. The behaviorist Konrad Lorenz points out that throughout literature what is praised as morally superior behavior is in fact behavior motivated by impulse rather than by reason, especially the impulse to defend one's mate in the wider sense, the group with which an individual identifies. He argues that even people's most rationalized behavior is governed to some extent by the urges inherent in the species, such as those of primitive man to defend the mate, a source of highly pleasurable emotions. He sees the "religious" shiver of the spine when the national anthem is intoned by a large crowd and the emotionally charged pledge of a group for action against a common enemy as examples of such emotions.[81] The frenzy overcoming spectators of team sports might well be another example that illustrates the point.

Successful socialization, however, demands to a large extent suppression of these primitive instincts and pleasurable emotions by submission to laws created by a superior and increasingly distant, impersonal authority.[82] As a token of these pleasures lost, most cultures cherish and celebrate the memory of some "outlaw," whether it be Robin Hood in England or the young, good-looking desperado of the American West. Although society could not function if all members conducted themselves in this fashion, the criminal conduct of these outlaws typically is justified by the "evil" of their enemies, usually portrayed as those administering the law of the central state.

In seventeenth-century Japan the policies of the fifth shogun amounted to a large-scale and unprecedented curtailment of the samurai's traditional privilege to be master over life and death. The emotionally charged and pleasurable bond to a master—not infrequently of erotic nature—that heightened the passion with which the samurai arbitrated over life and death, was to be replaced by submission to the laws of the central state. The pleasures of revenge, the satisfaction of setting things right, even at the price of one's own life, that edify the reader of *Hagakure* were to be forgone by accepting the impersonal verdict of a group of mostly anonymous officials.

The unbridled expression of emotions resulting in physical violence is the very antithesis of Tsunayoshi's Laws of Compassion. The elevation of violence, deception, and murder featuring prominently in both *Hagakure* and the Akō incident as manifestations of *bushidō*—the sacrosanct Way of the Warrior—was initially a protest against the policies of the fifth shogun. But the enduring popularity these stories have enjoyed to the present day seems based on the appeal to human beings' primitive emotions of the passionate bonding to mates and the godlike arbitration over life and death.

It is no coincidence that in the fictionalization of the Akō incident the enthusiastic plotting of the group is given extended coverage even though the various acts of trickery can hardly be seen as conforming to the samurai's code of honorable behavior. Moreover, Henry Smith has pointed out that a document in Ōishi Kuranosuke's hand rating the depth of commitment of the samurai he was leading in the vendetta throws doubt on whether group cohesion existed to the extent described by historians. Yet even though this document is contained in most compilations of material on the Akō incident, no scholar has dared to point out openly the obvious conclusions. Instead the document's value has been discounted, and one scholar has warned that it can properly be understood only by "true" scholars of the loyal retainers. Group cohesion is similarly challenged with Smith's argument that material documenting the expulsion of the forty-seventh member of the Akō samurai on account of his lowly status has purposely been overlooked. Such discrimination is seen as incompatible with the ideal of the righteous samurai *(gishi)* and hence has been ignored.[83] In line with Lorenz' argument, the ideal of the group must not be tarnished if the story is to touch the innermost human emotions.

Aware of the intensity and power of such emotions, governments have attempted to use them for political purposes. In the case of *Hagakure* and the Akō incident, it was easy for the wartime administration of Japan to turn the emperor into the personal lord to whom total devotion is due and the much-hated, cold central authority into the rest of the world trying to restrain this ideal emotional commitment. Although Japan's defeat and occupation broke the spell the government's appeal to these primitive emotions had cast, their power never totally subsided, as the popularity—in Japan and abroad—of Mishima Yukio's works dwelling on this theme testify.[84] To the contrary, such sentiments are continuously clothed in new garb, as the unity of the group is reaffirmed in global terms of cultural differences. Just as the samurai must kill to redeem his honor, it is argued that the "clash of civilizations" is unavoidable, since "for peoples seeking identity . . . enemies are essential."[85]

Although most of the economically advanced world prides itself on the freedoms of democracy, the individual's life is more than ever restricted by the impersonal laws of a central authority. This will guarantee that future warmongering will be justified as "reasonable," and works such as *Hagakure* and especially the visually sumptuous productions of the fictionalized Akō incident will continue to have their fans, as the audience indulges in the surrogate experience of paradise lost.

How much the glorification of the Akō samurai and especially their leader Ōishi Kuranosuke is based on sentiment rather than on reasoning and historical facts also becomes evident when matters of finance are examined. To make up its annual deficit, the Akō domain had issued paper money that on its demise was found to be backed only to some 60 percent by available cash. The fact that those who had placed—or were forced to place—their trust in the domain administration by accepting the paper money lost 40 percent of their assets finds little mention in historical writing. Yet the *bakufu*'s issue of a coinage with a nominal value not fully covered by its bullion content has become a major source of criticism by historians.

13

Financial Matters

Copper coins flow like currents of water, while silver piles up like drifting snow. Visible in the distance is Mt. Fuji, rising in all its magnificence against the horizon, while footsteps of people streaming across Nihon Bridge sound exactly like the passage of thousands of wagons along the highway. Every morning fish are sold in such quantities in the Funa Street market that one may well wonder whether or not the supply in the seas surrounding our fair islands has been exhausted.[1]

The words of the novelist Ihara Saikaku published in the fifth year of the Genroku period (1692) have a modern ring. Consumption at the time had reached a point where nature's supply seemed near exhaustion. Elsewhere in his novel *This Scheming World (Seken mune zanyō)* Saikaku expresses the fear that millstones are being sold in such quantities "that there's danger the very hills from which they are quarried will eventually disappear."[2] Edo, at the time perhaps the largest city in the world,[3] was booming. He noted: "Shops of every variety are open for business, and never a day passes but goods from every province in the country are shipped in by boat and packed on the backs of thousands of horses. No further proof is needed that there is an abundance of gold and silver in the world, and it would be a pity indeed if a merchant were unable to lay hands on at least a bit of it."[4]

The Genroku period (1688-1704) spanning the central part of the fifth shogun's government was one of the most prosperous in Japanese history before the post-World War II boom in the second half of the Shōwa era. Yet in spite of the well-acknowledged prosperity of the Genroku period, the financial policies of Tsunayoshi's government have been roundly condemned as the bankrupt machinations of a luxury-loving and spendthrift tyrant. The earlier part of his administration is recognized as one of financial sobriety and stringency, but these measures—generally referred to as the Tenna Government, since they took place during the brief Tenna period of 1681-1684—have been credited to his grand councilor Hotta Masatoshi. After Masatoshi's assassination in 1684, Tsunayoshi's chamberlains rose in political importance, and the financial policy during the ensuing years has been much censured by historians. However, on examining the relevant documentation it becomes evident that there was a continuation of policy and that the financial predicament in which Tsunayoshi found himself was not altogether of his making.

The Financial Foundations of the *Bakufu*

The first shogun Ieyasu cemented the foundations of the *bakufu* by amassing considerable wealth. Confiscating the domains of his defeated enemies, he created the so-called *tenryō* or *chokkatsuryō*, the land directly under the control of the *bakufu*. After the battle of Osaka in Genna 1 (1615), this land reached approximately 2,300,000 *koku*,[5] providing the administration with a steady income. A further source of Ieyasu's wealth was his direct engagement in trade, both domestic and foreign.[6] But the greatest source of wealth was undoubtedly the country's gold and silver mines. Indeed, some scholars maintain that the *bakuhan* system could not have been established without the great wealth derived from the mines in the first half of the seventeenth century.[7]

Mining is mentioned in Japanese sources as early as the seventh century, but it was only in the middle of the sixteenth century that techniques came to be known that permitted adequate exploitation of Japan's mineral resources.[8] From the late Ashikaga period onwards it became apparent that ownership of mines was an important factor in determining political supremacy. In Tenshō 17 (1589), one year after the minting of his large gold coin the Tenshō *ōban*, Toyotomi Hideyoshi began to confiscate the country's mines and declare them *tenka no yama*, the "ruler's (or government's) mountains." His reasoning was that in taking on the responsibility for the monetary system, the central government required bullion to mint the coinage.[9]

On establishing his political supremacy over the Toyotomi regime, Ieyasu similarly claimed possession of the country's mines. He was, moreover, fortunate in finding in Ōkubo Nagayasu (1545–1613) a skillful administrator who, by introducing Western methods of amalgamation and new management techniques, considerably increased the output of the mines.[10] Thus the productive gold and silver mines of Sado and the equally rich silver mines of Iwami and Izu came under Ieyasu's control and Nagayasu's supervision in Keichō 6 (1601). Under the latter's efficient management the Sado mines alone produced a steady 60 million *kan* of silver during the first twelve years of the seventeenth century, peaking at 100 million *kan* in Keichō 7 (1602).[11]

In the second half of the seventeenth century, foreign visitors such as the Dutch were given an obligatory tour of Kyoto's most prominent temples, including the large Buddha of Hōkōji—rivaling that of Nara—to impress them with Japan's wealth and culture.[12] In Ieyasu's time, however, it was the mines that were the country's pride. When the Jesuit vice provincial Francisco Pasio and his entourage visited Ieyasu in Suruga in 1607, Ieyasu urged his visitors to make a detour and inspect the mines at Izu on their way to Edo.[13] In 1609, when the Jesuit João Rodrigues visited Suruga, he reported that Ieyasu's treasurer had just made a count of the bullion stored there and that the silver alone amounted to 83 million taels and was still growing.[14] As neither the terminology nor exchange rates were unified and consistent at the time, it is difficult to determine the exact amount this represents.[15] If the tael is calculated at 10 *momme*, with 60 *momme* to the *ryō*, this would amount to nearly 14 million *ryō*. The supply of precious metals the foreigners observed in Japan was clearly extraordinary. The Spanish merchant Bernardino de Avila Girón, who lived in Japan at the beginning of the seventeenth century, wrote: "There are mines everywhere and the metal is of high quality; the gold ore is so rich that they obtain ten taels of gold from every spadeful. In the same way there is a great deal of copper and iron which they extract very easily."[16]

There is no complete record of the wealth Ieyasu left to his descendants when he died in Genna 2 (1616). Adding up the figures from various sources, scholars estimate that it amounted to nearly 2 million *ryō* in addition to a large amount of precious artifacts and valuable trade goods.[17] But this was only the cash and bullion stored by Ieyasu at Suruga. Initially his successor Hidetada intended to divide the whole of this bullion among the Three Related Houses, as he considered he had sufficient reserves at Edo. Only on the cautioning of Honda Masazumi was it decided to distribute merely 300,000 *ryō* each to Owari and Kii, and 150,000 *ryō* to the Mito domain, and retain the remainder in reserve at Suruga.[18] In light of Hidetada's initial claim that he did not need the funds from Suruga, Tsuji Tatsuya estimates that reserves at Edo most probably consisted of some 4 million *ryō* and that the total amount left by Ieyasu amounted to 6 million.[19] But there is no reason why the funds at Suruga might not represent an even smaller fraction of the wealth stored at Edo.

The Third Shogun's Extravagances and the Consequences

Scholars estimate that on his death in Kanei 9 (1632) Hidetada left some three and a half million *ryō* to his successor. The third shogun Iemitsu apparently did not consider himself short of funds, because he distributed a total of 600,000 *ryō* as legacy from his father to some six thousand people. These ranged from two thousand pieces of gold and ten thousand pieces of silver to Tōfukumon-in, Hidetada's daughter married to the emperor Gomizuno'o, down to gifts to his late father's sandal bearers.[20]

During the twenty-odd years of Iemitsu's rule, government expenditure reached a peak. No comprehensive figures of government disbursements are available, but Iemitsu's extraordinarily lavish spending is indicated in various contemporary records. The most famous of his projects was the rebuilding of the Tōshōgū at Nikkō, where the body of the first shogun had been laid to rest in Genna 3 (1617), turning it into the lavishly decorated mausoleum still admired today.[21] What has received less attention is that the *bakufu* also constructed some thirteen lesser Tōshōgū shrines throughout the country.[22] Among the more elaborate was the Tōshōgū of Edo castle's second enceinte, the construction of which began in Kanei 13 (1636). From Kanei 17 (1640) Iemitsu also began enlarging the original Tōshōgū at Kunōsan in Suruga. Finally in Keian 3 (1650), one year before his death, Iemitsu ordered the construction of a Tōshōgū at Tōeizan Kaneiji at Ueno.[23] Moreover, in his testament he decreed that he himself be buried at Nikkō, committing the *bakufu* to further building costs.[24]

The cost of construction of the so-called Kanei Tōshōgū at Nikkō by Iemitsu amounted to over 578,000 *ryō* at the time.[25] This was only the initial outlay of what was to prove a constant drain on the finances of all future governments. The finely constructed buildings with their extensive use of lacquer and painted carvings inside and out required constant maintenance and often major repairs. Earthquakes, fires, and even rats took their toll.[26] By the time of Tsunayoshi's government, the shrine complex was fifty years old and in need of a major overhaul. Over 62 percent of all government expenditure on temple repairs during the period from Genroku 1 to Genroku 9 (1688–1696) was allotted to the Nikkō Tōshōgū. If the expenses for repairs at the Kunō Tōshōgū are added, this amounts to nearly 65 percent.[27] The *bakufu*'s outlay for construction expenses had already risen earlier in Jōkyō 2 (1685), owing to a fire at the mausoleum and the surrounding settlements.[28]

Material presented by the scholar Ōno Mizuo shows that the Genroku government was burdened by an extraordinary heavy schedule of temple and building repairs outside Edo. In addition to Nikkō, these ranged from repairs at Sunpu, Nijō, and Osaka castles, to work at the grand shrines at Atsuta and Ise.[29] Such repairs were of no financial consequence during the first half of the seventeenth century, when the *bakufu* enjoyed great liquidity. By the time of the fifth shogun, however, building repairs came to represent a major part of the budget. Analyzing figures for Jōkyō 3 (1686), Ōno calculated construction expenses as 31.87 percent of the available budget figures.[30] Tsunayoshi has traditionally been criticized for his high expenditure on religious buildings, and scholars have neglected to point out that this was to maintain the buildings and traditions of his predecessors.

The early *bakufu*'s boom in temple building also committed its successors to the maintenance of a large number of clergy and regular ceremonial worship by the shogunal family. Iemitsu himself visited the Nikkō Tōshōgū some eleven times in stately procession.[31] At the time of the fifth shogun, the cost of a shogunal procession to Nikkō was estimated at 100,000 *ryō*. Tsunayoshi wanted to pay his respects at Nikkō some two years after his accession but decided that with recent bad harvests, this would have to be postponed. Thirteen years later he was still told that government finances did not permit this expenditure. He had visited the mausoleum with his elder brother in the spring of Kanbun 3 (1663) but never proceeded as shogun to what was arguably the most sacred site of the Tokugawa clan.[32] The cost of sending the shogun's representative on a regular basis, however, still had to be met.

Iemitsu's generosity also extended to a great many other places of worship. Government records are no longer extant, and to my knowledge no scholar has attempted to gain insight into this expenditure by extracting figures from *Edo bakufu nikki* or *Tokugawa jikki* and searching individual temple records. Such research is also beyond the scope of this volume, but even a casual glance at the histories of major temples, such as Kiyomizu, Chion-in, and Enryakuji in Kyoto reveals that all of them received funds for major building works from the third shogun.[33]

Another large drain on the *bakufu*'s treasury was Iemitsu's famous visit to Kyoto and Osaka with a procession of 307,000 people in Kanei 11 (1634), lasting for two months. It was the last and most lavish of his three journeys to the capital, the previous two having taken place together with his father, the second shogun Hidetada. Again, no financial records of the expenses remain, but the fact that Iemitsu distributed a total of 10,000 *kan* of silver among the citizens of Kyoto and Edo on this occasion must be taken to indicate that in other respects similarly no expense was spared.[34] Gifts were also distributed at Osaka and Sakai.[35] The stipend of the imperial household was increased threefold, and lesser nobles were granted additional income too.[36] One historian estimates that Iemitsu's three journeys to court cost the government one million *ryō* each, while the quelling of the Shimabara rebellion amounted to a further outlay of 400,000 *ryō*.[37]

The *bakufu* also acted with paternal generosity towards its *fudai* daimyo and liege vassals. A total of 508,700 *ryō* was distributed to them in Kanei 12 (1635), while at the same time they were ordered to practice frugality.[38]

It is said that Iemitsu was unable to understand "simple arithmetic" and had no conception of the value of money, arguing, according to one anecdote, that it did no good "shut up in a vault."[39] The relative lack of importance he accorded to financial management is also apparent in the bureaucratic structures created under his administration. Yet assuming that Iemitsu lacked all understanding of the value of money is, I believe, underestimating his political astuteness.

With the death of Hidetada in Kanei 9 (1632), the shogunate entered a new political phase. Until then Tokugawa rule rested on the principle of dual authority. Only two years after taking the title of shogun himself, Ieyasu resigned and passed it on to his son Hidetada, cementing Tokugawa hegemony with a dual seat of authority. Hidetada, similarly, handed over the title to his eldest son at an early stage and himself continued to act as a second source of political control.

On Hidetada's death there was for the first time since the inception of the Tokugawa regime no heir apparent, for Iemitsu had as yet no children. At the same time the cumulative effects of natural calamities causing poor harvests from the early 1630s were leading up to what is known as the Kanei famine a decade later, creating unrest at all levels of society. It made political sense that under these conditions Iemitsu would try to take his wealth and "transfigure" it—to use Herman Ooms' term—into political authority. Like his near contemporary the French Roi Soleil Louis XIV, Iemitsu employed the available funds to demonstrate his strength and supremacy. Marching with a retinue nearly three times the size of the combined armies of Sekigahara from Edo to Kyoto and distributing large sums of money to the people in the process could leave no doubt in anybody's mind what forces the *bakufu* would be able to muster if challenged. Large-scale temple building and the creation of elaborate religious rituals to worship the founder of the hegemony had similar propaganda value.

In the absence of sophisticated accounting practices and detailed financial forecasts, Iemitsu most probably believed that he could afford such lavishness. After all, the yield from Japanese mines in the early seventeenth century, according to some scholars, represented one-quarter or even one-third of the world's output of silver.[40] That the *bakufu* was, nevertheless, overspending its resources is perhaps indicated by the fact that between Kanei 9 (1632) and Kanei 13 (1636) funds from Ieyasu's legacy were moved from Suruga to Edo.[41]

Sliding into Red Figures

Yet when on Iemitsu's sudden death in Keian 4 (1651) the ten-year-old Ietsuna succeeded as the fourth shogun, the government was by no means bankrupt. The legacy distributed among the court, the shogunal family, *bakufu* vassals (*hatamoto*), and the large number of women in Iemitsu's *oku* amounted to some 526,428 *ryō* and was thus not much less than the sum distributed on the death of the previous shogun. Less than two decades later, however, in Enpō 4 (1676), the *bakufu* was bankrupt and to cover its annual deficit reluctantly started minting the ingots that Ieyasu had designated as emergency funds for military defense. What had brought government finances to such a rapid decline? Historians cite two major reasons: the declining output of Japan's mines and the large expense resulting from the devastation of the Meireki fire.

There is no complete record of the output of the mines, but we know that the production of the most important silver mine, that of Sado, suddenly dipped to less than one-third in Kanei 12 (1635). An uneven rate of decline continued from then on, and by Meireki 2 (1656) the annual yield was at times less than 10 million *kan* of silver, one-sixth of what it had been earlier in the century.[42] At the same time the *bakufu* was facing an unexpected drainage of funds.

The Meireki Fire

Six years after the fourth shogun's accession, in the first month of Meireki 3 (1657), a fire raging three days destroyed the greater part of the city of Edo and the shogunal castle. Exact figures differ according to sources, but *Tokugawa jikki* notes that some five hundred city wards, nine thousand rice granaries, sixty bridges, three hundred temples and shrines, five hundred buildings in daimyo compounds, as well as the main castle with its five-story keep, the second and third enceintes, were destroyed.[43] A total of 108,000 people are believed to have died in the flames.[44] The *bakufu*'s main reserve of bullion stored in the castle's keep had melted, but there were still enough funds to start immediate relief measures such as the distribution of rice gruel.[45] Less than a month later a detailed program of loans and grants to *hatamoto* and to daimyo with domains of less than 100,000 *koku* was announced. They were scaled according to the size of the domain and provided a daimyo with an income of 99,000 *koku* with a grant of 300 *kan* of silver, while the owner of 100 *koku* received 15 *ryō*. The town centers *(shisei)* within Edo were promised a total of 10,000 *kan* of silver.[46]

To pay for these relief measures, gold and silver were being distributed directly from the government treasuries at Suruga and Osaka, and transport of bullion was being organized.[47] (In the first three months after the fire, 10,000 *kan* of silver was sent in seven convoys from Suruga to Edo, while during the year 70,000 *ryō* in gold and 50,000 *kan* of silver was received from Osaka.) According to Kurita's calculation, the total amounted to some 979,090 *ryō*.[48] Thus by the beginning of the fifth month it was possible to pay out the first half of the 10,000 *kan* of silver promised to the citizens of Edo.[49] At the same time repairs to the second enceinte were progressing. The top rafter was raised by the fourth month and the construction completed by the eighth.[50] Reconstruction of the main castle *(hon maru)* had begun in the fifth month.[51]

The timing of the government's payouts and schedule of construction is important, for it supports the conclusion reached by Kurita that the government's expenses resulting from the Meireki fire were met from the reserves at Suruga and Osaka. The reminting of the bullion that had been stored in the keep of Edo castle and had melted during the fire began only at a later stage,[52] and Kurita argues that it was not used for disaster relief. Two different sources of Manji 2 (1659) and Kanbun 1 (1661) respectively record that the equivalent of some 3,900,000 *ryō* was obtained from the reminting, which Kurita believes remained after the expenses resulting directly from the fire had been met.[53] Still, just over a decade and half later the government was bankrupt. One must therefore ask why the *bakufu* that had so jealously promoted its supremacy previously permitted its finances to decline to a point of financial, and hence political, weakness.

The Bakufu's Balance Sheet

Iemitsu greatly extended the authority of the *bakufu*. He introduced the system of alternate attendance at Edo for his retainers, continued to confiscate domains with great vigor even though *bakufu* opposition had been quelled, and commanded the daimyo to provide large amounts of manpower and material to greatly enlarge the fortifications of Edo castle.[54] He set up new administrative structures and controls, expelled the Christian missionaries, and strictly regulated foreign trade and travel. Yet in his effort to increase the authority of the Tokugawa hegemony, Iemitsu also increased the *bakufu*'s financial responsibilities. The government's largesse became a symbol of its authority, and precedents were set for a progressively more generous maintenance of the court and places of worship as well as generous gifts and distribution of funds to samurai and commoners alike. Ceremonial functions and duties increased. As a perusal of the pages of *Tokugawa jikki* well demonstrates, by the time of the fourth shogun there was a heavy schedule of regular visits to a great number of mausoleums and temples as well as other ceremonies. If these ceremonial duties could not be discharged by the ruler himself, they still had to be performed by a deputy with suitable pomp and disbursement.

Under Iemitsu new traditions for *bakufu* expenditure were created and the overhead expense of conducting government was greatly increased. It might, nevertheless, have been possible to keep *bakufu* finances on an even keel if Iemitsu had been succeeded by a string of strong autocratic rulers intent on securing the political dominance and hence financial solvency of the administration. But he was not. With the succession of a minor in the person of the sickly Ietsuna, the personal authority of the shogun abruptly declined.

The change in the *bakufu*'s power structure was mirrored in the terminology of the Regulations for the Military Houses *(buke shohatto)*. While the document of Kanei 12 (1635) referred to "the shogun's command" *(jōi)* and his "personal adviser" *(kinju)*, the version of Kanbun 3 (1663) substituted terms such as "the office of the magistrates" *(bugyō sho)* and "the house" *(ie)*. This reflected the change from government by a single ruler to that by a group of officials with loyalties divided between the central government and their own house, from appointment by personal selection by the ruler to one largely determined by the inherited status of the individual and the family.[55] As a result, when a choice had to be made involving financial considerations, assuring the status, stability, and continuation of the house or family *(ie)* took precedence over maintaining the absolute authority of the shogunate.[56]

After the great fire, in which the *bakufu* itself probably suffered a proportionally much greater loss of buildings than did the daimyo, some daimyo were requested to assist with various repairs.[57] But on the whole scholars have noted a marked decrease of *bakufu* impositions for building projects during the government of the fourth shogun compared to those under his predecessor. Instead, grants and loans to daimyo and lesser vassals continued to be distributed by the *bakufu* over and above the initial large-scale relief measures.[58]

The historian Tokutomi Sohō views the *bakufu*'s fiscal problems as inherent in the initial structure set up by Ieyasu, accepting the *bakufu*'s financial responsibility for the administration of the whole country. He states emphatically that the financial distress of the daimyo and house vassals was the responsibility of the *bakufu*.[59] This view of the role and the obligations of the *bakufu* is well reflected in the policies of the government of the fourth shogun. But it was not the only possible solution. At the time of Ietsuna's accession, the *bakufu* was still in possession of considerable wealth. Under a strong, authoritarian ruler, the destruction of the Meireki fire could have served not to weaken the financial foundations of the *bakufu* but to strengthen them. The reserves the *bakufu* had stored at Osaka and Suruga could have been used to rebuild the castle in its former splendor and make the distance between the ruler and his vassals all the more apparent. Yet instead the shogunate chose to use its reserves to assist its vassals, itself forgoing the rebuilding of the castle's keep, the symbol of shogunal authority. The "loans" generously given by the *bakufu* under the fourth shogun to permit the daimyo to rebuild their mansions were still outstanding when the fifth shogun succeeded well over a decade later. Tsunayoshi not only demanded a return of outstanding monies but was also the first shogun who on accession made no distribution from the funds left by his predecessor; with these unpopular measures he set the tone for the financial policies of his government.[60]

Iemitsu had also distributed relief funds to the daimyo and *hatamoto*, but he did this at a time of financial liquidity, and, moreover, these funds had been limited to *fudai* daimyo.[61] It is doubtful whether Iemitsu would have bankrupted his own coffers to assist his vassals. As in other aspects of government, the shift in the distribution of power had resulted in a corresponding shift of political priorities. The early *bakufu*'s striving to solidify its authority, if necessary at the expense of its vassals, had changed to concern for the stability and well-being of the military houses at the expense of the *bakufu*.

Under the third shogun the financial responsibilities of the *bakufu* increased to reflect the authority and wealth of the ruler. Under the fourth shogun these obligations widened yet again to maintain the authority and standing of the military houses. When the fifth shogun succeeded in Enpō 8 (1680), he inherited a government with large financial obligations, depleted reserves, and a shrinking income. His attempt to turn back the clock and regain financial solvency and authority for the central government was not to prove popular.

Turning Back the Clock

Accounts of Tsunayoshi's government document the harshness of his policies by pointing out that the amount of domain land confiscated from his daimyo was considerably larger under his government than that appropriated by his predecessor or any of his successors. Indeed, under the fourth shogun Ietsuna, the *bakufu* confiscated an average of some 26,000 *koku* a year, under the sixth and seventh shoguns a combined average of some 18,000 *koku,* and this dropped under the eighth shogun to some 10,000 *koku* a year. In contrast Tsunayoshi confiscated an annual average of some 60,000 *koku* a year. However, this is a small figure when compared with annual averages of some 239,000, 240,000 and 198,000 *koku* of land confiscated during the governments of the first, second, and third shoguns respectively.[62]

Similarly Tsunayoshi's appointment of one senior councilor solely responsible for the administration of the farmers and their taxes was unprecedented since the creation of that office under Iemitsu. But in practical terms it was no more than a return to the control earlier shoguns had exercised over this important source of government income.

The Administration of the *Bakufu*'s Domain

The first shogun Ieyasu entrusted the administration of the *bakufu*'s domain to a small number of intendants *(daikan)* directly under shogunal control. Supervision was strict, and many lost their lives for embezzlement. On their dismissal or death, the regions under their control were broken up.

Thus Ōkubo Nagayasu had administered the greater part of the Kantō area. But on his death in Keichō 18 (1613) and posthumous discrediting, the region under his control was divided into eighteen separate districts. As the area under the jurisdiction of a single intendant was reduced, the importance of the office declined in proportion. While initially the intendants were on the same level as the directors of finance *(kanjō gashira),* an order of the first year of Shōhō (1644) indicates that they now had to report to this office.[63] Further steps to place the intendants firmly under the control of the directors of finance took place in the early 1660s.[64]

At the same time the office of director of finance was being downgraded. In Keichō 14 (1609) the daimyo Matsudaira Masatsuna (1576–1648) was appointed to take charge of the collection and accounting of tax for the whole of the *bakufu* domain and thus can be rightfully called the first director of finance. During the governments of the first two shoguns, Masatsuna is said to have been singly in charge of this office; he was closely associated with the rulers and wielded wide powers. As the bureaucratic structures of the *bakufu* increased in complexity, however, additional appointments were made to share the administrative load, and Masatsuna's powers declined.[65] Moreover, with Iemitsu's reorganization of the *bakufu*'s administration in Kanei 12 (1635), the office of director of finance fell under the jurisdiction of the senior councilors, who came to supervise financial affairs in monthly rotation.[66]

Previously the daimyo Matsudaira Masatsuna with an income of some 22,000 *koku* had been able to gain specialized knowledge by devoting himself solely to financial administration over a long period of time. In contrast, by the time of the fourth shogun Ietsuna, the intendants were administered by the directors of finance, officials of *hatamoto* status, with an income of some 2,000 to 3,000 *koku*.[67] The majority had no specialized training in financial affairs, many having previously been employed in various guard duties.[68] Nor were their superiors, the senior councilors, more knowledgeable. They were men of daimyo status, but being jointly responsible for the greater part of government affairs, they were unlikely to acquire any expertise in the administration of the country's finances. Since they were responsible for financial matters in monthly rotation, there was no incentive to tackle particular problem areas.[69]

The intendants themselves, however, were able to solidify their position and authority inasmuch as the office generally became hereditary, permitting the holder to exploit his position as quasi-feudal landlord. Often new areas of land were opened up, increasing the revenue and authority of the intendant, but not necessarily increasing payments to the *bakufu* accordingly.[70] Moreover, an order of Keian 5 (1652), one year after the death of the third shogun Iemitsu, accorded the intendants the privilege of delaying their final accounting and consequently the delivery of tax rice, giving them further opportunities to use government income for their own purposes in the interim.[71]

With Tsunayoshi's appointment of Hotta Masatoshi, the administration of the farmers and their taxes was vested again in a single individual of daimyo status on a permanent basis under the immediate control of the shogun. Yet that the stringent measures adopted during Masatoshi's tenure of this office were not dependent on his personal initiative is suggested by the fact that they continued unabated after his assassination in Tenna 4 (1684).

Early in Tenna 1 (1681) four finance officials and three assistants were appointed to investigate rice taxes still outstanding from the intendants.[72] The result was obviously not wholly satisfactory, for in the following year two officials were appointed as investigators, a development that scholars interpret as the establishment of the office of finance inspector *(kanjō ginmiyaku)*.[73] The appointees were well qualified for the office, one having been a finance group head *(kanjō kumi gashira)*, the other an intendant himself. An order for further financial inspections appears again five years later in Jōkyō 4 (1687).[74] A few months afterwards, an additional order addressed to the finance group heads and intendants exhorts both to keep detailed financial records and to pay particular attention to the prompt delivery of tax rice.[75]

The practical effects on the intendants of these administrative reforms were soon apparent. As early as the second month of Tenna 1 (1681), the intendant Ina Tadatoshi, the grandson of the intendant Ina Tadatsugu who had been much favored by Ieyasu, was relieved of his duties and placed in custody.[76] During the twenty-nine years of Tsunayoshi's government a total of thirty-four intendants were dismissed, many punished with death. While the exact number of intendants on Tsunayoshi's accession is not known, it is safe to say that this represented at least half of all officials.[77] There was no break in dismissals on Hotta Masatoshi's death. To the contrary, the greatest annual number appears five years after his death in Genroku 2 (1689), when twelve intendants were removed from office within the year.[78] Further, many hereditary intendants whose management of domain lands did not give cause for dismissal were rotated within the bureaucracy.[79] By these measures Tsunayoshi changed the pattern of administration of *bakufu* lands from hereditary officeholders governing in a quasi-feudal fashion to officials performing their duties under the strict control of the central government.

The Rise of Ogiwara Shigehide

The stringent supervision of the early years did not cease after the death of Hotta Masatoshi, and the pattern of frequent dismissal suggests that the shogun personally held the reins.[80] Of the ten appointments Tsunayoshi made to the office of director of finance during the first nine years of his government, only two were promoted to other *bakufu* positions. Of the rest, one died, two were excused on account of sickness, and four dismissed and punished for misadministration. While the man who died and one of the two who retired on account of illness succeeded in remaining in office for some ten years each, the others served an average of a mere two years before they lost their positions.[81]

When in the course of one day in the ninth month of Jōkyō 4 (1687) three directors of finance and one finance inspector were dismissed owing to incompetence, a lower finance group head was promoted as finance inspector. He was to outlast all others and eventually to carry the major responsibility for the country's financial policy not only during the government of the fifth shogun, but also, in spite of fierce criticism and opposition, for most of the administration of the sixth shogun Ienobu.[82] This was Ogiwara Shigehide (1658–1713), the second son of a middle-ranking finance official, who had begun his training in the financial administration as a clerk *(kanjō)* at the age of sixteen. In Tenna 3 (1683) he was promoted to finance group head, and four years later he replaced his dismissed colleague as finance inspector *(kanjō ginmiyaku)*.[83] This was a post Tsunayoshi had already established in the second year of his government. First known as *kanjō sashisoe yaku* (lit.: additional finance officials), the incumbents apparently were charged to inspect not only the intendants, but also the work of their superiors and colleagues.[84] This is also suggested by an entry in Toda Mosui's diary noting that the shogun had called Shigehide in by himself and instructed him to peruse not only the books of the intendants, but also all other matters he considered worth investigation, relying on his own judgment and wits.[85] The shogun's order that Shigehide rely on his own wits and judgment—rather than that of his immediate superiors, the senior councilors—purposely perverted the hierarchical structure of command. Binding individuals of lower standing in personal loyalty to him and asking them to report on their superiors, Tsunayoshi attempted to reestablish the autocratic authority exercised by the first three shoguns.

Ogiwara Shigehide obviously did well in the task assigned to him, for only three months after he became finance inspector, the shogun granted him the honor of wearing the ceremonial robes *(hoi)* reserved normally for holders of the fourth rank or higher.[86] In Genroku 9 (1696) Shigehide was promoted to the position of director of finance. From around this time the position became known as finance magistrate *(kanjō bugyō)*, placing it on a par with the important posts of magistrate of temple and shrines and city magistrate and reflecting the weight Tsunayoshi attached to it.[87]

The Genroku Land Survey

One way to increase income from agriculture was to resurvey the land in the hope that new methods of farming and new strains of rice had improved the yield and that newly opened, but as yet unregistered, fields as well as other taxable farm produce could be found.

Already much earlier, under the fourth shogun Ietsuna, Shigehide had won the ruler's praise and rewards for the part he played in land surveys of the Kinai region.[88] In Tenna 1 (1681) he had been a member of the team that confiscated the Numata domain, which the Sanada family had governed for a century. The ensuing land survey was so thorough that it resulted in organized protest against the payment of the additional taxes.[89]

Land surveys had also been conducted under previous shoguns, but under Tsunayoshi's government new rigor was introduced into the process. A seventeen-article document composed for the land survey of the Takatō domain in Shinano in Genroku 3 (1690), enforcing new levels of detail and accuracy, became the blueprint for all future surveys under his government.[90] As a result of the survey, the original 30,200 *koku* of the Takatō domain were reassessed at 39,300 *koku*, giving the *bakufu* an increase of nearly one-third. What is referred to by scholars as the Genroku land survey *(Genroku kenchi)*, however, can also be observed in the earlier part of Tsunayoshi's government. When the Echigo domain was confiscated in Tenna 1 (1681), similar measures were used to maximize *bakufu* revenue. The process of creating a detailed record of the tax responsibilities served not only to increase the government's revenue, but also to assure and reassert the independence of small cultivators who frequently had been forced into semi-servile status by large landholders.[91] Akin to the process of the shogun establishing direct control over his officials, this process aimed at removing an administrative layer to permit the government more direct and efficient control over producers.

Tsunayoshi's reforms in the agricultural sector were successful inasmuch as the *bakufu*'s landholdings increased and in Genroku 5 (1692) for the first time in *bakufu* history reached the 4 million *koku* level. However, the increased yield from the *bakufu* domain could not make up for the income that under previous governments had been added from the mines and later the reserves of bullion. Ogiwara Shigehide was to find a place in the annals of Japanese history by suggesting and supervising a temporarily effective but highly unpopular strategy to overcome the *bakufu*'s financial problems, namely, the debasement of the coinage.

14

Producing Currency

"Producing currency is a matter for the state. It would not make the slightest difference if rubbish were substituted for currency."[1] These words were put into the mouth of Ogiwara Shigehide by the author of *Sannō gaiki* not to show his progressive thinking in matters of finance, but to document his absolute depravity. They were written to mock Tsunayoshi's government and demonstrate the absurd extremes to which his financial policy of debasing the coinage would lead. The major debasement of the coinage, however, took place not under Tsunayoshi but under the government of his successor, the sixth shogun Ienobu, and the process was repeated some ten times during the remaining Tokugawa period.[2] Yet not just contemporaries but also later historians have singled out Tsunayoshi in their condemnation of this policy, some historians suggesting that it was one of the worst stratagems in feudal history.[3]

Typically it was the legacy of expenditure Tsunayoshi had inherited from his predecessors that precipitated the unprecedented measure of debasing the coinage. When well over ten years after his accession the shogun decided that he must finally pay his respects at the most sacred site of the Tokugawa clan, the mausoleums of his father and great-grandfather at Nikkō, the senior councilor in charge of finance, Ōkubo Tadatomo, informed him that the necessary funds were lacking. The 100,000 *ryō* considered necessary for the shogunal pilgrimage were simply not available. As to the solution of the problem, the shogun's senior ministers "were silent, as if dumb." It was at this time that Ogiwara Shigehide, though of relatively low official standing in his position as finance inspector, made the suggestion to melt down and remint the gold and silver coinage. By alloying it, the government would be able to increase the coinage and not only solve its financial problems, but also remedy the shortage of coinage in circulation. As a result, the gold content of the large coins known as Keichō *ōban* after the era (1596–1615) in which they were initially minted was reduced from 84.29 percent to 57.37 percent, while in the silver coins the proportion of silver was decreased from 80 to 64 percent. Eventually, in Hōei 5 (1708), the copper coins were also debased by minting the large coins known as *tōjū sen*.[4]

The Government's Explanation

The public was only told indirectly of the *bakufu*'s financial plight. The official order announcing the reminting in Genroku 8 (1695) stated that this had become necessary because the official imprint on the old coins had worn off with age and, owing to the decreasing output of the mines, available bullion was insufficient to mint enough coinage to meet the increasing need for currency.[5] Though not the whole story, these were valid reasons. The original coinage minted in Ieyasu's time had been in circulation for nearly one hundred years, and with its high purity it is likely that the imprint was wearing off. The financial boom of the Genroku period resulted in an expansion of trade and the increasing use of coinage in even the remoter parts of the country. Rapid population growth and the fast development of large urban centers further contributed to the shortage of legal tender. In addition there was a considerable outflow of coinage through the foreign merchants at Nagasaki. According to Engelbert Kaempfer, in 1641 the Dutch were still permitted to leave Japan with some eighty tons of gold and an equal amount in silver in exchange for the goods they had imported. Under Tsunayoshi the outflow was stemmed when in Jōkyō 2 (1685) a quota for the imports of the Dutch was set at ten and a half tons of gold (300,000 taels or 3,000 *kan me*, depending on the exchange rate), while the Chinese traders were permitted twice that amount.[6] In addition, large amounts of bullion left the Japanese islands through the trade conducted by the daimyo of Tsushima with Korea.[7]

To pay for its expenses and to satisfy the increasing demand for coinage, the *bakufu* had since its inception been minting coinage. The enterprises charged by the first shogun Ieyasu with the minting of coinage were still in constant operation some seventy years later.[8] However, some years after the Meireki fire, at the beginning of the Kanbun period (1661–1673), bullion began to be in short supply and the minting houses began petitioning the government to debase the gold coinage. Their requests were refused.[9] Only the gold content of the large *ōban* was slightly reduced from 68.11 to 67.27 percent.[10] Instead the administration of the fourth shogun preferred to dip into the *bakufu*'s last reserves, those set aside by Ieyasu for military emergencies. In Enpō 4 (1676) seven of Ieyasu's emergency ingots were minted to produce 57,800 *ryō*. In the following year some of the silver of the emergency fund was turned into coinage.[11]

By Genroku 5 (1692), however, these final reserves were also nearing their end, and the minting houses, again short of bullion, were petitioning the government to remint.[12] Two years previously the shogun had added the financial supervision of the Sado mines to the responsibilities of Ogiwara Shigehide, who inspected the site personally.[13] Under Shigehide's supervision the output of the Sado mines increased by over 10 percent during the following decade.[14] But the supply of bullion was still insufficient to support the *bakufu*'s traditional measure of minting new coinage to cover its deficit, and in the face of this unprecedented situation, there appeared to be no other choice but to solve the financial crisis with the unprecedented measure of reminting the old coinage. According to Arai Hakuseki, Ogiwara Shigehide later explained the situation to the sixth shogun Ienobu in the following terms:

> In the reign of the previous shogun [Tsunayoshi], the yearly expenditure had been twice the income. With national finances having already taken a downward turn, gold and silver coins were reminted from the ninth month of Genroku 8 [1695]. From then on, the yearly public profit amounted to a total of approximately 5 million *ryō*. This always covered the deficit. In the winter of Genroku 16 [1703], the damage caused by the great earthquake had to be repaired, and the profits accumulated over the years were immediately exhausted. After that, government finances again showed a deficit. They were in the same state as before, and therefore in the seventh month of Hōei 3 [1706] the silver coinage was again reminted. In spite of that, the yearly deficit could not be covered, and in the following spring a proposal of [the junior councilor] Tsushima no Kami Shigetomi was adopted and the *tōjū daisen* issued. (It is said that Ōmi no Kami did not approve of this *daisen*.)[15] Now that the situation has to be quickly remedied, there is no other way but to remint the coinage.[16]

Shigehide was well aware that his efforts to solve the unprecedented financial situation with unprecedented measures was regarded with deep suspicion by many of the shogun's traditionally minded officials. According to Arai Hakuseki, he tried to justify himself as follows: "Apparently people have been saying all sorts of things in private. Yet if we had not taken these measures, how, for instance, would we have been able to give relief in the case of an unforeseen disaster like that in the winter of Genroku 16 [1703]? In this way we can meet the needs of the times and when in future years the harvest is plenty and government finances show a surplus, it will be very easy to restore the coinage to its old state."[17]

Debasement under the Sixth Shogun

Under the sixth shogun Ienobu as well, Shigehide's proposal to debase the coinage found approval. Approval was not given because it was felt that changing conditions justified "breaking the laws of the forefathers" but simply because no one else had the technical knowledge to suggest alternative solutions. According to Hakuseki, the sixth shogun objected strongly. "Who knows, if the coinage had not been reminted in the first place, there might not have been one natural disaster after another," he speculated. Apparently he also voiced fear that continued debasement of the coinage was tantamount to inviting further calamities on the heads of the hapless population and might even lead to the end of the illustrious Tokugawa house.[18]

It is debatable whether the sixth shogun really had such apprehensions or whether Hakuseki later considered it his duty to convince posterity that his master had the virtue to condemn this immoral policy. Yet the philosopher's moral objections could no longer stop the rational decision that further devaluation was essential to meet government expenditure. Even though Hakuseki maintained that it happened without the sixth shogun's knowledge, it is more likely that the shogun—if he did not approve—simply turned a blind eye to the devaluation. After all, it not only provided the essential funds for the running of the country, but also paid for the construction of splendid new shogunal quarters consuming some 700,000 *ryō*, on which Tsunayoshi's successor insisted.[19] Three times the sixth shogun rejected Hakuseki's pleas to remove Ogiwara Shigehide, pointing out that there was no one else qualified to run the financial affairs of the country. Only when Ienobu was approaching death, after several months of incapacitating illness, did Hakuseki finally succeed in having Shigehide removed and the reminting stopped.[20] The official order to repeal the reminting was drafted by Hakuseki himself more than a year after Ienobu's death.[21] By then Ogiwara Shigehide was no longer alive, having died a mysterious death. Only at this point did Hakuseki manage to have him, his fiercest opponent, denounced as a criminal, guilty of one of the greatest of all crimes: that of violating the laws of the forefathers.[22]

As a last service to his master, Hakuseki strove to convince the world that the base act of recoinage had never been sanctioned by the sixth shogun but was carried out by Ogiwara Shigehide in secret. Previously he had decided that Ienobu's shameful dancing in *nō* performances should not go down in history.[23] Now he similarly saw to it that the shame of recoinage did not rest with his dead master and that its repeal be seen as Ienobu's last wish.[24] His efforts were successful. Historians even today maintain that the sixth shogun, while enjoying the profits of the monetary reform and repeatedly rejecting Hakuseki's proposals for dismissing Ogiwara Shigehide, was in fact wishing to restore the coinage to its original purity.[25]

The monetary reform resulted in inflation, including a steep rise in the price of rice, but this was beneficial to large sections of the community whose income fluctuated according to the crop's commercial value. Despite the chain of natural disasters that occurred towards the turn of the century, both samurai and peasants were financially better off during the years of repeated devaluation under the governments of the fifth and sixth shoguns than during the eighth shogun's government, when the price of rice fell, reducing their income.

The debasement also reduced the value in real terms of loans that daimyo and lesser samurai had contracted.[26] Why then did the monetary reform earn the fifth shogun harsh criticism and provoke a man like Hakuseki to such desperate attempts to deny the sixth shogun's knowledge of it?

Paradigm Change

The debasement of the coinage was yet another part of the much-resented paradigm change from quasi-feudal, decentralized government to autocratic administration that Tsunayoshi attempted to effect during his government. When the eighth shogun, Yoshimune—who, contrary to Tsunayoshi, has been greatly praised for his wise government—encountered financial difficulties, he attempted to solve this crisis by asking for special contributions from the daimyo. Like any government's effort to obtain funds, it was not a popular measure, but neither did it attract the criticism of being immoral, a crime. Yoshimune's measures conformed to the traditional feudal pattern in which a lord had the right to call for assistance from his vassals. The contributions of the daimyo to the shogunal purse were not voluntary. However, the matter was only concluded after ample discussion with all concerned, and the fact that the shogun himself made concessions to make up for the levy shows that here the daimyo had some control over financial arrangements.[27]

The debasement of the coinage was no more than a similar demand for the shogun's subjects to contribute to national finance. The way this contribution was levied, however, made it compulsory, not negotiable. Any decision of how much to contribute was firmly taken out of the hands of the daimyo. In that sense it was an early claim to the right of universal taxation. Somewhat akin to a modern tax, the debasement was in the first instance a charge proportionate to the individual's monetary wealth. It was considered immoral inasmuch as it implied that people—regardless of whether they lived in the shogunal or the daimyo domain—were equally the shogun's subjects on whose wealth he could draw. The daimyo, traditionally the intermediary between the people and the ruler, had been cut out. As never before in Tokugawa history, they were given to understand that matters of currency and national finance were being handled by the central government without their interference.

Rubbish Substituted for Currency: *Hansatsu*

Ogiwara Shigehide was mocked and condemned for producing coinage that did not represent its worth in bullion. That the real issue was not a question of the morality of issuing nominal coinage but of who should be accorded the privilege of issuing it becomes apparent when considering the circulation of *hansatsu*, paper money issued by individual domains. Typically this privilege, an encroachment upon the traditional monopoly of the *bakufu* to issue currency, had been accorded to the domains under the government of the fourth shogun. By the time the fifth shogun succeeded, fifteen domains were producing their own paper money. This number was permitted to increase by an additional eight domains, but after Hōei 1 (1704) no further permits were issued.[28]

It appears that earlier than the *bakufu*, the daimyo had hit upon the idea of boosting their ailing finances by issuing money that was not covered by the available supply of bullion. When on the death of Asano Naganori the Akō domain was confiscated by the *bakufu*, it was found that the paper money issued during the previous decade was covered only to 60 percent by bullion.[29]

This source of daimyo income abruptly came to an end, however, when an edict of 13.10.Hōei 4 (1707) decreed that, within fifty days of the order reaching local authorities, all issuance of paper money must be stopped and the currency newly minted by the government be used instead.[30]

Deprived by the shogun of their privilege to issue their own tender, the daimyo were not even permitted the freedom to stipulate whether on sale of their tax rice they were to be paid in silver or gold units. Orders that both silver and gold must be accepted were issued on a national scale and neither individual daimyo nor the area under their jurisdiction could claim exemption from these laws.[31] *Bakufu* interference was also apparent when an attempt was made to fix officially the exchange rate among gold, silver, and copper coins.[32] Orders decreeing that any difficulties encountered in enforcing the *bakufu*'s monetary policy should be reported to the finance inspector Ogiwara Shigehide further emphasized the authority of the shogun and his personal appointees.[33] And while the new laws were strictly policed by a man of lowly origin, another of the so-called upstarts was enfeoffed with a domain that by virtue of tradition was exempted from the *bakufu*'s attempts at financial centralization and permitted to continue minting its own currency. In Hōei 4 (1707) the grand chamberlain Yanagisawa Yoshiyasu was authorized by the shogun to mint gold coins in his domain of Kai.[34]

The Price of His Policies

Tsunayoshi had to pay dearly for his unpopular policies. Not only have Tokugawa authors criticized him harshly for measures that other rulers enacted without censure, even today historians are selective in what they quote, maintaining the picture of the wasteful, immoral shogun.

Thus Tsunayoshi's visits to daimyo mansions, especially a total of fifty-eight visits to that of his grand chamberlain Yanagisawa Yoshiyasu, are condemned as a heavy drain on *bakufu* finances.[35] Ignored is the fact that his father, the third shogun Iemitsu, made many more: forty-two visits to daimyo mansions in the space of just one year. In that same year Iemitsu set out on fifty-three hunting expeditions.[36] The latter were a much greater drain on *bakufu* finances since, in the case of the former visits, the daimyo honored with the shogun's visit had to bear the greater part of the expense.

When Tsunayoshi visited the mansion of Maeda Tsunanori in Genroku 15 (1703), the total expense is said to have amounted to 360,000 *ryō*, no doubt a source of financial hardship for the domain. Yet this complaint does not support the argument that the shogun's visits were a major drain on *bakufu* finances.[37] The shogun bestowed a large number of presents on such occasions, but the host had to provide gifts in return. Since most of these presents were recyclable or consisted of amounts of money, the expense for the *bakufu* would have been considerably less than a simple addition of the cost of presents would indicate. Moreover, to label these gifts as excessive, they must be compared with those bestowed by his predecessors and successors, a task that to my knowledge no historian has attempted. Even if it were found that, for instance, the fourth shogun bestowed fewer gifts upon his daimyo, it must be remembered that Tsunayoshi confiscated much greater amounts of lands from this same class of people and consequently cannot be accused of draining *bakufu* finances by his largesse to his retainers.

The third shogun Iemitsu placed great strain on daimyo finances not just with his frequent outings, but also by bestowing on the daimyo the dubious honor of regular attendance upon him at Edo. Historians have not condemned this practice as evil but seen it as a means calculated to strengthen central authority and in the process weaken those the *bakufu* wished to dominate. Tsunayoshi's visits to the mansions of his daimyo fall into the same category. They were a means to affirm shogunal authority with lavish entertainment (provided by the daimyo) within the financial constraints of *bakufu* finance. At the same time they ensured that those thus honored, like the powerful daimyo Maeda Tsunanori, would for years to come lack the finances to mount protest action against the *bakufu*.

Tsunayoshi's negative image in the sources reflects the pain he inflicted on the class responsible for the record. Modern historians frequently ignore this fact, and available material is interpreted with the a priori conviction that it must document the dissolute extravagances of a corrupt ruler. A good example is the conclusions the scholar Ōno Mizuo draws from two fragmentary sets of accounts detailing expenses under the fifth shogun.[38]

The Shogun's Accounts

Ōno compares figures of *bakufu* annual expenditure corresponding roughly to the early 1680s and early 1690s contained in two documents of different provenance. Turning these figures into percentages and grouping them under four headings, he notes that expenditure for official salaries amount to 48.3 percent for the earlier period and 36.5 percent for the later. Repairs to government buildings outside Edo, including those at Nijō, Osaka, Ōtsu, and Sunpu come to 28.4 percent in the early 1680s and 19.4 percent in the early 1690s. Shogunal household expenditures, among which Ōno includes the shogun's official presents and clothing expenses *(nando)*, reach 13.4 percent for the early period and 18.1 percent for the later. The final category comprises various construction costs amounting to 8.6 percent for the early period and 24.6 for the later. He then examines individual items and notes that expenditures for workmanship *(saiku kata)*, tatami, the shogun's presents and clothing, as well as payments to maids in the women's quarters *(gōryoku kin)* had increased by an average of over 44 percent. On the basis of this calculation, Ōno states: "There was a rapid increase in construction costs on account of the building of temples and Buddha statues and also, owing to Tsunayoshi's extravagances, an increase in the expenditures of the shogunal household. Finally, in the Genroku period, the [*bakufu*'s] income became insufficient."[39]

There are a number of problematic aspects to this argument. First, since no breakdown according to projects is supplied, the evidence presented appears insufficient to conclude that "building costs" represented the shogun's expenditures for temples and Buddha statues. After all, the *bakufu* was also responsible for bridges and a great variety of secular buildings, such as government storehouses and guard stations. In the large category of "building costs," Ōno includes *saiku kata* and tatami, and later points out that they showed a particularly large increase. *Saiku kata* included detailed repair work, such as that of shoji, but also the production of public signboards and other implements.[40] Ōno presents no evidence that these items pertained just to the shogunal quarters or to religious buildings, and one must therefore assume that they, similarly, covered all structures under government control in Edo. Thus, to conclude from an increase in construction costs, and particularly of the two items mentioned above, that this had something to do with the shogun's piety or love of luxury is problematic.

Second, Ōno fails to mention that the one item that can be most closely related to the standard of living of the shogunal family, foodstuffs *(go makanai kata)*, drops by roughly one-third from the early 1680s to the early 1690s, both in real and percentage terms.

Ōno makes his comparisons in percentage terms presumably to avoid the complex issue of inflation. But this raises the question of how complete the figures under examination are. The individual categories are very large, and there is no breakdown of what expenditures they contain. Moreover, there is no evidence that the two sets of figures represent the whole of the *bakufu*'s budget and that some expenditures included under headings in the later figures were not included and set out in a different budget in the case of the earlier figures and vice versa. Since accountancy practices had not reached a high degree of sophistication, such inconsistencies cannot be discounted. This is especially true since the two documents do not originate from the same source.

Finally one must question whether one can accuse the fifth shogun of spendthrift habits on the basis of an increase in expenditure within the period of his government. With no figures available for the government of the previous shoguns, one could also conclude that expenditures during the early 1680s reflected a period of extreme frugality—as also documented by *Yōgenroku*— while those of the early 1690s represented the norm. In other words, unless the expenditures of the fifth shogun are seen in the context of those of his predecessors and successors, as well as the sociopolitical events of the times, we can learn comparatively little.

Daimyo Assistance

Tsunayoshi's extravagances cannot be adequately documented. Yet what is well recorded is that he made demands on his daimyo that on occasion lacked precedents not only in the thirty-year government of his predecessor, but also in the preceding century of Tokugawa rule. Thus after one hundred years he revived the tradition of daimyo contributing with labor and funds to riparian projects.[41]

A rapid increase in population density had placed increasing stress on the river system of the Kinai region, leading to progressively more frequent flooding. Riverbeds had silted up, and in periods of heavy rain the dikes of major rivers, such as the Yodo and Yamato, would break, leading to loss of life and property. Attempts at remedying the situation had been made periodically under the fourth shogun, but it was only under the fifth that the *bakufu* made a concentrated effort to become acquainted with and solve the problem. In Tenna 3 (1683) a delegation of senior officials and experts, including the merchant entrepreneur Kawamura Zuiken, was led by the junior councilor Inanba Masayasu and sent on an extensive tour of the region. In the following year Zuiken was entrusted with a major riparian project, including the cutting of a new canal to ease water levels. At that time the daimyo holding land in Kōchi and Settsu provinces were merely charged with the responsibility of stopping the development of the mountainous area along the riverbeds and replanting forests to prevent further erosion.[42]

In this early project, newly cultivated fields were returned to nature both in the mountains and at the mouths of rivers in order to prevent silting. Yet when further riparian work along the banks of the Yamato river became necessary in Genroku 16 (1703), the *bakufu* decided to recoup part of the expense by opening up and selling new fields. When these funds proved insufficient, however, the daimyo were ordered to assist with the work. The last time the *bakufu* had requested such assistance from its senior vassals had been in 1604, under the first Tokugawa shogun Ieyasu.[43]

River projects in the Kantō region were initiated throughout the remaining period of Tsunayoshi's government, with seven major projects completed between Hōei 1 and Hōei 7 (1704–1710). Different from the *bakufu*'s later river projects in the Kanpō period (1741–1744), where the daimyo had to assist with manpower, here financial contribution was sought for civil contractors tendered for the projects under the direction of the finance magistrate Ogiwara Shigehide. It has been suggested that without the organizational talent of Ogiwara Shigehide, these projects imposing a considerable burden upon the daimyo could not have been executed.[44]

Ogiwara Shigehide similarly showed his ingenuity in ameliorating *bakufu* finance by establishing various taxes on the transport and turnover of commercial goods known as *unjōkin*. Like the monetary reform, the taxes were a countrywide measure and did not respect domain boundaries. Most famous and most resented was the tax on sake, but more lucrative was that on the Nagasaki trade. These commercial taxes only came into existence during the Genroku period but by the close of the period in Hōei 1 (1704) already represented 27.7 percent of the *bakufu*'s total income.[45]

Tsunayoshi was the first Tokugawa shogun to inherit the legacy of government expenditure created by his predecessors without the reserves they had relied upon. He attempted to solve the *bakufu*'s financial problems with autocratic measures enacted by his "upstarts." Naturally they proved highly unpopular, especially with the military class who bore the brunt of these stratagems and recorded their complaints in the sources historians rely on. Failure to distinguish between the expressions of resentment among the elite and the effect these measures had on the greater part of the population has resulted in two disparate images of the period: one of great financial hardship, the other of wealth unprecedented in Japanese history.

While in matters of finance the daimyo received their directions from the "upstart" Ogiwara Shigehide, in matters of political philosophy and Chinese learning, they were subjected to the debates of men who were often of equally low status. It is therefore perhaps not surprising that Tsunayoshi has been given little credit for his support of Confucianism, unprecedented in Tokugawa history.

The Two Wheels of a Cart

The Way of the Buddha and the Way of Confucius are based on compassion and require charity. They resemble the two wheels of a cart and both should be deeply revered. However, those who study the Way of the Buddha are affected by the teachings of the sutras. In their desire to master the Way of the Buddha, they part from their lords, send away their parents, leave their homes, and live in seclusion. Thus the Five Relationships tend to be violated.[1] We ought to be very much afraid of this. Those who study the Way of Confucius are affected by the sayings of the classics. At ceremonies it is common to use the meat of animals as food. They do not think it detestable to take the life of living creatures. Thus everybody will adopt the customs of the barbarians and neglect benevolence. We ought to be very much afraid of this too. In the study of Confucianism and Buddhism, people must not lose sight of the notions on which these teachings are based.[2]

This passage from a letter of the fifth shogun to his grand chamberlain Yanagisawa Yoshiyasu in Genroku 5 (1692) shows a politically motivated, utilitarian attitude towards religion. It stands in stark contrast to the blind devotion to both Buddhism and Confucianism of which Tsunayoshi is generally accused, but in terms of Japanese political history this type of attitude was not new.

Religion and Politics

From earliest times the Shinto gods were invoked to sanction the authority of the emperor, and the introduction of Buddhism in Japan had much to do with a political power struggle between two contending court factions. In the Tokugawa period, Buddhist temples were used to maintain a national registry of the population, and Ieyasu's deification as *gongen* at Nikkō—a reincarnation of the imperial ancestor Amaterasu—was unashamedly a political statement in religious garb.[3] Yet one cannot simply condemn this as a cynical use of religion for political purposes.

Although the popular use of words such as ideology and psychology is of a more recent date, the power of mental images and thought was understood throughout human history. One might even argue that they were better understood in the premodern period, when nonvisible elements were accorded greater powers than our society, oriented towards scientific verification, permits today. The political use of ideology—as well described by Herman Ooms—must be regarded as a legitimate concern of the Tokugawa *bakufu*.

There was, moreover, a firm belief at the time that the safety and well-being of the country depended on the protection of the gods and could be willed or refused by them. Historians cannot be content to discount this as superstition, for this conviction was considered realistic and rational at the time, much as armies and military equipment are considered effective tools for the protection of a country today. Future generations may well question the use of armies and military equipment for the protection of civilian populations, considering this as unrealistic as we today view the allocations of funds for religious projects to strengthen national security and well-being in the Tokugawa period.[4] Both views are subject to the belief and value system of the times, and historians can no more interpret the latter as unintelligent and misguided "squandering" of government funds as consider such terminology appropriate in discussing the former. Both must be viewed as serious government concerns, equally beset by the problem of how much finance is to be allocated to such protection and who is to foot the bill.

Footing the Bill

The governments of the first three Tokugawa shoguns saw a large investment in the religious sector that—though exact figures are lacking—is likely to have peaked under the third shogun with the large expense of the Tōshōgū shrines. Different from the construction of Edo castle, where daimyo were required to supply manpower and labor, here expenses were paid overwhelmingly out of government funds.[5] Under the fourth shogun, government expenditure was greatly reduced, and the daimyo were economically favored, as the reduction in attainder and the financial allocations after the Meireki fire have shown. Some three hundred temples and shrines were destroyed in the great fire, and some of these were moved by government order from their prime locations, but no systematic allocation of funds for rebuilding is found in the records.[6]

For Tsunayoshi, a pious man greatly committed to good government, there could have been no question as to the *bakufu*'s duty to support and maintain temples and shrines. Moreover, with reduced spending on religious structures of importance to the ruling house under the fourth shogun, repairs were likely to have assumed some urgency. Government finances, however, no longer permitted large financial allocations. Tsunayoshi solved this problem by encouraging—and if this failed forcing—others to contribute. Temples and shrines were officially given permission to collect donations, and the daimyo, as the largest landholders outside the *bakufu,* were expected to contribute accordingly. Should they fail to do so voluntarily, they were ordered to. A good example is the rebuilding of Tōdaiji.

The Great Buddha of Nara of the Tōdai temple was burned down in 1567 during the struggles of the Warring States period. Hideyoshi chose to build his own Great Buddha at Kyoto—which Engelbert Kaempfer admired and sketched—and subsequent shoguns also preferred to support other religious establishments.[7] Finally in Tenna 4 (1684) the monk Kōkei (1648–1705) was given permission by Tsunayoshi to collect funds countrywide, and in the third month of Genroku 5 (1692) a new Great Buddha was consecrated. However, collecting the additional funds for the large hall to house the statue presented problems, and the *bakufu* ordered that its intendants donate one *bu* of gold for each *koku* of *bakufu* domain. The daimyo were expected to follow suit voluntarily, but when this did not happen, they were commanded to provide funds at the same ratio.[8]

Daimyo Assistance

Another way for the *bakufu* to raise funds for building projects was the system of *tetsudai fushin,* literally "assistance with construction," where daimyo were required to furnish materials and labor for specific projects, discussed with regard to riparian work in the previous chapter. Tsunayoshi also used this system extensively with regard to religious buildings, it serving both to boost the ailing finances of the *bakufu* and to display his authority over the daimyo.

From Ieyasu's promulgation as shogun in 1603 to the fall of the *bakufu* 265 years later, the scholar Ōno Mizuo counted a total of 311 cases of *bakufu* requests for *tetsudai fushin.* If these are averaged out over the whole period, Tsunayoshi's government of twenty-nine years, stretching over some 17.6 percent of the total period, should have been responsible for some 54 requests, but in fact 67 requests were made. Of the total 311 requests by the *bakufu,* 84 cases were for assistance with castle construction and 143 for temples and shrines. In Tsunayoshi's case the record shows that 42 of 67 requests were made on behalf of temples and shrines. This amounts to some 78 percent of requests for assistance with temple and shrines, while the Tokugawa average is some 46 percent.[9] These figures reflect the fact that Tsunayoshi asked for more help from his daimyo than average and that a much larger proportion than the average was for temple construction or repair.

Ogyū Sorai well understood the political significance of *tetsudai fushin* when he noted that under the first three shoguns such assistance was requested to weaken the daimyo financially and prevent uprisings. Under Tsunayoshi, he observed, frequent requests bankrupted the daimyo, but nobody dared to refuse, fearing the shogun's authority.[10] By Tsunayoshi's time shogunal authority was no longer squarely based on military strength as in the case of the first shogun but to a large degree on the belief system created by his predecessors, one that assumed the hegemony favored and protected by the spiritual world. This spiritual world was focused in the ancestral temples of Zōjōji, Kaneiji, and the Nikkō Tōshōgū, as well as the latter's many branch temples in Edo and elsewhere, extensive structures costly to maintain.[11] Both within the framework of this belief system and in view of the fact that wealth would permit the daimyo to challenge a government lacking funds, it made political sense for Tsunayoshi to command the assistance of the daimyo in maintaining these places of worship when the *bakufu*'s budget could no longer afford to do so. It also made political sense that to these were added temples for priests such as Ryōken and Ryūkō, whose efficacy was proven by the shogun's safe birth and his recovery from illness as well as that of other family members in an age of high mortality.[12] By forcing the daimyo to contribute to the worship of gods and spirits protecting the Tokugawa clan in preference to those defending their own houses, Tsunayoshi strove to centralize authority not only in the secular world, but also within the spiritual realm.

The Buddhist Establishment

The author of *Hagakure* warned young samurai not to acquaint themselves with Buddhism since it might inhibit spontaneous attack and the taking of life.[13] Tsunayoshi, conversely, strove to promote Buddhism in order to reduce the violence within the society he had inherited. In terms of Tsunayoshi's worldview, the expenditure on Buddhism was legitimate and sound, but for the daimyo footing a large part of the bill, it was not. There was not only the financial burden, but as the early popularity of *Hagakure* indicates, the violence advocated in its pages was for many still the samurai ideal. Despised were "the monks of recent times [who] all entertain false ideas and desire to become laudably gentle."[14] It is therefore not surprising that the shogun was criticized for excessive piety.

The Buddhist establishment should have come out in praise of the shogun's ardent patronage, especially if he had been the blindly devoted believer, with uncritical respect for the clergy, that he is usually made out to be. But he was not. The strict supervision he imposed upon his officials was also reflected in the way he dealt with the Buddhist sects.

Like his predecessor, the fourth shogun, Tsunayoshi issued temples and shrines with a patent carrying his vermilion seal permitting them to operate under his government. But unlike his predecessor, he extended these permissions even to small temples and shrines with holdings below 50 *koku*, making their establishment and operation also subject to government control.[15] Later, in Genroku 5 (1692), Tsunayoshi confirmed 146 temples that had been newly established, but forbade the founding of more temples in the future.[16]

Sects were furnished with strict codes of behavior and reprimanded when these were not followed, a task his grand chamberlain Yanagisawa Yoshiyasu also pursued actively.[17] Quarrels within sects were punished: dissent among the clergy of Mount Koya caused the banishment of some one thousand monks in Genroku 5 (1692). Various monks were banned for false teachings, and in Tenna 3 (1683) the diverse group of religious known as *onmyōji* that included the difficult-to-control mountain priests was made subject to registration and control by the Tsuchimikado family in Kyoto.[18]

Tsunayoshi is frequently criticized for his overgenerous endowment of temples and shrines. Yet total revenue grants during the twenty-nine years of his government amounted to below 16,000 *koku*, less than 1 percent of the lands he added to the shogunal domain by confiscation from his daimyo.[19] Out of this amount the Gokoku temple (lit.: temple protecting the country) built for the monk Ryōken, whom Tsunayoshi's mother Keishō-in credited with her son's safe delivery, received 300 *koku* on its founding in Tenna 1 (1680). The temple's revenue was doubled some fourteen years later, and another 100 *koku* followed after three years. Only in Genroku 16 (1703), well over two decades after its founding, was the temple assigned a further 500 *koku*, giving it a total revenue of 1,200 *koku*, still a minor amount considering the monk's importance within the belief system of the times.

Historians make much of Tsunayoshi's expenditures on religious institutions but fail to compare this with the sums other shoguns invested in this sector. For instance, Tsunayoshi is often criticized for having spent lavishly on the ancestral Kaneiji at Ueno. Yet as the name indicates, the temple was founded in the Kanei period, namely, in Kanei 2 (1625), by the Tendai monk Tenkai, who had earlier functioned as the trusted adviser of the first shogun Ieyasu. Its purpose was to protect Edo as the temple complex of Hieizan protected Kyoto, and it was therefore also known as the Tōeizan (the Eastern Eizan). Initially built under the third shogun, it was also endowed by Ietsuna and Tsunayoshi, but the greatest donation came from the eighth shogun Yoshimune, who raised its landholdings to 12,000 *koku*, the size of a small daimyo domain.[20] Tsunayoshi ordered the building of an additional temple within the compound, the Konpon Chūdo, but part of the expense was borne by the Shimazu clan, which was ordered to assist with the construction.[21]

Further, it is frequently asserted that the allegedly misguided religious fervor of Tsunayoshi's mother, Keishō-in, led to uncontrolled expenditure on religious institutions.[22] That this was not so and that the monks his mother favored were subject to the same strict supervision as others within the orbit of the shogun is documented by a passage from the diary of the monk Ryūkō. In the eighth month of Genroku 6 (1683), Ryūkō was summoned by the shogun and questioned about a monk by the name of Jōju-in. The monk's prayers had apparently been efficacious in preventing fires, and Keishō-in had come to trust in his teachings. Yet her request that he be given *bakufu* funds to build a temple was firmly refused by the shogun. Moreover, officials, including the magistrate of temples and shrines, were charged with investigating the monk's background, with the result that his teachings were found unsuitable and he was put under house arrest.[23]

Rulers throughout history have used members of the clergy as their confidential advisers, so much so that Max Weber considered this an important pattern in the centralization of authority. The advantages of the clergy as learned men believed to have high ethical standards, not permitted to accumulate secular wealth, and not identifying themselves with the concerns of the military class are obvious. Like his predecessors the Ashikaga shoguns, Ieyasu took full advantage of the talents of the clergy, and the monk Sūden (1569–1633), whom Ieyasu entrusted with important political tasks and who served under the second and third shoguns, went down in history as the Black-Robed Prime Minister *(kokue no saishō)*.[24] Another monk upon whom the first three shoguns greatly relied was the long-lived Tenkai (1536–1643). It was he who secured the shogun's patronage for the Tendai sect and after Ieyasu's death created the cult of his deification, committing the *bakufu* to the erection of grand temple structures and elaborate worship for the remaining years of its hegemony.[25]

The two monks Ryōken and Ryūkō, whom Tsunayoshi is accused of having patronized with excessive religious fervor, played very minor roles in comparison. Ryūkō's temple Goji-in (lit.: Protective Temple) was not a grand establishment with its revenue of 1,500 *koku*.[26] The monk's diary reveals that he frequently attended Buddhist and Confucian lectures and discussions at the castle, and he was invited to *nō* performances as well as various ceremonies and entertainment of dignitaries. It does not reveal that he was greatly involved in the political sector, though the shogun's resolve to install his nephew Ienobu as his successor appears in the pages of Ryūkō's diary some days before the senior councilors and the Three Related Houses were informed of this important decision.[27] Known to enjoy the shogun's confidence, he was approached by those attempting to use the network of the clergy to bring their case before the shogun, such as the leader of the Akō samurai pleading for the reestablishment of the confiscated domain.[28] Perhaps his unpopularity stemmed from the fact that his advocacy was difficult to gain or that it did not achieve much. Yet no doubt it was as a result of his bad image that already at an early period he was held responsible for the shogun's much resented protection of animals, and particularly of dogs, even though no such evidence exists. Ryūkō's own diary does not

The monk Ryūkō (1649–1724). Reproduced courtesy of Gokokuji, Tokyo.

refer to these laws. If the monk had possessed such influence over the ruler that policies were based on his counsel, then surely such a fact would have been recorded in the diary with pride, and some details of the legislation would have found mention.[29]

Having earned the trust of the shogun, Ryūkō was permitted access to the *oku*, the women's quarters. Here he is said to have driven out fox spirits that adopted human shape and posed as ladies-in-waiting, but he was no Rasputin, as the historian Tokutomi Sohō has suggested. Such fox spirits also appeared in other parts of Edo, and it was part of the duties of the Buddhist clergy to drive them away with ceremonies and prayers.[30] Rather than calling on him to display occult powers, Ryūkō's diary reveals, the shogun placed great emphasis on debates. At Edo castle the monk was required to listen regularly to the shogun's lectures on the Confucian classics and the debates by others. Even when the shogun visited Ryūkō's temple, Goji-in, in the company of his mother, that was the course of events.

For instance on 3.10.Genroku 6 (1693), a rainy day, the shogun arrived at the fourth hour, between 10:00 and 12:00 in the morning. His mother had arrived some two hours earlier. After the appropriate ceremonies had been conducted, Ryūkō gave an exposition of the Buddhist scriptures, including a debate on the Three Mysteries, part of the esoteric teaching of the Shingon sect to which the monk belonged. After the shogun had listened to these explanations, he himself lectured not on Buddhism, but on the so-called Three Main Cords of the Confucian classic *The Great Learning*, dealing with self-cultivation and government.[31] Honjō Munesuke, Keishō-in's younger brother, and the chamberlain Yanagisawa Yoshiyasu in turn gave lectures on this theme. The visit finished with *shimai*, the enactment of scenes from *nō* plays, and the shogun returned at the seventh hour. Keishō-in, however, stayed on to exchange poems with the priest.[32] While the monk might have felt honored by the ruler's attention, there was also a painful aspect to his visit. In his *Ten Stages of the Religious Consciousness*, Kūkai (774–835), the founder of Shingon Buddhism, had ranked the various beliefs current in Japan and assigned Confucianism the second lowest position, only one step above the animal-like mind, ignorant of any form of religion.[33] The shogun demonstrated his censure of such sectarian upmanship by holding Confucian lectures at a Buddhist temple.

On another occasion, on 12.9.Genroku 10 (1697), Ryūkō was required to accompany the shogun on a visit to the Yanagisawa mansion, and there, again in front of the shogun's mother and a wider audience, he had to submit to being questioned on the Three Mysteries by the young Confucian scholar Ogyū Sorai.[34] For Ryūkō to have to defend the sacred teachings of his sect against an aggressive young Confucian and, moreover, to have to do so in front of a large general audience was a major challenge, if not an insult. It is consequently not surprising that though the occasion is mentioned in his diary, including the questioning of Zen monks by Confucian scholars, his own participation finds no mention.[35] If Ryūkō wanted to remain in his privileged position close to the shogun, he had no choice but to suffer such occasions and defend his beliefs as best as he could. It is not difficult to visualize how many in the audience would have been more interested—and perhaps amused—by the embarrassment these worthies had to suffer than by the content of the discussion.

No doubt it was the result of such skirmishes among the intellectuals of the day performed in front of a lay audience that earned Tsunayoshi the reputation of "trifling" with Confucianism. He might well have enjoyed these intellectual cockfights, but this does not permit the conclusion that he did not take the propagation of Buddhism and Confucianism seriously. Both were essential to his policy of producing a less violent and better-educated society. As even his strong critic the scholar Arai Hakuseki admitted, Confucianism greatly benefited under Tsunayoshi. "From the time of his administration the teaching known as Confucianism was officially established and even the lower classes in the distant provinces came to know of it."[36] In spite of the important role Confucianism played in Tsunayoshi's government and his sponsorship, in turn, played in the spread of this philosophy in Tokugawa Japan, little research has been done on what kind of Confucianism he adhered to.

Tsunayoshi's Confucianism

Ogyū Sorai's statement that, at the time of the judgment of the peasant Dōnyu, the shogun was a follower of the Chinese philosopher Chu Hsi (1130–1200) is well known.[37] Yet no research has been published on who introduced Tsunayoshi to the Chinese classics and guided him in his early Confucian studies. Standard sources are silent on this matter: they give the name of his instructor in fencing and also that in painting but do not tell us who guided him in his literary studies. As a seven-year-old, Tsunayoshi was presented by the twelve-year-old shogun with a copy book written in the latter's own hand. We do not know whether this was in appreciation of the younger brother's precocious fondness for the brush or to encourage diligent practice. Copy books were based on the sayings of the Confucian classics, and one can assume that they provided Tsunayoshi's introduction to Confucianism. Yet who supervised his studies and explained the intricacies and significance of the maxims contained in these works?

Only weeks after Tsunayoshi succeeded as shogun, he ordered two men to hold regular Confucian debates. One was, as might be expected, the head of the Hayashi family, Nobuatsu (Hōkō), who had just succeeded to the position on the death of his father Shunsai (Gahō). The other was the Confucian scholar Hitomi Yūgen.[38] Yūgen and his father had been frequent visitors to Tsunayoshi's Kanda mansion long before he became shogun.

Hitomi Yūgen

Hitomi Yūgen (also Chikudō, Yoshitaka, 1637–1696) was the son of the Kyoto physician Hitomi Gentoku (1604–1684). The latter, who had made a name as pediatrician, was consulted by the imperial family and called to Edo by the third shogun Iemitsu to treat his daughter Chiyohime as well as the often sick Ietsuna.[39]

Gentoku's son Yūgen was a precocious child. At age nine he was appointed by Iemitsu as attendant to the four-year-old Ietsuna and came to live with the future shogun in the third enceinte of the castle.[40] Yūgen's talent was recognized early by Hayashi Razan, and he was made a disciple of Razan's son Shunsai. In Kanbun 1 (1661), aged twenty-four, Yūgen was ordered "to do the same work" as Shunsai.[41] To fill this post he had to shave his head and take the Buddhist name of Yūgen, akin to other members of the Hayashi family. Later in the year he received the Buddhist title of *hōin,* and in Kanbun 12 (1672) he was honored with the higher Buddhist title of *hōgan*.[42] Together with Shunsai's sons he worked at the projects entrusted to the Hayashi house, such as making a copy of Fujiwara Teika's *Meigetsuki* or compiling the historical work *Zoku honchō tsugan* (Addition to the *General Mirror of Japan*), and was rewarded in equal terms.[43] Together with Shunsai's eldest son Harunobu he was entrusted with important functions within the shogun's secretariat, such as keeping the shogun's vermilion seal.[44] After the ceremonies of Iemitsu's seventeenth death anniversary at Nikkō, he was rewarded for his contribution to the successful conclusion of the event, with his name appearing at the top of the list, second only to the Kantō magistrate, Ina Tadatsune.[45] He was also jointly appointed with Hayashi Harunobu to keep a variety of official records. These included accounts of Buddhist ceremonies, such as those held at the mausoleum at Zōjōji.[46]

Yūgen also kept the records of Tsunayoshi's and Tsunashige's mansions, the above-cited *Kanda ki* and *Sakurada ki*. From the very first page, dated Keian 5 (1652), of Tsunayoshi's house record, we see Yūgen's father Gentoku calling on the young Tsunayoshi, perhaps in his capacity of pediatrician.[47] Later we see Gentoku being honored with the role of "fellow guest" *(shōban)* when Tsunayoshi is entertained by his brother Tsunashige, an indication of the high esteem in which he was held by the shogun's brothers.[48] Yūgen's home was conveniently located in the vicinity of Tsunayoshi's Kanda mansion,[49] and he must have been a constant visitor to collect information for his record. On various occasions he also accompanied Tsunayoshi to the castle and was present at important functions such as the New Year celebrations.[50]

With Tsunayoshi's accession, it was Yūgen and not the head of the Hayashi house who wrote the inscription on the stone casing surrounding the coffin of the fourth shogun.[51] He also played an important role in the reception of the Korean embassy of Tenna 2 (1682) and was lavishly praised by the envoys for his skill in poetry composition. In the following year he was entrusted with the composition of the new *Buke shohatto* (Regulations for the Military Houses), and, again on the order of the shogun, he completed the compilation of the historical work *Butoku taisei ki* (Great compilation of military virtue) in 1686 with Kinoshita Jun'an and Hayashi Nobuatsu. He was renowned as a poet and left a number of literary works. Had he found the time and reason to dwell at length in writing on all important meetings with the shogun and the work he did for his government, his record might well have outshone that of Arai Hakuseki. Unlike many others, he never fell out of grace with the shogun, and when he died in

The Chinese refugee scholar Chu Shun-shui (1600–1682). Reproduced courtesy of the Suifu-Meitokukai Foundation, Mito.

office in Genroku 9 (1696), he was succeeded by his son Yukimitsu, who like his grandson Noriari continued to serve the *bakufu* as a Confucian scholar.[52]

The diary of Hayashi Shunsai frequently shows Yūgen lecturing on the Chinese classics, and he is also known to have taught the sons of daimyo at several Edo mansions.[53] Yūgen believed that the Confucian classics should be taught in an easy-to-understand fashion, and he is said to have criticized the scholars of the Hayashi house as poor lecturers for their use of obscure terms and phrases. This apparently made his teacher Shunsai very angry. It was the duty of the Hayashi house to give scholars "a broad and solid education" and not to excel in lecturing like the Kimon School of Yamanzaki Anzai. If Yūgen's advice were followed and more attention were paid to lecturing, "our school and learning will go to ruin in no time," the scholar Ogyū Sorai later quoted Shunsai as saying.[54] The episode must have taken place before Tsunayoshi's succession in Enpō 8 (1680), for Shunsai died at that very time.

In the same way Yūgen was censured by Shunsai, Tsunayoshi was later criticized for attaching importance to lectures on the Confucian classics for a wide audience rather than patronizing more advanced forms of scholarship. With Yūgen nine years Tsunayoshi's elder, renowned as teacher, and a frequent visitor to the Kanda mansion, it seems highly plausible that it was Yūgen who introduced Tsunayoshi to the Chinese classics and that the future shogun's understanding of the role of Confucianism owed much to this scholar. Yet how did Yūgen come to develop the idea of Confucianism as moral education for the masses, a concept so very different from the narrow, exclusively scholarly approach of his teacher Shunsai? What could have emboldened him to challenge the teacher who had nurtured his studies? I would like to suggest that Yūgen's confidence to criticize Shunsai rested on his respect for an authority on Confucianism he considered higher. This was the Chinese refugee scholar Chu Shun-shui (1600–1682), who arrived in Edo in Kanbun 5 (1665) as the guest of Mito Mitsukuni.

The Confucianism of Chu Shun-shui

One of the hallmarks of the teaching of the Chinese refugee scholar Chu Shun-shui is the utilitarian approach to Confucianism that was to characterize Tsunayoshi's attitude later. Confucianism was primarily a moral teaching that would improve society if followed by everyone. To Yamaga Sokō, the Chinese scholar wrote: "What is learning? I will explain it to Sokō. Ardently seeking wisdom, ardently seeking saintliness. There is no limit to it. Become like Yao and Shun. This is possible for everybody. The Way of Confucius is not difficult. With self-cultivation virtue will increase."[55]

For Chu, Confucianism manifested itself in the practice of *jin* (benevolence) in government policies that provided for the needs of the commoners. The fall of the Ming Chu blamed on scholar-officials more interested in the form of their essays and abstract learning than the principles of good government. He was, as Julia Ching put it, "a Confucian scholar, not in a specialist sense as a classicist or philosopher, but rather as a 'universalist.'" In this he differed from the more academic approach of most Japanese scholars. Chu likened Ito Jinsai's learning to embroidery on silk and contrasted it with his own, which he described as wooden utensils. On account of these fundamental differences in their interests, Chu refused to meet the already famous Jinsai. While Chu politely praised Jinsai's scholarship, he nevertheless asserted that it was "quite useless to the service of the world." The Chinese scholar was emphatic on this point, stating that what Jinsai "considers to be the Way, is not my Way."[56] Chu was in all aspects a practical man, and his Japanese disciples would marvel that, besides being master of a wide range of scholarship, he also knew how to plow a field and build a house, and he even possessed knowledge about the preservation of food and wine.[57]

Like Tsunayoshi, Chu believed that Japan's samurai were much in need of a Confucian education, and it was on these grounds that he finally accepted Mitsukuni's offer. He gave public lectures at both Edo and the Mito domain, and took pride in the large crowds that came to hear him.[58]

Chu's Confucianism, both with regard to the content of its teaching and the audience he sought to address—as well as the fact that he styled himself "a faithful commoner"[59]—was at variance with the more academic and elitist approach of Hayashi Shunsai. The latter's student Hitomi Yūgen, however, made great efforts to befriend the foreign scholar as soon as he arrived in Edo.

Chu Shun-shui and Hitomi Yūgen

Chu Shun-shui arrived in Edo on 11.7.Kanbun 5 (1665). Within days of his arrival, even before Chu left his inn to move to the Mito mansion, Yūgen had made contact with the Chinese scholar. The correspondence between Yūgen and Chu portrays a quickly developing warm relationship, with Yūgen respectfully taking the position of the disciple. Mutual visits often lasted a full day, and discussions continued till deep into the night. "Our brushes became our tongues, and our eyes became our ears," Yūgen writes to the scholar Oyake Seijun at the Mito mansion, enthusiastically describing his meeting with the Chinese expatriate at which the lack of a common spoken language meant that the scholars had to communicate in writing. Yūgen asks the friend for assistance in overcoming physical barriers that were created once Chu moved into the Mito mansion, and the letter conveys a feeling of urgency about meeting the Chinese scholar again.[60]

Yūgen makes great efforts to please the foreigner with his presents, including a flask of horse's milk, a most unusual gift in Japan, no doubt deliberately chosen to match the taste of the Chinese scholar. As the relationship develops, Yūgen asks to borrow various items, ranging from clothes to silver chopsticks, which he has carefully copied. Special care is taken in copying the traditional Confucian clothes the Chinese is dressed in, and one might well speculate that when eventually Tsunayoshi permits the wearing of these, it was because of Yūgen's appeals and the knowledge he had obtained from Chu.[61]

But the main topic of discussion between the two men is the nature of Confucianism. After a long night of discussion—which Yūgen praises as more enlightening than the light of a lantern lasting ten years—he expresses his appreciation of Chu's teaching. The Chinese scholar had explained that the Confucian Way was not like the splendid feast the Chinese emperor offered ceremoniously to the gods *(tairō hacchin)* but like the five grains, essential for living, or like everyday green tea and rice cakes, playing a far more significant role in the world than the rarified food of the imperial court. Yūgen enthusiastically takes up the suggestion that Confucianism must be as much a part of a person's daily life as such humble, common food: "Precisely therefore the very essence of the Way is to savor its taste. Thank you so much! Thank you so much!" he writes excitedly.[62] On another occasion Yūgen expresses his gratitude for Chu's comments on *The Great Learning*'s maxim of "rectified heart, sincere thoughts" *(seishin sei'i)*. He is delighted with the practical applications explained by the Chinese scholar and their resulting "merit for daily life."[63] Yūgen was discovering a new kind of practical Confucianism, one that did not contain the highbrow sophistries valued by the Hayashi house.

Yūgen's enthusiasm for the teaching of the Chinese scholar did not escape the notice of his teacher Shunsai. The latter met Chu Shun-shui for the first time at Yūgen's house on 7.9.Kanbun 5 (1665), not long before the foreigner was to make his first trip to the Mito domain. In his diary Shunsai commented on how Yūgen was very much taken by Chu's Chinese style and was frequently inviting and meeting the expatriate scholar. "They are as close as if they were old friends," Shunsai wrote of the two men who had met for the first time just a month previously.[64] Six days later Shunsai sent his son Harunobu together with Yūgen to bid the foreign scholar farewell on his departure for Mito and noted in his diary: "Harunobu returned early; Yūgen stayed to talk."[65] The younger Hayashi was obviously not as interested in Chu's teaching as was Yūgen.

The special trust that quickly developed between Yūgen and Chu is also apparent when the former quite freely complains to the latter about his work under his teacher Shunsai. Yūgen bemoans the fact that the work in the historical institute of the Hayashi house does not leave him a free moment. He feels "like a fish on a hook."[66]

At Mito, Chu Shun-shui came to meet Yūgen's younger brother Hitomi Bōsai (Den), who had been adopted by his uncle Hitomi Hajime. There was only one year of difference in age between the brothers, yet Yūgen refers to Bōsai as if he were a mere student, by far his junior.[67] Scholars, however, generally refer to Bōsai rather than to Yūgen when mentioning Chu's connection with the Hitomi family.[68] An exception is Tokuta Takeshi, whose careful analysis of the correspondence between Yūgen and Chu has made it possible to assign dates to the letters and gain a clearer picture of the friendship between the two men. This analysis has drawn attention to an exchange of letters suggesting that Mito Mitsukuni's first visit to the lodgings of Chu Shun-shui took place only in Kanbun 7 (1667), two years after Chu's arrival at Edo. This assumption stands in contradiction to the findings of other studies, where Mitsukuni's first visit to Chu is dated a year earlier, in Kabun 6, and no evidence of a visit in Kanbun 7 has been discovered. The letters do not refer to the high-ranking visitor by name, and I would suggest that rather than Mito Mitsukuni, the visitor could well have been Tsunayoshi.

In the letters exchanged between Chu and Yūgen, the general appellation of "lord" *(jōkō)* appears, and scholars generally believe that this and similar titles of reverence always refer to Mitsukuni. Yet not only the date but also other parts of this particular exchange of letters suggest that the visitor to Chu's mansion on this occasion was somebody else. Replying to news from Chu about the high-ranking man's visit, Yūgen suggests that this event was not only of great significance for Chu personally, but also for the whole country. This visit might start a custom among the nobles and great lords of Japan promoting scholarship and nurturing saintliness, he rejoiced.[69] Such wording seems inappropriate for a visit by Mitsukuni, who was often in touch with the Chinese scholar he had employed and always treated him with considerable respect. Moreover, other daimyo had employed Chinese refugee scholars in the very same fashion before this, and it is difficult to see how a visit by Mitsukuni could be heralded as a sign of a new custom taking root in the country. The suggestion of a new custom would, however, make sense if the visitor had been the shogun's brother, a man of even higher status than Chu's employer Mitsukuni. In his reply Chu takes up the point made by Yūgen, that the visit was unprecedented and of significance for the whole country, and adds that "this present *(ima)* lord has great talent and wide-ranging learning." Again, with Chu being in Mitsukuni's employment for two years already at that time and the two scholars frequently in touch, it seems odd to describe Mitsukuni's virtues to Yūgen as if he had just discovered them. Moreover, with the meaning of the word *ima* including the sense of "new," it is more likely to refer to the "newly visiting lord," someone other than Mitsukuni. My suggestion, therefore, is that this could well refer to a visit by Tsunayoshi, who even by his critics was praised as a man of great intelligence and who would have been more familiar with Chinese scholarship than other daimyo.

Tsunayoshi was a man of great curiosity, and an impromptu, unofficial call on the house of the foreign refugee scholar about whom he must have heard from the frequently visiting Yūgen seems well within the possible. Such a visit would follow the pattern of Tsunayoshi's contact with the Dutch, where he surprised the envoys with his impromptu inspections before becoming shogun and after his accession arranged for a special, informal audience to examine them, an occasion so well described by Engelbert Kaempfer.

The available material strongly suggests that Tsunayoshi admired and visited Chu but does not furnish us with conclusive proof. We know for certain, however, that Yūgen greatly admired Chu and his advocacy of a simple, popular Confucianism, to the point of criticizing his teacher Shunsai for his arcane approach. We also know that Yūgen as page to the young Ietsuna was close to the shogunal brothers and frequently visited Tsunayoshi's mansion before he became shogun. Yūgen is also known to have taught Confucianism at various daimyo mansions. Moreover, from the day Tsunayoshi takes over the government, Yūgen is frequently given preference over the head of the Hayashi house, to the point of composing the official inscription on the stone sarcophagus of Ietsuna. Another of Chu's admirers and correspondents, the Confucian scholar Kinoshita Jun'an (1621–1698), is employed by Tsunayoshi two years later.[70] Finally the similarities between Chu's brand of practical Confucianism as a tool to improve morals and bring about stable government and Tsunayoshi's unprecedented use of this philosophy in Japan in the very fashion advocated by Chu can hardly be coincidental. For someone watching the political developments uneasily from the sidelines, as Tsunayoshi is reported to have done, Chu's warning about a government that had neglected to pay attention to the plight of the greater part of the population, the peasants, was unlikely to go unnoticed.

Tsunayoshi's patronage of Confucianism was much admired by a visitor such as Kaempfer but has rarely found the approval of historians. Tracing the connection to the teaching of the politically experienced Chu Shun-shui helps to explain the rationale behind Tsunayoshi's brand of Confucianism and demonstrates that its alleged simplicity was not the product of a simple mind. Further, the difference between the hands-on, political Confucianism to improve society that Chu quite happily propagated as "a faithful commoner" and the much more theoretical and elitist approach of his Japanese counterparts, concerned to maintain their social preeminence, foreshadows the opposition and criticism that Tsunayoshi's sponsorship of Confucianism was to encounter even among Confucian scholars.

The Confucian Scholars

Tsunayoshi's use of Confucianism as a moral teaching, propagated much like Christian morals in Sunday sermons from the pulpit, is reflected in his early order that Hitomi Yūgen and Hayashi Nobuatsu give lectures three times monthly to the assembled officials and dignitaries. His approach in this respect was fundamentally different from that of the daimyo Ikeda Mitsumasa, who had employed Kumazawa Banzan in a position akin to a house elder with a relatively high stipend of 3,000 *koku*.[71] In line with Tsunayoshi's view of Confucianism as moral instruction rather than a skill, he did not employ Confucians as administrators but used them as educators for his bureaucrats. Here their treatment resembled that of the Buddhist clergy, and this aspect of their duties was emphasized when they had to defend their moral principles and philosophical ideas against the arguments of the Buddhist priests in open debates.

Tsunayoshi's aim to make the Confucian classics more accessible to the lay person, much like the Buddhist scriptures, is also reflected in his early order that the punctuation of the Confucian Four Books and the Five Classics as well as Chu Hsi's *Chin ssu lu (Kinshi roku)* and his *Little Learning (Shōgaku)* be revised.[72] The annotated books, together with Chu Hsi's commentary on the Four Books, were printed and copies presented to temple and shrines as well as to those who attended the lectures at Edo castle.[73]

Shortly afterwards Tsunayoshi made his attendant Yanagisawa Yoshiyasu his disciple in the study of Confucianism.[74] This can be interpreted as the shogun's vainglorious thinking that he had reached the level of a qualified Confucian teacher, ready to pass on his knowledge. But it can also be understood as an indication that the shogun saw the need for a new kind of Confucian learning, suitable for those who—unlike the Hayashi scholars and their disciples—were not able to devote their entire life to the study of the Chinese classics. The shogun's intent to show that knowledge of the Confucian classics was not to be limited to professional scholars was similarly demonstrated by his order that at the New Year's celebration of Tenna 2 (1682) Yoshiyasu read from *The Great Learning*. Yoshiyasu would perform the task of reading from the Confucian classics at New Year's throughout the remainder of the fifth shogun's government.[75]

Chu Hsi, whose teaching the shogun was said to have followed, saw remote antiquity as the Golden Age, successful because of the prevailing high standard of moral education.[76] Tsunayoshi attempted to re-create this Golden Age in his own country, educating not only his officials but also the population as a whole. One attempt in this direction was the countrywide issuance of placards exhorting the population to practice filial piety.

The Filial Piety Placards

Tsuji Tatsuya has pointed out that the wording on Tsunayoshi's famous placards was not altogether new. Comparing the placards the fifth shogun issued in Tenna 2 (1682) with those issued under the fourth shogun in Kanbun 1 (1661), he notes that only the first four orders were new, namely, those concerning filial piety, frugality, the honest practice of one's profession, and the reporting of crime. Yet though these first four orders had not appeared on public placards before, they were contained in similar wording in the *Shoshi hattō*, the regulations for the behavior of the *bakufu*'s direct retainers *(hatamoto)* of Kanbun 3 (1663). What Tsunayoshi had done in unprecedented fashion was to erase the distinction between lower samurai and commoners by issuing the same orders to both.

But Tsunayoshi went one step further. He also erased the distinction between the *hatamoto* and the daimyo with regard to the law by abolishing the *Shoshi hattō* and making the *Buke shohatto*, the Regulations for the Military Houses, previously applicable only to the daimyo, binding for both the *bakufu*'s *hatamoto* and daimyo. The fact that the rules of behavior previously furnished only to the military class were now directly issued to the commoners, together with the tenor of the *bakufu*'s order to the intendants of Enpō 8 (1680) on the governance of the farmers, leads Tsuji to conclude that an important shift in the assessment of the common people was taking place. While previously they were referred to as *gumin*, "the foolish people" who must simply be controlled and supervised by officials, they are now seen as people capable of education.[77]

Tsunayoshi's filial piety placards were accompanied by four further placards dealing with a host of regulations, ranging from the fees for packhorses, forged currency, and the sale of drugs, to fire precautions and the reporting of Christians.[78] One could interpret this promulgation as a tightening of *bakufu* control under the fifth shogun, but it is also possible to see it as an emancipation of the commoner. Such regulations existed before and were enforced when considered necessary, but there had been little attempt to explain the details of the laws to the *gumin*, the foolish commoners. Max Weber has pointed out that legal norms guarantee the right that punishment "does not depend upon questions of expediency, discretion, grace, or arbitrary pleasure."[79] Yet if these legal norms are unknown to those regulated by them, the authorities retain arbitrary powers, permitting them to terrorize their subjects with the constant fear of transgression. Tsunayoshi's placards not only acknowledged the commoners' intelligence to understand these laws, but also furnished them with the right to know what was permitted and whether convictions were just. In this sense the placards reduced the authority of officialdom.

One of the orders of the placards, however, is believed to be totally unprecedented, namely, the prohibition of publishing unauthorized books.[80] Print had always been subject to strict *bakufu* control, and cases of punishment before the government of the fifth shogun are numerous. The fact that such a law was now made public to commoners indicates the extent to which the use of books—and consequently learning—was spreading.

Under Tsunayoshi the spread of "learning" became a political measure.[81] The study of the Confucian classics was no longer the preserve of the scholar. Confucian-based rules of conduct were no longer applicable only to "gentlemen," but also to the common people.

Yet for Tsunayoshi Confucianism was but one wheel of a cart, and while on his placards he called for Confucian filial piety, he added that servants must be treated with compassion *(renmin)*.[82] The placards were followed by the Laws of Compassion, inspired by the Buddhist teaching of the sanctity of life. The enforcement of Buddhist compassion, however, was not to prove easy in the warrior society of the day, as the frequent repetition of the laws—indicating their ineffectiveness—demonstrated. One reason was the lack of cooperation from officials. It is perhaps no coincidence that after issues of insubordination by officials reached a peak around 1687, Tsunayoshi again turned to Confucianism and decided to give it greater visibility and emphasis as an educational tool for his administrators. With the lectures held at Edo castle apparently not having produced the desired effect, he now decided to throw the weight of his authority behind a Confucian establishment outside the castle walls.

In the eleventh month of Genroku 1 (1688), Tsunayoshi proceeded with his courtiers to the Confucian hall of Hayashi Nobuatsu at Shinobu ga Oka in Ueno for the celebration of Confucian ceremonies. It was the first time a shogun had visited the Hayashi school and Confucian shrine since Iemitsu had paid a short visit on his return from Kaneiji well over half a century previously and the first time a shogun officially celebrated ceremonies in honor of Confucius and his disciples.[83] It took eight years after his accession as shogun for this event to take place, a further indication that for Tsunayoshi the utilitarian educational nature of the philosophy, rather than the ceremonial aspects of Confucianism, was a priority. The impression this visit made on contemporaries must have been significant, judging from an effusive letter of Mito Mitsukuni to Hayashi Nobuatsu celebrating the fact that finally the light of Confucianism was also illuminating Japan.[84]

Tsunayoshi, too, must have been pleased with the effect, for only three months later, on 21.2.Genroku 2 (1689), he paid a repeat visit. He might well have come to realize at that time the importance of his personal involvement, for on 21.8 of the following year he personally lectured to his high officials, including the senior councilors, on the *Great Learning*, an event that thereafter was to take place monthly, with the Four Books being discussed in turn.[85] A month later he had a wider circle of men, all those above the sixth rank, including the heads of guard units, magistrates of temples and shrines, and so on, assemble in his presence. He reminded them that both literary and military learning had always been considered the ingredients of the way of government. From now on they were to set their hearts on literary learning and apply themselves to scholarship. For the practical implementation of this directive, he ordered that a room next to the official audience chamber at Edo castle be set aside and that there all officials—except the highest-ranking attending his own lectures—should monthly listen to a lecture by Hayashi Nobuatsu.[86]

The Yushima Seidō

The establishment of the Yushima Seidō, ordered in the seventh month of that same year (1690), must be seen in this context. If learning was to take place on a wider scale, it was preferable to move it out of the castle. Yet the facilities of Shinobu ga Oka were small, the original shrine having been built for the Hayashi family by Owari Yoshinao, though it was enlarged with *bakufu* funds in Kanbun 1 (1661).[87] The private school of the Hayashi family was to become a public

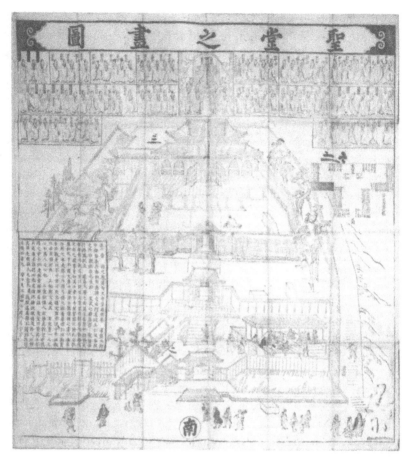

The Yushima Confucian Shrine on its completion in 1691. Reproduced courtesy of Daitōkyū Kinen Bunko, Tokyo.

institution of learning, and for this purpose a site in Kanda, much closer to the castle, where the Yushima Seidō is still located today, was made available. The edict of 9.7.Genroku 3 (1690) ordering the construction of the Confucian complex explained that, with the shogun's devotion to Confucianism, the private facilities of the Hayashi house were insufficient, and the old location at close proximity to Buddhist temples did not permit further expansion. Tsunayoshi's trusted attendant Matsudaira Terusada was put in charge of the construction, while the daimyo Hachisuka Hida no Kami Takeshige had to supply the necessary laborers.[88] Tsunayoshi personally wrote the characters for the tablet over the entrance of the main hall. The location was renamed Shōhei Saka in memory of Confucius' birthplace. Before the year ended, construction was completed.[89]

An order early in the following year permitting Confucian scholars to distinguish themselves from the Buddhist clergy by adopting the hairstyle and dress of samurai was a further indication of the new importance the shogun attached to raising the public image of the philosophy. As mentioned above, this might well have been at the instigation of Hitomi Yūgen. Most likely at the behest of Chu Shun-shui, Mito Mitsukuni had much earlier, in Enpō 4 (1676), decried the custom of imposing the tonsure and Buddhist dress upon Confucian scholars as an evil remnant of the Warring States period and had permitted his own scholars to adopt secular dress.[90] To further enhance the status of the Hayashi establishment, Tsunayoshi conferred upon Hayashi Nobuatsu the title of Rector of the University *(daigaku no kami)* and had him promoted to the lower fifth court rank.[91]

On 7.2.Genroku 4 (1691) the images of the original Hayashi shrine were moved in an elaborate procession, while images of the ten sages were newly produced, and paintings of the seventy-two worthies were ordered from the Kanō house.[92] The shogun's first visit to the new premises took place three days later. It was a grand formal occasion in which the traditional Confucian ceremony of *sekiten* was performed with due pomp. In line with the shogun's emphasis on the sanctity of life, vegetables were sacrificed instead of animals. Later the shogun lectured personally to a large audience on the Confucian classics. Entertainment with sake and the performance of *nō* scenes followed.[93]

The same ceremonies were repeated in the following year, and it was apparently then that the Dutch were told of these events. Kaempfer, who was a member of the Dutch delegation to Edo in 1692, wrote later:

> Around this time we heard that last year the shogun had built a *miya* [shrine] in honor of the wonderful Chinese politician Confucius, who taught the art of government, and that this year he had built the lecture hall of this same *miya*, which he visited the day before our arrival. The day before yesterday the shogun came to speak on the subject of the art of government in the presence of his councilors, and on the spot gave such an excellent discourse or lecture that those prostrated in his presence were overwhelmed with emotion.[94]

Kaempfer's informants were the Nagasaki interpreters and his student Imamura Gen'emon, whom he was training in Western medicine, all men whose learning had begun with the Chinese classics. They were familiar with the wide scope of Confucian learning, and the emphasis on politics and government in the information transmitted to Kaempfer is therefore noteworthy. As a reflection of the observation and understanding of the shogun's aims by his contemporaries, it confirms the shogun's own pronouncement that the study of Confucianism was crucial for the conduct of government. This essentially utilitarian attitude stands in contrast to later claims that Tsunayoshi's interest in Confucianism was devotional.[95] It is also reflected in the shogun's relatively small endowment of the large complex and its important mission as national educational institution with a revenue of 1,000 *koku*. When the earthquake of Genroku 16 (1703) destroyed many of its buildings, they were, moreover, reconstructed on a smaller scale, while the *onari goten*, the building for the private use of the shogun, was never reconstructed.[96]

The government's relatively limited financial commitment stands in contrast to the shogun's personal dedication to lectures on the Confucian classics. Beginning with his first address to his officials in the summer of 1690, we see an increasing number of lectures delivered by the ruler with rising numbers of listeners. They take place not only at the castle and at the Yushima Confucian hall, but also on his visits to his retainers, which in turn occur with increasing frequency. In Genroku 6 (1693) the shogun started lectures on the Chinese classic of *The Book of Changes (I ching;* Jap.: *Eki kyō)* eight times monthly, and the record tells us that until Genroku 13 (1700) he gave 240 lectures on this subject. His lecture on *The Doctrine of the Mean (Chung yung;* Jap.: *Chūyō)* in the second month of Genroku 7 was given to an audience of 342, including many daimyo, while in the third month of the following year he addressed 414 people on the *Book of Changes*. Finally, on 29.12.Hōei 5 (1708), the shogun's lecture had to be cancelled on account of illness: it was eleven days before his death.[97]

That Tsunayoshi's dedication to lecturing on the Confucian classics was more than a fascination with hearing his own voice is suggested by the fact that a number of other men were always called upon to similarly lecture and engage in debate. These were not only professional Confucian scholars; daimyo and even Buddhist prelates were also required to demonstrate their knowledge of the Confucian classics by lecturing in front of the shogun and the assembled court. Thus, for instance, in the third month of Genroku 5 (1692), the prelate *(monseki)* of Kyoto's Nishihongan temple on his visit to Edo had to present a lecture on *The Great Learning*,[98] while on 3.6 of that year, the country's highest-ranking daimyo assembled to lecture for their ruler. Tsunayoshi's brother-in-law Owari Mitsutomo and his son Tsunanari; Kii Mitsusada and his son Tsunanori; Tsunayoshi's nephew, the future Ienobu; and Mito Mitsukuni's heir Tsunaeda as well as Matsudaira Tsunanori of Kaga each presented an exposition on a passage from the *Great Learning*. Matsudaira Tsunanori was accorded the honor of also discussing the first chapter of *The Doctrine of the Mean*. After these lectures had been concluded, the dignitaries were entertained with a banquet and the performance of passages from nō plays *(shimai)*.[99]

Evaluating the above event, one must keep in mind that the fathers of most of these men, Tsunayoshi's senior relatives, had been ardent patrons of Confucianism much earlier. Thus Mitsutomo's father, Tokugawa Yoshinao, had invited prominent Confucians, including the Chinese refugee scholar Ch'en Yüan-pin, and (as explained in chapter 5) had already much earlier established a Confucian hall in his domain. Mitsusada's father Yorinobu had similarly been an early patron of Confucianism, much guided by the Confucian scholar Nawa Katsusho (1595–1648). Mito Mitsukuni patronized the scholar Chu Shun-shui, who assisted with the education of the young Tsunaeda. Maeda Tsunanori was Mitsukuni's nephew and himself a great patron of learning, famous for his collection of books, inviting scholars such as Kinoshita Jun'an and Muro Kyūsō to his house.[100]

For these men, debating the Confucian classics was nothing new; unprecedented, though, was the fact that Confucian education and debates were sponsored by the ruler. The previous generation had been curbed by the *bakufu* in their sponsorship of Confucianism and denied the right to establish schools in their domains to spread Confucian education, for Confucianism, with its ideal of the benign autocrat assisted by administrators chosen for ability, challenged the decentralization of authority and advancement according to birth right that had progressed under the fourth shogun. Tsunayoshi's patronage of Confucianism was a political measure to effect the paradigm change resisted by the government of his predecessor. Its use as an educational tool was designed to produce a large pool of officials participating in the political process not to further their own, regional interests, but on account of the service Confucians believed they owed to their lord and humanity. Buddhism would inculcate in these officials and their subjects compassion to produce the ideal political world order.

Tsunayoshi saw his mission in remedying the ills of society. For him neither Buddhism nor Confucianism was the path to personal salvation; they were two wheels of a cart named politics. Failure to understand Tsunayoshi's political use of Confucianism has obscured the fact that the writings of arguably Japan's greatest political philosopher, Ogyū Sorai, owe much to the apprenticeship he served under the government of the fifth shogun.

16

The Apprenticeship of Ogyū Sorai

"Since the shogun Tsunayoshi was fond of learning, it spread throughout the country, and people holding lectures on various books appeared in towns like clouds in the sky,"[1] wrote the Confucian scholar Ogyū Sorai, documenting the shogun's success in raising popular interest in learning and particularly Confucianism. Sorai himself was one of those who "appeared in towns like clouds." In Genroku 5 (1692), when his father, the physician Ogyū Hōan, was included in a shogunal pardon and permitted to end his exile of over a decade in the provinces, Sorai returned to Edo to make a living lecturing in front of the large temple Zōjōji.[2] It is unlikely that the young scholar would have attempted to earn his keep as a Confucian teacher if such lecturing had not suddenly come into demand with the shogun's sponsorship. Nor would he have found ready employment in the Yanagisawa mansion some years later. Sorai himself explained that his employment was due to the recommendation of the abbot of Zōjōji, a claim scholars have met with skepticism, suggesting that Sorai's father Hōan's reinstatement as physician to Tsunayoshi was the decisive factor.[3] No doubt this was necessary to clear the way for Sorai's employment in the Yanagisawa mansion, but it is difficult to imagine that this alone would have qualified him to join the elite group of scholars that were gathered at the house of the shogun's most powerful minister. It is more likely that the abbot noticed that this young scholar's approach to the Confucian classics well matched that favored by the shogun.

Returning to the city of Edo at around the age of twenty-six after having spent over a decade of the most formative years of his life in the provinces, Sorai found himself out of tune with the sophistication of the city samurai. Throughout his life he would refer to his rustic way of thinking.[4] It was, however, this largely untutored approach to and understanding of the Chinese classics that secured Sorai not merely employment, but also quick promotion in the Yanagisawa mansion and, in turn, the attention of the ruler. The reason for Sorai's early promotion from the "lowermost seat of the hall" was the judgment of the peasant Dōnyu.[5]

The Judgment of the Peasant Dōnyu

Dōnyu was a peasant of the Yanagisawa domain who was so poor that he first divorced his wife and later abandoned his ailing mother. He was now charged with unfilial conduct. Sorai later described how Yoshiyasu asked his scholars to investigate precedents to determine the appropriate punishment, but neither the law codes of Ming China nor other writings contained information on this topic. Since Dōnyu had been so poor that several days earlier he had divorced his wife, the scholars decided that he ought to be considered an outcast. For an outcast his behavior of taking his mother along with him until he could no longer support her was commendable. As originally he had no intention of abandoning his mother, he should not be charged with this crime. Yet Yoshiyasu was not satisfied with this verdict, insisting that even among the poorest, abandoning one's parents could not be tolerated. Since somehow the matter had come to the shogun's notice, Yoshiyasu decided it would be wise to consult him. The shogun was, according to Sorai, at that time a follower of the Chinese philosopher Chu Hsi, believing in the latter's theory that everything in the world was infused with its own particular *li* (Jap.: *ri*) or principle.[6]

According to Chu Hsi, every person shares the same *li*, or characteristic essence of humankind, but the nature of *ch'i* (Jap. *ki*) an individual is endowed with varies and determines the state of the person's heart or mind. Evil is thus explained as a heart polluted by evil *ch'i*.[7] According to Sorai the shogun was particularly concerned with the investigation of the heart, which in this context must be taken to mean the search for the source of evil, here the evil of abandoning one's parent. Yet, Sorai explained, Yoshiyasu was a follower of Zen Buddhism, who normally did not give much credence to the theory of *li* or principle. Under these circumstances, Sorai decided to take a practical approach and voiced the following opinion:

> If a famine is to occur, such people will also appear from other domains. Abandoning one's parents cannot be tolerated. If you consider this case a matter of a parent having been abandoned, then, regardless of the punishment, other domains will adopt this [thinking] as their model. In my opinion the fact that circumstances reach a point where such a person comes forth is firstly the fault of the intendant *(daikan)* and the district magistrate *(gun bugyō)*. Further up, it is the fault of the house elders. And people still further up ought also to be considered guilty. [In comparison] Dōnyu's offense is extremely light.

Though Sorai spoke from the lowest seat of the hall, Yoshiyasu for the first time said: "I entirely agree."[8]

Sorai explained his success on this occasion by three facts. First, he had personally experienced the hardships of the population in the countryside. Second, as a rustic he was blunt in speech, and third, having been away from Edo for over a decade, he was aware of the political changes that had taken place in the interim, changes others ignored.[9] These circumstances made Sorai eminently qualified to understand the fifth shogun's change in political direction, and the judgment he suggested was no more than a faithful application of the ruler's political principles.

In one of his earliest and most important orders, Tsunayoshi had stated that "all intendants must always bear in mind the hardships of the people and must govern them so that they do not suffer from hunger and cold." Sorai had personally witnessed "the hardships" of the people in the country and, unlike his colleagues, with his rustic bluntness was not afraid to put the blame on those above his own station. But perhaps even more important was that he had fully grasped the change of direction in government policies. Much earlier Hotta Masatoshi had found it difficult to comprehend that he as the shogun's highest minister should consider himself responsible for even the most wretched street urchin. Masatoshi's untimely end might even have come about because he never fully came to terms with this radical change in government policy.

The view that the state must alleviate the suffering of the people also formed the background of laws holding officials responsible for abandoned children, sick travelers, and others in need. Yet for the samurai this role of "civil servant" was an uncomfortable notion to accept, and the scholars whom Yoshiyasu had asked for an opinion had also turned a blind eye to the responsibilities of the officials in this case. Sorai had grasped the fact that the shogun's sponsorship of Confucianism was not concerned with finding precedents in ancient Chinese classics for particular cases but with using the authority of the classics to break the traditional pattern of samurai dominance over the commoners on the basis of the sword.

Although Sorai considered his judgment of the peasant Dōnyu instrumental in attracting his lord's attention, his name finds no mention when the same story appears in *Genkō jitsuroku*, the record of Yabuta Shigemori, a retainer of the Yanagisawa house. This work similarly notes that the incident had reached the shogun's ears but has the addition that Hayashi Nobuatsu had been asked for an opinion and judged this to be a case of abandoning one's parents, a crime usually punished severely by the shogun. It also notes that Yanagisawa Yoshiyasu had already taken measures to have relief rice shipped to the province. Here it is Yoshiyasu himself who points out that abandoning one's parents cannot be tolerated, and if this were to be judged the peasant's crime, such cases would increase when famine hit other regions. In other words, officials needed to be held responsible to prevent further occurrences, an opinion all the more reasonable considering that relief rice had been shipped to the area.¹⁰

Although differing in certain points, the two accounts do not contradict but complement each other. The task of the scholars of the Yanagisawa mansion was to offer advice to their lord so that he might reach an informed decision, much like today's bureaucrats tender advice to and write speeches for their ministers on the basis of government policy. For Ogyū Sorai it was noteworthy that on this occasion his lord accepted his opinion, even though he was a newcomer. But for Yabuta Shigemori what counted were the principles his lord chose to follow and that Yoshiyasu had defended his opinion against a man as learned as Hayashi Nobuatsu. Sorai's advice contained nothing new but simply was in tune with Yoshiyasu's thinking, which, in turn, was in line with the shogun's policies. The omission of Sorai's name in *Genkō jitsuroku* suggests as much.

Sorai's understanding of the paradigmatic changes that had occurred since the succession of the fifth shogun secured him a meteor-like rise to fame. Within half a year the vagrant lecturer outside the temple gate had become a scholar whose presence the shogun requested at his own lectures. Instead of selling his knowledge and instruction to the ignorant, he now had the honor of debating with some of the most learned and famous men in the country in front of the ruler and his court. Even the shogun's mother heard of the rise of this new star in the scholarly firmament and requested that he join senior scholars to debate in her presence. The penniless young man who only months previously had relied on a charitable beancurd seller for his fare was now participating at shogunal banquets, invited to theatrical entertainment, and rewarded with presents.¹¹

Sorai and the Confucianism of the Fifth Shogun

Scholars generally describe Tsunayoshi's involvement with Confucianism as amusement or genteel accomplishment. This judgment is made not on the basis of the scholarly discussions that took place—which have remained largely unexamined—but with reference to the entertainment that generally followed such occasions.¹² Sorai himself, however, did not see it that way. For him the shogun was not a half-crazed dilettante, as he is popularly known,¹³ but a much-revered ruler worthy of comparison with those of ancient China.

In two letters addressed to his disciple Yamagata Shunan (1687–1752), Sorai speaks in the most effusive terms about the fourteen years during which he regularly appeared in the shogun's presence, was permitted to lecture in front of the ruler, and answered his questions. The honorifics and symbolism used in these letters addressed to a disciple and friend give evidence of the awe with which he looked up to the ruler and the high regard in which Sorai held him. Like Yanagisawa Yoshiyasu's concubine Machiko in her *Matsukage nikki*, he refers to the shogun's death in terms of the Chinese legendary Yellow Emperor's ascent to heaven. When speaking of the honors conferred upon him, he demonstratively uses vocabulary appropriate for an emperor, something that later earned Sorai the strong criticism of proimperial factions.[14] It is important to note that there could be no ulterior motives for the use of such high-flown vocabulary. These were not letters to officials, where the expression of deep admiration for the shogun was considered good practice or necessary to obtain favors. What we see here is a simple outpouring of grief over the loss of a much-valued and admired patron, heightened no doubt by fears Sorai harbored for the future. Later, when he became famous as a scholar independent of shogunal patronage, Sorai's view of his service under Tsunayoshi might have lost some of the overenthusiastic admiration expressed in these letters. Yet even at the end of his life, when he spoke with pride about the significance of his own scholarship, he never denigrated the Confucianism or government of the fifth shogun.

Light is shed on the relationship between Sorai and the shogun in *Shinruigaki yuishogaki* (Record of the family and lineage), the family's official record of the scholar's life. On two occasions when listening to the shogun's lecture, Sorai showed doubts or a lack of understanding *(futoku shin)* on his face. The shogun immediately called Sorai to his side and inquired about the problem. When Sorai stated in detail the reasons for his disagreement with the shogun's position, the latter was pleased, and on both occasions Sorai was awarded with special personal gifts.[15] We see here the otherwise autocratic shogun genuinely interested in sponsoring debate, even at the risk of being proved wrong. The fact that Sorai dared to give expression to his disagreement with this ruler much feared for quick punishment indicates that scholars were used to voicing contrary opinions in his presence without trepidation. Moreover, Sorai, by expressing his disagreement on these two occasions, demonstrates a genuine interest in the contents of the shogun's lecture. The episode also shows that times when Sorai did not agree with the shogun were rare. In other words, Sorai considered such events to be occasions for true academic debate, rather than a "show" staged for the enjoyment of the shogun, as they are frequently described.

The fact that this information was included in the otherwise terse record of *Shinruigaki yuishogaki* also indicates that neither Sorai, who made this information available, nor his descendants who composed the record were ashamed to associate Sorai's learning with that of the fifth shogun. This stance is at variance with that of later scholars who have made considerable efforts not to connect the scholarship of Sorai with the government of the much-criticized and often ridiculed shogun, and hence have overlooked otherwise obvious continuities. For example, Tsunayoshi is often ridiculed for the 240 lectures he gave on *The Book of Changes,* but this work was also of utmost importance for Sorai and was considered to teach the very foundation of Confucian government.[16] I do not argue that Sorai was consistently in agreement with the policies of the fifth shogun, but his criticism—as detailed later—does not concern those areas generally criticized by scholars.

Historians must evaluate sources with due attention to their purpose, time, and place. When this is done, it becomes evident that Sorai's references to the Confucianism of the fifth shogun are not of censorial nature as they are generally interpreted to be.

For instance, in his mature work Sorai greatly criticized Neo-Confucianism, a philosophy he elsewhere reported the shogun subscribed to at the time of the Dōnyu incident. Yet Sorai made no secret of the fact that until Shōtoku 4 (1714), some five years after the shogun's death, he himself was an adherent of Neo-Confucianism.[17] Moreover, one must note Sorai's deliberate addition of the words "at that time" when referring to the shogun's belief in Neo-Confucianism. This must lead to the conclusion that the shogun was not always a supporter of Neo-Confucianism and suggests that, much like Sorai himself, he changed his position.

Shogunal Lectures and Ignorant Scholars

In their assertion that Sorai was highly critical of the government of the fifth shogun, scholars point to a recurring phrase in his writing seemingly condemning the lecturing Tsunayoshi inaugurated. For instance in *Seidan* Sorai states:

> However, from the time that the shogun before the last two [Tsunayoshi] made lecturing the most important thing, scholars have not engaged in other learning and it has come to the point that they look upon lecturing as their assigned duty. Now they are all unlearned, of no use in government service. Moreover, since only Naiki [Hayashi Nobuatsu] and his sons are ordered to engage in government business and since they are given special preference, the other Confucian scholars have no government business to attend to, and this might be the reason why they do not engage in scholarship.[18]

Maruyama Masaso cites this passage as an example of Sorai's "severe criticism" of the shogun's "half-dilettante interest in these lectures." No doubt as a consequence of Maruyama's interpretation of Sorai's words, his translator, Hane Mikiso, gives the honorific verb *asobasu* in the original text the modern meaning of "to play," translating the first part of the passage cited above as: "During Shogun Tsunayoshi's regime, the Shogun amused himself by listening to lectures, so that the Confucian scholars neglected all other learning and literature and behaved as if it was their sole duty to lecture on Confucianism."[19]

The a priori assumption that Sorai must be criticizing the fifth shogun has also influenced the rendering of this passage in other respects. The text is ambiguous as to whether the process of scholars neglecting other learning began during or after the fifth shogun. The ensuing phrase "it has come to the point" *(koto ni narite)* followed by "now" *(ima)* favors the latter interpretation. Such a reading is also supported by Sorai's complaint that only the Hayashi house is being consulted on government affairs. This was not the case in Tsunayoshi's time, when Sorai's rather than Hayashi Nobuatsu's judgment was accepted in the politically important case of the Forty-Seven Rōnin. It is not *then* but *now* that the only duty scholars outside the Hayashi house are assigned by the government is lecturing, with the logical consequence that, as Sorai states, they consider it their sole duty. This interpretation is confirmed in the last sentence of the passage, where Sorai questions whether the lack of scholarship is not the result of the fact that no other demands are now being made on scholars.

The Danger of Criticism

To grasp the full meaning of the passage quoted above, one must not only carefully examine the words for any intentional ambiguity, but also consider the environment in which they were written and their purpose. In this case it is important to note that *Seidan* was a secret document addressed to the eighth shogun Yoshimune in which Sorai was making suggestions for improvements in government policies and the administration. The basis for "improvement" is criticism of the status quo. Such criticism, however, was a dangerous undertaking in Tokugawa Japan. When this is kept in mind, Sorai's blunt criticism on the subject of learning becomes trenchant indeed: "As to scholarship, thanks to the care of the shogun [Yoshimune], Confucian scholars give lectures at Shōhei Saka [Yushima Confucian shrine] and at the Takakura mansion. However, no samurai of *hatamoto* rank come to listen; just some daimyo retainers, doctors, and city people attend in small numbers. For the shogun to cater only to those kind of people is useless. Since this approach is bad, it will not accomplish the shogun's aims."[20]

Yoshimune had extended the scope of lecturing far beyond that of Tsunayoshi. Shortly after his accession, he had commanded that Hayashi Nobuatsu give lectures daily at the Yushima Confucian shrine. In unprecedented fashion he ordered that everybody, even farmers and merchants, be permitted to attend these lectures and do so without further training *(kokoro no mama ni)*. At the end of the month the list of attendance was handed to the shogun.[21] Two years later, in Kyōhō 4 (1719), Yoshimune extended this program of educating samurai and commoners together by opening up the Takakura mansion for lectures. Three Confucian scholars outside the Hayashi house, including Muro Kyūsō, were ordered to give public lectures there, again to people without regard to their

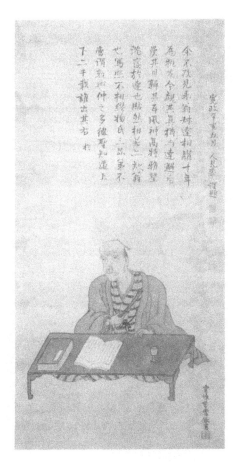

The Confucian scholar Ogyū Sorai (1666–1728). Painting of Kansei 3 (1789). Reproduced courtesy of Chido Museum, Tsurugaoka, Yamagata.

status.[22] How much this lecturing to an audience regardless of station would have grieved Sorai can be estimated when one considers how status-conscious he was, permitting only people of samurai status to remain in his presence. Even among his own students, those who were not of samurai status had to listen to his instructions from outside his room.[23]

The Devaluation of Cultural Goods

Yoshimune had much changed and greatly lowered the social standing and academic contents of the lectures Tsunayoshi had inaugurated, including in the audience not only lower samurai, but also commoners. Yet he failed to participate in person. Lecturing on the Confucian classics was no longer conducted at the highest level of government with some of the country's most respected dignitaries engaging in debate. Now it was relegated to the dull masses. The sport of the ruler was again hawking. Scholarship was no longer a status symbol; its worth was devalued. Confucian lectures were no longer "cultural goods" in Bourdieu's sense. Sorai alludes to this idea when he says: "Even if expense is involved, if people believe in their teacher and thus put their heart into learning their lesson, they will learn their lesson. This is human nature."[24]

When the fifth shogun personally listened to the lectures of Confucian scholars, their words were vested with authority. Since Tsunayoshi had made learning a priority, people believed in the importance of it and made progress. Now they no longer did. Yet is this interpretation compatible with another passage in Sorai's work, apparently suggesting to Yoshimune that poetry meetings were far superior to the lecturing the fifth shogun had engaged in?

Shogunal Poetry Meetings

> The shogun before the last two [Tsunayoshi] was very keen on learning. As a result, scholarship became popular. However, people have placed emphasis on lecturing, and because poetry and prose are not popular, people are not concerned with literary skills and hence are useless. From this point on, the *bakufu*'s Confucian scholars have also all been men of little learning. However, if there were things like shogunal poetry meetings, that would be far better than the lecturing of the shogun before the last two [Tsunayoshi].[25]

In translating the above passage from Sorai's *Seidan*, attention must be paid to the fact that the Japanese text uses no honorifics in "placed emphasis on lecturing," "poetry and prose are not popular," and "not concerned with literary skills." This indicates that it is not the action of the fifth shogun that is referred to but that of others, and the word "people" has consequently been supplied in translation. The time element, moreover, is vague and does not permit placing these events firmly into the period of the fifth shogun. There is much that speaks against such an interpretation.

Sorai was well aware that Tsunayoshi's scholarly interests were not confined to lecturing and that he would not have tolerated anybody lacking scholarship in his presence. Sorai's emphatic protest about the evil of lecturing to an uneducated audience in other passages as well suggests the interpretation that the misunderstanding of what scholarship was all about had occurred in Yoshimune's time. Could Sorai be trying to tell Yoshimune that he had drawn the wrong conclusion and that, by simply extending lecturing to a much wider audience, he was in no way bettering the fifth shogun? This theory finds support in Sorai's rather odd suggestion that, if Yoshimune wanted to outdo the fifth shogun, he should try poetry meetings. It was not only odd considering that Tsunayoshi had taken the unprecedented step of creating an official *bakufu* position for the Kyoto poet Kitamura Kigin, but also inasmuch as in the preceding passage Sorai had explained that, though the composition of Chinese poetry was often criticized as frivolous, it was in fact a good way of learning Chinese, a preparatory step for reading the Confucian classics.[26] Describing the composition of poetry as a first step towards reading the classics reveals Sorai's statement that in this way Yoshimune could outdo the fifth shogun to be no more than a ruse to persuade this ruler with no ambition of personally engaging in scholarship to try at least the more entertaining forms of Chinese studies.

The Sage Emperors

The change from the shogun, often in person, consulting Confucian scholars on government business to scholars being ordered by the government to lecture to the broad masses—much like monks—was an enormous drop in status for them. It is not surprising, therefore, that the topic appears repeatedly in Sorai's writings.

In his work *Taiheisaku* (A proposal for a great peace) Sorai again makes the point that public lectures to an ignorant audience was an evil of the present day and complains that respect for scholars is now so low that some gentlemen even make them squat outside their room while listening to the lectures inside. It was the very reverse situation he himself adopted for students not of samurai status. Sorai contrasts this kind of behavior with that of the sage emperors, who visited the mansions of the scholars from whom they sought advice and did not summon them in such undignified fashion.[27] Nobody at the time would have failed to remember that Tsunayoshi frequently visited the mansions of his retainers to hear their scholars lecture and debate. But just to ensure that this meaning was fully understood, Sorai added rather explicitly:

> And suddenly it has became the custom that among monks, even average ones are venerated, and the rules laid down by a previous ruler, when Confucian scholars were respected for their virtue, have become unknown. To the contrary, Confucians have become common people and are not given any special treatment. Hence Shigenori [Sorai] and others have concluded that an event like facing the ruler and his ministers and explaining to them the Way is certainly not going to happen in these present times.[28]

So irked was Sorai by the demand that scholars spread their scholarship to the undeserving masses that he recalled nostalgically an ideal he himself had never experienced: namely, the situation under Hayashi Shunsai, when a select circle of disciples lived with their teacher from morning to night, when scholars were bad at lecturing, and the language they used was so complex that outsiders were unable to follow their discourse.[29] Ironically such an education would not have permitted Sorai to acquire the knowledge of life beyond the classroom and independence of thought that distinguished him from others and propelled him to fame. Yet it was an ideal Sorai attempted to create towards the end of his life, when he made every effort not to spend time with people beyond the small circle of his students and learned friends.[30]

There was also a personal reason. Sorai suffered from a physical condition, most probably excessive nervousness, which made lecturing difficult for him. "After one day in official robes, I was ill in bed for another three," he would later write. Speaking publicly did not come easy. "When inspiration came, any number of words quickly bubbled out of my mouth," but he found it difficult to "explain these matters in front of the lords of the world." He makes no secret of the fact that he enjoyed the favor of the fifth shogun and blames this "peculiar illness" from preventing his rise to a high office at the time.[31]

Yet the question remains whether without this handicap he would indeed have been appointed to such a position. Tsunayoshi made no attempt to turn Confucian scholars into *bakufu* officials; his aim was to have *bakufu* officials adopt the moral norms of Confucianism. No Confucian scholar was rewarded with a large stipend, a fact that might have prompted Sorai to lament on Tsunayoshi's death, "It was once said that the Han emperor's favors were scanty."[32]

For scholars such as Ogyū Sorai and Hayashi Shunsai, Confucianism was a complex field of full-time study, requiring a good knowledge of Chinese, honed by extended devotion to subjects such as poetry and literary composition. Tsunayoshi was not devoid of wider scholarly interests, as his patronage of Chinese monks as well as the much-acclaimed poet Kitamura Kigin and his son Koshun (1648-1697) showed.[33] Yet for the shogun such scholarly ideals had to give way to the practical necessities of government, and these required that the moral standards rather than the scholarship associated with Confucianism be adopted by his administrators. There was no time or necessity for bureaucrats—or the shogun for that matter—to acquire the scholarship necessary to read the Chinese classics in the original. It was the task of scholars to produce easily readable versions. All that was required was that those in government had the right frame of mind when dealing with their duties. Akin to today's mass education, this meant a lowering of academic standards, which a full-time scholar such as Sorai would naturally deplore, even though it was the very notion that secured him a living.

Sorai's view of the role of the Confucian scholar differed fundamentally from that of the fifth shogun. But any complaints on Sorai's part must be interpreted against the background of his employment in the Yanagisawa mansion and his sudden rise under Tsunayoshi. This would not have taken place if Confucianism had remained confined to lectures unintelligible to outsiders as given by Hayashi Shunsai. And without this employment—and the facilities for scholarship and the challenges to excel among equals before the ruler that it provided—it is doubtful whether Sorai would have been able to write the works that later secured his fame.

Sorai's Chinese Scholarship

Fundamental to Sorai's scholarship and writing was his knowledge of modern and ancient Chinese, and this knowledge was acquired at the Yanagisawa mansion. The scholar Imanaka Kanshi is emphatic that the neglect with which this aspect of Sorai's career has been treated is a serious mistake and a great defect. Imanaka and in his wake Olof Lidin detail how scholars from Nagasaki fluent in Chinese employed at the Yanagisawa mansion as well as visiting Chinese dignitaries, many of them prelates of the Obaku sect, provided Sorai with instruction in Chinese during his service. Later in life he used these earlier connections to extend his circle of Chinese friends and acquaintances to continue his Chinese studies.[34]

Yanagisawa Yoshiyasu had been a follower of Zen Buddhism from early in his life,[35] but his particular interest in the Obaku branch of Zen, with many Chinese refugee monks in its ranks, also had much to do with the shogun's interest in China and its language. Both Japanese and Chinese prelates of that sect were invited and requested to lecture before the shogun. Yoshiyasu himself attempted to master the Chinese language, and, the record notes, on occasions when lectures were presented in Chinese, he was able to understand the contents before a Japanese translation had been supplied.[36] One of these prelates was the Chinese monk Yüeh-feng Tao-chang (1635–1734), known as Eppō Dōshō in Japan, who became the eighth abbot of the Obaku Manpuku temple in Kyoto and received the high imperial distinction of the purple robe in Hōei 3 (1706). He came several times to Edo, was invited to debate in front of the shogun, and was also asked to stay at Rikugien, the Yanagisawa retreat at Komagome, so Yoshiyasu could spend more time with him.[37] In a letter addressed to the abbot after his first meeting with him at the Yanagisawa mansion in Hōei 4 (1707), Sorai expresses in superlatives the overwhelming experience and great privilege it had been for him to meet and converse with a man of such lofty disposition, learning, and station.[38] In a number of other letters to Obaku dignitaries as well, Sorai speaks effusively of how the sound of their speech was music to his ears or how grateful he was for their instruction in the Chinese language. Writing to the priest Kōkoku, he proudly describes how in their use of Chinese many of his fellow scholars at the Yanagisawa mansion "were so exceptional and rare that people applauded and beat the table every time they listened to them."[39]

The presence of such "exceptional and rare" scholars made it possible that on occasion lectures in front of the shogun were given in Chinese. *Tokugawa jikki* sometimes mentions these debates in *tōon*, colloquial Chinese, but often does not, and they are not referred to in the later version of the record of Tsunayoshi's government known as *Jōken'in dono jikki* (The true record of Lord Jōken'in) or *Kenbyō jitsuroku* (The true record of Kenbyō). This record was compiled with the help of scholars of the Yanagisawa mansion from records kept at Edo castle. The final, clean copy was written by Sorai, but a letter of a fellow scholar at the mansion, Hattori Nankaku, claims that the work was composed by Yanagisawa Yoshiyasu with Nankaku's assistance.[40] The manuscript was completed in Shōtoku 4 (1714) but did not please the eighth shogun Yoshimune, and an altered version was produced shortly after his accession in Kyōhō 2 (1717). This is the facsimile version available in print today.[41]

There was, however, yet another record kept at the Yanagisawa mansion, known as *Rakushidō nenroku* (The chronology of Rakushidō). According to the introduction, after a fire in Genroku 15 (1702) destroyed many documents, Yoshiyasu ordered that a new record of past events be assembled, and a detailed daily account was kept from then on. Here, for instance, we find a verbatim record of a question and answer session Ogyū Sorai carried on with his disciple Kuraoka Sozan (Motoyoshi, 1679–1750) in colloquial Chinese on the occasion of the shogun's visit to the Yanagisawa mansion on 5.2.Hōei 2 (1705). The Chinese pronunciation is carefully noted in *kana*.[42] Sozan, the son of a Nagasaki interpreter, spoke Chinese and was even rumored to be of Chinese parentage.[43] The fact that the debate was held in Chinese appears neither in the description of the event in *Tokugawa jikki*—where the presents distributed are given major weight—nor in the published version of *Kenbyō jitsuroku*.[44] In other words, the commonly used records do not adequately describe the full academic content of the events that took place on the shogun's visit to the Yanagisawa mansion. The fact that these records detail every box of fish and every roll of cloth distributed, presents that were a matter of routine on shogunal visits, further tends to encourage the interpretation that these were social events where scholarship was mere pretense and ornamentation. Yet before judgment is passed on the level of scholarship on these occasions, one needs to reflect on how many members of institutions of higher learning would be able to conduct similar debates in a foreign language today.

Olof Lidin suggests that the early program of Sorai's own Ken'en School was merely "an extension and continuation of the studies which were pursued in the Yanagisawa mansion." The Chinese debates in front of the shogun, in turn, prepared the ground for Sorai's Chinese conversation group, the Ken'en Tōwa.[45]

Moreover, the foundation of Sorai's School of Ancient Learning, with its claim that the interpretations of the Chinese classics by the scholars of Sung China were incorrect, was a thorough knowledge of Chinese. This Sorai acquired in the course of duty at the Yanagisawa mansion. The main purpose of the scholars' employment was to shine with their knowledge of the Chinese classics in front of the shogun and the dignitaries who accompanied him. Hence Sorai had to immerse himself deeply in probing their meaning. The scholar Hiraishi Naoaki points out that there is nothing novel in Sorai's discussion, held at the Yanagisawa mansion in Hōei 2 (1705), of the definition of the Mean in the so-called Doctrine of the Mean.[46] Yet it is not difficult to see how frequent discourse on this topic for well over a decade would eventually lead to the more sophisticated explanations of this term offered in *Bendō* (Distinguishing the Way). Only an intense occupation with the meaning and usage of Confucian terminology could eventually lead to the confidence of suggesting—as Sorai does in this work—that not only the Japanese philosopher Itō Jinsai, but also the luminaries of Sung China had misinterpreted this important concept.[47] Sorai might well not have found the leisure to devote himself to such studies had they not been part of his duties at the Yanagisawa mansion.

Sorai's claim of superior knowledge also extended to the composition of Chinese poetry, where he criticized the Sung poets as having "gone astray with too much didacticism" and lack of lyricism.[48] Here too he had honed his skills in frequent poetry sessions with the "exceptional and rare" Chinese speakers at the Yanagisawa mansion, where on occasion the famous *waka* poet Kitamura Kigin was also present, since he had accepted Yanagisawa Yoshiyasu as his disciple.[49] The Sōdō Shōshū, the poetry group of the "Grassy Pavillion" Sorai set up later, is again in many ways the continuation of a genteel habit he had learned to appreciate during his employment at the mansion.

Sorai complained that his service "in official robes" exhausted him physically, yet he never voiced any criticism about the scholarship he encountered on such occasions. Although his own scholarship would eventually exceed that of the men he had met at the Yanagisawa mansion, there can be no doubt that the foundations were laid at that time. The question consequently arises whether Sorai's political theories similarly owe a debt to these years of his apprenticeship.

Sorai's Political Thought

In his survey of Ogyū Sorai's political philosophy, Maruyama Masao points out that the judgments of the peasant Dōnyu and of the Forty-Seven Loyal Samurai reveal "the unique character of Sorai's thought," foreshadowing "the primacy of the political that runs like a *leitmotif* through Sorai's later thought." Maruyama goes on to explain that, for Sorai, Confucianism does not consist of abstract speculations about heaven. The "Way of the Sages" is simply "the way to govern the land."[50]

This utilitarian approach to religion and philosophy was fundamental to Tsunayoshi's weltanschauung, and it has been argued above that both of Sorai's famous judgments were no more than the correct application of the established policies of Tsunayoshi's government. Both cases hinge on the concept that the characteristically violent samurai behavior of the Warring States period required change so that not the sword but *jinsei*, compassionate government, would reign.

The Need for Change

Sorai expressed this idea clearly in *Tōmonsho*, his replies to questions of two young domain officials, a work known in English as *Master Sorai's Responsals*.[51] During the Warring States period, he states, the literary virtues were abandoned and the country was ruled solely by military means. Yet even when the fighting stopped, these methods did not change. "Officials were allotted the same duties as in wartime, and the government did not revise wartime laws. Military force was used to subdue." Sorai explains that the character *bu*, military, came to be misunderstood in Japanese as meaning simply pacifying revolts. However, its true meaning is "to pacify revolts by letting the kind of compassion reign that brings contentment to the people and peace to the country."[52]

At the end of the original version of *Kenbyō jitsuroku*, the motivation for Tsunayoshi's policies is explained in much the same terms: "The traditions of the Warring States period became the way of the samurai and senior officials. Brutality was permitted and considered to be *bu* (military [virtue]). Spirited behavior was considered righteous, and there was much conduct lacking benevolence, violating the principles of humanity."[53]

Similarities between the characteristics of Tsunayoshi's government as summarized at the end of the original version of *Kenbyō jitsuroku* and Sorai's political thought can also be noted in other respects. Thus the scholar Haraishi Naoaki has pointed out the resemblance between the terms in which Tsunayoshi's respect for the imperial institution is described here and Sorai's thoughts on these topics in his mature works.[54]

One could argue that the similarities between *Kenbyō jitsuroku* and Sorai's later work were due to the fact that they were written by the same hand and that they were no more than Sorai's first expression of principles that later became fundamental to his political thought. Yet Sorai was responsible only for the "fair copy" *(seisho)* of this document. This might include style and expression but not the underlying principles expressed. Moreover, on account of its importance, the document, if not composed by Yanagisawa Yoshiyasu, at least would have been subject to his close perusal, and Yoshiyasu would not have tolerated any characterization of the fifth shogun's government that was not in line with actualities. One might well explain the similarities by crediting Sorai with the theoretical formulation of the political principles underlying

Tsunayoshi's policies. Yet this explanation documents that Sorai considered these principles to be in accord with his own thinking, principles to be developed and elaborated in his later works.

Jinsei, Compassionate Government

For Sorai, the key to peacetime policies is *jinsei,* compassionate or benevolent government. He emphasizes this term in the first letter of *Tōmonsho,* explaining its meaning in some detail. The term *jin,* humanity, is generally glossed as compassion *(jihi),* but for Sorai the best definition is "the father and mother of the people."[55] These explanations are also reiterated at some length in his work *Taiheisaku.*

In Tsunayoshi's policies the term *jinsei* finds frequent mention, but in view of his laws heavily punishing people for mistreating animals, such utterances are generally considered empty protestations. As if to forestall such argument, Sorai continues his discussion in *Taiheisaku* with the role of punishment within the framework of benevolent government. Punishment was not inflicted out of hatred for the criminal but because the criminal's conduct inflicted great damage on the customs of the people. He maintained that punishment meted out to bring peace to the people was benevolent government and even asserted that such benevolence always entailed killing people.

Tsunayoshi had from the beginning of his government instructed his officials to judge cases not merely on the basis of right or wrong but so that the behavior of the people would be improved.[56] This was also the aim of his Laws of Compassion. Tsunayoshi had inherited a society where brutality was sanctioned as military virtue. For the value system to be changed rapidly required the legal enforcement of nonviolent behavior. Yet on account of the high level of tolerance for arbitrary, personal violence, legal enforcement was possible only when backed by the accustomed forms of heavy punishment. This led to the paradox of new norms of nonviolence being enforced by traditionally violent forms of punishment. In terms of the social conditions existing in seventeenth-century Japan, the heavy punishments of the Laws of Compassion were well within the orbit of measures Sorai considered necessary and benevolent for "bringing peace to the people." As if referring to these laws, he concludes his discussion stating: "The ruler of the people must carry out all measures, even if they conflict with just principles and become the object of ridicule, so long as this brings peace to the people."[57]

It would be difficult to find a better example of laws conflicting "with just principles" and becoming "the object of ridicule" than those that inflicted heavy punishment for harming dogs. Sorai was well aware of the contradictions inherent in the policy he advocated, contradictions for which the fifth shogun was severely criticized. In *Bendō* Sorai justifies such apparent contradictions as follows: "The government prohibits violence but uses military law to execute people. Can this be called benevolence? The essential fact is, however, that it brings peace to the world."[58]

Political expediency cannot exist side by side with the lofty and pure ideals of absolute morality. As Tsunayoshi put it well over thirty years before Sorai expressed his ideas in writing, "in the purest water, fish cannot exist."[59] For both Tsunayoshi and Sorai, the government's priority was the well-being of the people. The concerns of the individual were of secondary importance. The ruler and his ministers as well as individual members of society at times had to sacrifice their personal morality, honor, and reputation for the common good. This was not only the principle making possible the laws for the protection of animals but also the one underlying the judgment of the Forty-Seven Loyal Samurai. Yet here, as also in the judgment of Dōnyu, Sorai was simply applying the government's existing policy and not introducing novel ideas. These would hardly have been acceptable to a ruler such as Tsunayoshi, whose ideas of good government were firmly established. If we accept Maruyama's assertion that these judgments contain the guiding principle of Sorai's later thought, we must also accept that the political doctrine underlying the government of the fifth shogun provided the guiding principles for Sorai's political philosophy.

The Meaning behind the Words

Sorai's political writings were composed under the government of the eighth shogun Yoshimune. Although Yoshimune recalled many of Tsunayoshi's officials and readopted some of his policies, as will be explained in the final chapter, he also took care not to identify with his much-resented autocratic measures. In the face of these circumstances, Sorai was beset by the problem of how to advocate the political concepts of the fifth shogun without appearing to praise his unpopular government. He resorts to various tactics to deal with this dilemma. For instance, discussing the monetary reform, Sorai does not praise it but condemns the reversal of this policy. Moreover, he expresses beliefs that fully justify the debasement of the coinage. He maintains, for instance, that the value of metal contained in the coinage is completely irrelevant to its value and questions why tax is levied from farmers only and not from the rest of the community.[60] It has been argued earlier that the debasement of the coinage under Tsunayoshi was akin to a flat tax on cash assets throughout the country. It thus answered Sorai's request for a broader base for taxation, as did also the tax on various goods known as *unjōkin*, introduced on a countrywide basis by Tsunayoshi's government. Both the debasement of the coinage and the monetary reform would eventually be used in Yoshimune's government to ease the *bakufu*'s financial problems.

While it would have been politically unwise to praise the recent government of the fifth shogun, such restraint did not exist when it came to the actions of the deified first shogun, Ieyasu. Sorai, however, employs a literary device that must raise doubts in the mind of the reader about whether he was indeed referring to Ieyasu. Before recording any praise, he invariably first cites criticism, somewhat inappropriate when referring to a man who had joined the ranks of the gods. Thus Sorai rejects those censuring Ieyasu for permitting Ōkubo Nagayasu, a man of exceptional ability, to carry out his policies, all the while ignoring his misdeeds:

> Uninformed people say that various misdeeds went without punishment because he was one of the shogun's favorites. However, that is not so. He was not punished because, if you do not overlook small mistakes, people are unable to make full use of their talents. That afterwards this man committed a serious crime is a different matter. It is simply that the way people are used and treated by the shogun becomes an example for future generations and is by no means an insignificant matter. The approach used here should become a model for a thousand generations. Among later generations a strong inclination to be small-minded developed, and people had no idea how to do things profitably. This is where Ieyasu's talent differed greatly.[61]

Contemporaries would remember that the situation described here closely resembles the much more recent past, namely, Tsunayoshi's patronage of Ogiwara Shigehide, the low-ranking finance official who conceived and supervised the reminting of the coinage. Like Nagayasu, Shigehide had been in charge of government mines and minting, an area where personal profit could easily be made. Yet particularly in the case of Ogiwara Shigehide, the country's desperate financial problems were solved through his then totally new and untried stratagem of reminting the existing coinage. Thanks to his innovative measures, relief funds were available when shortly afterwards the country was beset by natural catastrophes. The words "later generations"—Sorai's text is ambiguous as to whether "generation" is singular or plural—could well refer to the government of the sixth shogun Ienobu, in which Arai Hakuseki greatly intrigued against Shigehide and, as Ienobu was lying on his deathbed, succeeded in bringing about Shigehide's fall. Interesting is the claim that people of low origin were promoted not because of shogunal favoritism but because of their talents, a topic Sorai also discussed elsewhere with particular reference to the fifth shogun.

The next paragraph in Sorai's text is even more revealing. He starts with an apology for yet again expressing his great admiration for Ieyasu, an apology that would be gratuitous if indeed he was referring to the man officially revered as avatar and divine being. What Sorai considers so praiseworthy about

Ieyasu is that he called even lower officials into his presence and consulted with them about government affairs, conduct that is well attested to for Tsunayoshi. Ieyasu is further praised for according people of lower rank the honor of being served sake as well as for his wide-ranging interests even in small matters, down to rocks from the garden. Elsewhere Sorai had eulogized that even he, a mere lowly *baishin* retainer, was honored with just such conduct on the part of the fifth shogun. That the fifth shogun was a man of wide-ranging curiosity is well documented by, for instance, his unprecedented request to inspect the Dutch delegation at close range at a second, informal audience. On these occasions the utensils of the Dutch, such as watches and pens, had to be handed behind the shogunal screen for careful inspection by Tsunayoshi. The shogun's own environment received his close attention as well. Examples for this range from his inviting festival parades into the castle grounds to his inspecting the castle's moat in person. Sorai further speaks admiringly of Ieyasu's impromptu conduct, contrary to all conventions, calling on even the lower orders on the spur of the moment. Similar conduct is related by the Dutch, who encountered Tsunayoshi on two occasions in just this impromptu fashion before he became shogun.

Sorai follows this passage with another citing malicious gossip about Ieyasu only to, yet again, justify his conduct: "There are some people who judge him with their glib tongues, saying, 'Since he came to rule the country from a humble position, he was not conversant with shogunal etiquette,' but I reverently feel that it was merely an expression of his great genius."[62]

By this time the deified Ieyasu had been credited with an illustrious ancestry, and if Sorai had merely wished to make the point that Ieyasu's example should be followed, citing the criticism of "glib tongues" was surely unnecessary and indeed irreverent. Ieyasu needed no justification. But Tsunayoshi did. Sorai's reference to a humble position *(go shōmi)* that resulted in lack of knowledge of shogunal etiquette could well refer to the fact that Tsunayoshi was born as only the fourth son of Iemitsu and not trained to succeed as ruler. But it might also refer to the lowly origins of his mother.

In Sorai's *Shinruigaki yuishogaki* reference to Tsunayoshi's mother Keishō-in is followed by an explanation of her origin. Yet while in official records she is normally said to have been from the house of Honjō, a family of lower aristocratic standing into which she was adopted, here she is plainly described as the daughter of a greengrocer. While the maternal origin was not accorded much importance in Tokugawa Japan, the prominent role Keishō-in played, however, was a constant reminder that Tsunayoshi had the blood of a greengrocer in his veins. His fraternization with men of lower birth might well have been explained at the time by—and might indeed have been due to—his love and admiration for his mother, who was of this background.

Men of Humble Status

Sorai concludes his discussion by asking how a ruler who only consults high officials can make decisions on matters about which he knows little. How can he decide whom to call into his presence on various matters, he questions, and once again he praises Ieyasu for having been on friendly terms with even men of low *hatamoto* status.[63]

From the very beginning of his government, Tsunayoshi followed the policy of personally consulting officials of lower standing, which was so highly praised by Sorai. While Tsunayoshi is frequently criticized by historians for promoting favorites and homosexual partners, Sorai saw the matter differently. He openly speaks out in defense of Tsunayoshi's employment of people of lower rank. The daimyo did not even have the learning of an ordinary person, he claims. He approves of Tsunayoshi employing his pages *(koshō)*, castle servants or attendants *(konando)*, and even priests *(bōzu)* to assist in the administration and praises their contribution. "All those who were employed in the Shogunal Inner Secretariat were trained and experienced, and today many of them occupy important posts."[64]

Yoshimune's famous suggestion boxes are no replacement for employing talented men. Sorai is explicit: "It is thought that if the people that have been at the top until now were left in their positions and the good suggestions from the lower orders were put into effect, this would be as good as the sages' demand to raise men of talent."[65]

A few paragraphs later, Sorai again cites Tsunayoshi as an example. At the beginning of his government, *hatamoto* with traditional rights to certain offices showed little enthusiasm for their work. Consequently he promoted people such as actors, who did well and advanced to higher offices. Yet Sorai notes: "At the present time, however, the shogunal policy has changed, and there is no point in showing energy or exerting oneself." Nowadays some people think that those who have risen from lowly positions under Tsunayoshi should be stripped of their ranks, but, Sorai argues, "the fact is that lowly commoners are often more talented than nobles."[66]

Sorai repeatedly makes the point that family status should not be a criterion for high office. Instead those who acquired some learning should be promoted. If that were done, "learning would become fashionable."[67] Though he continues with examples from the Heian period, it must have been fairly obvious to the contemporary reader whose example Sorai was praising, since only a few paragraphs later he attributes the desirable situation in which learning has become "fashionable" to Tsunayoshi's government, using the very same expression.[68]

Sorai's ideal government must conform to a detailed set of conditions to which even that of Tsunayoshi did not live up. But he repeatedly makes the point that in essence the fifth shogun's administration met with his approval. Sorai wrote:

> From the time of the shogun before the last two [Tsunayoshi], it was considered proper that people employed in the government attune themselves to their colleagues, make efforts to inquire about precedents, and in every aspect be conscientious. Ostentatious clothes and swords, and even conspicuous hairstyles were disliked, and it was considered proper to attune oneself to what was usual in society and take a moderate stance. Accordingly matters such as rules of etiquette and manners have been largely newly established.[69]

Speaking about the shogun's senior ministers he writes: "Until Genroku [1688-1704] they were all prudent, and their speech and appearance was excellent. From about Shōtoku [1711-1716] onwards this declined, and I have heard that now there are no more dignified people."[70]

Sorai's favorable opinion has been explained away as being based on the fact that the senior minister during the Genroku period was Yanagisawa Yoshiyasu, of whom Sorai was a retainer.[71] But that does not prove that his statements are spurious. *Seidan* was a secret document addressed to the eighth shogun, to be burned after perusal, and there was no need to praise the by now deceased Yoshiyasu.[72] To the contrary: it is much more likely that the author of the document was fearful of expressing praise for the government and people under whom he had achieved a status within government circles that was largely denied to him under the eighth shogun. In view of this fact, scholars' a priori assumption that, since Tsunayoshi's government was widely criticized by posterity, such criticism must also appear in Sorai's writing is not tenable.

If Sorai's works are not read with the preconceived idea that the government of the fifth shogun was corrupt and must therefore be condemned by the scholar, the examples of implicit praise for Tsunayoshi's government become too frequent to enumerate. A constant theme in Sorai's political discourse is the present ruler's lack of involvement in government affairs. Up to Iemitsu's time the shogun would personally consult with even the officers of the guard of Edo castle, Sorai wrote. But since Ietsuna was a minor on becoming shogun, the senior councilors did not think such conduct suitable for him. Hence men of lower station, the *hatamoto*, became separated from the shogun by a gulf of formality. On account of this estrangement between the high and the low, Sorai argues, men no longer put their hearts into their duty.[73] Sorai does not mention here what happened during the ensuing government of the fifth shogun, but it would have been well known that a constant theme of Tsunayoshi's orders was that no distance ought to exist between the high and the low.

Indeed, the extent to which Tsunayoshi attempted to close the gap between high and low at times exceeded Sorai's level of tolerance. Thus when Sorai was first called to the castle to listen to the shogun's lecture on *The Book of Changes*, he appeared in the dress proper for his status as lowly retainer. But when he looked around the hall, he saw that senior councilors and junior councilors, daimyo and *hatamoto*, people in office and out of office, were all dressed exactly like him. "Seeing this was just too much; tears filled my eyes and I was struck dumb," he wrote, describing his distress at the sight of so much unaccustomed equality in *Seidan*. Sorai also expresses dissatisfaction with the fact that, as long as people have the money to do so, even common people can dress like daimyo.[74] Although on other occasions he pleads that the common people not be despised and that there be no discrimination according to status, here, it appears, the fifth shogun had taken the matter of equality and economy too far for Sorai's taste.

Autocratic Government

Unlike historians, Sorai does not criticize Tsunayoshi for his spendthrift habits. He does, however, censure him for depleting the finances of his daimyo. The numerous calls for daimyo contribution to various building projects *(o tetsudai)* had daimyo borrowing money from the merchants of Osaka and Kyoto far beyond their means. The reason they did this regardless of the consequences was because "they were in such fear of the awesome power of the shogun."[75]

Yet the autocratic powers of the shogun were for Sorai an essential prerequisite for good government. "Unless the affairs of the entire land can be dealt with as the shogun wishes, the course of government will from time to time be obstructed," Sorai wrote, a notion Maruyama Masao interprets as an "'equalization' of subjects under a Tokugawa absolutism."[76] Tsunayoshi's autocratic policies did not include all the measures that Sorai favors, such as limiting the size of daimyo fiefs and reducing the status of the samurai by resettling them on the land. Yet Tsunayoshi greatly increased shogunal authority after the weak rule of the fourth shogun and commanded more authority than any of his successors. There can be no question that the underlying political ideals of the shogun and the scholar—the ruler likening himself to the sun in the skies lightening even the farthest corner of the empire—are identical.

Sorai did not totally approve of Tsunayoshi's government, and criticism can be found on a number of issues. But his disapproval is limited to minor points, such as that Tsunayoshi misinterpreted the text of *The Great Learning* on the subject of petitions.[77] Criticism of such details serves to indicate that, with regard to overall issues, he was in agreement. Nowhere do we find as sweeping a condemnation of the government of the fifth shogun as Sorai reserves for the administration of the eighth, when he predicts somberly, "Because those at the top lack learning and are ignorant of the Way of the Sages, the world has rapidly decayed. In the future, power will pass to those at the lower levels of society."[78]

In his basic principles of autocratic government with emphasis on the good of the commoners, on shogunal involvement in the details of government, as well as on the ruler's personal selection of officials regardless of rank, Sorai was in agreement with the government of the fifth shogun. There is no criticism of corruptness, unethical conduct, spendthrift habits, or the like, which historians see as a hallmark of Tsunayoshi's government, especially after the assassination of Hotta Masatoshi. To the contrary, Tsunayoshi went too far in his measures of economy and equality and, in his effort to bestow benevolent government on the people, even permitted them luxuries previously limited to the daimyo. As can be expected of a man whose rise from humble origins to unparalleled fame as a scholar owed much to the ruler's promotion of scholarship, Sorai expresses his praise and admiration for Tsunayoshi openly when the occasion permits or couched in language sufficiently transparent to contemporaries when it does not.

Although Tsunayoshi is criticized by historians for his autocratic behavior, for Sorai he did not go far enough in curbing the authority of the daimyo. It was fortunate for the eighth shogun that he ignored Sorai's suggestions in this respect. Had he dared to follow them, he would, no doubt, have been even more unpopular than the fifth. Since the military who wrote history did not have to suffer Sorai's radical policies, his good name remained unblemished, and he is proudly spoken of as the Japanese Machiavelli.

Sorai and Dazai Shundai

Sorai's great respect for the fifth shogun, however, might paradoxically have been responsible for the most frequently cited work on the evils of his government. It could well have been Sorai's reference to Tsunayoshi in honorifics appropriate for the rulers of China that persuaded one of his disciples, Dazai Shundai, to write *Sannō gaiki,* the "Unofficial Record of the Three Kings." Shundai entered Sorai's school shortly after its establishment on Tsunayoshi's death at the relatively advanced age for a student of thirty-one. The master-disciple relationship was always an uneasy one. Shundai's parody of the ruler under whose government Sorai came to fame was perhaps also a send-up of his teacher, whom Shundai later sought to rival but never quite managed to outshine.

One of the characteristics of Sorai's philosophy is his continual reference to the "Way of the Early Kings," the three legendary sage emperors Yao, Shun, and Yü. His demand that Confucian government must be based on the "Way of the Early Kings" and not on later interpretations of the Confucians classics is also one of the main themes of his work *Bendō*. An important aspect of his criticism of later commentators is the concept of *naisei gaiō*, translated by Lidin as "sageliness within and kingliness without."[79] Sorai explains that later Confucians, influenced by the writings of Lao Tzu and Chuang Tzu, erroneously believed that self-cultivation was of primary importance, mistakenly asserting that as long as the ruler was saintly, government would take care of itself. It is on this point that Sorai criticizes Itō Jinsai for his emphasis on personal development and that Sorai in turn has been criticized by other scholars.[80] Related to this question is the issue of political expediency versus absolute morality, discussed above with reference to the Laws of Compassion. In the final instance this issue also forms the basis of the judgement of the Forty-Seven Loyal Samurai, where again the question of the personal morality of the samurai was judged less important than political concerns.

Sorai's rejection of *naisei gaiō* moreover finds expression in his evaluation of the fifth shogun, justifying reference to him in terms of the Chinese emperors. Under Tsunayoshi's government the country experienced unprecedented wealth, and, though the samurai were treated harshly, there were no large-scale riots, plots, or other popular disturbances. For Sorai this fulfilled the most important duty of government, namely, that of bringing peace to the world. According to Sorai's philosophy, the man who presided over this government correctly followed "the Way of the Early Kings" regardless of the morality of his actions. It is perhaps no coincidence that the title Shundai chose for his send-up not only includes reference to the "three kings" of ancient China *(san ō*, an alternate romanization of *sannō)*, whom Sorai as well as Tsunayoshi considered so important, but also a jumbled version of two of the four characters that make up the term *naisei gaiō*. While the refutation of this concept permitted Sorai to admire Tsunayoshi, with this word play Shundai might well be insinuating in reverse that he was describing the possible conduct of the three rulers if the principle of *naisei gaiō* was totally rejected.

The gods seemed to have smiled upon the country during the greater part of Tsunayoshi's government, making possible the "good life" the Genroku period is famous for. With the close of the century, however, the powers of nature were again unleashed upon the hapless population. Within the space of four years, Edo and the surrounding countryside was hit by Japan's worst earthquake and tsunami to date, followed by an eruption of Mount Fuji, covering large areas with a thick blanket of hot ash, first causing fires and later floods, and destroying large tracts of agricultural land. In line with Ogyū Sorai's observations on the efficiency of Tsunayoshi's administration, the government succeeded in dealing with these unprecedented disasters without famines or riots occurring. Perhaps this achievement under the fifth shogun stood in too stark a contrast with the great famines and riots later in the century for samurai historians to want to dwell on the details of government measures at the time. As a result official historical records are sparse, and these socioeconomically significant events are more or less ignored in most history books, their analysis and description remaining generally the preserve of seismologists.[81]

Yet while the administrational reforms Tsunayoshi had instituted proved their worth in this time of crisis, for the shogun personally these natural catastrophes could not but have been a sign of disapproval from the gods. Gloom spread over the final years of his life, as not only large numbers of his people died in these natural disasters, but also his closest family members and friends passed away, until he too finally fell victim to illness.

17

The Final Years

"To describe the recent earthquake as very, very terrifying would be a silly understatement. It occurred in the early hours around the twentieth day of the eleventh month when it was extremely cold, but one could not remain inside. The feeling of horror was beyond compare. I have heard of such things in the past, but I have never experienced heaven and earth collapsing in this fashion in front of my very eyes. What incomparable misery, I thought in great bewilderment."[1] The genteel world of the aristocratic Machiko seems to be lacking the vocabulary to describe adequately the horrors of the 8.2 magnitude earthquake that hit Edo around 2:00 a.m. on 22.11.Genroku 16 (1703).

Heaven and Earth Collapsing

The scholar Arai Hakuseki found his house "tossing like a small boat in a heavy sea," and, after having his family squat outside on some broken shutters in case the ground below opened up, he rushed to the mansion of his lord, the shogun's nephew, the future Ienobu. Heavy tremors continued and progress was difficult with chasms opening as the earth crumbled, water gushing forth and walls collapsing, the whole nightmare scene wrapped in clouds of dust. The material from houses "fell across the roadway like strips of silk curling in the breeze." Fires were starting here and there, and their light revealed the injured and dying as they were dragged from beneath the rubble. Nevertheless, as dawn broke, Ienobu decided he had to make his way to the castle to inquire after the shogun's safety.[2]

The castle and its fortifications had suffered greatly. Most of the gates and guard stations as well as the stone walls and buildings were badly damaged. The moat embankment had cracks up to two inches wide; major destruction was reported at some thirty-seven places within the castle. There were rumors that the guard unit especially created by Tsunayoshi, the *kirinoma ban*, had been totally wiped out and even that the shogun himself had died. In fact Tsunayoshi had fled to the safety of the shogunal gardens with his entourage.[3]

The devastation in Edo was great, but the news from the provinces was even worse. Odawara castle and town were nearly totally destroyed, first by the quake and then by fire, with few survivors. A tidal wave had swept inland from the southeast and washed away houses and even whole villages along the coast of Awa, Kazusa, and Shimoosa, present-day Chiba, and Izu and Sagami, today's Shizuoka and Kanagawa prefectures respectively. The number of dead seemed impossible to calculate. Documents and memorials erected later in their memory indicate that over 90 percent of the population along the Chiba coastline perished. Even villages 2 kilometers inland were assaulted by repeated waves the size of "a high mountain" moving up rivers. No earthquake approaching this scale had been experienced since Keian 2 (1649), and this one, to all appearance, was twice as strong, the *bakufu*'s daily record noted.[4]

Contemporary perceptions were correct. With an estimated magnitude of 8.2, the earthquake is the strongest recorded in Japanese history. Scientists have discovered many similarities with the Great Kanto Earthquake of 1923 in both strength (magnitude 7.9) and location of the epicenter in Sagami Bay. Yet of the two the Genroku earthquake and the tsunami that followed were in all respects worse.[5] The Dutch first heard of a death toll of 380,000, but when they visited Edo three months later this estimate was revised down to 270,000. The figure, however, excluded the large number of victims residing within the outer walls of Edo and Odawara castles, the numbers of which were kept secret by the government. The contemporary Asahi Shigeaki noted a toll of some 226,000.[6] Curiously, however, this most destructive of all natural disasters in Japanese history rarely finds a mention in school textbooks, reflecting the fact that historians in general have paid little attention to it. Although the earthquake's location is virtually identical with that of 1923, the name Great Kanto Earthquake *(Kantō dai jishin)* is reserved for the latter, in which some 140,000 people died, even though the devastation and death toll of the 1703 predecessor was far greater.

Government Response

At this time of crisis, concentration of authority in the hands of the shogun was an advantage, for it permitted swift action on the part of the government and flexibility of policy to meet the demands of the catastrophe. Even as aftershocks were continuing with great frequency day and night, and the shogun with his entourage was housed in temporary accommodation in the gardens, orders were issued and appointments were made personally by Tsunayoshi with detailed delegation of tasks. Had the first duty of guards and officials previously been to man their posts, they were now instructed that their prime responsibility was to ensure their own safety. Further, they were to fight fires without waiting for instructions, demonstrate initiative beyond the limits of their orders when making their rounds of inspection, and without fear or hesitation seek refuge in the shogunal gardens at times of tremors. Officials whose homes had been damaged heavily were given leave. Prayers were ordered at shrines and temples throughout the realm. Arrangements were made for those whose homes had been destroyed, including the shogun's daughter Tsuruhime, as the mansion of her husband, the Lord of Kii, had suffered heavy damage.[7]

Some of the detailed reports received from the provinces were copied into the house record of the Yanagisawa mansion and are still preserved today. The dead and the material damage are listed for each district, and the expression "total destruction" *(nokorazu tsuie)* appears all too often. In the town of Odawara alone, the earliest reports already spoke of 2,291 dead.[8]

Yet as the *bakufu* was making efforts to assess and contain the damage, worse was to come. Towards the evening of 29.11, fire broke out in the Koishikawa mansion of the Mito house and fanned by strong winds quickly spread across Hongo to Ueno, Asakusa, Yushima, Ochanomizu, Kanda, and then onto Hirokōji, Ryōgokubashi, up to Fukagawa. Machiko recorded that more than one-third of Edo was destroyed; the Dutch in Nagasaki heard that two-thirds of the city lay in ruins. Large temples, such as Yushima Tenjin, Kanda Myōjin, and the shogun's newly erected Confucian hall at Shoheizaka, fell victim to the flames. Even Kaempfer back in his native Lemgo in Germany heard of the earthquake and fire and received the information that over two hundred thousand people had died. But the greatest human tragedy occurred when Ryōgoku bridge collapsed under the weight of fleeing crowds and hundreds died in the water that had reached boiling temperatures with the burning debris.[9]

The economic havoc these events created soon became apparent. In Kyoto trade came to a standstill as merchants refused to sell at the much-reduced prices their goods were now fetching. In Edo, in contrast, food, building material, and labor were impossible to obtain. Edo's water supply system, with its intricate network of wooden pipes bringing fresh water from the surrounding mountains, had been heavily damaged, and the Dutch heard that water was sold at a premium. The government ordered the daimyo to send provisions, building materials, and carpenters to Edo from their domains. Yet since stretches of the Tōkaidō, especially the section between Hakone and Odawara, were heavily damaged and blocked by landslides, travel posed a problem.[10]

With extreme cold and earthquakes even at Nagasaki, and the news that the daimyo in Edo were still camping in "tents of oiled paper" because of continuing aftershocks, the Dutch were reluctant to set out on their annual journey to Edo. They also heard the news that many towns and inns along the route had been destroyed. Yet since permission had officially been granted for the journey, they had little choice.

The delegation reached the Hakone Pass on March 28, 1704, corresponding to 22.2.Genroku 17 in the Japanese calendar. Three months after the event, the damage in the little village was still very much apparent. "Everything was upside down, and most houses had burned down," their record notes. Those structures that had been spared by the flames had collapsed. The inn where the Dutch normally took their midday meal had also totally collapsed, killing the children of the innkeeper. In the village of Hakone alone, four hundred people had died.[11]

The road down the mountains to Odawara was difficult to negotiate. Parts had been destroyed by landslides; elsewhere trees had fallen across. Other sections were blocked by large boulders. Too large and heavy to remove in one piece, workmen were busy splitting them into smaller parts.

At Odawara, where the foreigners normally spent the night, the inn had also been destroyed, and they had to proceed to Ōiso. The locals were living in temporary huts and tents. The government kept the numbers of those that perished within castle walls secret, but it was believed that in the castle of Odawara alone forty thousand men, women, and children had died.[12] Also large parts of the inn at Ōiso had been damaged. Travelling the next day, the Dutch could not take their midday meal at Fujisawa as usual, for that town as well as the previous highway station of Hiratsuka lay in ruins. Lunch was obtained at Totsuka, where only half the houses had collapsed. At Kanagawa, where the foreigners spent the night, the damage was comparatively light, but the town of Hodogaya, which they had passed before reaching Kanagawa, similarly lay in ruins.[13]

"Edo was a pitiful sight. Everywhere one saw areas completely flattened where the houses had collapsed with the earthquake and burned to the ground," the Dutch noted. Their inn was damaged, and even before entering the city, they felt earth tremors. These were to continue with varying strength throughout their two-week stay, with periodic fires causing further destruction. On these occasions their luggage was packed in case flight became necessary. It is perhaps not surprising that under these conditions the visitors felt like neither eating nor sleeping.[14]

The Dutch heard that initially the shogun had refused to have them proceed to the castle, considering it "a great loss of face *(een grote Schande)* for the foreigners to see the castle so badly damaged that in many places it was no more than a heap of rubble," and asked that the presents be delivered to the shogunal representative in Kyoto. However, eventually the shogun relented, since a number of high officials, including the governor of Nagasaki, pleaded that the audience take place as usual. Perhaps they feared that, after the great material loss from the earthquake, they would also have to go without the presents the Dutch customarily delivered after the shogunal audience. Though some of the dignitaries had to excuse themselves from entertaining the foreigners, since their mansions were destroyed, they nevertheless suggested that the interpreters deliver the gifts.

The fortifications of the castle were indeed a sorry sight. The leader of the delegation, the Opperhoofd G. Tant, noted:

We could not proceed along the normal route because the bridges and guard stations at the entrance to the castle had broken and collapsed with the earthquake. Areas farther away along the first moat of the castle were also destroyed so that people in private are saying that only one continuous section of these very big, strong, and heavy walls is still standing. Could be, for very many areas are no more than a heap of rubble, with everything upside down, and many sections have collapsed into the moat.[15]

Crossing over a temporary bridge and proceeding through a gate that had partly fallen down, the Dutch reached the area between the outer and inner moat, where "thousands of workmen" were carrying out repairs. It was here that the important daimyo had their splendid mansions, but now the walls had broken and many houses had collapsed. The Dutch marveled at the strength of an earthquake that could create such havoc of solid walls and great buildings. The main guardhouse within the second moat, where the Dutch were normally entertained until invited to proceed farther, had been entirely destroyed, and the mansion of the lord of Shimabara was used for this purpose instead. Later, after they had crossed the second castle moat also on a temporary bridge, they were shown the place where the great guardhouse had once stood. Now laborers were busy piling up the large stones that had been part of the building and a nearby gate. Here as well much lay in ruin; those structures that had survived the earthquake had large cracks and were tilting, propped up everywhere by supports. Finally the delegation proceeded up the large broad path that led to the shogunal residence, passing through an only recently constructed gate with equally new doors before entering the building.

Under these conditions the ceremonies accompanying the audience were much abbreviated. After the brief presentation of presents to the shogun, there was no time for the Dutch to receive the usual extended congratulations on the successful conclusion of the audience from high officials. Instead the foreigners were told to leave at once, since the shogun wished to visit his mother and had to use the same corridor.[16] Parts of the main building, the *hon maru*, were unusable.

Heavenly Punishment

As the first news of the terrible destruction at Edo castle arrived at Nagasaki, the Dutch heard that people considered this disaster a punishment from Heaven, inflicted upon the shogun and his ministers for reminting and circulating bad coinage.[17] Machiko implies the existence of such rumors when she points out that, since the government was not at fault, these disasters must have come about accidentally. And, she repeats emphatically, since government policy was beyond reproach, "wise people" were saying that things could not get any worse.[18] Apparently there were some people whom Machiko would not term "wise" voicing opinions to the contrary.

There were also rumors that the shogun's astronomer Shibukawa Shunkai (1639–1715) had discovered an unusual constellation of stars and interpreted this as a display of Heaven's displeasure with a person of the highest rank. This was taken to refer to the shogun's mother Keishō-in, who, in accordance with the wishes of the shogun, had been greatly honored with the highest imperial court rank in the previous year. Heaven was said to be angered that a common woman was thus elevated. It was rumored that a particularly large number of Keishō-in's entourage had lost their lives, a further indication of Heaven's anger at her promotion. The *bakufu* quickly took action and made the spreading of rumors punishable.[19]

It is important to note that the gossip and verses ascribed to "the people" are from the diary of samurai and reflect the feelings of this class and not necessarily of the whole population. The commoners, of course, also suffered great loss. Yet reconstruction offered employment and increased wages to the survivors, and many a merchant made his fortune in the wake of such disasters.[20] After the 1855 earthquake, popular prints showed the *namazu*, the giant catfish below the Japanese islands held responsible for the tremors, as the hero of the poor. On one print a construction worker observes: "With your help, Mr. Namazu, we make such a lot of money at present that we don't know how to thank you for it."[21] After the devastation of Edo a century and a half earlier, sentiments were unlikely to have been much different.

With the unprecedented loss of life and destruction, the shogun must, nevertheless, have harbored fears that the gods were displeased with some aspect of his government. As tremors and fires continued, an attempt was made to break the chain of disasters by changing the era name, and in the third month, the year Genroku 17 was renamed Hōei 1.[22]

Perhaps it was the belief that Heaven might be disapproving of the severity of his punishments that he issued pardons and lightened the restrictions for those under house arrest at this time. Attendance at the castle was reduced and some ritual gifts to the shogunate were temporarily abolished as well.[23] The ruler, however, was not persuaded to change his expressions of esteem for his mother or his direct financial impositions upon the military. As a humanitarian gesture he suspended the tax levied for the dog pounds and the recently introduced tax on a variety of goods *(unjōkin)*. Yet the tax on sake, perhaps one of the most resented by the military, was maintained.[24] Of greater consequence for the ranks of the upper military was the continuation of the shogun's policy of requiring the daimyo to assist with construction projects. Coming at the very time when the daimyo were attempting to repair their own mansions, these impositions were a major burden, and no doubt much resented, especially when assistance was ordered for repairs at the temple of the shogun's favorite priest or the reconstruction of the Confucian hall at Yushima.[25] The shogun's reputation of being pious to the point of madness might well reflect the daimyo's vexation at that time.

Yet if such policies are analyzed from the point of view that strong central authority is indispensable for efficient government, they demonstrate anything but madness. According to current beliefs, religion and learning were considered essential for the welfare of the state. Although such requests meant reduced living standards for the daimyo, for the government they were an effective method of widening the gap between its own authority and that of its subjects.

Comparing the *bakufu*'s handling of the devastation of Genroku with that of the Meireki fire, a sharp change in government policy becomes apparent. After the fire of Meireki 3 (1657), large sums of money were distributed to daimyo and *hatamoto*, as well as to Edo citizens, to assist with reconstruction. Reserves of bullion were shipped from the government treasuries at Suruga and Osaka to meet these costs. Help was demanded from the daimyo for the repair of Edo castle on a limited scale, and the reconstruction of the most prominent and expensive building, the castle's keep, was abandoned.[26]

After the Genroku devastation, distribution of funds was limited to few daimyo, such as Ōkubo Tadamasu, who as lord of Odawara castle had suffered a loss far beyond any other daimyo, and the head of the Mito house.[27] The government itself took an active part in repairs, with Ogiwara Shigehide, the architect of the monetary reform, surveying the damage, while lower officials from within the shogunal entourage were given temporary appointments as shogunal repair magistrates *(goshuri no kari bugyō)* to supervise the various projects.[28] Daimyo were required to supply material and labor from their domains for public works.[29] Stringent, detailed sumptuary laws regulated daily living, down to materials used in religious ceremonies; monetary or other valuable presents to officials were made an offense.[30]

Such changes are indicative of the transfer of government authority from a collective of daimyo to an autocratic shogun, and the displeasure and criticism of the military is not surprising. In the wake of such criticism, the *bakufu*'s efficiency in dealing with the unprecedented crisis is given no praise in the record, for that would have entailed praising the shogun's promotion of well-skilled men of lower ranks and sanctioning the burden imposed on the daimyo to assist with reconstruction. Yet there can be no doubt that the *bakufu*'s success in maintaining law and order and preventing the outbreak of famine and disease in Edo, a city of around a million inhabitants and of extreme population density, was a major administrative achievement. Local records describe in gruesome detail how for weeks corpses were washed up on beaches, and they give some indication of, for instance, the sanitary problems that had to be tackled to ensure the health of a population whose nourishment depended to a large extent on the produce of the sea.[31]

Installing a Successor

Had the shogun been concerned that the gods were indicating their anger by inflicting such large-scale devastation upon the country he was attempting to govern as model ruler, then such misgivings must have been strengthened when he came to suffer great personal loss. Just a month after the government attempted to break the chain of disasters by having the era name changed to Hōei, the shogun's only daughter, Tsuruhime, died.[32]

Tsuruhime had been born in Enpō 5 (1677) to Tsunayoshi's concubine Oden, who two years later also gave birth to his son, Tokumatsu. As a child she was suitably betrothed to the heir of the house of Kii, Tsunanori. After the early death of her brother Tokumatsu and in the absence of any more children being born to the shogun, a son from this union had constituted the only hope for a successor. The death of Tsuruhime was therefore not only a personally painful loss of an only child, but also a political defeat. It could well lead people to suspect that Heaven did not want Tsunayoshi's descendants to rule the country.

Approaching his sixtieth year, the shogun decided to adopt and install as successor his nephew, the son of his older brother Tsunashige, the only remaining grandson of the third shogun Iemitsu. Tsunashige's death, it will be remembered, had been shrouded in mystery. Although he was a sickly man, there were rumors that he had committed suicide as a result of a confrontation between his elder brother, the fourth shogun, and the latter's powerful ministers over monetary matters.[33] He had been buried at Dentzū-in, where Ieyasu's mother and other shogunal relatives of lesser rank were laid to rest, but now, with the installment of his son as shogunal successor, he was reburied at Zōjōji.[34] Ienobu, his only son, had been born early in his life, before the official betrothal to a woman of suitably high station. The birth had therefore been kept secret, and the child had been brought up by a retainer. Only in Kanbun 10 (1670), after the death of Tsunashige's aristocratic wife, was the child recognized as his son and successor. As has been pointed out above, the story has similarities with a rumor contained in *Sannō gaiki*, where it is claimed that the shogun had similarly concealed the birth of a son and had him brought up as Yanagisawa Yoshiyasu's son.

Like many episodes in this spurious piece of writing, fact and fiction are cleverly interwoven to project a semblance of truth. Yanagisawa Yoshiyasu was much involved in installing Tsunayoshi's successor but did not install his own son. The person chosen, as the third shogun's only remaining grandson, must have won the approval of the military. Yet the way in which the matter was handled no doubt did not, and *Sannō gaiki*'s version is a clever parody of the shogun's exquisite praise and rewards for Yoshiyasu on this occasion. Yoshiyasu had accomplished the important matter of installing the successor single-handedly, the shogun stated, and in return was to be rewarded with the castle and lands in Kai previously held by Ienobu. These lands had until then been in the possession of the shogunal family, but, the shogun explained, since he considered Yoshiyasu to be like a member of his family, he was bestowing them upon him.[35] The enfeoffment and accompanying statement were an affront to the Three Related Houses, the shogun's real relatives. *Sannō gaiki* criticized and ridiculed the shogun's statement that the upstart chamberlain was like a member of the Tokugawa clan by imaginatively showing what the consequences would be if these words were taken literally.

Contemporaries would have been painfully aware of the difference between the installation of Tsunayoshi as shogunal successor some twenty-four years ago and the process then taking place. Previously it had been the shogunal ministers, the established, most powerful daimyo of the realm, who argued among themselves regarding who was to succeed. Now the shogun consulted no one and, to add insult to injury, told his mother and favorite priest of this important political decision before informing the heads of the Three Related Houses and the daimyo, for whom the choice had serious long-term implications.[36] The total elimination of the traditional powerholders from this process was indicative of the shift in political authority under the government of the fifth shogun.

In contrast, Tsunayoshi's treatment of the Kyoto aristocracy was more generous than that by his predecessors. At the beginning of Hōei 2 (1705), he increased the stipend of the imperial family by 10,000 *koku*.[37] It was no coincidence that the shogun received the imperial title of minister to the right *(udaijin)* and Ienobu that of chief councilor of state *(dainagon)* around that time.[38]

Death's Toll

But hardly had the celebrations of these felicitous events been concluded than death took its toll again. In the fifth month of that year Kii Tsunanori, the husband of the shogun's recently deceased daughter, also passed away.[39]

A month later the poet and scholar of classical literature Kitamura Kigin died. Tsunayoshi had called him to Edo, together with his son Koshun, in Genroku 2 (1689) at the age of sixty-five, when he already had a high scholarly reputation and had a number of works to his name. The shogun established for him an official position as scholar of poetry *(kagakukata)*, and like other scholars and artists in the employ of the *bakufu*, he was ranked with the Buddhist clergy. His initial stipend of 200 *hyō* was in line with that of scholars such as Muro Kyūsō but was raised in the following year. In Genroku 4 (1691) he was given a major increase of 500 *koku* and the Buddhist title of *hōgan*. Kigin was part of the shogun's inner circle of retainers, frequently asked to lecture for him on poetry and literature, and eventually honored with the title of *hōin*. He died at age eighty-one, but he was actively teaching even in his later years, for he had accepted Yanagisawa Yoshiyasu as his student only five years previously, and three years before his death he was still visiting the Yanagisawa mansion.[40]

The ultimate personal loss for the shogun occurred only a week later, when his mother Keishō-in died at age seventy-eight. Her health had given concern for some time. In the autumn of the previous year, she had suddenly suffered from paralysis in her left hand and foot, perhaps an indication of a mild stroke. The shogun had considered the matter serious enough to visit her daily for some five days.[41]

When half a year later Tsunayoshi was informed of his daughter's death in the morning of a scheduled visit to Keishō-in, he was greatly concerned that the sad news would adversely affect her health. After consulting the monk Ryūkō, he decided that he would excuse himself that morning on account of a slight cold and that his mother be told first that her granddaughter was seriously ill to slowly prepare her for the bad news.[42]

The diary of the monk Ryūkō, called upon to pray in times of ill health and to provide solace in times of sadness, gives a rare personal glimpse of the warm relationship between the shogun and his mother. When Tsunayoshi learned that his mother particularly enjoyed having her stomach and back massaged, he personally massaged her on his visits, once for four and a half hours as she lay in bed, while music to relax her was played in the next room.[43] He would often attempt to entertain her by performing scenes from *nō* plays, and when she was well enough, they would play the game of *go* together. He would consult with her doctors and invariably personally serve her food during his visits. Frequently the now seventy-one-year-old Makino Narisada, the man whom Kaempfer described as acting like Tsunayoshi's foster father, visited Keishō-in's chambers at the same time.[44]

Tsunayoshi was in the habit of calling on his mother in the third enceinte of Edo castle about every third day. But from the beginning of the sixth month, when with the onset of the rainy season her health deteriorated, he increased his visits to every second day. Yet Keishō-in did not want her son to see her in the hour of her death, and she died in his absence on the twenty-second of that month surrounded by priests praying for her soul.[45] The shogun was devastated, and according to *Matsukage nikki*, the whole country was gripped with sorrow.[46] Those who had blamed Keishō-in's promotion to the highest court rank for the unprecedented earthquake no doubt thought otherwise. But if they believed that the gods were now appeased, then they were to be proven wrong.

The Eruption of Mount Fuji

The early years of Tsunayoshi's government had been marked by natural disasters. Storms and excessive rainfall caused floods, destroyed the harvest, and led to famine. A strong earthquake in Tenna 3 (1683) toppled stone lanterns at Ieyasu's shrine at Nikkō and caused destruction at the fortifications of Edo castle at some twenty places. But then there had followed relative calm for over a decade, until Genroku 7 (1694), when the country was again plagued by calamities.[47]

Not that Japan had been earthquake free in the interim. During the two years Engelbert Kaempfer lived in Japan (1690–1692), he experienced several "terrible" earthquakes, one of which shook his inn at Edo "with a loud sound" and another that was strong enough to cause the ship's pilot at the roadstead of Nagasaki to fall out of his bed. But for the Japanese such tremors were a common occurrence and given no more attention than Westerners paid to thunderstorms. "There, again, is a whale creeping below the earth: it's of no significance," people would say on such occasions.[48]

An earthquake in Genroku 10 (1697) that caused large-scale damage at Kamakura and also in Edo could not be ignored as being "of no significance."[49] The years that followed saw floods and storms causing failed harvests and famine but no extraordinary tremors.

In Genroku 15 (1702) the scholar Toda Mosui saw ominous white steam rising from Mount Fuji and floating to the east. The thin bands of clouds were also visible at Edo after dark until late into the evening. The same phenomenon could be observed again at the end of the second month, when the white bands of steam were this time floating to the west.[50] Yet in the next year when the Kantō region was devastated by the strongest earthquake recorded in Japanese history, Mount Fuji remained quiet. The epicenter was out at sea in Sagami Bay, and a fireball rising out of the sea sighted from Shinagawa indicated that an underwater eruption may have taken place.[51]

Some four years later, in the morning of 4.10.Hōei 4 (1707), the samurai Asahi Shigeaki at Nagoya noted strange red clouds to the northeast: like a summer sunset, he thought. That evening at dinner, as the first round of sake was being served, there was an enormous roar from the northeast, and the house began shaking. It became impossible to walk, yet his companions somehow fled the scene, for Shigeaki had three further cups of sake by himself before he went to inspect the damage. This was considerable. Since Kanbun 2 (1662) there had been nothing comparable at Owari, and this earthquake had been stronger and longer than the earlier one.[52]

The effect of this seismic activity had been weaker at Edo, but soon news reached the city of the havoc tremors and tidal waves had caused throughout the western part of the country down to Tosa, Bungo, and Nagato.[53] Damage was also reported at Sunpu castle and at Ieyasu's mausoleum on Mount Kuno. The junior councilor Inagaki Tsushima no Kami Shigetomi was immediately dispatched with a team of officials to report on the destruction, and priests were ordered to pray.[54]

Nobody at Edo, however, was aware of signs of worse to come that were appearing at Mount Fuji. On the twenty-first of the tenth month, a large, apparently bottomless hole opened near the base of the mountain. Curious peasants cast down a rope of some 500 meters, but it failed to reach the bottom. Roaring noises could be heard.[55]

A month later, on the morning of 23.11, the daimyo assembled at Edo castle for the usual confirmation and awarding of titles. On this occasion Yanagisawa Yoshiyasu's fourth and fifth sons, born to his aristocratic concubine Machiko, the thirteen-year-old Tsunetaka and the eleven-year-old Tokichika, were, despite their young age, honored with imperial titles.[56]

From early morning on the monk Ryūkō noticed the sliding doors and shoji of his residence rattling, as if shaken by wind, though there was none. He thought it might be an earthquake, but the ground was not shaking. The priest went to the castle in expectation of the scheduled *nō* performances on this felicitous day, but here also doors and shoji were rattling inexplicably. Eventually tremors began to be felt. Shortly after noon, black clouds appeared in the sky, and it became dark as if evening was approaching. The shogun cancelled the theatrical performances and sent the priests to pray instead.

By two in the afternoon it was raining sand, with some 7 centimeters collecting on the roofs of houses. Noise like the roaring of thunder could be heard, and flashes of lightning were seen, followed by gray ash, settling everywhere, like snow. The small pebbles that rained from the sky at that time still show up clearly in archaeological deposits.[57]

There are many contemporaneous reports of these events that signaled the onset of Mount Fuji's greatest recorded eruption, creating the so-called Hōei hump that still disfigures the otherwise perfect cone of the mountain today. Scientists estimate that the eruption resulted in pyroclastic fall deposits of 456 million cubic meters in areas east of Mount Fuji. While the average thickness of ashes is calculated at 76 centimeters, at the eastern foot of the mountain at Mikuriya, areas were buried under a blanket of as much as 3 meters of fallout.[58]

The belching eruptions and rain of ash lasted until the beginning of the twelfth month. When snow finally covered the deposits of ash at Edo on 9.1.Hōei 5 (1708), there was, according to Arai Hakuseki, "no one who was not suffering from a cough."[59] Today we know that breathing pollutants contained in volcanic smoke causes long-term harm to health beyond a cough, a fact historians have so far given little consideration when looking at the historical record.

While the roughly one million people that made up the population of

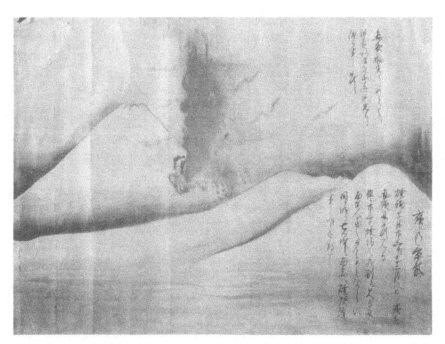

Night view of the 1707 eruption of Mount Fuji. Reproduced courtesy of the owner, Mr. H. Tsuchiya, and the Rekishi Bunka Jōhō Sentaa, Shizuoka Kenritsu Chūō Toshokan, Shizuoka. The painting depicts the eruption as seen from the vicinity of Numazu in Shizuoka. The inscription states that, from the twenty-third day of the eleventh month to the eighth day of the twelfth month, every night red fire was seen like lightning but that it was particularly fierce on the first night, when ash fell on the inn where the painting was made.

Edo, some 100 kilometers distant from Mount Fuji, had to cope with the effect of smoke on their health, they were nevertheless able fairly easily to sweep up the ash that was covering the ground. Areas closer to the mountain were much harder hit. Here houses had been ignited by glowing rocks, and areas were blanketed with ash meters deep. As reports of the disaster reached the shogun, he sent a team of investigators *(kachi metsuke)* to inspect not only the damage in government lands, but also that in daimyo domains.[60] General inspectors and building inspectors were also sent to assess damage to the Kuno shrine and the post stations along the Tōkaidō. Both needed repairs, and daimyo were immediately ordered to assist.[61]

As in the disaster of 1703, relatively low-level *hatamoto* officials advised the shogun on the extent of repair work required and determined the amount of assistance to be requested from the daimyo. The shogun, no doubt, selected the daimyo, but the work itself was, once again, subject to the supervision of men of *hatamoto* status. The authority and status of the daimyo were further compromised by the government's move to survey the damage that had occurred in their domains to determine whether appropriate relief action was being taken to alleviate suffering among the commoners.

Samurai sources contain little material on this subject, but as the documents preserved by farming communities are being researched, tales of unprecedented suffering under the government of the fifth shogun become apparent. Those who suffered were not the commoners, however, but the daimyo and their senior ministers who had to cope with farmers well aware that their protests would have dire consequences for both the lord and his administrators.

He Would Sell His Most Treasured Sword

How commoners took advantage of this government policy, forcing officials to give in to their demands, is illustrated by the negotiations for compensation between the farmers of Ashigara *gun* of the Odawara domain, heavily hit by the eruption, and the officials of their domain lord, the senior councilor Ōkubo Tadamasu (1656–1713). Since this process is generally given no attention in discussions of the government of the fifth shogun, this sample case, well documented by correspondence underlying the negotiations, will be examined in some detail.

The first petition for compensation in the twelfth month of Hōei 4 (1707) is in the name of three villages only. It states that the valleys around Mount Fuji are covered with fallout of up to some four and a half meters, that many people have lost their homes, that the harvest of barley is destroyed, and that food and even drinking water are lacking. The exact day of the petition is unknown, but when by the middle of the month the official Yanagida Kyūzaemon was sent by the domain lord to inspect the damage, it might well have been in response. In this case the villagers had acted soon after the eruptions ended on 8.12, perhaps even before. By 26.12 the request for relief had widened considerably: the official representatives, the *nanushi*, of 104 villages were now joining a petition to the domain lord, which the official Yanagida Kyūzaemon was to take back to Edo on 28.12.

Apparently there was no immediate response from the domain lord, and the farmers were not inclined to tolerate any delay over the New Year celebrations. Only five days later, on 3.1.Hōei 5, the 104 village representatives assembled and decided to march to Edo in protest. On the following day they gathered outside Odawara castle and handed the local domain official a letter announcing their departure for Edo on the morrow and the reasons for such action. Aware that domain finances were in a precarious state with the earthquake four years earlier and failed harvests, the farmers nevertheless insisted that they could not survive without help to remove the ash. Hence they were putting their request to the *bakufu*.[62]

The local domain officials were desperate to stop the march, bargaining for every day of delay. They offered relief food supplies on behalf of the domain, but the farmers insisted that this was not enough; they also needed help to remove the ash. This was urgent: otherwise the planting of the new crop would be delayed. Hence they were going to request relief directly from the Edo authorities. The village representatives could finally be persuaded to wait for a response at Odawara, but the farmers could not. When domain officials woke up on 8.1.Hōei 5, they found that some four to five thousand farmers were setting out for Edo, some having left during the night and already well on their way. Domain officials chased after them and promised immediate relief of five *gō* of rice for every man and two for every woman if the protesters would delay until 10.1. The village representatives thought this was a good offer, but the farmers scoffed at the rather small amount of 0.9 liter of rice for each man and even less for each woman, and with a great amount of noise and clamor continued on their way to Edo. The farmers obviously knew how to strike fear in the hearts of the officials: a noisy disturbance at Edo would invariably result in heavy punishment for the officials who had permitted it to occur. Finally a bargain was struck; it was agreed that only the village representatives would proceed to Edo to plead the case, while the thousands of noisy farmers would return to their homes.[63]

When the delegation of village officials reached Chigasaki village in Takaza *gun* of Sagami province on 9.1, they were met by Takatsuki Kansuke as the daimyo's representative from Edo. Joined by local domain officials, he attempted to persuade the village representatives to return to Odawara. The team of officials brought the message that their lord was fully aware of the difficulties the farmers were facing and felt compassion for them. He had ordered distribution of food, but only when they had returned to Odawara would they be given the details of the domain lord's relief program. To further placate the representatives, they were told that the official Yanagida Kyūzaemon who had conducted the initial survey and unsatisfactory negotiations had not transmitted the lord's messages correctly and was suspended from dealing with the matter.

Yet the village representatives were not so easily cowed into obedience. After some consultation, they replied that, though they would willingly follow the lord's order, they were afraid that, if they returned empty-handed, the farmers would set out on their march to Edo again, causing a great disturbance. If they could not be informed of the relief program on the spot, they would proceed to Edo to listen to the lord's order there. With that pressure, the domain officials conceded relief rice to the amount of 20,000 *hyō*, even though this meant that the lord himself would very much have to curb his lifestyle, for this was all he had in store. On the matter of the removal of the fallout, however, the representatives were assured only of the lord's compassion for the farmers.[64]

The village representatives gratefully accepted the 20,000 *hyō* of relief rice but argued that if they returned without assurances concerning the removal of ash, the farmers would set out again on their noisy protest, and hence they would proceed to the Tōkaidō post station of Fujisawa. It was only when they had reached Fujisawa that another official from Edo, Kanō Gōsuke, finally offered the sum of 270,000 *ryō* for the removal of ash and the proviso that locations needing even greater support could later again petition for help.

Upon receiving this offer, the representatives returned on 10.1.Hōei 5 to Odawara, where during the evening and night all the farmers assembled. By 11.1 they had drawn up a detailed record of the negotiations, specifying the terms of the agreement: the domain lord's offer of 20,000 *hyō* of relief rice, the sum of 270,000 *ryō* for the removal of ash, and assurance that the official Yanagida Kyūzaemon would no longer be handling the matter. This document was addressed to Katatsuki Kansuke and Kanō Gōsuke as representatives of the daimyo at Edo.[65]

The next day, however, the village representatives were summoned and informed by Kanō Gōsuke that they had misunderstood the offer. The sum of 270,000 *ryō* for the removal of ash was simply an estimate and not a promise. Noisy and violent protest by the farmers followed, and the representatives resolved to set out for Edo again. They were finally intercepted at Shinagawa with the most dramatic messages of sympathy and promises from the domain lord. He would sell his most treasured sword, forgo his evening meal, and if need be himself petition the shogun on behalf of the farmers for funds to clear the ash. He swore to all this by his samurai honor and a number of deities. The representatives felt sufficiently reassured by these dramatic pledges to leave Shinagawa on 15.1.Hōei 5 and return to Odawara.[66]

The day after the village representatives had left Shinagawa, the government issued a statement complaining that no progress had been made on removing the heavy fallout in the provinces of Musashi, Sagami, and Suruga. Action by local officials (*jitō*) was urgently needed to clear the land for spring planting. Farmers should be exhorted to remove the ash themselves, but, in areas where this was impossible, help should be given. In the meantime care should be taken to prevent famine. Details were to be obtained from the finance magistrate, Ogiwara Shigehide.[67]

This was open interference in domain administration, all the more significant since the daimyo in whose domain the worst damage had occurred, Ōkubo Tadamasu, held the position of senior councilor. The shogun's right to control the administration of the whole country was even more clearly expressed when in the following month he took the unprecedented step of temporarily placing the worst hit areas directly under *bakufu* control, assigning the three daimyo in question to different areas. The funds to finance the relief action were levied from the whole country, again without distinction between *bakufu* and domain lands. A flat tax of 2 golden *ryō* per 100 *koku* of assessed harvest was to be contributed by landholders. Only the areas hit by the eruption and temple lands were excepted.[68]

The restoration of the areas suffering from the eruption was entrusted to the Kantō magistrate Ina Tadanobu, in whose honor grateful farmers later erected a shrine at which he is still venerated today.

The Kantō Magistrate Ina Tadanobu

The man acclaimed for his great compassion and efficiency in helping the desperate farming population suffering from the fallout of Mount Fuji's worst recorded eruption had performed well under the fifth shogun.

Ina Tadanobu was born as the second son of the Kantō magistrate Ina Tadatsune. He began his career as a member of the *shoin-ban,* the guard unit generally responsible for the safety of the shogun. He must have performed his duties to the satisfaction of the shogun, for he was progressively selected for the *kirinoma* guard, a unit Tsunayoshi had personally established, and the shogun's bodyguard, the *kinju ban.* Later he was promoted to shogunal attendant. In Genroku 10 (1697) he was adopted by his elder brother on his deathbed and thus came to inherit the position of Kantō magistrate. Though Tadanobu's year of birth is not known, his elder brother died in Genroku 10 (1697) at the age of twenty-eight, so he would have been younger than that.[69] With an area of nearly 250,000 *koku* under his supervision, he was by far the most powerful and important of the *bakufu's* regional magistrates.[70]

Tsunayoshi obviously had great faith in the young man, for after his appointment as Kantō magistrate he was soon assigned important tasks in the *bakufu's* public works program. Barely three months after taking up his duties, he was put in charge of building a bridge over the Fukakawa river, high enough for boats to pass underneath.[71] The bridge, known as Eidai Bashi, was completed in only four months, and Tadanobu was duly rewarded by the shogun.[72]

As Kantō magistrate, Tadanobu had wide powers, including the assignment of land for public projects and samurai residences. In this capacity he worked closely with the later much-maligned Ogiwara Shigehide, who had been appointed finance magistrate at about the same time Tadanobu had inherited his powerful position. The two men also cooperated in major public works projects to prevent flooding of the rivers that drain into present-day Tokyo Bay.[73]

Cooperation between Ina Tadanobu and Ogiwara Shigehide was also at the basis of the government's program to restore the areas hit by the eruption of Mount Fuji. While Tadanobu toured the stricken areas to determine what needed to be done, Shigehide was active at the center of government. The order of 16.1.Hōei 5 expressing dissatisfaction with the domain's handling of the emergency mentioned above as well as later orders confirm that Shigehide was charged with handling the matter. The strategy of imposing a levy upon the whole country to finance the restoration similarly bears his imprint. Shigehide was also responsible for collecting the levy, which he did with detailed instructions, down to specifying dates of payment and even the labeling of the boxes in which the money was to be presented. All landholders, including the most powerful daimyo, were subject to his bidding.[74]

The task of restoring the mountainous area with its intricate rivers system draining into Sagami Bay was not an easy one. Ash removed from one area was washed down into valleys and streams by rain, causing riverbeds to be clogged repeatedly, dikes to break, and floods to occur. Only in Kyōhō 1 (1716) were the first areas ready to be handed back to the domains, and it took over another two decades before all the land was returned as agriculturally viable.[75] Both Ina Tadanobu and Ogiwara Shigehide were by then long dead. They passed away under somewhat mysterious circumstances some six months apart, three years after the death of the fifth shogun.

Shigehide's financial management has come under strong attack in the writings of Arai Hakuseki, who, after the death of the fifth shogun, acted as scholarly adviser to the sixth shogun's grand chamberlain Manabe Akifusa. Falling out of favor a decade later on the succession of the eighth shogun Yoshimune, Hakuseki lived nearly another decade to reminisce and record his involvement in government affairs. This he did at length, making him perhaps the single most cited source on the period.[76] It must not be forgotten, however, that Hakuseki's writings present only one side of the story; they are recollections and opinions of a man vehemently opposed to the policies of the fifth shogun and the officials who executed them, especially Ogiwara Shigehide. That Ienobu was loath to dismiss the ingenious financier and efficient administrator is evident from the duties Shigehide continued to be charged with and the rewards he received under the sixth shogun, comprising an increase in salary of 500 *koku*.

Shigehide's duties included taking charge of the large Korean delegation congratulating Ienobu on his succession. This was an important matter of foreign diplomacy, an area where Hakuseki as Confucian scholar felt he ought to be heard. Yet, however much Hakuseki tries to assert in his memoirs that his instructions were instrumental in arranging the visit of the envoys, there can be little doubt that the orders of the *bakufu*'s magistrate of finance carried much greater weight, a matter of further resentment on Hakuseki's part. In the seventh month of Shōtoku 1 (1711), Shigehide was promoted to sit on the supreme court *(hyōjōsho)* and was rewarded with ceremonial garments by the sixth shogun. The ceremonial first shogunal audience of Shigehide's thirteen-year-old younger son in the twelfth month of that year also indicates that he still was in favor with the ruler. Only when Ienobu lay on his deathbed in the ninth month of Shōtoku 2 (1712) did Hakuseki succeed in bringing about Ogiwara Shigehide's fall.[77] A contributing factor may have been that in the second month of that year Ina Tadanobu had suddenly died, it is not clear why and how. Only some two months previously, Tadanobu had been received by the sixth shogun together with fifteen of his intendants to be praised for his successful handling of the Korean delegation.

Although both Ogiwara Shigehide and Ina Tadanobu remained in office after the death of Tsunayoshi, there are indications that within one month *bakufu* financing for the areas hit by the eruption of Mount Fuji had been stalled. One complaint states that food rations had been supplied only from the third month of Hōei 5 (1708) to the second month of Hōei 6 (1709) and that afterwards there had only been sporadic supplies. Villagers were forced to leave their homes and hire themselves out as day laborers or were reduced to begging, with only the very old, the sick, and children remaining in the villages.[78] Ina Tadanobu and Ogiwara Shigehide were still involved in the restoration, for the record shows that on a number of occasions both were rewarded by the sixth shogun for successfully completing river dredging and other restorative work.[79] Tadanobu's personal involvement is apparent, as he took village delegates to Ogiwara Shigehide's mansion at Edo to discuss with him personally the financial aid necessary.[80] Finally, however, Tadanobu apparently did not think that the help forthcoming from the government was sufficient for the people in his charge. Local tradition has it that in the end, when there was the threat of widespread famine, he opened government rice stores at Konyamachi in Sunpu and distributed 13,000 *koku* of rice to the starving masses without *bakufu* authorization. This earned him the gratitude of the local farming population, but it is said that he was removed from office in punishment and committed *seppuku*.[81] The fact that the shrine honoring his memory was only erected in Keiō 3 (1867), when the fall of the Tokugawa *bakufu* was imminent, may be an indication that Tadanobu had fallen out of grace with the regime.

Bakufu records are silent on this matter. They are also surprisingly silent about the successful restoration of the area without any major uprisings or famine. The *bakufu*'s administrative achievement at that time stands in stark contrast to the events accompanying the eruption of Mount Asama seventy-six years later. In the latter case the *bakufu* acted only after desperate farmers rioted and caused large-scale destruction *(uchi kowashi)*. Even though petitioned to do so, the government refused to take charge of the stricken areas.[82] In contrast, Tsunayoshi placed the devastated lands under direct government control; even before this move he had kept a close watch on the actions of domain officials. The knowledge that the government would punish officials who permitted riots to occur gave the farming population unprecedented bargaining power. With this power having reached the degree that the senior councilor Ōkubo Tadamasu promised to sell his most treasured sword to appease his farmers, it is not surprising that such humiliating circumstances have no place in samurai records.

It might well have been for the same reason that no record has been preserved of the government's successful relief program following the eruption of Mount Fuji. Though apparently not continued as originally planned after the death of the fifth shogun, the program was administered during the early, most crucial period by officials who lived up to Tsunayoshi's conviction that the population had a right to be supported by the state in time of crisis.

It is only natural that this policy, endowing commoners with a new importance, was violently opposed by most of the samurai population. A man such as Arai Hakuseki, who proudly related in his memoirs how he would have cut down an old couple to escape detention and fight for his honor, could not but be horrified at the spectacle of the senior councilor Ōkubo making promises to the villagers that they then recorded. Hakuseki's opposition to Ogiwara Shigehide, the official who enacted the shogun's injurious policies, can well be understood. More difficult to understand, however, is why historians' presentation of the events today remains in line with Hakuseki's criticism of Shigehide. Thus it is suggested that either Shigehide or the *bakufu* embezzled most of the 488,770 *ryō* collected for the relief program, since the extant records of payment to villagers add up only to some 60,000 *ryō*.[83] Yet even Hakuseki's figure for the amount spent by the government on relief within the first year adds up to 160,000 *ryō*, making it obvious that extant records of expenditure are not complete.[84] Moreover, since removal of the extraordinarily heavy fallout was not a matter to be accomplished in a year, it was only to be expected that the total amount had not been spent by the death of the fifth shogun in early Hōei 6 (1709). Surprisingly, the historians who charge Ogiwara Shigehide and the government of the fifth shogun with squandering the relief funds voice no criticism at the sixth shogun spending some 700,000 *ryō* on the building of a new residence. This was equal to the amount spent on rebuilding the imperial palace in Kyoto, with all its various buildings, that had been gutted by fire in the previous year. Even Hakuseki is critical of this extravagance, and his assertion that the construction of Ienobu's residence went ahead owing to Shigehide's encouragement must surely be recognized as an effort to whitewash the reputation of his lord.[85] In other words, a large part of the money collected for the relief program went into the new residence for the sixth shogun, and this might well have been why Ina Tadanobu finally saw no alternative but to feed the starving population by opening up the government's grain stores at Sunpu. In contrast the fifth shogun on his accession moved into the quarters of his predecessor, requesting only a new toilet, but he even offered to fast while the change was being made so as not to incur the expense of building an additional facility.[86]

The efficient response to the eruption of Mount Fuji demonstrates how well the fifth shogun had succeeded in the course of his three-decade government in enacting his political ideal pronounced early in his administration that the ruler was responsible for every one of his subjects, whether samurai or commoner, resident in *bakufu* or daimyo domains. It was a policy approaching the notion of "'equalization' of subjects under a Tokugawa absolutism" that Maruyama Masao detected in Ogyū Sorai's writings.[87] For the samurai it signaled the decline of their authority and standing, in both economic and social terms. It is not surprising, therefore, that when the fifth shogun finally passed away, there was great rejoicing, or at least according to the record furnished by those men proficient in wielding the brush.

The Death of the Shogun

"As the autumn winds turned chilly, an illness called measles appeared in Japan," wrote Machiko in the mansion of the grand chamberlain Yanagisawa Yoshiyasu. Yoshiyasu's eldest son, Yoshisato, fell ill but recovered, as did the youngest son Rokurō. Yoshiyasu himself became unwell and could not attend to his duties. By the twelfth month, however, he had recovered sufficiently to supervise the arrangements for the delivery of a child by one of Ienobu's aristocratic concubines. But just at the time when the baby was expected any day, Ienobu contracted measles; then his wife came down with the same illness. Neither case was serious, but the stream of visitors to their sickbeds threw the castle into confusion and did little to stop the spread of the disease. Finally, before the year had ended, a healthy son was born to Ienobu.[88]

The birth of the child was kept secret for some time to stop the flow of people feeling obliged to call and congratulate on the auspicious event. The monk Ryūkō was secretly told of the birth but took his cue and did not call, congratulating the shogun instead. With some of the high-ranking samurai and priests afflicted by the illness, Ryūkō's daily schedule was a busy one. He visited the sick, joined prayer gatherings with other clerics, and also attended as usual upon the shogun.[89]

There was a rumor that the contagious illness had been brought to Japan and spread by priests from China. It was said that in Nagasaki, their point of arrival, some ten thousand people had already died from measles.[90] It is not unlikely that in Edo, where people's health was already damaged by the noxious fumes from Mount Fuji's eruption just over a year before, the infection was also spread by priests, who like Ryūkō daily were in contact with a large number of people, attending to both the sick and the healthy. The shogun's entourage was no exception. First one of Tsunayoshi's concubines contracted measles and then, on 28.12.Hōei 5 (1708), the shogun came down with a headache and fever. The monks immediately began incantation of the appropriate sutras, praying that the symptoms might not indicate the onset of measles. This seemed to have been efficacious, for on the following day the shogun felt better, even though the fever had not subsided. He was, at any rate, well enough to present the monks with their seasonal presents. The next day, the last of the year, Tsunayoshi was able to receive the congratulations of the most important lords of the country. It was after noon by the time clerics such as Ryūkō were finally received in groups. Yet the strain on the shogun was beginning to show. "The color of his face looked worse than yesterday," the monk noted. The fact that Tsunayoshi still had a headache and soon started to cough made the monk fear that he had indeed caught the infection. The afternoon was spent with incantations to banish the illness.

On New Year's day of Hōei 6 (1709), the shogun felt better but not strong enough to attend the lengthy ceremonies of the day, and they were carried out by his nephew Ienobu. On the following day, too, there was some improvement, giving hope that the sickness had after all been only a simple cold. But on the morning of the third day, the fever had returned, and the news soon circulated that the telltale red spots had finally appeared. On the fourth and fifth days, Ryūkō was not permitted direct contact with the shogun and had to perform his incantations behind closed shoji doors. Yet by the sixth he was again received in audience and observed the shogun's skin covered with measles. But the illness seemed to be passing lightly, and by the ninth day Tsunayoshi was given the traditional hot sake bath *(sakayu)* celebrating recovery. It was therefore completely unexpected when his condition suddenly took a serious turn on the morning of the tenth. Ienobu was immediately alerted at his residence in the western enceinte of the castle, but before he arrived, the shogun had passed away.[91]

Since the illness had appeared to be mild, the news of his sickness had not been made public, and the country was completely unprepared for the shogun's death. At first there was widespread disbelief. Machiko noted in her diary: "As people were not properly informed on what had happened, rumors soon emerged and people were saying: How strange! This is impossible to believe! Some fool is making up such stories to alarm people."[92] Yet nobody had been able to ignore the measles epidemic with its heavy toll. In Owari the cause of the shogun's death was noted by Asahi Shigeaki, who heard not only that he had passed away suddenly the day after the bath marking recovery, but also that he had died "with the knee of a maidservant as his pillow." Shigeaki also claimed to know that the shogun had been inflicted with syphilis early in life and that, for people with this illness, measles were fatal. An irreverent quip on how the shogun's collection of money for the removal of ash had presaged his demise expressed the samurai's resentment of the shogun's financial imposition and their lack of grief on his death.[93] *Sannō gaiki*'s story of the shogun's murder by his wife to prevent an illegitimate son raised in the Yanagisawa mansion from succeeding as shogun went only one step further in ridiculing the ruler's passing. With the epidemic raging and the nephew officially installed as successor carrying out the shogun's duties during his illness, the suggestion had no credibility. For contemporaries it would have been no more than a witticism lambasting the end of political dominance by the powerful grand chamberlain.

The mood was altogether different in the Yanagisawa household, where there was great bewilderment and sadness at the sudden death of the ruler. Reminiscing, Machiko wrote:

> If I am to put it into words, he bestowed upon us a blessed reign, committing not a single error in the thirty years of his far-reaching government of this country of Japan. Even on mornings of fog and deep snow, he would rise early, and with the people his first concern, he never neglected to see that they suffered neither hunger nor cold. In the dark of the night, he did not sleep either, but untiringly devoting himself to the study of government, he went over volume after volume of the writings of the ancient sages. And all that to care and provide for this country of ours.[94]

18

The Legacy

"The left wing of his mansion contained an iron depository filled with some 300,000 *ryo* of gold coins. But he had a taste for art too. The right wing he called the 'silver room.' Here the lower portions of the panels and sliding doors . . . were decorated with beautiful paintings. And in this wing he assembled pretty women entertainers from Kyoto." Thus described Ihara Saikaku, the popular novelist of the Genroku period, the life of one of his protagonists.[1]

The Genroku Period

The Genroku era (1688–1704), spanning the greater part of the fifth shogun's government, is famous for a popular cultural flowering unmatched in Japanese history. Most of the cultural icons of Japanese tradition, shaping the country's image in the world today, were perfected in this era. The name Genroku conjures up the magnificent screens of Ogata Kōrin, the highly original and strikingly modern pottery of his student Kenzan, and the gorgeously dyed robes of Miyazaki Yūzen, establishing the intricate patterns known as *yūzen some*. It calls to mind lavish kabuki performances entertaining boisterous commoners and colored woodblock prints pioneered by Hishikawa Moronobu (1618–1694) portraying the stars of the stage and the famous beauties of the entertainment quarters. Genroku invokes *ukiyo*, the fleeting world, when for the first time in Japanese history entertainment was affordable by the masses.

The colorful subject of Genroku culture, both popular and elite, has been treated in many volumes and is too complex to do justice here. Brief mention need only be made of three writers, who are credited with the "Genroku Renaissance," for each in turn transformed older elements of Japanese culture into fashionable entertainment for the broad mass of commoners.[2] What is important here is that the popular entertainment they provided for ordinary men and women was based on the written and spoken word. That is, it required a basic level of literary education to be enjoyed. The three men, the novelist Ihara Saikaku, the playwright Chikamatsu Monzaemon, and the haiku poet Matsuo Bashō, were all students of Kitamura Kigin, the poet promoted to an official *bakufu* position by Tsunayoshi.

Most historians attribute the flowering of Genroku culture to the pax Tokugawa, prevailing with only a few localized interruptions from the beginning of the seventeenth century. The absence of wars brought about population increase, commercial development, and hence prosperity. But why did it take some eight decades for this flowering of popular culture to manifest itself? Why did it not occur under the government of the third shogun Iemitsu (1623–1651), when Japan's mines were still producing large quantities of ore, and the ruler could afford extravaganzas such as marching with some 300,000 followers to Kyoto, distributing gold coins to the spectators. The formal establishment under Iemitsu of the system of alternate attendance by the daimyo at Edo (*sankin kōtai*) resulted in an upsurge of road development and brought new commercial opportunities to rural areas through which the elaborate road system passed. Thereafter daimyo regularly had to spend a considerable part of their wealth on travel, providing employment and profit for commoners servicing the processions of up to two thousand people en route. Alternate attendance also meant some 250 daimyo families and retainers were housed at Edo, with families often running three mansions in different locations in and on the outskirts of the city, again providing new sources of income for commoners. Surely, the effects should have been visible at least by the government of the fourth shogun Ietsuna (1651–1680).

In his work *How Societies Change*, Daniel Chirot makes the point that the progress in Europe leading to the Enlightenment was not due to "any inherent superiority among Europeans" but to "a different structure of opportunity." That is, "there was more room for and more reward for independent thinkers, just as there was more leeway for commerce and independent urban life."[3] Independent thought was not welcome in Tokugawa Japan. But analogously I would argue that the Japanese of the Genroku period were not more gifted than those of other ages, but "there was more room and more reward" for education, scholarship, and the arts, as well as commercial opportunity to bring about a cultural flowering. For the first time in Japanese history, there were sufficient monetary rewards for an increasing number of poets, playwrights, and novelists catering not just to the elite but to the great mass of the common populace, to permit them to concentrate solely on their craft and perfect it.

There occurred what has been called the Genroku revolution in publishing, when the number of books available increased rapidly. In Kanbun 10 (1670) the total annual number of volumes printed was 3,826, but by Genroku 5 (1692), just over two decades later, the number had nearly doubled to 7,181. The demand for books was not limited to urban centers. Sales in the countryside indicate that here also there was an increased ability and leisure to read and the money to afford books. More farming families could now spare the labor of their children to send them to local temple schools for some education. It was under the government of the fifth shogun that books were written by farmers and for farmers, such as *Saizōki* (Treasury of sagacity) and the fifteen-volume *Hyakushō denki* (Farmers' record), explaining the intricacies of farming and irrigation. *Nōgyō zensho* (Complete book on farming), incorporating much learning from Chinese sources, was published in Genroku 10 (1697) by Miyazaki Yasusada (1623–1697), a samurai turned farmer. Now even those with a scholarly bent did not consider the subject of agriculture beneath their dignity. There was also the mathematical genius Seki Takakazu (1642–1708), rivaling with his discoveries his British contemporary Newton, and the astrologer Shibukawa Shunkai (Harumi), whose revised calendar was adopted from Jōkyo 2 (1685) and who was raised to the position of government astrologer.[4]

It seems difficult to ignore the fact that these developments coincide with the fifth shogun's policies emphasizing learning and the welfare of the commoners. Scholars question the scholarly nature of debates held by the fifth shogun, but Ogyū Sorai's observation that the demand for learning was increasing as fast as clouds in the sky cannot be ignored. Sources suggest that the shogun's instructions to govern the commoners so that they would not suffer from hunger or cold were no empty words. The increased purchasing power for non-essentials, such as books, appearing suddenly during the Genroku period even in rural areas, suggests that he was successful in raising living standards there.[5]

From Military to Civil Society

While increased prosperity and leisure for the commoners took some eight decades to appear, the change from warrior to civil society inherent in the long Tokugawa peace manifested itself much earlier. Already in the early 1620s the author of *Mikawa monogatari* (Tale of Mikawa) complained that the old-fashioned warrior was being replaced by new glib administrators.[6]

By the fiftieth anniversary of Ieyasu's death, in Kanbun 5 (1665), the *bakufu* acknowledged these changes by proclaiming that the times had come to differ greatly from the period of the Warring States, and hence new policies were required. With peace now reigning for many generations, the military custom of following one's lord into death was to be prohibited and the daimyo's rendering of hostages to the government formally abolished. These changes the *bakufu* considered "a great and excellent accomplishment" *(mottomo ichi dai biji)*. Historians have followed the *bakufu*'s praise of its own policy and refer to "the three excellent accomplishments" *(san dai biji)*, adding the permission for deathbed adoptions to the previous two.[7]

To account for this process in a scholarly fashion, Kurita Mototsugu developed the theory of change from militarism *(budan shugi)* to civil society *(bunji/bunchi shugi)*. For him the essential features of this change were the *bakufu*'s rejection of hostility in favor of friendship and esteem, of oppression in favor of enlightened education, of military force in favor of rites and music, and the rule of might in favor of the rule of right. As the *bakufu* itself had done, he locates the beginnings of this trend under the government of the fourth shogun Ietsuna, when policies such as permission for deathbed adoptions and reduction in the confiscation of domains characterized government policy, showing unprecedented leniency towards the military. He sees this trend continuing under the fifth shogun Tsunayoshi but declares any policy injurious to the military, such as the Laws of Compassion, as aberration caused by the evil personality of the shogun.[8]

The problem with the militarism to civil society theory is that the pace of change is being measured by merely examining the policies the *bakufu* exercised towards the roughly 7 percent of the population that made up the military. It ignores the fact that the development from military to civil society demanded changes increasing the rights of commoners and, in turn, requiring considerable sacrifice from the ruling samurai elite, depriving them of the arbitrary authority over the commoners vested in every single one of their class. Consequently the Laws of Compassion, robbing the samurai of the right to kill instantly, are considered evil and not recognized as a "civilizing" measure.

As is the norm under a totalitarian regime, records of opposition to the government are few. Yet that protest was increasing is evidenced by antigovernment plots and criticism from even a prominent daimyo shortly after the death of the third shogun Iemitsu that could not escape the record.[9] The response by the daimyo exercising shogunal authority on behalf of the young Ietsuna was a hardening of government control. What Kurita terms "civilizing" policies, such as deathbed adoptions, the prohibition of following one's lord into death, and a decrease in the confiscation of domains were, in fact, a strengthening of the established military order. Together with restricting *bakufu* offices to established families, these policies were concessions to the "in group," those in power, designed to prevent and not encourage any change in the status quo.

A further measure in this direction was the enforcement of the Laws for the Examination of Sects in the 1660s, strengthening control over the common populace by providing the government with a complete register of every person. That this was for the purpose of military control rather than devising measures of education or welfare is documented by the conflict between the government's strongman, Sakai Tadakiyo, and Ikeda Mitsumasa.

Hawks and Doves

Even before Tsunayoshi's succession, the political leadership was divided on how to cope with the problems facing the country, into what one might term the hawks and the doves: those who believed that samurai authority could be preserved in the face of changes by increasing military control and those convinced that the samurai's sway over the commoner would have to give way to a benign autocracy Confucian-style, to which all were subject. As with the division into the political right and left, such lines cannot be drawn neatly, with feuds taking place among individuals and factions and personal convictions combining elements of both, as in the case, for instance, of Kumazawa Banzan. Nevertheless, the division between those who resented the passing of the old order, so vividly described in *Hagakure,* and others who considered a change in the function of the samurai essential cannot be ignored.

The latter political orientation meant a destruction of the traditional military way of life and the prerogatives attached to it. Injurious to the ruling elite, such a policy was unlikely to find large-scale samurai support. It was a quirk of fate that the position of fifth shogun went to a man who was not only part commoner by birth, but was also permitted to become closely attached to a woman of this class. As a result Tsunayoshi developed a worldview critical of the chauvinism that dominated the society of his predecessors and was prepared to endorse and work to accelerate the process of change that was so painful for the samurai.

The Yin and Yang of Men and Women

"In the practice of medicine there is a differentiation of treatment according to the Yin and Yang of men and women. There is also a difference in pulse. In the last fifty years, however, men's pulse has become the same as women's. . . . Thus I knew that men's spirit had weakened and that they had become the same as women, and the end of the world had come."[10] Thus wrote the author of *Hagakure,* around the time of Tsunayoshi's death, in response to the changes that were taking place in Japanese society.

In the medieval period the move of political authority to warrior clans had increasingly reduced the status of women within the ruling elite and had come to shape moral ideals. Centuries of warfare had elevated the male to overwhelming importance within the ethos of society; even the ancestral sun goddess Amaterasu came to be worshipped as the male god Tenshō Daijin.[11] Within this belief system, which *Hagakure* attempted to enshrine in words, women were of importance only inasmuch as they produced the male. Except for the firstborn, daughters should be killed on birth, the work advised.[12] As reflected in the praise for the Akō samurai, what counted within this value system was the personal honor of the privileged male, narcissistically redeemed by killing, regardless of the cost to society.

There had been several strong, politically active women within the Tokugawa orbit before this period. There was Yodogimi, the mother of Toyotomi

Hideyori, holding out against the machinations of Ieyasu; as well as her younger sister, apparently much feared by her husband, the second shogun Hidetada; and also Kasuga no Tsubone, the famous nursemaid of the third shogun Iemitsu who is credited with securing his succession as shogun. But in the case of Tsunayoshi, we have for the first time a government that did not simply on occasion cede to the wishes of a woman but that was fundamentally shaped in its policies by elements of female thinking. Tsunayoshi did not simply strive to fulfill his mother's wishes in a material sense. Because he was left in her care, his value system was influenced from the earliest stage by typically female characteristics such as compassion and the need to protect and nurture the weak. Such concepts were the very antithesis of dominance by military strength and "might makes right" that was fundamental to the establishment of the Tokugawa order. Iemitsu's neglect of Tsunayoshi's education had inadvertently permitted his mother to raise a rebel within this male-dominated society. With strong mother-child bonding, Keishō-in and Tsunayoshi created and shared a vision of the ideal ruler who would set right the inequities she as the daughter of a common greengrocer had suffered as a child.

Tsunayoshi found the ideal of the ruler as champion of the oppressed to be confirmed in the Confucian classics. In the world of the ancient Chinese sage rulers Yao and Shun, there were no samurai threatening the life of commoners and no daimyo opposing the ruler's plans. It was an agricultural society, where efficient bureaucrats executed the commands of the benevolent yet autocratic ruler. Tsunayoshi's study of the Chinese classics and ardent patronage of Confucianism must be seen within the framework of achieving the ideal that mother and son had created at an early stage. His fervor was directed towards the utopia of the ideal state, rather than Confucianism itself, a mere tool to achieve his vision. This made possible his equally ardent patronage of Buddhism, the second wheel to balance the cart, as he explained in a letter to Yanagisawa Yoshiyasu. Temple building and maintaining clergy to pray for the state were political actions to achieve his goal within the belief system of the times, when the protection of the gods was viewed as an effective deterrent against adversity. The Laws of Compassion protecting all animate creation fall into a similar category. The Buddhist precept of not taking life was greatly at variance with the practices of Japan's warrior society, and Tsunayoshi's laws did no more than attempt to enforce with this-worldly punishment what priests had always sought to achieve by threatening retribution in the afterlife.

Tsunayoshi saw sanction of his political ideals not only in the Confucian classics and Buddhist teachings, but also in the political events unfolding during his childhood and youth. During this period the imperial Ming government of China was brought to fall, largely because a dissatisfied peasantry denied support to their ruler against the invaders. The prolonged military struggle on the continent, with Chinese scholars seeking refuge in Japan describing eloquently the evils of the Ming's oppression of the commoners, validated Tsunayoshi's policy of according them greater rights.

Under the tutelage of his mother, Tsunayoshi had mapped out for himself an ambitious goal. Presumably it was the combination of two very different genetic streams that gave him the physical energy and mental agility that distinguished him as a child from his brothers and caused his father to fear that these qualities might induce him to challenge their rule. Once he became shogun, these attributes permitted him to devise complex stratagems and policies and, with neither financial reserves nor military force to back his commands, bring about a significant paradigm change to the detriment of the traditional holders of authority.

Minerva Arising from the Head of Jupiter

If one takes the level of domain confiscation as a yardstick, Tsunayoshi was not the most severe of the fifteen Tokugawa rulers. The first three shoguns exceeded him by far in this respect. He was, however, exceptional among the Tokugawa rulers in that he claimed the right to interfere personally in even detailed matters of government. He was, as Kumazawa Banzan criticized, "through ability and intelligence . . . over-scrupulous in conducting investigations" into the workings of his administrators.[13] While Tsunayoshi's claim to this right is exceptional in terms of Japanese premodern history, it is not in terms of that of Europe. There Frederick the Great declared in 1752:

> Just as Newton could not have discovered the Laws of Gravity in joint research with Leibniz and Decartes, it is impossible to establish and successfully execute a political system unless it is the brainchild of a single individual. It must be conceived by the ruler, like Minerva in full armor arising from the head of Jupiter. That is to say, the sovereign must design his own political system and personally supervise its execution. Since his own ideas are more important to him than those of others, he will ensure the success of his stratagems with the necessary fervor, and the self-absorption that binds him to his enterprise will also profit his country.[14]

Well over two hundred years previously, Niccolò Machiavelli had advised the ruler how to obtain the independence in government that Frederick the Great was seeking. He was to choose advisers from among men who were unable to develop their own base of power, and to honor and enrich them. With their newfound position and wealth completely dependent upon the ruler, they would, motivated by self-interest, be totally loyal and oppose any change of regime.[15]

In his *Treasures among Men*, Harold Bolitho suggests that if the Tokugawa had followed such a policy and "kept recruiting their officials from modest backgrounds, rewarded them generously, given them domains in the Kantō, close to the center of Tokugawa influence, and made clear to them that continued tenure of those domains depended upon their participation in Bakufu administrative duties," centralization of government powers would have been likely.[16] One of the exceptions Bolitho lists is Yanagisawa Yoshiyasu. Tsunayoshi to all intents and purposes followed Machiavelli's counsel by recruiting men without powerful family connections, rewarding them highly, and placing them into a position where their subsistence depended upon his favors.

In Europe, especially during the so-called Age of Absolutism, this process in which the ruler attempted to divest himself of the political interference of powerful estate holders occurred so frequently that the sociologist Max Weber saw it as a universal pattern.

Political and Financial Expropriation according to Max Weber

Asserting that political domination is based on control of manpower and material goods, Weber differentiates between the state where the material goods are partly or entirely owned by the individuals who administer them and that where the material goods are owned by the central authority and are administered by agents on its behalf. The former, his *"ständisch" gegliederter Verband* (association based on estate holdings), is not termed feudal but shares many features with the feudal pattern. His *Stände* (estate holders) are defined as private owners of military and other administrative means, functioning only selectively and not permanently in the central administration. The ruler divides his authority with the estate holders, who independently administer parts of his realm. In the second type of state, the ruler uses agents solely dependent on himself to administer material goods totally owned by him. Weber sees this form of political domination as characteristic of states that are patriarchal, patrimonial, and despotic, and also of the modern bureaucratic state.[17]

The process of change is set in motion by the ruler's ambition to function no longer as primus inter pares and his attempt to concentrate authority in his own person. To assist him, he recruits men who for socioeconomic reasons are barred from obtaining authority or wealth on their own account and consequently are prepared to fight with unconditional loyalty for the ruler's aggrandizement, recognizing that it will reflect favorably on their own position. To divest local powerholders and extend government authority over new areas, the development of a sophisticated administrative apparatus becomes essential. The increasingly complex technical knowledge required to operate it necessitates specialized bureaucrats. Since their promotion depends on their monopoly of mastering the intricacies of central government, they will gladly assist in the development of its complexity.

The political process finds its parallel in the centralization of wealth. It is increasingly wrested from the estate holders and administered by professionals subservient to the ruler. Under their expert guidance, personal and ad hoc financial contributions to the ruler are replaced by fixed, nationwide levies. Lack of specialized knowledge prevents the estate holders from maintaining their traditional role in the government of the country and from stemming the tide of political developments that run counter to their interests. Instead their authority is usurped by "professional politicians," new men nurtured by the ruler. Their background varies and may include clergy and literati as well as the impoverished aristocracy and gentry. For Weber these men constitute the ruler's "most important tool in his struggle for power and political expropriation."[18]

In the premodern period Weber sees the above model as applying to patriarchal patrimonialism, where the "father of the people" (*Landesvater*) administers his subjects as benevolent autocrat. He explains:

> Feudalism [in all its forms] is always domination by the few who have military skills. Patriarchal patrimonialism is mass domination by one individual; as a rule it requires officials, whereas feudalism minimizes the demand for these. As far as it does not rely on alien patrimonial troops, it strongly depends upon the subjects' good will, which feudalism can afford to forgo to a large extent. Against the dangerous aspirations of the privileged status groups, patriarchalism plays out the masses who everywhere have been its natural following.[19]

When the policies of the fifth shogun are examined through the prism of Weber's models, it becomes evident that they are not the haphazard stratagems of a crazed individual but follow the rules of a universal paradigm change.

Max Weber's estate holders are the daimyo of Tokugawa Japan. On his accession Tsunayoshi immediately stripped the most powerful, the grand councilor Sakai Tadakiyo, of his authority. Cautiously he replaced him with another estate holder more likely to do his bidding, Hotta Masatoshi, but when the latter was assassinated four years into his government, Tsunayoshi felt confident enough to appoint men of low socioeconomic status. It has been discussed in chapter 9 above how Tsunayoshi demanded a high level of professionalism from his appointees, and a man such as Yanagisawa Yoshiyasu, in the final years supervising the whole of the administration, can well be compared to Weber's "professional politicians." In men such as Ogiwara Shigehide we find the technically skilled bureaucrat, whose expert knowledge permits him to develop policies that increasingly bring the wealth of the estate holders, the daimyo, under the control of the central government. Despite their high rank, lack of knowledge prevents them from challenging these financial policies of the much lower placed administrators (chapter 14). In accordance with Weber's model, the government's wealth is controlled by skilled bureaucrats of lowly status.

Clergy and literati too played a role in the fifth shogun's subordination of the daimyo. When the shogun endowed debates on the Buddhist scriptures and Confucian classics with social value and status by his presence, the daimyo, having to compete with these professionals, were shown up as inferior in learning and debating skills. Whether as administrators or educators, the new men of lowly background also in Tsunayoshi's case become the ruler's "most important tool in his struggle for power and political expropriation."

Tsunayoshi's ideal of the ancient Chinese sage kings Yao and Shun personally governing their people as benign autocrat well fits Weber's model of the *Landesvater* heading the patrimonial state. Again, Weber's finding that the quasi-feudal, decentralized state relies on military strength, while the patrimonial state attempts to forgo conflict by benign administration of the masses, accords with the changes under the fifth shogun. Tsunayoshi has been accused of great cruelty, but when such charges are examined, it becomes evident that this harshness is directed towards the military rather than the commoners. The amount of daimyo attainder and punishment of officials fall into this category. When Kumazawa Banzan accused the shogun of being "inhumane," he referred to his close supervision of samurai administrators and not to any policy towards the commoners.

It is in his perception of this paradigm change under the fifth shogun that Ogyū Sorai distinguished himself. Asserting that it was not the peasant so poor that he had to abandon his mother who was guilty, but the officials who had permitted such abject poverty to occur, he demonstrated his grasp of the shogun's policies that eluded others. The changes the shogun's "inhumane" policies towards officialdom brought about become evident after the eruption of Mount Fuji in 1707. The farmers, aware that officials permitting protest marches were investigated and punished, cleverly use this government policy to press their demands. When the senior councilor Ōkubo Tadamasu finally sees no other avenue but to offer selling his prized sword so that he can accede to the demands of the farmers, then this takes on greater symbolic meaning. The samurai's most prized possession was about to be sacrificed to the demands of the shogun's Realpolitik of providing for the great mass of the population, the commoners.

Weber's model also accounts for the controversial Laws of Compassion. Early in his government Tsunayoshi had startled Hotta Masatoshi with the demand that, as the shogun's minister, he consider himself responsible even for the most wretched street urchins. True to the *Landesvater* ideal, Tsunayoshi devised laws protecting pregnant women from the demand to abort and children from being abandoned or murdered. The protection of animals and particularly dogs was in line with those ideals. The enforcement of the laws was a power struggle for authority over samurai privilege with regard to the administration as well as the observance of the laws. Being punished for killing a dog was abhorrent to the samurai by signifying both the samurai's absolute submission to shogunal authority and the loss of their right to use their swords as they pleased. As with the abolition of hawking, the commoners are likely to have profited, though the records are mostly silent on this matter. Occasionally some evidence comes to light indicating that the local citizens welcomed the government's action, such as a petition that the stray dogs of the area be removed to the pound. When, moreover, a law becomes necessary to forbid jeering at samurai dog catchers, since the latter are now unable to use their swords against those ridiculing them in their new, menial duties, then the emotional pain the laws inflicted upon these men becomes apparent.[20]

Tsunayoshi was without doubt harsh and "inhumane" in his treatment of the samurai. Yet Weber's model indicates that concentration of authority in the hands of the ruler and, in the process, divesting the military of their authority and privileges while improving the government of the commoners was no more than the normal course of a paradigm change. Moreover, Weber asserts that this shift from military to bureaucratic rule is essential for the birth of the modern state. The complex administrative machinery the ruler creates to govern the country without sharing his authority with the traditional estate holders is the same as that required by the modern nation, regardless of the extent of democracy that might exist.

"Whether It Is Better to Be Loved Than Feared, or the Reverse"

Discussing the question of whether it is better to be loved than feared,[21] Machiavelli firmly comes down on the side of the latter. Especially a new prince, he warns, "finds it impossible to avoid a reputation for cruelty because of the abundant dangers inherent in a newly won state."[22]

The first three shoguns had established their power and governed the country by fear. The fourth shogun, who succeeding as child had been unable to install this fear in the hearts of his retainers, had to pay the price of becoming the "*sayō sama*," the Lord So-Be-It, on account of his compliance with the wishes of his ministers. In terms of loyalty to the principles of his ancestors, Tsunayoshi's actions of reestablishing the fear of the hegemon cannot be faulted. Kaempfer's remarks that the daimyo were just waiting in the wings to seize power rings true, considering that Tokugawa rulers chose to live until the very end of the regime behind a maze of high walls and moats, separating them not only from the commoners, but also from the residences of their retainers. The Tokugawa rulers never felt secure enough to permit large avenues providing visual and physical access to their residence, as did the European monarchs. The long avenues flanked by trees, gates, and lanterns at shrines and temples indicate that the visual effect of exalting an object by placing it at the end of a long vista was well understood. Yet at Edo castle the so-called *masugata* gates, forming part of a boxlike structure, did not even reveal the area behind when the doors were open.[23] Kumazawa Banzan's suggestion that Tokugawa rulers, and particularly Tsunayoshi, would do better to be loved than feared lacked practicality. Moreover, Banzan's forced retirement from domain administration on account of protests against his policies indicates that he himself had been unsuccessful in living up to this advice.[24]

The very fact that Kumazawa Banzan dared to put such pointed criticism of the ruler in writing indicates how times had changed since the government of the third shogun. Had Tsunayoshi succeeded his father rather than his older brother, Lord So-Be-It, there would no doubt have been far less criticism. A sharp decrease, rather than an increase, in domain confiscation would then have been apparent, and the promotion of new men to high office would have been nothing new. Harold Bolitho has made the point that other criticism of Tsunayoshi, such as that of his alleged "sexual deviance," was also no more than anger at his promotion of new men at the expense of the old guard who had assumed that the privileges of the previous thirty years were permanent. In other shoguns such faults went unnoticed.[25] Yet while the anger of contemporary daimyo at the loss of their privileges is easy to comprehend, the fact that historians have continued to make the same claims is not.

There is, for instance, no evidence of Tsunayoshi's sexual mores or of sexual conduct of any form beyond that contained in the obviously spurious *Sannō gaiki*. Homosexual tendencies the shogun might well have had; homosexuality was commonly accepted behavior, even eulogized by the novelist Ihara Saikaku. Yet historians' conclusion that it affected the choice of officials and ultimately government standards is not warranted when there is no evidence of such behavior. As a man who detested alcohol and entertained his guests with the sermons of priests and Confucians, Tsunayoshi is an unlikely candidate for sexual revelries. Moreover, reports on the sexual excesses of the daimyo, as found in *Dokai kōshūki*, are unlikely to have been assembled on his orders had he himself considered such practices normal. Although there is evidence of Iemitsu's sexual liaison with his senior ministers and although on his death some three thousand women he had collected in the *oku* of Edo castle had to be resettled, such conduct is generally ignored.[26]

Although precise documents are lacking for the early Tokugawa period, there can similarly be no doubt that Iemitsu's spending habits far outweighed those of his son Tsunayoshi. Yet Iemitsu's large-scale consumption of Tokugawa financial reserves is rarely held responsible for the regime's financial plight, while Tsunayoshi's measures of frugality, as, for instance, contained in the otherwise frequently cited works of Ogyū Sorai, rarely appear in the pages of history books. Tsunayoshi's fondness of *nō* is criticized, while equal devotion to this theatrical art by other shoguns generally remains without censure. Similarly his promotion of Confucianism is often ridiculed even though a scholar personally opposed to Tsunayoshi, Arai Hakuseki, admitted its importance. Again, specialists in the field have recognized that Tsunayoshi's newcomers were no different from the men the first three shoguns used in their government and promoted to daimyo status. Yet Yanagisawa Yoshiyasu is still popularly described as an undeserving upstart, even though his grandfather fought for Tokugawa supremacy at Osaka. In contrast, the sixth shogun's chamberlain Manabe Akifusa, a former *nō* actor, has generally escaped such criticism. This negative image of Tsunayoshi is contained in the sources, but it is the task of historians to give due consideration to their nature.

Paring Away the Unedifying and *Tokugawa jikki*

"Surely you have heard that in antiquity Confucius 'pared away the unedifying' in basing the Ch'un Ch'iu on the records of Lu. And as is also said, the actions of the ruler become a precedent for later ages. Thus, it is incumbent upon those who act as historians to take care. How can it reflect well upon the nation to transmit these events to later ages?" Thus wrote the Confucian scholar and historian Arai Hakuseki about the compilation of history as practiced in his age.[27] With the actions of past rulers becoming "a precedent for later ages," historians shouldered a heavy responsibility. They could not simply compile facts but had to take heed of the consequences. At times paring away the unedifying was not advisable. A case in point is the fifth shogun, where *Tokugawa jikki*, the official history of the *bakufu* written by its Confucian scholars some hundred years after the event, emphatically criticizes his government and warns firmly: "No future ruler must ever look up to and revere him." Modern scholars have consequently concluded that with such negative appraisal even by those who followed the principle of "paring away the unedifying," his government must have been extraordinarily bad.[28]

Since *Tokugawa jikki* is accorded a high degree of reliability and historians' appraisal of the period is based predominantly on its record, any study of the fifth shogun must take into consideration the criticism the compilers voiced about him. The compilation of the greater part of *Tokugawa jikki*, covering the first ten shoguns, is ascribed to the Confucian scholar and *bakufu* official

Narushima Motonao (1778-1862). This first part of the work was supervised by the official head of the government's Confucian academy, Hayashi Jussai (1768-1841). The compilation began in Bunka 6 (1809), and a first version was completed in Tenpō 14 (1843), two years after Jussai's death. In the same year Motonao was disciplined for undefined reasons. The final version was presented to the *bakufu* six years later, in Kaei 2 (1849). The work completed at that time was known as *Gojikki* (Honorable true record), covering the government of the first ten Tokugawa rulers in 447 Japanese volumes *(maki)*. At a later date, the period of the last five shoguns was covered in 68 volumes, bringing the work to a total of 515 Japanese volumes, and it became known as *Tokugawa jikki*.[29]

The greater part of the work is organized as a daily record, collating material from various sources. The convenience for historians of being able to check at a glance what events occurred on a specific day is obvious. This is especially so since the work includes entries from the *bakufu*'s official daily record, known accordingly as *Ryūei hinami ki* or *Edo bakufu nikki*, which is available only in manuscript form, in beautiful yet for most scholars difficult to read cursive writing, and copies are expensive to obtain. Also in this volume references to *Tokugawa jikki* are frequent.

Yet with the convenience offered by *Tokugawa jikki*, it is easy to overlook that the record is shaped by editorial policy not only with regard to what topics needed covering, but also regarding what works and which parts of a certain work should be cited. Thus while *Buya shokudan* is cited extensively on the nature of Tsunayoshi's early education, the fact that this work considers the beginning of the Laws of Compassion to be the abolition of hawking, a sport described as causing great suffering to farmers, finds no mention. Again, this supposedly reliable work cites, without further warning or qualification, the very unreliable *Sannō gaiki* in its claim that the daimyo were so afraid of the fifth shogun that they did not dare to lift their eyes in his presence. The daimyo's fear of the shogun is also documented elsewhere, but that they never looked at him seems unlikely since he performed in *nō* plays and lectured to them. Yet *Tokugawa jikki* does not consistently paint a negative picture of the fifth shogun: it also contains high praise in unexpected places. To understand this work's portrayal of the fifth shogun, some consideration must be given to the editorial policy shaping its composition.

Matsudaira Sadanobu: Pulling the Historical Strings

Tokugawa jikki's composition took place under the unusually long government period of the eleventh shogun Ienari (1773-1841). Ienari's government as thirteen-year-old minor had begun under the stern guidance of Matsudaira Sadanobu (1758-1829), a grandson of the eighth shogun Yoshimune. Sadanobu is well known for wide-sweeping political changes, the so-called Kansei Reforms, that included a revival of Tsunayoshi's Confucian shrine and school at Yushima.

How much this establishment had declined in status is apparent from an event reported to have taken place before Sadanobu entered office. During a government economy drive, the office responsible for public buildings *(sakuji bugyō)* suggested that the useless buildings at Yushima be pulled down. On formulating the petition to the shogun, officials tried to determine their original purpose, wondering whether they were housing a Shinto or Buddhist deity. Finally someone warned that it had something to do with a certain Chinese by the name of Confucius, the author of a lot of books, and destruction of the building might sour relations with China. The story is contained in a work by Sadanobu's associate Matsuura Seizan and might well have been somewhat exaggerated to show off the merits of Sadanobu's reforms.[30] Yet it cannot be denied that Sadanobu's changes at Yushima, placing the establishment directly under government control and renewing its mandate as a place of learning and instruction, were far-reaching. The budget for scholars' salaries was increased, but these were now paid by the *bakufu* and no longer under the control of the Hayashi house. A number of outside scholars were appointed to join the Hayashi school, and when in Kansei 5 (1793) the incumbent head of the Hayashi family died without an heir, the younger son of a daimyo, Matsudaira Kumakura, was installed by Sadanobu as the eighth successor under the name of Hayashi Jussai. In Kansei 9 (1797) the establishment was brought entirely under government control, to become the Shōheizaka Gakumon Jo, the official *bakufu* school that until the end of the Tokugawa period trained and examined government officials. An edict of Kansei 2 (1790), forbidding unorthodox teachings of Confucianism, ensured that a politically correct form of Neo-Confucianism was being taught here.[31] It was in this atmosphere that *Tokugawa jikki* was compiled.

The debt Sadanobu's establishment of Confucianism as a state-sponsored philosophy owed to Tsunayoshi is well reflected in *Tokugawa jikki*. After the daily entries for each government, *Tokugawa jikki* has two sections presenting an overview of the particular shogun's rule. The first provides a summary of the ruler's life based on sources, while in the second the compilers express what appears to be their personal opinions. In the case of the fifth shogun, the second section is so much at variance with the opinions generally cited that I have translated parts at length.

> The lord much respected Confucian learning. From time to time he visited the Confucian temple and performed the ceremonies in person. Again, he personally lectured on the Confucian classics. The daimyo and officials below them were made to listen to his lectures, and therefore at that time

when the various lords went to the shogunal palace they would carry the Confucian classics in their pockets. It is even said that lectures were included in the duties of the guards of the shogun's quarters. Learning came to be valued throughout the country. The old customs of the Warring States period were changed. Even today there is no one who is not profiting from his [Tsunayoshi's] august virtue. Yūtoku-in [Yoshimune] was the lord who revived the Tokugawa house. Moreover he kept many of the laws of that earlier period. He did not neglect all the talented people who had been promoted at that time. Considering that over half of the ordinances and laws of that period have remained, it is obvious that the lord's [Tsunayoshi's] virtue was not of the ordinary kind.[32]

Although seldom referred to in more popular history books, Yoshimune's indebtedness to Tsunayoshi as outlined in this paragraph is also well documented elsewhere. In his work on the Kyōho Reform conducted by Yoshimune, Tsuji Tatsuya devotes a large section to the government of the fifth shogun to show the continuities. As the passage above states, many of the laws were continued, the most famous example being the Regulations for Military Houses (*Buke shohatto*). These ordinances had been rewritten under the fifth shogun but were altered at the instigation of Arai Hakuseki under the sixth shogun. Yoshimune changed the text back to that of Tsunayoshi, and this version was used for the remainder of the Tokugawa period. But not only were Tsunayoshi's policies continued under the eighth shogun; as *Tokugawa jikki* states, many officials trained and promoted during Tsunayoshi's government were also called back to office.

The most prominent was perhaps Yanagisawa Yoshiyasu's assistant and son-in-law, the grand chamberlain Matsudaira Terusada (1666–1747). As Yoshiyasu's duties increased and his health weakened, Terusada took on many of his responsibilities. Being placed in charge of the construction of the Confucian shrine at Yushima in Genroku 3 (1690) demonstrated the shogun's trust in his abilities.[33] Five years later the shogun began visiting his mansion, and by Hōei 2 (1705) Terusada had reached a position where he was permitted to sign all government documents on behalf of Yoshiyasu.[34] He was removed from office on Tsunayoshi's death, and his domain of Takazaki went to Ienobu's chamberlain Manabe Akifusa. But soon after Yoshimune's succession, he was reinstalled with duties and privileges equivalent to a senior councilor, and his domain was returned to him.[35]

When Yoshimune's government is praised for bureaucratic efficiency, it must be kept in mind that new standards were set by Tsunayoshi. Yoshimune, recalling many of those who had served under Tsunayoshi, indicates that this was well recognized at the time. This is also evident from Ogyū Sorai's writings, where the discipline of Tsunayoshi's bureaucracy is praised, and a decline of standards in the ensuing period is criticized.[36] The very fact that Sorai, a man who had won Tsunayoshi's praise as a retainer of the Yanagisawa mansion, was asked for political guidance again demonstrates the esteem in which the administration of the fifth shogun was held by Yoshimune.

The Evil of Tsunayoshi's Government

Tokugawa jikki's high praise of Tsunayoshi, however, is not sustained. "He was too brilliant," the commentary notes. In his later years he increasingly occupied himself with the conjecture of the Buddhists and patronized monks, the work complains, revealing the commentator's anti-Buddhist sentiments as a Confucian scholar. "Finally prohibitions to take life were enforced severely, and it came to the point where people took the place of birds and beasts." The Laws of Compassion, which most historians see as the greatest flaw in Tsunayoshi's government, are criticized with one short sentence. What irked the commentator much more and is given far greater attention is Tsunayoshi's fondness for *nō* and his promotion of *nō* actors. "He promoted such entertainers greatly, inflicting harm on his fellow samurai."

The commentator shared his distaste for *nō* actors with Arai Hakuseki. It is perhaps no coincidence that Matsudaira Sadanobu greatly admired Arai Hakuseki's writings, to the point of petitioning his descendants to donate some of his papers to the *bakufu*.[37] But the question remains, why did Hakuseki and other commentators so much oppose the ruler's fondness for *nō*, a serious and demanding form of art, studied and performed even by the illustrious first shogun Ieyasu. The answer lies in the fact that *nō* actors could not afford to be dilettantes. The texts they were required to study were already archaic at the time, most of them having been written some three hundred years earlier by the famed Zeami and his disciples. Hence *nō* actors were men with a solid literary education. That was the problem. As Ogyū Sorai pointed out, many were more educated and intelligent than the senior councilors. Arai Hakuseki's intense dislike of *nō* is attributed to his rivalry with the erstwhile *nō* actor Manabe Akifusa, who as chamberlain commanded all access to Hakuseki's patron, the sixth shogun Ienobu.[38] As educated men of lowly status, they were well suited not just to display their talents on the stage, but also to act in the role of what Max Weber termed the ruler's "most important tool in his struggle for power and political expropriation."

"Extraordinary rulers are prone to such blunders," the commentator of *Tokugawa jikki* concludes his condemnation of Tsunayoshi's promotion of actors, and then warns sternly: "No future ruler must ever look up to and revere him."[39]

The evaluation of Tsunayoshi's government is an extraordinary mixture of high praise and strong condemnation. Such praise, it must be noted, was not a convention. The fourth shogun Ietsuna, for instance, was described as just a very ordinary man. The commentator seems to be aware of the contradictions in Tsunayoshi's appraisal, for the shogun's faults are explained as "one side of his brilliant talent," and the account ends with apologies that he was simply trying to discuss the merits and failures of this ruler for the instruction of posterity.

The passage well reflects the personal sentiments of Matsudaira Sadanobu and those under his influence. Yet, while in Confucian circles at Yushima orthodoxy reigned under a head appointed by Sadanobu even after Sadanobu's retirement from government, political developments showed signs of reverting to the pre-Sadanobu years.

Sadanobu is well known for reversing the policies of Tanuma Okitsugu (1719–1788), the allegedly corrupt strongman of the tenth shogun Ieharu (1737–1786). Like Tsunayoshi's grand chamberlain Yanagisawa Yoshiyasu, Tanuma Okitsugu is criticized as an upstart, usurping the authority of the shogun and in the process infringing upon the prerogatives of the daimyo. He had risen in rank under Sadanobu's father, the ninth shogun Ieshige (1711–1761), a sickly man with a speech defect who relied in his government on another "upstart," Ōoka Tadamitsu (1709–1760). Harold Bolitho well describes how "a new onslaught on daimyo prerogatives" characterized the governments of the ninth and tenth shoguns, "two most unpromising rulers."[40] The compilers of *Tokugawa jikki* certainly had a low opinion of them, especially of the ninth shogun Ieshige, for whom the unusually short appendix merely dwells on his ill health and love of flowers and gardens.[41]

For Matsudaira Sadanobu the ideal government was that of his grandfather, the eighth shogun Yoshimune, a ruler selected by the daimyo from the collateral Owari branch, after the seventh shogun had died in childhood and there was no candidate in the main Tokugawa line. When he was invited to become the country's ruler as a thirty-two-year-old daimyo, Yoshimune's policies towards his erstwhile equals differed greatly from those of the authoritarian fifth shogun and those of the sixth, who in his brief three-year government still profited from the shogunal authority restored by his uncle. It is not surprising that Yoshimune's administration, though including periods of unprecedented popular unrest and a major famine, has been written up as the ideal government.

In the eyes of Matsudaira Sadanobu, the limited authority the eighth shogun exercised was a virtue, and he strove to restore the conditions of these times. As leader of the administration, he took great pains to govern in consultation with fellow officials and to restore to the daimyo some of the independence they had lost under the two infamous strongmen of the ninth and tenth shoguns. This applied especially to the *bakufu*'s fiscal policy. He attempted to curb expenditure by reducing the size of government and, when funds were needed, sought these only from the merchants and peasants of the land under direct *bakufu* control and not the daimyo. He was against any government impositions upon the daimyo and instead assisted them with government funds. In his distaste for central authority, Sadanobu went so far as to assert that the emperor had appointed the daimyo to govern the people, totally ignoring the position of shogun. Sadanobu resigned from government in Kansei 5 (1793), but the administration of the country continued in this spirit under his associate and disciple Matsudaira Nobuaki.[42]

Yet as the eleventh shogun was reaching manhood, a new shogunal favorite appeared who threatened to upset the government's policy of largesse and laissez-faire towards the daimyo. This was Mizuno Tadaakira (Tadanari, 1762–1834), eleven years the shogun's senior, who, like other much-maligned favorites, had served him as page from childhood on. Through adoption Tadaakira had been raised to the position of daimyo, but his priorities clearly differed from other men of this status. On the illness and death of Matsudaira Nobuaki in 1817, the shogun appointed Mizuno Tadaakira to Nobuaki's position of senior councilor, thus inaugurating a new era of government by shogunal favorites. A jingle circulating at the time in wordplay unique to the Japanese language associating the ascendancy of Mizuno Tadaakira with the government of Tanuma Okitsugu and Yanagisawa Yoshiyasu indicates that contemporaries had not forgotten the government of the fifth shogun.[43]

Sadanobu's distaste not just for upstarts but for any politician attempting to centralize authority at the cost of the daimyo is clearly expressed in the section of *Tokugawa jikki* where the fifth shogun's government is summarized on the basis of sources and concrete political events.

After the statement that there had never been a ruler in Japan or abroad who used rewards and punishment to the same extent in governing the country, the reader is unexpectedly treated to a survey of Japanese history from the time of the Heian emperor Montoku (ruled 850–858).[44] Montoku was the father of Emperor Seiwa, and Ieyasu claimed descent from the Seiwa-Genji line of the imperial house. Thus *Tokugawa jikki*'s summary of Ieyasu's government starts with this ruler. So does also Arai Hakuseki's historical work *Tokushi yoron* (Arguments beyond reading history), indicating that it was an accepted reference point for the origins of the Tokugawa line. Yet, except for Ieyasu, in whose case the claim of descent from the imperial line required such explanation, the compilers of the events under the first ten shoguns appended no such historical survey to the accounts. Why change the format in the case of Tsunayoshi?

It appears the compilers had discovered enough similarities between these earlier events and the government of the fifth shogun to make the political lesson they were about to teach more poignant. Emperor Montoku passed over three elder sons to appoint the fourth by a daughter of Fujiwara no Yoshifusa as crown prince, the future Emperor Seiwa. This permitted the outsider Yoshifusa to usurp the authority of the ruler, and with this, as Hakuseki also claimed, began the decline of good government.[45] While in Ieyasu's biography the transfer of authority to the Fujiwara is dealt with in one brief sentence, quickly passing on to the twelfth-century emperor Toba, in Tsunayoshi's account the point is labored. Several additional sentences elaborate how all affairs were dealt with by the Fujiwara, while Emperor Seiwa, cloistered in the far end of his palace, did nothing whatsoever. Clearly this passage served to remind the reader that Tsunayoshi too was merely the fourth son and suggested that under his government as well affairs were taking a turn for the worse owing to the evil presence of a mother from outside ruling circles. But there is also a second theme. This becomes abundantly clear when the historical account prefacing the write-up of Tsunayoshi's government finally arrives at the time of the fourth shogun Ietsuna. Tsunayoshi is praised for removing the fourth shogun's strongman Sakai Tadakiyo, of whom it was said that "both the high and the low stood in awe of the dust of his carriage." This is a surprise, for Tadakiyo was of impeccable daimyo provenance. The author apparently wants to warn against outsiders usurping the power of the legitimate ruler to wield power at the center, whatever their status.

But, having praised the fifth shogun's political acumen and talents for promptly eliminating Sakai Tadakiyo, the coin is quickly reversed. Tsunayoshi is not to be admired, for he also brought about the fall of illustrious houses such as that of Matsudaira Mitsunaga. With strict application of the law, many domains were confiscated or reduced. What the author criticizes most is the unprecedented fashion in which Tsunayoshi rewarded certain men either on account of duties performed or because of ties of an earlier period. Some ten low-ranking men came to acquire daimyo status with domains of over 10,000 *koku*. People of even lower status were given no end of stipends and presents. With this extreme policy of rewards and punishment, he governed the country for thirty years, while the daimyo of the sixty provinces could do nothing but watch. In his later years the shogun, moreover, lost interest in government and left everything to his chamberlain Yanagisawa Yoshiyasu. This made possible the rise of an evil retainer such as Ogiwara Shigehide, who devalued the coinage and made the country suffer under new taxes and other abhorrent policies. To dispel any doubt about the moral to be drawn from the story, the passage ends with the pointed phrase: "Is this not an excellent warning for posterity?"[46] There is no attempt to hide the fact that the account was written as instruction on how to govern the country rather than as historical record.

In this evaluation of Tsunayoshi's government, *Tokugawa jikki* focuses its criticism on issues that for Max Weber are essential elements of the paradigm shift from military and quasi-feudal rule to bureaucratic central rule, changes ultimately required for the birth of the modern state. The establishment's fear of determined, intelligent men of lower social origin exercising political authority in the name of the ruler was not unfounded. With the Meiji Restoration the question of who should administer the country was decided in favor of those *Tokugawa jikki* condemned, men who made their way to the top not on account of their birth, but through dedication and intelligence. True to Weber's model, the country and its wealth came to be administered not by those who claimed ownership to it, but by specialized officials prepared to serve a higher authority, now called the modern state. By using the fifth shogun's government to teach a political lesson, the compilers of *Tokugawa jikki* and their mentors accorded recognition to the important role Tsunayoshi's thirty-year government played in accelerating this paradigm shift that was so painful for the ruling elite.

Historians have mostly turned a blind eye to what *Tokugawa jikki* states quite openly, namely, that it is not a straightforward record of political events, but a document with a political message. Closer attention to this fact might show other periods of government in a new light as well.

Abbreviations

Discourse	Ogyū Sorai, *Ogyū Sorai's Discourse on Government (Seidan)*, trans. Olof G. Lidin
NKBT	*Nihon koten bungaku taikei*
NST	*Nihon shisō taikei*
Oritaku	Arai Hakuseki, *Oritaku shiba no ki*, *NKBT*, vol. 95
Seidan	Ogyū Sorai, *Seidan*, *NST*, vol. 36
Shokafu	*Kansei chōshū shokafu*
TJ	Kuroita Kasumi et al., eds., *Tokugawa jikki*
Told	Arai Hakuseki, *Told Round a Brushwood Fire*, trans. Joyce Ackroyd

Notes

Chapter 1: Prologue

1. *TJ*, 5:376, 6.urū8.Enpō 8; 5:377, 14.urū8, Enpō 8; Nakajima Yōichirō, *Kikin*, p. 8; Endō, *Kinsei*, p. 110.
2. Toda Mosui, p. 11. The Sanō shrine is known today as Hie Shrine and located at Nagata chō, Chiyodaku (p. 12, note 6).
3. Arai Hakuseki, *Arai Hakuseki nikki*, 2:79; *Ryūkō sōjō nikki*, 3:256-257.
4. *Bunrosō*, 18.1.Hōei 6.
5. *Matsukage nikki*, p. 285.
6. Konoe Motohiro, *Motohiro kōki*. Also cited in Endō, p. 153.
7. Segawa, pp. 98, 101. Motohiro was finally appointed *kanpaku* in Genroku 3 (1690). Ibid., p. 113.
8. *Deshima Diaries: Marginalia 1700-1740*, p. 109; *Deshima Dagregisters*, ms., 15 April 1709, folio 172.
9. The author of *Sannō gaiki* is given as Tōbu Yashi. The characters of this name can be translated as "a popular account of the Eastern warriors" and was quite obviously a joke. In 1880 the work was published by Hokiyama Kageo. In this publication the names of historical personages appear that probably were absent in the original version. Pages are numbered on the face only, with no numbers on verso. An alternate spelling of the title is *Sanō gaiki*, but that used by *Kokushi sō mokuroku* has been adopted here.
10. *Sannō* refers to the three sage kings Yao, Shun, and Yü, featured as model rulers in the Confucian classics.
11. Matsuura Seizan, pp. 252-253. For the multiple meaning of Matsukage, see "Conventions."
12. Nakase, *Edo jidai no wairo hishi*, pp. 10, 14, cites *Sannō gaiki* next to Ogyū Sorai's work *Seidan*. For further discussion of the topic, see chapters 9 and 18. *Sannō gaiki* even finds mention in the *Cambridge History of Japan* (Hall, p. 431, but here with the qualification that the work "is not the most reliable."
13. Wakita, p. 65.
14. For a translation of Kaempfer's work, see *Kaempfer's Japan*. For a discussion on how the word *sakoku* entered the Japanese language with the Japanese translation of Kaempfer's work on the closure of the country, see p. 19. On how closed Japan was during this period, see Toby, *State and Diplomacy in Early Modern Japan*.
15. Sakata Morotō, "Kai shōshō Yoshiyasu ason jikki," manuscript completed in 1897.

16. Ikeda, "Tokugawa shi shisei no chōshi o hyō su." The article is also discussed in Tsuji Tatsuya, *Kyōhō kaikaku no kenkyū*, pp. 3-4.
17. For details of these works, see the bibliography.
18. Tokutomi, 17:78-79, 512.
19. Irizawa, pp. 1-12.
20. Shinshi, pp. 172-173.
21. Kurita Mototsugu, "Inu kubō ron" and "Yanagisawa Yoshiyasu ron." For reference to *Sannō gaiki*, see, for instance, Kurita Mototsugu, *Edo jidai shi*, 1:436-437 and p. 439, note 25, and further discussion of Kurita's work in chapter 9 below.
22. Hayashi Yawara, *Yangisawa Yoshiyasu*.
23. Tsuji Zennosuke, "Yanagisawa Yoshiyasu no ichimen."
24. Tsuji Tatsuya, *Kyōhō kaikaku no kenkyū*, pp. 39-80.
25. Tsuji Tatsuya, "Politics in the Eighteenth Century"; Shively, "Tokugawa Tsunayoshi"; Bolitho, "The Dog Shogun."
26. Ienaga, p. 140.
27. Tsukamoto, *Tokugawa Tsunayoshi*, pp. 289-297. For his other publications, see the bibliography.
28. Skinner, p. 209.
29. Erikson, p. 404.
30. For further discussion of this issue, see chapter 18.
31. Ōishi Shinzaburō, *Nihon keizai shi ron*, pp. 76-77, 86; Ōishi, *Genroku jidai*, pp. 139-140, 161, 186-187.

Chapter 2: The Inheritance

1. De Vivero, p. 184 (my own translation from the French).
2. Cooper, *They Came to Japan*, p. 140.
3. Ibid., p. 46.
4. Hayashiya Shinsaburō, *Tenka ittō*, p. 323.
5. Sadler, p. 140. Totman, *Tokugawa Ieyasu*, pp. 48-49. Tokutomi, 13:524.
6. Hayashiya, *Tenka ittō*, p. 488.
7. Tokutomi, 11:16-17.
8. Ibid., 11-12.
9. Hayashiya, *Tenka ittō*, p. 509.
10. *Kaempfer's Japan*, p. 49. Later (p. 182) he refers to Hideyoshi's "illegal successor Ieyasu."
11. Cooper, *They Came to Japan*, p. 120.
12. Tsuji Tatsuya, *Edo kaifu*, p. 145.
13. Ōkubo Hikosaemon, cited in Inagaki, p. 45; *Buya shokudan* as cited in *TJ*, 3:699. The fact that Tadanaga was the brighter child is, however, not mentioned in any of the printed versions of *Buya shokudan* available today. *TJ* has Kunisendai instead of Kunimatsu for Tadanaga's name.
14. See, for instance, Kōronsha Shuppan Kyoku, pp. 22-37; *Kasuga no Tsubone Tōshō daigongen shukushi*, cited in Ōmaru, pp. 78-79.
15. *TJ*, 3:699.

16. *TJ*, 2:155–156, 9.10.Genna 4.
17. *TJ*, 2:374, 21.7.Kanei 3; Watanabe Kazutoshi, p. 170.
18. Tokutomi, 15:355; *Korō zatsudan*, cited in Hayashi Ryōshō, *Tokugawa shi to Edo bakufu*, pp. 119–120; Nakamura, *Hoshina Masayuki*, p. 12.
19. Hayashi Ryōshō, *Tokugawa shi*, pp. 118–119, 121. Hayashi believes that the story is reliable, since it is contained in a record of Hoshina Masayuki's life *(Sen tose no matsu)* and hence was not written to eulogize Tadanaga.
20. Fujino, *Oneiroku haizetsuroku*, p. 66; *Kokushi daijiten*, 10:291–292.
21. Tokutomi, 15:356–357.
22. Yamamoto Hirofumi, *Asobi o suru shōgun, odoru daimyō*, pp. 112–113.
23. The correspondence between Tadanaga and the monks Tenkai and Sūden, who were asked to intervene on his behalf, is cited in Tokutomi, 15:361–390.
24. Fujino, *Oneiroku haizetsuroku*, p. 251. Yamamoto, *Asobi o suru shōgun*, states that Tadanaga was ordered to commit suicide by a secret messenger from Iemitsu (p. 111) but does not give a source.
25. Tsukamoto, "Kaisetsu," p. 465.
26. *TJ*, 3:357, 24.5.Shōhō 1; 3:392, 3.5.Shōhō 2.
27. Compare *TJ*, 3:358, 1.6.Shōhō 1, for Tsunashige with 3:385, 5.3.Shōhō 2, for Kamematsu and 3:428, 14.1.Shōhō 3, for Tsunayoshi. See also Tsukamoto, *Tsunayoshi*, pp. 10–11.
28. *TJ*, 3:358, 1.6.Shōhō 1.
29. *TJ*, 3:427, 11.1.Shōhō 3, for Tsunashige; *TJ*, 3:508, 27.11.Shōhō 4, for Tsunayoshi.
30. *TJ*, 3:428, 13.1.Shōhō 3.
31. *TJ*, 3:525, 25.3.Keian 1; 3:572, 11.12.Keian 1, and so forth.
32. *Kenbyō jitsuroku*, p. 534. Kenbyō refers to Tsunayoshi's Buddhist death name Jōken-in.
33. *Buya shokudan*, ed. Murakami Tadashi, pp. 8, 13. See unnumbered preface for the date of creation.
34. *TJ*, 6:727.
35. Ibid.
36. *TJ*, 3:504–506, 13.11.Shōtoku 4.
37. Nakae Tōju, *Okina mondō*, pp. 57–58, 85. A similar opinion was expressed by the scholar Kumazawa Banzan. See Watanabe Hiroshi, *Kinsei nihon shakai to sōgaku*, p. 12.
38. Nakae Tōju, *Tōju sensei nenpu*, p. 287; also cited in Watanabe, *Kinsei*, p. 12.
39. Arai Hakuseki, *Oritaku shiba no ki* (hereafter *Oritaku*), pp. 187–188. See also the translation by Joyce Ackroyd, *Told Round a Brushwood Fire* (hereafter *Told*), pp. 61–62.
40. Tsukamoto, *Tsunayoshi*, pp. 12–13. Moreover, these two passages are, to my knowledge, not found in the printed versions of *Buya shokudan* available today: *Kokushi sōsho*, part 2 (1917); *Nihon meicho taikei*, part 1 (1925); *Nihon zuihitsu taisei*, ed. Murakami (1967). However, this might well indicate that the compilers had a manuscript at their disposal that in later versions was altered to exclude the cited passages. Later

versions of *Buya shokudan*, such as the *Okina gusa* version, appear to have undergone a screening process whereby material critical of Tsunayoshi was added, while that detrimental to Iemitsu's reputation was eliminated. For instance the *Okina gusa* version in *Nihon zuihitsu taisei* (ed. Murakami), p. 189, has the added information that dogs were to be called *o'inusama*. See also note 13 above.

41. *Go kiryō nashi* (for Japanese characters, see the glossary).
42. *Buya shokudan*, ed. Murakami, p. 87.
43. Tokutomi, 17:30.
44. Suzuki Hisashi, pp. 27-33.
45. Varenius, p. 106. Varenius brought together a number of Western accounts of Japan contained in reports and letters of the early Western visitors.
46. Kagan, p. 41.
47. Ibid., p. 42.
48. Ibid., p. 59.
49. References are found throughout *TJ*, 4.
50. *TJ*, 4:204, 25.12.Meireki 2.
51. Tsukamoto, *Tsunayoshi*, p. 36.
52. *Kenbyō jitsuroku*, translated in Shively, p. 113. Though there is no evidence of Tsunayoshi actually speaking these words, they appear in the summing up of his government, indicating that he transmitted such thoughts to his retainers.

Chapter 3: When a Child's Nurse Ought to Be Male

1. *Kenbyō jitsuroku*, p. 527. Also cited in Urabe, p. 104.
2. The outcasts (*hinin* or *eta*) were not considered a class.
3. *Kaempfer's Japan* has "according to a proclamation that has recently been renewed, no commoners, but only proper soldiers, are permitted to carry two swords" (p. 241). The necessity to renew the proclamation indicates that at times it was ignored.
4. *Kaempfer's Japan* explains that while the height of the curve of the carrying pole of a palanquin was fixed by law according to the social status of the passenger and was strictly enforced in the case of men, this law did not apply to women (p. 246).
5. Hosokawa Tadaoki even claimed in a letter that the children of Hidetada's daughter Kazuko (Tōfukumon-in), who had been made consort of Emperor Gomizuno'o, were being killed to prevent a grandchild of the shogun from succeeding to the throne. Finally, however, a daughter briefly succeeded as Meishō Tennō. Izumi Hideki, p. 13.
6. Inagaki, pp. 58-59.
7. *Deshima Dagregisters* (Viallée and Blussé), p. 273, entry 20.1.1647. One might also suspect that the interpreters thought it wiser not to mention this fact to the authorities to keep the peace, but they could only make this decision without incurring guilt because Japanese society offered them a ready excuse for such omission.
8. Terashima Ryōan, 2:124.
9. Varenius, p. 107.
10. Akiyama, pp. 42-48. (For the characters for *menoto*, see the glossary.)
11. She was, moreover, an extraordinary choice since Iemitsu was the grandson

of Oda Nobunaga's sister, and Kasuga no Tsubone was the daughter of Saitō Toshimitsu, a loyal retainer of Akechi Mitsuhide, the assassin of Oda Nobunaga.

12. Fujii Jōji, *Tokugawa Iemitsu*, pp. 15-16.
13. Tsuji Tatsuya, *Edo kaifu*, pp. 383, 433-434.
14. *Ryūei fujodensō*, pp. 153-154. Ogyū Sorai, *Shinruisho yuishogaki* (cited in Imanaka, p. 65), confirms the fact that her father was a Kyoto greengrocer but cites the name as Niuemon.
15. *Ryūei fujodensō*, p. 3.
16. *Tokugawa shoka keifu*, 2:77, 2:75.
17. Mano, p. 96; Josei Shi Kenkyūkai, p. 219.
18. *Tokugawa shoka keifu*, 2:78, *TJ*, 3:130, 7.3.Kanei 16; *Gyokuyo ki* in *Ryūei fujodensō*, pp. 38-39. Gyokuyo, The jeweled palanquin, refers to lowly women rising to high status through marriage.
19. *TJ*, 3:385, 29.2.Shōhō 2; Fujii, *Tokugawa Iemitsu*, p. 230.
20. Tsukamoto, *Tsunayoshi*, p. 7; Josei Shi Kenkyūkai, p. 219.
21. Suzuki Hisashi, *Hone wa kataru*, pp. 127-130; Suzuki, Yajima, and Yamanobe, pp. 194-200, 260-262.
22. After Iemitsu's death, over 3,700 female servants of the *oku* were dismissed. *TJ*, 4:4, 24.4.Keian 4.
23. The secrecy was such that only in the Meiji period did the conditions become known. Nagashima and Ōta, Introduction, p. 1.
24. Ibid., pp. 92-94.
25. See, for instance, ibid., pp. 95-100.
26. For an overview of the seasonal ritual, see ibid., pp. 23-70.
27. *The Confucian Analects*, book 2, ch. 3: "The Master said, 'If the people be led by laws, and uniformity sought to be given them by punishments, they will try to avoid the punishment, but have no sense of shame. If they be led by virtue, and uniformity sought to be given them by the rules of propriety, they will have the sense of shame, and moreover will become good.'" Legge, *Four Books*.
28. Toda Mosui, pp. 62-64.
29. Ibid., p. 67.
30. *Shinruisho yuishogaki*, cited in Imanaka, p. 65.
31. *TJ*, 6:208, gives the date as 25.8.Genroku 7.
32. *Buya shokudan*, ed. Murakami, pp. 103-104. The priest Yūten was not head priest at Zōjōji at the time, as Kurita citing *Zoku meiryō kōhan* (*Edo jidai*, 1:438) states. For the career of Yūten, see chapter 10 below.
33. Urabe, p. 104.
34. *Kenbyō jitsuroku*, p. 532, 15.8.Keian 1.
35. *TJ*, 3:561, 15.8.Keian 1. In *Kenbyō jitsuroku*, p. 532, the date of the stipend is given as 10.9.Keian 1.
36. Fukai, pp. 155, 163.
37. Ibid., p. 164. The question of Tsunayoshi's early staff is discussed in greater detail in chapter 4.
38. Esser et al., pp. 246-264.

39. Wolf, p. 42.
40. Johnson, p. 5.
41. This subject is discussed at length in Erikson, *Childhood and Society.*
42. There is an extensive literature covering the debate. See, for instance, Rose, pp. 625–654; Plomin et al., pp. 32–43; Lamb, p. 751.
43. Suzuki, *Hone wa kataru,* pp. 27–33.
44. Tsuji Tatsuya, however, suggests that Ietsuna was not as passive a ruler as is generally suggested. See Tsuji Tatsuya, *Edo bakufu seijishi kenkyū,* pp. 212–218.
45. See chapter 18.
46. *Kaempfer's Japan,* p. 49.
47. *Sōhonzan Hasedera,* pp. 106, 158. The painting appears on the cover and frontispiece of the book.
48. Kraft, p. 29.
49. Locurto and Freeman, p. 8.
50. See chapter 8.
51. See chapter 15.
52. See chapter 9.

Chapter 4: Lord of Tatebayashi

1. *Kenbyō jitsuroku,* p. 534. *TJ,* 3:689, 3.4.Keian 4.
2. *TJ,* 4:17, 18.7.Keian 4; 4:29, 12.9.Keian 4; 4:35, 13.12.Keian 4, respectively.
3. *TJ,* 4:30, 29.9.Keian 4.
4. *TJ,* 4:34, 8.12.Keian 4.
5. Tsukamoto, *Tsunayoshi,* p. 19.
6. *Kenbyō jitsuroku,* p. 535.
7. *TJ,* 4:89, 19.8.Jōō 2.
8. *TJ,* 4:396, 9.urū8.Kanbun 1; *Kenbyō jitsuroku,* p. 535.
9. *TJ,* 4:536, 15.10.Kanbun 3, and 4:512, 19.9.Kanbun 4, respectively; *Kenbyō jitsuroku,* p. 536; Tsukamoto, *Tsunayoshi,* pp. 37–38.
10. Tanno, "Tokugawa shōgun ke to chōtei," p. 95.
11. *TJ,* 7:1–2.
12. *Kenbyō jitsuroku,* p. 537; Tsukamoto, *Tsunayoshi,* p. 41.
13. *Kenbyō jitsuroku,* p. 537; *TJ,* 5:311, 6.5.Enpō 7.
14. *Kanda ki,* undated entry prior to the first month of Enpō 3. *Kanda ki* is classified at Naikaku bunko as volume 13 of *Hitomi shiki,* though *Hitomi shiki* is also the name of another set of documents within this collection of manuscripts by Hitomi Yūgen. This has made it difficult to find, and I thank Professor Tsukamoto Manabu for advising me on its location. The collection also contains *Sakurada ki* and *Mita roku,* which like *Kanda ki* will hereafter be referred to by these names.
15. *Kanda ki,* ms., 26.10.Jōō 2; 1.1.Enpō 5; 5.5.Enpō 4, and so on.
16. Tsukamoto, *Tsunayoshi,* p. 299; *TJ,* 4:234, 12.7.Meireki 3.
17. *Kanda ki,* ms., 3.5.Enpō 4.
18. For instance, *Kanda ki,* ms., 8.2.Enpō 4, 25 and 26.4.Enpō 4, and so on.
19. *TJ,* 4:212, 25.1.Meireki 3; Tsukamoto, *Tsunayoshi,* p. 299.

20. Tsukamoto, *Tsunayoshi*, p. 16.
21. *TJ*, 3:693, 20.4.Keian 3.
22. The change of policy has been well described by Bolitho in *Treasures*, 164–169. For financial considerations see Bodart-Bailey, "The Economic Plight of the Fifth Tokugawa Shogun," pp. 50–51.
23. *TJ*, 4:33, 22.11.Keian 4; Fukuda Chizuru, *Sakai Tadakiyo*, p. 41.
24. *TJ*, 4:81, 5.urū6.Jōō 2.
25. E.g., *Kanda ki*, ms., 22.10.Keian 5.
26. The *bakufu* guard consisted of five units, each commanded by an officer with the title of *bangashira*. The five units were *ōban, shoinban, shinban, kojūninban,* and *koshōban. Sekai dai hyakka jiten*, entry *kojūnin gumi*.
27. *TJ*, 3:524, 14.3.Keian 1; *Kansei chōshū shokafu* (hereafter *Shokafu*), 6:276, has "Norinari."
28. *TJ*, 3:524, 14.3.Keian 1; *Shokafu*, 4:272.
29. *Kenbyō jitsuroku*, p. 532, 15.8.Keian 1.
30. *TJ*, 3:561, 15.8.Keian 1. In *Kenbyō jitsuroku*, p. 532, the date of the stipend is given as 10.9.Keian 1. While *TJ* says he had the lower fourth court rank, *Shokafu* gives the court rank as lower fifth (21:104).
31. Fukai, pp. 160–161.
32. *Kanda ki*, ms., 24.4.Enpō 4.
33. *Kenbyō jitsuroku*, p. 536; *TJ*, 4:465, 15.5.Kanbun 3; Tsukamoto, *Tsunayoshi*, pp. 36–37. Once Tsunayoshi became shogun, there were insufficient funds to finance the appropriate procession. See chapter 14 below.
34. Kumazawa Banzan, cited in McMullen, *Idealism*, p. 158.
35. Morita, pp. 142–143.
36. *Sannō gaiki*, p. 3.
37. *Shokafu*, 6:276.
38. *Kaempfer's Japan*, p. 357.
39. *TJ*, 2:539, 28.2.Kanei 9; 2:546, 10.4.Kanei 9.
40. *Kanda ki*, ms., 19. 9, 6.10, 13.10, 19.10.Enpō 6; *Shokafu*, 11:371; Tsukamoto, *Tsunayoshi*, p. 51.
41. *Kanda ki*, ms., 20.9.Enpō 7.
42. For a discussion of the larger issue, see Bodart-Bailey, "Urbanisation and the Nature of the Tokugawa Hegemony."
43. See, for instance, Takayanagi Kaneyoshi, *Shiryō*, 406–409.
44. Foucault, 2:378.
45. Ibid.
46. Yamaguchi Kazuo, "Kinsei shoki buke kan'i no tenkai to tokushitsu ni tsuite," pp. 134–135; see also Tsuji, *Edo kaifu*, pp. 29–31.
47. Tokutomi, 13:108–109. See Ooms, p. 167, on the problems of Ieyasu's legitimacy.
48. Yamaguchi, "Kinsei shoki," p. 135.
49. Kaempfer mentions Ieyasu's usurpation of authority a number of times; see, for instance, *Kaempfer's Japan*, pp. 49, 182.

50. Asao Naohiro, "Buke shohatto"; Ooms, p. 53.
51. Foucault, 2:377.
52. Tokutomi, 13:109–111; Futaki, p. 2; Ueshima, "Shosatsu rei."
53. Futaki, p. 3.
54. For examples under Hidetada and Iemitsu, see Yamaguchi, "Kinsei shoki," pp. 127–134.
55. Ooms, pp. 58–61.
56. Cassirer, pp. 84–85.
57. Thus Tsunayoshi attended the fiftieth death anniversary of Sūgen-in, the wife of Hidetada, his grandmother, on 15.9.Enpō 3.
58. For the schedule of regular ceremonies, see Takayanagi, *Shiryō*, pp. 281–430.
59. *TJ*, 6:730.
60. Six: Kaempfer ms., British Library, Sloane 3061, folio 97; Brevinck: Kraft, p. 29.
61. Nesaki, p. 69.
62. Ōtomo Kazuo, *Nihon kinsei kokka no ken'i to girei*, p. 216.
63. Nesaki, p. 19; Endō, p. 31.
64. For a record of the granting of hawking grounds *(takaba)* by the first four shoguns, see Nesaki, p. 175.
65. Ōtomo, p. 38.
66. Nesaki, p. 58.
67. Lorenz, 2:188–189.
68. Cleland, *The Institution of a Young Noble Man*, cited in Thomas, p. 145.
69. Thomas, p. 162.
70. *TJ*, 4:59, 5.9.Jōō 1/Keian 5.
71. Nesaki, p. 175.
72. Ibid., pp. 68–69.
73. See Eliade, 3:154, where this is discussed with reference to the laws of ritual purity of Judaism, which separated the faithful from the rest of the population.
74. While *Kulturgüter* has been rendered as "culture goods" by the translators of Weber's work, an equally good, if not better, translation would be "cultural goods." Weber's manuscript is uncompleted and ends abruptly shortly after the introduction of the concept of *Kulturgüter* (*Wirtschaft und Gesellschaft*, p. 530).
75. Weber, *Wirtschaft und Gesellschaft*, p. 537; Weber, *Economy and Society*, p. 935. Weber's German terms are difficult to translate. The translations used here are those found in *Economy and Society*, even though they are not perfect.

Chapter 5: Confucian Governance
1. *TJ*, 1:339, translation by Mikiso Hane in Maruyama, *Studies in the Intellectual History of Tokugawa Japan*, p. 15 (corresponding to Maruyama, *Nihon seiji shisōshi kenkyū*, p. 12).
2. The secretary-cum-astrologer Yeh-lu Ch'u-ts'ai (Jap. Yaritsu Sozai) (1189–1243) advised Genghis Khan as follows: "Although the empire has been conquered on horseback, it cannot be administered on horseback." Ch'u-ts'ai was quoting a saying contained in Ssu-ma Ch'ien's *Book of History* (*Shih chi*, 97, 7b, Po-na ed.) where Lu Chia,

expounding the Confucian Odes and Annals to Kao-tsu, was rebuked by the latter, saying, "I conquered [the empire] on horseback, why should I bother about the Odes and the Annals?" Lu replied, "You conquered it on horseback, but you cannot administer it on horseback." (I thank my colleague Igor de Rachewiltz for this reference.)

3. *Kaempfer's Japan,* p. 133.
4. Hayashi Razan, *Seika sensei gyōjō* (The conduct of Master Seika), cited in Maruyama, *Studies,* p. 15.
5. Kinugasa, p. 179; Kurita, *Edo jidai,* 1:564.
6. *Buya shokudan,* ed. Murakami, p. 110.
7. Minamoto, pp. 527-529; Kaempfer, *Flora Japonica,* p. 11.
8. Yokoyama, p. 44; Monbushō, pp. 211-212.
9. Hori, pp. 201-202; Ooms, p. 74.
10. Satō Seijitsu, *Nihon kyōiku shi,* 1:133.
11. Monbushō, pp. 210-211; Hori, p. 252; Ooms, p. 74.
12. Ooms, p. 59.
13. Hori, p. 253.
14. For the extent of Razan's involvement in the administration, see Ooms, pp. 73-76.
15. Hara, p. 8.
16. Tokutomi, 14:123-124.
17. Naramoto, *Kinsei nihon shisō to bunka,* p. 414.
18. See Ooms, pp. 57, 75; also Gerhart, pp. 7-9.
19. Ishii, *Tokugawa kinrei kō,* 6:78-80. While some places of worship had both Buddhist and Shinto affiliation, scholars maintain that Shinto clergy *(shinshoku)* too were required to register with a Buddhist temple (Takano, *Kinsei nihon no kokka kenryoku to shūkyō,* p. 296). The extent to which religious establishments had both Buddhist and Shinto affiliations in the seventeenth century awaits further investigation. The contemporaneous observer Kaempfer clearly distinguishes between Buddhist and Shinto clergy. Also the *aratame* for Kyoto, referred to below, makes the distinction between "*negi* people, servants of the Shinto gods," of which there were some 9,000 and "*shukke,* Buddhist priests," of which there were some 37,000 in Kyoto.
20. For the usefulness of the registers to establish population figures, see Hayami and Cornell, pp. 105-114.
21. Kaempfer somehow managed to obtain the *aratame* for Kyoto and have it translated. It is likely to have dated from the time of his visit to Japan, 1690-1692 (*Kaempfer's Japan,* pp. 323-324).
22. *Honsaroku* is attributed to Honda Masanobu (1538-1616).
23. Arai Hakuseki, *Honsaroku kō,* pp. 549-550. For further details see Bodart-Bailey, "The Persecution of Confucianism in Early Tokugawa Japan," pp. 299-301.
24. Arai Hakuseki, *Honsaroku kō,* pp. 550-551. The "Western barbarian" Hakuseki met was the Italian priest Giovanni Battista Sidotti (1668-1714), in 1709.
25. *Kaempfer's Japan,* p. 133.
26. See Ōtsuki, p. 5.
27. An example is the astronomer Mukai Genshō (1609-1677). Numata et al., p. 695.

28. *Kaempfer's Japan*, p. 28.
29. Numata et al., p. 705.
30. *Honsaroku*, p. 278.
31. See, for example, *Kana shōri*, p. 249.
32. See Tyler, p. 93.
33. See Gerhart, pp. 6-9.
34. Nishimura, pp. 56-57, 59, 88, 90.
35. Ibid., pp. 54-55, 73-77, 89, 130-131; *Buya shokudan*, ed. Murakami, pp. 109-110.
36. Nishimura, pp. 206-207.
37. Ibid., pp. 209-215.
38. Tokutomi, 16:416-417.
39. Nishimura, pp. 86, 87; *Kokushi daijiten*, 10:695.
40. Nishimura, pp. 208; Aichiken Kyōiku Kai, p. 5.
41. Tokutomi, 16:453, 476-480.
42. Ibid., pp. 595-607; Ching, "Chu Shun-shui, 1600-82," p. 188. A photo of the epitaph faces p. 184. An extended version of this article can be found in Ching, "The Practical Learning of Chu Shun-shui (1600-1682)." Here the Chinese romanized spelling used by Julia Ching is adopted for the Chinese scholar rather than the Japanese romanized spelling Shu Shun-sui. The scholar is referred to by his family name of Chu when the name is abbreviated, rather than the personal name, as done for Japanese names.
43. Tokutomi, 16:519.
44. Noguchi, *Tokugawa Mitsukuni*, p. 169; Tokuta, pp. 71-72.
45. Tamamuro, "Danka seido no seiritsu," p. 115; Nishiwaki, pp. 23-24; Takano, *Kinsei nihon*, p. 296.
46. Tamamuro, "Danka seido," p. 120; *Kokushi daijiten*, 7:312.
47. Ooms, p. 192.
48. Tokutomi, 16:558-559; Ching, "Chu Shun-shui, 1600-82," pp. 183-185.
49. Tokutomi, 16:467.
50. Order dated 23.8.Kanbun, cited in *Ikeda Mitsumasa kō den*, 1:802-803; Tamamuro, *Edo bakufu no shūkyō tōsei*, pp. 116-120.
51. Wajima, "Kanbun igaku no kin," p. 1241; Maeda, pp. 28-29; Ooms, p. 192.
52. Naitō, 2:1078; Gotō, p. 477.
53. Gotō, pp. 468-470, 475-476; Tokutomi, 14:502.
54. Gotō, p. 482; McMullen, *Idealism*, pp. 92-95.
55. Shibata, pp. 45-46; Gotō, p. 481.
56. Gotō, p. 479.
57. Ibid., pp. 477-479.
58. Hirao, pp. 86-89, 93-95; Kensha, pp. 56-64.
59. Kinugasa, pp. 10-11.
60. *Ikeda Mitsumasa nikki*, p. 157.
61. Gotō, pp. 482-483; *Ikeda Mitsumasa nikki*, p. 176; McMullen, *Idealism*, 117-118.
62. Gotō, p. 582.

63. *Ikeda Mitsumasa nikki*, p. 242.

64. See chapter 8 below. Similarities in the government of Ikeda Mitsumasa and the fifth shogun Tsunayoshi have also been pointed out by James McMullen, for instance, *Idealism*, p. 133.

65. McMullen, *Idealism* 116–117; quotation from *Ikeda Mitsumasa nikki*, p. 250, translated in McMullen; Gotō, pp. 484–487.

66. Gotō, pp. 489–490; Kumazawa Banzan, p. 373: *bungaku shite sangyō to suru mono wa shōjin no ju nari;* "book-reading monks" is *mono yomi bōzu* (for Japanese characters see the glossary).

67. "*Seiji ni amari ari to sezu tote,*" cited in Taniguchi Sumio, *Ikeda Mitsumasa*, p. 54.

68. *Kokushi daijiten*, 12:718.

69. On Tenju-in see Urabe, pp. 33–35.

70. *Kaempfer's Japan*, p. 133; square brackets indicate words added.

71. *Ikeda Mitsumasa kō den*, 1:1.

72. Ibid., 1:780; Shibata, p. 49.

73. Shibata, p. 56; Sanyō Shinbun Shuppan Kyoku, pp. 86, 90–91.

74. *Ikeda Mitsumasa kō den*, 1:801; Shibata, p. 50.

75. *Ikeda Mitsumasa kō den*, 2:903; Shibata, pp. 48–49; Shizutani Gakkō Shi Hensan Iinkai, pp. 31–32. For details see also Bodart-Bailey, "Persecution of Confucianism," pp. 309–312.

76. Cited in Taniguchi, *Ikeda*, pp. 66–69.

77. For example, Taniguchi, *Ikeda*, p. 65; Bolitho, *Treasures among Men*, p. 125.

78. For example, Taniguchi, *Okayama han*, p. 216; Hall, *Government and Local Power in Japan*, p. 408; *Shizutani gakkō shi*, p. 24.

79. *Shizutani gakkō shi*, pp. 32–35.

80. See Shibata, pp. 52–54, for primary sources and discussion of whether the initial order of Kanbun 10 applied to a temporary school. The domain record referred to is *Biyō koku gakkō kiroku*.

81. Hall, *Government and Local Power*, pp. 408–409. The issue of whether these changes were specifically requested by Edo requires further investigation.

82. Cited in Taniguchi, *Ikeda*, p. 194; Taniguchi does not provide the date of the letter, but the text suggests that it falls within the period of Sakai Tadakiyo's administration.

83. Hall, *Government and Local Power*, p. 408; Taniguchi, *Ikeda*, p. 195.

84. Shibata, pp. 55–56. See *Shizutani gakkō shi*, p. 24, for Tsunamasa's achievements.

85. Tokutomi, 14:505; Iwao, 402–405.

86. Ching, "Practical Learning," p. 197. See also Ching, "Chu Shun-shui, 1600–82," p. 184.

87. Kumazawa Banzan's opinion appears in writing only much later in his *Daigaku wakumon* (likely to have been composed 1686–1691), but this work contains reflections and description of events of the earlier period. McMullen, *Idealism*, pp. 92–93, 420–421.

88. *Honsaroku*, p. 289. See also chapter 8 below.

89. McMullen, *Idealism*, p. 120.

90. Hayashi Gahō, pp. 10, 12, and so forth.

91. For Hayashi Shunsai's (Gahō) complaints about this work and the ignorance of the senior councilors, see Nakai, "Tokugawa Confucian Historiography," p. 71.

92. See below, chapter 16. For Confucian compassion, see Ching, "Practical Learning," p. 205.

Chapter 6: A Great and Excellent Lord

1. Kaempfer, *Amoentitatum exoticarum*, p. 502; A German translation of the original Latin appears in Kaempfer, *Geschichte und Beschreibung von Japan*, 2:414.

2. *Kaempfer's Japan*, pp. 407–408.

3. Claudius, pp. 258–259. This subject is discussed in Kapitza, p. 31.

4. Kaempfer, ms, British Library, Sloane 3061, 109v–110. *Keyser* (emperor) has been translated as shogun, *Konig* [sic] (king) as daimyo, and *Konigin* [sic] (queen) as the wife of the daimyo. The spelling of names has been modernized.

5. *TJ*, 5:295. Usually *Tokugawa jikki* includes a brief life history on this occasion.

6. *Sannō gaiki*, p. 10; Tokutomi, 17:256–257.

7. Coolhaas, p. 366.

8. *Kanda ki*, ms., 2.13.Enpō 7.

9. Tsukamoto, *Tsunayoshi*, p. 49. For the high price of fish in winter, see *Kaempfer's Japan*, p. 357.

10. *Sakurada ki*, ms., 2.12.Enpō 4.

11. *TJ*, 5:277, 14.1.Enpō 6.

12. Tsukamoto, *Tsunayoshi*, p. 49; *Sakurada ki*, ms., 6.6.Enpō 6.

13. Tsukamoto, *Tsunayoshi*, p. 42.

14. For instance *Sakurada ki*, ms., 1.5.Enpō 4; 30.9.Enpō 4; 1.1.Enpō 5.

15. *Sakurada ki*, ms., 1.1.Enpō 6.

16. The festival in question was that of *jōshi*, now known as *hina matsuri* or the Dolls Festival. It was originally a purification ceremony. For details on the ceremonies at Edo castle, see Takayanagi, *Shiryō*, pp. 358–360. For Tsunashige see *Sakurada ki*, ms., 12.2.Enpō 6, 3.3.Enpō 6.

17. *TJ*, 5:292, 25.7.Enpō 6; *Sakurada ki*, ms., same date.

18. *Sakurada ki*, ms., Tsukamoto, *Tsunayoshi*, p. 48.

19. *Sakurada ki*, ms., 12–13.9.Enpō 6. Iseki Gensetsu was officially appointed the shogun's physician the following year (*TJ*, 5:329, 18.12.Enpō 7) but had already been used by the *bakufu* on prior occasions (*TJ*, 4:498, 598, 5:65, 91, 143, 219, 233, 304). See also Tachibana, pp. 95–96.

20. *TJ*, 5:553, 5.8.Jōkyō 2; Tachibana, pp. 98–99.

21. *Sakurada ki*, ms., 14.9.Enpō 6.

22. *TJ*, 5:299, 12.12.Enpō 6.

23. *TJ*, 5:382, 16.9.Enpō 8.

24. *TJ*, 5:391, 9.12.Enpō 8.

25. *TJ*, 5:355.

26. Toda Mosui, p. 14.

27. Fukuda Chizuru, *Sakai Tadakiyo*, p. 178.

28. Toda Mosui, p. 13; lit.: "many crimes against the ancestors": *akugyaku no*

onkoto tsumori. *Akugyaku* was one of the ten crimes *(jū aku)*, namely, that of harming or murdering one's ancestors. In a wider sense it meant to act contrary to what was accepted as benevolent.

29. Coolhaas, p. 366.
30. Endō, *Kinsei*, p. 109.
31. *TJ*, 5:331, 12.1.Enpō 8. Sakai Tadakiyo received 20,000 *koku*; Inaba Masanori and Ōkubo Tadatomo received 10,000 *koku* each.
32. For these verses see Kodama, *Genroku jidai*, p. 205.
33. *TJ*, 5:333, 4.3, and 7.3.Enpō 8; *Sekai dai hyakka jiten*, entry "Arisugawa no miya."
34. *TJ*, 5:333, 10.3.Enpō 8; Toda Mosui, p. 220, 18.1.Genroku 4.
35. *Deshima Dagregisters*, ms., entry March 29, 1680.
36. *TJ*, 5:337, entry following 29.4.Enpō 8.
37. Matsudaira Naonori, p. 561. This report contradicts the suggestion by Fukuda Chizuru that the seriousness of Ietsuna's state of health was not recognized by Sakai Tadakiyo (Fukuda, *Sakai Tadakiyo*, p. 178).
38. *TJ*, 5:335, 10.4.Enpō 8.
39. *TJ*, 5:336, 18.4.Enpō 8.
40. *TJ*, 5:336, 27.4.Enpō 8.
41. Matsudaira Naonori, p. 568.
42. Tsukamoto (*Tsunayoshi*, p. 56–57) points out that *Hitomi shiki (Genyū kōki)* has the time of assembly as the hour of the sheep (about 3:00 p.m.), while according to the diaries he kept for Tsunayoshi's and Tsunatoyo's mansion *(Kanda ki* and *Sakurada ki)*, Tsunayoshi and Tsunatoyo were called in the hour of the monkey (roughly 5:00 p.m.). However, *Yamato no kami nikki* (Matsudaira Naonori, p. 569) specifies the later hour for the assembly of the senior councilors.
43. *Buya shokudan*, ed. Murakami, p. 82. The story appears in *TJ*, 5:354–355.
44. I thank my colleague Hanada Fujio for assistance in deciphering this.
45. *Buya shokudan*, ed. Murakami, p. 83.
46. *TJ*, 5:337, 6.5.Enpō 8.
47. Tsukamoto, *Tsunayoshi*, pp. 55–56; a photo of the document is on p. 55.
48. *Kenbyō jitsuroku*, p. 6, entry 6.5.Enpō 8.
49. Matsudaira Naonori, p. 570.

Chapter 7: The First Year of Government

1. Literally: was still *shōkō*.
2. *Buya shokudan*, ed. Murakami, p. 86. See unpaginated preface for the date of composition.
3. Kaempfer, ms., Sloane 3061, folio 110.
4. Ibid.
5. Toda, p. 10.
6. *Kaempfer's Japan*, p. 370.
7. See *Dokai kōshūki*, ed., and ann. Kanai Madoka; *The Works of Mencius*, book 4, part 2, ch. 3:1; Legge p. 181 (pagination of the Mencius section).

8. *TJ*, 5:359, 28.5.Enpō 8, between 1:00 and 2:00 p.m. Since throughout the year the time between sunrise and sunset was divided into equal periods, in summer the hours of the day were longer than in winter. See Bodart-Bailey, "Keeping Time," pp. 15, 18.

9. *Hagakure* (10:105) gives the date as 24.5.Enpō 8, *Kenbyō jitsuroku* (p. 9) has 26.6.Enpō 8, while *TJ* (5:363) only notes the incident under 9.7.Enpō 8. Since Ietsuna died on 8.5 and was laid to rest in his coffin on 13.5 (*TJ*, 5:338), *Hagakure* appears to be correct. Yamamoto Tsunetomo, *Hagakure*, ed. Watsuji and Furukawa, 2:144.

10. *TJ*, 5:364. *Kenbyō jitsuroku*, pp. 11-12. The grand ceremony of installment took place on 23.8.Enpō 8. *TJ*, 5:370.

11. *TJ*, 5:363.

12. *TJ*, 5:366, 25.7.Enpō 8.

13. Kurita Mototsugu, *Edo jidai*, 1:207-208; Sasama, pp. 254, 353.

14. *TJ*, 5:366; Kodama, et al., *Nihonshi sōran*, 4:49, 58, 63.

15. Ōishi, *Genroku jidai*, p. 86.

16. Momose, pp. 116-117.

17. *Sekai dai hyakka jiten*, entry "Matsudaira Tadanao"; Momose, p. 117.

18. *TJ*, 5:417, 26.6.Tenna 1. See also Yamamoto Hirofumi, *Tokugawa shōgun to tennō*, pp. 236-238.

19. Momose, p. 117.

20. Hayashi Ryōshō, *Tokugawa shi*, p. 144.

21. See, for example, *Kenbyō jitsuroku*, p. 10, 10.7.Enpō 8; p.23, 4.urū8.Enpō 8.

22. *TJ*, 5:414, 19.6.Enpō 8.

23. Momose, pp. 127-129.

24. Ibid., p. 124.

25. Ibid., pp. 120-123.

26. Ibid., pp. 129-131; *TJ*, 5:325, 19.10.Enpō 7.

27. Toda Mosui, pp. 15-16.

28. *Buya shokudan*, ed. Murakami, pp. 305-306; Yamamoto, *Tokugawa shōgun to tennō*, pp. 250-251.

29. Matsudaira Naonori, 27.5.Tenna 1; Fukuda Chizuru, *Bakuhan seiteiki chitsujo to oie sōdō*, pp. 324-325.

30. *TJ*, 5:417, 26.6.Tenna 1.

31. *TJ*, 5:416, 22.6.Tenna 1.

32. Fukuda Chizuru, *Bakuhan*, pp. 322-323, 327; Bolitho, *Treasures*, p. 176.

33. *Watakushi no saiban no yō ni oboshimesu*.

34. Sasama, p. 224.

35. *TJ*, 5:415-416, 21.6.Tenna 1.

36. E.g., Momose, p. 134.

37. Fukuda Chizuru, *Bakuhan*, pp. 316-318; Fukuda Chizuru, *Sakai*, pp. 199-200.

38. Fukuda Chizuru, *Bakuhan*, p. 314, citing *Tokugawa shoka keifu*.

39. *TJ*, 5:391, 9.12.Enpō 8.

40. Fukuda Chizuru, *Sakai*, pp. 193-194.

41. Ibid., pp. 195-196.

Notes for Pages 86-94   315

42. *Kaempfer's Japan*, p. 162.
43. *TJ*, 5:397, 12.1 and 15.1.Enpō 9 respectively. However, Fukuda Chizuru (*Sakai*, p. 197), citing *Eidai nikki*, has the confiscation of Tadakiyo's villa on 12.1 and the order of the confiscation on 8.1.
44. Fukuda Chizuru, *Bakuhan*, p. 315, cites a letter from the lord of Tosa, Yamanouchi Tadatoyo, dated 22.urū8.Enpō 8. Since Tadatoyo died in Kanbun 9, this must surely be a letter from his son Toyomasa.
45. Fukuda Chizuru, *Bakuhan*, p. 327.
46. For details see ibid., p. 323.
47. "Toriatsukai fuchō ni oboshimesare ni tsuke." Matsudaira Naonori, p. 597, 1.7.Enpō 9.
48. Sakai Tadakiyo's son, Tadataka (here Tadaaki), explained Tadakiyo's retirement in terms of the shogun establishing his authority to the retainers in his domain. Fukuda Chizuru, *Sakai*, p. 196.
49. Yoshikawa Machi Kyōiku Iinkai, p. 7.
50. Kodama, *Genroku jidai*, p. 281.
51. Fukuda Chizuru, *Sakai*, pp. 179-180.
52. Ibid., p. 201.
53. Ibid., pp. 203, 207.
54. Ibid., pp. 206-208.
55. For instance Itō, 2:109.

Chapter 8: The Rise and Fall of Hotta Masatoshi

1. Nakajima Yōichirō, p. 8. Endō, p. 110.
2. *TJ*, 5:368, 7.8.Enpō 8; *Kenbyō jitsuroku*, p. 15.
3. *TJ*, 5: 369, 16.8.Enpō 8. The word *narabini* signifies that they were placed next to and not under him.
4. Tsuji Tatsuya, *Kyōhō kaikaku*, p. 63.
5. *TJ*, 5:370.
6. *TJ*, 5:367-368.
7. Tsuji Tatsuya, *Kyōhō kaikaku*, p. 37, n. 6.
8. *Yōgen roku*, p. 33. I would like to acknowledge the assistance of the late Julia Ching in reading this document many years ago.
9. See *The Book of Mencius*, book 7, pt. 2, ch. 14:1; Legge, p. 333.
10. *Honsaroku*, p. 289.
11. Paku, p. 66. (I thank my student Chiba Yasumi for this information.)
12. Tokutomi, 17:48-49.
13. Morohashi, 12:353.
14. While the pronunciation is "Atake," the characters are those for *an* (safety) and *taku* (house, residence). The suffix *maru* denotes a vessel.
15. *Yōgen roku*, pp. 33-34; Toda Mosui, pp. 45-46, 49; A good description of the festivities as well as a drawing of the ship can be found in Yamamoto Hirofumi, *Asobi*, pp. 152-155.
16. *Yōgen roku*, p. 34. The text refers to the reduction of *dōshin* officials.

Those rotated were of the *yoriki* and *dōshin* class. Also *TJ*, 5:465, 11.11.Tenna 2; Nesaki, p. 72.

17. *Yōgen roku*, p. 34.
18. Toda Mosui, pp. 33-35.
19. *Yōgen roku*, pp. 31, 34. *Kaempfer's Japan* (p. 209) states that only cloth without gold or silver threads was imported.
20. Kawano, p. 82. E. S. Crawcour makes the same inference (p. 46).
21. *Yōgen roku*, p. 34.
22. Ibid., p. 33.
23. Ibid., pp. 30-31.
24. For a discussion of this subject, see Bolitho, *Treasures*, pp. 166-169. Also Asao, "Shogun seiji no kenryoku kōzo," pp. 35-36.
25. See Sasama, p. 186, for a chart of offices below the city magistrates.
26. For Hotta Masamori's rise under Iemitsu, see Fujii Jōji, *Edo bakufu rōjūsei keisei katei no kenkyū*, pp. 267-275. See also Hesselink, pp. 62-63.
27. Kasuga no Tsubone was a distant relative of Hotta Masatoshi, his great-grandmother and Kasuga no Tsubone being wives of the same man, Inaba Masanari. *Sekai dai hyakka jiten*, entry "Hotta Masamori."
28. *TJ*, 5:250-251, 28.8.Jōkyō 1.
29. See the Hotta family tree in Kodama, *Genroku jidai*, p. 289.
30. Toda Mosui, pp. 80-84; Tokutomi, 17:68 citing Muro Kyusō.
31. *TJ*, 5:250, 28.8.Jōkyō 1.
32. Tokutomi, 17:59-60.
33. Toda Mosui, pp. 80-84.
34. Ibid., p. 84. Tsukamoto's note 5, p. 86, indicates that the gift of books to Masayasu also appears in Itō Jinsai's diary.
35. *TJ*, 5:522; Tokutomi, 17:62-63; Kurita, *Edo jidai*, 1:441.
36. Tokutomi, 17:61-63, Toda Mosui, p. 81.
37. Tokutomi, 17:60, citing Muro Kyusō.
38. *TJ*, 5:521-522.
39. Kurita, *Edo jidai*, 1:440; Ōishi, *Genroku jidai*, p. 112.
40. Kodama, *Genroku jidai*, pp. 184-186, 193.
41. Ōishi, *Genroku jidai*, p. 111.
42. Kuwata, p. 61, citing Matsuura Shigenobu. Tokutomi, 17:66-67.
43. Kaempfer, ms., Sloane 3061, folio 111.
44. For instance Kuwata, p. 63.
45. Toda Mosui, p. 85, note 2. On Kaneda Masakatsu see Fukai, pp. 170-171, 327.
46. Toda Mosui, p. 111.
47. *Shokafu*, 11:2. The poverty of the Hotta family had a negative effect on the career of Arai Hakuseki, who became one of the fifth shogun's most cited critics.
48. Tokutomi, 17:73-74.
49. *Yōgen roku*, p. 38.
50. Noma, pp. 498, 600, 624; *Hagakure*, 1:24, ed. Watsuji and Furukawa, p. 32; trans. Wilson, p. 23.

Chapter 9: The Shogun's New Men

1. Nicholson, p. 26.
2. Ogyū, *Seidan* (hereafter *Seidan*), p. 351; my translation. An English translation by Olof Lidin is found in *Ogyū Sorai's Discourse on Government (Seidan)* (hereafter *Discourse*), pp. 197-198. Where I have used my own translation, references to Lidin's are given in parentheses.
3. Ōishi, *Genroku jidai*, p. 144.
4. Tokutomi, 17:73-74.
5. Endō, p. 124; and, for instance, *TJ*, 6:30, 20.12.Genroku 1; 6:31, 24.12.Genroku 1.
6. Toda Mosui, p. 105, entry 21.7.Jōkyō 2.
7. *Kaempfer's Japan*, p. 357.
8. *TJ*, 5:363, 9.7.Enpō 8, and 5:432, 11.12.Tenna 1; *Shokafu*, 6:277; *Ryūei bunin*, 1:22. Arai Eiji notes that the latter work does not always agree with other sources (p. 272). See also the table in this chapter.
9. *Oritaku*, 424-425.
10. Tsuji Tatsuya, *Kyōhō kaikaku*, pp. 60-61, note 1.
11. The information on the promotion and background of chamberlains and grand chamberlains has been taken from *Ryūei bunin*, 1:96-99 and 1:22-24 respectively.
12. Ibid., 1:65-68.
13. Toda Mosui, p. 158, 18.5.Genroku 1, and p. 160, date not specified; *TJ*, 6:13, 18.5.Genroku 1. See also Ōishi, *Genroku jidai*, p. 19.
14. *Matsukage nikki*, p. 285. For Ogyū Sorai see below.
15. *TJ*, 6:244-245, 29.11.Genroku 8.
16. Morita, p. 33.
17. *Rakushidō nenroku*, ms., vol. 3, 25.4.Tenna 1.
18. Ibid., vol. 3, 3.6.Tenna 1. *Rakushidō nenroku* merely states that he became Tsunayoshi's disciple, but *Genkō jitsuroku* (p. 47) and *Yanagisawa ke hizō jikki* (p. 76) make it clear that Tsunayoshi was his teacher in Confucian learning. First reading: *TJ*, 5:435, 1.1.Tenna 2.
19. *Rakushidō nenroku*, ms., vol. 3, 11.1.Tenna 2. For the two characters of *makoto*, see the illustration of Tsunayoshi's holograph.
20. *Rakushidō nenroku*, ms., vol. 3, 25.6.Tenna 3 and 11.11.Jōkyō 1, respectively.
21. *Ryūei bunin*, 1:119-120.
22. Hōgetsu and Iwasawa, 5:423-424.
23. *Matsukage nikki*, pp. 203-204.
24. Ueno Yōzō notes that her mother came to Edo as an attendant of Tsunayoshi's aristocratic wife Takatsukasa Nobuko and that Machiko was called to Edo on the recommendations of her mother. Ueno, p. 520.
25. *Matsukage nikki*, p. 125.
26. E.g., *TJ*, 6:721-723.
27. *Sannō gaiki*, pp. 4, 9; *Gokoku onna taiheiki*, pp. 154-168. The name of the latter work refers to the fourteenth-century war epic *Taiheiki*, where a total of 2,140 men committed ritual suicide (Ikegami, p. 105). In this version of *Taiheiki*, a woman *(onna)* commits suicide to protect the country *(gokoku)*.

28. E.g., Morita, p. 137.
29. See chapter 10.
30. Naramoto, *Machibito no jitsuryoku*, pp. 27-30.
31. *Genkō jitsuroku*, p. 8; *Yanagisawa ke hizō jikki*, p. 45.
32. Kodama, *Jinbutsu nihon no rekishi*, 13:39. The author of this section, Gomi Yasuke, is also wrong in stating that Yoshisato's title of *yakata sama* was limited to shogunal offspring (ibid., p. 40).
33. *Matsukage nikki*, p. 125.
34. *Rakushidō nenroku*, ms., vol. 3, 12.11.Genroku 1, records the order that Yoshiyasu was to work alongside the shogun's grand chamberlains, while *TJ*, 6:26, of this date notes that Yoshiyasu was appointed to grand chamberlain.
35. Sasama, p. 368.
36. *Osoba ōsetsukerare soraedomo* is ambiguous, as *osoba* could also be an abbreviation of *osoba yōnin* or *sobashū*. Yet later in the text this phrase is used for Saitō Hida no Kami, who only served as *koshō*. It has therefore been translated literally as "serving at the shogun's side."
37. *Genkō jitsuroku*, pp. 85-86; *Yanagisawa ke hizō jikki*, p. 102; on the importance of seating, see Kasaya, pp. 154-156.
38. *TJ*, 6:34, 26.1.Genroku 2; Toda Mosui, p. 179, 6.urū1.Genroku 2; *Shokafu*, 4:113. Perhaps Naomasa was found to have syphilis—the same ideogram being used for "boil" and that illness—and therefore was not employed again. The statement that "he did not measure up to the shogun's expectations" could then be taken to mean that he was spending his time on amusement rather than devoting himself fully to his work.
39. *Matsukage nikki*, pp. 121, 125, 126, 132-133, 136, 162, 172.
40. E.g., *Rakushidō nenroku*, ms., vol. 7, 26.3.Genroku 4.
41. *Rakushidō nenroku*, ms., vol. 50, 3.11.Genroku 10. The Senmyō calendar, which had been in use for over eight hundred years showed considerable discrepancy with the natural seasons. Shibukawa Shunkai calculated the appropriate adjustments, and his calendar became known as the Jōkyō calendar. See also Shively, p. 121.
42. See chapter 16 below.
43. *Seidan*, p. 316.
44. *Genkō jitsuroku*, pp. 39, 58-59; *Yanagisawa ke hizō jikki*, p. 84.
45. Yan Ying (Jap.: Anei) was prime minister during the Spring and Autumn period in China. His charioteer, proud of his master's position, handled his horses with such exuberance that his wife requested a divorce.
46. *Matsukage nikki*, pp. 215-216.
47. Toda Mosui. p. 323, 11.7.Genroku 9.
48. Nakase, *Edo jidai*, p. 12.
49. *Kaempfer's Japan*, pp. 240, 368, 415. On Makino Narisada's gifts to the shogun, see p. 357.
50. As for instance in Nakase, *Edo jidai*, pp. 15-17, citing Toda Mosui, p. 447, entry 5.4.Genroku 15.
51. Cited in Bolitho, *Treasures*, p. 173. The Dutch record for the year 1706 states that Yoshiyasu refused all gifts. (*Deshima Diaries: Marginalia 1700-1740*, p. 76, April 7, 1706).

52. Tokutomi, 17:403, citing *Kenzan hisaku*. As Ōishi (*Genroku jidai*, pp. 137–138) has pointed out, because of the personal antagonism that existed this accusation should not be taken seriously.

53. *Seidan*, p. 358. (*Discourse*, p. 209 has "Until Genroku . . . all rōjū Elders paid attention to their behaviour" [p. 209], but the words "all *rōjū* Elders" are not contained in the original. "Their behavior" refers to the behavior of *shissei no shin* (lit.: officials of the government), the subject of the previous paragraph.

54. *Matsukage nikki*, p. 304.

55. Kurita, *Edo jidai*, 1:436–437, 439, note 25; Toda Mosui, pp. 272–273. Lidin, *The Life of Ogyū Sorai*, p. 168, citing *Kansan yoroku, kan* 2, in *Nihon bunko*, 1:37. On Yamana's adoption: *Meiryō kōhan*, p. 363.

56. *Kaempfer's Japan*, p. 408.

57. Male prostitution, ibid., p. 339; male servants, p. 366.

58. *Matsukage nikki*, p. 202.

59. Hiraishi, pp. 189–194.

60. Yamamoto, *Asobi*, pp. 124, 129–130, 152–153.

61. Ibid., p. 154.

62. *Kaempfer's Japan*, pp. 407–408.

63. *Matsukage nikki*, pp. 159–160; *TJ*, 6:312, entry 14.11.Genroku 10; Toda Mosui, pp. 365–366, same date.

64. See chapter 16 below.

65. Yoshiyasu's appointment: *TJ*, 6:214, 25.11.Genroku 7; Narisada's appointment: *TJ*, 5:376, 6.urū8.Enpō 8; for the composition of the *hyōjōsho*: Sasama, p. 224.

66. *Kanrosō*, ms., vol. 3, 10.7.Genroku 9; Naitō, 6:120.

67. *TJ*, 6:336, 21.7.Genroku 11; *Matsukage nikki*, pp. 152, 162–163, 180.

68. Tokutomi, 17:187–191; *Matsukage nikki*, p. 163.

69. The exact date is not known, but on her father's death in the second month of Genroku 16 (1703), Machiko wrote that she had been over ten years in the Yanagisawa mansion (*Matsukage nikki*, p. 204).

70. *Matsukage nikki*, p. 183; *Rakushidō nenroku*, ms., vol. 87, 13.9.Genroku 14.

71. *Rakushidō nenroku*, ms., vol. 102, 12.7.Genroku 15.

72. *Matsukage nikki*, p. 201.

73. *TJ*, 6:365–367, 29.4.Genroku 12; *Matsukage nikki*, p. 171; Morita, pp. 158–168.

74. Takayanagi Kaneyoshi, *Tokugawa fujinden*, p. 53; Kurita, *Edo jidai*, 1:429.

75. *Rakushidō nenroku*, ms., vol. 95, 9.3.Genroku 15; *Matsukage nikki*, pp. 191–192.

76. *Matsukage nikki*, pp. 212–215.

77. Ibid., pp. 215, 222, 227.

78. *TJ*, 6:336, 21.7.Genroku 11; *Matsukage nikki*, p. 163.

79. *TJ*, 6:374, 14.7.Genroku 12.

80. For Sakai Tadakiyo: *TJ*, 5:15, 17.4.Kanbun 8; for Hotta Masatoshi, 5:469, 8.1.Tenna 3; for Ii, 5:535, 17.1.Jōkyō 2; for Hoshina, 5:551, 8.1.Jōkyō 2.

81. *TJ*, 6:397, 2.3.Genroku 13.

82. Toda Mosui, p. 422, third month, Genroku 13.

83. His last increment had been on 26.7.Genroku 10, bringing his stipend to 92,030 *koku; TJ,* 6:303.
84. *TJ,* 6:432, continuation of entry 5.3.Genroku 14 from previous page; *TJ,* 7:146, 13.2.Shōtoku 2. For Shigehide see chapter 17.
85. *Rakushidō nenroku,* ms., vol. 93, 26.11.Genroku 14.
86. *Matsukage nikki,* pp. 191-192.
87. Toda Mosui, p. 447, 5.4.Genroku 15.
88. *TJ,* 6:559, 21.12.Hōei 1.
89. *Matsukage nikki,* p. 237.
90. *Ryūkō sōjō nikki,* 3:290, 1.12.Hōei 1; *Matsukage nikki,* p. 237.
91. *Genkō jitsuroku,* p. 9; *Yanagisawa ke hizō jikki,* p. 46. *Gyōbu shō:* deputy vice minister of law; *shikibu shō:* deputy vice minister of ceremonies. These imperial titles no longer implied the holding of office.
92. *Matsukage nikki,* p. 238.

Chapter 10: The Laws of Compassion

1. Ōishi, *Genroku jidai,* p. 20; Kitajima, *Kinseishi no gunzō,* p. 204.
2. Irizawa, pp. 1-12.
3. Shinshi, pp. 172-173, citing *Korō chawa (Nihon zuihitsu taisei)* (Yoshikawa Kōbunkan, 1927-1931), 6:72-73. See also Tsukamoto, "Shōrui awaremi no seisaku to Saikaku-bon," p. 4, for a discussion of the uncritical dramatization of the subject.
4. Kurita, "Inu kubō ron," p. 113.
5. Tsukamoto's books on this subject include *Shōrui meguru seiji* (1983), *Edo jidai hito to dōbutsu* (1995), and *Ikiru koto no kinseishi* (2001).
6. Naoki Kōjirō et al., p. 179.
7. *Sannō gaiki,* p. 2; Tokutomi, 17: 204-205.
8. Matsuura Seizan, pp. 252-253. See chapter 1 above.
9. Miyazaki Eiga, p. 3.
10. *Discourse,* pp. 86-87; *Seidan,* p. 272.
11. *Hagakure,* 4:47, 7:14 (ed. Watsuji and Furukawa, 1:191, 2:161; trans. Wilson, pp. 92, 102). The Japanese original mentions the age of fourteen or fifteen, which in Western reckoning corresponds to thirteen or fourteen, since traditionally the infant is counted to be one year old on birth.
12. Miyamoto Musashi, *The Book of Five Rings.*
13. *Kaempfer's Japan,* p. 223.
14. *Hagakure,* 8:55, 7:31 (Watsuji, 3:50, 2:171; Wilson, 117, 106-107) respectively.
15. Ibid., 2:66 (Watsuji, 1:115; Wilson, p. 75).
16. Ibid., 9:20 (Watsuji, 3:85; Wilson, 131-132).
17. *Told,* pp. 64-65.
18. See, for instance, the string of murders in Kaga, pp. 157-205.
19. *Kaempfer's Japan,* pp. 342-343.
20. Tsukamoto, *Ikiru koto no kinseishi,* p. 74; *Dokai kōshūki,* pp. 118-119.
21. *Hagakure,* 11:77, 6:18 (Watsuji 3:189, 2:93; Wilson, pp. 160, 195) respectively.
22. Tsukamoto, *Shōrui o meguru seiji* (1993), p. 198.

23. *Shokafu*, 10:412.
24. *Deshima Dagregisters* (Viallée and Blussé), p. 225.
25. Tsukamoto, *Edo jidai hito to dōbutsu*, p. 46; Tsukamoto, *Shōrui o meguru seiji* (1993), pp. 198-199.
26. *Honchō shokkan*, cited in Tsukamoto, *Edo jidai hito to dōbutsu*, p. 47.
27. Tsukamoto, "Seikun to shite no inu kubō," p. 68.
28. Edo Kiseki Kenkyūkai, p. 400.
29. An example of forty dogs being transported by the daimyo to Nagoya and set free in the city is documented in Tsukamoto, *Shōrui o meguru seiji* (1993), p. 215.
30. Tsukamoto, *Edo jidai hito to dōbutsu*, pp. 117-118; Takigawa, p. 164.
31. The former is from *Edo zu byōbu*, National Museum of Japanese History, Sakura, Chiba; The latter is from *Edo meisho zu byōbu*, Idemitsu Museum of Arts. See illustrations, p. 135.
32. *TJ*, 3:435, 7.4.Shōhō 3.
33. *TJ*, 3:504-506, 13.11.Shōhō 4. See also Takayanagi, *Shiryō*, pp. 444-445.
34. *Kenbyō jitsuroku* (original *sōsho* version).Warring States refers to the period between the beginning of the Ōnin war in 1467 and Nobunaga's entry into Kyoto in 1568.
35. There are no exact figures available for this early period, since the temple registers *(shūmon aratame jō)* available for other locations have largely been destroyed by earthquakes and fire in the case of Edo. Hayami, *Rekishi jinkō gaku de mita nihon*, pp. 127-128.
36. Matsuo Bashō, "Travelogue of Weather-Beaten Bones," p. 40. Original text: Matsuo, *Bashō bunshū*, 46:36-37.
37. Tsukamoto, *Edo jidai hito to dōbutsu*, pp. 117-122.
38. Jorissen, pp. 123, 189, 284-285; Frois, pp. 127-128.
39. Tsukamoto, *Shōrui o meguru seiji* (1993), pp. 254-256.
40. Takada, pp. 219-220; *Shōhō jiroku*, 2.5. Kanbun 7.
41. Ishii, *Oshioki saikyochō*, p. 425, no. 974 of 6.8.Hōei 8; Takada, pp. 220-221.
42. Takada, pp. 28-43.
43. Ibid., pp. 209-218. Takada cites various sources on the incident, including material on the background of the Takano family.
44. Such as *modoshi, kogaeshi, oshikaeshi*, and so on. Takada, pp. 225-226.
45. *Kaempfer's Japan*, p. 344; Takada, pp. 225-227.
46. *Hagakure*, 2:116 (Watsuji, 1:116; Wilson, p. 84). Wilson translates *suteru* rather weakly as "disregard".
47. Blacker, pp. 307, 312-313.
48. Takada, p. 158.
49. Ibid., pp. 221-224.
50. Ibid., pp. 150-152; *TJ*, 6:357, 4.2.Genroku 12. *Kenbyō jitsuroku*, same date, has a short entry describing Yūten's appointment as an "unprecedented promotion" *(hakaku no shusse)* on account of Keishō-in's request. The temple in question is Oimi (also Oyumi) Daiganji in present-day Chiba, one of the *Kantō jūhachi danrin* or eighteen teaching temples of the Jōdo sect in the Kantō area that functioned as seminaries for the training of priests.

51. Takada, p. 153; *Sekai dai hyakka jiten*, entry "Denzū-in." Keishō-in, however, was buried at Zōjōji.

52. *TJ*, 7:203, 6.12.Shōtoku 1.

53. *TJ*, 7:361, 3.12.Shōtoku 3.

54. Takada, pp. 24–28. Later Hakuseki's dislike of Yūten is likely to have been the cause of the *bakufu*'s refusal to restore the Ankoku temple within the precincts of Zōjōji. *Told*, pp. 235–237. See also Ōkawa, pp. 36–55.

55. *TJ*, 5:598, 11.4.Jōkyō 4.

56. *Shōhō jiroku*, laws 775, 776, pp. 280–281.

57. Ibid., laws 846, 847, 935, 1025, 1040, pp. 310, 311, 337, 365, 369, respectively.

58. *TJ*, 8:664, 15.9.Kyōhō 19.

59. *Discourse*, Lidin, p. 71.

60. *Kaempfer's Japan*, p. 372.

61. *Shōhō jiroku*, p. 245, order 698 of 20.12.Jōkyō 2; *TJ*, 6:23–24, 9.10.Genroku 1. The topic had already been treated in 1920 in Kurita Mototsugu, "Inu kubō ron," p. 13.

62. Vaporis, pp. 231–232.

63. *Discourse*, p. 252.

64. *TJ*, 5:586, 27.9.Jōkyō 3; 6:750.

65. *TJ*, 6:15, 19.6.Genroku 1.

66. *Kenbyō jitsuroku*, p. 406, 21.2.Genroku 15; *TJ*, 6:464, same date. Masayuki's appointment as senior councilor had taken place in the first month of Genroku 14 (*TJ*, 6:427).

67. *Hagakure*, 1:36 (Watsuji, 1:36–37; Wilson, p. 24). The reference to fifty years ago indicates the time before Tsunayoshi's government.

Chapter 11: The Dog Shogun

1. *Kaempfer's Japan*, p. 146.

2. Ibid., pp. 408, 433, respectively. The *shu* was a silver monetary unit, worth one sixteenth of a *ryō*.

3. Compare ibid., p. 72 and p. 146.

4. Ibid., pp. 160–161; on taxes: pp. 164–167; on smuggling: p. 221.

5. See chapter 6 above.

6. *Kaempfer's Japan*, p. 149.

7. *Discourse*, pp. 84, 86–87; *Seidan*, pp. 270–272.

8. *Sannō gaiki*, p. 4.

9. Tsukamoto, *Shōrui o meguru seiji* (1993), p. 238.

10. Fukuda Toyohiko et al., p. 106, with illustration.

11. *Told*, p. 91.

12. Kaga, pp. 162, 168, 213, 227.

13. Toda Mosui, pp. 138–139. Calculated correctly the figure should be 162. Mosui also fails to take into account that dogs generally do not reproduce six months after birth.

14. Tsukamoto, *Shōrui o meguru seiji* (1993), pp. 98–99, quoting *Kyōhō sewa* and *Kenzan hisaku* respectively.

15. Tsukamoto, *Shōrui o meguru seiji* (1993), pp. 174–177. One *bu* was a gold coin and contained 15 *momme* (*Kaempfer's Japan*, pp. 445–447).

16. Tsukamoto, *Shōrui o meguru seiji* (1993), p. 178. Tsukamoto states 2 *to*, 4 *shō*, 5 *gō*, and this has been converted into *koku*. (One *koku* of rice was considered the ration of one man per year.)

17. Ibid., pp. 177–178.

18. Ibid., p. 103, quoting Asai Ryōi, *Ukiyo monogatari: gyakusei*, unjust/unreasonable government, but no doubt also alluding to the homophone meaning "tyranny."

19. Tsukamoto, *Shōrui o meguru seiji* (1993), p. 102; Asai Ryōi, pp. 306–307. The case of hunting samurai trampling rice fields and thus destroying the harvest is also mentioned in *Hagakure*, 4:41 (Watsuji, 1:189). Here, however, the lord makes up the damage on the complaint of an old peasant woman.

20. On details of the elimination of hawking, see Tsukamoto, *Shōrui o meguru seiji* (1993), p. 122; Nesaki, pp. 68–69.

21. *Buya shokudan*, ed. Murakami, p. 85. On the limitations of the use of firearms to ward off dangerous animals *(teppō aratame)*, see Tsukamoto, *Shōrui o meguru seiji* (1993), pp. 10–95.

22. Nesaki, p. 70, citing *Kyōrei ruisan*.

23. *TJ*, 5:392, 16.12.Enpō 8; 5:441, 21.3.Tenna 2; Tsukamoto, *Shōrui o meguru seiji* (1993), pp. 115–116, 126–136; Nesaki, pp. 69–71.

24. *Shōhō jiroku*, order 696, p. 244.

25. Toda Mosui, pp. 107–108; *TJ*, 5:553, 6.8.Jōkyō 2; Tsukamoto, *Shōrui o meguru seiji* (1993), pp. 205–206.

26. For instance Kimura, pp. 172–176.

27. Asai Ryōi, pp. 323–324.

28. *Shōhō jiroku*, pp. 230–232, order 662; p. 240, order 681; p. 243, order 691; *TJ*, 5:465, 11.11.Tenna 2.

29. *Atake maru*: see *Shōhō jiroku*, order 644, p. 225; houseboats: *Shōhō jiroku*, order 683, p. 240; Falconers' tools: *Edo machi bure shūsei*, order 2409, p. 122, 28.1.Jōkyō 3.

30. Gambling, daimyo's luggage: *Shōhō jiroku*, orders 692, 693, p. 243; palanquins: orders 620, 621, pp. 212–213.

31. Dicussed in chapter 8.

32. *TJ*, 5:379, urū 8, Enpō 8; *Shōhō jiroku*, p. 245, order 697 of 18.9.Jōkyō 2; Ishii, *Gotōke reijō*, orders 475, 477 of 23.2.Jōkyō 3 (p. 241). In the latter order the inspector general *(ōmetsuke)* is held responsible, indicating that the order applies to daimyo.

33. *Shōhō jiroku*, p. 242, order 689; *TJ*, 5:558, 7.11.Jōkyō 2.

34. Even the scholar Tsukamoto Manabu, who has researched the shogun's Laws of Compassion in great detail and published his findings in many books and articles, calls it a mad obsession, and this is even more so the opinion of other historians.

35. *Shōhō jiroku*, order 704, p. 250; *Edo machi bure shūsei*, order 2477, p. 140.

36. *Shōhō jiroku*, order 714, p. 254.

37. Ibid., order 715, p. 254.

38. Tsukamoto, "Seikun to shite no inu kubō," p. 68.

39. *TJ*, 5:595, 24.2.Jōkyō 4.

40. *Shōhō jiroku*, order 726, pp. 257-258.

41. For details on the number of orders see Bodart-Bailey, "The Laws of Compassion," p. 171.

42. Ishii, *Gotōke reijō*, p. 246, order 499; p. 248, order 511, and so on.

43. Ibid., p. 248, order 508. The translation is from Shively, p. 113.

44. *Oritaku*, p. 239, my own translation (see also *Told*, p. 106).

45. Tsukamoto, *Shōrui o meguru seiji* (1993), pp. 207, 231, note 28.

46. *Kenbyō jitsuroku* (manuscript Kokuritsu Kokkai Toshokan), vol. 30 (corrected in manuscript to vol. 34.) Also quoted in Tokutomi, 17:240.

47. *TJ*, 6:753.

48. *Kenbyō jitsuroku*, vol. 30 (manuscript: vol. 34); also in Kurita, *Edo jidai*, 1:450.

49. *Oritaku*, p. 239 (*Told*, pp. 105-106).

50. *Oritaku*, p. 241 (*Told*, p. 107).

51. For enforcement of the laws in daimyo domains, see Tsukamoto, *Shōrui o meguru seiji* (1993), p. 207; for greater detail of this argument Bodart-Bailey, "Laws of Compassion," pp. 182-183.

52. Tsukamoto, *Shōrui o meguru seiji* (1993), pp. 209; Ishii, *Oshioki saikyo chō*, pp. 285-286, orders 673-676; pp. 295-298, orders 673-707.

53. Toda Mosui, p. 135; Ishii, *Oshioki saikyo chō*, p. 295, order 696; *TJ*, 5:612, 13.10.Jōkyō 4; change of title: *TJ*, 5:614, 21.10.Jōkyō 4.

54. Maruyama, *Intellectual History*, p. 133.

55. *Shōhō jiroku*, 1:357, order 994.

56. *Genkō jitsuroku*, p. 19; *Yanagisawa ke hizō jikki*, p. 53.

57. *Kaempfer's Japan*, pp. 222-223, 258-259.

58. For example, Ishii, *Oshioki saikyo chō*, pp. 93, 370; Ishii, *Genroku gohōshiki*, p. 460; Asahi Shigeaki, *Ōmurō chūki*, 2:76.

59. *Kaempfer's Japan*, pp. 258-259.

60. Toda Mosui, p. 137.

61. *Shōhō jiroku*, pp. 308, 313, orders 838 and 854 respectively. The tax was suspended when earthquakes and fires created considerable hardship (*Shōhō jiroku*, p. 361, order 1014).

62. Tsukamoto, *Shōrui o meguru seiji* (1993), pp. 212-214, 232, note 39; *TJ*, 6:231, 1.6.Genroku 8; 6:248.

63. Tsukamoto, *Shōrui o meguru seiji* (1993), pp. 214-216.

64. Asahi Shigeaki, *Ōmurō chūki*, 1:195, 26.6.Genroku 10.

65. Tsukamoto, *Shōrui o meguru seiji* (1993), p. 218.

66. *Shōhō jiroku*, p. 337, order 933.

Chapter 12: The Forty-Seven Loyal Samurai

1. Genroku Chūshingura no Kai, pp. 228-238. With forty-seven characters in the kana syllabary, the number alludes to completeness and wholeness, while "copy book" stands for the exemplary action of the samurai. Bell, p. 30. The play has been translated into English and commented on in Donald Keene, trans., *Chushingura*, and James R. Brandon, ed., *Chushingura*.

2. *Kanadehon chūshingura*, program, 231st November kabuki performance, Tokyo, November 2002.

3. For a listing of films, TV productions, and novels, see Genroku Chūshingura no Kai, pp. 170-176.

4. Bell, pp. 37-43, 118-139. Authors of popular humorous books like Shikitei Sanba (1776-1822) also poked fun at the Chūshingura plot. Totman, *Early Modern Japan*, p. 421.

5. Marcon and Smith, pp. 449-461.

6. See, for instance, Nakajima Yasuo, *Ōishi Kuranosuke, saigo no misshi*. For new material discovered in the 1930s, see Smith, "The Trouble with Terasaka," p. 36.

7. For a listing of historical sources and nonfiction publications, see Genroku Chūshingura no Kai, pp. 178-227.

8. Miyazawa, *Kindai nihon to "Chūshingura" no gensō*.

9. In addition to those given above, these are Smith, "The Capacity of Chūshingura"; Bitō, "The Akō Incident"; and McMullen, "Confucian Perspectives," in *Monumenta Nipponica*, vol. 58, nos. 1, 2, 3, respectively. See also Ikegami, pp. 223-240.

10. Smith, "The Trouble with Terasaka," pp. 37-38.

11. See also ibid., p. 48, on this point.

12. Though generally personal names are used for abbreviation, the custom of referring to Asano, Ōishi, and Kira (rather than Naganori, Kuranosuke, and Yoshinaka) is adhered to here.

13. *Kajikawa shi hikki*, cited in Bitō, *Genroku jidai*, pp. 298-299. For an edited translation, see Smith's translation of Bitō, "The Akō Incident," pp. 150-151. *Okado denhachirō jikki*, the record of the inspector who questioned Asano Naganori, is believed by Bitō to have been composed later and is considered unreliable. However, here as well no further reasons are given for Asano Naganori's slaying of Kira Yoshinaka.

14. *Kenbyō jitsuroku*, pp. 394-395, entry 14.3.Genroku 14.

15. The problem of what happened to the forty-seventh is the subject of Smith, "The Trouble with Terasaka."

16. Izumi Hideki, "Chūshingura no shinjitsu," p. 12, citing *Motohiro kōki*, entry 20.3.Genroku 14; Tanno, "Godai Tokugawa Tsunayoshi," p. 95, referring to *Motohiro kōki*.

17. This point was made early by the Confucian scholar Satō Naokata in "Yonjūroku nin no hikki," p. 379.

18. Tahara, *Akō yonjūrokushi ron*, p. 64; Kōsaka, pp. 180-182; Asahi Shigeaki, *Ōmurō chūki*, 1:255, 1:304. Details of the attack on Kira's mansion are supposed to be contained in *Jintenroku*, written by Asahi Shigeaki and his father. Despite scholars' ardent search for further primary sources on this incident, this document has never been printed. The manuscript is held at Nagoya Shi Tsurumai Chūō Toshokan, which has advised that parts are no longer extant and that there is no information on whether the critical material is still contained in those volumes that have been preserved. This is odd considering the ardency with which this subject has otherwise been researched.

19. *Arai Hakuseki nikki*, 1:146, 170-181; Toda Mosui, p. 433. The point that the events attracted relatively little public interest has also been made by Bito Masahide in "The Akō Incident," p. 156.

20. *Dokai kōshūki*, p. 350. For the work's reliability, see below.
21. *TJ*, 5:205, 23.3. Enpō 3.
22. Tokutomi, 18:38-39.
23. Tsunoda et al., 1:385-386.
24. *Hagakure*, describing the event, puts nearly the same words Asano spoke in the mouth of his uncle, namely, "Remember [the incident] the other day?" *Hagakure*, 10:105 (Watsuji, 2:144); Genroku Chūshingura no Kai, p. 51. The event is also described in chapter 7.
25. *TJ*, 6:186, 22.12.Genroku 6.
26. Satō Naokata, "Yonjūroku nin no hikki," p. 379.
27. Cited and explained in Bitō, *Genroku jidai*, p. 306; in English: "Akō Incident," p. 156.
28. *Kōseki kenmonki*, cited in Tahara, *Ako yonjūrokushi ron*, p. 11; see also p. 23.
29. *Dokai kōshūki*, p. 349.
30. Cited and explained in Bitō, *Genroku jidai*, p. 311; "Akō Incident," p. 160.
31. Bitō, *Genroku jidai*, p. 303; "Akō Incident," pp. 153-154.
32. This point was discussed early on by Satō Naokata in "Yonjūroku nin no hikki," p. 385. See also Bitō, *Genroku jidai*, p. 312; "Akō Incident," p. 160.
33. Tokutomi, 18:43-45.
34. *TJ*, 4:445-446, 13.1.Kanbun 3; 4:449, 19.2.Kanbun 3; Tokutomi, 18:47.
35. *TJ*, 4:505, 5.6.Kanbun 4.
36. *TJ*, 5:155, 287.
37. *TJ*, 5:387, 28.10.Enpō 8.
38. Tokutomi, 18:51.
39. Ibid., p. 57.
40. See *Kaempfer's Japan*, pp. 204-205.
41. See chapter 4.
42. Satō Naokata, "Yonjū roku nin no hikki," 27:379.
43. Bito, "Akō Incident," p. 152.
44. Tokutomi, 18:61.
45. Hayashi Ryōshō, "Jikken no hottan," p. 13.
46. Tahara, *Akō yonjūrokushi ron*, pp. 62-63.
47. Ibid., pp. 109-110. On the removal of Ogyū Sorai's essay, see also McMullen, "Confucian Perspectives," p. 299, note 25.
48. Tahara, *Akō yonjūrokushi ron*, pp. 106-107. For an exposition of Asami Keisai's thought on the subject, see Watanabe Hiroshi, pp. 84-87.
49. Satō Naokata, "Yonjūroku nin no hikki," 27:378-380.
50. McMullen, "Confucian Perspectives," pp. 300-301.
51. For instance in Kanai, pp. 60-73; Ōishi, "Genroku Kyōhō ki," 4:52-55.
52. Tahara, *Akō yonjūrokushi ron*, p. 22.
53. *TJ*, 6:478, 18.7.Genroku 15.
54. Genroku Chūshingura no Kai, p. 56.
55. Bito, "Akō Incident," p. 161.
56. Kurita, *Edo jidai*, 1:582.

57. *TJ*, 6:499, 4.2.Genroku 16. Few historians mention this, but it appears in Tahara, *Akō yonjūrokushi ron*, p. 111, and Takeuchi, *Genroku ningen moyō*, p. 67. The possibility of the mistaken character was explained to the author by Professor Takeuchi Makoto in a conversation of April 4, 2005.

58. Nihon Daijiten Kankō Kai, entry *naginata* (8:218).

59. Miyamoto, Musashi, *The Book of Five Rings*, pp. 58–65.

60. The samurai's "calculating" also found mention in *Hagakure*, as discussed below. Also see Smith, "Trouble with Terasaka," p. 48, on this point.

61. Sakata Morotō, ms., vol. 30, 23.12.Genroku 15.

62. Ibid.; also reprinted in Iio, pp. 266–268.

63. Nobuatsu's original verdict is quoted by Iio on p. 269. After the sentence had been pronounced, he wrote another commentary on the incident, this time justifying the *bakufu*'s judgment.

64. E.g., *TJ*, 6:750, quoting *Zoku meiryō kōhan*.

65. Sakata Morotō, *Kai shōshō ason jikki*, ms., vol. 30; Kuwata, pp. 246–247.

66. Asano had received precisely this punishment. For another example, see *TJ*, 6:305, 13.8.Genroku 10. Henry Smith in "The Trouble with Terasaka" (pp. 43, 47–48) suggests that the forty-seventh, Terasaka Kichiemon, was sent away by his comrades after the attack because he was not of samurai status, and they feared that this might influence the *bakufu*'s decision.

67. *Yanagisawa ke hizō jikki*, 3:64. Translation Lidin, *Ogyū Sorai*, pp. 48–49.

68. As explained above, Uesugi Tsunanori was Kira's real son adopted into the Uesugi family as an infant.

69. *Sorai giritsu sho*, cited in Maruyama, *Nihon seiji*, p. 75. Though the text is in the translation of this work (*Intellectual History*, p. 74) and has also been translated by Lidin (*Ogyū Sorai*, p. 50), I have translated it again. Both these translations render *gi* as "righteousness." *Gi*, however, does not mean righteousness in the Western sense of a public righteous judgment but includes the proper fulfillment of personal duty (see, for instance, Tsunoda et al., pp. 386, 425). This distinction is essential here since the very point Sorai is making is that personal duty conflicted with public law and that the latter must be given precedence.

70. Lidin, *Ogyū Sorai*, p. 50.

71. For discussion see chapter 16.

72. Tahara, *Akō yonjūrokushi ron*, pp. 68–69.

73. Reprinted in Maruyama, *Intellectual History*, p. 73.

74. Lidin, *Ogyū Sorai*, p. 50.

75. Iio, pp. 258–266.

76. Ikegami, p. 285; *Hagakure*, trans. Wilson, pp. 141–142.

77. Ikegami, pp. 293–294.

78. *Hagakure*, 1:45, no. 55; translation: Ikegami, p. 287.

79. Smith, "Capacity of Chūshingura," p. 10.

80. Ikegami, p. 288.

81. Lorenz, pp. 164, 186–190.

82. Ibid., pp. 188–189.

83. Henry D. Smith, handout for presentation. "The Problem of the 47th Ronin: A New Look at the Ako Incident and the Chushingura Legend" (International Christian University, December 13, 2001), p. 3, and "The Trouble with Terasaka."

84. Miyazawa's work *Kindai nihon to chūshingura gensō* gives a detailed analysis of the use of the Akō incident for political purposes. On Mishima and *Hagakure* see also Ikegami, p. 279.

85. Huntington, p. 20.

Chapter 13: Financial Matters

1. Ihara Saikaku, *This Scheming World*, trans. Stubbs and Takatsuka, p. 126.
2. Ibid., p. 31.
3. For a comparison of the population of European cities, see Bodart-Bailey, "Urbanisation and the Nature of the Tokugawa Hegemony," pp. 100–101.
4. Ihara Saikaku, trans. Stubbs and Takatsuka, p. 126.
5. *Kokushi daijiten*, 9:1043; Ōno, p. 31, has 2,300,000 to 2,400,000 *koku*.
6. Tokutomi, 13:190–192; Kurita, *Edo jidai*, 1:234; Ōno, p. 33.
7. Yamaguchi Keiji, p. 20.
8. *Kokushi daijiten*, 5:354–355.
9. Sasaki and Watanabe, p. 212. Tokutomi, 13:177.
10. Tokutomi, 13:177–181; Kurita, *Edo jidai*, 1:149–150.
11. Kurita, *Edo jidai*, 1:149–150; Hasegawa Riheiji, p. 62. One *kan* is 3.75 kilograms.
12. *Kaempfer's Japan*, pp. 378–384, 424–428.
13. Cooper, *Rodrigues the Interpreter*, p. 213.
14. Cooper, *This Island of Japon*, p. 53.
15. For some of the difficulties encountered in determining exchange rates, see Kobata, "The Production and Uses of Gold and Silver," especially pp. 250–255.
16. Cooper, *They Came to Japan*, p. 10. The tael is usually considered equivalent to 10 *momme*, which would make this 37.5 grams. However, at the time measurements frequently varied and were applied loosely.
17. Tsuji Tatsuya, *Edo kaifu*, pp. 173–176. Kurita Mototsugu's calculations (*Edo jidai* 1:226) amount to 1,930,000 to 1,940,000 *ryō*; Ōno, p. 31, also has 1,940,00 *ryō*. George Sansom (*A History of Japan*, 3:5) gives 1,950,000 *ryō* but does not state his source.
18. Ōno, p. 31, introduces different source material, giving the amount to Owari and Kii as 400,000 *ryō* each and that to Mito as 260,000 *ryō*.
19. Tsuji Tatsuya, *Edo kaifu*, pp. 176–177; Kurita, *Edo jidai*, 1:226.
20. Tsuji Tatsuya, *Edo kaifu*, pp. 176–177; Kurita, *Edo jidai*, 1:230.
21. Nikkō Shishi Hensan Iinkai, 2:223, 342–345.
22. *Kokushi daijiten*, 10:110–113.
23. Fujii Jōji, *Tokugawa Iemitsu*, pp. 199–201.
24. Tanabe, pp. 105–106, 109–115; Nikkō Shishi Hensan Iinkai, 2:418–423.
25. *Tōshō daigongen sama gozōei gomokuroku*, cited in Fujii Jōji, *Tokugawa Iemitsu*, p. 194; Nikkō Shishi Hensan Iinkai, 2:392.
26. Tanabe, pp. 44–47; Nikkō Shishi Hensan Iinkai, pp. 424–437.
27. *Takebashi yohitsu besshū*, as cited in Ōno, pp. 210–211.

28. Ōno, pp. 199–200.
29. Ibid., pp. 204, 210.
30. Ibid., p. 199. For figures not included, see p. 201.
31. Kurita, *Edo jidai*, 1:230. Fujii, *Tokugawa Iemitsu*, p. 194, has nine times.
32. *TJ*, 4:463, 4.5.Kanbun 3; 5:443, 28.3.Tenna 2; Bodart-Bailey, "A Case of Political and Economic Expropriation," pp. 179–180.
33. *Kokushi daijiten*, Kiyomizu: 4:412; Chion-in: 9:368; Enryakuji: Aoki, 1:960, 962. See also Nikkō Shishi Hensan Iinkai, 2:342–343.
34. Kurita, *Edo jidai*, 1:230; Tsuji Tatsuya, *Tennō to shōgun*, pp. 110–113. Based on Tsuji's calculation this amounts roughly to 172,000 *ryō*.
35. Tokutomi, 19:15–16.
36. Tsuji Tatsuya, *Tennō to shōgun*, 111–112.
37. Mikami Ryūzō, p. 150.
38. *TJ*, 2:685, 7.7.Kanei 12.
39. Sansom, 3:26.
40. Yamaguchi Keiji, p. 19. Iwao Seiichi believes that the silver that left Japan through the foreign trade alone, was equal to 30 or 40 percent of the total world silver production outside Japan (p. 10).
41. Kurita, *Edo jidai*, 1:230.
42. Hasegawa Riheiji, pp. 62–64. See also the tables in Ōishi, p. 75, showing the amount of precious metals from the Sado mines between 1613 and 1693.
43. *TJ*, 4:209, 19.1.Meireki 3.
44. *TJ*, 4:217, 29.2.Meireki 3.
45. *TJ*, 4:212, 29.1.Meireki 3.
46. *TJ*, 4:214–215, 9.2.Meireki 3.
47. *TJ*, 4:215, 217, 221, and so on.
48. *Takebashi yohitsu besshū*, cited in Kurita Mototsugu, "Genroku izen ni okeru Edo bakufu no zaisei ni tuite," p. 1159 (1 *kan*=1,000 *momme*; 66 *momme*=1 golden *ryō*; however, the exchange rate between *momme* and *ryō* varied).
49. *TJ*, 4:227, 11.5.Meireki 3.
50. *TJ*, 4:225, 20.4.Meireki 3; 4:238, 15.8.Meireki 3.
51. *TJ*, 4:227, 9.5.Meireki 3.
52. Officials were appointed on 9.4.Manji 1. *TJ*, 4:264.
53. Kurita Mototsugu, "Genroku," 1150–1158.
54. For a description of the building works at Edo castle, see Fujii Jōji, *Tokugawa Iemitsu*, pp. 114–117.
55. Asao, "Shōgun seiji," pp. 35, 39–40; Tsuji Tatsuya, "Geba shōgun seiji no seikaku," p. 30.
56. Asao, "Shogun seiji," pp. 41–42; Bolitho, *Treasures*, pp. 166–167.
57. E.g., *TJ*, 4:258, 5.2.Manji 1; 4:259, 15.2.Manji 1; and so on.
58. Bolitho, *Treasures*, p. 168; Kurita, "Genroku," p. 1159; *TJ*, 4:259, 26.2.Manji 1; 4:262, 15.3.Manji 1; 4:265, 18.4.Manji 1; 4:266, 23.4.Manji 1; 4:273, 3.7. and 4.7.Manji 1; and so on.
59. Tokutomi, 17:245–253.

60. *TJ*, 5:431, 24.11.Tenna 1.

61. Compare *TJ*, 2:685, 7.7.Kanei 12, with 4:214, 9.2.Meireki 3.

62. These figures are calculated on the basis of those given in Fujino, *Bakusei to hansei*, p. 42. The period for the first shogun is calculated from 1600 to 1615 (where attainders amounted to 3,594,640 *koku*) and for the second shogun from 1616 to 1631 (3,605,420 *koku*.). A breakdown of these figures can be found in ibid., pp. 3-9. Variations from figures by other scholars occur depending on whether land later enfeoffed again to members of the same family is counted. See also Hall, "The Bakuhan System," p. 152, using these figures.

63. Kitajima, *Edo bakufu no kenryoku kōzō*, pp. 348-349. For a discussion of the change of the intendants' role after Ieyasu, see Izumi Seiji, pp. 403-412.

64. Fujii Jōji, "Ietsuna seiken ron," p. 59.

65. Kitajima, *Edo bakufu*, pp. 346-347.

66. Fujii Jōji, *Edo bakufu rōjūsei*, p. 545.

67. Sasama, pp. 211-212.

68. Tsuji Tatsuya, *Kyōhō kaikaku*, pp. 63-64.

69. Ibid., p. 63.

70. Ōishi, *Genroku jidai*, p. 116; Ōishi, *Kyōhō kaikaku no keizai seisaku*, p. 80; Kitajima, *Edo bakufu*, pp. 349-350.

71. Tsuji Tatsuya, *Kyōhō kaikaku*, p. 68, citing *Gotōke reijō*, section 23 (*Kinsei hōsei shiryō sōsho*, 2:158).

72. *TJ*, 5:401, 18.2.Tenna 1.

73. Sasama, p. 240; Ōishi, *Kyōhō kaiku*, p. 81, 84, note 7; Nakase, *Tokugawa bakufu no kaikei kensa seido*, p. 95; *TJ*, 5:451, 14.6.Tenna 2.

74. *TJ*, 5:603, 21.6.Jōkyō 4.

75. Nakase, *Tokugawa bakufu*, pp. 145-146, citing *Okattegata osadame gakki*.

76. *TJ*, 5:400, 9.2.Tenna 1; Tsuji Tatsuya, *Kyōhō kaikaku*, p. 66. On Tadatsugu see Murakami, *Edo bakufu no daikan*, pp. 19-40.

77. Tsuji Tatsuya, *Kyōhō kaikaku*, p. 65. Following *Kojiruien*, Tsuji estimates that there were between forty and fifty intendants. Murakami (*Edo bakufu*, unpaginated appendix) lists seventy-five for Enpō 1 (1673).

78. Tsuji Tatsuya, *Kyōhō kaikaku*, pp. 64-65.

79. Ibid., p. 67.

80. Though no appointment to replace Hotta Masatoshi appears in the record, at the time of the reminting of the coinage, the senior councilor Ōkubo Tadatomo is said to have been in charge of finance (Bodart-Bailey, "A Case of Political and Economic Expropriation," p. 185).

81. Kodama, *Nihonshi sōran*, 4:63.

82. *TJ*, 5:610, 9.9.Jōkyō 4.

83. *Shokafu*, 10:143; *TJ*, 5:610, 10.9.Jōkyō 4.

84. Matsudaira Tarō, p. 640; Sasama, p. 240; Tsuji Tatsuya, *Kyōhō kaikaku*, p. 63.

85. Toda Mosui, p. 148.

86. *TJ*, 5:621, 25.12.Jōkyō 4; *Shokafu*, 10:143. The granting of *hoi* for the holders of this position later became common in view of the heavy responsibilities vested in it (Sasama, p. 240).

87. *Shokafu*, 10:143; Sasama, p. 211.
88. *Shokafu*, 10:143.
89. Ibid.; Fujino, *Oneiroku haizetsuroku*, p. 286; *Sekai dai hyakka jiten*, entry "Haritsuke Mozaemon."
90. Hasegawa Masatsugu, p. 28.
91. Ibid., pp. 38 and 29 respectively.

Chapter 14: Producing Currency
1. *Sannō gaiki*, p. 5 verso.
2. Itō, 2:134.
3. For instance, Naitō, 6:106; Tokutomi, 17: 266.
4. Sakata Morotō, *Kai shōshō ason jikki*, ms., vol. 19, 11.8.Genroku 8. According to Ogyū Sorai, Ogiwara Shigehide suggested this measure to permit not only the pilgrimage to Nikkō, but also a visit to the emperor at Kyoto. *Seidan*, p. 332. In *Discourse*, pp. 171-172 "Ogiwara" is mistakenly rendered as "Hagiwara." A literal translation of the passage would be "Ogiwara Ōmi no kami said: I have a humble proposal that would result in the shogun's pilgrimage and his procession to the imperial capital not being curtailed by [the *bakufu*'s insufficient] receipts."
5. Ōkurashō, 2:568-569, translated in Bolitho, "Dog Shogun," p. 135.
6. *Kaempfer's Japan*, pp. 213, 215-216.
7. Totman, *Early Modern Japan*, pp. 142-143.
8. For Ieyasu's appointment of minting houses, see Kobata, *Nihon kahei ryūtsū shi*, pp. 472-475.
9. Kodama et al., *Nihonshi sōran*, 4:516.
10. *Sankazui*, cited in Tokutomi, 17:254-255, and Kurita, "Genroku," p. 1161.
11. Kurita, "Genroku," p. 1160; *TJ*, 6:672, 13.10.Enpō 4.
12. Taya, pp. 162-164.
13. *Shokafu*, 10:143; *TJ*, 6:101, 15.2.Genroku 4.
14. Ōishi, *Genroku jidai*, p. 75.
15. Parentheses are in the original. Ōmi no Kami=Ogiwara Shigehide.
16. *Oritaku*, p. 233.
17. Ibid., p. 234.
18. Ibid., pp. 234-235.
19. Ibid., pp. 238, 300, 305.
20. Ibid., pp. 300, 308; *TJ*, 7:245, 11.9.Shōtoku 2.
21. *Oritaku*, p. 361; *TJ*, 7:378-379, 15.5.Shōtoku 4. See *Oritaku*, pp. 319-320, for rumors that Hakuseki was responsible for stopping the reminting.
22. *Oritaku*, pp. 360-363.
23. Ibid., p. 251.
24. While we have no proof that the laws were not repealed by Ienobu as publicly stated or that their repeal was only issued as his order after his death, Hakuseki described how this kind of measure had been adopted for the repeal of the Laws of Compassion. *Oritaku*, pp. 226-227.
25. Tsuji Tatsuya, "Politics," p. 439.

26. Sakudō, pp. 96-97, 122; Yamamura, p. 43; Tsuji Tatsuya, "Politics," p. 436.

27. The contribution levied in Kyōhō 7 (1722), known as *agemai*, called for 100 *koku* of rice for each 10,000 *koku* of a daimyo's revenue. In return for the contribution, the period of residence at Edo stipulated by the *sankin kōtai* system was halved. Daimyo whose duties within the *bakufu* required them to be present at Edo paid only one-third of the levy. Itō, 2:122-123.

28. Taya, p. 184; Nihon Ginkō Chōsa Kyoku, pp. 23-24. For a listing of domains issuing paper money and corresponding dates, see p. 21. It was not until Kyōhō 15 (1730) that the daimyo were again permitted to issue paper money (Kitajima, *Edo bakufu no kenryoku kōzō*, p. 624).

29. Tokutomi, 18:92; Kodama, *Genroku jidai*, p. 348.

30. *TJ*, 6:672.

31. Ōkurashō, 2:574, twelfth month, Genroku 14; Tokutomi, 17:282-283, 291.

32. Ōkurashō, 2:573, eleventh month, Genroku 13; 2:581, *urū* first month, Hōei 5.

33. For instance Ōkurashō, 2:571, first month, Genroku 11.

34. Ibid., 2:576-580.

35. For instance, Kodama, *Genroku jidai*, p. 216.

36. Fujii Jōji, *Tokugawa Iemitsu*, p. 208, table.

37. For a description of the expenses on a shogunal visit see Kodama, *Genroku jidai*, pp. 380-381.

38. This is also pointed out by Fujita Satoru, "Genroku ki bakufu zaisei no shin shiryō," p. 64 (1544).

39. Ōno, pp. 200-202.

40. Sasama, pp. 244-245.

41. Ōtani, p. 273.

42. Fukuyama, pp. 62-71.

43. Ōtani, p. 273; Bolitho, *Treasures*, p. 178.

44. Ōtani, pp. 281-282. For details on the Kantō river projects in the Hōei period, see the rest of Ōtani's article.

45. Ōno, p. 223; Tsukamoto, *Kinsei saikō*, p. 180.

Chapter 15: The Two Wheels of a Cart

1. The Five Relationships of Confucianism are between father and son, ruler and subject, husband and wife, older and younger brother, and between friends.

2. *Rakushidō nenroku*, ms., vol. 13, 22.9.Genroku 5. Also quoted in Kurita, *Edo jidai*, 1:590.

3. See Ooms, pp. 175-177, for an elaboration of this topic.

4. It is interesting to note that Tsunayoshi is criticized as superstitious for his belief in the efficacy of the gods, while scholars holding similar views such as Arai Hakuseki and Ogyū Sorai are viewed as "rational" thinkers. For Hakuseki see, for instance, chapter 14 above. For Sorai, see Ogyū Sorai, *Master Sorai's Responsals*, p. 50.

5. Fujii Jōji, *Tokugawa Iemitsu*, p. 194.

6. The sum of 300 *ryō* was allocated through the magistrate of temples and

shrines, but this was for burial services for the over one hundred thousand people who died. *TJ*, 4:218, 29.2.Meireki 3.

7. For the Kyoto Great Buddha, see *Kaempfer's Japan*, pp. 380–384; Kurita, *Edo jidai*, 1:98. For Tōdaiji, see Takano, *Kinsei nihon*, p. 119.

8. Tsukamoto, *Tsunayoshi*, p. 197.

9. Ōno, p. 212.

10. *Seidan*, pp. 321-322; *Discourse*, p. 159. The original does not refer to the first three shoguns but to the Keichō and Kanei eras (1596–1644) when they governed.

11. For an analysis see Ōno, pp. 210–211.

12. Tsukamoto, *Tsunayoshi*, pp.185–187.

13. *Hagakure*, trans. Wilson, p. 95.

14. Ibid.

15. Ōno, p. 220; *TJ*, 4:579, 18.6.Jōkyō 3.

16. *TJ*, 6:141, 9.5.Genroku 5; Tsukamoto, *Tsunayoshi*, p. 192.

17. Tsukamoto, *Tsunayoshi*, p. 192; *Matsukage nikki*, p. 151; *Yanagisawa Yoshiyasu kō sanzen roku*, pp. 14–15, 28.

18. Takano, *Kinsei*, p. 281. For a description of the mountain priests, see *Kaempfer's Japan*, 123–126.

19. Ōno, pp. 218–219, 223.

20. *Sekai dai hyakka jiten*, entry "Kaneiji."

21. Toda Mosui, pp. 384, 388; Kodama, *Genroku jidai*, p. 385.

22. See, for instance, Tokutomi, 17:193–200.

23. *Ryūkō sōjō nikki*, 1:76, 8.8.Genroku 6; Tsukamoto, *Tsunayoshi*, p. 188; *TJ*, 6:175, 12.8.Genroku 6. Here the monk is referred to as Hachiōji Jōju-in.

24. Tsuji Tatsuya, *Edo kaifu*, pp. 275–277, 288.

25. For elaboration of this topic see ibid., pp. 292–303; and Ooms, pp. 59–60, 173–186. For a book-length treatment of this topic, see Sonehara, *Tokugawa Ieyasu shinkakuka e no michi*.

26. Ōno, p. 218; *TJ*, 6:220, 25.1.Genroku 8.

27. *Ryūkō sōjō nikki*, 3:290.

28. See chapter 12.

29. See chapter 10.

30. Toda Mosui, pp. 181–182; see also Tsukamoto's comment in *Tsunayoshi*, pp. 185–186; Tokutomi, 17:194.

31. Fung Yu-Lan, p. 182.

32. *Ryūkō sōjō nikki*, 1:81.

33. Tsunoda et al., 1:136.

34. *TJ*, 6:307; Hiraishi, p. 45.

35. *Ryūkō sōjō nikki*, 1:260.

36. Arai Hakuseki, *Honsaroku kō*, 6:551. See also chapter 5.

37. See chapter 16 below.

38. *TJ*, 5:381, 11.9.Enpō 8; *Kenbyō jitsuroku*, same date.

39. Kurita Naomi, p. 9.

40. *TJ*, 3:704.

41. *Shokafu*, 17:218; *TJ*, 4:396, 6.uru8.Kanbun 1; Kurita Naomi, p. 10.
42. *Shokafu*, 17:218.
43. *Meigetsuki: TJ*, 4:429, 11.7.Kanbun 2; *Zoku honchō tsugan: Shokafu*, 17:218. On the composition of *Honchō tsugan*, see Nakai, "Tokugawa Confucian Historiography," pp. 71-72; Ooms, pp. 212-213, and Kornicki, p. 385.
44. *TJ*, 4:495, 17.3.Kanbun 4; 4:506, 28.6.Kanbun 4.
45. *Shokafu*, 17:218; *TJ*, 4:610, 4.5.Kanbun 7.
46. *TJ*, 4:490, 16.1.Kanbun 4. The information that the ceremony was held at Zōjōji is contained in *Hitomi shiki*, ms., vol. 6 *(Genyū kōki)*, under this date.
47. *Kanda ki*, ms., 15.9.Keian 5; 28.10.Keian 5; 7.11 and 11.11.Keian 5, and so forth.
48. *Hitomi shiki*, ms., vol. 6, 11.8.Kanbun 7.
49. Ishikawa et al., p. 324.
50. For instance *Kanda ki*, ms., 3.3, 5.5.Enpō 3; 1.1, 3.3.Enpō 8.
51. *TJ*, 5:338, 9.6.Enpō 8.
52. *Shokafu*, 17:218-219.
53. Hayashi Gahō, *Kokushikan nichiroku*, pp. 2:75, 91, and so on; Ishikawa, p. 324.
54. *Discourse*, p. 321; *Seidan*, pp. 442-443. Sorai discusses this subject in greater detail in *Gakuryō ryōken sho*, pp. 566-567.
55. Letter from Chu Shun-shui to Yamaga Sokō, cited in Tokutomi, 16:565.
56. Ching, "Practical Learning," pp. 192, 197, 200, 204, 208, 214.
57. Tokutomi, 16:568.
58. Ching, "Practical Learning," pp. 198, 200; Ishihara, pp. 142, 152.
59. Ching, "Practical Learning," p. 191.
60. Tokuta, pp. 40-45.
61. Ibid., pp. 47, 59.
62. Ibid., pp. 46-47.
63. Ibid., pp. 67-68.
64. Hayashi Gahō, 1:122, 7.9.Kanbun 5.
65. Ibid., 1:123, 13.9.Kanbun 5; also Tokuta, p. 59.
66. Tokuta, p. 60.
67. Ibid., pp. 62, 64.
68. Ishihara, pp. 241, 243; Ching, "Practical Learning," p. 211.
69. Letter from Hitomi Yūgen, cited in Tokuta, pp. 81-82. Yūgen used the expression *kuni no kyō taifu* (the country's nobles and great lords), which is from *The Spring and Autumn Annals*.
70. Ōishi, *Genroku jidai*, p. 93; Ching, "Practical Learning," p. 213; For Jun'an's career under Tsunayoshi, see *TJ*, 5:455, 28.7.Tenna 2; 5:468, 23.12.Tenna 2; 5:499, 12.11.Tenna 3; 5:585, 18.9.Jōkyō 3; 6:283, 28.1.Genroku 10; 6:183, 5.2.Genroku 6, and so forth.
71. See chapter 5 above.
72. *Kenbyō jitsuroku*, p. 35, last entry second month, Tenna 1. The Five Books are *The Great Learning, The Doctrine of the Mean, The Confucian Analects,* and *The Works of Mencius*. The Five Classics are *The Book of Changes, The Book of Poetry, The Book of History, The Spring and Autumn Annals,* and *The Book of Rites*.

73. Tokutomi, 17:120. Also *TJ*, 6:25, 1.11.Genroku 1.
74. *Rakushidō nenroku*, ms., 3.6.Tenna 1.
75. *TJ*, 5:435.
76. Julia Ching, *To Acquire Wisdom*, pp. 15-16.
77. Tsuji Tatsuya, "*Seidan* no shakaiteki haikei," pp. 778-781. For Tsunayoshi's order to the intendants, see chapter 8 above.
78. *TJ*, 5:449-450, end of fifth month of Tenna 2.
79. Weber, *Economy and Society*, 1:315; Weber, *Wirtschaft und Gesellschaft*, p. 184.
80. Konta, p. 61.
81. See Tsuji Tatsuya, "*Seidan* no shakaiteki haikei," p. 781.
82. Ibid., p. 778. *TJ*, 5:449, uses the word *jinjo*, the meaning of which is also "compassion."
83. *TJ*, 6:27, 21.11.Genroku 1; Tokutomi, 17:125-127; Tsukamoto, *Tsunayoshi*, pp. 164-165.
84. Tokutomi, 17:127-128.
85. *Kenbyō jitsuroku*, 21.8.Genroku 3, has *shissei shitsuji nado no tame ni*. *TJ*, 6:82, same date, does not have this explanation.
86. *Kenbyō jitsuroku*, 21.9.Genroku 3; *TJ*, 6:84, same date.
87. Hashimoto, no pagination. For an illustration, see section F, no. 2; Wajima, *Nihon sōgakushi no kenkyū*, pp. 500-501.
88. *TJ*, 6:79.
89. *TJ*, 6:90, 21.11.Genroku 3; 6:92, 16.12.Genroku 3; 6:93, 22 and 23.12.Genroku 3 respectively.
90. Tokutomi, 16:517-519.
91. *TJ*, 6:95, 13.1.Genroku 4.
92. *TJ*, 6:97.
93. *TJ*, 6:98-100.
94. *Kaempfer's Japan*, pp. 407-408.
95. Tokutomi, 17:521.
96. Hashimoto, no pagination.
97. Tsukamoto, *Tsunayoshi*, pp. 168-169.
98. *TJ*, 6:136, 28.3.Genroku 5; Tsukamoto, *Tsunayoshi*, p. 168.
99. *Kenbyō jitsuroku*, p. 238, 3.6.Genroku 5; *TJ*, 6:143; Tsukamoto, *Tsunayoshi*, pp. 168-169. The interpretation of *seidōkyō*, the subject of the first chapter of *The Doctrine of the Mean*, differs among scholars. Legge translates the first article, which contains the definition, as "What Heaven has conferred is called The Nature; an accordance with this nature is called The Path of duty, the regulation of this path is called Instruction (Legge, p. 2 of chapter "The Doctrine of the Mean"). Fung Yu-lan (pp. 174-175) has "What Heaven confers is called the nature. The following of this nature is called the Way (Tao). The cultivation of this Way is called spiritual culture." In his explanation Fung emphasizes "the importance of the common and ordinary," a concept well fitting Chu's as well as Tsunayoshi's interpretation.
100. Kodama, *Genroku jidai*, p. 312.

Chapter 16: The Apprenticeship of Ogyū Sorai

1. Ogyū Sorai, *Yakubun sentei*, p. 546. Also Ogyū Sorai, *Nihon no meichō*, p. 241.
2. *Kenbyō jitsuroku*, p. 237, 2.6.Genroku 5; *TJ*, 6:143, same date; Iwabashi, p. 117. Controversy exists over whether Sorai returned with his father or two years previously. For discussion of this point, see Tsuji Tatsuya, "*Seidan* no shakai teki haikei," p. 602; and Hiraishi, pp. 173-174. *Kanda ki*, ms., 20.9.Enpō 6, confirms that his father was banished in 1678, but Sorai refers both to thirteen years and fourteen years of banishment.
3. For Sorai's statements, see Lidin, *Ogyū Sorai*, pp. 34-35; for skepticism, Imanaka, pp. 64-65.
4. Hiraishi, pp. 40-41.
5. *Seidan*, p. 290.
6. *Seidan*, p. 289. For an explanation of Chu Hsi's theory of *li*, see Fung Yu-Lan, pp. 296-297; Noguchi, *Ogyū Sorai*, pp. 46-48. Since Chu Hsi's theory of *li* (Jap. *ri*) would have been familiar to Sorai's readers, I do not think *rigaku* should be translated as "rationalistic" as it is in Maruyama, *Intellectual History*, p. 70, and *Discourse*, p. 115. See also the editor's (Tsuji Tatsuya) note on the text in *Seidan*, p. 289.
7. Fung, p. 301. See also Minamoto, p. 73. The relationship between "principle" and "heart" was a topic also debated by Kumazawa Banzan (Minamoto, p. 237).
8. *Seidan*, pp. 289-290.
9. Ibid., p. 290; *Discourse*, pp. 115-116.
10. *Genkō jitsuroku*, pp. 34-35.
11. Hiraishi, pp. 42-44; Lidin, *Ogyū Sorai*, pp. 32-33.
12. For instance Imanaka, p. 67. A short extract is cited in Hiraishi, pp. 177-178.
13. For instance Noguchi, *Ogyū Sorai*, p. 59.
14. Bitō Masahide, "Kokka shugi no sokei to shite no Sorai," pp. 22-23; Ogyū Sorai, *Sorai shū*, pp. 221-222; Lidin, *Ogyū Sorai*, pp. 77-78, 80. (What Lidin translates as "a lovely cinnabar time" on p. 77 is an honorific referring to the death of the shogun, as Bito explains on p. 22.) See also *Matsukage nikki*, pp. 285-286.
15. *Shinruigaki yuishogaki*, as cited in Imanaka, pp. 65-66; Lidin, *Ogyū Sorai*, p. 175.
16. Tahara, *Sorai gaku no sekai*, pp. 90-99.
17. Letter to Yabu Shin'an cited in Imanaka, p. 114.
18. *Seidan*, p. 443 (my translation; *Discourse*, p. 322).
19. Maruyama, *Nihon seiji shisō*, p. 118; Maruyama, *Studies in the Intellectual History*, p. 114.
20. *Seidan*, p. 439 (my translation; *Discourse*, p. 316).
21. *TJ*, 8:82, entry at the end of the seventh month, Kyōhō 2. See also Tsuji Tatsuya, *Tokugawa Yoshimune*, p. 165.
22. *TJ*, 8:174, 28.10.Kyōhō 4. Also Tsuji Tatsuya, *Yoshimune*, p. 167. Wai-ming Ng's translation stating that when Tsunayoshi lectured "anyone interested was welcome to attend" (p. 66) seems to suggest that such an audience was also welcomed by Tsunayoshi. However, the original text (*Kenbyō jitsuroku*, p. 247) makes it clear that this welcome was only extended to members of the select groups specified.
23. *Ken'en zatsuwa*, cited in Iwabashi, p. 149. Only when one of the students of common status turned blind did Sorai feel pity and admit him to his room.

24. *Seidan*, p. 443.
25. Ibid., p. 442 (*Discourse*, p. 320).
26. *Seidan*, p. 442 (*Discourse*, p. 320); on poetry as a preparatory step, see also Lidin, *Ogyū Sorai*, p. 162, citing *Bunkai zakki, kan* 2.
27. Ogyū Sorai, *Taiheisaku*, pp. 455–456; McEwan, pp. 133–135.
28. Ogyū Sorai, *Taiheisaku*, p. 456.
29. Ogyū Sorai, *Gakuryō ryōken sho*, pp. 566–567.
30. Lidin, *Ogyū Sorai*, pp. 137–138, translating a letter to priest Kōkoku; Ogyū Sorai, *Sorai shū*, pp. 324–325.
31. Lidin, *Ogyū Sorai*, pp. 79–80, translating a letter to Yamagata Shūnan (Ogyū Sorai, *Sorai shū*, p. 222).
32. Lidin, *Ogyū Sorai*, p. 72, translating Sorai's poem; Ogyū Sorai, *Sorai shū*, p. 47; also in Iwabashi, p. 128. On the topic of low remuneration for Confucian scholars, see also Nakai, *Shogunal Politics*, pp. 32–33.
33. Tokutomi, 17:124–125.
34. Imanaka, pp. 76–90; Lidin, *Ogyū Sorai*, pp. 112–130.
35. *Matsukage nikki*, p. 138. *Yanagisawa Yoshiyasu kō sanzen roku*, pp. 16–17.
36. Lidin, *Ogyū Sorai*, pp. 114–116; Baroni, p. 78.
37. *TJ*, 6:619, 28.4.Hōei 3. Baroni, p. 237, note 46, dates his appointment to 1707; see also Jansen, *China in the Tokugawa World*, p. 57; Jansen, *The Making of Modern Japan*, p. 89; *Matsukage nikki*, pp. 272–273, 276–277.
38. Ogyū Sorai, *Sorai shū*, p. 314; Lidin, *Ogyū Sorai*, pp. 116–117. Part of the letter is also cited in Jansen, *The Making of Modern Japan*, p. 89; *Matsukage nikki*, pp. 272–273, describes the visit to the Yanagisawa mansion.
39. Lidin, *Ogyū Sorai*, pp. 118–119.
40. Hiraishi, p. 210; letter of Hattori Nankaku, cited in Hino, p. 182.
41. *Kenbyō jitsuroku*, p. 4; Hiraishi, pp. 210–213. An earlier version is available as microfilm at the National Diet Library, Tokyo. The entry of 13.2.Genroku 16 mentioned by Lidin (*Ogyū Sorai*, p. 113) is not contained in the version published in 1982.
42. *Rakushidō nenroku*, ms., 5.2.Hōei. Hiraishi, pp. 177–178, cites the question and answers but not the final summing up of the subject by Sorai that follows.
43. Imanaka, p. 80.
44. *TJ*, 6:567; *Kenbyō jitsuroku*, p. 458. The latter entry is extremely short, stating only that the shogun visited the Yanagisawa mansion.
45. Lidin, *Ogyū Sorai*, p. 115.
46. Hiraishi, p. 178.
47. Ogyū Sorai, *Ogyu Sorai's Distinguishing the Way*, pp. 10, 22.
48. Lidin, *Ogyū Sorai*, p. 128.
49. For Chinese poetry, see example cited in Hiraishi, p. 53. For Kitamura Kigin, see *Rakushidō nenroku*, ms., vol. 87, entry 13.9.Genroku 14, and also chapter 9.
50. Maruyama, *Intellectual History*, pp. 75, 81.
51. Ogyū Sorai, *Master Sorai's Responsals*, trans. Samuel Hideo Yamashita.
52. *Ogyū Sorai zenshū*, 1:465, my translation. Yamashita's translation (pp. 85–86)

is less literal. Moreover, I do not see any justification for translating *seiji* as "provincial governments."

53. *Kenbyō jitsuroku*, ms., original *sōsho* version.
54. Hiraishi, p. 212.
55. Ogyū Sorai, *Responsals*, pp. 35–36; *Ogyū Sorai zenshū*, 1:426.
56. *Yōgen roku*, p. 32.
57. Ogyū Sorai, *Taiheisaku*, p. 467. Translation in Maruyama, *Intellectual History*, p. 82.
58. *Ogyu Sorai's Distinguishing the Way*, p. 47, for the Japanese text; Hane's translation (Maruyama, *Intellectual History*, p. 82) has been used partially here.
59. See chapter 8.
60. McEwan, p. 100.
61. *Seidan*, pp. 388–389 (my translation; *Discourse*, p. 244).
62. *Seidan*, p. 389 (my translation, *Discourse*, p. 244).
63. *Seidan*, p. 389. (In *Discourse*, p. 245, the phrase *omae e deru hito kiwamaru toki wa*, "when it is a matter of deciding who is to enter the shogunal presence," is rendered rather differently.)
64. *Discourse*, pp. 197–198; *Seidan*, p. 351.
65. *Seidan*, pp. 368–369 (my translation; *Discourse*, p. 223).
66. *Discourse*, p. 225; *Seidan*, p. 370.
67. *Discourse*, p. 318; *Seidan*, p. 440.
68. *Discourse*, p. 320; *Seidan*, p. 441.
69. *Seidan*, p. 316 (my translation; *Discourse*, p. 151).
70. *Seidan*, p. 358 (my translation; *Discourse*, p. 209).
71. Editor Tsuji Tatsuya's note, *Seidan*, p. 385.
72. Sorai makes the request that the work be burned (*Seidan*, p. 445; *Discourse*, p. 325).
73. *Discourse*, pp. 241–242; *Seidan*, p. 386.
74. *Seidan*, p. 314 (my translation; *Discourse*, p. 149).
75. *Discourse*, p. 159; *Seidan*, p. 322.
76. Maruyama, *Intellectual History*, p. 133 (Maruyama, *Nihon seiji shisō*, p. 137), citing *Seidan* (p. 411). Reading Lidin's translation (*Discourse*, pp. 275–276), one might get the impression that Sorai is anticipating the Meiji Restoration, something that is not in the original.
77. *Discourse*, pp. 269–270; *Seidan*, p. 407.
78. Ogyū Sorai, *Taiheisaku*, p. 454, translation in Maruyama, *Intellectual History*, p. 134.
79. *Ogyu Sorai's Distinguishing the Way*, p. 14. For Japanese characters *naisei gaiō*, see the glossary.
80. Tahara, *Sorai gaku no sekai*, pp. 135–137.
81. One of the few exceptions is Matsuo Mieko's "Fuji san funka to Asama san funka," pp. 147–176. Takano Toshihiko's one and a half pages (pp. 69–70) in his *Genroku no shakai to bunka* is also more than most historians are prepared to devote to the subject. For the writings of seismologists, see the next chapter.

Chapter 17: The Final Years

1. *Matsukage nikki*, p. 223.
2. *Told*, pp. 79-81.
3. Asahi Shigeaki, *Ōmurō chūki*, 1:332-334, 337. There is frequent reference to men being transferred to the *kirinoma ban* from 10.7.Tenna 1 (1681; *TJ* 5:419). When the unit was abolished on 18.5.Shōtoku 3 (1713) after the death of the sixth shogun Ienobu, it comprised sixty-six men. (*Nihon kokugo daijiten*, 3:936, is mistaken in stating that it was abolished on Tsunayoshi's death.)
4. *Edo bakufu nikki*, ms., 23.11.Genroku 16; *Rakushidō nenroku*, ms., same date (also printed in Kantō Chiku Saigai Kagaku Shiryō Sentaa, p. 1); *TJ*, 6:520, 22.11.Genroku 16; Koyama Yutaka, pp. 125-127.
5. Tsuji Yoshinobu "Genroku jishin, tsunami (1703-XII-31) no Shimoda isei no shiryō jōkyō," p. 410; Tsuji Yoshinobu, "Jishin kazan saigai bumon."
6. *Deshima Diaries, Marginalia 1700-1740*, pp. 40, 45, entries January 19 and March 30, 1704, respectively; *Deshima Dagregisters*, ms., March 30, 1704, folio 212, gives the figure of 270,000 for the area of death between Odawara and Edo. The foreigners seem unaware of the extensive damage and loss of life along the Chiba coast. The *Marginalia* is not a complete translation of the manuscript, and the manuscript has been used as necessary. See also Asahi Shigeaki, *Ōmurō chūki*, 1:340. *Odawara jishin oboegaki* records a toll of 207,313 dead; cited in Takano, *Genroku no shakai to bunka*, p. 69.
7. *Edo bakufu nikki*, ms., 24-29.11.Genroku 16. *TJ*, 6:520-521, 24-29.11.Genroku 16.
8. *Rakushidō nenroku*, ms., 23.11.Genroku 16; Kantō Chiku Saigai Kagaku Shiryō Sentaa, p. 2.
9. *Matsukage nikki*, p. 223; *The Deshima Diaries, Marginalia 1700-1740*, p. 39, entry January 17, 1704; Kaempfer, ms., Sloane 3063, folios 56, 58; Kaempfer, *Briefe*, pp. 585, 588.
10. *Deshima Diaries, Marginalia 1700-1740*, pp. 39-43, covering the period January 15-March 14, 1704.
11. *Deshima Dagregisters*, ms., March 28, 1704, folio 204.
12. Ibid., folios 205-206. This figure is far higher than that in *Rakushidō nenroku*, which is limited to the wards of the town, though the latter figure might have gone up by this time. Also, a large part of Odawara's population lived within the outer walls of the castle. That these included families follows from the specific reference to women and children. Kaempfer estimated in 1690-1691 that the city had one thousand houses, but he also described the population as "high-ranking and rich, living off stipends," having settled there because of the city's "pleasant situation and healthy air" (*Kaempfer's Japan*, pp. 346-347). This again seems to suggest a large samurai population.
13. *Deshima Dagregisters*, ms., April 28, 29, 1704, folios 207-208.
14. Ibid., March 30, 1704, folios 208-209; April 1, 1704, folios 216, 221; April 4, 1704, folio 235.
15. Ibid., April 1, 1704, folios 217, 219-220; April 2, 1704, folio 222.
16. Ibid., April 2, 1704, folios 222-227. *The Deshima Diaries, Marginalia 1700-*

1740, p. 47, much abbreviates the text. For a description of the castle before the earthquake, see *Kaempfer's Japan*, pp. 353–354, 358–359.

17. *Deshima Dagregisters*, ms., January 16, 1704, folios 117–118.
18. *Matsukage nikki*, p. 223.
19. Asahi Shigeaki, *Ōmurō chūki*, 1:343, 346.
20. Ōishi, *Genroku jidai*, p. 204.
21. Totman, *Early Modern Japan*, p. 446; Miyazaki, "Namazue wa nanio gataru no ka," pp. 142–151.
22. *TJ*, 6:534, 30.3.Hōei 1.
23. *TJ*, 6:542, 30.6.Hōei 1 and following entry for the sixth month; 6:543, 6.7.Hōei 1.
24. Asahi Shigeaki, *Ōmurō chūki*, 1:347.
25. *TJ*, 6:540, 29.5.Hōei 1, and 6:543, 4.7.Hōei 1, for Goji-in and Yushima Confucian shrine respectively.
26. Discussed in Bodart-Bailey, "Economic Plight," pp. 46–47.
27. *TJ*, 6:521, 29.11 and 1.12.Genroku 16.
28. *TJ*, 6:521, 29.11.Genroku 16.
29. See, for example, *TJ*, 6:520, 25.11.Genroku 16; 6:521, 2.12.Genroku 16; 6:529, 22.1.Hōei 1, and so on; *Deshima Diaries, Marginalia 1700–1740*, p. 40, January 26, 1704.
30. *TJ*, 6;531, 13.2.Hōei 1; *Edo machi bure shūsei*, 2:486, order no. 3856.
31. Koyama Yutaka, p. 128. Some villages lost their livelihood because of the environmental damage caused by the disaster. See Ōta, p. 33.
32. *TJ*, 6:535, 13.4.Hōei 1; a more detailed description of her illness and death can be found in *Matsukage nikki*, pp. 230–233.
33. See chapter 6.
34. *TJ*, 6:578, 14.urū4.Hōei 2.
35. *TJ*, 6:559, 21.12.Hōei 1.
36. *Ryūkō sōjō nikki*, 2:290, 1.12.Hōei 1.
37. *TJ*, 6:567, 28.1.Hōei 2.
38. *TJ*, 6:569, 5.3.Hōei 2; on the system of awards of imperial titles to the military aristocracy at Edo as practiced at that time, see Matsuzawa, particularly p. 305.
39. *TJ*, 6:581, 19.5.Hōei 2.
40. *Jōken-in dono go jikki* (*Kenbyō jistsuroku*, ms.), quoted in Tokutomi, 17:124–125; Toda Mosui, p. 229; *Matsukage nikki*, p. 248; Ishikura, pp. 19–21; Takeuchi, *Edo to Ōsaka*, p. 67.
41. *Ryūkō sōjō nikki*, 2:231; Tsukamoto, *Tsunayoshi*, p. 253.
42. *Ryūkō sōjō nikki*, 2:258–259, 13.4.Hōei 1; Tsukamoto, *Tsunayoshi*, p. 254.
43. *Ryūkō sōjō nikki*, 3:26, 21.4.Hōei 2; Tsukamoto, *Tsunayoshi*, p. 257.
44. *Ryūkō sōjō nikki*, 3:26–33.
45. Ibid., 3:36, 22.6.Hōei 2.
46. *Matsukage nikki*, p. 248.
47. Nishiyama, pp. 468–470.
48. *Kaempfer's Japan*, p. 56; Edo earthquake, p. 356, Nagasaki earthquake, p. 394. Kaempfer's experience of other earthquakes is described on pp. 395, 408, and 416.
49. *Edo machibito no kenkyū*, 5:470; *TJ*, 6:309, 12.10.Genroku 10.

50. Toda Mosui, p. 444.
51. Asahi Shigeaki, *Ōmurō chūki*, 1:336.
52. Ibid., 2:90-92.
53. Kantō Chiku Saigai Kagaku Shiryō Sentaa, pp. 23-77; *Matsukage nikki*, 273; Nishiyama, p. 473.
54. *Ryūkō sōjō nikki*, 3:125; *TJ*, 6:671, 4.10 and 6.10.Hōei 4.
55. *Itō Shimano no kami nikki*, 15.12.Hōei 4, cited in Koyama Masato et al., "Fujisan Hōei funka no sui," p. 87. This story can also be found in Tsuji Yoshinobu, *Fuji san no funka*, pp. 197-198. However, the author appears to be unaware of the detailed information in *Itō Shimano no Kami nikki* referring to a rope of 300 *hiro* (1 *hiro* = 1.82 meters). Tsuji gives the measurement of approximately 450 meters.
56. *Matsukage nikki*, p. 273; *TJ*, 6:675, 23.11.Hōei 4.
57. *Ryūkō sōjō nikki*, 3:168, 23.11.Hōei 4 (the diary has layers of sand of 23 *bu*; this has been calculated at 1 *bu* = 3.03 millimeters); *Itō Shimano no Kami nikki*, cited in Koyama Masato et al., "Fujisan Hōei funka no sui," p. 83; Koyama Masato et al., "Fujisan no Hōei funka," p. 65.
58. Sumiya et al., pp. 133-134; for descriptions of the earthquake, see also Asahi Shigeaki, *Ōmurō chūki*, 2:98-101; *Told*, p. 90 (*Oritaku*, pp. 222-223). Shinsai Yobō Chōsakai, pp. 93-96, contains a summary of primary sources. *Matsukage nikki* ignores the event, presumably because it could lead later generations to believe that the gods looked unfavorably on the promotion of Machiko's sons.
59. *Told*, p. 90; the translator has transposed Japanese dates into the Western calendar. For the original text, see *Oritaku*, p. 223.
60. *TJ*, 6: 675, 25.11.Hōei 4. For an explanation of the post of *kachi metsuke*, see Sasama, p. 357.
61. *Fushin bugyō* and *kobushin bugyō* were sent to Kuno shrine on 26.11 and returned on 28.11.Hōei 4 (*TJ*, 6:675). Two *metsuke* were sent to inspect the post stations on 1.12.Hōei 4 (*TJ*, 6:675). The daimyo ordered to help with the repair of the post stations were Sakai Tadazane, Honda Tadataka, and Sanada Yukimichi.
62. Suzuki Rizaemon, pp. 34-42. The reference to the 1703 earthquake as six years previously instead of four might be a mistake in the transcription (p. 41).
63. Ibid., pp. 42-44.
64. Ibid., pp. 44-46.
65. Ibid., pp. 46-53.
66. Ibid., pp. 54-59.
67. *TJ*, 6:679, 16.1.Hōei 5, reproduces the order except for the reference to Ogiwara Shigehide. The complete order is found in Takayanagi Shinzō and Ishii Ryōsuke, *Ofuregaki kanpō shūsei*, 25:745-746, *Bunrosō*, ms., Naikaku bunko, vol. 5, 21.1.Hōei 5; also reproduced in Murakami, "Bakufu seiji no tenkai to Kantō gundai," p. 328.
68. *TJ*, 6:681, 3. *urū*1.Hōei 5; 6:682, 7.*urū*1.Hōei 5.
69. *Shokafu*, 15:44.
70. See Fujino, *Shihai taisei*, pp. 22-23, for a listing of the areas controlled by the *gundai*.
71. Toda Mosui, p. 374.

72. *Shokafu*, 15:44; *TJ*, 6:338. 28.7.Genroku 11.
73. Murakami, "Bakufu seiji," pp. 316-322; Ebihara, *Kantō gundai Ina shi*, p. 102.
74. *TJ*, 6:683, 14.urū1.Hōei 5. For further orders referring to Ogiwara Shigehide, see Murakami, "Bakufu seiji," pp. 328-329.
75. Murakami, "Bakufu seiji," p. 336; Ebihara, *Ina ke no gyōseki*, p. 52, differs.
76. The standard Western source on Arai Hakuseki is Nakai, *Shogunal Politics*.
77. *Shokafu*, 10:143; examples of Ogiwara Shigehide being rewarded by the sixth shogun can be found in *TJ*, 7:32, 7.5.Hōei 6; 7:48, 21.7.Hōei 6; 7:67, 25.11.Hōei 6; 7:111, 28.7.Hōei 7; 7:138, 11.12.Hōei 7; Arai Hakuseki frequently refers to the Korean envoys in his *Oritaku shiba no ki*, but especially on pp. 130-141 and 143-146 of *Told*; Ogiwara Shigehide's dismissal: *TJ*, 7:245, 7.9.Shōtoku 2. Rumors of Ienobu's ill health and expected death are recorded from the third month (April of the Western calendar) of Shōtoku 12. Asahi Shigeaki, *Omuro chūki*, 2:210; *Deshima Diaries, Marginalia 1700-1740*, p. 145, April 5, 1712.
78. Ebihara, *Ina ke*, p. 42.
79. *TJ*, 7:48, 21.7.Hōei 6; 7:111, 28.7.Hōei 7; 7:138, 11 and 15.12.Hōei 7.
80. Matsuo Mieko, p. 160.
81. Honma, p. 189; Ina Jinja homepage.
82. Matsuo Mieko, pp. 172, 174-175.
83. For instance Ōtomo, 66:77; Takano, *Genroku Kyōhō no jidai*, p. 207.
84. *Arai Hakuseki nikki*, 2:83; *Told*, pp. 100-101.
85. *Told*, pp. 100-101. For the extent of the destruction in Kyoto: *TJ*, 6:690, 11.3.Hōei 5; Endō, p. 152.
86. *Yōgen roku*, p. 33.
87. Maruyama, *Intellectual History*, p. 133.
88. *Matsukage nikki*, p. 279.
89. *Ryūkō sōjō nikki*, 3:239-244.
90. Asahi Shigeaki, *Ōmurō chūki*, 2:138-139. Ann Bowman Jannetta in her *Epidemics and Mortality in Early Modern Japan* (p. 126), independent of this evidence, comes to the conclusion that the illness died out between epidemics and was reintroduced repeatedly in Japan via Nagasaki and Tsushima.
91. *Ryūkō sōjō nikki*, 3:246-253; *Matsukage nikki*, pp. 280-282. Tsunayoshi's symptoms follow closely the normal course of the illness. The cough especially is symptomatic and therefore led Ryūkō to suspect that the shogun was suffering from measles before the rash appeared. His sudden death after the measles had subsided well accords with Bowman Jannetta's explanation of a secondary infection (pp. 111-112).
92. *Matsukage nikki*, p. 282.
93. Asahi Shigeaki, *Ōmurō chūki*, 2:144, 146. The quip ignores the fact that shoguns were not cremated but interred in stone coffins. Hence there were no ashes.
94. *Matsukage nikki*, p. 285.

Chapter 18: The Legacy
1. Ihara Saikaku, *The Life of an Amorous Man*, p. 63.
2. Suzuki Toshio, 1:114.

3. Chirot, p. 68.

4. Suzuki Toshio, 1:119–124. Kornicki, p. 52, points out that the blocks of 1697 were used for reprints for the next ninety years. This serves as testimony to their value. Satō Tsuneo et al., *Nihon nōsho zenshū*, contains all of the three cited works: *Saizōki*, vol. 28; *Hyakushō denki*, vols. 16 and 17; and *Nōgyō zensho*, vols. 12 and 13. For Seki Takakazu and Shibukawa Shunkai (Harumi), see *Sekai dai hyakka jiten*, entries under the respective names.

5. Suzuki Toshio, 1:124, citing Imada Yōsan.

6. Ōkubo, pp. 426–427.

7. *TJ* 4:541, 13.7.Kanbun 5; Hayashi Ryōshō, *Tokugawa shi to Edo bakufu*, pp. 161–162, has *san dai biji*. *Biji* is literally "beautiful thing" but used in the sense of "accomplishment; something to be praised." Nihon Daijiten kankō kai, 8:1391, entry "biji."

8. Kurita, *Edo jidai*, 1:419–420, 616–617.

9. The protest is treated in some detail in Kodama, *Genroku jidai*, pp. 2–36. *TJ*, 4:15–16, 10.7.Keian 4, reports the protest of the daimyo Matsudaira Sadamasa, who returned his holdings and entered religious life with his son.

10. *Hagakure*, 1:36, trans. Wilson, p. 24 (Watsuji, 1:36–37).

11. *Kaempfer's Japan*, p. 52.

12. *Hagakure*, 2:116 (Watsuji, 1:116; Wilson, p. 84).

13. Cited in McMullen, *Idealism*, p. 158.

14. Neuhaus, pp. 211–212.

15. Machiavelli, pp. 124–125.

16. Bolitho, *Treasures*, p. 150.

17. Weber, *Wirtschaft und Gesellschaft*, pp. 823–824, 827. This part of Weber's work is not included in the standard translation.

18. Ibid., pp. 826–827.

19. Weber, *Economy and Society*, 2:1106–1107; Weber, *Wirtschaft und Gesellschaft*, p. 651. The text in square brackets has been added by me, since the English translation cited is not faithful to the original in this respect. Weber has "der Feudalismus in all seinen Formen." This, I feel, permits us to pass over the much-debated question of whether Japan was feudal in the strict sense of the term.

20. *Shōhō jiroku*, 1:337; for the petition, see chapter 11 above.

21. The quotation above is from Machiavelli, *The Prince*, chapter 17, p. 95.

22. Ibid., pp. 95–96.

23. For details see Bodart-Bailey, "Urbanisation and the Nature of the Tokugawa Hegemony," pp. 120–124.

24. McMullen, *Idealism*, p. 423; Gotō, p. 493.

25. Bolitho, *Treasures*, p. 171.

26. One of the exceptions is Hesselink, for instance, pp. 62–63.

27. Nakai, "Apologia pro Vita Sua," p. 182.

28. *TJ*, 6:725; Tsuji Tatsuya, "Politics," pp. 435–436.

29. Fujino Tamotsu, *Tokugawa seiken ron*, p. 145; *Sekai dai hyakka jiten*, entries "Narushima Motonao" and *"Tokugawa jikki."* Following common usage the name *Tokugawa jikki* will also be used for the early part.

30. Matsuura Seizan, p. 56.
31. Hashimoto, pages unnumbered; Tsunoda et al., 1:493-494.
32. *TJ*, 6:724-725.
33. *TJ*, 6:79, 9.7.Genroku 3.
34. *Matsukage nikki*, pp. 146, 251-252.
35. *TJ*, 8:88, 25.9.Kyōhō 2. For Takazaki domain: *Sekai dai hyakka jiten*, entry "Takazaki han."
36. See, for instance, *Discourse*, pp. 197-198. See also chapter 16 above.
37. Kurita Mototsugu, *Arai Hakuseki no bunchi seiji*, p. 15.
38. Nakai, *Shogunal Politics*, pp. 15, 57; chapter 16 above.
39. *TJ*, 6:725. Tsuji Tatsuya, "Politics," pp. 435-436, erroneously has "excesses" for Japanese *kashitsu*, meaning blunder, unpremeditated crime, negligence.
40. Bolitho, *Treasures*, pp. 191-194.
41. *TJ*, 9:766, 769-771.
42. Bolitho, *Treasures*, pp. 198-205, has an excellent description of Sadanobu's policies. The quote is from p. 199.
43. Ibid., pp. 205-208.
44. *TJ*, 6:723.
45. *TJ*, 1:131; Nakai, *Shogunal Politics*, p. 184.
46. *TJ*, 6:724. The perception that Tsunayoshi's government set a dangerous precedent was shared by the lord of Mito, Tokugawa Nariaki, when he likened the Genroku period to "people's power at full tide" and held this responsible for the popular uprisings at the end of the Tokugawa period (Fujita, *Kindai no taidō*, p. 67).

Glossary

The English equivalent given is that appropriate for the period and context in which the words and expressions are used in this volume. For additional meanings, a dictionary should be consulted.

akugyaku no onkoto tsumori 悪逆の御事つもり. Many crimes against the ancestors
bakufu 幕府. Government of a military ruler, here that of the Tokugawa shogun
ban kata 番方. Member of a guard unit
bu 武. Military/military arts
bu 分. Monetary unit, equivalent to 15 *momme* or one-quarter of one *ryō*
budan shugi 武断主義. Militarism
bugyō sho 奉行所. Commissioner/magistrate's office
bugyō 奉行. Commissioner/magistrate
buke shohatto 武家諸法度. Regulations for the Military Houses
bun 文. Literature/literary skills
bungaku shite sangyō to suru mono wa shōjin no ju nari 文学して産業とするものは小人の儒也. Those who turn the study of books into a trade are Confucians of low stature
bunji/bunchi shugi 文治主義. Principle of civil administration
bōzu 坊主. Buddhist priest
chokkatsuryō 直轄領. Land directly under the control of the *bakufu* (same as *tenryō*)
ch'i (Jap. *ki*) 気. Life force
daigongen 大権現. Great Avatar; title given to the first shogun Ieyasu after his death
daikan 代官. District intendant
daimyō 大名. Territorial lord, Tokugawa vassal with landholding of above 10,000 *koku* (in this text the Westernized spelling of daimyo has been adopted)
dainagon 大納言. Imperial councilor
dōshin 同心. Lower official, below the *yoriki,* mainly acting as patrol and police
Edo machi bugyō 江戸町奉行. Edo city magistrate
fudai daimyō 譜代大名. Daimyo families supporting Tokugawa Ieyasu before the battle of Sekigahara in 1600
fuju fuse 不受不施. Lit.: no giving, no receiving; Buddhist sect refusing contact with mainstream Buddhism
fukyō 不矜. No arrogance
futoku shin 不得心. Lack of understanding
gakusō 学僧. Acolyte studying the scriptures

geba 下馬. Lit.: "dismount"; order posted at castle gates

geba shōgun 下馬将軍. Nickname for Sakai Tadakiyo, whose mansion stood next to the sign "dismount" and was said to wield shogunal powers

gekokujō 下克上. "Inferiors overthrowing superiors"

genpuku 元服. Coming-of-age ceremony for boys of the military class

gi 義. Righteousness (here: devotion to duty)

go 御. Honorific; prefix for many offices/matters pertaining to the shogun

gō 合. 0.18 liter

go kiryō nashi 御器量無し. Has not the qualification/ability

gokonando 御小納戸. Shogunal servant

gokoshō 御小姓. Shogunal page

go makanai kata 御賄方. (The office responsible for) shogunal food

go nainai nite 御内々二而. A secret matter

gonaisho 御内書. Official responsible for handling the shogun's correspondence with his vassals, primarily the daimyo

gōryoku kin 合力金. Here: salary of maids

gosanke 御三家. The Three Related Houses, eligible to provide successors should the Tokugawa main line lack an heir

goshoin no bangashira 御書院の番頭. Commander of the guard of Edo castle

goshōmi 御小身. Humble position

goshuri no kari bugyō 御修理の仮奉行. Temporary appointments as shogunal repair magistrates

gosoba 御側. Shogunal chamberlain

goyōnin beya 御用人部屋. Room where the senior councilors habitually assembled

gumin 愚民. The foolish commoners

gun bugyō 郡奉行. District magistrate

gun'yō 軍用. Items/finance used by the military

gyakusei 逆政. Unjust/unreasonable government

gyōbu shō 刑部少輔. Imperial court title: deputy vice minister of law

hakaku no shusse 破格の出世. Unprecedented promotion

hansatsu 藩札. Paper money issued by individual domains

hatagashira 旗頭. Head of the troops

hatamoto 旗本. Bannerman, Tokugawa vassal with landholdings and income of less than 10,000 *koku*

hōgan (hōgen) 法眼. Buddhist title below *hōin* but also used for Confucians, doctors, poets, and so on, employed by the *bakufu* and treated like priests

hoi 布衣. Ceremonial robes normally reserved for holders of the fourth rank or higher

hōin 法印. Title for Buddhist priests but also used for Confucians, doctors, poets, and so on, employed by the *bakufu* and treated like priests

hon maru 本丸. The main building, here of Edo castle

hyō (tawara) 俵. Bales of rice equivalent to 0.4 to 0.45 *koku*

hyōjōsho 評定所. Supreme court

ie 家. House, here in the sense of family

inu kubō 犬公方. Dog shogun, nickname for the fifth shogun Tsunayoshi

inu ōu 犬追う. Lit.: chasing dogs; traditional sport of the military
jihi 慈悲. Compassion
jijū 侍従. Imperial court title: gentleman-in-waiting
jin 仁. Humanity, benevolence
jinjo 仁恕. Compassion
jinsei 仁政. Benevolent government
jisha bugyō 神社奉行. Magistrate of temples and shrines
jitō 地頭. Local officials of the provinces
jōi 上意. The shogun's command
jōkō 上公. Lord
jui 儒医. Combined profession of Confucian and doctor
junshi 殉死. Following one's lord into death
kachi metsuke 徒目付（徒歩目付）. Below the inspectors, on twenty-four-hour duty at Edo castle
kamioki 髪置. Childhood ceremony of dressing the hair
kan 貫. 3.75 kg
kana zōshi 仮名草子. Works published in phonetic script
kanjin 姦人. Villain
kanjō bugyō 勘定奉行. Magistrate of finance
kanjō gashira 勘定頭. Director of finance
kanjō ginmiyaku 勘定吟味役. Finance inspector
kanjō kumi gashira 勘定組頭. Finance group head
kanjō sashisoe yaku 勘定差添役. Lit.: (the office of) additional finance official
kanpaku 関白. Regent to an adult emperor
Kantō 関東. Lit.: east of the barrier, referring to the area east of the Hakone pass. It included the eight provinces of Hitachi (Ibaraki), Shimotsuke (Tochigi), Kōzuke (Gunma), Musashi (Saitama and the city of Tokyo), Sagami (Kanagawa), and Shimōsa, Kazusa, and Awa (all three Chiba).
Kantō gundai 関東郡代. Kantō magistrate
karō 家老. Senior retainer
ki 気. Life force
kinju 近習. Personal advisor
kinju ban 近習番. Shogun's bodyguard
kinju shuttōnin 近習出頭人. Official in direct contact with the shogun
kirinoma ban 桐之間番. Guard unit created by the fifth shogun
kodomo mitate 子供見立. Selection of children
ko jū nin gashira 小十人頭. Commander of a guard unit of ten men
kōke 高家. Lit.: high families, families responsible for ceremonial matters
kokoro aru mono 心有者. Lit.: people with a heart; right-minded people
kokoro no mama ni 心のままに. Without further training/education
koku 石. Measurement mainly for grain: 180 liters, 47.654 U.S. gallons
kokuyō 国用. National finance
konando 小納戸. Attendant
koshō kumi gashira 小姓組頭. Senior/head page

kosode 小袖. Traditional garment
kōyō 公用. Items/expenditure used for public purposes
kuni no kyō taifu 国の卿大夫. The country's nobles and great lords
Kyōto machi bugyō 京都町奉行. Kyoto city magistrate
Kyōto shoshidai 京都所司代. Kyoto deputy, *bakufu* representative in Kyoto
li (Jap. ri) 理. Here: essence of mankind
maki 巻. A volume (of books, writing)
masugata 枡形. Style of gate, forming a boxlike structure
menoto 乳母夫, 乳母父. Male nurse assigned to a young child
metsuke 目付. Inspector
mitate e 見立て絵. Picture showing classical subject as parody
momme (monme) 匁. Monetary unit, usually 60 *momme* to 1 *ryō*
mono yomi bōzu ものよみ坊主. Book-reading monks
mottomo ichi dai biji 尤一大美事. A great and excellent accomplishment
myōdai 名代. Representative, here of the shogun
naisei gaiō 内聖外王. Sageliness within and kingliness without
nando 納戸. Clothing or the room where clothing was kept
nanushi 名主. Village representative
nokorazu tsuie 不残潰. Total destruction
ōban 大判. Large gold coin
oku 奥. Lit.: the back of the manor; place in the house where the women resided
okuzume 奥詰. Personal adviser
ōmetsuke 大目付. Senior inspector/inspector general
onari goten 御成御殿. Building for the private use of the shogun
onmyōji 陰陽師. Religious, frequently acting as soothsayer
o shichi ya 御七夜. Celebrations held seven days after birth
o tetsudai 御手伝. Daimyo contribution to various building projects
ōtemon 大手門. Great gate leading to the inner castle compound
renmin 憐愍. Compassion
ri 理. Here: essence of humankind
ryō 両. Monetary unit, usually 60 *momme*
rōjū 老中. Senior councilor
rōnin 浪人. Masterless samurai
saiku 細工. Workmanship
sakayu 酒湯. Traditional hot sake bath celebrating recovery from illness
sakon'e no shōshō 左近衛少将. Imperial court title: lesser commander of the guards
sa ma no kami 左馬の守. Imperial court title: commander of the stables to the left
san dai biji 三大美事. The three excellent accomplishments
san kenkō 三賢候. Three wise lords
sankin kōtai 参勤交代. Compulsory alternate attendance at Edo established by the third shogun Iemitsu
san no maru 三の丸. Third enceinte, here of Edo castle
seiji ni amari ari to sezu tote 政治に余りありとせずとて. It is said, not good for government

seishin sei'i 正心誠意. Rectified heart, sincere thoughts
sekiten 釈奠. Confucian ceremony
sendō 先導. Herald
seppuku 切腹. Self-immolation
sesshō 摂政. Imperial regent to a child emperor
shikibu shō 式部少輔. Imperial court title: deputy vice minister of ceremonies
shimai 仕舞. Passage from a *nō* play performed by a single actor
shimoyashiki 下屋敷. Suburban villa
shin'i dōfuku 深衣道服. The traditional garment of the Confucian scholar
shisei 市井. Town center
shōban 相伴. Fellow guest
shogun 将軍. Abbreviation for *sei i taishōgun* 征夷大将軍, great barbarian-quelling general; here head of the Tokugawa government (in this text the Western spelling of shogun has been adopted)
shoin ban 書院番. The guard unit generally responsible for the safety of the shogun
shōkō 相公. Honorific form for 宰相 *saishō*, high imperial court title
shōrui awaremi no rei 生類憐れみの令. Laws of Compassion
shoshi hattō 諸士法度 Regulations governing the behavior of the *bakufu*'s direct retainers
shu 朱 (銖). Silver monetary unit, one-sixteenth of a *ryō*
shūmon aratame no jō 宗門改め条. Laws for the Examination of Sects
shūmon ninbetsu aratame chō 宗門人別改帳. Temple register of worshippers
sobashū 側衆. Chamberlains
soba yaku 側役. Office of chamberlain
sōshaban 奏者番. Master of shogunal ceremony
tairei 大礼. Grand ceremonies of shogunal succession
tairō 大老. Grand councilor
tairō hacchin 大牢八珍. Splendid feast the Chinese emperor offered ceremoniously to the gods
takaba 鷹場. Hawking ground
tenarai 手習い. Primary school
tenka no yama 天下の山. The ruler's (or government's) mountains
Tenna no chi (ji) 天和の治. The Tenna Government
tenryō 天領. Land under direct *bakufu* control (same as *chokkatsuryō*)
tenshi 天子. Lit.: son of heaven; the emperor
Tenshō ōban 天正大判. Large gold coin of the Tenshō period (1573–1591)
tera koya 寺小屋. Primary Buddhist temple school
tetsudai fushin 手伝普請. Assistance with *bakufu* building projects
tōjū sen 当十銭. Copper coin of the Hōei period
tōta 淘汰. "Weeding out," elimination, here of Buddhist clergy
tozama daimyo 外様大名. Lit.: outside lord, daimyo families supporting the Tokugawa only after the battle of Sekigahara of 1600
tsubone 局. Room in a palace, imperial court title for women
tsuji kiri 辻斬り. Street murder
tsuki ban 月番. Official in charge for the month on a rotational system

tsukiban rōjū. 月番老中. Senior councilor in charge for the month on a rotational system
uchi kowashi 打壊し. Destruction caused by people rioting
u ma no kami 右馬の守. Imperial court title: commander of the stables of the right
unjōkin 運上金. Tax on the transport and turnover of commercial goods
wakadoshiyori 若年寄. Junior councilor
yashiki 屋敷. Mansion
yoriki 与力. Lower official of the Tokugawa *bakufu,* commanding the *dōshin*

Bibliography

Unpublished Sources

Deshima Dagregisters. Ms. Algemeen Rijksarchief, The Hague.
Edo bakufu nikki 江戸幕府日記. Naikaku Bunko 内閣文庫, Tokyo.
Hitomi Yūgen 人見有元. *Hitomi shiki* 人見私記. Ms. Naikaku Bunko 内閣文庫 27090. The ms. includes *Genyū kōki* 厳有公記, *Jōken kōki* 常憲公記, *Sakurada nikki* 桜田記, *Mita roku* 三田録, *Kanda ki* 神田記.
Kaempfer, Engelbert. Ms. Sloane 3061, 3063. British Library, London.
Kanrosō 甘露叢. Kokuritsu Kokkai Toshokan 国立国会図書館, Tokyo.
Kenbyō jitsuroku 憲廟実録 (*sōsho* version). Kokuritsu Kokkai Toshokan 国立国会図書館, Tokyo.
Konoe Motohiro 近衛基煕. *Motohiro kōki* 基煕公記. Yōmei Bunko 陽明文庫, copy Shiryō Hensanjo 史料編纂所, Tokyo University.
Rakushidō nenroku 楽只堂年録. Yanagisawa Bunko 柳沢文庫, Yamato Kōriyama 大和郡山.
Sakata Morotō 坂田諸遠. *Kai shōshō Yoshiyasu ason jikki* 甲斐少将吉保朝臣実記. Ms. Yanagisawa Bunko 柳沢文庫, Yamato Kōriyama 大和郡山; copy Shiryō Hensanjo 史料編纂所, Tokyo University.

Published Works

Aichiken Kyōiku Kai 愛知県教育会, ed. *Aichiken ijin den* 愛知県偉人伝. Nagoya, 1972.
Akiyama Kiyoko 秋山善代子. "Menoto ni tsuite" 乳父について. *Shigaku zasshi* 史学雑誌, 99:7 (July 1990).
Albin, Mel., ed. *New Directions in Psychohistory*. Toronto: Lexington Books, 1980.
Aoki Kazuo 青木和夫, ed. *Nihonshi daijiten* 日本史大事典. Tokyo: Heibonsha, 1992.
Arai Eiji 荒居英次. *Nihon kinsei shi kenkyū nyūmon* 日本近世史研究入門. Tokyo: Komiyama Shuppan 小宮山出版, 1974.
Arai Hakuseki 新井白石. *Arai Hakuseki nikki* 新井白石日記. Ed. Tōkyō Daigaku Shiryō Hensanjo 東京大学史料編纂所. *Dai nihon ko kiroku* 大日本古記録. Tokyo: Iwanami Shoten 岩波書店, 1953.
———. *Honsaroku kō* 本左録考. In *Arai Hakuseki zenshū* 新井白石全集, vol. 6. Tokyo: Kokusho Kankōkai 国書刊行会, 1907.
———. *Oritaku shiba no ki* 折りたく柴の記. *NKBT*, vol. 95, reprint 1967.
———. *Told Round a Brushwood Fire*. Trans. Joyce Ackroyd. Tokyo: University of Tokyo Press, 1979.

Asahi Shigeaki 朝日重章. *Ōmurō chūki* 鸚鵡籠中記. Ed. Tsukamoto Manabu 塚本学. 2 vols. Tokyo: Iwanami Bunko 岩波文庫, 1995.
Asai Ryōi. *Ukiyo monogatari.* 浮世物語 *NKBT,* vol. 90.
Asao Naohiro 朝尾直弘. Entry "Buke shohatto" 武家諸法度. In *Sekai dai hyakka jiten* 世界大百科事典.
———. "Shogun seiji no kenryoku kōzō" 将軍政治の権力構造. *Iwanami kōza Nihon rekishi* 岩波講座日本歴史, vol. 10, *Kinsei* 近世2. Iwanami shoten, reprint 1971.
Baroni, Helen J. *Obaku Zen: The Emergence of the Third Sect of Zen in Tokugawa Japan.* Honolulu: University of Hawai'i Press, 2000.
Bell, David. *Chushingura and the Floating World.* Folkestone: Japan Library 2001.
Bitō Masahide 尾藤正英. "The Akō Incident, 1701–1703." *Monumenta Nipponica,* 58:2 (Summer 2003).
———. *Genroku jidai* 元禄時代. Vol. 19 of *Nihon no rekishi* 日本の歴史. Tokyo: Shōgakukan 小学館, reprint 1981.
———. "Kokka shugi no sokei to shite no Sorai" 国家主義の祖型としての徂徠. In *Nihon no meicho* 日本の名著, vol. 16. Tokyo: Chūō Kōronsha 中央公論社, 1974.
Blacker, Carmen. *The Catalpa Bow.* London: George Allen and Unwin, 1975.
Bodart-Bailey, B. M. "A Case of Political and Economic Expropriation: The Monetary Reform of the Fifth Tokugawa Shogun." *Papers on Far Eastern History,* March 1989.
———. "The Economic Plight of the Fifth Tokugawa Shogun." *Kobe University Economic Review 44* (1998).
———. "Keeping Time—Now and Then" 時を刻む今昔物語. *Springer Science,* 12:3 (Fall 1997).
———. "The Laws of Compassion." *Monumenta Nipponica,* 40:2 (Summer 1985).
———. "The Persecution of Confucianism in Early Tokugawa Japan." *Monumenta Nipponica,* 48:3 (Autumn 1993).
———. "Urbanisation and the Nature of the Tokugawa Hegemony." In Nicolas Fiévé and Paul Waley, eds., *Japanese Capitals in Historical Perspective: Place, Power and Memory in Kyoto, Edo and Tokyo.* London: Routledge Curzon, 2003.
Bolitho, Harold. "The Dog Shogun." In Wang Gungwu, ed., *Self and Biography.* Sydney: Sydney University Press, 1975.
———. *Treasures among Men.* New Haven: Yale University Press, 1974.
Brandon, James R., ed. *Chūshingura: Studies in Kabuki and the Puppet Theatre.* Honolulu: University of Hawai'i Press, 1982.
Bunrosō 文露叢. Facsimile. *Naikaku bunko shozō shiseki sōkan* 内閣文庫所蔵史籍叢刊, vol. 48. Tokyo: Kyūko Shoin 汲古書院, 1985.
Buya shokudan 武野燭談. Edited and annotated by Murakami Tadashi 村上直. Tokyo: Jinbutsu Ōraisha 人物往来社, 1967.
———. *Kokushi sōsho* 国史叢書, part 2. Kokushi Kenkyūkai 国史研究会, ed. and publisher. Tokyo, 1917.
———. *Nihon meicho taikei* 日本名著大系, part 1. Sanshima Saiji 三島才二, ed. Tokyo: Shūhōkaku 聚芳閣, 1925.

Cassirer, Ernst. *An Essay on Man.* New Haven: Yale University Press, 1992.
Ching, Julia. *To Acquire Wisdom: The Way of Wang Yang-ming.* New York: Columbia University Press, 1976.
———. "Chu Shun-shui, 1600–82, a Chinese Confucian Scholar in Tokugawa Japan." *Monumenta Nipponica,* 30:2.
———. "The Practical Learning of Chu Shun-shui (1600–1682)." In W. T. de Bary and I. Bloom, eds., *Principle and Practicality: Essays in Neo-Confucianism and Practical Learning.* New York: Columbia University Press, 1979.
Chirot, Daniel. *How Societies Change.* Thousand Oaks, Calif.: Pine Forge Press, 1994.
Claudius, Matthias. *Ein Tropfen aus dem Ozean: Ausgewählte Werke und Briefe.* Ed. Gunter Albrecht. Berlin: Rutten and Loening, 1975.
Cleland, James. *The Institution of a Young Noble Man.* Oxford, 1607.
Coolhaas, W. Ph., ed. *Generale Missiven van Gouverneurs-Generaal en Raden aan Heren XVII der Verenigde Oostindische Compagnie,* IV: 1675–1685. The Hague: Martinus Nijhoff, 1971.
Cooper, Michael. *Rodrigues the Interpreter: An Early Jesuit in Japan and China.* Tokyo: Weatherhill, 1974.
———, trans. and ed. *They Came to Japan.* Berkeley: University of California Press, 1965.
———, trans. and ed. *This Island of Japon: João Rodrigues' Account of 16th-Century Japan.* Tokyo: Kodansha International, 1973.
Crawcour, E. S. "Kawamura Zuiken." *Transactions of the Asiatic Society of Japan,* 3rd series, vol. 9, May 1966.
The Deshima Dagregisters. Volume 11 (1641–1650). Ed. and trans. Cynthia Viallé and Leonard Blussé. Intercontinenta No. 23. Leiden, 2001.
The Deshima Diaries: Marginalia 1700–1740. Ed. Paul Van der Velde and Rudolf Bachofner. Tokyo: The Japan-Netherlands Institute, 1992.
Dokai kōshūki 土芥寇讎記. Ed. and ann. Kanai Madoka 金井円. In *Edo shiryō sōsho* 江戸史料叢書. Tokyo: Jinbutsu Ōraisha 人物往来社, 1967.
Ebihara Kei 海老原恵. *Ina ke no gyōseki* 伊奈家の業蹟. Suikaidō 水海道: Shinshindō Insatsujo 新々堂印刷所, 1961.
———. *Kantō gundai Ina shi* 関東郡代伊奈氏. Tsuchiura 土浦: Tsukuba shorin 筑波書林, 1980.
Edo Kiseki Kenkyūkai 江戸遺跡研究会 (The Edo Site Research Association), ed. *Zusetsu Edo kōkogaku kenkyū jiten* 図説江戸考古学研究辞典. Tokyo: Kashiwa Shobō 柏書房, 2001.
Edo machi bure shūsei 江戸町触集成. Vol. 2, ed. Kinsei Shiryō Kenkyū Kai 近世史料研究会. Tokyo: Hanawa Shobō 塙書房, 1994.
Eliade, M. *A History of Religious Ideas.* Chicago: University of Chicago, 1985.
Endō Moto'o 遠藤元男. *Kinsei seikatsu shi nenphyō* 近世生活史年表. Tokyo: Yūzankaku 雄山閣, 1982.
Erikson, Erik H. *Childhood and Society.* Reprint. New York: W. W. Norton, 1963.
Esser, Gunther, et al. "Bedeutung und Determinanten der frühen Mutter-Kind-Beziehung." *Zeitschrift für Psychosomatische Medizin und Psychoanalyse,* 39:3 (1993).

Foucault, Michel. *Aesthetics, Method and Epistemology*. Trans. Robert Hurley and others. New York: New Press, 1998.

Frois, Luis, S.J. *Kulturgegensätze Europa-Japan* (1585). Ed. and trans. Josef Franz Schütte, S.J. Monumenta Nipponica Monographs. Tokyo, 1955.

Fujii Jōji 藤井譲治. *Edo bakufu rōjūsei keisei katei no kenkyū* 江戸幕府老中制形成過程の研究. Tokyo: Azekura Shobō 校倉書房, 1990.

―――. "Ietsuna seiken ron" 家綱政権論. In Matsumoto Shirō 松本四郎 and Yamada Tadao 山田忠雄, eds., *Kōza nihon kinsei shi* 講座日本近世史, 4, *Genroku, Kyōho ki no seiji to shakai* 元禄・享保期の政治と社会. Tokyo: Yūhikaku 有斐閣, 1980.

―――. *Tokugawa Iemitsu* 徳川家光. Tokyo: Yoshikawa Kōbunkan 吉川弘文館, 1997.

Fujii Shun 藤井駿 et al., eds. *Ikeda Mitsumasa nikki* 池田光政日記. Tokyo: Kokusho Kankōkai 国書刊行会, 1983.

Fujino Tamotsu 藤野保. *Bakusei to hansei* 幕政と藩政. Tokyo: Yoshikawa Kōbunkan 吉川弘文館, 1979.

―――. *Oneiroku haizetsuroku* 恩栄録廃絶録. Tokyo: Kondō Shuppan sha 近藤出版社, 1970.

―――, ed. *Shihai taisei to gaikō, bōeki, tenryō to shihai keitai* 支配体制と外交・貿易天領と支配形態. *Ronshū bakuhan taisei shi* 論集幕藩体制史, series 1, vol. 4. Tokyo: Yūzankaku Shuppan 雄山閣出版, 1994.

―――. *Tokugawa seiken ron* 徳川政権論. Tokyo: Yoshikawa Kōbunkan 吉川弘文館, 1991.

Fujita Satoru 藤田覚. "Genroku ki bakufu zaisei no shin shiryō" 元禄期幕府財政の新史料. *Shigaku zasshi* 史学雑誌 90:10 (October 1981).

―――. *Kindai no taidō* 近代の胎動. *Nihon no jidaishi* 日本の時代史, vol. 17. Tokyo: Yoshikawa Kōbunkan 吉川弘文館, 2003.

Fukai Masaumi 深井雅海. *Tokugawa shōgun seiji kenryoku no kenkyū* 徳川政治権力の研究. Tokyo: Yoshikawa Kōbunkan 吉川弘文館, 1991.

Fukuda Chizuru 福田千鶴. *Bakuhan seiteiki chitsujo to oie sōdō* 幕藩制的秩序と御家騒動. Tokyo: Azekura Shobō 校倉書房, 1999.

―――. *Sakai Tadakiyo* 酒井忠清. Tokyo: *Jinbutsu Sōsho* 人物叢書, 2000.

Fukuda Toyohiko 福田豊彦 et al. *Kōtōgakkō seisen nihonshi B* 高等学校精選日本史 B. Tokyo: Daiichi Gakushūsha 第一学習社, reprint 2003.

Fukuyama Akira 福山昭. *Kinsei nihon no suiri to chiiki: Yodogawa chiiki o chūshin ni* 近世日本の水利と地域：淀川流域を中心に. Tokyo: Yūzankaku 雄山閣, 2003.

Fung Yu-Lan. *A Short History of Chinese Philosophy*. New York: The Free Press, reprint 1967.

Futaki Kenichi 二木謙一. "Edo bakufu shōgun haietsu girei to daimyō no kakushiki" 江戸幕府将軍拝謁儀礼と大名の格式. *Nihon rekishi* 日本歴史, 11:4 (1999).

Genkō jitsuroku 源公実録. By Yabuta Shigemori 薮田重守. *Yanagisawa shiryō shūsei* 柳沢史料集成, vol. 1. Yamato Kōriyama: Yanagisawa Bunko Hozonkai 柳沢文庫保存会, 1993.

Genroku Chūshingura no Kai 元禄忠臣蔵の会, ed. *Genroku chūshingura deeta fairu* 元禄忠臣蔵データファイル. Tokyo: Shinjinbutsu Ōrai Sha 新人物往来社, 1999.

Gerhart, Karen M. "Visions of the Dead: Kano Tan'yū's Paintings of Tokugawa Iemitsu's Dreams." *Monumenta Nipponica*, 59:1 (Spring 2004).
Gokoku onna taiheiki 護国女太平記. Ed. Tsukamoto Tetsuzō 塚本哲三. Tokyo: Yūhōdō Shoten 有朋堂書店, 1927.
Gotō Yōichi 後藤陽一. "Kumazawa Banzan no shōgai to shisō no keisei" 熊沢蕃山の生涯と思想の形成. In *Kumazawa Banzan* 熊沢蕃山, NST 30. Tokyo, 1971.
Hagakure 葉隠. Attributed to Yamamoto Tsunetomo 山本常朝. Ed. Watsuji Tetsurō 和辻哲郎 and Furukawa Tetsushi 古川哲氏. 32nd reprint. Tokyo: Iwanami Shoten 岩波書店, 2003.
Hagakure: The Book of the Samurai. Attributed to Yamamoto Tsunetomo. Trans. William Scott Wilson. Tokyo: Kodansha International, paperback edition, 1983.
Hall, John Whitney. "The Bakuhan System." In Hall, ed., *The Cambridge History of Japan*, vol. 4: *Early Modern Japan*. Cambridge: Cambridge University Press, 1991.
———, ed. *Cambridge History of Japan*, vol. 4: *Early Modern Japan*. Cambridge: Cambridge University Press, 1991.
———. *Government and Local Power in Japan, 500–1700*. Princeton: Princeton University Press, 1966.
Hara Nensai 原念斎. *Sentetsu sōdan* 先哲叢談. Vol. 1 of *Dai nihon bunko* 大日本文庫. Tokyo: Shunyōdō Shoten 春陽堂書店, 1936.
Hasegawa Masatsugu 長谷川正次. *Daimyō no zaisei* 大名の財政. Tokyo: Dōseisha 同成社, 2001.
Hasegawa Riheiji 長谷川利平次. *Sado kinginzan shi no kenkyū* 佐渡金銀山史の研究. Tokyo: Kondō Shuppan 近藤出版社, 1991.
Hashimoto Teruhiko 橋本昭彦. "Edo jidai no kyōiku 江戸時代の教育." In Uchiyama Chinari 内山知也 and Honda Tetsuo 本田哲夫, eds., *Yushima seidō to Edo jidai* 湯島聖堂と江戸時代. Tokyo: Shibunkai 斯文会, 1990.
Hayami Akira 速水融. *Rekishi jinkō gaku de mita nihon* 歴史人口学で見た日本. *Bunshun shinsho* 文春新書 vol. 200. Tokyo, 2001.
Hayami Akira, and Laurel L. Cornell. "Shūmon aratame chō: nihon no jinkō kiroku" 宗門改帳：日本の人口記録. In Hayami Akira et al., eds., *Tokugawa shakai kara no tenbō* 徳川社会からの展望. Tokyo: Dōbunkan 同文館, 1989.
Hayashi Gahō 林鵞峯. *Kokushikan nichiroku* 國史館日録. Ed. Yamamoto Takeo 山本武夫. *Shiryō sanshū* 史料纂集, vol. 117. Tokyo: Zoku Gunsho Ruijū Kanseikai 続群書類従完成会, 1999.
Hayashi Ryōshō 林亮勝. "Jikken no hottan" 事件の発端. In Genroku Chūshingura no Kai, ed., *Genroku chūshingura deeta fairu*. Tokyo: Shinjinbutsu Ōraisha, 1999.
———. *Tokugawa shi to Edo bakufu* 徳川氏と江戸幕府. Tokyo: Ningensha 人間, 2003.
Hayashi Yawara 林和. *Yangisawa Yoshiyasu* 柳沢吉保. Tokyo: Jiggyō no Nihonsha, 実業之日本社, 1921.
Hayashiya Shinsaburō 林屋辰三郎. *Tenka ittō* 天下一統. Vol. 12 of *Nihon no rekishi* 日本の歴史. Tokyo: Chūkō Bunko 中公文庫, 1974.
Hesselink, Reiner H. *Prisoners from Nambu: Reality and Make-Believe in 17th-Century Japanese Diplomacy*. Honolulu: University of Hawai'i Press, 2002.

Hino Tatsuo 日野龍夫. *Sorai gakuha: jugaku kara bungaku e* 徂徠学派：儒学から文学へ. Tokyo: Chikuma Shobō 筑摩書房, 1975.

Hiraishi Naoaki 平石直明. *Ogyū Sorai nenpu kō* 荻生徂徠年譜考. Tokyo: Heibonsha 平凡社, 1984.

Hirao Michio 平尾道雄. *Nonaka Kenzan to sono jidai* 野中兼山と其の時代. Kōchi: Kōchiken Bunkyō Kyōkai 高知県文教協会, 1970.

Honma Kiyotoshi 本間清利. *Kantō gundai; Ina shi no keifu* 関東郡代：伊奈氏の系譜. Urawa 浦和: Saitama Shinbunsha 埼玉新聞社, 1983.

Honsaroku 本左録 Attributed to Honda Masanobu 本田正信. In Ishida Ichirō 石田一郎 and Kanaya Osamu 金谷治, eds., *Fujiwara Seika, Hayashi Razan* 藤原惺窩林羅山, *NST*, vol. 28.

Hori Isao 堀勇雄. *Hayashi Razan* 林羅山. Tokyo: Yoshikawa Kōbunkan 吉川弘文館, 1964.

Huntington, Samuel P. *The Clash of Civilizations and the Remaking of the World Order*. New York: Touchstone, 1997.

Hōgetsu Keigo 宝月圭吾 and Iwasawa Yoshihiko 岩沢愿彦. *Keizu san'yō* 系図纂要. 18 vols. Tokyo: Meicho Shuppan 名著出版, 1973–1976.

Ienaga Saburō 家永三郎 et al., eds. *Shin nihon shi B* 新日本歴史B. Tokyo: Sanseidō 三省堂, reprint 2001.

Ihara Saikaku. *The Life of an Amorous Man*. Trans. Kenji Hamada. Tokyo: Tuttle, reprint 2001.

———. *This Scheming World*. Trans. David C. Stubbs and Masanori Takatsuka. Tokyo: Tuttle, 1965.

Iio Kuwashi 飯尾精. *Genroku chūshingura: sono omote to ura* 元禄忠臣蔵：その表と裏. Akō: Ōishi Jinja Shamusho 大石神社々務所, 1975.

Ikeda Kōen 池田晃淵. *Tokugawa bakufu jidai shi* 徳川幕府時代史. Tokyo: Waseda Daigaku Shuppan 早稲田大学出版, 1904.

———. "Tokugawa shi shisei no chōshi o hyō su" 徳川氏施政の張弛を評す. *Shigaku zasshi* 史学雑誌, 4:40 (1893).

Ikeda Mitsumasa kō den 池田光政公伝. Ed. and pub. Ishizaka Zenjirō 石坂善次郎. Tokyo, 1932.

Ikeda Mitsumasa nikki 池田光政日記. Ed. Fujii Shun 藤井駿 et al. Tokyo: Kokusho Kankōkai 国書刊行会, 1983.

Ikegami, Eiko. *The Taming of the Samurai: Honorific Individualism and the Making of Modern Japan*. Harvard: Harvard University Press, 1995.

Imanaka Kanshi 今中寛司. *Soraigaku no kisoteki kenkyū* 徂徠学の基礎的研究. Tokyo: Yoshikawa Kōbunkan 吉川弘文館, 1966.

Ina Jinja home page. http://www.wbs.ne.jp/bt/kankooyama/kanko/kansubasiri/inajinja.htm.

Inagaki Fumio 稲垣史生. *Buke no fujintachi* 武家の夫人たち. Tokyo: Jinbutsu Ōraisha, 人物往来社, 1967.

Irizawa Tatsukichi 入沢達吉. "Tokugawa Tsunayoshi no seishin jōtai ni tsuite" 徳川綱吉の精神状態について. *Kokka igakkai zasshi* 国家医学会雑誌, 189 (1903).

Ishihara Michihiro 石原道博. *Shu Shunsui* 朱舜水. Tokyo: Yoshikawa Kōbunkan 吉川弘文館, 1961.

Ishii Ryōsuke 石井良助, ed. *Genroku gohōshiki* 元禄御法式. In *Kinsei hōsei shiryō* 近世法制史料, vol. 1. Tokyo: Sōbun Sha 創文社, reprint 1981.

———, ed. *Gotōke reijō* 御当家令状. In *Kinsei hōsei shiryō* 近世法制史料, vol. 2. Tokyo: Sōbunsha 創文社, reprint 1981.

———, ed. *Oshioki saikyochō* 御仕置裁許帳. In *Kinsei hōsei shiryō* 近世法制史料, vol. 1. Tokyo: Sōbunsha 創文社, reprint 1981.

———, ed. *Tokugawa kinrei kō* 徳川禁令考. Tokyo: Sōbunsha 創文社, 1959.

Ishikawa Yō 石川洋 et al., eds. *Edo bunjin jiten* 江戸文人辞典. Tokyo: Tōkyōdō Shuppan 東京堂出版, 1996.

Ishikura Shigetsugu 石倉重継. *Kitamura Kigin den* 北村季吟伝. Sanshōdō 三松堂, 1897. reprint Tokyo: Kuresu Shuppan クレス出版, 1995.

Itō Tasaburō 伊東多三郎. *Nihon kinseishi* 日本近世史. Vol. 2. Tokyo: Yūhikaku 有斐閣, 1952.

Iwabashi Junsei 岩橋遵成. *Sorai kenkyū* 徂徠研究. Tokyo: Seki Shoin 関書院, 1934.

Iwao Seiichi 岩生成一. *Sakoku* 鎖国. *Nihon no rekishi* 日本の歴史, vol. 14. Tokyo: Chūkō Bunko 中公文庫, reprint 1988.

Izumi Hideki 泉秀樹. "Chūshingura no shinjitsu" 忠臣蔵の真実. *Kyōsai dayori* 共済だより, 7:5 (1999).

Izumi Seiji 和泉清司. *Tokugawa bakufu seiritsu katei no kisoteki kenkyū* 徳川幕府成立過程の基礎的研究. Tokyo: Bunken Shuppan 文献出版, 1995.

Jannetta, Ann Bowman, *Epidemics and Mortality in Early Modern Japan*. Princeton: Princeton University Press, 1987.

Jansen, Marius B. *China in the Tokugawa World*. Cambridge, Mass.: Harvard University Press, 1992.

———. *The Making of Modern Japan*. Cambridge, Mass.: Harvard University Press, 2000.

Johnson, Randal. "Editor's Introduction." In P. Bourdieu, *The Field of Cultural Production*. New York: Columbia University Press, 1993.

Jorissen, Engelbert. *Das Japanbild im "Traktat" (1585) des Luis Frois*. Münster, Westfalen: Aschendorffsche Verlagsbuchhandlung, 1988.

Josei Shi Kenkyūkai 女性史研究会, ed. *Nihon shi josei hyaku sen* 日本史女性 100 選. Tokyo: Akita shoten 秋田書店, 1973.

Kaempfer, Engelbert. *Amoentitatum exoticarum politico-physico-medicarum fasciculi V*. Lemgo, 1712.

———. *Briefe, 1683–1715*. Ed. Detlef Haberland. Munich: Iudicum, 2001.

———. *Flora Japonica*. Trans. and ann. Wolfgang Muntschick. Wiesbaden: F. Steiner Verlag, 1983.

———. *Geschichte und Beschreibung von Japan*. Trans. C. W. Dohm. 2 vols. Lemgo, 1777–1779. Facsimile, Stuttgart: Brockhaus, 1964.

———. *Kaempfer's Japan: Tokugawa Culture Observed*. Ed., trans., and ann. B. M. Bodart-Bailey. Honolulu: University of Hawai'i Press, 1999.

Kaga Kishirō 加賀樹芝朗, ed. *Genroku kakyū bushi no seikatsu* 元禄下級武士の生活. Tokyo: Yūzankaku Shuppan 雄山閣出版, 1966.

Kagan, Jerome. *Personality Development*. New York, Chicago, San Francisco, Atlanta: Harcourt Brace Jovanovich, 1971.

Kanai Madoka 金井円. *Hansei* 藩政. Tokyo: Shibundō 至文堂, 1962.

Kana shōri 仮名性理. Attributed to Fujiwara Seika 藤原惺窩. In *NST*, vol. 28.

Kansei chōshū shokafu 寛政重修諸家譜. Ed. Hotta Masaatsu 堀田正敦. 26 vols. Tokyo: Zoku Gunsho Ruijū Kansei Kai 続群書類従完成会, 1964–1967.

Kantō Chiku Saigai Kagaku Shiryō Sentaa 関東地区災害科学史料センター, ed. *Rakushidō nenpō* 楽只堂年報. Tokyo, 1981.

Kapitza, Peter. *Engelbert Kaempfer und die Europäische Aufklärung*. Munich: Iudicum, 2001.

Kasaya Kazuhiko 笠谷和比古. *Kinsei buke shakai no seiji kōzō* 近世武家社会の政治構造. Tokyo: Yoshikawa Kōbunkan 吉川弘文館, 1993.

Kawano Kyōsuke 川野京輔. *Genroku hijō monogatari: Yanagisawa sokkin seiji no hikari to kage* 元禄非常物語：柳沢側近政治の光と影. Tokyo: Nami Shobō 波書房, 1975.

Keene, Donald, trans. *Chūshingura (The Treasury of Loyal Retainers): A Puppet Play by Takeda Izumo, Miyoshi Shoraku and Namiki Senryu*. New York: Columbia University Press, 1971.

Kenbyō jitsuroku 憲廟実録 (*Jōken-in zōdai shōkokukō jikki* 常憲院贈大相国公実記). Facsimile of *kaisho* ms. *Naikaku bunko shozō shiseki sōkan* 内閣文庫所蔵史籍叢刊, vol. 17. Tokyo: Kyūko Shoin 汲古書院, 1982.

Kensha Ō 懸車翁. "Nonaka Kenzan shikkyaku no genin" 野中兼山失脚の原因. *Tosa shidan* 土佐史談, 43.

Kimura Motoi 木村礎. "Tokugawa Tsunayoshi." In Kitajima Masamoto 北島正元, *Tokugawa shōgun retten* 徳川将軍列伝. Tokyo: Akita Shobō 秋田書房, 1974.

Kinugasa Yasuki 衣笠安喜. *Kinsei nihon no jukyō to bunka* 近世日本の儒教と文化. Tokyo: Hōsei Daigaku Shuppan 法政大学出版, 1990.

Kitajima Masamoto 北島正元. *Edo bakufu no kenryoku kōzō* 江戸幕府の権力構造. Tokyo: Iwanami Shoten 岩波書店, 1964.

———. *Kinseishi no gunzō* 近世史の群像. Tokyo: Yoshikawa Kōbunkan 吉川弘文館, 1977.

———. *Tokugawa shōgun retten* 徳川将軍列伝. Tokyo: Akita Shobō 秋田書房, 1974.

Kobata Atsushi 小葉田淳. *Nihon kahei ryūtsū shi* 日本貨幣流通史. Tokyo: Tōkō Shoin 刀江書院, 1943.

———. "The Production and Uses of Gold and Silver in Sixteenth- and Seventeenth-Century Japan." *Economic History Review*, 2nd ser., 18:1–3 (1965).

Kodama Kōta 児玉幸多. *Genroku jidai* 元禄時代. *Nihon no rekishi* 日本の歴史, vol. 16. Tokyo: Chūkō Bunko 中公文庫, reprint 1990.

———, ed. *Jinbutsu nihon no rekishi* 人物日本の歴史, vol. 13. Tokyo: Shōgakukan 小学館, 1976.

Kodama Kōta et al., eds. *Nihonshi sōran* 日本史総覧. Tokyo: Shinjinbutsu Ōraisha, 新人物往来社, 1984.

Kokushi Daijiten Henshū Iinkai 国史大事典編集委員会, comp. *Kokushi daijiten* 国史大事典. 14 vols. Tokyo: Yoshikawa Kōbunkan 吉川弘文館, 1979–1993.
Konta Yōzō 今田洋三. *Edo no kinsho* 江戸の禁書. Tokyo: Yoshikawa Kōbunkan 吉川弘文館, 1981.
Kōronsha Shuppan Kyoku 広論社出版局, ed. *Kasuga no Tsubone to Tokugawa ke* 春日局と徳川家. Tokyo: Kōronsha 広論社, 1989.
Kornicki, Peter. *The Book in Japan: A Cultural History from the Beginnings to the Nineteenth Century.* Honolulu: University of Hawai'i Press. 2001.
Kōsaka Jirō 神坂次郎. *Genroku gotatami bugyō no nikki* 元禄御畳奉行の日記. Tokyo: Chūkō Shinsho 中公新書, 1984.
Koyama Masato 小山真人 et al. "Fujisan Hōei funka no sui o kiroku suru ryōshitsu no shiryō Itō Shima no Kami nikki" 富士山宝永噴火の推移を記録する良質資料『伊東志摩守日記』(English title supplied: Historical Document "Itō-Shimanokami Nikki" as a Detailed Record of the 1707 Hoei Eruption of Fuji Volcano, Japan). *Rekishi jishin* 歴史地震, no. 17 (2001).
———. "Fujisan no Hōei funka" 富士山の宝永噴火. In National Museum of Japanese History, ed., *Documenting Disaster.* Sakura-shi, Chiba, 2003.
———. "Bohi ga akashita genroku jishin tsunami higai" 墓碑が明かした元禄地震津波被害. *Kagaku asahi* 科学朝日, 1988:6 (June).
Kraft, Eva S., ed. *Andreas Cleyer: Tagebuch des Kontors zu Nagasaki auf der Insel Deshima.* Bonn: Bonner Zeitschrift für Japanologie, 1985.
Kumazawa Banzan 熊沢蕃山. *Shūgi washo* 集義和書. *NST*, vol. 30.
Kurita Mototsugu 栗田元次. *Arai Hakuseki no bunchi seiji* 新井白石の文治政治. Tokyo: Ishizaki Shoten 石崎書店, 1952.
———. *Edo jidai shi* 江戸時代史. 2 vols. Tokyo: Kondō Shuppansha 近藤出版社, 1976.
———. "Genroku izen ni okeru Edo bakufu no zaisei ni tuite" 元禄以前における江戸幕府の財政に就いて. *Shigaku zasshi* 史学雑誌, 38:12 (December 1937).
———. "Inu kubō ron" 犬公方論. *Chūō shidan* 中央史壇, 1:3, 1:5 (1920).
———. "Yanagisawa Yoshiyasu ron" 柳沢吉保論. *Chūō shidan* 中央史壇, 2:5 (1921).
Kurita Naomi 栗田直躬. Preface to *Hitomi Chikudō shibun shū* 人見竹洞詩文集. Tokyo: Kyūko Shoin 汲古書院, 1991.
Kuroita Katsumi 黒板勝美 and Kokushi Taikei Henshūkai 国史大系編修会, eds. *Tokugawa jikki* 徳川実實記. Tokyo: Yoshikawa Kōbunkan 吉川弘文館, reprint 1976.
Kuwata Tadachika 桑田忠親. *Tokugawa Tsunayoshi to Genroku jidai* 徳川綱吉と元禄時代. Tokyo: Akita Shoten 秋田書店, 1975.
Lamb, Michael E. "Heredity, Environment, and the Question 'Why?'" *Behavioral and Brain Sciences,* 17:4 (December 1994).
Legge, James. *The Four Books.* Hong Kong: Wei Tung Book Store, n.d.
Lidin, Olof. *The Life of Ogyū Sorai, a Tokugawa Confucian Philosopher.* Scandianvian Institute of Asian Studies Monograph Series, 19. Lund, 1973.
Locurto, Charles, and Mark Freeman, "Radical Behaviorism and the Problem of Nonshared Development." *Behavior and Philosophy,* 22:1 (Spring/Summer 1994).

Lorenz, Konrad. *Über tierisches und menschliches Verhalten, Gesammelte Abhandlungen.* Munich: Piper, 1984.

Machiavelli, Nicolò. *The Prince.* Trans. George Bull. Harmondsworth: Penguin, 1961.

Maeda Kōji 前田恒治. *Aizu han ni okeru Yamazaki Ansai* 会津藩に於ける山崎闇斎. Tokyo: Nishizawa Shoten 西沢書店, 1935.

Mano Echū 真野恵澂. *Shōgun no onna* 将軍の女. Nagoya: Chūnichi Shinbun Honsha 中日新聞本社, 1981.

Marcon, Federico, and Henry D. Smith II. "A Chūshingura Palimpsest: Young Motoori Norinaga Hears the Story of the Akō Rōnin from a Buddhist Priest." *Monumenta Nipponica*, 58:4 (Winter 2003).

Maruyama Masao 丸山真男. *Nihon seiji shisōshi kenkyū* 日本政治思想史研究. Tokyo: Tōkyō Daigaku Shuppan Kai 東京大学出版会, 1952.

———. *Studies in the Intellectual History of Tokugawa Japan.* Trans. Mikiso Hane. Princeton and Tokyo: Princeton University Press and University of Tokyo Press, 1974.

Matsudaira Naonori 松平直矩. *Matsudaira Yamato no kami nikki* 松平大和守日記. In *Nihon shomin bunka shiryō shūsei* 日本庶民文化史料集成, vol. 12. Tokyo: Sanichi Shobō 三一書房, 1977.

Matsudaira Tarō 松平太郎. *Edo jidai seido no kenkyū* 江戸時代制度の研究. Tokyo: Kashiwa Shobō 柏書房, reprint 1993.

Matsukage nikki 松蔭日記. By Ōgimachi Machiko 正親町町子. Ed. Kai Sōsho Kankō Kai 甲斐叢書刊行会. Vol. 3 of *Kai sōsho* 甲斐叢書 (12 vols.). Tokyo: Daiichi Shobō 第一書房, 1974.

Matsuo Bashō 松尾芭蕉. *Bashō bunshū* 芭蕉文集. *NKBT,* vol. 46.

———. "Travelogue of Weather-Beaten Bones." In Sam Hamill, trans., *Narrow Road to the Interior and other Writings.* Boston and London: Shambhala, 2000.

Matsuo Mieko 松尾美恵子. "Fujisan funka to Asamasan funka" 富士山噴火と浅間山噴火. In Ōishi Manabu 大石学, ed., *Kyōhō kaikaku to shakai henyō* 享保改革と社会変容. Vol. 16 of *Nihon no jidai shi* 日本の時代史. Tokyo: Yoshikawa Kōbunkan 吉川弘文館, 2003.

Matsuura Seizan 松浦静山. *Kasshi yawa* 甲子夜話. In *Zoku zoku gunsho ruijū* 続々群書類従, vol. 76. Tokyo: Kokusho Kankōkai 国書刊行会, 1910-1911.

Matsuzawa Katsuyuki 松澤克行. "Kinsei zenki no buke kan'i jonin tetsuzuki to chōtei" 近世前期の武家官位叙任手続きと朝廷. In Hashimoto Masanobu 橋本政宣, *Kinsei buke kan'i no kenkyū* 近世武家官位の研究. Tokyo: Zoku Gunsho Ruijū Kanseikai 続群書類従完成会, 1999.

McEwan, J. R., *The Political Writings of Ogyū Sorai.* Cambridge, 1962.

McMullen, James. "Confucian Perspectives on the Akō Revenge: Law and Moral Agency." *Monumenta Nipponica*, 58:3 (Autumn 2003).

———. *Idealism, Protest, and the Tale of Genji.* Oxford: Oxford Oriental Monographs, Clarendon Press, 1999.

Meiryō kōhan 明良洪範. By Sanada Zōyo 真田増誉. Tokyo: Kokusho Kankōkai 国書刊行会, 1912.

Mikami Ryūzō 三上隆三. *Edo no kahei monogatari* 江戸の貨幣物語. Tokyo: Tōyō Keizai Shinhōsha 東洋経済新報社, reprint 1997.

Mikami Sanji 三上参次. *Edo jidai shi* 江戸時代史. 2 vols. Tokyo: Fuzambō 富山房, 1943-1944.
Minamoto Ryōen 源了圓. *Kinsei shoki jitsugaku shisō* 近世初期実学思想. Tokyo: Sōbunsha 創文社, 1980.
Miyamoto Musashi 宮本武蔵. *The Book of Five Rings* 五輪書. Trans. William Scott Wilson. Tokyo: Kodansha, 2001.
Miyazaki Eiga 宮崎英華. "Gojiin Ryūkō sōjō no nikki ni tsuite" 護持院隆光僧正の日記について. *Rekishi chiri* 歴史地理, 30:3 (1917).
Miyazaki Fumiko 宮崎ふみ子. "Namazue wa nanio gataru no ka" 鯰絵は何を語るのか. In National Museum of Japanese History, ed., *Documenting Disaster*. Sakurashi, Chiba, 2003.
Miyazawa Seiichi 宮澤誠一. *Kindai nihon to "Chūshingura" no gensō* 近代日本と「忠臣蔵」の幻想. Tokyo: Aoki Shoten 青木書店, 2001.
Momose Meiji 百瀬明治. *Go ie sōdō* 御家騒動. Tokyo: Kōdansha 講談社, 1993.
Monbushō 文部省. *Nihon kyōikushi* 日本教育史. Tokyo: Kōdōkan 弘道館, 1910.
Morita Yoshikazu 森田義一. *Yanagisawa Yoshiyasu* 柳沢吉保. Tokyo: Jinbutsu Ōraisha 人物往来社, 1975.
Morohashi Tetsuji 諸橋轍次. *Dai kanwa jiten* 大漢和辞典. Vol. 12. Tokyo: Daishūkan Shoten 大修館書店, 1968.
Murakami Tadashi 村上直. "Bakufu seiji no tenkai to Kantō gundai: Ina Hanzaemon Tadanobu o chūshin ni" 幕府政治の展開と関東郡代—伊奈半左衛門忠順を中心に— (English title supplied: *Tokugawa Shōgun's* Politics and the *Kantō* Magistrate: With Special Reference to Ina Hanzaemon). *Bulletin of the Tokugawa Institute for the History of Forestry* 徳川林政史研究所, March 1972.
———. *Edo bakufu no daikan* 江戸幕府の代官. Tokyo: Kokusho Kankōkai 国書刊行会, reprint 1983.
Nagashima Imashirō 永島今四郎 and Ōta Yoshio 太田贇雄, eds. *Teihon Edo jō ō oku* 定本江戸城大奥. Tokyo: Shinjinbutsu Ōraisha 新人物往来社, reprint 1995.
Naitō Chisō 内藤耻叟. *Tokugawa jūgodaishi* 徳川十五代史. Tokyo: Jinbutsu Ōraisha 人物往来社, reprint 1968.
Nakae Tōju 中江藤樹. *Okina mondō* 翁問答. In *NST*, vol. 29. Tokyo, 1974.
———. *Tōju sensei nenpu* 藤樹先生年譜. In NST, vol. 29. Tokyo, 1974.
Nakai, Kate Wildman. "Apologia pro Vita Sua." *Monumenta Nipponica,* 36:2 (Summer 1981).
———. *Shogunal Politics: Arai Hakuseki and the Premises of Tokugawa Rule.* Harvard East Asian Monographs 134. Cambridge, Mass., 1988.
———. "Tokugawa Confucian Historiography: The Hayashi, Early Mito School and Arai Hakuseki." In Peter Nosco, ed., *Confucianism and Tokugawa Culture.* Princeton: Princeton University Press, 1984.
Nakajima Yasuo 中島康. *Ōishi Kuranosuke, saigo no misshi* 大石内蔵助 最期の密使. Tokyo: Sangokan 三五館, 2000.
Nakajima Yōichirō 中島陽一郎. *Kikin nihonshi* 飢饉日本史. Tokyo: Yūzankaku Shuppan 雄山閣出版 1996.

Nakamura Akihiko 中村彰彦. *Hoshina Masayuki* 保科正之. Tokyo: Chūkō Shinsho 中公新書, no. 1227, 1995.

Nakase Katsutarō 中瀬勝太郎. *Edo jidai no wairo hishi* 江戸時代の賄賂秘史. Tokyo, 1989.

———. *Tokugawa bakufu no kaikei kensa seido* 徳川幕府の会計検査制度. Tokyo: Chikuchi Shobō 築地書館, 1990.

Naoki Kōjirō 直木孝次郎 et al. *Nihon rekishi B* 日本歴史B. Tokyo: Jikkyo Shuppan 実教出版, 2001.

Naramoto Tatsuya 奈良本辰也. *Machibito no jitsuryoku* 町人の実力. *Nihon no rekishi* 日本の歴史, vol. 17. Tokyo: Chūō Kōronsha 中央公論社, 1966.

———. *Nihon kinsei nihon shisō to bunka* 日本近世の思想と文化. Tokyo: Iwanami Shoten 岩波書店, 1978.

Nesaki Mitsuo 根崎光男. *Shōgun no taka kari* 将軍の鷹狩り. Tokyo: Dohsei Publishing Co. 同成社, 1999.

Neuhaus, Helmut, ed. *Deutsche Geschichte in Quellen und Dartstellung*, vol. 5: *Zeitalter des Absolutismus 1648–1789*. Stuttgart: Reclam, 1997.

Ng, Wai-ming. *The I Ching in Tokugawa Thought and Culture.* Honolulu: Hawai'i University Press, 2000.

Nicholson, Harold. *The Age of Reason (1700–1789).* Reprint Panther History, 1971.

Nihon Kokugo Daijiten Kankō Kai 日本国語大辞典刊行会, ed. *Nihon kokugo daijiten* 日本国語大辞典. Tokyo: Shōgakukan 小学館, reprint 1980.

Nihon Ginkō Chōsa Kyoku 日本銀行調査局, ed. *Hansatsu gaiyō* 藩札概要. Tokyo: Ōkurashō Insatsukyoku 大蔵省印刷局, 1964.

Nihon koten bungaku taikei 日本古典文学大系. Tokyo: Iwanami Shoten 岩波書店, 1957–1969.

Nihon shisō taikei 日本思想大系. Tokyo: Iwanami Shoten 岩波書店, 1970–1982.

Nikkō Shishi Hensan Iinkai 日光市史編纂委員会, ed. *Nikkō shishi* 日光市史. Tokyo: Nikkō, 1979–1986.

Nishimura Tokihiko 西村時彦. *Owari keikō* 尾張敬公. Nagoya: Nagoya Kaifu Sanbyaku Nen Kinennkai 名古屋開府三百年記念会, 1910.

Nishiwaki Osamu 西脇修. "Kinsei jidan seido no seiritsu ni tsuite 近世寺檀制度の成立ついて. In Tamamuro Fumio et al., eds., *Kinsei bukkyō no shomondai* 近世仏教の諸問題. Tokyo: Yūzankaku 雄山閣, 1979.

Nishiyama Matsunosuke 西山松之助, ed. *Edo machibito no kenkyū* 江戸町人の研究, vol. 5. Tokyo: Yoshikawa Kōbunkan 吉川弘文館, 1978.

Noguchi Takehiko 野口武彦. *Ogyū Sorai, Edo no don-kiho-te* 荻生徂徠、江戸のドン・キホーテ. Tokyo: Chūkō Shinsho 中公新書, 1993.

———. *Tokugawa Mitsukuni* 徳川光圀. Tokyo: Asahi Shinbunsha 朝日新聞社, 1976.

Noma Shōichi 野間省一. *Chūgoku koten meigenjiten* 中国古典名言辞典. Tokyo: Kōdansha 講談社, 1972.

Nosco, Peter, ed. *Confucianism and Tokugawa Culture.* Princeton: Princeton University Press, 1984.

Numata Jirō 沼田次郎 et al., ed. *Yōgakushi jiten* 洋学史辞典. Tokyo: Yushodo Co. 雄松堂出版, 1984.

Ogyū Sorai 荻生徂徠. *Gakuryō ryōken sho* 学寮了簡書. Shimada Kenji 島田虔次, ed., *Ogyū Sorai zenshū* 荻生徂徠全集, vol. 1. Tokyo: Misuzu Shobō, みすず書房, 1973.
———. *Master Sorai's Responsals*. Trans. S. H. Yamashita, Honolulu: Hawai'i University Press, 1994.
———. *Ogyū Sorai's Discourse on Government (Seidan)*. Ann. and trans. Olof Lidin. Wiesbaden: Harrassowitz Verlag, 1999.
———. *Ogyu Sorai's Distinguishing the Way: An Annotated English Traslation of the Bendo*. Trans. Olof G. Lidin. Monumenta Nipponica Monograph. Tokyo, 1970.
———. *Sorai shū* 徂徠集. Annotated by Hiraishi Naoaki 平石直昭. Vol. 3 of *Kinsei juka bunshū shūsei*, 近世儒家文集集成. Tokyo: Perikan Sha ぺりかん社, 1985.
———. *Taiheisaku* 太平策. *NST*, vol. 36.
———. *Seidan* 政談. *NST*, vol. 36.
———. *Sorai sensei tōmon sho* 徂徠先生答問書. *Ogyū Sorai Zenshū* 荻生徂徠全集, vol. 1. Tokyo: Misuzu Shobō みすず書房, 1973.
———. *Yakubun sentei* 訳文筌蹄. *Nihon no meicho* 日本の名著, vol. 16. Tokyo: Chūō Kōronsha 中央公論社, 1974.
———. *Yakubun sentei* 訳文筌蹄. *Ogyū Sorai zenshū* 荻生徂徠全集, vol. 2. Tokyo: Misuzu Shobō みすず書房, 1974.
Ōishi Shinzaburō 大石慎三郎. *Genroku jidai* 元禄時代. *Iwanami shinsho* 岩波新書, no. 755. Tokyo 1970.
———. "Genroku Kyōhō ki no kezai dankai" 元禄・享保期の経済段階. In Furushima Toshio 古島敏雄, ed., *Nihon keizai shi taikei* 日本経済史大系. Tokyo: Tōkyō Daigaku Shuppan 東京大学出版, 1965.
———. *Kyōhō kaikaku no keizai seisaku* 享保改革の経済政策. Tokyo: Ochanomizu Shobō 御茶の水書房, 1961.
———. *Nihon keizai shi ron* 日本経済史論. Tokyo: Ochanomizu Shobō 御茶の水書房, 1967.
Ōkawa Makoto 大川真. "Arai Hakuseki no kishinron saikō 新井白石の鬼神論再考. *Nihon rekishi* 日本歴史, no. 674 (July 2004).
Ōkubo Hikozaemon 大久保彦左衛門. *Mikawa monogatari* 三河物語. In Ono Shinji 小野信二, ed., *Ieyasu shiryō shū* 家康史料集. *Sengoku shiryō sōsho* 戦国史料叢書, vol. 6. Tokyo: Jinbutsu Ōraisha 人物往来社, 1965.
Ōkurashō 大蔵, ed. *Nihon zaisei keizai shiryō* 日本財政経済史料. Tokyo: Zaisei Keizai Gakkai 財政経済学会, 1922-1923.
Ōmaru Isao 王丸勇. *Byōseki gaku kara mita Matsudaira Tadanao, Tokugawa Iemitsu, Tokugawa Tsunayoshi* 病跡学から見た松平忠直・徳川家光・徳川綱吉. Tokyo: Rekishi Toshosha 歴史図書社, 1970.
Ōno Mizuo 大野瑞男. *Edo bakufu zaisei shiron* 江戸幕府財政史論. Tokyo: Yoshikawa Kōbunkan 吉川弘文館, 1996.
Ooms, Herman. *Tokugawa Ideology: Early Constructs, 1570-1680*. Princeton: Princeton University Press, 1985.
Ōta Naohiro 太田尚宏. "Edo jō osakana jōnō no tenkai to Kantō gundai" 江戸城「御肴」上納制度の展開と関東郡代. *Chihō shi kenkyū* 地方史研究, 40:2 (April 1991).

Ōtani Teifu 大谷貞夫. "Hōei ki no kawa fushin joyaku ni tsuite" 宝永期の川普請助役について. *Kokugakuin zasshi* 国学院雑誌, 80:11 (November 1979).

Ōtomo Kazuo 大友一雄. *Fujisan sunafuri sogan kiroku* 富士山砂降り訴願記録. *Nihon nōsho zenshū* 日本農書全集, vol. 66. Tokyo: Nōsan Gyōson Bunka Kyōkai 農山漁村文化協会, 1994.

———. *Nihon kinsei kokka no ken'i to girei* 日本近世国家の権威と儀礼. Tokyo: Yoshikawa Kōbunkan 吉川弘文館, 1999.

Ōtsuki Akira 大月明. *Kinsei nihon no jugaku to yōgaku* 近世日本の儒学と洋学. Kyoto: Shinbunkaku Shuppan 思文閣出版, 1988.

Paku Chonmyon 朴鐘鳴, ed. *Kanyōroku: chosen jusha no nihon yoku ryūki* 看羊録：朝鮮儒者の日本抑留記. *Tōyō bunko* 東洋文庫 440. Tokyo: Heibonsha 平凡社, 1984.

Plomin, Robert, David Riess, E. Mavis Hetherington, and George, W. Howe. "Nature and Nurture: Genetic Contributions to Measures of the Family Environment." *Developmental Psychology,* 30:1 (January 1994).

Rose, Richard J. "Genes and Human Behavior." *Annual Review of Psychology,* vol. 46 (1995).

Ryūei bunin 柳営補任. Ed. Negishi Moriisamu 根岸衛奮. In *Dai Nihon kinsei shiryō* 大日本近世史料. Tokyo: Tōkyō Daigaku Shuppankai 東京大学出版会, 1963.

Ryūei fujodensō 柳営婦女伝双. Ed. Kokusho Kankōkai 国書刊行会. Tokyo: Meicho Kankōkai 名著刊行会, 1965.

Ryūkō sōjō nikki 隆光僧正日記. By Gojiin Ryūkō Sōjō 護持院隆光僧正; ed. Nagashima Fukutarō 永島福太郎, Hayashi Ryōshō 林亮勝. 3 vols. *Shiryō sanshū* 史料纂集. Tokyo: Zoku Gunsho Ruijū Kanseikai 続群書類従完成会, 1970.

Sadler, A. L. *The Maker of Modern Japan: The Life of Tokugawa Ieyasu.* London: George Allen and Unwin, 1937.

Sakudō Yōtarō 作道洋太郎. *Kinsei nihon kaheishi* 近世日本貨幣史. Tokyo: Kōbundō 弘文堂, 1958.

Sannō gaiki 三王外記. By Tōbu Yashi 東武野史. Tokyo: Hokiyama Kageo 甫喜山景雄, 1880.

Sansom, George. *A History of Japan.* Stanford University Press, 1963.

Sanyō Shinbun Shuppan Kyoku 山陽新聞出版局, ed. and pub. *Shizugatani gakkō* 閑谷学校. Okayama, 1990.

Sasaki Junnosuke 佐々木潤之助 and Watanabe Norifumi 渡辺則文. "Sho sangyō no gijutsu to rōdō keitai" 諸産業の技術と労働形態. In *Iwanami kōza Nihon rekishi* 岩波講座日本歴史, vol. 11. Tokyo: Iwanami Shoten 岩波書店, 1976.

Sasama Yoshihiko 笹間良彦. *Edo bakufu yakushoku shūsei* 江戸幕府役職集成. Tokyo: Yūzankaku 雄山閣, 1965.

Satō Naokata 佐藤直方. "Yonjūroku nin no hikki" 四十六人の筆記. *NST,* vol. 27.

Satō Seijitsu 佐藤誠実. *Nihon kyōiku shi* 日本教育史. 1909. Reprint Naka Arata 仲新, Sakai Yutaka 酒井豊, eds., *Tōyō bunko* 東洋文庫 231. Tokyo 1973.

Satō Tsuneo 佐藤常雄 et al., eds. *Nihon nōsho zenshū* 日本農書全集, vol. 66. Tokyo: Nōsan Gyōson Bunka Kyōkai 農山漁村文化協会, 1994.

Segawa Yoshiko 瀬川淑子. *Ōjo shina no miya no nichijō seikatsu* 皇女品宮の日常生活. Tokyo: Iwanami Shoten 岩波書店, 2001.

Sekai dai hyakka jiten 世界大百科事典. CD-ROM. Tokyo: Hitachi Degitaru Heibon Sha 日立デジタル平凡社.
Shibata Hajime 柴田一. "Okayama han no hangaku to kyōgaku" 岡山藩の藩学と郷学. In *Shizugatani gakkō kenkyū* 閑谷学校研究, 1997:5 (vol. 1).
Shinsai Yobō Chōsakai 震災予防調査会. *Nihon funka shi* 日本噴火志. Tokyo: Yūmei Shobō 有明書房, 1991 (reprint of 1918 edition).
Shinshi Yoshimoto 進士慶幹. "O-inu sama" お犬さま. In *Nihon rekishi* 日本歴史, 260.
Shively, Donald H. "Tokugawa Tsunayoshi." In Albert M. Craig and Donald H. Shively, eds., *Personality in Japanese History*. Berkeley: University of California Press, 1970.
Shizutani Gakkō Shi Hensan Iinkai 閑谷学校史編さん委員会, ed. *Shizutani gakkō shi* 閑谷学校史. Okayama: Shizutani Gakkōshi Kankōkai 閑谷学校史刊行会, 1971.
Shōhō jiroku 正宝事録. Ed. Kinsei Shiryō Kenkyū Kai 近世史料研究会. 3 vols. Tokyo: Nihon Gakujutsu Shinkōkai 日本学術振興会, 1965.
Skinner, B. F. *Beyond Freedom and Dignity*. New York: Knopf, 1971.
Smith Henry, D. II. "The Capacity of Chūshingura." *Monumenta Nipponica*, 58:1 (Spring 2003).
———. "The Trouble with Terasaka: The Forty-Seventh Rōnin and the Chūshingura Imagination." *Japan Review*, 2004:16.
Sōhonzan Hasedera 総本山長谷寺, ed. *Hasedera meihōten* 長谷寺名宝典. Tokyo: Sankei Shinbunsha 産経新聞社, 1992.
Sonehara Satoshi 曽根原理. *Tokugawa Ieyasu shinkakuka e no michi* 徳川家康神格化への道. Tokyo: Yoshikawa Kōbunkan 吉川弘文館, 1996.
Sumiya Hitomi 角谷ひとみ et al. "Fujisan Hōei funka (1707) ato no dosha saigai" 富士山宝永噴火 (1707) 後の土砂災害 (English title supplied: Distribution of Sediment Disasters after the 1707 Hoei Eruption of Fuji Volcano in Central Japan, Based on Historical Documents). *Rekishi jishin* 歴史地震, no. 18 (2002).
Super nihongo daijiten スーパー日本語大辞典. CD-ROM (ISBN 4-05-700017-8). Tokyo: Gakken 学研.
Suzuki Hisashi 鈴木尚. *Hone wa kataru Tokugawa shōgun, daimyō no hitobito* 骨は語る徳川将軍・大名の人びと. Tokyo: Tōkyō Daigaku Shuppan 東京大学出版, 1985.
Suzuki, H. 鈴木尚, K. Yajima 矢島恭介, and T. Yamanobe, 山辺知行, comps. *Studies on the Graves, Coffin Contents and Skeletal Remains of the Tokugawa Shoguns and Their Families at the Zōjōji Temple* 増上寺徳川将軍墓とその遺品・遺体. Tokyo: Tōkyō Daigaku Shuppan 東京大学出版, 1967.
Suzuki Rizaemon 鈴木理衛門. "Fujisan sunafuri sogan kiroku (Sagami)" 富士山砂降り訴願記録 (相模). In *Nihon nōsho zenshū* 日本農書全集, vol. 66. Tokyo: Nōsan Gyōson Bunka Kyōkai 農山漁村文化協会, 1994.
Suzuki Toshio 鈴木敏夫. *Edo no honya* 江戸の本屋. Tokyo: Chūkō Shinsho 中公新書, reprint 1993.
Tachibana Terumasa 橘輝政. *Kodai kara bakumatsu made Nihon igaku senjin den* 古代から幕末まで日本医学先人伝. Tokyo: Iji Yakugyō Shinpōsha 医事薬業新報社, 1969.

Tahara Tsuguo 田原嗣郎. *Akō yonjūrokushi ron* 赤穂四十六士論. Tokyo: Yoshikawa Kōbunkan 吉川弘文館, 1978.

———. *Sōrai gaku no sekai* 徂徠学の世界. Tokyo: Tōkyō Daigaku Shuppan 東京大学出版, 1991.

Takada Mamoru 高田衛. *Edo no ekusoshisuto* 江戸の悪霊祓い師. Tokyo: Chikuma Bunko, 筑摩書房 reprint 2000.

Takano Toshihiko 高埜利彦. *Genroku Kyōhō no jidai* 元禄・享保の時代. Vol. 13 of *Nihon no rekishi* 日本の歴史. Tokyo: Shūeisha 集英社, 1992.

———. *Genroku no shakai to bunka,* 元禄の社会と文化. *Nihon no jidaishi* 日本の時代史, vol. 15. Tokyo: Yoshikawa Kōbunkan 吉川弘文館, 2003.

———. *Kinsei nihon no kokka kenryoku to shūkyō* 近世日本の国家権力と宗教. Tokyo: Tōkyō Daigaku Shuppan 東京大学出版, 1989.

Takayanagi Kaneyoshi 高柳金芳. *Shiryō: Tokugawa bakufu no seido* 史料・徳川幕府の制度. Tokyo: Jinbutsu Ōraisha 人物往来社, reprint 1976.

———. *Tokugawa fujinden* 徳川夫人伝. Tokyo: Jinbutsu Ōraisha 人物往来社, 1967.

Takayanagi Shinzō 高柳真三 and Ishii Ryōsuke 石井良助, eds. *Ofuregaki kanpō shūsei* 御触書寛保集成. Tokyo: Iwanami Shoten 岩波書店, 1958.

Takeuchi Makoto 竹内誠. *Edo to Ōsaka* 江戸と大坂. Vol. 10 of *Taikei nihon no rekishi* 大系日本の歴史. Tokyo: Shōgakukan 小学館, 1989.

———. *Genroku ningen moyō* 元禄人間模様. Tokyo: Kadokawa Shobō 角川書房, 2000.

Takigawa Masajirō 滝川政次郎. "Inu ni kansuru ritsuryō no hōsei" 犬に関する律令の法制. *Nihon rekishi* 日本歴史, 260 (1970).

Tamamuro Fumio 圭室文雄. "Danka seido no seiritsu 檀家制度の成立. In *Rekishi kōron* 歴史公論, vol. 2. Tokyo: Yūzankaku Shuppan 雄山閣出版, 1985.

———. *Edo bakufu no shūkyō tōsei* 江戸幕府の宗教統制. Tokyo: Hyōronsha 評論社, 1971.

Tanabe Yasshi 田辺泰. *Nikkō byō kenchiku* 日光廟建築. Tokyo: Shōkokusha 彰国社, 1944.

Taniguchi Sumio 谷口澄夫. *Ikeda Mitsumasa* 池田光政. Tokyo: Yoshikawa Kōbunkan 吉川弘文館, 1960.

———. *Okayama han* 岡山藩. Tokyo: Yoshikawa Kōbunkan 吉川弘文館, 1964.

Tanno Shirō 淡野史良. "Godai Tokugawa Tsunayoshi: Reigen tennō, Higashiyama tennō" 5代徳川綱吉・霊元天皇、東山天皇. In *Rekishi dokuhon* 歴史読本, 44:7 (June 1999).

———. "Tokugawa shōgun ke to chōtei: godai Tokugawa Tsunayoshi" 徳川将軍家と朝廷・5代徳川綱吉. *Rekishi dokuhon* 歴史読本, 44:7 (June 1999).

Taya Hirokichi 田谷博吉. *Kinsei Ginza no kenkyū* 近世銀座の研究. Tokyo: Yoshikawa Kōbunkan 吉川弘文館, 1963.

Terashima Ryōan 寺島良安. *Wakan sansai zue* 和漢三才図会. Tokyo: Heibonsha 平凡社, 1985.

Thomas, Keith. *Man and the Natural World: Changing Attitudes in England 1500–1800*. Harmondsworth: Penguin Books, 1984.

Toby, Ronald P. *State and Diplomacy in Early Modern Japan*. Princeton: Princeton University Press, 1984.

Toda Mosui 戸田茂睡. *Gotōdaiki* 御当代記. Ed. Tsukamoto Manabu 塚本学. Tōyō-bunko 東洋文庫 643. Tokyo: Heibonsha 平凡社, 1998.
Tokugawa shoka keifu 徳川諸家系譜. Ed. and pub. Gunsho Ruiju Kanseikai 続群書類従完成会. Tokyo, 1974.
Tokuta Takeshi 徳田武. "Hitomi Chikudō Shu Shunsui ōfuku shotoku nenji kōshō" 人見竹洞・朱舜水往復書牘年時考証 (English title supplied: A Study of the Chronology of the Correspondence between HITOMICHIKUDO and SHUSHUNSUI). *Meiji daigaku kyōyō ronshū* 明治大学教養論集, *Nihon bungaku*, no. 259 (1993).
Tokutomi Iichiro 徳富猪一郎. *Kinsei nihon kokuminshi* 近世日本国民史. Vol. 11: *Sekigahara yaku* 関原役. Vol:13: *Ieyasu jidai gaikan* 家康時代概観. Vol. 14: *Tokugawa bakufu jōki: sakoku hen* 幕府上期：鎖国篇. Vol. 15: *Tokugawa bakufu jōki: tōsei hen* 徳川幕府上期：統制篇. Vol. 16: *Tokugawa bakufu jōki: shisō hen* 徳川幕府上期：思想篇. Vol. 17: *Genroku jidai: seiji hen* 元禄時代：政治篇. Vol. 18: *Genroku jidai: gishi hen* 元禄時代：義士篇. Vol. 19: *Genroku jidai: sesōhen* 元禄時代世相篇. Tokyo: Minyūsha 民友社, 1935-1936.
Totman, Conrad. *Early Modern Japan*. Berkeley: University of California Press, 1993.
———. *Tokugawa Ieyasu: Shogun*. Torrance: Heian International 1983.
Tsuji Tatsuya 辻達也. *Edo bakufu seijishi kenkyū* 江戸幕府政治史研究. Tokyo: Zoku Gunsho Ruijū Kanseikai 続群書類従完成会, 1996.
———. *Edo kaifu* 江戸開府. Vol. 13 of *Nihon no rekishi* 日本の歴史. *Chūkō bunko* 中公文庫, vol. 660. Reprint Tokyo, 1990.
———. "Geba shōgun seiji no seikaku" 「下馬将軍」政治の性格. In *Yokohama shiritsu daigaku ronsō jinbunkagaku keiretsu* 横浜私立大学論叢人文科学系列, 30:2-3 (August 1979).
———. *Kyōhō kaikaku no kenkyū* 享保改革の研究. Tokyo: Sōbunsha 創文社, 1963.
———. "Politics in the Eighteenth Century." Trans. Harold Bolitho. In John Whitney Hall, ed., *The Cambridge History of Japan*, vol. 4: *Early Modern Japan*. Cambridge: Cambridge University Press, 1991.
———. "*Seidan* no shakaiteki haikei" 「政談」の社会的背景. In Ogyū Sorai 荻生徂徠, *Seidan, NST*, vol. 36.
———. *Tennō to shōgun* 天皇と将軍. Vol. 2 of *Nihon no kinsei* 日本の近世. Tokyo: Chūō Kōrosha 中央公論社, 1991.
———. *Tokugawa Yoshimune* 徳川吉宗. *Jinbutsu sōsho* 人物叢書. Tokyo: Yoshikawa Kōbunkan 吉川弘文館, 1958.
Tsuji Yoshinobu つじよしのぶ. *Fuji san no funka* 富士山の噴火. Tokyo: Tsukiji Shokan 築地書館, 1992.
Tsuji Yoshinobu 都司嘉宣. "Genroku jishin, tsunami (1703-XII-31) no Shimoda isei no shiryō jōkyō 元禄地震・津波 (1703-XII-31) の下田以西の史料状況 (English title supplied: Documents of the 1703 Genroku Tsunami along the Coasts of the Tokai District, the Kii Peninsula, and the Shikoku Island). *Jishin* 地震, vol. 34 (1981).
———. "Jishin kazan saigai bumon" 地震火山災害部門. *Nisen nendo jishin kenkyū kōkai kōgi (1): Genroku 16 nen (1703 nen) no Kantō shinsai* 2000 年度地震研究

公開講義（１）元禄 16 年（1703）の関東震災. Internet site: http://www.eri.u.-tokyo.ac.jp/KOHO/KOHO/30/30-3.html (2003/10/11).
Tsuji Zennosuke 辻善之助. "Yanagisawa Yoshiyasu no ichimen" 柳澤の一面. *Shirin* 史林, 10:3 (1925). Reprint *Nihon bunka shi, betsuroku* 日本文化史 別録. Tokyo: Shunjūsha 春秋社, 1953.
Tsukamoto Manabu 塚本学. *Edo jidai hito to dōbutsu* 江戸時代人と動物. Tokyo: Nihon Editaa Sukuuru Shuppanbu 日本エディタースクール出版部, 1995.
———. *Ikiru koto no kinseishi* 生きることの近世史. Tokyo: Heibonsha Sensho 平凡社選書, 2001.
———. "Kaisetsu" 解説. In Toda Mosui 戸田茂睡, Gotōdaiki 御当代記, ed. Tsukamoto Manabu 塚本学. Tōyōbunko 東洋文庫, 643. Tokyo: Heibonsha 平凡社, 1998.
———. *Kinsei saikō* 近世再考. Tokyo: Nihon Editaa Sukuuru Shuppanbu 日本エディタースクール出版部, 1986.
———. "Seikun to shite no inu kubō" 聖君としての犬公方. In *Rekishi to jinbutsu* 歴史と人物, July 1980.
———. "Shōrui awaremi no seisaku to Saikaku-bon" 生類憐れみの政策と西鶴本. In *Jinbun kagaku ronshū* 人文科学論集, 14 (1980).
———. *Shōrui wo meguru seiji* 生類をめぐる政治. Tokyo: Heibonsha Sensho 平凡社選書, 1983.
———. *Shōrui o meguru seiji* 生類をめぐる政治. Tokyo: Heibonsha Raiburarii 平凡社ライブラリー, 1993.
———. *Tokugawa Tsunayoshi* 徳川綱吉. Tokyo: Jinbutsu Sōsho 人物叢書, Yoshikawa Kōbunkan 吉川弘文館, 1998.
Tsunoda. R., et al., comps. *Sources of Japanese Tradition*. New York: Columbia University Press, reprint 1968.
Tyler, Royall. "The Tokugawa Peace and Popular Religion." In Peter Nosco, ed., *Confucianism and Tokugawa Culture*. Princeton: Princeton University Press, 1984.
Ueno Yōzō 上野洋三. "Ōgimachi ke keizu" 正親町家系図. In *Matsukage nikki* 松蔭日記. Tokyo: Iwanami Bunko 岩波文庫, 2004.
Ueshima Tamotsu 上島有. Entry "Shosatsu rei" 書札礼. In *Sekai dai hyakka jiten*.
Urabe Noriko 卜部典子. *Jinbutsu jiten: Edo jō ō oku no onnatachi* 人物事典：江戸城大奥の女たち. Tokyo: Shinjinbutsu Ōraisha 新人物往来社, 1988.
Vaporis, Constantine Nomikos. *Breaking Barriers*. Cambridge, Mass.: Harvard University Press, 1994.
Varenius, Bernhardus. *Beschreibung des Japanischen Reiches*. Amsterdam, 1649. Trans. Ernst Christian Volkmann. Darmstadt: Wissenschaftliche Buchgesellschaft, 1974.
de Vivero, Rodrigo. *Du Japon et du bon gouvernement de l'Espagne et des Indes*. Trans. and ed. Juliette Monbeig. Paris: S.E.V.P.E.N., 1972.
Wajima Yoshio 和島芳男. "Kanbun igaku no kin: sono rinmon kōryū no kankei" 寛文異学の禁：その隣門交流の関係. In *Ōtemae joshi daigaku ronshū* 大手前女子大学論集, 8 (1975).
———. *Nihon sōgakushi no kenkyū* 日本宋学史の研究. Tokyo: Yoshikawa Kōbunkan 吉川弘文館, reprint 1988.

Wakita Osamu 脇田修. *Genroku no shakai* 元禄の社会. Tokyo: Hanawa Shobō 塙書房, 1980.
Watanabe Hiroshi 渡辺浩. *Kinsei nihon shakai to sōgaku* 近世日本社会と宋学. Tokyo: Tōkyō Daigaku Shuppan 東京大学出版, reprint 1987.
Watanabe Kazutoshi 渡辺和敏. *Kinsei kōtsū seido no kenkyū* 近世交通制度の研究. Tokyo: Yoshikawa Kōbunkan 吉川弘文館, 1991.
Weber, Max. *Economy and Society*. Ed. Guenther Roth and Claus Wittich. Berkeley, University of California Press, 1978.
———. *Wirtschaft und Gesellschaft*. Tübingen: J. C. B. Mohr, 1976.
Wolf, Ernest S. "Psychoanalytic Selfobject, Psychology and Psychohistory." In Mel Albin, ed., *New Directions in Psychohistory*. Toronto: Lexington Books, 1980.
Yamaguchi Kazuo 山口和夫. "Kinsei shoki buke kan'i no tenkai to tokushitsu ni tsuite" 近世初期武家官位の展開と特質について. In Hashimoto Masanobu 橋本正宣, ed., *Kinsei buke kan'i no kenkyū* 近世武家官位の研究. Tokyo: Zoku Gunsho Ruijū Kanseikai 続群書類従完成会, 1999.
Yamaguchi Keiji 山口啓二. *Sakoku to kaikoku* 鎖国と開国. Tokyo: Iwanami Shoten 岩波書店, 1993.
Yamamoto Hirofumi 山本博文. *Asobi o suru shōgun, odoru daimyō* 遊びをする将軍踊る大名. Tokyo: Kyōiku Shuppan 教育出版, 2002.
———. *Tokugawa shōgun to tennō* 徳川将軍と天皇. Tokyo: Chūō Kōron Shinsha 中央公論新社, 1999.
Yamamura Kozo. *A Study of Samurai Income and Entrepreneurship*. Cambridge, Mass.: Harvard University Press, 1974.
Yanagisawa Yoshiyasu 柳沢吉保. *Yanagisawa Yoshiyasu kō sanzen roku* 柳澤吉保公参禅録. Yamato Kōriyama 大和郡山: Eikeiji 永慶寺, 1973.
Yanagisawa ke hizō jikki 柳澤家秘蔵実記. Vol. 3 of Kai Sōsho Kankō Kai 甲斐叢書刊行会, ed., *Kai sōsho* 甲斐叢書 (12 vols.). Tokyo: Dai Ichi Shobō 第一書房, 1974.
Yōgen roku 颺言録. By Hotta Masatoshi 堀田正俊. In vol. 13 of *Zoku zoku gunsho ruijū* 続々群書類従. Tokyo: Kokusho Kankōkaikai 国書刊行会, 1906–1909.
Yokoyama Tatsuzō 横山達三. *Nihon kinsei kyōikushi* 日本近世教育史. Tokyo: Dōbunkan 同文館, 1904.
Yoshikawa Machi Kyōiku Iinkai 吉川町教育委員会. *Shūmon aratame chō, Tenna sannen kenchi chō* 宗門改帳・天和三年検地帳. Niigata: Yoshikawa Machi Kyōiku Iinkai 吉川町教育委員会, 1993.

Index

abortion, 137–142
Akō, 163, 166; castle, 165, 167, 178; castle museum, 172
alternate attendance (*sankin kōtai*), 45, 190, 203, 279, 332n. 27
Arai Hakuseki, 17, 99, 105, 116–117, 131, 141, 146, 148, 155–157, 165, 216, 255, 266, 272–274, 290, 293, 294, 296–297; and Confucianism, 53–55, 60, 68, 290; and reminting, 199–201, 247
Arisugawa no Miya Yukihito, 74–75, 88
Asahi Shigeaki, 131–132, 146, 157–158, 160, 165, 265, 276
Asai Ryōi, 149–150
Asano Nagahiro, 166, 171
Asano Naganori, 164–171, 173, 175, 202, 325n. 13
Ashikaga: academy 51; shogunate, 45, 52, 212; Takauji, 58; Yoshiaki, 45
Atake maru, 94, 120, 151
attendant (*konando*), 110, 249; senior (*konando jōza*), 109, 113
authority, political, 285–286, 288, 297–298; *bakufu*, 187, 190–191; shogunal, 8, 40, 195, 210, 251–252, 261, 275

bakufu domain (*tenryō, chokkatsuryō*), 90–91, 184, 192–194, 196; and domain confiscation, 42, 81, 192, 281, 284, 289
bakufu finance, 184–185, 188–191, 196, 201–203, 206, 208; expenditure, 185–186, 189–190, 199, 203–205. See also *bakufu* impositions; currency
bakufu impositions, 190–191, 205–206, 209–210
benevolence (*jin*) 29, 245, benevolent/compassionate government (*jinsei*), 62, 67, 90, 218, 244–246, 252

Blacker, Carmen, 140
Bolitho, Harold, 6, 285, 289, 295
Book of Five Rings (*Gorin sho*), 131, 172
books, publishing of, 224, 279–280
Bourdieu, Pierre, 31, 48–49, 238
Brevinck, Albert, 33, 46
bridges, 92; Edai Bashi, 271
Buddhism, 50–53, 132, 139–140, 207, 210–215, 283, 294; confrontation with Confucianism, 53–57, 59–60, 64, 214
Buddhist clergy, 2, 130, 294; Obaku sect, 241; sects, 53, 59, 211
Buke shohatto. See Regulations; for the Military Houses
Buya shokudan, 16–17, 20, 23, 76–77, 79, 84, 149, 291, 303n. 40

chamberlain (*sobashū, soba yaku, go soba*), 60, 81–82, 101, 104–107, 109
Ch'en Yüan-pin (Jap.: Chin Genpin), 57, 229
Chikamatsu Monzaemon, 3, 278
children, 117, 137; abandoned (*sutego*), 35, 137, 139, 141–142; child-rearing, 18–19, 31–32; education, 18, 35, 139–142. See also abortion; infanticide; samurai: children of
China, 7–8, 241–243, 275, 292. See also Ming dynasty
Chinese emperors/kings, 3, 252–253; Kao-tsu, 50; sage emperors, 239; Shun, 94; Wen 1; Wu, 101; Yellow Emperor (*huang-ti*), 234. See also Yao and Shun
Chiyo hime, 39, 70, 215
Christianity, 47, 53–55
Chu Hsi, 215, 223, 231
Chu Shun-shui (Jap.: Shu shun-sui), 58–59, 136, 218–222, 227, 229

371

Chūshingura, 161–163, 324n. 1
Confucian: burial, 60–61, 64, 66; ceremony, 57, 225, 227; hall/shrine (*senseiden*), 57, 66, 69; ideal government, 56; school, 51, 64–66, 229. *See also* benevolence: government
Confucian classics, 7, 17, 35, 52, 110, 119, 217–218, 223–224, 239, 283, 292–293; *The Book of Changes*, 52, 228, 234; *The Confucian Analects*, 27; *The Doctrine of the Mean*, 228; *The Great Learning*, 220, 223, 225, 228, 251;*The Works of Mencius*, 93
Confucian scholars, 2, 8, 55, 222; as "book-reading monks," 63; shed Buddhist robes, 59, 69, 219, 226–227. *See also* Yanagisawa mansion and names of individual scholars.
Confucianism, 17, 207, 215–229, 283; Confucius, statue of, 57, 66; lack of sponsorship, 50–53; practice of, 53–56
currency, 184, 188, 197, 201–202; debasement, 197–201, 246–247, 259, 297, 331n. 4

daikan. *See* intendant
daimyo, 153, 159–160, 189, 190–191, 201–202, 223, 263, 279, 286–287, 295; assistance, 205–206, 209–210, 251, 260–261, 267, 272, 296; ignorance of, 103, 118, 249, 287
Dazai Shundai, 3, 70, 170, 172, 176, 252–253
death, 2, 5; death sentence, 3
director of finance (*kanjō gashira*), 82, 90–91, 192–195
dogs, 2, 8, 16, 35, 288; astral Year of, 2–3, 6, 110, 128–129, 144, 146; attacking and killing people, 133–134, 136–137, 152, 154, 157, 159; breeding of, 132; dog meat, 148–149; dog pounds, 158–160, 260; and hunting, 47, 132; orders concerning, 150–154; treatment of, 130, 133, 134, 144, 154. *See also* Laws of Compassion
Dokai kōshūki, 80, 166, 167, 171, 289
Dutch, 95, 104, 116, 132, 158, 168, 221, 248, 257–259; East India Company, 4, 198; reports of, 70–71, 74–75, 80; rulers, 22.

earthquake, 1, 83, 186, 199, 255–260, 265
Echigo *sōdō* (succession dispute), 82–88
Edo bakufu nikki, 43, 70, 76–77, 187, 291
Edo castle, 1, 10, 40, 96, 186, 189, 190–191, 255, 258–259, 261, 265, 289; guard of, 40, 106, 256, 293; *kirinoma* guard (*ban*) of, 255, 271, 339n. 3
Edo city magistrate (*Edo machi bugyō*), 82, 94, 97, 121, 154, 173, 195
emperor, 23, 44, 56–58, 123–124, 148, 168, 181; Godaigo, 58; Gomizuno'o, 185; Gosai, 74, 88; Gotsuchimikado, 122; Higashiyama, 122, 164; Montoku, 296; Nintoku, 46; Reigen, 38, 168; Seiwa, 296–297; Taishō, 123; and hawking, 46–47. *See also* imperial
exorcism, 138–140

famine, 90, 188, 231, 253, 265, 270, 273, 295
farmers, 279–280; administration of, 90–93, 224; demand for relief, 268–270, 287; hardship of, 149–150, 232, 291
filial piety, 21, 29, 34, 172, 175, 178; placards, 34, 223–224
finance: group head (*kanjō kumi gashira*), 193–194; inspector (*kanjō ginmiyaku*), 193–195. *See also* magistrate of finance
Foucault, Michel, 43–45
fudai daimyo, 39, 107, 124, 187, 191; punishment of, 81, 87
Fuji, Mount, 183; eruption, 265–267, 268, 271, 273–274, 275, 287
Fujiwara Seika, 51, 56–57, 93

Genghis Khan, 50, 308n. 2
Genkō jitsuroku, 114, 126–127, 176, 232–233
Genroku period, 4, 183, 198, 204, 253, 278–280, 344n. 46
gift-giving, 116–117, 168–169, 258, 261
Gokoku onna taiheiki, 112–113, 317n. 27
Gosanke. *See* Three Related Houses
Gotōke reijō, 92
grand chamberlain, 104–109, 113–115, 125. *See also* Makino Narisada; Yanagisawa Yoshiyasu
grand councilor (*tairō*), 124–125. *See also* Hotta Masatoshi; Sakai Tadakiyo

Index

Hagakure, 101, 130–132, 139, 178–181, 210, 282
Hatakeyama Motoharu, 109, 114
hatamoto, 82, 110, 188, 189, 191, 193, 223, 249, 250
Hattori Nankaku, 115, 242
hawks, 148–149; damage caused to farmers, 147–148; grounds, 47–48, 149–150, 159; hawking, 43, 46–48, 151, 291
Hayashi Harunobu, 216, 220
Hayashi house, 17, 55, 58, 67, 120, 220, 236, 292. *See also* Yushima Confucian shrine
Hayashi Jussai, 291, 292
Hayashi Nobuatsu (Hōkō), 173–174, 176, 215, 216, 222, 225, 227, 232–233, 235–236
Hayashi Razan, 17, 51–53, 56, 63, 216
Hayashi Shunsai (Gahō), 215, 216, 217–221, 239–240
Hiraishi Naoaki, 119, 243, 244
Hitomi Bōsai (Den), 220
Hitomi Gentoku, 215, 216
Hitomi Yūgen (Chikudō), 93, 215–222
Honda Masanobu, 56, 93
Honda Masazumi, 185
Honjō Michika, 30, 40
Honsaroku, 53, 56, 93; *Honsaroku kō,* 53
Hori Kyōan, 56–57
horses, 19, 35, 146–147, 151
Hoshina Masayuki, 13–14, 39, 60, 63–65
Hosoi Kōtaku, 115, 123
Hosokawa family, 175–177
Hotta Masamori, 97, 105, 127, 132
Hotta Masanobu, 99–100
Hotta Masatoshi, 5, 27, 34, 70, 76–77, 81–82, 85, 87–89, 124, 146, 150–151, 232, 252, 286, 287; and administration of farmers, 90–92, 193–194; assassination, 98–101, 104, 165, 167; and *Yōgen roku,* 93–98, 100
hunting, 16, 132. *See also* hawks
hyōjōsho. See supreme court

Ihara Saikaku, 4, 137, 140–141, 183, 278, 289
Ii Naomori, 124–125
Ikeda Mitsumasa, 60–68, 222, 281
Ikeda Tsunamasa, 65–66
imperial: envoys, 164; finance, 187, 263; institution, 122–123; palace, 274; tombs, 123. *See also* emperor

Ina Tadanobu, 271, 273, 274
Ina Tadatsune, 216, 271
Inaba Masanori, 69–71, 75, 97–98
Inaba Masayasu, 98–100, 165, 167, 205
Inaba Masayuki, 143
Inagaki Shigetomi, 266
infanticide, 35, 139–142, 304n. 5. *See also* children
inspector (*metsuke*), 82, 91; general (*ōmetsuke*), 106, 173
intendant (*daikan*), 90–93, 192–194, 209, 224, 231–232
Iseki Gensetsu, 72
Itakura Shigemune, 60–62
Itō Jinsai, 53, 98–99, 218, 243, 253

Jesuits, writings of, 137, 184–185
jin, jinsei. See benevolence
jisha bugyō. See magistrate of temples and shrines
junior councilor (*wakadoshiyori*), 82, 105–107, 109, 121
junshi (following one's lord into death), 40, 87–88, 96, 100, 280, 281

kabuki, 138, 161, 278
Kaempfer, Engelbert, 4, 12, 33, 44, 77, 79–80, 86, 100, 104, 118, 142, 158, 198, 209, 221, 257, 264, 265, 288; and Confucianism, 50, 55–56, 63–65, 69, 120, 131, 222, 227; on dogs, 144–146; and Tsunashige's death, 69–71, 73
Kai, 126–128, 202, 263
Kamakura, 265; bakufu, 57; period, 16, 22
Kanda ki, 38, 43, 216
Kaneiji, 33, 53, 101, 104, 122, 124, 186, 210, 211
Kang Hang (Kyōkō), 93
kanjō gashira. See director of finance
kanpaku (senior regent to the emperor), 44, 123
Kansei chōshū shokafu, 107, 109
Kantō magistrate (*Kantō gundai*), 271. *See also* Ina Tadanobu
Kasshi yawa, 3, 88
Kasuga no Tsubone, 22–23, 97–98, 283, 304n. 11
Kawagoe, castle 116, 119

Kawamura Zuiken, 99, 205
Keishō-in, 7-8, 16, 20-21, 27, 126-127, 142, 264, 283-284; ambitions, 26-28, 30; and Buddhism, 129, 138, 142, 211-212, 214; childhood, 31-32, 136; and Confucianism, 27-29, 233; court rank, 112, 123, 125, 260; family background, 23-24, 248; physical appearance, 25, 33. *See also* mother.
Kenbyō jitsuroku, 15, 77, 242, 244
Kii Tsunanori. *See* Tokugawa Tsunanori
kinju, 190; *kinju shuttōnin*, 105-106
Kinoshita Jun'an, 216, 222, 229
Kira Yoshinaka, 164-165, 166-172, 175-176, 178, 179
Kitami Shigemasa, 104, 109, 114
Kitamura Kigin, 122, 238, 240, 243, 263-264, 278
Kōfu, 14, 38, 119
kōke (master of court ceremonies), 114, 168. *See also* Kira Yoshinaka
konando. See attendant
Konoe Motohiro, 1-2, 301n. 7
Korean Embassy, 216, 272, 273
koshō. See page
Koyake Seijun, 59
Kumazawa Banzan, 57, 60-63, 67, 222, 282, 284, 287, 289
Kuraoka Sozan, 242
Kurita Mototsugu, 6, 117, 128, 189, 280-281
Kusunoki Masashige, 58
Kuze Hiroyuki, 87
Kyōhō Reform, 6, 293
Kyoto, 187-188; *aratame*, 53; aristocracy, 44, 45-46; deputy (*Kyōto shoshidai*), 106, 109; magistrate (*Kyōto machi bugyō*), 91

lampoons, 2, 8, 74, 167, 276, 296
land survey, 88, 195-196
Laws for the Examination of Sects (*shūmon aratame no jō*), 52, 59-60, 64-65, 281
Laws of Compassion, 4, 6, 9, 93, 112, 129-130, 136, 149, 151, 180, 224, 245, 253, 281, 283, 287-288, 291, 294; children and pregnant women, 141-142; dogs, 146-148; and officials, 153-156, 160; punishments, 156-158; travelers and prisons, 142-143. *See also* dogs; horses
Lidin, Olof, 241, 242, 252

Lorenz, Konrad, 47, 180-181
Louis XIV of France, 96, 103, 188

Machiavelli, Niccolò, 69, 252, 284-285
Machiko, 1, 3, 111-113, 115-117, 121, 122-125, 127, 233-234, 255, 257, 259-260, 266, 275-277
Maeda Tsunanori, 203, 229
magistrate of finance (*kanjō bugyō*), 195, 271, 272
magistrate of temples and shrines (*jisha bugyō*), 82, 107, 121, 195, 212
Makino Narinori (also Norinari), 30, 40, 42-43
Makino Narisada, 2, 27, 41-42, 76, 104-105, 108, 109, 121-122, 146, 153, 264; appointment, 81-82
Manabe Akifusa, 105, 272, 290, 293, 294
Maruyama Masao, 157, 235, 243, 246, 251, 275
master of shogunal ceremony (*sōshaban*), 107
Matsudaira Masatsuna, 192-193
Matsudaira Mitsunaga, 82-86, 88, 297
Matsudaira Naonori, 75-77, 84-85, 87
Matsudaira Nobuaki, 296
Matsudaira Nobutsuna, 61, 63, 67
Matsudaira Nobutsune, 109
Matsudaira Sadanobu, 291-292, 295-296
Matsudaira Tadachika, 104, 109
Matsudaira Tadanao, 83
Matsudaira Terusada, 109, 122, 155, 226, 293
Matsudaira Tsunakata, 84
Matsudaira Tsunakoku, 84
Matsudaira Tsunanaga, 171
Matsudaira Tsunanori, 228
Matsukage nikki, 3, 108, 113, 115-117, 121, 127, 233-234, 264
Matsuo Bashō, 137, 141, 278
Matsuura Seizan, 3, 292
measles, 3, 275-276, 342nn. 90-91
Meireki fire, 39-40, 96, 188-189, 191, 261
menoto. See nurse
metsuke. See inspector
Mikado, The (opera), 145
militarism, 6; change to civil society, 280-284, 297-298; prewar, 179

Index 375

military (*bu*), 244; arts, 16–17; values, 19–20; virtue, 134, 245
mines, 184–185, 188, 196, 198–199, 279
Ming dynasty, 231; fall of, 8, 67, 218, 283–284
Mishima Yukio, 181
Mito Mitsukuni, Yorifusa. *See* Tokugawa Mitsukuni
Miyamoto Musashi, 131, 172
Miyazaki Eiga 3, 6, 129
Mizuno Tadaakira, 296
Momijiyama, 104, 124–125
mother, 2–3, 6–8, 297; mother-child bonding, 7, 22, 29–31, 34, 283. *See also* Keishō-in
Motoki Ryōi, 55
Motoori Norinaga, 162
Muro Kyūsō, 99, 117, 169, 229, 236, 263; on hawking, 147–148, 157
Muroka Masatoshi, 30, 40
Muromachi period, 16, 58

Nabeshima Mitsushige, 130
Nagai Naokatsu, 45
Nagoya, 57, 160, 165, 265
Naitō Tadakatsu, 81, 166
Nakae Tōju, 17, 60–61
Nakatsukasa Nobufusa, 24
Nanbu Naomasa, 109, 114–115, 318n. 38
nanushi. See village representative
Narushima Motonao, 291
Nawa Katsusho, 229
Neo-Confucianism, 51, 235, 292
Nikkō, mausoleum at, 27, 41, 42, 186, 210, 216, 265; procession to, 186–187, 197
nō, 21, 118, 200, 227, 228, 264, 266, 290, 291, 294; actor, 2, 249, 294
Nonaka Kenzan, 61
nurse, 22; wet nurse, 23, 137–138

O Ume, 23–24
Oda Nobunaga, 11, 304n. 11
Odawara, 255–258, 261; domain, 268–270
Oden, 38, 262
Ofuregaki kanpō shūsei, 92
Ōgimachi Dainagon Sanetoyo, 1, 111
Ōgimachi Machiko. *See* Machiko
Ogita Shume, 83–84
Ogiwara Shigehide, 125, 195–196, 197–202, 206, 247, 261, 270, 271–274, 286, 297

Oguri Masanori, 83–86
Ogyū Hōan, 42–43, 230
Ogyū Sorai, 9, 42, 68, 95, 103, 108, 115, 117, 119, 121, 143, 145, 170, 209–210, 214, 217, 230–253, 275, 280, 287, 290, 293–294; *Bendō*, 243, 246, 252; and Chinese scholarship, 241–243; and Dōnyu, 231–233, 243, 246; and Forty-Seven Loyal Samurai, 174–177, 236, 243, 246; and Keishō-in, 28, 233, 248; *Seidan*, 142, 235–236, 238, 250–251; *Taiheisaku*, 239, 245; *Tōmonsho*, 244–245
Ōishi Kuranosuke, 162, 163, 167, 171, 177, 181
Ōishi Shinzaburō, 8–9, 103
oku, 122, 213; women of, 21, 25–26, 188, 289
Ōkubo Masatomo, 42
Ōkubo Nagayasu, 184, 192, 247
Ōkubo Tadamasu, 261, 268–270, 273–274, 287
Ōkubo Tadatomo, 75, 197
okuzume. See personal adviser
ōmetsuke. See senior inspectors
Ōno Mizuo, 186, 203–204, 209
Ooms, Herman, 50, 188, 208
Osaka, 187, 189; battle of, 45, 83, 85, 110, 112, 127, 184, 191; castle, 186
Owari Mitsutomo. *See* Tokugawa Mitsutomo
Oyake Seijun, 219

page (*koshō*), 105, 108, 109, 110, 249; senior head page (*koshō kumi gashira*), 106
personal adviser (*okuzume*), 107, 109

Rakushidō nenroku, 110, 111, 127, 242
Regulations (*shohatto*), 45, 51–52; for the Military Houses, 190, 216, 223–224, 293
river works, 99, 150–151, 205–206, 271–272, 273
rōjū. See senior councilors
rōnin (masterless samurai), 27, 32, 43
Rouvroy, Louis de, 103
Ryōken, 210, 211, 212
Ryūei bunin, 107, 109, 111
Ryūei fujodensō, 23
Ryūei hinami nikki. See Edo bakufu nikki
Ryūkei, 33

Ryūkō, 126, 129, 171, 210, 212–214, 264, 266, 275–276

Saitō Hida no Kami, 114
Sakai Tadakatsu, 40, 62, 63, 68, 97, 119
Sakai Tadakiyo, 40–41, 68–71, 81, 97, 124, 286, 297; and Echigo dispute, 84–89; and Ikeda Mitsumasa, 63–67, 281; and shogunal succession, 73–75, 77–78, 100
Sakurada ki, 38, 43, 72, 216
samurai, 274, 275, 281–282; birthright, 59, 61, 67, 143; children of, 22; class/status, 8, 236–237, 251, 327n. 66; honor, 131, 178, 179, 180, 282; and killing, 130–132, 134, 136, 145, 180–181, 282; and learning, 17; prerogatives, 153, 160, 288; revenge, 167, 174, 180; training, 130–131
sankin kōtai. See alternate attendance
Sannō gaiki, 2–4, 70, 112–113, 117–118, 129, 146, 150, 197, 252–253, 262–263, 276–277, 289, 291, 301nn. 9, 10, 12
Satō Naokata, 166, 169–173, 178
schools, 58–59; Confucian, 64–66; Hanabatake, 61, 63–64; Shizugatani, 66
Seiwa Genji, 44, 110, 168, 296
Sekigahara, 45, 188
Sengakuji, 163, 164, 177
senior councilors (*rōjū*), 82, 90–92, 101, 104–107, 116, 121, 125, 126, 173, 193, 250; and dogs, 152–153, 156
senior inspectors (*ōmetsuke*), 82
seppuku (disembowelment), 161, 164, 174, 175–177, 273. See also *junshi*
Shibukawa Shunkai (Harumi), 115, 260, 280, 318n. 41
Shimabara: lord of, 259; rebellion, 187
Shimazu Mitsuhisa, 16, 134
Shinto, 52, 57, 60, 64, 207, 309n. 19
shogunal succession, 12, 15–16, 18
shohatto. See Regulations
Shūmon aratame no jō. See Laws for the Examination of Sects
Six, Daniel, 46
Smith, Henry D., 162, 178, 181
sobashū. See chamberlain
Someko, 112–113
Sūden, 45, 52, 56, 212
Sūgen'in, 12–13, 283

Sugiyama Wa'ichi, 72
supreme court (*hyōjōsho*), 84–85, 87, 121, 158, 173, 175, 272
Sunpu, 10, 14, 53, 186, 266, 273, 274
superintendent of finance (*kanjō bugyō*), 106, 121, 173
Suruga, 10, 41, 126, 186, 188, 189, 191
Suzuki Hisashi, 24–25, 33

Tahara Tsuguo, 169, 176
Takada: castle, 82–83; princess of, 83
Takeda Shingen, 52
Tanuma Okitsugu, 295, 296
Tatebayashi, 38, 41
tax, 194, 201, 206, 246, 260, 271, 297
temple/shrine construction/repairs, 186–188, 204, 208–210, 261
Tenju-in, 12, 15, 37, 39, 62–63
Tenkai, 52–53, 56, 211, 212
tenryō. See *bakufu* domain
Three Related Houses, 12, 39, 41, 56–57, 73, 76–77, 83, 85, 88, 126, 185, 263
tidal wave. See tsunami
Toda Mosui, 17, 27, 73–74, 80, 84–85, 94–95, 98–101, 104, 106, 115–117, 124–125; on dogs, 146–147, 157, 159, 165, 265
Tōkaidō, 13–14, 132, 257–258, 267, 270
Tokugawa Hidetada, 10–14, 40, 42, 45, 83, 110, 185, 187–188
Tokugawa Iemitsu, 13–20, 22–24, 32–33, 35, 39, 42, 83, 94, 96, 119–120, 127, 289; and Confucianism, 53; death, 36–37, 61, 281; expenditure, 185–188, 279, 290; and hunting, 47, 132, 134
Tokugawa Ienari, 291–292, 296
Tokugawa Ienobu, 2, 38–39, 55, 73, 113, 125, 126, 141, 228, 255, 262–263; and reminting, 199–201, 247, 272–274, 275, 276
Tokugawa Ietsuna, 15, 19–20, 33, 39, 69–71, 84, 106, 215, 281; finances under, 188–191; and hawking, 47–48, 149; illness and death, 74–77
Tokugawa Ieyasu, 10–14, 22, 49, 82–83, 96, 132, 187, 198, 296–297; and ceremony, 44–45; Confucianism, 50–53; and farmers, 67, 93; and Ogyū Sorai, 247–248; wealth of, 184–185. See also Nikkō, mausoleum at

Tokugawa jikki, 3, 13, 16, 24, 33, 43, 45, 48, 50, 70, 83, 92, 107, 109, 111, 124, 141, 169, 187, 241–242, 290–298
Tokugawa Kamematsu, 15, 24
Tokugawa Mitsukuni (Mito), 58–60, 64–65, 68, 77, 99, 132, 218–221, 225, 227–229; and dog pelts, 148
Tokugawa Mitsusada (Kii), 228–229
Tokugawa Mitsutomo (Owari), 39, 84–85, 228
Tokugawa Nobuyasu, 11
Tokugawa Tadanaga, 13–15, 18, 20, 32, 41, 110
Tokugawa Tadateru, 82
Tokugawa Tokumatsu (Tsunayoshi's son), 27, 38, 76–77, 150, 262
Tokugawa Tsunaeda (Mito), 228, 229
Tokugawa Tsunanari (Owari), 228
Tokugawa Tsunanori (Kii), 126, 228, 262, 263
Tokugawa Tsunashige, 15–16, 18–19, 33, 37–39, 113, 216, 262; financial problems, illness, and suicide, 69–73; and hawking, 47–48
Tokugawa Tsunayoshi: and autocratic government, 96–98, 126–127, 136, 195, 201, 251–252; death, 1, 112, 273, 274, 275–277, 342n. 93; as Dog Shogun, 2, 128; education, 16–18, 20, 23, 34, 136, 283; financial problems, 71–73, 149, 186–187; frugality, 95, 115, 250–251, 274, 290; intelligence, 16–17, 33, 221, 284, 294, 295; involvement in administration, 90–93, 108, 143, 249–250, 256, 284; madness, 6, 29, 128; physical appearance, 33; relative morality, 101–102, 253; sexual mores, 117–118, 289; succession, 1, 70, 73–78; type of Confucianism, 120, 215, 221–223, 227–229, 232–236, 283, 292–293; value system, 152. *See also subjects and persons pertaining, such as* authority, benevolence, etc.
Tokugawa Yorifusa, 14, 57
Tokugawa Yorinobu (Kii), 61, 229
Tokugawa Yoshikatsu, 57
Tokugawa Yoshimune, 6, 103, 155–156, 201, 211, 242, 246, 250–252, 293–295; and Confucianism, 236–239, 291; and hawking, 147–148, 237

Tokugawa Yoshinao, 51, 56–59, 68, 228; and Hayashi family, 57, 225
Tokutomi Ichirō (Sohō), 5, 14, 18, 93, 168
Toyotomi Hideyori, 11–12, 15, 45, 283
Toyotomi Hideyoshi, 11–12, 44, 123, 184, 209
tozama daimyo, 82
Tsuji Tatsuya, 6, 92, 105, 185, 223–224, 293
Tsukamoto Manabu, 6, 17, 27–28, 39, 71, 128, 132, 137, 150
tsunami, 1, 256, 265
Tsuruhime, 38, 126, 257, 262

Uesugi Tsunanori, 168, 175
Ukiyo-e (woodblock prints), 162, 278

Valignano, Alessandro, 10–11
village representative, 268–270
Vivero y Velasco, Rodrigo de, 10
Vizcaino, Sebastian, 12

wakadoshiyori. See junior councilor
Warring States period, 10, 209, 227, 244, 280, 293, 321n. 34
Weber, Max, 9, 48–49, 212, 224, 285–288, 294, 297–298

Yabuta Shigemori, 126–127, 232–233
Yamaga Sokō, 56–57, 166, 218
Yamagata Shunan, 233–234
Yamamoto Tsunetomo, 130–132, 177–178
Yamazaki Ansai, 53, 56, 60, 170, 217
Yanagisawa ke hizō jikki, 174–177
Yanagisawa mansion, 28, 230; court proceedings at, 120–121; scholars and lectures at, 115, 118–121, 214, 241; shogunal visits to, 117–119, 242
Yanagisawa Yoshisato, 112–113, 275
Yanagisawa Yoshiyasu, 1, 4, 6, 20, 109, 110–127, 146, 173, 175–177, 202, 244, 250, 262–263, 266, 275–277, 285, 286, 293, 296; and Chinese, 241–242; and Confucianism, 110, 214, 223; and Dōnyu, 231–233; and emperor, 112, 123–124; and gifts, 116–117, 122, 318n. 51; and laws, 155–156; and poetry, 122–124, 264; and protest, 124–127; Rikugien,

116, 241. *See also* Machiko; Someko; Yanagisawa mansion; Yanagisawa Yoshisato
Yao and Shun, 35, 57, 96, 98, 136, 155, 218, 252–253, 283, 287
Yodogimi, 11–12, 282–283
Yui Shōsetsu, 62

Yūki Hideyasu, 11, 83
Yushima Confucian shrine (*seidō*), 29, 120, 225–228, 236, 257, 261, 292
Yūten, 138–142

Zōjōji, 81, 138, 140–141, 166, 230; mausoleum of, 18, 24, 73, 104, 210, 216, 262

About the Author

Beatrice M. Bodart-Bailey received her postgraduate degrees from the Research School of Pacific and Asian Studies of the Australian National University. She has published books, book chapters, and articles on a wide range of topics on early Tokugawa Japan in several languages, including her translated work *Kaempfer's Japan: Tokugawa Culture Observed* (University of Hawai'i Press, 1999). She is professor of Japanese history and a founding member of the Department of Comparative Culture at Otsuma Women's University, Tokyo.

Production Notes for Bodart-Bailey/*The Dog Shogun*

Cover design by Santos Barbasa Jr.

Text design by Lucie Aono in Minion with display
in Bernard MT Condensed.

Composition by inari information services.

Printing and binding by the Maple-Vail Book Manufacturing Group.